P9-DTR-207

THE CAMBRIDGE HISTORY OF LATER GREEK AND EARLY MEDIEVAL PHILOSOPHY

THE CAMBRIDGE HISTORY OF LATER GREEK AND EARLY MEDIEVAL PHILOSOPHY

EDITED BY A. H. ARMSTRONG

CAMBRIDGE
AT THE UNIVERSITY PRESS
1967

PUBLISHED BY
THE SYNDICS OF THE CAMBRIDGE UNIVERSITY PRESS

Bentley House, 200 Euston Road, London N.W.1
American Branch: 32 East 57th Street, New York, N.Y. 10022

Printed in Great Britain at the University Printing House, Cambridge
(*Brooke Crutchley, University Printer*)

LIBRARY OF CONGRESS CATALOGUE
CARD NUMBER: 66–12305

CONTENTS

Contents

PART III PLOTINUS

by A. H. Armstrong

PART IV THE LATER NEOPLATONISTS

by A. C. Lloyd, Professor of Philosophy in the University of Liverpool

PART V MARIUS VICTORINUS AND AUGUSTINE

by R. A. Markus, Senior Lecturer in Medieval History in the University of Liverpool

PART VI THE GREEK CHRISTIAN PLATONIST TRADITION FROM THE CAPPADOCIANS TO MAXIMUS AND ERIUGENA

by I. P. Sheldon-Williams, formerly Assistant Representative, The British Council in Greece

Contents

PART VIII EARLY ISLAMIC PHILOSOPHY

by R. Walzer, Reader in Arabic and Greek Philosophy in the University of Oxford

PREFACE

The Cambridge History of Later Greek and Early Medieval Philosophy was originally planned in connexion with W. K. C. Guthrie's *History of Greek Philosophy*, but has developed on rather different lines, and is not exactly a continuation of that work. It is an independent survey designed to show how Greek philosophy took the form in which it was known to and influenced the Jews, the Christians of East and West and the Moslems, and what these inheritors of Greek thought did with their heritage during, approximately, the first millennium A.D. The length of the period and the extreme variety and complexity of the subject-matter made it impossible for any one man to deal adequately with the whole, so it was decided to return to the older Cambridge pattern of a composite history by several hands, and I was asked by the Syndics to undertake the planning and editing of the whole work, and to write the Part on Plotinus.

The period covered extends from the fourth century B.C. to the beginning of the twelfth century A.D., from the Old Academy to St Anselm. All divisions of the history of philosophy into periods are somewhat arbitrary, but the points chosen for ending the later Parts of this volume appeared to us good stops in themselves, and the thought covered in the volume as a whole does seem to have a certain degree of unity, as is more fully explained in the introductory chapter. It is hoped that the philosophy of the thirteenth century and the later Middle Ages in the West, with later Jewish, Moslem, and Byzantine developments, will some day be dealt with in another Cambridge volume. As for the beginning, there is a good deal of chronological overlapping with Professor Guthrie's work, but little real overlapping of subject-matter. In order to explain the genesis of the Neoplatonism of Plotinus, the central and dominant form of Greek philosophy in our period, it was necessary to go back to Plato. But a reading of Professor Merlan's chapters will soon show that in dealing with Plato, the Old Academy, Aristotle and the Stoics, he has confined his attention to their influence on the thought of Plotinus, and has considered other questions about their philosophies only in this context. It was agreed that Merlan should only deal with the Greek background of the thought of Plotinus, excluding Philo the Jew and the Gnostics, whose influence on Neoplatonism has sometimes been thought to be considerable. Philo and the Gnostics are treated in what seemed to me a more appropriate context in Professor Chadwick's Part, and the question of the relationship between Gnosticism and the philosophy of Plotinus is touched upon incidentally in my own Part. The decision to deal with it in this way is perhaps the most controversial of the many decisions which I have had to take about what to include and what to exclude and where particular subjects are to be treated, and I must take full editorial responsibility for it (I arrived at it, of course, because I do not consider that the influence of the Gnostics, or of Philo, on Plotinus was of great importance).

In a composite work of this kind, everything depends on the degree of co-operation and understanding which can be established between those taking part in the work. No editor could have had more willing and intelligent collaboration than I have had from the other contributors to the volume. Its virtues are mostly due to them; for its defects, which I am sure are many, I am responsible. I am most grateful to all concerned at the Cambridge University Press, and especially to Mr A. L. Kingsford, for their continual help at every stage in the preparation of this volume; they have made the task of an inexperienced and naturally inefficient editor easier than I ever expected. I am also very grateful to the Abbot and community of Downside Abbey, who allowed me to do much of my editorial work in their excellent theological library. And I most sincerely thank the successive secretaries of the School of Classics in the University of Liverpool for all their help with typing and correspondence.

A. H. A.

Liverpool

1965

ABBREVIATIONS

The following abbreviations are used in the notes throughout the volume:

CC	*Corpus Christianorum*
CSEL	*Corpus Scriptorum Ecclesiasticorum Latinorum*
PG	Migne, *Patrologia Graeca*
PL	Migne, *Patrologia Latina*
RE	*Realencyclopädie der klassischen Altertumswissenschaft*
SC	*Sources Chrétiennes*
SVF	*Stoicorum Veterum Fragmenta*

The abbreviations used in the notes of each Part will be found at the beginning of each Part.

References to Plotinus throughout the volume are in the following form: Ennead and treatise number [number in Porphyry's chronological order] chapter number and, where appropriate, Bréhier–Henry–Schwyzer line number, e.g. II 9 [33] 9, 35–9. References to *PG*, *PL* and *RE* are by volume and column number.

CHAPTER I

INTRODUCTORY

What we are trying to do in this volume is to provide a wide-ranging and fairly detailed survey of the philosophy of the period when thought in the Mediterranean lands, and later in Europe north of the Alps, took forms which deeply influenced our literature, art, social behaviour and institutions at least down to the seventeenth century and, to some extent and in some quarters, to the present day. We set out to show how Greek philosophy reached its latest, and perhaps most influential, phase, that which modern historians of ancient philosophy call Neoplatonism; and how this was taken over and adapted in various ways to suit their own purposes by Jews, Christians and Moslems. Whatever the relationship of this late Platonism to the real thought of Plato may have been (here Merlan has some interesting suggestions in the first chapter of his section), it is certain that it is this, rather than the Platonism of the dialogues as understood by modern scholars, which we encounter whenever there is a question of Platonic influence on art, literature, theology or philosophy before the nineteenth century, and sometimes even later. It, and its various theological transformations, therefore seem worth studying, and in recent years they have been vigorously studied. There is a great deal going on, in particular, in the fields of Neoplatonic and patristic studies: so much, in fact, that inevitably a good deal in this volume will be out of date by the time it is published. But it still seems worth while attempting a comprehensive survey, because much of the scholarly material is rather inaccessible except to specialists in the various fields, and also because the study of this period, lying as it does across the frontiers of so many disciplines, has suffered rather more than most from academic compartmentalization.

One object of this volume is to make generalization about the thought of the period more difficult. This is particularly necessary, because there is no period about which sweeping and ill-founded generalizations have been more common. So we have tried to show its philosophies and theologies in all their complexities and variations, and in particular to give some idea of how many different things 'Platonism', or 'Christian Platonism' can mean. There has, of course, been no attempt to impose any uniformity of outlook on the contributors, or a rigid pattern of treatment on the very varied subject-matter of the several contributions. Inevitably, the same or closely related topics have occasionally been treated in different Parts in different ways and from different points of view. Where this has happened, or where it seemed to me that for any reason it would be interesting and useful for the reader to compare passages from different Parts, I have inserted editorial cross-references in the notes. This deliberate refusal to over-simplify or impose a superficial tidiness has made the task of writing an introductory chapter a good deal harder. All I shall try to do in the rest of it is to provide a kind of rough sketch-map of the contents of the volume and to try to indicate the dominant preoccupations and attitudes of the philosophers and theologians of the period, and the more interesting convergences and divergences in their ways of thinking. If in doing this I slip back into just the kind of generalization which the volume was designed to make more difficult, at least the corrective will be ready to hand: a reading of the relevant chapters will soon supply the qualifications which my general statements need.

The first Part, by P. Merlan, tells the complex story of the developments in Greek philosophy which led up to Plotinus, from Plato and Aristotle onwards. Here there is a full account of Middle Platonism and late Pythagoreanism, philosophies whose influence, direct and indirect, was perhaps wider than that of Plotinus himself. Something of this influence can already be seen in the next Part, by H. Chadwick, on Philo and the beginning of Christian thought, where we find Jews and Christians taking over Greek ideas and adapting them to their own purposes and ways of thinking long before Plotinus: the section ends with an account of the great pagan philosopher's older contemporary, the Christian Origen, probably a pupil of the same master, Ammonius Saccas, whose thought has points of contact with that of Plotinus in some ways, but is utterly different in many others. Part III, of which I am the author, deals with Plotinus himself, the central and dominant figure and greatest philosopher of the whole period; though this does not mean that all its later philosophies can simply be classified as forms of Plotinian Neoplatonism. Merlan in his section has sufficiently shown the degree of his dependence on earlier Greek philosophy (the assumption underlying the whole treatment of Plotinus in this volume is that he was a genuine Greek philosopher, not an Orientalizer or a Gnostic). So in my section I have tried to give a self-contained outline of his philosophy with little reference to earlier or later thought, prefaced by some account of the man himself, and his way of living and teaching: for Plotinus was a complete and consistent character in whom life and thought were so closely related that it is not easy to understand the one without knowing something about the other. With Plotinus we have reached the third century A.D. The next Part, by A. C. Lloyd, carries on the story of pagan Neoplatonism to its end in the sixth century. It is, perhaps, of all the contributions in the volume the one which will be most interesting to those professionally concerned with philosophy (in the modern sense) rather than theology; and it shows good reasons for revising some earlier judgements on those, till recently, rather neglected and despised philosophers, Iamblichus and his successors.

The later Neoplatonic schools were pagan enclaves in a world which was becoming wholly Christian, at least officially. They survived into the age in which the first great Byzantine churches were built at Ravenna and Constantinople. The next three Parts are concerned exclusively with Christian thought. The first of them (v), by R. A. Markus, deals with Marius Victorinus and Augustine. It may surprise some readers to find that the former, who generally appears as a minor figure in biographies of Augustine, is given a chapter to himself. Till recently he was neglected, because very few people indeed had taken the very considerable trouble necessary to understand him. But the great edition of Henry and Hadot[1] has revealed him as one of the most original and interesting of the philosophical theologians who adapted Neoplatonic speculations to serve Christian purposes. The important place given to Augustine in the volume, of course, needs no explanation or defence. In the chapters devoted to him, though no artificial and anachronistic attempt has been made to separate his 'philosophy' from his 'theology' attention has been concentrated on those parts of his

[1] Marius Victorinus, *Traités Théologiques sur la Trinité*. Texte établi par P. Henry. Introduction, traduction et notes par P. Hadot (Sources Chrétiennes, 68–9) (2 vols. Paris, 1960).

wide-ranging and many-sided thought which are likely to be of interest to philosophers. Augustine's influence was immense, but did not extend to the Christian East, with which he had little contact, and which from the fourth century onwards followed paths of speculative theology increasingly divergent from those of the West. The next Part, by I. P. Sheldon-Williams, tells the story of Greek Christian Platonism from the fourth to the ninth century. It contains much that will be new to all but a handful of specialists, particularly about the developments after the Pseudo-Dionysian writings came into circulation. In the last chapter of this section that isolated and mysterious figure of the Carolingian age, Johannes Scottus Eriugena, is shown in his most appropriate context, that of post-Dionysian Greek Christian theology, which makes him a good deal less mysterious. The Latin background of Eriugena, and his contribution to distinctively Western controversies, is dealt with in the last of these three sections on Christian thought, by H. Liebeschütz, which traces the history of Western Christian philosophy from Boethius to Anselm. The ground traversed here will, in part at least, be more familiar to many readers than that covered in the section before, but there are few so well informed that they will not find their understanding, especially of the Carolingian and immediately post-Carolingian periods, increased by these chapters. Finally Part VIII, by R. Walzer, gives a sketch of early Islamic philosophy: for reasons which he makes clear, no more than a preliminary survey can be attempted. He has concentrated his attention on the great, and rather neglected, tenth-century philosopher al-Fārābī, whom he shows to be a thinker of exceptional importance and interest, not least because he developed and adapted to the conditions of the Islamic world of his time an otherwise unknown late Greek tradition of political philosophy based on the *Republic* and *Laws* of Plato. Plotinus and the other Neoplatonists whom we know at first hand show very little interest in Plato's political and social thought: so here, as at other points, a study of Islamic philosophy not only is worth while for its own sake and in view of its later influence, but can enlarge our understanding of the Greek thought from which it derives.

Perhaps a good starting-point for considering what, if any, common characteristics the thought of these many and diverse philosophers and theologians had is to observe what they meant by philosophy. It was something very different from what modern philosophers understand to be their professional activity: though perhaps even today the ordinary man sometimes, in a vague sort of way, expects them to provide him with philosophical guidance of the older sort, and is annoyed and disconcerted when they tell him, very properly on their own presuppositions, that this is none of their business, and goes to look for what he wants where he can find it, in East or West, sometimes in very odd and unacademic quarters indeed. Philosophy for most of the ancients, after Plato at any rate, and certainly for the men of our period, was as Markus puts it, speaking of Augustine, 'an all-embracing activity concerned with everything relevant to the ultimate purpose of human life'.[1] This accounts for the strong ethical emphasis and, to the modern mind, disconcertingly close connexion between philosophy and religion which we find in nearly all the thinkers of the period, in the Greek pagans just as much as in the adherents of revealed religions. This was of course compatible with a great variety of attitudes towards religious revelations and religious practices, and generalization here is particularly risky. Even the later Neoplatonists, Iamblichus and his successors, cannot just be dismissed, as is still often done, with a few general observations about superstitition and the decline of rationalism. Lloyd's observations on the relationship of their philosophy to their religion, which are among the most enlightening pages in the volume on this whole question, make this clear.[2] But the strong moral and religious concern of most of the philosophers of the period makes it easier to understand, for instance, why the Christians saw what we should call theology as a superior form of philosophy, and why in consequence it was quite impossible in planning this volume to make a tidy separation of the two and leave theology out of it. Only at one place and one time, in the towns of the Lombard plain in the earlier Middle Ages, do we find, for reasons which Liebeschütz makes clear,[3] logicians whose attitude to their studies was entirely secular and in whose writings, as he says, 'questions of religion and theology appear to be removed to an isolated corner of the discussion'. This local attitude, the

[1] Part v. ch. 21, p. 344.

[2] See Part iv, chs. 17 and 18 C.

[3] Part vii, ch. 37 B, p. 596.

importance of which for the later direction of Western medieval thought Liebeschütz shows, is rather different from the way in which many earlier philosophers and theologians, pagan and Christian, regarded Aristotelian logic as a kind of neutral preliminary study to religious speculation, though it ultimately derives from it.

The close connexion of philosophy and religion in our period leads us naturally to consider another aspect of its thought which is often misunderstood, the attitude to authority. At first sight it seems a period of servile authority-mindedness, among pagans as well as Christians. Whatever their attitude to religious revelations, the pagan philosophers regarded the great men of the past, above all Plato, with unbounded veneration. They disapproved of originality and devoted their lives to expounding what they thought to be the authentic teaching of the ancient masters, and commenting on their works. And the Jews and Christians were of course dominated by the authority of the religious revelation they accepted: though here again we find an exception to our generalization in the early medieval West, the championing of the claims of reason against authority by Berengar of Tours.[1] The Christian West saw, much more clearly than the Christian East seems to have done, that there was a problem about the relationship of reason to religious authority, as early as Augustine,[2] and at the end of our period Anselm is still very much concerned with it.[3] In the Moslem world the problem was still more clearly seen,[4] and the philosophers offered an interesting variety of solutions. Al-Kindī's[5] subordination of philosophy to revelation follows a familiar pattern, and Avicenna's[6] identification of the two is, perhaps, not so very far from the position of Philo. But it would be difficult to find parallels among Jews or Christians in our period for ar-Rāzī's[7] resolute dismissal of revealed religion as superstition, or for the most interesting solution of all, that of al-Fārābī,[8] who carried on into his own very different world the attitude of the Greek philosophers to their traditional cults and myths by interpreting the various religions of his time, including Islam, as more or less imperfect symbolic representations of philosophical truth.

[1] See Part VII, ch. 37 C.
[2] See Part V, ch. 21.
[3] See Part VII, ch. 38.
[4] See Part VIII, ch. 39.
[5] *Ibid.* ch. 39 B.
[6] *Ibid.* ch. 40 B.
[7] *Ibid.* ch. 39 B.
[8] *Ibid.* ch. 40 B.

But when we look at the thinkers of our period more closely, we find that in fact they managed to combine great freedom of speculation with their respect for authority. There is surprisingly little 'textbook scholasticism', parrot-like repetition of consecrated formulae without further thinking, even among the later Neoplatonists. One reason for this, rather disconcerting at first to the modern scholar, was their thoroughly unscholarly and unhistorical approach to the documents which they regarded as authoritative. The way in which Plotinus used Plato, and Philo's exegesis of the Jewish Scriptures, are good examples of this.[1] Another was the bafflingly unsystematic character of the authoritative documents themselves, the dialogues of Plato and the Jewish and Christian Scriptures—to say nothing of the Chaldaean Oracles, which are, to put it more mildly than they deserve, decidedly oracular. Within our period as a whole one kind of philosophy, later Platonism, dominates (Merlan's chapters show the interrelationship of 'Middle' Platonism and later Pythagoreanism, and the continuity of Neoplatonism with both). But at few points do we find mere conformism, disciples simply reproducing the thought of their master. The later pagan Neoplatonists were perhaps the most conformist. They were certainly more dependent on Plotinus than some scholars have thought, as Lloyd shows.[2] But Plotinus was not for them an 'authority'—less so than Iamblichus. This volume makes clear his central importance and wide-ranging influence on the thought of the whole period. But his prestige and reputation in later centuries (when and where he was remembered at all) were comparatively moderate. Nor was his influence due simply to doctrinal innovation; he can hardly be said to have taken a completely new line in philosophy. Merlan's chapters show the continuity of his thought with that of his predecessors. Certainly the superior clarity and coherence of his philosophy counted for a great deal. But perhaps his influence was still more due to the colour and passion which he brought into Platonism by thinking it through in the light of his own experience—not only the experience of union with the One, but the equally intense experience which transforms his account of the intelligible world, his experience of the transcendent self in

[1] See Part III, ch. 13, pp. 213–14 and Part II, ch. 8, pp. 137–9.

[2] See Part IV, ch. 17.

union with the archetypal reality of all things. It is this double experience which makes him a unique force in European thought, and, though there is no good evidence for any Indian influence on his philosophy, seems to bring him close at some points to the thought of India.

When we turn to the Jews and Christians within our period we find another help to originality, the tension between Platonic philosophy and revealed religion. Some good examples of the varied ways in which this worked can be seen in the chapters of Chadwick on Philo, of Markus on Marius Victorinus, and of Sheldon-Williams on Greek Christian Platonism.[1] This tension accounts, to a great extent, for the extraordinary range and variety of what is loosely called 'Christian Platonism', a variety which is amply displayed in our volume. There are continual divergences and reactions, often of great importance. One which is particularly interesting, and not very well known, is the reaction against the influence of Proclus in the Christian East described by Sheldon-Williams.[2] Greek Christian Platonism is more varied than Latin. There is no one great dominating figure. But even in the West, though Augustine towered over all the others and had an influence deeper and wider than that of any single Greek Christian thinker, he did not totally dominate the thought of Latin Christendom. Liebeschütz's account of Boethius[3] shows us another, quite different and very influential, form of Latin Christian Platonism.

There is one particularly interesting kind of divergence within Christian Platonism, leading to a good deal of original speculation and springing from tensions which go deep and far back in both the Platonic and Christian traditions, which deserves special mention. This is the divergence, apparent at several points in our volume, between the tendency to make a very sharp division between 'spirit' and 'matter' or 'soul' and 'body' and the concern to give a real religious and moral value to body, the material world, time, change and history. Generalization here is particularly difficult and dangerous. Augustine can be quoted on both sides, and does not fit tidily into this or any other general scheme of classification, though his influence in the West worked, on the whole, on the dualist side. Among the Greeks the

[1] See Part II, ch. 8; Part V, ch. 20; Part VI, ch. 28.

[2] Part VI, ch. 31.

[3] Part VII, ch. 35.

Cappadocians generally made the opposition between spiritual and material very sharp. But the post-Dionysian Greeks, and above all St Maximus, made the most sustained effort which is apparent anywhere in our period to find a place for body, physical motion and time in the movement of return to God and to show them as sacred. This seems to be closely bound up with their concern to show clearly what they regarded as an implication of the doctrine of creation, that things have no completely separate reality apart from God, that their whole existence is a participation in his being, so that Eriugena, the inheritor of this tradition, can even say that he creates himself in creating them.[1] In Liebeschütz's account of the *Libri Carolini*[2] we can see theologians influenced by the two tendencies clashing in a most interesting way, with a political and social background and implications to the controversy which will repay study but defy generalization. On one side, the Byzantine, we have the idea of the sacred cosmos of images and the intimate presence of God in human acts and works. On the other, the Carolingian, we have an over-simplified Augustinianism sharply separating body and soul and leading to a curiously modern conception of a non-sacred material world which, as Liebeschütz says, is 'a stage for human action only'.

The post-Dionysian Greeks made much use of Aristotle in constructing their more positive view of the material world. And this leads us to one last point about the thought of our period which it is important to make if we are to avoid a kind of particularly superficial and misleading generalization which used to be very fashionable in certain circles, that which opposes the 'Christian Aristotelianism' of the thirteenth century to the 'Platonism' of earlier Christian thinkers. Merlan's chapters show how close, if sometimes uneasy, the interrelationship of Platonism and Aristotelianism was from the beginning. There is a strong Aristotelian element in Neoplatonism, though Plotinus often criticizes Aristotle severely. And throughout the sections dealing with Christian and Islamic thought we find the direct or indirect influence of Aristotle at work again and again. In fact the interaction of Platonism and Aristotelianism is one of the main themes of this history.

[1] See Part VII, chs. 32 and 34.

[2] Part VII, ch. 36 A. Sheldon-Williams's chapter on 'The Philosophy of Icons' (Part VI, ch. 33) should be compared.

PART I

GREEK PHILOSOPHY FROM PLATO TO PLOTINUS

BY P. MERLAN

ABBREVIATIONS

ARISTOTLE

Anal. post.	*Analytica posteriora*
De an.	*De anima*
Eth. Nic.	*Ethica Nicomachea*
De gen. anim.	*De generatione animalium*
De gen. et corr.	*De generatione et corruptione*
Hist. anim.	*Historia animalium*
De div. per somn.	*De divinatione per somnium*
Met.	*Metaphysica*
Meteor.	*Meteorologica*
De partibus anim.	*De partibus animalium*
Phys.	*Physica*
De resp.	*De respiratione*
Top.	*Topica*

PLATO

Polit.	*Politicus*
Rep.	*De republica*
Soph.	*Sophistes*
Theaet.	*Theaetetus*

PLUTARCH

De Is. et Os.	*De Iside et Osiride*
De Ei	*De E apud Delphos*
De Pythiae or.	*De Pythiae oraculis*
De def. or.	*De defectu oraculorum*
De sera	*De sera numinis vindicta*
De genio Socr.	*De genio Socratis*
Cons. ad ux.	*Consolatio ad uxorem*
Qu. conv.	*Quaestionum convivalium libri IX*
Ad princ. iner.	*Ad principem ineruditum*
De facie	*De facie quae in orbe lunae apparet*
Plat. qu.	*Platonicae quaestiones*
De an. pr.	*De animae procreatione in Timaeo*
Adv. Col.	*Adversus Colotem*
Quomodo	*Quomodo adolescens poetas audire debeat*
De lib. et aegr.	*De libidine et aegritudine*

THEOPHRASTUS

Met.	*Metaphysica*

CHAPTER 2

THE OLD ACADEMY

A. *Introduction*

Neoplatonism is a term usually designating Plato's philosophy as reinterpreted by Plotinus and post-Plotinian Platonists. The term is slightly misleading,[1] in that to some it may suggest a more radical difference between the philosophies of Plato and Plotinus than is warranted, in that it tends to obscure the debt of Plotinus to Platonists before him, particularly the Old Academy and the Platonism of the period between the first century B.C. and his time (today often designated as pre-Neoplatonism or Middle Platonism), and finally in that it suggests that all post-Plotinian Platonism bears the stamp of Plotinus' philosophy, whereas in many cases his influence on other Platonists was only limited.[2]

However, in what follows we shall, in the main, limit ourselves to indicating those Platonic and post-Platonic philosophic doctrines which were probably of major importance for Plotinus, and the knowledge of which helps us to place his philosophy in historic perspective. No attempt will be made to ascertain the primary sources of these doctrines or to reconstruct systems of which only fragments have survived, nor do we plan to compete with an *apparatus fontium*. We shall simply present those major philosophic doctrines which we, in explicit form, still possess and which Plotinus knew, or in all likelihood knew.[3] The framework of our presentation is provided by four passages in Porphyry's *Vita Plotini*. In the first, Porphyry says that Plotinus' writings contain Stoic and Peripatetic doctrines, and that all of Aristotle's *Metaphysics* is present there in condensed form.[4] Secondly, Porphyry tells us that in the school of Plotinus these writers were read:

[1] It is a modern term anyway. Plotinus claimed to be an orthodox Platonist (*Enn.* V 1 [10] 8; VI 2 [43] 1; VI 3 [44] 5), and for centuries this claim went uncontested.

[2] Cf. Ueberweg–Praechter, *Grundriss* (1926), p. 601.

[3] Cf. H.-R. Schwyzer, 'Plotinos', *RE*, XXI/1 (1951), esp. col. 547–54, 572–81; W. Theiler, 'Plotin und die antike Philosophie', *Museum Helveticum*, 1 (1944), pp. 209–25.

[4] *Life*, ch. 14.

Severus, Cronius, Numenius—whom we should call either Platonists or Pythagoreans; Gaius and Atticus—whom we should designate as Platonists; and, of the Peripatetics, Aspasius, Alexander—obviously Alexander of Aphrodisias—and Adrastus.[1] Thirdly, Porphyry quotes Longinus' opinion of Plotinus, according to which Plotinus was superior to other expounders of Pythagorean and Platonic doctrines, such as Numenius, Cronius, Moderatus, and Thrasyllus.[2] Fourthly, Porphyry tells us that Plotinus often used to refute gnosticism.[3]

B. *Aristotle's presentation of Plato's philosophy*

The main aspects of Platonism leading to the system of Plotinus can best be seen if we start from what Aristotle presents as the main features of Plato's philosophy.[4] According to this presentation, instead of the dichotomy sensibles–intelligibles (ideas), to which dichotomy the dichotomy of two modes of cognition—one, sensation, resulting in mere opinion, the other, *noein*, resulting in truth—belongs, a dichotomy fully accepted by Plotinus,[5] which seems to underlie most of the Platonic dialogues, Plato divides all reality into three spheres: ideas (intelligibles), mathematicals, and physicals (sensibles). This 'horizontal' trichotomy is accompanied by a 'vertical' dualism of supreme principles, the One and the Indefinite Dyad. The interaction of these principles 'produces' the ideas (themselves in some way designated as numbers), and, as the ideas are the causes of everything else, the two principles become universal causes.[6] They are likened by Aristotle to the formal and the material cause of his own system:[7] and in some way they are also identified with the principles of good and evil.[8]

[1] *Life*, ch. 14.

[2] *Life*, ch. 20. Unfortunately we know next to nothing of the philosophic opinions of Gaius, Aspasius, and Thrasyllus (on the life of the latter, see F. H. Cramer, *Astrology in Roman Law and Politics* [Philadelphia, 1954], pp. 92–108).

[3] *Life*, ch. 16. [For Plotinus and gnosticism see Part III, ch. 12, pp. 205–6; ch. 15, pp. 243–5.]

[4] Most passages are now collected in K. Gaiser, *Platons ungeschriebene Lehre* (1963). Together with H. J. Krämer, *Arete bei Platon und Aristoteles* (1959), Gaiser centres his interpretation on Aristotle's presentation of Plato. Very instructive and somewhat neglected is the discussion in R. Heinze, *Xenokrates* (1892), pp. 10–47.

[5] *Enn.* I 1 [53] 7; III 6 [26] 6; IV 8 [6] 4; V 3 [44] 3. On sensation as constrasted with thinking see IV 4 [28] 12.

[6] *Met.* A 6, 987b14–29; Z 2, 1028b18–32.

[7] Parallel passages are listed in W. D. Ross, *Aristotle's Metaphysics* (1924), *ad* 987b14.

[8] *Met.* A 6, 988a7–15; Λ 10, 1075a35–6; N 4, 1091b32; cf. below, p. 26.

No longer as a mere report, but rather as his criticism, Aristotle explains that the assumption of these two principles seemed to Plato and Platonists necessary to account for plurality. Specifically, without the assumption of the Indefinite Dyad as one of the supreme principles, all being, they thought, would be frozen in the Parmenidean One.[1] Plotinus explicitly recognizes the derivation of plurality as an old and fundamental problem.[2]

The order ideas–mathematicals–sensibles is by no means arbitrary. Mathematicals mediate between ideas and sensibles in that they share changelessness with the former, multiplicity with the latter. Thus, if ideas are themselves designated as numbers, these numbers must differ from the numbers belonging to intermediate mathematicals. Perhaps the term idea-numbers or ideal numbers would indicate this difference.[3] One of the characteristic qualities of ideal numbers would be that each is unique and does not consist of unities, so that ideal numbers would be qualitative rather than quantitative and therefore inaddible.

Whatever the sources of Aristotle's presentation of Plato's philosophy, nobody in pre-Plotinian antiquity doubted its correctness. Nor was it ever doubted that he (and Theophrastus) correctly attributed these doctrines not only to Plato but also to Speusippus, Xenocrates, Hestiaeus, and other Platonists left unnamed. Finally, it was assumed that the main source of Aristotle's presentation was an *akroasis*,[4] a *synousia*,[5] *agraphoi synousiai*,[6] i.e. a lecture or a course of lectures delivered by Plato under the title *The Good* (or: *On Goodness*), the text of which was edited by Aristotle himself, Speusippus, Xenocrates, Hestiaeus, Heraclides, and other Platonists.[7] Not that all these Platonists held entirely identical doctrines. They differed, for example, in the explanation of the relation between the realm of ideas and mathe-

[1] *Met.* N 2, 1088b35–1089a6; here the Indefinite Dyad is called non-being.

[2] *Enn.* VI 3 [44] 3.

[3] *Met.* M 9, 1086a5; N 2, 1088b34; 3, 1090b35; M 7, 1081a21; 8, 1083b3; N 3, 1099b33; A 8, 990a30; M 6, 1080b22; 8, 1083a31; N 4.

[4] Aristoxenus, *Harmonics*, p. 39 Da Rios; Simplicius, *In Phys.* 151, 10 Diels.

[5] Simplicius, *In Phys.* 454, 18 Diels; *De anima* 28, 7 Hayduck.

[6] Simplicius, *In Phys.* 542, 11 f.; 545, 23 f. Diels; Philop. *In Phys.* 521, 10. 14 Vitelli; *De an.* 75, 34 ff. Hayduck.

[7] Alexander Aphrodisias, *In Met.* 56, 33 Hayduck; Simplicius, *In Phys.* 151, 6; 453, 28; 454, 19; 247, 30 – 248, 15 Diels; cf. Speusippus, *fr.* 33A, 51 Lang; Theophrastus, *Met.* 11. The lecture is referred to in *Enn.* V 1 [10] 5 and V 4 [7] 2.

maticals; also their terminology relating to the two supreme principles varied almost from author to author. But what they had in common was the assumption of a realm of being mediating between whatever they assumed the supreme sphere of being to be (ideas or mathematicals, and the latter either ideal mathematicals or mathematicals in the usual sense of the word, or finally, ideas identified with mathematicals) and sensibles. An interesting variant of this tripartition is provided by Aristotle himself when he divided all reality into the realm of the unchangeable, astronomicals, and sensibles.[1] What these Platonists had further in common was the assumption of the One and the Indefinite Dyad (in Aristotle's terms, matter; by others called by other names) as supreme principles, though among them disagreement started early as to whether the two should have absolutely equal status.[2] For quite a while even Aristotle himself must have shared the derivation of all reality from two opposite principles, sometimes referred to by him as Being and Non-being.[3]

The introduction of the mathematical as an intermediate realm between ideas and sensibles will perhaps appear a little less striking if we remember that the artificer in Plato's *Timaeus*, when imposing order (*kosmos*) on chaos (the receptacle agitated by irregular change), while using an ideal cosmos for his archetype, 'creates' the universal soul—this creation described by Plato in such a way that it is not easy to decide whether Plato speaks of what ordinarily would be called soul, or rather of some mathematical entity (or at least of an entity having a strictly arithmetico-geometrical structure). Indeed, Crantor, roughly a contemporary of Polemo, who succeeded Xenocrates as the head of the Academy, interpreted the 'psychogony' of the *Timaeus* as being simply 'arithmogony', i.e. the 'derivation' of numbers as the first sphere of reality from some superior principles obviously related to the One and

[1] *Met.* Λ 1, 1069a30–6. Cf. P. Merlan, 'Aristotle's Unmoved Movers', *Traditio*, IV (1946), pp. 1–30, esp. pp. 4 f. Essentially, this is also the tripartition of Xenocrates (*fr.* 4 Heinze), who accordingly replaced Plato's epistemic dualism αἴσθησις–νόησις by a tripartition: αἴσθησις, δόξα, νόησις (*fr.* 5 Heinze).

[2] Hermodorus being probably the first witness to it (Simplicius, *In Phys.* 247, 31 — 248, 15 Diels); cf. A. J. Festugière, *La Révélation d'Hermès Trismégiste*, IV (²1954), pp. 307–14. It is important to realize that a monistic interpretation of the Two-opposite-principles doctrine is rendered impossible if the Indefinite Dyad is identified with evil.

[3] Cf. P. Merlan, *From Platonism to Neoplatonism* (²1960), pp. 204 ff.

the Indefinite Dyad.[1] In other words, a peculiar approximation of the mathematical and the (universal) soul appears within the orbit of Platonism; and both Speusippus and Xenocrates defined or described the soul in terms suggesting that it was a kind of mathematical entity. Thus, Speusippus spoke of the soul as a form of that which extends in all directions, this form being constituted according to mathematical ratios;[2] Xenocrates defined the soul as a self-changing number.[3] In short, the *Timaeus* and the doctrines of Speusippus and Xenocrates seem to point to some kind of equation between mathematicals and the soul, whether we take soul to mean cosmic or individual soul.[4] Either of the two could be assumed to mediate between ideas (the intelligible) and the physicals (the sensible).

What is the relation of the several realms of being? Aristotle seems to assume that the lower ones were in some sense of the word derived from or generated by the higher. This is particularly striking with regard to sensibles. As most moderns see it, ideas, mathematicals, the supreme principles themselves—if they exist at all—have only an ideal existence and can therefore not cause anything to come into spatio-temporal existence (most moderns are Aristotelians in this respect that, in addition to, or instead of, these ideal principles and causes, they would demand a moving cause, without which by no stretch of imagination something 'real', i.e. existing in time and space, could evolve from them). But it is impossible to escape the impression that the Academic system of 'derivation' in some way was meant to explain the coming-into-being of everything, including the spatio-temporal, without intervention of an efficient moving cause.[5] Theophrastus[6] blames Platonists who failed to show this derivation in detail while praising Plato and Hestiaeus for having attempted it.

It seems obvious that this Academic system of derivation is in many respects similar to the Plotinian system of emanation.[7] The most important differences are two. Though obviously, in the Academic system, the One is *a* supreme principle, it does not seem to be *the*

[1] Plutarch, *De an. pr.* 2, 1012 D.

[2] *Fr.* 40 Lang.

[3] *Fr.* 60 Heinze.

[4] Zeller, *Phil.* II/1 (⁵1922), pp. 780–4.

[5] P. Merlan, *From Platonism to Neoplatonism* (²1960), pp. 197–201. See, for example, *Met.* Z 2, 1028b18–27; *De caelo* III 1, 299a2–300a19; Theophrastus, *Met.* 12–13.

[6] *Met.* 11.

[7] L. Robin, *La Théorie platonicienne des Idées et des Nombres d'après Aristote* (1908), p. 600.

supreme principle, as it is always spoken of in connexion with the Indefinite Dyad, whether the latter is fully coordinated to the former or not. Secondly, whereas the supreme sphere of being, ideas (ideal numbers, intelligibles), roughly corresponds to Plotinus' second hypostasis, i.e. intelligence,[1] and the sphere of the sensible to the corresponding hypostasis in his system, the Plotinian hypostasis between these two is that of the soul, never that of mathematicals.

C. *Some aspects of the theory of ideas in Plato's dialogues: the One and the Good*

It is not easy to recognize the ideas as presented in Plato's dialogues (eternal paradigms, which the soul has seen before her incarnation) in the ideas presented by Aristotle as derived from the two supreme principles, thus containing the Indefinite Dyad (matter), etc. Neither do the former have any principle superior to them, nor do they exhibit any kind of structure or order. But there is an exception to this: in the *Republic*,[2] the idea of the Good is elevated above other ideas. And one aspect of this superiority is expressed in the formula that this supreme idea is 'beyond' (or 'above') the realm of being (*ousia*). This expression is striking, because, on the whole, all ideas are presented in the Platonic dialogues as truly being—in opposition to things belonging to the realm of the sensible. However, it remains an isolated passage in Plato. Needless to say, it is of prime importance for Plotinus. He equates his One with the Good and elevates it above being.

Foreign to Plato also seems to be the derivation of the sensible from the intelligible. Again there is one exception to this. In the *Nomoi*,[3] we read a peculiar description of the process of becoming (genesis). Genesis of all existents takes place whenever 'the principle' starts increasing, so that it steps into the second dimension, from there on into the next, and, after having reached three dimensions, becomes a sensible to those capable of sensation. This is the kind of change and alteration constituting all genesis. Here, it seems, Plato indeed derives the sensible from the mathematical and does so, strangely enough, as a matter of course. But the passage also remains isolated in Plato's

[1] This is the way in which the word νοῦς will be translated here. Accordingly, νοεῖν will be translated by 'to intelligize'.

[2] VI 509C.

[3] X 894A.

written work, and it does not seem that it was ever mentioned by Plotinus.[1]

When Plato says that the ideas are truly being, he always implies that they are changeless (unmoved). But there is again an exception to this, viz. in the *Sophist*. Here the main speaker suddenly turns against those who assume ideas to lack intelligence (*nous*), change (movement), and life.[2] Again, the passage remains isolated in Plato's writings (and many contemporary scholars try to deprive it of its startling character by assuming that the passage really means that change [movement] must be included within the realm of existence, this realm comprising both ideas and sensible reality).[3] For Plotinus (and, indeed, for most of his successors) the passage is of prime importance. The three fundamental qualities of the second hypostasis become being (ideas), intelligizing (*noein*, i.e. non-discursive or intuitive thinking), and living[4]—a triad which one could, incidentally, also derive from Aristotle's 'intelligence at work is life'[5] when we remember that for Aristotle intelligence in its activity is identical with intelligibles, and that for Plotinus intelligibles would equal ideas, thus that which is.[6]

Having attributed movement, intelligence, and life to that which truly is, Plato proceeds to enumerate the five fundamental qualities constitutive of ideas, viz. being, movement, rest, identity, and diversity.[7] These five 'categories' Plotinus suggests instead of Aristotle's ten as fundamental for the realm of the intelligible *sensu latiori*.[8]

One more passage of the *Sophist* is of some importance for Plotinus. To introduce life, intelligence, and movement into the realm of the truly being, Plato asks the rhetorical question: Is it possible to assume that the truly being is lifeless, does not intelligize, is solemnly im-

[1] The passage is discussed, for example, in F. M. Cornford, *Plato and Parmenides* (1939), pp. 14 f. and 198. Perhaps philosophers sympathetic towards Bergsonism will also be in sympathy with the principle of derivation; matter (material, spatio-temporal reality) is the result of spirit's loss of its élan.

[2] 248E–249B.

[3] See, for example, F. M. Cornford, *Plato's Theory of Knowledge* (1935), pp. 244–7. *Contra*: C. J. de Vogel, 'Platon a-t-il ou n'a-t-il pas introduit le mouvement dans son monde intelligible?', *Actes du XIe Congrès International de Philosophie*, XII (1953), pp. 61–7.

[4] E.g. *Enn.* I 6 [1] 7; III 6 [26] 6; V 4 [7] 2; V 6 [24] 6.

[5] *Met.* Λ 7, 1072b27.

[6] Cf. P. Hadot, 'Être, Vie, Pensée, chez Plotin et avant Plotin', *Les Sources de Plotin, Entretiens*, V (1960), pp. 107–57.

[7] 254B–255E.

[8] *Enn.* VI 2 [43] 7–8.

mobile (*semnon kai hagion*)?[1] Surprisingly, Plotinus interprets this passage as meaning that the qualities which, Plato says, cannot be attributed to the truly being are by him meant to describe the nature of that which is above being.[2]

We have said above that it is difficult to recognize the ideas as presented in Plato's dialogues in ideas as derived from the One and the Indefinite Dyad. There is, however, one dialogue which could conceivably serve as a bridge between the two. In the *Philebus*[3] ideas seem to be first introduced as henads or monads (this is at least one possible interpretation, while another would be that the terms monad and henad refer to all existents). This reminds us that, indeed, Plato has always represented ideas as one over many sensibles and one is inclined to interpret the terms monad and henad as applied to ideas in this sense of the word. But Plato then also introduces the terms 'limit' and 'the unlimited' and speaks of them in a way permitting an interpretation of the passage as implying that these two are the supreme principles of everything and thus even of ideas themselves. If we now identify 'limit' and 'the unlimited' with the One and the Indefinite Dyad, the *Philebus* would, indeed, make it possible to show some similarity between the two aspects of the idea theory.[4]

Plotinus is, of course, as intimately familiar with Aristotle's presentation of Plato[5] as he is with Plato's *Philebus* (see Bréhier's index). There is no sign that he rejects the former outright, though its apparent dualism must, as we said, have been unacceptable to him. We shall see this better on the occasion of a discussion of Plotinus' concept of matter (below, p. 27). But there is no doubt that he tried to incorporate it in some way into his system. He does it, for example, by assigning the role of the Indefinite Dyad to the whole second hypostasis, leaving the role of Plato's One to his own One.[6] Thus, he reinterprets in some

[1] 248E–249A.

[2] *Enn.* VI 7 [38] 39. This interpretation by Plotinus is discussed by K.-H. Volkmann-Schluck, *Plotin als Interpret der Ontologie Platos* (²1957), pp. 130–5.

[3] 15A–C; 23C.

[4] See, for example, *Plato, Philebus and Epinomis*, tr.... by A. E. Taylor (1956), pp. 48 f. It seems that Porphyry, in his *Philebus* commentary, indeed tried this very thing (Simpl. *In Phys.* 453, 22 – 454, 16 Diels).

[5] Just as is Alexander Aphrodisias (*In Met.* 52, 10 – 56, 35 Hayduck; cf., for example, Simplicius, *In Phys.* 454, 19 – 455, 11 Diels).

[6] *Enn.* V 4 [7] 2. And he also derives numbers and ideas from the One and the Indefinite Dyad (*ibid.*).

way Plato's dualism. We shall also see (and we have already hinted at it; cf. above, p. 17) that he was not the first to do it.

Furthermore, the concept of the One appears in both the *Nomoi*[1] and the *Epinomis* (the problem whether the latter is genuine is of no interest in the present context, as it was considered such by many in the period between the time of Plato and Plotinus; others saw in it a work by Philip of Opus and thus sufficiently authoritative). It is not quite clear whether it refers to the unity of the idea as opposed to the plurality of sensibles or whether it means some kind of unity (a One) superior to ideas. Thus, when the *Epinomis* enjoins us to look, in whatever we study, for the One and promises us that when we ourselves shall have become one we shall be able to see the One, which is the supreme task of man,[2] we have the impression that the concept of the One plays, in Plato's philosophy, a major role not limited to being a quality of ideas as opposed to sensibles.

In the *Parmenides*,[3] the concept of the One plays certainly the main role.[4] In this dialogue it is proved that whatever we assert the One to be (or not to be), we shall find ourselves entangled in contradictions and paradoxes. One of the latter turns out to be that the One, if it exists, can in no wise be named or known; and that to assume this is impossible. However, the discussion of the One is conducted in the *Parmenides* in such a baffling way that the whole could be considered just an exercise in eristics, dealing with empty concepts rather than any realities. Plotinus is the first (or among the first; see below, p. 93) to interpret the *Parmenides* as containing a serious presentation of the One as the highest reality.[5] Thus, the above statement regarding the unknowability of the One would express genuine agnosticism commensurate with the nature of the One.[6]

[1] XII 962E–965E.

[2] 986D; 991E–992B. The passage is quoted by Plotinus: *Enn.* VI 9 [9] 3. Another quotation from the *Epinomis*: VI 7, 11 (*pace* H.-R. Schwyzer, 'Plotinos', *RE*, XXI/1 [1951], p. 551).

[3] Esp. 137D–142A.

[4] Full light was thrown on the *Parmenides* as the source of Plotinus' notion of the One by E. R. Dodds, 'The *Parmenides* of Plato and the Origin of the Neoplatonic "One"', *Classical Quarterly*, XXII (1928), pp. 129–42. His key passages are: 137D–E; 138A; 139B; 139E; 140B; 140D; 141A; 141E; 142A; 144B; 145A; 145B; 145E; 146A. Cf. also Bréhier ad *Enn.* V 3 [49]; V 5 [32]; VI 4–5 [22–3]; VI 7 [38].

[5] Albinus is still treating this dialogue as preliminary to philosophic study proper (*Isag.* ch. 3; *Didasc.* ch. 4).

[6] See e.g. *Enn.* VI 7 [38] 32.

In summa we could say: the One appears in Plato's dialogues, but it is a somewhat ghostlike appearance.[1] Plotinus breathes life into the ghost. And it does not seem possible to reject this as entirely illegitimate.

The *Parmenides* is of prime importance for Plotinus in one more respect, viz. in that it introduces the concept (and the problem) of the undivided presence of the idea in that which is multiple.[2]

Plato's *akroasis* on goodness has already been mentioned (above, p. 16). There is one particular passage, the culminating or the concluding one, which must be mentioned; it is not easy to say how it was connected with the Two-opposite-principles doctrine. Towards the end of the *akroasis* (or, to top it all: see below, p. 102), so we hear, Plato declared that the good (goodness) is the One.[3] Here again the concept of the One appears in a significant way. We shall speak of this passage later.

D. *Plato's cosmogony and psychology*

Let us now turn to some other doctrines of the Platonic dialogues. Of these, only the *Timaeus* is fully devoted to one of the central topics of pre-Socratic philosophers, viz. cosmogony. According to the *Timaeus*, world order (or, our orderly world) is the work of a god, whom Plato calls artificer. He is called good, and it is said of him that when he decides to create an orderly world, he looks at an ideal model, called live or animated being, containing in itself ideas (and in this act of looking he is referred to as intelligence), and now proceeds to make an image of it out of a pre-existing chaos, called by him space, nurse, or receptacle.[4] As the image is also to be animated and intelligent and as intelligence cannot exist except in a soul, the artificer fashions a cosmic soul out of a stuff, the ingredients of which are called 'the indivisible' and 'that which is divisible about bodies', 'the identical', and 'the different'. He now creates the elements by imposing geometrical forms on their rudiments already present in the chaos, builds of them the body of the world, and wraps the cosmic soul around it, creating an orderly world which is an animated being.[5]

[1] But cf. H. J. Krämer, *Arete bei Platon und Aristoteles* (1959), pp. 487–505.

[2] *Parm.* 131B; cf. Plotinus, *Enn.* VI 4 and 5.

[3] Aristoxenus, *Elem. harm.* 44, 6 Marqu., pp. 39 f. Da Rios.

[4] 28C–30D; 39E.

[5] 34B–35A.

As he proceeds to create all kinds of beings which shall inhabit the cosmos, he particularly also fashions individual souls; and he fashions them out of the same kind of stuff of which he had fashioned the cosmic soul, though the mixture constituting the stuff of the individual souls is less perfect than that of the cosmic soul.[1] In due time he enjoins his sub-gods to add to these individual souls which (as created by him) are immortal, other parts which, however, will be mortal.[2] After their first incarnation, all human souls will be subject to transmigration into bodies of other men or of beasts.[3]

All these doctrines (a world soul and individual souls, all incorporeal; their immortality, i.e. pre- and post-existence of individual souls; reincarnation, including transmigration of human souls into bodies of beasts—Plotinus adds plants) appear with some modifications in the system of Plotinus.[4] One of these modifications is the stress on the doctrine that all souls, though different, are only one soul, though Plato to some extent anticipated this doctrine when he, in the *Timaeus*,[5] has the world soul and the individual souls consist of the same basic 'stuff' or when he says that our souls are derived from the cosmic soul,[6] or when he, to Plotinus, seems to deny the existence of individual souls leaving only one cosmic soul.[7] Only, Plotinus rejects any interpretation of these Platonic passages which would make our souls *parts* of the world-soul; all the souls—the cosmic and the individual ones—are one.[8] And this doctrine of the unicity of the souls plays a very important role in Plotinus.[9] It guarantees the unity of the cosmos; it explains that all its parts are in sympathy with each other, which, in turn, explains what we today should call occult phenomena, such as action at a distance, magic, efficacy of prayers (the latter in spite of the fact that the gods do not 'listen' to man, or exercise any kind of voluntary action).

Highly puzzling is the description of the stuff of which the soul is fashioned.[10] It is a mixture which obviously is meant to ensure an inter-

[1] 31 D–E. [2] 41 C–D. [3] 41 E–42 E.

[4] *Enn.* IV 7 [2]; III 6 [26] 6—here against the doctrine of bodily resurrection; IV 3 [27] 13; III 2 [47] 13; III 4 [15] 2; VI 7 [38] 6, etc. (main passages in Plato: *Phaedo* 82 A; *Tim.* 91 D; *Rep.* X 617 D–621 A; *Nomoi* IX 872 E).

[5] 41 D. [6] *Philebus* 30 A.

[7] *Phaedrus* 246 B; cf. Plotinus, *Enn.* IV 3 [27] 1; 7.

[8] *Enn.* IV 3 [27] 1–8; IV 9 [8].

[9] *Enn.* III 5 [50] 4; III 7 [45] 13; IV 3 [27] 4; 5; 7. [10] *Tim.* 35 A.

mediate position to the soul, mediating between the realm of the immutable and the realm of the changing. But the meaning of the terms describing the factors of the 'stuff' (the key terms being 'indivisible', 'divisible', 'the same', 'the other') is not clear, though the idea of the soul's intermediacy is. Ever since Crantor wrote the first commentary on the *Timaeus*,[1] the identification of the terms mentioned above has been attempted time and again.[2] Plotinus offers several interpretations of the whole *Timaeus* passage.[3] However, there is a perceptible change in perspective. Though in his philosophy soul can be said to be intermediate between the realm of intelligence and the sensible, it is much closer to the former than the latter.

In addition to being intermediate, the soul in Plato's philosophy has to perform another all-important function: by being self-moved (or, as it would perhaps be better to say, by being self-motion),[4] the soul is the source of all motion (change) in the universe. And this theory of the soul is connected with another important problem—that of the origin of evil.

According to the testimony of Aristotle, the Indefinite Dyad is at the same time the principle of evil.[5] Is there in the Platonic dialogues any kind of entity which could be compared to the Indefinite Dyad on the one hand, and considered to be the principle of evil on the other?

More than once Plato recognizes in his dialogues that the orderly motions of the universe are counteracted by disorderly ones. But whence the source of disorder? The question becomes complicated by Plato's doctrine, mentioned above, that the soul is the only source of motion. This seems to leave no other possibility except to assume the existence of an 'evil' soul or 'evil' souls responsible for disorder, and, indeed, this is the doctrine of the *Nomoi*[6] and the *Epinomis*.[7] On the other hand, as Plato speaks of the disorderly motion of the 'receptacle' in the *Timaeus*, it is possible to argue that this 'receptacle' is essentially identical with what, in Aristotle's philosophy, is called matter, and that

[1] Procl. *In Tim.* vol. I, p. 277, 8 Diehl.

[2] A survey of the main solutions can be found in Plutarch's *De animae procreatione in Timaeo.*

[3] *Enn.* III 4 [15] 6; IV 1 [21]; IV 2 [4] 1; IV 3 [27] 19; IV 9 [8] 3.

[4] *Nomoi* X 896A.

[5] *Met.* A 6, 988a14–15; Λ 10, 1075a32–6; M 8, 1084a35; N 4, 1091b13–1092a3; cf. Eudemus, *fr.* 49 Wehrli.

[6] X 896C; 898C; 904A.

[7] 988D–E.

(irregular) motion is its inherent quality, in other words, that matter is the origin of evil.[1] Thus, the Indefinite Dyad, an evil soul, and the disorderly self-agitated receptacle can claim to have been considered by Plato the source of evil.[2]

For Plotinus the concept of an evil cosmic soul is entirely unacceptable. For this, the soul, as we have said before, is much too close to the realm of intelligence. But as Plotinus, no less than Plato, admits the existence of evil, he is left with only two claimants: the Indefinite Dyad and the receptacle.

Now, Aristotle undoubtedly identified these two with what, in his own system, is called matter, though his matter differs from either in very important respects. From the former, it differs in that it has no opposite, but rather is that which underlies opposites: from the latter, in that it is that of which, not that into which, the sensible world is fashioned. Besides, it is as a rule treated as an entirely relative concept, i.e. always being only potentially this or that, but being always actually something else, so that there would exist something like proximate matter, whereas prime or ultimate[3] matter would be a very dubious concept—a border concept at best. And, above all, Aristotle's matter is on the whole neutral, thus not the source of evil (the existence of which Aristotle minimizes anyway, tending to replace it by the concept of imperfection).[4]

Plotinus, as did virtually all Platonists and Stoics, took over the term 'matter' from Aristotle. He in some way also identified it with

[1] See Arist. *Met.* A 6, 988a14; *Phys.* I 9, 192a14; cf. above, p. 15.

[2] In addition, in one dialogue, the *Politicus* (269C–270A), there is an alternation of periods of cosmos and chaos, due to something like an inborn inertia of the universe, under the effect of which, when not 'steered' by the originator of order, the universe lapses into disorder—and this doctrine (myth) will be used by Plutarch and Severus to teach the periodical destruction and recurrence of the cosmos, a doctrine accepted also by Pythagoreans, Stoics (Zeller, *Phil.* III/1 [⁵1909], p. 157 n. 2), and Plotinus (*Enn.* V 7 [38] 1–3; IV 3 [27] 12); see below, p. 79. Other passages indicative of an element of resistance to order: *Tim.* 48A; 56C (cf. Theophr. *Met.* 33). And the amount of evil in the universe is greater than that of good: *Rep.* II 379C; *Polit.* 273D; *Theaet.* 176A. Cf. Zeller, *Phil.* II/1 (⁵1922), p. 765 n. 5.

[3] See, for example, Zeller, *Phil.* II/2 (⁴1921), p. 320 n. 2; W. Wieland, *Die aristotelische Physik* (1962), pp. 209–11; L. Cencillo, *Hyle* (1958), p. 39. Plotinus speaks of ἁπλῶς ὕλη: *Enn.* II 4 [12] 11, 24. Cf. H. R. King, 'Aristotle without Prima Materia', *Journal of the History of Ideas*, XVII (1956), pp. 370–89; F. Solmsen, 'Aristotle and Prime Matter', *ibid.* XIX (1958), pp. 243–52. Cf. below, p. 27 n. 5.

[4] But Aristotle himself speaks of the κακοποιόν of matter (*Phys.* I 9, 192a15). Cf. Zeller, *Phil.* II/2 (⁴1921), pp. 331; 427–36.

both the Indefinite Dyad and Plato's receptacle.[1] But he could not accept from Aristotle the concept of a neutral matter, or he would have been left without the possibility of explaining evil. For him, therefore, matter became the principle of evil.[2]

However, this assumption involved him in a great difficulty. Aristotle had identified his matter with the Indefinite Dyad. But the Indefinite Dyad was one of the factors present in ideas (intelligibles).[3] Therefore, evil would be present in ideas themselves, or, in the system of Plotinus, in the realm of the intellect. Plotinus tried to get out of this difficulty by assuming a double matter,[4] one corresponding to the Indefinite Dyad and thus present in ideas,[5] the other present only in sensibles. Only the latter was supposed to be the source of evil.[6] But by so doing, he created for himself another difficulty. How were the two matters to be related to each other? Plotinus presented the first as the ideal paradigm of the other,[7] but this made it all the more incomprehensible why the lower matter could be the source of evil. Furthermore, the assumption of a double matter involved him in the assumption of a double origin of matter. Lower matter appeared only at the end of the emanative process[8] either as a product of the soul or as the realm where the realm of the soul stops—just as darkness begins where a cone of light ends; but higher matter seemed to emerge directly from the One. In Plotinus and in many later Platonists (e.g. in Syrianus and in Proclus),[9] the problem of the (single or double) origin of matter appears time and again; it does not seem that it has ever been satisfactorily solved.[10]

[1] *Enn.* II 4 [12] 7; 11; III 6 [26] 16–18.

[2] *Enn.* I 6 [1] 5; I 8 [51] 3, 35–40. 14. 10–14; II 4 [12] 16.

[3] It is a well-known problem for interpreters of Plato: was Aristotle correct in presenting Plato as assuming that *the same* matter which is present in sensibles is (under the designation of Indefinite Dyad) present also in ideas (*Phys.* III 4, 203a9–10; IV 2, 209b33; *Met.* A 6, 988a7–14; cf. Zeller, *Phil.* II/1 [51922], pp. 750–60)?

[4] *Enn.* II 4 [12].

[5] In so doing he was greatly helped by Aristotle's term of an intelligible matter. However, Aristotle used the concept, designated by it, for purposes entirely different from those of Plotinus.

[6] *Enn.* I 8 [51] 3; I 8 [51] 8.

[7] *Enn.* II 4 [12] 3.

[8] *Enn.* I 8 [51] 7, 20; IV 3 [27] 9, 25; V 8 [13] 7, 22.

[9] See K. Praechter, 'Syrianos', *RE*, IV/2 (1932), esp. col. 1754 f.; R. Beutler, 'Proklos', *RE*, XXIII/1 (1957), esp. col. 242 f. Cf. C. J. de Vogel, 'La théorie de l' ἄπειρον chez Platon et dans la tradition platonicienne', *Revue philosophique*, CXLIX (1959), pp. 21–39.

[10] On other difficulties inherent in Plotinus' notion of matter, see J. M. Rist, 'Plotinus on Matter and Evil', *Phronesis*, VI (1961), pp. 154–66.

The psychology of the *Timaeus* connects it with a number of other Platonic dialogues which teach the doctrines of immortality and reincarnation. But, as Plato's statements concerning the nature of the soul are inconsistent (why modern interpreters devote so much effort to proving the opposite, is incomprehensible), it is not easy to say what is actually immortal, according to Plato. In the *Phaedo*[1] the soul is supposed to have no parts; therefore, all of it must be immortal. In the *Phaedrus*[2] even the discarnate souls have parts roughly corresponding to the same three parts which the *Republic* attributes to incarnate souls, i.e. a reasonable, an indignant (irascible), and a concupiscent part,[3] and thus the whole soul including these parts would be immortal. In the *Timaeus* the two lower parts of the soul are explicitly declared as mortal (see above, p. 24); thus only the reasonable part of the soul would survive. It is by no means sure that Plato wants to teach one consistent doctrine concerning the nature of the soul and its immortality. And the same is true concerning the problem of reincarnation. Sometimes[4] Plato speaks of reincarnation as the result of some universal law which orders a never-ending cycle of reincarnations. Sometimes only some souls are supposed to become incarnate due to some failing during their discarnate existence when they contemplated ideas, resulting in a 'fall'.[5] This fall starts a cycle of reincarnations from which, however, permanent escape is possible.[6] And finally, sometimes the first incarnation is ordered by a divinity and is not the result of any fault or fall.[7] Though Plato often refers to the body as soul's impediment or grave,[8] this obviously cannot be applied to the incarnation of the type just described. The same lack of consistency we find in Plato with regard to the condition of the soul after death. On the whole, some intermediate condition between one incarnation and the next is assumed (reward, punishment, resumption of discarnate existence),[9] but at least once Plato assumes that the souls which were not 'clean' when they left their body are immediately attracted to another.[10]

On the whole we could say that incarnation and reincarnation in

[1] 78C.
[2] 246A–B.
[3] IV 438E–441B.
[4] *Rep.* X 617D.
[5] *Phaedrus* 248C.
[6] *Phaedrus* 248C–249A; cf. *Timaeus* 42C.
[7] *Timaeus* 41E.
[8] *Phaedo* 66B–67B, 79C; *Gorgias* 493A.
[9] *Rep.* X 613E–621B; *Phaedo* 113D–114C; *Gorgias* 524A–526C; *Phaedrus* 248A–249D.
[10] *Phaedo* 81B–E.

Plato's work exhibit a 'neutral', an 'optimistic', and a 'pessimistic' aspect. Most certainly the incarnation of the cosmic soul is conceived by Plato as something good.

However, consistent or not, generally Plato's theories of immortality and incarnation, and the attendant doctrine of anamnesis, are considered central to his doctrine. One notable exception is *De anima mundi* by Ps. Timaeus Locrus in which one passage,[1] not quite consistent with the rest, states flatly that the whole doctrine is a *pia fraus* for those who without it could not be persuaded to live a life given to pursuit of perfection (*aretê*). For Plotinus, however, it most certainly is a central doctrine. But, because of Plato's inconsistencies, he feels left in the lurch by him when it comes to explaining the reason for incarnation of individual souls (that of the cosmic soul needs none in him, just as it does not need any in Plato), precisely because he tries to make it a consistent doctrine.[2] In the context of his cosmology he is inclined to accept an optimistic point of view: incarnation is a 'natural' event and, therefore, one not to be blamed. However, in the context of his ethical theories he is a pessimist and sees the condition of incarnation as one of misery for the soul. In the end, he devises a theory which, as he himself says, is original with him: the soul is not actually fallen but, even when in us, continues its life on a higher plane, that of intelligence—only we are not conscious of it.[3] Furthermore, immortality for him means even immortality of the soul of plants,[4] whereas Xenocrates and Speusippus limited immortality to souls of beasts.[5]

We can now return to Plato's cosmogony.

The description of the cosmogonic process is preceded by a question: has this cosmos existed always or has it come to be? And the answer is: it has come to be.[6]

Of this aspect of Plato's doctrines we shall speak later (p. 47).

[1] 104D–E.

[2] *Enn.* IV 8 [6] 1.

[3] IV 8 [6] 8. On this question, whether the soul has actually fallen or not, his followers are divided (see, for example, Iamblichus in Simpl. *De an.* 5, 38 – 6, 17 Hayduck).

[4] *Enn.* IV 7 [2] 14.

[5] Olympiodorus, *Phaedo*, p. 124, 16 Norvin, i.e. section D.

[6] *Tim.* 28D.

E. *Plato's Letters*

So far we have discussed, as the three main sources of our knowledge of Platonism, the presentation by Aristotle, the dialogues, the reports on the *akroasis* on the good (goodness). One remains, viz. Plato's *Letters*, particularly the *2nd*, *6th*, and *7th*.[1] The *2nd* contains a kind of secret formula obviously meant to convey some very important aspect of Plato's thought, saying that everything is related to the king, on behalf of whom all exists and who is the reason of beauty, second things to the second, third things to the third.[2] The *6th* contains a reference to a god who is the ruler of the universe, and to another, his father, obviously above him.[3] The *7th* teaches that what is obviously the core of Plato's thought cannot be taught in the same manner in which all other branches of knowledge can, but, as a result of long endeavours, something like a spark is kindled in the soul and the flame thus engendered goes on burning by itself.[4] In other words, the *7th Letter* suggests that the access to Plato's philosophy can be obtained only in some kind of satori, a supra-rational experience.[5]

None of these three utterances fits easily into the context of Plato's doctrines as we know them from the other three sources.[6] At the same time all three passages are sufficiently unclear to permit a number of interpretations. But obviously all could easily be adopted by Plotinus: the *2nd*, to find his three hypostases in Plato; the *6th*, to elevate a god above the artificer; the *7th*, to teach an ineffable union with the One.

F. *The Two-opposite-principles doctrine in Speusippus*

We noticed that the Two-opposite-principles doctrine was professed by pupils of Plato. Particularly remarkable is the case of Speusippus.

[1] At the time of Plotinus, nobody doubted their authenticity. Plotinus quotes the *2nd* (I 8 [51] 2; III 5 [50] 8; V 1 [10] 8; V 3 [44] 17; VI 7 [38] 42), the *6th* (VI 1 [42] 8) and the *7th* (V 3 [44] 17; VI 9 [9] 4; II 6 [17], 1—*pace* H.-R. Schwyzer, 'Plotinos', *RE*, XXI/1 [1951], col. 551).

[2] 312E. [3] 323D. [4] 341C–D.

[5] It should be stressed, the sooner the better, that whatever Plato is describing here is obviously not what we could call a mystical ecstasy. For the hallmark of the latter is that it is a passing experience, whereas Plato describes a permanent change—an insight acquired and from then on possessed. However, Plotinus uses the passage when he explains mystical ecstasy (V 3 [44] 28–9).

[6] The *Phaedrus*, however, seems to express similar doubts as to the possibility of communication of philosophical truths in writing (275C–277A); the *7th Letter*, however, does not distinguish between the spoken and the written word. Cf. P. Merlan, 'Form and Content in Plato's Philosophy', *Journal of the History of Ideas*, VIII (1947), pp. 406–30, esp. pp. 426 f.

Speusippus

As Aristotle seems to present it, Speusippus spoke of the One as not even being, as a kind of seed out of which that which is more perfect—in this case, being—comes into existence.[1] But such an interpretation leaves us with the difficulty of interpreting the opposite of the One, the Indefinite Dyad (or, as Speusippus used to call it, multitude). Shall we say that it is not even non-being? Furthermore, according to Aristotle, from the supreme principles Speusippus derived a number of entities, the first being mathematicals, with the soul coming next.[2] Mathematicals thus replaced Plato's ideas.[3] Now, it is obvious that the entities which came after the mathematicals were of a lower order—down to sensibles. It is difficult to imagine that Speusippus conceived the transition from the One to mathematicals as an ascent, but the transition from mathematicals to the rest of existents as a descent. It therefore rather seems that Aristotle expressed himself ambiguously and that the One in Speusippus was meant to be non-being in the sense of better (higher) than being. Once we have encountered in Plato the phrase 'beyond (above) being', it is not difficult to assume that the concept was incorporated by Speusippus in his own variant of the Two-opposite-principles doctrine. This assumption can particularly be defended in the light of a quotation from Speusippus recently found in the lost part of Proclus' commentary on Plato's *Parmenides*.[4] According to this quotation, Speusippus explicitly placed the One above being and saw it as a kind of super-principle, thus stressing its absolute transcendence. Moreover, it seems that one of the chapters of Iamblichus' *General Mathematics* is a kind of excerpt from Speusippus, and in this chapter the doctrine of the One as above being is clearly enunciated.[5] Thus, in all likelihood this is the way in which we should interpret Speusippus' doctrine of the One. It is obvious how closely such a doctrine is related to that of Plotinus.[6] Moreover, it seems obvious that Plotinus, who found his One in Plato, and his doctrine that

[1] *Fr.* 34A, E, F Lang.

[2] *Fr.* 33E, 42G Lang.

[3] The existence of which Speusippus came to deny: *fr.* 42A, C, D, E Lang.

[4] R. Klibansky, C. Labowsky,... *Procli Commentarium in Platonis Parmenidem* (1953), pp. 38, 33–41, 10.

[5] See P. Merlan, *From Platonism to Neoplatonism* (²1960), pp. 96–140.

[6] Cf. E. R. Dodds, 'The *Parmenides* of Plato and the Origin of the Neoplatonic "One"', *Classical Quarterly*, XXII (1928), pp. 129–42, esp. p. 140, with n. 5.

intelligibles are within intelligence in Parmenides,[1] must have interpreted Aristotle's report on Speusippus' One in this sense.[2]

This One Speusippus distinguished both from the good[3] and from intelligence.[4] The latter is precisely what Plotinus did; as to the former, he, on the whole, follows Plato in calling his supreme principle good or the good (goodness), but sometimes he warns us that this rather means that the One is the source of all goodness than that it is good itself. On the other hand, while Speusippus refused to identify his second principle with evil[5]—thus making it easier to interpret the Two-opposite-principles doctrine monistically (see below, p. 36), Plotinus did identify it so—but only if it was equated with the matter of sensibles (see below, p. 129).

Speusippus was among the first to distinguish a double One, a higher and a lower, the latter constitutive of number.[6] This, in another way, prepares us for Plotinus' notion of an absolutely transcendental One.

G. *Theology and Demonology: Plato and Xenocrates*

We said that it is difficult to find a bridge linking the Two-opposite-principles doctrine with the doctrine of ideas as it appears in Plato's dialogues. But the juxtaposition of these two doctrines reveals another, even more radical, difficulty. It can safely be said that, from the beginning to the end of Plato's literary activity, the world of gods plays a prominent role in very many of his dialogues. These gods are presented as persons. But where do gods (or a god, or God) find a place in a system in which the One and the Indefinite Dyad are supposed to be the supreme principles from which everything is derived? Three possibilities present themselves. Either Plato's gods, as they appear in the dialogues, are sheer myth (and who would not be inclined to see in the Zeus of the *Politicus*, or in the procession of the gods in the *Phaedrus*, a

[1] *Fr.* 5 Diels; *Enn.* V 1 [10] 8; V 9 [5] 5; etc.

[2] But the point of view could be defended that Plotinus accepted Aristotle's interpretation according to which Speusippus conceived of his One as a mere seed or sperma, by pointing out that Plotinus himself, who usually accepts the Aristotelian point of view that actuality (perfection) precedes potentiality (imperfection), sometimes speaks of his One as a seed (*Enn.* III 3 [48] 7; IV 8 [6] 5; 6; V 9 [5] 6). Cf. A. H. Armstrong, *The Architecture of the Intelligible Universe in the Philosophy of Plotinus* (1940), pp. 61–4.

[3] *Fr.* 35 A, B, D, E Lang.

[4] *Fr.* 38 Lang.

[5] *Fr.* 35 D Lang.

[6] *Fr.* 42 D Lang.

myth only? or to side with many scholars who see in the artificer in the *Timaeus* nothing but a literary device, really identical with ideas?);[1] or they themselves are indeed in some way 'derived' from these two principles; or these principles and what is derived from them (notably numbers) must be 'theologized', i.e. changed from abstract principles into persons. It seems that in all Neoplatonists we find something like a combination of the second and the third alternatives. In Plotinus, indeed, we find the strange structure of the second hypostasis: it contains ideas, intellects, and *gods*—in other words, abstract principles, semi-persons, and persons.

There is, however, one strong obstacle to either of the alternatives. If the gods (or god) are not persons, what becomes of providence?

Plato devoted a considerable section of the *Nomoi*[2] to the problem of theology and particularly of providence. In the light of the foregoing, this section can be read either as a popular presentation of the philosophic point of view that providence is simply identical with the reasonable structure of the universe, or that, indeed, the gods exercise some kind of personal providence. In Plotinus, his insistence on emanation as an involuntary and non-premeditated process excludes personal providence[3] and his providence, indeed, coincides with the natural order of things (which includes the inevitability of imperfection and moral evil, while suffering is no true evil for the truly wise man). However, this still does not definitely answer the question whether Plato's and Plotinus' gods are persons, myths, or abstract principles. For an answer we must turn from the topic of gods to that of demons.

Demonology is the doctrine teaching the existence of some entities (demons, spirits, angels, devils, jinns, etc.) in some way superior to men but not gods either. We should call them supernatural, but for a Platonist, as for many other Greeks, the concept of nature was much wider than for us and simply included such entities. We must not forget that in the philosophy of Democritus and Epicurus even gods become 'natural' entities and are simply nature's products. In Plato and in the

[1] For example, Zeller, *Phil.* II/1 (⁵1922), pp. 926–34 and 710.

[2] X 899 D–905 D.

[3] *Enn.* IV 4 [28] 6; IV 4, 39; VI 7 [38] 1, 31; III 2 [47] 1; VI 8 [39] 17.

Academy, including Aristotle,[1] interest in demons had always existed. It is well known that Plato's *Apology* is in great part based on the assumption that Socrates had some special *rapport* with an entity (or quality) to which he referred as 'the demonic'.[2] And when Plato represented Diotima as the teacher of Socrates, he attributed to her a full-fledged demonology.[3] The *Epinomis*, whoever its author,[4] presents another elaborate system of demonology.[5]

Now, the same Plato who, as it seems, as a matter of course assumed the existence of demons (spirits, angels), was violently critical of false opinions concerning the nature of the gods. He considered it particularly impious to attribute to them any kind of changeability (i.e. appearance in a form other than their own) and, quite particularly, to see in them originators of evil. It is obvious that in so doing he was denying the truth of generally accepted religious convictions. But were these convictions entirely baseless? Xenocrates utilized his belief in the existence of spirits (demons) to explain the origin of these convictions and, at the same time, to accept fully Plato's doctrines concerning the true nature of the gods. He did so by distinguishing good spirits from evil spirits. To the latter he attributed everything 'immoral' believed to have been done by the gods. And everything which was wrong in

[1] In fact, in *De gen. anim.* Aristotle provides us with an excellent example of what could be called 'natural' demonology. After having assigned plants, fish, and 'footed' animals, i.e. birds *and* land animals, to the elements of earth, water, and air respectively, he states that there must be a fourth kind of living beings, living in fire. However, it must not be terrestrial fire (which does not exist in pure condition here on earth and appears only in disguise—something is burning, not fire itself; the same problem in Theophrastus, *fr.* III 1 Wimmer), but pure fire as it exists on the moon (III 11, 761b8–23). What else would Aristotle call these living beings, if not demons (cf. Plotinus, *Enn.* II 2 [14] 6)? It should be obvious how greatly Aristotle is straining his classification of animals, precisely to be able to find a 'natural' place for demons—he assigns not only birds but *all* 'footed' animals to the air, so as not to run out of elements (the fifth element, ether, is of course the habitat of heavenly bodies, i.e. divinities). And in *De div. per somn.* (463b12–15), while he denies that dreams are god-sent, he asserts that they are sent by demons, and it does not seem that we have the right to tone down the words 'though not divine, nature is demonic', as if this would not mean 'full of demons'. On all this see W. Lameere, 'Au temps où F. Cumont s'interrogeait sur Aristote', *Antiquité Classique*, XVIII (1949), pp. 279–324. M. Detienne, *La notion de Daimôn dans le Pythagorisme ancien* (1963), esp. pp. 140–68. Cf. below, p. 39; Zeller, *Phil.* II/2 (⁴1921), p. 553. The distinction between two kinds of fire appears also in the Stoa and in Plotinus (*Enn.* II 1 [40] 7); cf. Zeller, *Phil.* III/1 (⁵1923), pp. 188 f.; below, p. 72.

[2] One of the reasons for the continued interest in Socrates exhibited by Platonists, was precisely the fact that he seemed to have had a guardian angel (demon). Plutarch (*De genio Socratis*) and Maximus of Tyre, *Or.* XV 7, remind us of this. For Socrates the aporeticist Platonism, after its return to dogmatism, had little use.

[3] *Symp.* 202E–203A.

[4] Plotinus quoted it as Platonic: VI 7 [38] 11.

[5] 984E–985C. P. Moraux, 'quinta essentia', *RE*, XXIV/1 (1963), pp. 1188 f.

human ideas concerning gods and the manner in which they should be worshipped was simply the effect of the nature and activities of these evil spirits. Thus all religious cults, rites, convictions, etc., of the Greek religion could, with this one modification, continue to be maintained. The belief in Plato's 'moral' gods could be harmonized with the belief in 'immoral' spirits.[1]

From the time of Xenocrates on, the belief in good and evil spirits became universal among Platonists.[2] Plotinus is no exception. Only, for him the existence of evil demons is hardly acceptable. But how should we interpret his belief in demons?

For everybody who denies that for Plato the gods of the Greeks were anything but myths it follows that he will also deny that Plato actually believed in demons (although remembering what we said about Greek beliefs in demons as 'natural' beings, we should admit the possibility of not believing in gods while believing in demons, just as a spiritist might be an atheist). Now the same could be said of Plotinus.

Xenocrates distinguished three kinds of demons. Some had simply always existed as demons. A second class consisted of souls of men which, after death had separated them from their bodies, became demons. And finally, Xenocrates also recognized demons in us identical with our soul. In so doing, he followed Plato, who, in the *Timaeus*,[3] explicitly equated the intelligence in us with a demon, whereas in other works he recognized the existence of demons outside us. Now, in Plotinus we find the same three classes of demons.[4] But we cannot take this to mean that he actually believed in demons only in the third of the meanings enumerated above, while otherwise speaking of demons in a purely mythical sense. What we know of his life should incline us to assume that he believed in the existence of demons in a quite literal sense of the word.[5]

Xenocrates' religious interests were not limited to demonology. He

[1] *Fr.* 23–5 Heinze.

[2] See T. Hopfner, *Griechisch-ägyptischer Offenbarungszauber*, 2 vols. (1921–4), esp. vol. I, pp. 10–26, 43 f.; also K. Svoboda, *La Démonologie de Michel Psellos* (1927). P. Boyancé, 'Les dieux de noms personnels dans l'antiquité gréco-latine', *Revue de Philologie*, LXI (1935), pp. 189–202, interprets Menander, *fr.* 714 Körte (κακὸν γὰρ δαίμον' οὐ νομιστέον εἶναι...) as protest of a pupil of Theophrastus against Xenocrates.

[3] 90 A.

[4] III 4 [15]; III 5 [50] 6; IV 3 [27] 18; IV 4 [28] 43; V 8 [31] 10; VI 7 [38] 6.

[5] Cf. *Enn.* II 1 [40] 6. P. Merlan, 'Plotinus and Magic', *Isis*, XLIV (1953), pp. 341–8.

identified a number of what we should consider abstract concepts (or merely conceptual entities) with divinities, and, accepting the Two-opposite-principles doctrine,[1] especially the One with Zeus, equal intelligence; the Dyad[2] with the mother of gods, equal cosmic soul.[3] It is not easy to see whether by so doing he tried to 'theologize' concepts or to 'conceptualize' gods. It is also striking that he in some way associated parts and elements of the universe with the Olympic divinities.[4] But, above all, the identification of the Indefinite Dyad with the cosmic soul is particularly interesting. It seems that at times Xenocrates, in his way, tried to mitigate the dualism of the two opposite principles by identifying one of them with intelligence, the other—subordinated to it—with the cosmic soul. In so doing he perhaps characterized the Indefinite Dyad as sheer receptivity (the female principle) rather than the principle of evil. Strangely enough, in Plutarch's *Isis and Osiris*[5] we find an Egyptian myth which, as he tells us, has also been interpreted by Eudoxus. According to this myth, the three fundamental principles are Osiris, Isis (sheer receptivity), and Typhon as the representative of evil. One wonders whether Eudoxus did not contribute to the intramural discussions concerning the relation of the two supreme principles to each other and to the problem of the omnipresence of evil if the Indefinite Dyad is identified with evil. As Eudoxus was most likely, in the Academy, the main source of the knowledge of both Egyptian religion and Zoroastrianism, it is reasonable to assume that he compared Plato's dualism of supreme principles with the religious dualism of Persia,[6] just as he compared it with Egyptian religion. In any case, by identifying (sometimes only?) the One with intelligence, and the Dyad with the soul,[7] Xenocrates, perhaps influenced by Eudoxus, belongs to those who prepared the subordination of the latter to the former. We shall see later that Plutarch also in his way, but perhaps under the influence of Xenocrates, separated the two rather sharply.

[1] *Fr.* 15; 28; 34 Heinze.

[2] *Fr.* 15 Heinze.

[3] We assume that this Dyad is actually identical with what Xenocrates otherwise called the Indefinite Dyad. For the opposite point of view see R. Heinze, *Xenokrates* (1892), p. 35 n. 1 and now particularly H. J. Krämer, *Der Ursprung der Geistmetaphysik* (1964), pp. 39–41.

[4] *Fr.* 15 Heinze.

[5] 45–60, 369 A–375 D.

[6] Aristotle did it as a matter of course: *Met.* N 4, 1091 b 10. Cf. Diog. Laert. *Pr.* 8 (*fr.* 6 Rose) and Eudemus, *fr.* 150 Wehrli.

[7] *Fr.* 15 Heinze.

In any case, the way in which Xenocrates equated divinities with abstract principles reminds us that this was done by Neoplatonists in general. It is virtually impossible to decide whether, as in the case of Xenocrates, we should speak of their 'detheologizing' the gods or 'theologizing' concepts.

H. *The problem of dialectic and of categories*

Almost from the very beginning of his literary activity,[1] Plato attached great importance to a particular kind of logic and discussion, viz. dialectic.[2] It seems that it is best described as a kind of non-formal logic, i.e. a logic which reveals the structure of reality. The relation between dialectic and rhetoric on the one hand, and particularly between dialectic and logic, as it was created by Aristotle, on the other, has been explicitly and implicitly stated by different authors in different ways. Very often dialectic and logic have been equated. Plotinus is still aware of the difference between the two and considers dialectic to be by far superior to formal logic. But he firmly connects dialectic with the Platonic theory of love.[3]

Another field related to logic in which the Academy seems to have become interested early was a system of categories which would permit a classification of everything that exists. One of such attempts is connected with the names of Xenocrates[4] and Hermodorus.[5] They divided existents into absolutely and relatively existing (a division already found in Plato but used by him only incidentally). Another we find in the so-called *Divisiones Aristoteleae*. In each case the next step is the subdivision of the category of the relatively existent. Speusippus approached the problem of categories in a different way—by a division of concepts rather than their objects, making use of the terms 'homonyms' and 'synonyms'.[6] Aristotle's *Categories* (again the genuineness of their first part was not questioned in the period here under consideration) apply both approaches. Though the category of the relative (*pros ti*) appears along with nine other categories, it is obvious that all nine

[1] At least if the usual chronology is correct, and the *Euthydemus* is early: 290C.

[2] *Rep.* VII; *Phaedrus* 265C–266D.

[3] *Rep.* VII 403C; *Enn.* I 3 [20].

[4] *Fr.* 12 Heinze.

[5] In Simpl. *In phys.* 247, 33 – 248, 20 Diels; cf. A. J. Festugière, *La Révélation d'Hermès Trismégiste*, IV (^{2}1954), pp. 307–14.

[6] *Fr.* 32A Lang.

are opposed to his first category, that of substance (entity, *ousia*),[1] in that only this entity, whether it means a first or a second substance (*ousia*), has a non-relative existence, while all the other nine are 'in', 'between' substances, 'conditions', or 'affections' of substances. In other words, these nine could be subsumed under a higher kind of relative being, of which the relative being within the nine categories would only be a special case. On the other hand, Aristotle uses precisely the terms used by Speusippus, viz. homonymy and synonymy (whether with precisely the same meaning does not concern us here).[2] Thus, from the point of view of content, the doctrine of categories is on the confines of the Academy and the Peripatos. But whatever the reason, it seems that Aristotle's little treatise very soon displaced all other Academic presentations and was considered almost the only one of its kind. Plotinus refused to accept any doctrine of categories which would apply the same concepts to the world of the intelligence and that of the sensible. When he developed his own doctrine of categories,[3] he applied Aristotelian categories only to the realm of the sensible. As categories of the world of the intellect, he applied the five genera of the *Sophist*. Porphyry did not follow Plotinus; nor did other Platonists. And we shall see later to what extent Aristotle's categories were controversial among predecessors of Plotinus.[4,5]

[1] *Anal. post.* I 22, 83b11; *Phys.* I 7, 190a34.

[2] On this problem see P. Merlan, 'Beiträge zur Geschichte des antiken Platonismus. I.', *Philologus*, LXXXIX (1934), pp. 35–53.

[3] *Enn.* VI 1–3 [42–4].

[4] In *Enn.* VI 7 [38] 4 we find objections to other aspects of Aristotle's logic (definition).

[5] It is worth mentioning that Plato's philosophy of *erôs* (as a strictly personal passion rooted in sex) is entirely neglected by Plotinus despite a passage like *Enn.* VI 7 [38] 33, 20–30 or *Enn.* III 5 [50] (on Eros). Cf. W. Theiler, 'Plotin zwischen Plato und Stoa', *Les Sources de Plotin, Entretiens*, V (1960), pp. 63–86 and R. Harder's contribution to the discussion, pp. 90, 92. Of the ascent imagery in Plato's *Symposium* Plotinus makes frequent use (*Enn.* I 6 [1]; I 3 [20]).

CHAPTER 3

ARISTOTLE

A. *Cosmology, Noetic and Psychology*

From the consideration of a writing which might have been Aristotelian but could equally well have been Academic, we now pass to doctrines undoubtedly belonging to Aristotle. We concentrate mainly on those which seem to have been particularly controversial between pre-Plotinian Platonists and Aristotelians and single out six concerning: psychology, cosmology, noetic, cosmogony, ideas, and matter, and add a few words on his ethics and some special points.

Though probably not from the beginning, Aristotle denied the substantial character of the soul and, therefore, any pre- or post-existence of it, any kind of incarnation or reincarnation (transmigration). He also objected to any kind of astral psychology, i.e. to any doctrine teaching either the existence of a cosmic soul[1] or the animation of celestial bodies. To those who did the latter he mockingly replied that the fate of a soul causing the rotatory motion of a celestial body by being present in it reminded him of the fate of Ixion.[2] How, then, did he explain these motions? We find three answers in his writings;[3] whether they are consistent will be left undecided. First, we find the notion that the circular movement of the celestial bodies is caused by their attraction to a being (or, if there were several independent motions, to beings) described by him as a changeless changer (or changeless changers), this circular movement being the way in which they could satisfy their attraction.[4] Secondly, he attributed the circular motion to the nature of

[1] *De an.* I 3, 406b25; *Met.* Λ 6, 1071b37.

[2] *De caelo* II 1, 284a35.

[3] Cf. P. Merlan, 'Ein Simplikios-Zitat bei Pseudo-Alexander und ein Plotinos-Zitat bei Simplikios', *Rheinisches Museum*, LXXXIV (1935), pp. 154–60; Idem, *Philologische Wochenschrift*, LVIII (1938), pp. 65–9, esp. 68 f.; W. K. C. Guthrie, *Aristotle's 'De Caelo'* (Loeb, 1939), pp. xxxi–xxxvi; H. Cherniss, *Aristotle's Criticism of Plato* (1944), vol. I, pp. 540–5; H. A. Wolfson, 'The Problem of the Souls of the Spheres from the Byzantine Commentaries on Aristotle through the Arabs and St Thomas to Kepler', *Dumbarton Oaks Papers*, XVI (1962), pp. 64–93; P. Moraux, 'quinta essentia', *RE*, XXIV/1, col. 1198–1204; 1208 f.

[4] *Met.* Λ 7, 1072a30.

the body of which they consist, viz. ether,[1] whose natural (physical) motion is circular, just as the natural motion of other elements is upwards and downwards.[2] His third explanation, that the celestial bodies[3] should be considered as animated,[4] seems strangely out of tune with his criticism of Plato on this very score.

For Aristotle's cosmology, the ether theory is of prime importance.[5] Ether constitutes the supra-lunar sphere of the divinely changeless.[6] But we must not forget that it might also have played an important part in his psychology and noetics. It is reported that he made *astra mentesque* consist of ether.[7] Not so very different is the identification of the uppermost heavens with god.[8] It seems now very likely that at some time he referred to the soul as *endelecheia* rather than *entelecheia*, and if soul consisted of ether, this would immediately explain why it is permanently moving. In other words, the ether theory would represent something like a materialistic (or, considering the very special character of Aristotle's ether, a semi-materialistic) tendency present in Aristotle.[9]

[1] Though the word appears in the *Epinomis* (981 C, 984 B), here ether is located between fire and air and has none of the other qualities which Aristotle attributes to it. But Xenocrates (*fr.* 53 Heinze) enumerates the five elements in an order (ether first, fire second) which seems to indicate that he thinks of ether in Aristotelian terms. Cf. P. Moraux, 'quinta essentia', *RE*, XXIV/1, col. 1187 f., 1191 f.

[2] *De caelo* I 2, 269 b 18.

[3] Be it the stars themselves, or their respective spheres; cf. Zeller, *Phil.* II/2 (⁴1921), p. 456 n. 1; but cf. p. 466.

[4] Cicero, *De nat. d.* II 44; Arist. *De caelo* II 1, 285 a 29; 12, 292 a 18.

[5] P. Moraux, 'quinta essentia', *RE*, XXIV/1 (1963), col. 1196–1231.

[6] *De caelo* I 3, 269 b 18–270 a 35; *Meteor.* I 3, 339 b 16–30.

[7] Cicero, *Academ.* I 26; 39; *Tusc.* I 22; 41; 65–7; *De nat. d.* I 33; cf. *De fin.* IV 12.

[8] Cicero, *Somnium* VI 17.

[9] It is usual to assume that Aristotle's maximum of concessions to materialism in psychology is his doctrine of the *pneuma*, and it is usual to assume that *pneuma* means only something like a peculiar kind of body (analogous to ether) in which the soul permanently resides or which is its organ (*De gen. anim.* II 3, 736 b 29–737 a 12; III 11, 762 a 18; cf. Zeller, *Phil.* II/2 [⁴1921], p. 483 n. 4; p. 569 n. 3; A. L. Peck, *Aristotle, De gen. anim.* [Loeb, 1943], Appendix B; P. Moraux, 'quinta essentia', *RE*, XXIV/1, col. 1205). But the possibility cannot be discounted that at some phase of his philosophic career Aristotle *identified* the soul with ether, thus explaining why it is permanently moved (*endelecheia*). It was particularly H. v. Arnim, *Entstehung der aristotelischen Gotteslehre* (1931), who asserted (p. 12) that there must have been a materialistic phase in Aristotle's psychology, as in a way was asserted before him by F. F. Kampe, *Die Erkenntnis-theorie des Aristoteles* (1878), pp. 12–49 (identification of pneuma, ether, soul). E. Bignone, *L'Aristotele perduto e la formazione filosofica di Epicuro*, 2 vols. (1936), vol. I, pp. 195–7; 227–72 is inclined to accept this theory; so was W. K. C. Guthrie, to change his mind as indicated in his edition of *Aristotle, De caelo* (Loeb, 1939), p. xxxii. But others reject it entirely (see, e.g., A. Mansion in F. Nuyens, *L'Évolution de la Psychologie d'Aristote* [1948], pp. xii–xiv; E. Berti, *La filosofia di primo Aristotele* (1962), pp. 392–401; H. J. Easterling, 'Quinta Natura', *Museum Helveticum*, XXI (1964), pp. 73–85; P. Moraux, *op. cit.* col. 1195, 1213–31). Much in the history of the Peripatos can better

Undoubtedly, ether was meant to replace the astral soul and be elevated to be the only cause of the circular movements of the celestial bodies; and it is reasonable to assume that at times, at least, it was also meant to replace (or to explain) the human soul.[1] Thus, acceptance or rejection of the ether theory had far-reaching consequences. Plotinus himself did not accept it; we shall see, later on, that in this he was preceded by some Platonists and Aristotelians, while others accepted it. But this, of course, imposed on him the duty of explaining how the celestial beings, composed as they are of soul and body, could remain eternal.[2] In any case, the problem of ether remained a live issue and not only in physics.[3]

The materialism or semi-materialism of Aristotle is less surprising if we remember that Heraclides (sometimes referred to as Aristotle's student, but in any case with him among the 'eligibles' to succeed Speusippus) also seems to have at least toyed with the idea of a corporeal soul: he defined it as possessing the nature of light and as an ethereal body.[4] He even spoke of the soul as a mere quality of the body.[5]

be understood if we side with Kampe and Arnim and take into account that the materialistic interpretation of Aristotle was in antiquity very frequent and started very early. Cf. W. Jaeger, 'Das Pneuma im Lykeion', *Scripta minora*, 2 vols. (1960), vol. 1, pp. 83 f.; P. Moraux, *op. cit.* col. 1206; 1213–26; 1233 f.; 1245 f.; 1248 f. However, the evidence in favour of their interpretation cannot be presented here. Cf. G. Luck, *Der Akademiker Antiochos* (1953), pp. 37–40.

[1] We cannot overlook the psychological materialism of the Pythagoreans of Alexander Polyhistor (Diog. Laert. VIII 28; see below, p. 88).

Very instructive is the discussion of another aspect of Aristotle's 'materialism' (blood as determining man's intelligence, sensitivity and character according to *De partibus anim.* B 2, 648a3–13) in F. Solmsen, 'Tissues and the Soul', *The Philosophical Review*, LXIX (1950), pp. 435–68, esp. pp. 466–8. Solmsen contrasts Aristotle with Plato—but does he not forget *Tim.* 86B–87B with its strangely materialistic interpretation of the 'nobody fails on purpose'? It is worthwhile to read the discussion of this passage in A. E. Taylor, *A Commentary on Plato's Timaeus* (1928), with his attempt to exonerate Plato by asserting that he only presents Pythagorean doctrine. I am not quite sure that F. M. Cornford, *Plato's Cosmology* (1937), succeeded in disproving the materialistic character of the passage. *In summa* therefore one could say: materialism emerges as a possibility within the orbit of both Platonism and Aristotelianism. But on the whole the *Timaeus* passage remains entirely isolated in the *corpus Platonicum* and also in later Platonism. On the other hand, Solmsen pays no attention to the discussion in Zeller, *Phil.* II/2 (⁴1921), p. 489 n. 2, with its references to other 'materialistic' passages in Aristotle (*De gen. anim.* II 6, 744a30; *De partibus anim.* II 4, 651a12; IV 10, 686b22; *De resp.* 13, 477a16; *De an.* II 9, 421a22). Zeller tries to transcend the alternative materialistic–immaterialistic. Cf. P. Moraux, 'quinta essentia', *RE*, XXIV/1 (1963), col. 1212 f.

[2] *Enn.* II 2 [14] 2; 3.

[3] Well aware of its paradoxical character Plotinus defends his own interpretation of quasi-matter (intelligible matter), present in the realm of intelligibles, by comparing it with Aristotle's concept of ether as σῶμα ἄυλον (*Enn.* II 5 [25] 3, 18).

[4] *Fr.* 98A–100 Wehrli.

[5] *Fr.* 72 Wehrli. We see the same problem emerging here, as emerges with regard to the relation between *pneuma*, or ether, and soul in Aristotle. That Heraclides should have been a materialist seemed so incredible that many asserted that the work in which it was expounded

This, of course, Plotinus would have rejected, though perhaps he might have accepted it as a description of the soul's astral body.[1]

Be it as it may, in addition to or instead of ether, Aristotle introduced the concept of the changeless changer as ultimate source of all movement, and this changer he called intelligence. The motions caused by him were primarily celestial motions; and as he assumed the existence of several independent celestial motions, he attributed them to a number of changeless changers.[2] Though Aristotle himself does not do it, it seems permissible to call all these changers intelligences.

Now, the concept of intelligence plays an all-important role in Aristotle's philosophy.[3] It appears mainly in two complexes, which we shall call the psychological and the theologico-astronomical.

It is somewhat surprising that after having denied the transcendence of ideas and the substantial character of the soul, introducing instead the concept of soul as immanent form of a living body (entelechy), Aristotle in his psychology introduces intelligence in terms clearly indicative of its transcendental nature with regard to the soul and, therefore, to man.[4] It is equally surprising that after having established the mortality of the soul, Aristotle proceeds to assert the immortality of the intelligence.[5] Unfortunately, his description of the nature and activity of intelligence is brief to the point of obscurity. He expects us to apply to it his ubiquitous terms of potentiality and actuality[6] and thus distinguish an intelligence which becomes everything from another which acts or activates everything (we shall refer to them as passive and active intelligence). Of this latter intelligence, he says that it is active permanently.[7] And its activity needs no bodily organ; it is, therefore,

(περὶ τῶν ἐν Ἅιδου) was not his; U. von Wilamowitz (*Der Glaube der Hellenen* [²1956], vol. II, p. 525 n. 1) thinks of the possibility that it was a dialogue in which the materialistic point of view of one of the characters was, in the long run, refuted by Heraclides. Cf. Wehrli's commentary *ad loc.*; P. Moraux, 'quinta essentia', *RE*, XXIV/1, col. 1194.

[1] *Enn.* IV 3 [27] 15.

[2] The difficulties following from the assumption of either a single changer or a plurality of them have been discussed by Theophrastus in his so-called *Metaphysical Fragment* 4–7 (see below, p. 108).

[3] W. Kranz, 'Platonica', *Philologus*, CII (1958), pp. 74–83, reminds us of a poem of the *Anthologia Palatina* (*Appendix Planudea*) XVI 330 reading: Νοῦς καὶ Ἀριστοτέλους ψυχή, τύπος ἀμφοτέρων εἷς.

[4] First introduced in *De an.* I 4, 408b25–30; next in II 2, 413b24–6; cf. Plotinus IV 7 [2] 8, 15.

[5] *De an.* III 5, 430a23.

[6] Zeller, *Phil.* II/2 (⁴1921), pp. 324f.

[7] *De an.* III 5, 430a22.

not bound to the body and is immortal. It enters man from without.[1]

Great as the role of intelligence is in the context of Aristotle's psychology, it is even greater within the context of his astronomy-theology. For the changeless changer of whom we spoke above is the supreme principle of the universe, or, in plainer language, god. The only object of his activity (intelligizing) is he himself; he is intelligence intelligizing itself.

The idea of an intelligence which is its own object is not foreign to other aspects of Aristotle's epistemology. More than once he enunciates the principle that, as far as immaterial objects are concerned, the act of their cognition is not different from them.[2]

As already indicated, some aspects of Aristotle's noetic are, as far as psychology is concerned, difficult to reconcile with some other of its aspects. The same is true in the context of Aristotle's ontology (or metaphysics). On the whole, the pair of concepts which is of fundamental importance to Aristotle is the pair 'form–matter'. And, as Aristotle usually presents it, these two are entirely correlative: no matter without form, no form without matter. Two things are, therefore, striking. First, when speaking of his supreme deity (changeless changer), Aristotle refers to him as pure (immaterial) form. But what is a form which is not a form of something? Secondly, when speaking of the intelligence which is 'separable' from the rest of the soul and from man and his body, Aristotle again leaves us with an entity for which the framework of his concepts otherwise does not provide: an immaterial entity. Did it pay to deny the existence of 'separate' ideas only to introduce a 'separate' (or 'separable') intellect?

In other words, in almost all its aspects Aristotle's noetic stands out against the rest of his philosophy and so poses a *prima facie* problem whether the two can be reconciled. Just for this reason—no matter whether and how we can solve the problem—it must attract the atten-

[1] *De gen. anim.* II 3, 736b28. I cannot here discuss the recent attempts to dissociate this passage from the doctrines in *De anima*. Cf. the commentaries on *De anima* by A. Trendelenburg (1877), R. D. Hicks (1907), G. Rodier (1900), and W. D. Ross (1961). Alexander Aphrodisias, as is well known, identified the νοῦς θύραθεν with active intelligence and god.

[2] *De an.* III 4, 430a3–5; *Met.* Λ 7, 1075a2–5.

tion of every reader of Aristotle.[1] And many a Platonist will be attracted to Aristotle's noetic precisely because of its Platonic flavour.[2]

But this noetic leaves us with one more problem. Is the intellect dealt with in his psychology identical with the intellect as which Aristotle describes the supreme deity? Or is the intellect, which in some way is present in man and survives him, only related to the god-intellect? These questions, for which even today no generally accepted answer has been found, were discussed already in pre-Plotinian times. We shall see this later in our discussion of Aristocles and Alexander Aphrodisias.

Aristotle's psychology, into which these two disparate entities, viz. the soul as mere entelechy of the body, and intelligence entering it from without and separable from it, were included, encounters difficult problems. After having rejected the notion that the soul is cause of motion by being self-moved,[3] Aristotle asserts that the soul, being form, is unmoved.[4] But if the soul is unmoved, i.e. changeless, how can sensation which seems clearly to imply the soul's passibility be explained?[5]

The difficulties increase as Aristotle tries to explain in what way intelligence participates in man's mental life. For, most certainly, intelligence is supposed to be impassible, and its activity is not bound up with the body as the soul's is.[6] How, then, can intelligizing (or whatever we call its activity, e.g. intuitive thinking) be explained? As far as activities like love and hatred, memory, and discursive thinking are concerned, Aristotle asserts that these activities are not activities of the intelligence but of man, the composite of intelligence, soul, and body.[7] It is especially impossible to attribute desire to intelligence, for desire is caused by fantasies—and fantasy is an activity presupposing a body. To

[1] The simplest explanation would, of course, be that, in Aristotle's writings as we read them today, Platonic and anti-Platonic passages occur side by side—either as a residue of his original adherence to Plato or as a revival of it. Cf. Zeller, *Phil.* II/2 (⁴1921), pp. 175 f. For a different explanation see, e.g., E. v. Ivánka, 'Zur Problematik der aristotelischen Seelenlehre', *Autour d'Aristote* (1955), pp. 245–53.

[2] Cf. Zeller, *Phil.* II/2 (⁴1921), p. 196.

[3] *De an.* I 3, 404a21; 4, 408a30; 5, 409b19; 3, 406b15; 2, 403b28.

[4] And, as is well known, according to him all movement is ultimately caused by that which is unmoved: *Met.* Λ 6, 1071b4.

[5] Zeller, *op. cit.* pp. 596 f.

[6] *De an.* III 4, 429a18–29.

[7] *De an.* I 4, 408a30–b24; *Phys.* VII 3, 246b1; 247a28.

a certain extent the difficulty is lessened by the assumption of a double intelligence, of which the lower part, the 'passible' ('passive') intelligence, is indeed considered to be changeable, to possess memory, etc.[1] But wherein, then, does its similarity to the higher 'acting' intelligence consist?

Furthermore, Aristotle's 'active' intelligence is quite obviously not individualized. But, on the other hand, Aristotle says that intelligence is man's true self.[2] And a particular problem emerges in connexion with memory. Does intelligence remember? Aristotle denies this explicitly;[3] but, if so, it is obvious that the survival of the intelligence implies no survival of the former life.

Now, it can safely be said: no other part of Aristotle's system attracted Plotinus more than its noetic in all its aspects.[4] With some over-simplification we can say: to his second hypostasis Plotinus applied a number of concepts taken over from Aristotle. Particularly important was the doctrine that immaterial entities (Aristotle's intelligibles, identified by Plotinus with ideas, though in addition to these there were still other intelligibles in Plotinus' system) are identical with the acts by which they are cognized.[5] In Plotinus this doctrine developed into the thesis that ideas do not subsist outside the intelligence.[6] At the same time, Plotinus identified Aristotle's god, a self-centred intelligence, with the second of his own hypostases[7] and very often with Plato's artificer.[8] These two identifications permitted him to keep the number of hypostases to three and so to do full justice to the 'trinity' in Plato's *2nd Letter*. But as, for Plotinus, undoubtedly the same intelligence which forms the second hypostasis is also man's intelligence,[9] the

[1] *De an.* III 5, 430a23.

[2] *Eth. Nic.* IX 4, 1166a16–22; X 7, 1178a7; 8, 1178b28; cf. Plotinus, *Enn.* V 3 [49] 3.

[3] *De an.* III 5, 430a23.

[4] To which also the epistemological belongs: see *Anal. post.* II 19, 100b8, which, however, interested Plotinus less than the other.

[5] Arist. *De an.* III 4, 430a3; 5, 430a19; 7, 431a1; *Met.* Λ 7, 1072b21; 9, 1075a2.

[6] *Enn.* V 3 [49] 5; V 5 [32] 1. He quotes the Aristotelian doctrine: II 5 [25] 3, 25–6; V 9 [5] 2, 22; VI 6 [34] 6, 20; VI 7 [38] 37, 3–5; VI 9 [9] 7–8. Cf. H.-R. Schwyzer, 'Plotinos', *RE*, XXI/1 (1951), col. 555; P. Merlan, *Monopsychism, Mysticism, Metaconsciousness* (1963), pp. 7–16; A. H. Armstrong, *The Architecture of the Intelligible Universe in the Philosophy of Plotinus* (1940), pp. 39 f.; idem, 'The Background of the Doctrine that the Intelligibles are not outside the Intellect', *Les Sources de Plotin, Entretiens*, V (1960), pp. 391–413, esp. pp. 406–end.

[7] *Enn.* II 2 [14] 3; II 9 [33] 1; V 9 [5] 5.

[8] *Enn.* V 9 [5] 3.

[9] *Enn.* IV 7 [2] 85, 15.

psychological and theological aspects of Aristotle's noetics blend in Plotinus.[1] However, having now to reconcile Aristotle's statement that active (divine) intelligence acts unintermittently (a statement which Plotinus quite obviously accepts) with the fact that this is not true of human intelligence, Plotinus introduces the concept of unconsciousness: even when in us, intelligence continues its uninterrupted activity, only we are not conscious of it.[2] For the second time, then, the concept of the unconscious appears (see above, p. 29), this time to meet an Aristotelian difficulty.

But there were some more difficulties inherent in Aristotle's psychology which Plotinus had to face. He treats them, however, from an angle different from that of Aristotle. This is the result of two facts. First, Plotinus entirely rejects the idea of the soul being entelechy, and at the same time, with much greater vehemence than Aristotle, he rejects the idea that the soul is passible,[3] because for Plotinus, as noted before, the soul, much more so than even for Plato, belongs to the realm of the intelligence, which is the realm of the changeless.[4] He tries to extricate himself from the difficulty sometimes by assuming a higher and a lower soul, only the latter being changeable;[5] sometimes by asserting that what is really present in the body is not the soul itself but only its image or trace.[6] Secondly, whereas in Aristotle, as already noticed, it is not entirely clear whether the intelligence of which he speaks in *De anima* is the same as the intelligence of which he speaks in *Metaphysics*, it is obvious for Plotinus that the intelligence operative in us is identical with the intelligence forming the second hypostasis.[7] But of course, in such a case, it is simply impossible to assume that intelligence in us should be changeable. How then does intelligence participate in man's mental life? One of the answers given by Plotinus is that all the changes taking place in such activities as sensing, desiring, etc., are

[1] While he denies of the One that it is intelligence or intelligizes (e.g. *Enn.* v 6 [24] 2; 4; 5) or that it is νοῦ ἐνέργεια (*ibid.* 6), he applies to it Aristotle's categories εἰς ὃ πάντα ἀνήρτηται and οὗ πάντα ἐφίεται (*Enn.* I 7 [54] 1); I 8 [51] 2; VI 7 [38] 34; VI 5 [23] 10.

[2] *Enn.* V 1 [10] 11. Cf. P. Merlan, *Monopsychism, Mysticism, Metaconsciousness* (1963), pp. 4–84.

[3] *Enn.* III 6 [26] 1–5.

[4] But even in Aristotle these difficulties are present: see Zeller, *Phil.* II/2 (^{4}1921), p. 600.

[5] I 1 [53] 3; IV 3 [27] 26–32.

[6] *Enn.* I 1 [53] 7–8; VI 2 [43] 22; VI 4 [22] 15.

[7] *Enn.* I 2 [19] 4; V 3 [49] 3; VI 2 [43] 20; 22; VI 7 [38] 13.

actually changes in the body, which intelligence simply 'notices'.[1] And even this 'noticing' is not something like a change in the intelligence; it is rather something like a changeless change.[2] We shall see later that a similar idea was suggested by Theophrastus.[3] It is ultimately rooted in the well-known distinction made by Aristotle between perfective and destructive change.[4]

And just as did Aristotle, Plotinus asks the question whether memory is the function of the composite of soul and body, to decide to attribute memory to the soul.[5] Therefore, to a certain extent at least, survival is personal.[6]

So much about Aristotle's cosmology, noetic, and psychology. Let us now turn to his cosmogony (cf. p. 29). Central to it is the assertion that the cosmos has no origin in time and is imperishable.[7] As he interprets Plato's *Timaeus*, Plato taught the opposite (though the cosmos will not actually perish due to the will of its creator). In other words, Aristotle takes the words 'it has come to be' literally. This doctrine of Plato Aristotle rejected most vehemently; not only did he consider it false, but, inasmuch as the temporal origin implies the possibility of an end, even impious.[8] Now, it seems that all first-generation pupils of Plato became convinced by Aristotle that the cosmos is eternal. But many, instead of admitting that Plato was wrong, preferred to disagree with Aristotle's interpretation of the text. 'It has come to be', they said, was not to be taken in any temporal sense; Plato only used temporal language for pedagogic purposes, translating into the language of a story what is timeless. Aristotle, however, remained unconvinced and insisted that only a literal interpretation was possible.[9]

As we shall see, very many Platonists[10] accepted this or a similar kind

[1] *Enn.* I 1 [53] 6; 7; III 6 [26] 1; 2; IV 4 [28] 18; 19; 23. Cf. Zeller, *Phil.* III/2 (⁵1923), pp. 636–40.

[2] III 6 [26] 2; cf. I 1 [53] 13.

[3] Cf. pp. 109 f.

[4] *De an.* II 5, 417b2; III 5, 429b22; 7, 431a5.

[5] *Enn.* IV 3 [27] 26–32; IV 4 [28] 5; IV 6 [41] 3.

[6] Aristotle seems to deny personal survival in *De an.* III 5, 430a23. However, the interpretation of this passage is not certain: cf. Zeller, *Phil.* II/2 (⁵1921), p. 574 n. 3 and p. 604 n. 4. Much clearer is another passage (*De an.* I 4, 408b25–30), where the *nous* is explicitly exempt from διανοεῖσθαι, φιλεῖν, μισεῖν, and μνημονεύειν—all these activities belonging to man as a composite being, after whose death the *nous* therefore is no longer involved with any of them.

[7] *De caelo* I 10, 280a28; IV 2, 300b16; *Phys.* VIII 1, 251b17; *Met.* Λ 3, 1071b31–7.

[8] *Fr.* 18 Rose.

[9] *De caelo* I 10, 279b22.

[10] Among them Plotinus: *Enn.* II 1 [40] 1–4; II 9 [33] 3; III 2 [47] 1; IV 3 [27] 9; VI 7 [38].

of interpretation of Plato, or professed the eternity of the cosmos as their own doctrine.[1] By so doing, they established the concept of a non-temporal 'process'. It was easy for Plotinus to adapt this concept to his interpretation of the emanative process constituting the hypostases—ultimately even the hypostasis of the sensible world. We shall see later that a number of other interpretations were suggested, all having in common the denial that *gegone* was used by Plato literally.

It is striking that Aristotle refused even to recognize that, when Pythagoreans and Platonists spoke of derivation of numbers (mathematicals) from supreme principles, they did so only *didaskalias charin* (or *theôrêsai heneken*). He insisted that they could not have meant anything but genesis in the temporal sense of the word—because they, after all, spoke of the origin of the cosmos and *qua* physicists.[2]

Just as he did in matters of cosmogony, so Aristotle convinced many Platonists as to the theory of ideas. Whereas Plato seems to have continued professing it,[3] Speusippus[4] abandoned it.[5] They, however, replaced ideas by mathematicals (or identified the two), while Aristotle replaced them by immanent forms. In any case, the theory of ideas after the death of Plato seems to have played no major role in Platonism before the time of Antiochus (see below, p. 54). When it re-emerged, it often concentrated on the problem of defining ideas and determining of what Plato assumed ideas. In both respects a sentence of Xeno-

[1] Xenocrates, *fr.* 54. 68 Heinze (cf. p. 71 n. 2 of his Introduction); Crantor and Eudorus in Plutarch, *De an. pr.* 3, p. 1013 A–B; Taurus in Philop. *De aet. m.* VI 8, 21, 27, pp. 145–7, 186–9, 223 Rabe. Theophrastus discussed such an interpretation of Plato, but rejected it (*fr.* 28; 29 Wimmer); he himself professed the eternity of the cosmos. This was also the position of Alexander Aphrodisias in Philop. *De aet. m.* VI 27, pp. 213–16 Rabe. Plutarch, *De an. pr.* ch. 3–10, 1013 A–1022 E (see below, p. 59), and Atticus in Eus. *PE* XV 6 insisted on the literal interpretation; they, at the same time, professed the doctrine of the temporal origin of the cosmos as their own. With them sided Galenus (*Compendium Timaei Platonis*, ed. P. Kraus and R. Walzer [1951]). Cf. C. Baeumker, 'Die Ewigkeit der Welt bei Plato', *Philosophische Monatshefte*, XXIII (1887), pp. 513–29; A.-J. Festugière, 'Le Compendium Timaei de Galien', *Revue des Études grecques*, LXV (1952), pp. 97–116, esp. pp. 101–3. For a survey of modern interpretations, see W. Spoerri, 'Encore Platon et l'Orient', *Revue de Philologie*, XXXI (1957), pp. 209–33, esp. p. 225 n. 44.

[2] *Met.* M 3, 1091 a 12; *De caelo* I 10, 279 b 32; cf. P. Lang, *De Speusippi Academici scriptis* (1911), pp. 30–2.

[3] Cf. P. Merlan, 'Form and Content in Plato's Philosophy', *Journal of the History of Ideas*, VIII (1947), pp. 406–30, esp. p. 412 n. 24.

[4] *Fr.* 42 E Lang.

[5] Why they did so need not be discussed here.

crates[1] provided an answer: ideas, he said, are eternal paradigms (probably meaning: paradigmatic causes) of everything that is natural. Such a definition seemed to exclude any interpretation of ideas as mere concepts, and also implied that there were no ideas of what is unnatural (disease, etc.) or of artefacts. It was easily reconcilable with the doctrines of the *Timaeus* and could lead to a presentation of Plato according to which he taught a triad of supreme principles, viz. God, ideas, and matter. This, of course, would amount to presenting a philosophic system very much different from the Two-opposite-principles doctrine.

And now, some other points.

B. '*Dynamis–Energeia*', *etc.*

For Aristotle the couple *dynamis–energeia* is of fundamental importance, particularly to replace the Two-opposite-principles doctrine. Opposites, he insists, cannot act on opposites. Therefore the concept of the Indefinite Dyad,[2] which itself is one of the opposites, must be replaced by the concept of matter as something underlying the opposites.[3] Matter, in other words, is potentially that which it can actually become, for example A or non-A. Thus it is never sheer negation or sheer indefiniteness; it is always determined negation or indefiniteness.[4]

Plotinus does not have much use for either of the two concepts of actuality and potentiality. Matter, as he sees it, is not a relative concept as it is in Aristotle (whose concept of prime matter is only a *Grenzbegriff*);[5] only in a very special sense can it be called *dynamei* because in truth matter can never become anything and remains unaffected.[6] This is about the opposite of what Aristotle attributes to matter and much closer to Plato's concept of space (comparable to a mirror or a screen).

In addition, Plotinus is more careful than Aristotle to distinguish between potency as power (*dynamis*) and potency as weakness, viz.

[1] *Fr.* 30 Heinze, probably from the period when he still professed that theory.

[2] Taken by Aristotle to have been introduced by Plato to perform the same function as his (Aristotle's) concept of matter, viz. to explain becoming: *De caelo* III 8, 306b17.

[3] *Met.* Λ 10, 1075a32; N 4, 1091b30; *Phys.* I 9, 192a6.

[4] *Phys.* I, 6–10; *Met.* Λ 2, 1069b9–34; 4, 1070b11, 18; 5, 1071a8.

[5] *Phys.* III 5, 204b32; *De gen. et corr.* II 1, 329a8, 24; I 5, 320b12; cf. Zeller, *Phil.* II/2 (^{4}1921), p. 320 n. 2. Cf. the discussion in C. Baeumker, *Das Problem der Materie in der griechischen Philosophie* (1890), pp. 247–61.

[6] *Enn.* II 5 [25] and III 6 [26].

something not yet realized, whereas Aristotle often does not distinguish between these two meanings; and Plotinus, furthermore, prefers to refer to something actual as an *energeia* rather than *energeiai* (with an iota *adscriptum*) *on*.[1]

Ultimately, Plotinus' relative lack of interest in the above-mentioned pair stems from the fact that Aristotle introduced it to account for the problem of becoming in the sphere of the physical, to which problem Plotinus devotes hardly any attention. Still, Plotinus on the whole (but cf. p. 32 n. 2) accepts Aristotle's assertion[2] that energy always precedes potency (potentiality). And he uses the concept of *energeia* in a highly significant manner to describe the nature of the One.[3]

However, we know that Aristotle himself was ready to treat the concept of matter in an analogical way: the genus is matter for the species, the 'lower' of the five elements matter for the 'higher', the female is matter for the male.[4] With this use of the concept of matter Plotinus obviously agrees, when he, for example, speaks of the soul as matter of intelligence.[5]

Potentiality and actuality in Aristotle's philosophy are often identical with form and matter. And this latter pair of concepts Plotinus uses constantly and unhesitatingly.[6]

Of other metaphysical concepts of Aristotle, the principle that there are beings in whom essence and being coincide[7] is of considerable importance for Plotinus, when he tries to describe the nature of the One.[8]

C. *Ethics*

Aristotle's ethics exhibits three main aspects. It distinguishes perfections of character (ethical perfections), which consist in subordinating the unreasonable part of the soul (passion) to the rule of reason, from

[1] Cf. V 9 [5] 4, 12 and IV 8 [6] 3 on the one hand; IV 4 [28] 18–27 and III 6 [26] 1–5 on the other. Zeller, *Phil.* II/1 (⁴1921), p. 320 n. 1; p. 321 n. 1. Cf. above, p. 46, n. 1.

[2] *Met.* Θ 8, 1049b5; IV 7 [2] 8; II 5 [25] 3; V 9 [5] 4; V 1 [42] 26.

[3] *Enn.* VI 8 [39] 20.

[4] *Met.* Λ 4, 1070b17; 5, 1071a3, 25; *De caelo* IV 3, 310b15; 4, 312a12; *De gen. et corr.* I 3, 318b32; II 8, 335a16; *De gen. anim.* I 2, 716a7; II 1, 732a5; 4, 738b20, etc.; *Met.* A 6, 988a5; Δ 28, 1024a35.

[5] E.g. *Enn.* II 5 [25] 3, 10; III 9 [13] 5.

[6] On the whole section, cf. C. Rutten, 'La doctrine de deux actes dans la philosophie de Plotin', *Revue Philosophique*, LXXXI (1956), pp. 100–6.

[7] *Met.* Z 6, 1031a32. Cf. I 1 [53] 2, 12.

[8] *Enn.* VI 8 [39] 14.

perfections of the intelligence,[1] the activity of which consists in contemplation[2]—either of truth or of God.[3] This contemplation is accompanied by pleasure (joy), as is every unimpeded exercise of a natural faculty (in this case, of intelligence). And though happiness essentially depends on perfection, external goods are to a certain extent indispensable.[4]

For Plotinus, perfections are above all means of purification (i.e. the soul turning away from the body), this purification leading ultimately to man becoming godlike, or as Plotinus says, god.[5] Happiness for him consists in living the life of reason, which is the perfect life, and this life is accompanied by pleasure (joy) *sui generis* (*hêdy*, *hileôn*). This life of reason is actually the very essence of man, for the true ('higher') man is his intelligence.[6] To this extent Plotinus agrees with Aristotle. But he rejects the assertion that happiness should depend on external goods.[7] He also criticizes his concept of perfection, as it always includes passion (subdued by reason) and prefers to identify perfection with intelligence alone.[8] Only lower (social) perfections moderate passions.[9] In other words, in some respects he sides with the Stoa rather than with Aristotle (see below, p. 130); in certain ways even with the Kepos, in that he denies that supreme pleasure (joy) is becoming,[10] or that happiness increases with temporal duration.[11] He even agrees with the famous Epicurean assertion that the sage will be happy even when undergoing tortures; he only denies that Epicurus has a right to assert this, as he does not distinguish between the 'higher' man for whom the assertion holds and the 'lower' for whom it does not.[12]

D. *Being* qua *being*

One more aspect of Aristotle's doctrines must be presented. In defining what he calls first philosophy, Aristotle seems to determine its subject-matter in at least two different ways. Sometimes he says that it is the divine, sometimes that it is being *qua* being. Among modern

[1] Dianoetic perfections; *Eth. Nic.* II 1, 1103a14–b 2.
[2] *Eth. Nic.* X 7, 1177a12–1178a8.
[3] The divine: VI 7, 1141a18–b3.
[4] *Eth. Nic.* X 8, 1178a23–4.
[5] *Enn.* I 1 [53] 2; 3; 6; 7; I 6 [1] 6.
[6] *Enn.* I 4 [46] 4; 9.
[7] *Enn.* I 4 [46] 6.
[8] *Enn.* VI 8 [39] 6.
[9] *Enn.* I 2 [19] 2.
[10] *Enn.* I 4 [46] 12.
[11] *Enn.* I 5 [36].
[12] *Enn.* I 4 [46] 13.

interpreters of Aristotle there is much dissension as to whether these two designations can be reconciled, and, if so, in what way.[1] But it does not seem that this was ever a problem for the ancient readers of Aristotle up to the time of Plotinus. In some way, all seem to assume that being *qua* being does not designate something that is common to everything that exists in the sense of 'common' in which we usually take it. To be is not, in this case, something which can be said of the divine as well as of anything else that is not nothing. To translate this into modern terms: the ancient readers of Aristotle do not seem to distinguish between being *qua* being and the divine by assuming that the former refers to something that later was called *metaphysica generalis*, while the latter would refer to a *metaphysica specialis* (dealing with God, but not with everything that is). Thus, when Aristotle speaks of being *qua* being, ancient readers up to the time of Plotinus seem to take this to mean: only of God can it be said that he is, whereas everything else is not only being but also becoming. Right or wrong, they seem to take the phrase 'being as being' as a kind of definition of the divinity.[2] Therefore, they do not see any essential difference between Plato and Aristotle in this respect.

Thus, on the whole, Plotinus took over from Aristotle some very important doctrines. But he remained critical of him.[3]

[1] See, e.g., P. Merlan, *From Platonism to Neoplatonism* (²1960), pp. 160–220; V. Décarie, *L'Objet de la Métaphysique selon Aristote* (1961); J. Owens, *The Doctrine of Being in the Aristotelian Metaphysics* (²1963).

[2] This can be seen particularly in Syrianus: *In Met.* 5, 9–27; 54, 24–55, 33 Kroll; Asclepius, *In Met.* 361, 28–32 Hayd. See K. Kremer, *Der Metaphysikbegriff in den Aristoteles-Kommentaren der Ammonius-Schule* (1961), pp. 211 f.

[3] Cf. K. A. H. Steinhart, *Meletemata Plotiniana* (1840), esp. pp. 24–35 (*Plotinus Aristotelis et interpres et adversarius*). Steinhart especially investigates: *Enn.* VI 1 [42] 3 (against the doctrine of categories); IV 5 [29] (on Aristotle's theory of vision); IV 6 [41] (on Aristotle's doctrine of memory); III 7 [45] (on Aristotle's 'subjectivistic' theory of time) and I 4 [46] (on happiness). According to Bréhier's index, Plotinus quotes *Categories*, *De anima*, *Physics*, *Metaphysics*, *Nicomachean Ethics*, *De gen. et corr.*, *Meteorologica*, *De partibus animalium*; H.-R. Schwyzer, 'Plotinos', *RE*, XXI/1 (1951), col. 572, adds *De caelo*.

CHAPTER 4

THE LATER ACADEMY AND PLATONISM

A. *Antiochus and other Platonists of the first century* B.C.

Speusippus, Xenocrates, Polemo, and Crates were the successive heads of the Academy. It seems that the successor of Crates, Arcesilaus (fourth/third century), completely changed its character, teaching a kind of non-dogmatic, Socratic, in some sense of the word, sceptical Platonism.[1] This sceptical phase (it continued under Carneades and Philo of Larissa, first century B.C.) seems to have exercised very little influence on later Platonists. A return to dogmatism, from which Platonists from then on never deviated,[2] was initiated by Philo's successor, Antiochus of Ascalon (b. *c.* 130–120, d. *c.* 68 B.C.), one of Cicero's teachers.[3] Convinced that the Stoic philosophy was essentially derived from the Old Academy, that Aristotle, in at least one phase of his activity, was a Platonist, and that the Peripatos (which, according to him, originated only after the death of Speusippus), though it modified particularly Plato's ethics, was essentially identical with the Academy,[4] Antiochus incorporated many of their teachings in his own system; and this eclecticism, according to many scholars, paved the way for the Neoplatonic one. But it does not seem that he had any use for the Platonic Two-opposite-principles doctrine. In other words, his return to the Academy did not mean that he returned to all of its teachings.

Where did he stand on the theory of ideas? Speusippus, in some way

[1] There are some traces (e.g. Cicero, *Lucullus* 60) that scepticism was not the last word of Arcesilaus (see, e.g., O. Gigon, 'Zur Geschichte der sogenannten Neuen Akademie', *Museum Helveticum*, I [1944], pp. 47–64). But the traces (the strangest: the classification of gods, attributed to him and compared with that of Xenocrates, by Tertullian, *Ad nat.* II 2, p. 97 Wiss.; cf. R. Heinze, *Xenokrates* [1892], pp. 155 f.) are too faint to make it certain that his scepticism was ultimately in the service of dogmatism.

[2] Though a semi-Platonist like Philo of Alexandria makes occasional use of sceptic arguments (*Ebr.* chs. 41–9, 166–205), to recommend ἐποχή.

[3] On him in general, see A. Lueder, *Die philosophische Persönlichkeit des Antiochos von Askalon* (1940); G. Luck, *Der Akademiker Antiochos* (1953), with collection of fragments; K. Reinhardt, 'Posidonios', *RE*, XXII/1 (1953), col. 618–20, esp. col. 820 f.; M. Pohlenz, *Die Stoa* (²1959, 1955), I, pp. 208–38; II, pp. 104–22. On him specifically as a precursor of Neoplatonism: W. Theiler, *Die Vorbereitung des Neuplatonismus* (1930), pp. 34–55; Pohlenz, *op. cit.* I, pp. 391 f.; II, p. 190.

[4] Cicero, *Acad. post.* I 17; 22; *Lucullus* 15; 136; *De finibus* V 7; 14; 21; IV 5; *De legibus* I 38 f.

Xenocrates, and Aristotle had at a certain moment of their careers abandoned it. But Antiochus blames Aristotle for having 'weakened' it,[1] and indeed seems to have adopted it.[2] But he did so with considerable modifications. First of all, as he denied any radical difference between intelligence and the senses (despite 30–1 with its assertion that only *mens* is *rerum index*, because only *mens* can perceive ideas; see *Lucullus* 30: *mens ipsa sensus*), obviously ideas could not retain their paramount importance[3] nor their transcendent status despite the fact that their knowledge was still considered the prerogative of intelligence. Perhaps he identified them with the common notions of the Stoics,[4] helped by a certain ambiguity of the latter term. 'Common notions' may mean either inborn notions (and in this sense the phrase was used by Cicero, according to whom, in matters of theology and moral standards, all men are born with the same notions) or notions which all men cannot help forming on the basis of their sense-experiences. Probably Antiochus' ideas had something of both of these qualities. This, of course, would considerably weaken the importance of anamnesis; either everybody would, by and by, acquire the knowledge of ideas or he would have to remember them in the sense of ordinary recollection of what he knew at his birth but has now forgotten.[5]

To this modification he may have added another. It is possible that Antiochus tried to reconcile Aristotle's concept of immanent forms with Plato's concept of transcendent ideas. Surprisingly, in a singular passage, even Aristotle himself, in enumerating his four causes, adds a fifth, the paradigmatic cause, as if he had never criticized Plato's theory of ideas.[6] Thus, the formal cause which quite obviously was meant to replace Plato's idea was juxtaposed with it. Later Platonists (e.g. Albinus; see below, p. 65) operate with a five-causes series without any hesitation, thus reconciling Plato with Aristotle even as far as idea theory is concerned. Whatever the basis of this interpretation, it is

[1] Cicero, *Acad. post.* I 33.

[2] Cicero, *Acad. post.* I 30. So cf. Luck, p. 28; Theiler, pp. 40 f. For the opposite point of view see C. J. de Vogel, *Greek Philosophy* (1959), III, 1200 with notes.

[3] Cicero, *De finibus* IV 42.

[4] H. Strache, *Der Eklektizismus des Antiochos von Askalon* (1921), pp. 12 ff.; W. Theiler, *Die Vorbereitung des Neuplatonismus* (1930), p. 41. Ideas = thoughts: *SVF* I 65.

[5] Cf. *Lucullus* 21 f. as opposed to *Tusc. Disp.* I 57.

[6] *Phys.* II 3, 144b23.

possible that this reconciliation was started by Antiochus.[1] Its clearest expression can be found in Seneca. To explain the term idea (which he defines in terms of Xenocrates, *fr.* 30 Heinze), Seneca says that the form of the statue exists first in the mind of the artificer, secondly in the matter of the statue,[2] and he suggests the use of idea for the former, *eidos* for the latter.

At the same time, this way of explaining what is meant by an idea turns our attention to the fact that we have here a third modification of the idea theory. Ideas are thought of as existing in the mind of the artificer. According to Seneca's example, the artificer is human. But the same Seneca says that ideas are paradigms of everything, and that they subsist in God's mind.[3] Thus, Antiochus might have initiated the doctrine of ideas as God's thoughts.

A stronger proof that the reduction of ideas to (divine) thoughts was begun by Antiochus is provided by Cicero's interpretation of the difference between ideal and actual rhetoric, in the course of which the statement occurs that in the *mens* of the *artifex* is present the *species pulchritudinis*, which is only imperfectly expressed in the actual work of art.[4] It is difficult to give Cicero credit for this un-Platonic theory of art, and it is not impossible, though by no means certain, that it was originated by Antiochus.[5]

In Plotinus the doctrine of ideas plays a much less prominent role than in Plato. He deals with it *ex professo* mainly from two points of view: to deny that they exist outside intelligence,[6] and to assert that there are ideas of singulars.[7] For the first point of view Antiochus

[1] On its roots in Plato, see W. Theiler, *Die Vorbereitung des Neuplatonismus* (1930), p. 11.

[2] *Ep.* 58, 21; cf. *Ep.* 65, 7.

[3] *Ep.* 65, 7. On these two letters see E. Bickel, 'Seneca's Briefe 58 und 65', *Rheinisches Museum*, CIII (1960), pp. 1–20. He, however, asserts that the source of Seneca is Posidonius, *via* Annaeus Amicus (*Ep.* 58, 8—here read *Amicus*, not *amicus*; 77, 6), who used to work with Posidonius. He thus contradicts W. Theiler, *Die Vorbereitung des Neuplatonismus* (1930), pp. 15–55, esp. p. 36. Cf. also E. Norden, *Agnostos Theos* (1913), p. 348.

[4] *Orator* 7; cf. 101. Elsa Birmelin, 'Die kunsttheoretischen Gedanken in Philostrats Apollonios', *Philologus*, LXXXVIII (N.F. XLII), 1933, pp. 149–80, 392–414, esp. pp. 402–6; W. Theiler, *Die Vorbereitung des Neuplatonismus* (1930), p. 17; E. Panofsky, *Idea* (²1960), pp. 10 f.

[5] Varro seems to have interpreted the origin of Athena = insight out of the head of Zeus in this sense (*fr.* XV 4, p. 188 Agahd = August. *De Civ. dei* VII 28); cf. Theiler, p. 19, but also M. Pohlenz, *Die Stoa* (²1959, 1955), II, p. 132. Cf. J. M. Rist, *Eros and Psyche* (1964), pp. 61–6; J. H. Waszink, 'Bemerkungen zum Einfluss des Platonismus im frühen Christentum', *Vigiliae Christianae*, XIX (1965), pp. 129–62, esp. p. 139 n. 21.

[6] *Enn.* V 5 [32].

[7] *Enn.* V 7 [18] despite *Enn.* V 9 [5] 12, 3.

seems to provide us with an appropriate background. The second seems to be entirely original with Plotinus (but see below on Albinus). It is characteristic that in this context he adopts the Stoic doctrine of periodic destructions of the cosmos. As to anamnesis, Plotinus in favour of the doctrine of the unconscious virtually denies it.[1]

Did Antiochus believe in the existence of ether? Did he believe that it is the stuff of which not only stars but also souls (intelligences) consist? No clear answer can be found in our texts. He notices, without criticism, that Aristotle professed such a doctrine,[2] and that the Stoics rejected ether,[3] and he refers to it as a much debated question.[4] It is obvious that any theory making the soul (or intelligence) a material or even semi-material entity must have been anathema for Plotinus. He rejected the ether theory even in physics; but by now we know that, by so doing, he rejected it *a fortiori* in psychology.

Other aspects of Antiochus' philosophy could hardly have been of interest to Plotinus. Antiochus based his ethics on the concept of self-preservation.[5] This imposed the duty on him of explaining what he meant by the self. And Antiochus answered by pointing out that man consists of both soul and body, so that no matter which of the two is superior, self-preservation meant preservation of both.[6] This kind of anthropology could not have been attractive to the man who gave the impression that he was ashamed of having a body, and taught that only intelligence is man's true self.[7] Furthermore, Antiochus insisted that from the very beginning man's self was a social self;[8] his system of ethics was, therefore, a system of individual and social ethics. Above all, he derived the moral standard from nature.[9] These aspects of the doctrines of Antiochus could hardly attract Plotinus either. The same is true of Arius Didymus, who, though a Stoic, professed doctrines essentially identical with those of Antiochus.[10]

[1] *Enn.* I 2 [19] 4, 18–27; IV 3 [27] 25, 30–45; despite V 9 [9] 5.
[2] Cicero, *Acad. post.* I 26.
[3] *Ibid.* 39.
[4] *De finibus* IV 12.
[5] *Ibid.* IV 3–18; V 24–33.
[6] *Ibid.* 34–75.
[7] Porphyry, *Life of Plotinus*, ch. 1; *Enn.* V 3 [49] 1–5. Cf. P. Merlan, *Monopsychism, Mysticism, Metaconsciousness* (1963), pp. 77–81.
[8] *De finibus* V 65–7; *Acad. post.* I 21; cf. Zeller, *Phil.* III/2 (⁵1923), p. 629 n. 1.
[9] *De finibus* V 26. Cf. *Enn.* I, 4 [46] 14; 16, with its insistence that man is not a συναμφότερον of body and soul; this could be directed against Antiochus; against all attempts to derive standards from nature, see *ibid.* 1.
[10] Zeller, *Phil.* III/2 (⁵1923), pp. 636–9.

However, there was one aspect of the doctrine of self-preservation which could have appealed to Plotinus. Antiochus granted a self not only to man and beast, but even to plants. In so doing he was obviously influenced by Stoic monism and pantheism. Plotinus explicitly included plants in his schema of pananimism,[1] though he was not sure whether to derive plant life from the animated earth rather than from their own soul.[2] It could be that Antiochus (rather than Posidonius; see p. 128) inspired him with this idea.

But we should not overlook the possibility that in the first century B.C. there might have been Platonists who represented a point of view different from either that of the New Academy or that of Antiochus. Such Platonism seems to have found its expression in the source of Cicero's *Tusculan Disputations*, Book I.[3] On the whole, this Platonism is strictly dualistic (51), and knowledge through senses is thoroughly depreciated (46). Philosophy is preparing for death (74 f.); death is not to be feared, if or because the soul is immortal (41; 51; 21; 25). Belief in immortality, i.e. immortality of the intelligence (*mens*) alone (20; 80), first thought of by Pherecydes and his pupil, Pythagoras (38), is one of the hall-marks of Plato's philosophy (in comparison with which all other systems are of no consequence: 55; 79). The Platonist is at the same time a great admirer of Aristotle (22)—obviously the Aristotle *exotericus* (94; 114), and thus he remains indifferent to the problems of whether the soul consists of ether or *pneuma* or is immaterial (60; 65; 70), whether the cosmos had an origin in time or not, whether God is an effector or only a moderator of it.[4] In this kind of Platonism there is much that would have had a strong appeal to Plotinus. If it represents a Platonist unknown to us rather than Cicero's free composition, it

[1] *Enn.* IV 7 [2] 8⁵.   [2] *Enn.* IV 4 [28] 22.

[3] Whether this source was Posidonius or Antiochus is one of the major controversies in contemporary scholarship. From my review of its contents in the text, it will be seen, I trust, why I can accept neither of these two hypotheses. For the former, it is too contemptuous of the Stoa (55, 79 f.); for the latter, too dualistic and ascetic. This leaves it possible that some ideas are derived from Antiochus (e.g. the exceptional praise of memory [57]; see above, p. 54), others from Posidonius (e.g. the history of civilization [62]). Also, Crantor, whose *On Grief* was the model for Cicero's *Consolation*, might have contributed much. Cf. O. Gigon, 'Die Erneuerung der Philosophie in der Zeit Ciceros', *Entretiens Hardt*, III (1955), pp. 23–59, esp. pp. 51 ff.

[4] He equates intelligence with ether and once more uses the term *endelecheia* (*continuata motio et perennis*); once more souls and gods consist of ether (41, 56); a particular problem is posed by the formula *sensus communis* (46) as applied to intelligence (*mens*). Could this refer to Aristotle's doctrine of the unicity of intelligence rather than to the κοινὸν αἰσθητήριον of *De anima*?

would be a reminder that much in the history of Platonism may have been lost, and that we cannot hope to draw a full picture of its pre-Plotinian aspects.[1]

One more work by Cicero deserves special mention: the *Somnium Scipionis*. A strong case was made out for Antiochus as its source.[2] It is particularly the elevation of the life of action, i.e. of statesmanship, to a status guaranteeing the statesman the same immortality which a life of contemplation promises, which makes us think of Antiochus. Other passages, particularly the formula 'our life is actually death', the depreciation of glory, the stress on the puniness of the earth, etc., seem to many scholars to betray the influence of Posidonius. It seems most likely that we have before us a rather personal combination of Antiochus, Posidonius, Crantor, and Cicero, to much of which Plotinus would have remained indifferent.

B. *Plutarch and Taurus*

Of Antiochus' successors to the scholarchate (Aristus and Theomnestus) we know next to nothing. But the name of the scholarch (?) at the time of Nero and Vespasian, that of the Egyptian (!) Ammonius of Alexandria, has been immortalized by his student, Plutarch of Chaeronea (from *c*. 50 to *c*. 120 or later). He was obviously in sympathy with the 'orientalizing' and particularly 'Egyptianizing' tendencies of the Old Academy; under his influence Plutarch devoted his *On Isis and Osiris* to an interpretation of Egyptian myths and cults to find in them much philosophic wisdom, in fact, the main features of Plato's philosophy, and made Pythagoras, Plato, and Eudoxus students of 'barbaric' wisdom.[3]

If we now assume that Plutarch's writings, at least partly, not only express his own views but also reflect the interests of the Academy, some points deserve our attention.

[1] In this context it is appropriate to note that Cicero is the first author who mentions the Platonic *Letters*, and that he is still familiar with the Aristotle *exotericus*—much more so than with the *esotericus* (in fact, it is virtually certain that his *Hortensius* was patterned on Aristotle's *Protrepticus*).

[2] G. Luck, 'Studia divina in vita humana. On Cicero's Dream of Scipio and its Place in Graeco-Roman Philosophy', *Harvard Theological Review*, XLIX (1956), pp. 207–18.

[3] *De Is. et Os.* 10, 354E–F. One is reminded of Plotinus' recognition of the wisdom of the hieroglyphic script: *Enn.* V 8 [31] 6.

Plutarch is familiar with both the Aristotle *esotericus* and *exotericus*. He seems to have written on his *Categories* and on the *Topics*.[1] He objects to *De caelo* when it teaches the uniqueness of the cosmos[2] and, on the other hand, at times at least, accepts the existence of ether as a fifth element, not simply identical with fire,[3] on which he even wrote a special essay.[4] He also refers and objects to Aristotle's self-centred god of *Met.* Λ.[5] He is also familiar with the fact that Aristotle, in a number of his writings, criticized the idea theory,[6] but he also seems to know that he originally adhered to it, to change his mind later.[7] And when it comes to the description of the ultimate goal of philosophy,[8] he quotes both Plato and Aristotle as having proposed that this goal is reached in a kind of sudden illumination or a 'touching' of the divinity, comparable to that received by initiates of mystery religions,[9] thus obviously deriving his information concerning Aristotle from some of his exoteric writings. In the controversy regarding the interpretation of Plato's cosmogony,[10] he interprets Plato as teaching that the cosmos had a temporal origin, thus siding with Aristotle; but he is quite obviously not at all inclined to consider such a doctrine as false.[11] The receptacle he describes in terms of matter agitated by an evil soul;[12] matter itself he—with Aristotle[13]—describes as neutral[14] and, at the same time, desiring the good,[15] sometimes as evil,[16] for which he could also have referred to Aristotle.[17] On the whole, Aristotle is treated with sympathy and used freely; but no systematic attempt is made to reconcile him with Plato. This, in general,

[1] The former he found in Plato, *Tim.* 37A; *De an. pr.* 23, 1023E; for the latter see *Lamprias Cat.* no. 192. 156.

[2] *De def. or.* 24–30, 423C–426E.

[3] *De def. or.* 31–4, 426F–428C; 37, 430C–D; *De Ei* 11, 389F–390A.

[4] *Lamprias Cat.* no. 44.

[5] *De def. or.* 30, 426C.

[6] *Adv. Col.* 14, 1115A.

[7] *De virtute morali* 7, 448A; 3, 442B; cf. G. Verbeke, 'Plutarch and the Development of Aristotle', *Aristotle and Plato in the Mid-Fourth Century* (1960), pp. 236–47.

[8] Which he takes to be theology: *De def. or.* 2, 410B.

[9] *De Is. et Os.* 77, 382D–E.

[10] *De animae procreatione in Timaeo.*

[11] *De an. pr.* 4–10, 1013D–1023D; *Plat. qu.* IV, 1003A.

[12] *De Is. et Os.* 46–9, 369E–371E; *De an. pr.* 7, 1015D–E; cf. 5, 1014B; 6, 1014D; 9, 1016C, 1017A–B. It is this evil soul which Plutarch identifies with one of the ingredients of the cosmic soul, viz. the divisible (5, 1014D). Plotinus (*Enn.* IV 2 [4]) identifies the indivisible with the intelligible, the divisible with the sensible.

[13] *Met.* Λ 10, 1075a34.

[14] *De an. pr.* 6, 1014F.

[15] *De Is. et Os.* 53, 372E; 57, 374D.

[16] *De def. or.* 9, 414D.

[17] *Phys.* I 9, 192a15; *Met.* Λ 9, 1051a20; cf. Zeller, *Phil.* II/2 (^{4}1921), p. 338 n. 1.

is also the attitude of Plotinus, though by and large he finds more that is objectionable in Aristotle than does Plutarch.[1]

The way in which Plutarch tries to elevate God above everything else is to say of him that only he truly is and is truly one, whereas everything else becomes rather than is and is many rather than one. God is simple, free of all otherness.[2] But Plutarch's God[3] exercises providence[4] (which is why Plutarch[5] finds Aristotle's self-centred god unacceptable) and is, therefore, a far cry from the first or second divinity of Plotinus. In fact, in some passages Plutarch speaks like a Stoic of the cosmos and the cosmic soul as parts of God,[6] though in others[7] he objects to Stoic pantheism.

Between gods and men are demons; and in his demonology Plutarch, by and large, follows Plato and Xenocrates, with his three classes of them (see also below, p. 72). Of his demons, some have always been demons; some are souls of deceased men. And sometimes he speaks as if 'demon' would equal our intelligence; only, whereas Plato[8] seems, by such an equation, to deny the existence of demons as independent beings, Plutarch speaks as if he believed that intelligence really does not belong to man but *is* a demon.[9] And some of these demons are good, some are evil. Except the last point, all this—including the wavering between the 'internal' and 'external' interpretation of demons—we find in Plotinus (cf. above, p. 35).[10]

Of other aspects of Plato's philosophy, Plutarch is familiar with the Two-opposite-principles theory. But strangely enough, he quotes it in the Pythagorean rather than the Platonic form, in that he derives from these principles numbers rather than ideas.[11] He obviously prefers to

[1] In *De virtute morali*, Plutarch follows Aristotle to the extent that he accepted the Platonic division of the soul into a reasonable and an unreasonable part (he therefore rejects Stoic intellectualism). But it is precisely this writing in which Plutarch indicates that Aristotle changed his opinions (see above, p. 59). The problem whether the source of Plutarch was Posidonius, Andronicus, or Xenocrates cannot be discussed here; on it, see K. Ziegler, 'Plutarchos', *RE*, XXI/I (1951), col. 769 f.: M. Pohlenz, *Die Stoa* (²1959, 1955), I, pp. 255–358; II, pp. 132, 175.

[2] *De Ei* 17, 391 E; 19, 392 E; *De Is. et Os.* 77, 382 C.

[3] Or gods: in *De def. or.* 24, 423 C–D he even proves the necessity of there being more than one.

[4] *De Is. et Os.* 67, 377 F.

[5] *De def. or.* 30, 426 C.

[6] *Plat. qu.* II I. 2, 1001 A–C.

[7] *De def. or.* 29, 426 B; *Ad princ. iner.* 5, 781 F.

[8] *Tim.* 90 A.

[9] *De genio Socr.* 22, 591 E.

[10] One other passage on demons deserves mention: the assertion that some demons are homonymous with some gods: *De def. or.* 21, 421 E. Cf. *Enn.* VI 7 [38] 6.

[11] *De def. or.* 35, 428 E.

interpret Plato in terms of the triad 'artificer–ideas–matter'.[1] And he is willing to apply to matter not only the Aristotelian term *hylê*, and the Platonic *hypodochê*, *tithênê*, etc., but also the Pythagorean dyad.[2]

Significant is his attitude towards Socrates. He is aware of the tension between 'Socratics' and 'Pythagoreans'[3] and introduces, in *De genio Socr.* 9, a character who objects to the fantastic rantings of Pythagoreans, extolling, instead, Socrates' sobriety.[4] But the Pythagoreans Lummias and Theanor carry the day; Socrates remains a Socrates after their heart. It can safely be said: only a Pythagorean Socrates could have been of interest to Plotinus (but see below, p. 97).

It has already been indicated that Plutarch tends to separate sharply intelligence from the soul.[5] He even toys with the idea that intelligence always remains outside the body.[6] With this Plotinus would be in sympathy; just as with Plutarch's body–soul dualism, according to which the soul is sullied by its prolonged contacts with the body.[7] Reincarnation[8] is adopted by Plutarch as a matter of course; but we find in him some of the same contradictions concerning the fate of the soul after death and the reasons of incarnation as we found in Plato. In at least one of the passages incarnation (with subsequent reincarnation) seems assumed to be the result of a universal law, which would be tantamount to an 'optimistic' view of it.[9] But, as we have seen, when occasion demands, he presents incarnation as an evil for the soul. The body–soul dualism would, of course, contradict Antiochus (and agree with the source of Cicero's *Tusc. Disp.* I; see above, p. 57), thus proving the limited range of the former's influence on Platonists. In fact, Plutarch even has kind words for the scepticism of the New Academy,[10] though, for himself, scepticism means simply cautiousness in committing oneself to a definite solution of a difficult matter.[11] Furthermore, Plutarch is of the

[1] *Qu. conv.* VIII 2. 4, 720B.

[2] *De Is. et Os.* 48, 370E; *De an. pr.* 5, 1014D; 6, 1014E; 7, 1015D; 24, 1024C, etc.

[3] Of which Aeschines of Sphettus seems to be the first spokesman. Cf. H. Dittmar, *Aeschines von Sphettos* (1912), p. 213.

[4] 579F.

[5] *De facie* 28, 942E.

[6] Strangely enough, in one place in him we find the series: Monad, Intelligence, Physis (*De genio Socr.* 22, 591B). Cf. H. Dörrie, 'Zum Ursprung der neuplatonischen Hypostasenlehre', *Hermes*, LXXXII (1954), pp. 331–42, esp. p. 332.

[7] *Cons. ad ux.* 10, 611E–F; cf. Περὶ ψυχῆς 6, vol. VII, 21–7 Bernard.

[8] Also into beasts: *De sera* 32, 567E.

[9] *De facie* 27–30, 942C–945C.

[10] *Adv. Col.* 26, 1121E–1122A; 29, 1124B.

[11] *De sera* 4, 549D.

opinion that there has always been one Academy only[1] and that the Academy differed from Pyrrhonianism.[2] For Plotinus the New Academy simply does not exist.

We have already quoted the passage[3] in which Plutarch says that theology is the goal of philosophy, and that this goal can be reached only in a moment of sudden 'enlightenment'. A number of other passages[4] agree with this one; in them Plutarch describes how god can take possession of man's soul (the classic examples are, of course, the Pythia) which has made itself entirely receptive of him. As Zeller[5] says, we here see some roots of the Neoplatonic doctrine of ecstasy; but we should say that they are very feeble. In many respects here Plutarch again agrees with the Stoic theory of natural mantic.[6]

We have said that Plutarch is familiar with the Two-opposite-principles doctrine.[7] But it does not seem that he ever was interested in the 'horizontal' tripartition of reality into ideas, mathematicals, and sensibles. Yet he preserved for us an interpretation of the *Timaeus* done by Posidonius in which this tripartition is presented in a highly significant way. The role of Posidonius in paving the way for Plotinus is very problematic. Of one thing we can be sure: this interpretation of the horizontal tripartition provides Plotinus with a scaffolding of prime importance to his system. According to Posidonius, the passage in the *Timaeus* in which Plato assigns to the soul an intermediate position between the realm of the intelligible and that of the sensible is essentially identical with Aristotle's presentation of the philosophy of Plato as teaching the tripartition into ideas, mathematicals, and sensibles. For, so Posidonius asserts, essentially, soul equals mathematicals.[8] It is easy to see that the tripartition now emerging (ideas, *soul*, sensibles) is very similar to the well-known series of Plotinus.[9]

[1] *Lamprias Cat.* no. 63.
[2] *Ibid.* no. 64.
[3] *De Is. et Os.* 77, 382D–E.
[4] *De Pythiae or.* 21–3, 403E–405E; *Amatorius* 16, 758E.
[5] *Phil.* III/2 (⁵1923), p. 210.
[6] Cic. *De div.* I 64 (Posidonius), 110: 113; 115; 129; II 26; 34; 35.
[7] Cf. *De an. pr.* 2, 1012E; *De def. or.* 35, 428E—from these, we said, numbers are derived, not ideas.
[8] An equation to which Plutarch, who preserved this interpretation of Posidonius, objects: *De an. pr.* 23, 1023D.
[9] Cf. P. Merlan, *From Platonism to Neoplatonism* (²1960), pp. 34–9.

A number of Plutarch's works are dominated by religious interest. How can the delay of divine punishment be justified? Why are oracles no longer given in metric form? What did Socrates mean when he spoke of his daimonion? Why the decline of oracles? The answer to all these questions implies activities of spirits (demons). One can say: with Plutarch demonology continues playing its conspicuous role in Platonism.

In a number of writings Plutarch criticized not only the Epicureans[1] but also the Stoics. In other words, he certainly did nothing to promote syncretism (eclecticism) consciously.[2] And we have already mentioned the fact that he was fully aware of Aristotle's opposition to Plato (not only as far as the idea theory was concerned, but also as to the problem of a plurality of *kosmoi*, the possibility of which, as we know, Aristotle denied and Plato admitted). A similarly anti-eclectic attitude is found in Calvisius Taurus, Plutarch's pupil or younger friend,[3] teacher of Herodes Atticus and of Aulus Gellius, most likely scholarch of the Athenian Academy. He also criticized Epicureans and the Stoa and seems to have opposed those who tried to harmonize Plato and Aristotle.[4] On the other hand, his teacher obviously did not convince him that Plato taught a temporal origin of the cosmos,[5] and he also rejected Aristotle's theory of ether.[6] Once more we see that Antiochus' influence on the Academy was limited.

Disagreement between Plutarch and Taurus exists also on the problem of the soul's incarnation. Plutarch was sometimes inclined to take

[1] It is worth remembering that Antiochus (*De fin.* v 45) was not ready to commit himself to an anti-Epicurean position with regard to the question whether pleasure (*hêdonê*) belongs to the goods nature wants us to appropriate (οἰκειοῦσθαι). On the whole, however, his syncretism does not include Epicureanism. We meet a different situation in Seneca, many of whose writings have a strongly Epicurean flavour. Within the orbit of Platonism, Porphyry's *Letter to Marcella* includes a number of ethical doctrines of Epicurus.

As to Plotinus, whereas nothing in the theoretical philosophy of Epicureanism is acceptable to him, there is one particular doctrine of its practical philosophy that is, viz. the doctrine that happiness does not increase with the length of time. Of course Plotinus has to qualify this statement because of the Epicurean hedonism; but if perfection instead of *hêdonê* is accepted as man's goal in life, Plotinus would agree with it (*Enn.* I 5 [36]). However, in the very same essay Plotinus also denies the Epicurean doctrine that memory contributes to happiness. The *communis opinio* that Epicureanism is not included in late Greek syncretism needs some qualification.

[2] On his opposition—but also indebtedness—to Stoic ethics cf. Zeller, *Phil.* III/2 (⁵1923), pp. 201–4; cf. R. M. Jones, *The Platonism of Plutarch* (1916), pp. 9; 21.

[3] A. Gellius, *N.A.* I 26. 4. On him see K. Praechter, 'Taurus', *RE*, v/1 (1934).

[4] Gellius, *N.A.* IX 5, 8; XII 5, 5; *Suda S. V.* Tauros.

[5] Philop. *De aet. m.* VI 21, p. 186, 17 Rabe.

[6] *Ibid.* XIII 15, p. 520, 4 Rabe.

the pessimistic point of view that incarnation is an evil for the soul (see above, pp. 28–9); Taurus opted for the optimistic interpretation.[1]

We shall speak later of Atticus, whom some scholars consider to have succeeded Taurus as scholarch of the Academy. Anticipating what will be presented in detail, we can say that Atticus sides partly with Taurus in denying the harmony of Plato with Aristotle, partly with Plutarch in asserting the temporal origin of the world and the existence of an evil world soul.

C. *Albinus and Apuleius*

But in the same second century and outside of the Academy we also find a Platonism different from that of Plutarch, or Calvisius Taurus. It so happens that we are particularly well informed on the Platonism of Albinus.[2]

Albinus represents an entirely syncretistic Platonism. Free and full use is made of Aristotelian and some Stoic doctrines—obviously Aristotle is seen simply as a Platonist, the Stoa as a branch of Platonism.[3] Albinus divides philosophy into physics, ethics, and logic,[4] which is the division usually traced to Xenocrates but familiar also to Aristotle,[5] and adopted by the Stoa—though the order of these three parts is stated in different ways by different authors, and though sometimes the term logic is replaced by that of dialectic. Physics, in this case, includes theology. But occasionally Albinus speaks as if he distinguished physics on the one hand, ethics, politics, and economics on the other,[6] which would correspond to the Aristotelian division of

[1] Iambl. in Stob. *Ecl.* I 39, vol. I, p. 378, 25 Wachsmuth.

[2] In 151/2 he taught Galenus in Smyrna. On his doctrines, in addition to older literature listed in Ueberweg–Praechter, *Grundriss* (1926), see particularly: W. Theiler, *Die Vorbereitung des Neuplatonismus* (1930), *passim*; R. E. Witt, *Albinus and the History of Middle Platonism* (1937); J. H. Loenen, 'Albinus' Metaphysics', *Mnemosyne* ser. 4, vol. IX (1956), pp. 296–319; vol. X (1957), pp. 35–56; P. Merlan, *Monopsychism, Mysticism, Metaconsciousness* (1963), pp. 62–76. As to his identity, see below, p. 70 n. 3. The subsequent quotations without title refer to his *Didaskalikos*, while those from the *Isagoge* are indicated by the title. The text of both: in the sixth volume of the Plato edition by K. F. Hermann or in the third volume of Didot's *Plato* (English tr. by G. Burges in the sixth volume of the Bohn Library translation of Plato's works). The text of the *Isagoge* can also be found in J. Freudenthal, *Der Platoniker Albinos und der falsche Alkinoos* (1879); French translation by R. le Corré, *Revue Philosophique*, LXXXI (1956), pp. 28–38. The standard edition of the *Didaskalikos* (with French tr.) is by P. Louis, *Albinos, Epitome* (1945).

[3] *Didaskalikos*, ch. 12 is essentially identical with Arius Didymus in Euseb. *PE* XI 23 and Stob. *Ecl.* I 12, vol. I, p. 135, 20 Wachsmuth; cf. H. Diels, *Dox.* (²1929), pp. 76 f., 447.

[4] *Isag.* ch. 3.

[5] *Top.* I 14, 105b19.

[6] *Isag.* ch. 6.

philosophy into a theoretical and a practical part (whereas Albinus omits the third Aristotelian division, viz. poetic).[1] Again, when Albinus subdivides the theoretical part (ch. 7), he enumerates, as its first part, theology, defined as the study of that which is unmoved, of first principles, and of the divine (*ibid.*). This is, of course, entirely Aristotelian. The second part, physics, he describes as dealing with the motions of heavenly bodies (see below, p. 69) and the constitution of the visible world, with mathematics as the third part (*ibid.*)—thus combining two Platonico-Aristotelian tripartitions, viz. into theology, astronomy, and physics and into theology, mathematics, and physics.[2]

So much for the divisions of philosophy. A similar picture of a complete blend of Aristotle and Plato is found in a number of specific doctrines. Let us begin with the doctrine of ideas.

By designating them as intelligibles, Albinus combines Plato's doctrine of ideas with Aristotle's noetic. He assumes the existence of disembodied intelligibles which he equates with Plato's ideas and intelligibles which are inseparable from matter (ch. 4). In other words, whereas in Aristotle the forms-in-matter were meant to replace ideas, Albinus treats ideas and forms-in-matter just as two kinds of ideas (cf. above, p. 54; below, p. 117).

To the two kinds of intelligibles–ideas, two kinds of 'intelligizing' correspond—roughly speaking, the discursive and the intuitive. But the intuitive itself is divided into two kinds: before our soul has become embodied and afterwards. This latter intelligizing (or its objects: act and object begin to blend) can be called *physikê ennoia* (*ibid.*). Thus, the Stoa is included into Albinus' syncretism—and, at the same time, it becomes somewhat dubious whether the concept of anamnesis (though he clings to it: ch. 5) still has its full Platonic force. In any case, Albinus firmly rejects any theory of abstraction. Ideas can be termed 'common properties'. But we cannot abstract that which is common from particulars. We cannot do so from all particulars, because there are infinitely many of them. But we cannot abstract them from a few or

[1] However, in a different context, he treats rhetoric as allied to logic (ch. 6).

[2] On the problem of the two orders: theology–physics–*mathematics* as against theology–*mathematics*–physics, see P. Merlan, *From Platonism to Neoplatonism* ([2]1960), pp. 75 f., 84.

we should constantly be making mistakes. Rather, a light touch (*aithygma*) releases our anamnesis (ch. 25).[1]

The doctrine that ideas are God's thoughts is enunciated without any hesitation; it has obviously by now become accepted doctrine (ch. 9). But stress is also laid on the paradigmatic character of ideas, and it is not made entirely clear whether they are paradigms only in the sense that God looks at them when fashioning the cosmos or whether they actually have a causality of their own. In any case, the supreme principles of Plato are assumed to be God, ideas, and matter.

Accepting Xenocrates' definition of ideas,[2] Albinus rejects ideas of artefacts, worthless things, and individuals (*ibid.*). We must assume that some discussion as to the existence of ideas of individuals must have taken place in Platonism preceding Albinus, for he explicitly says that in this rejection he sides with the *majority* of Platonists; in other words, when Plotinus decides to prove that there are ideas of individuals,[3] he takes a stand within an already existing frame of reference (ch. 9; cf. ch. 12).

From Aristotle's noetics Albinus takes over not only the concept of intelligibles, but also some of the most characteristic doctrines concerning the nature of the intelligence. First of all, he distinguishes between potential and actual intelligence and characterizes the latter by saying that it intelligizes incessantly and simultaneously (ch. 10). The actual intelligence he identifies sometimes with the supreme god, but sometimes he distinguishes a god who is the cause of intelligence and, instead of, or along with, the triad god–ideas–matter establishes another: first god, intelligence, soul. This, of course, would completely anticipate the Plotinian triad. But hardly has Albinus said of his first god that he is the cause of the active intelligence (or, of the incessant activity of the intelligence [ch. 10]) when he again calls him intelligence (*ibid.*; cf. ch. 27). In other words, Albinus is on the way to elevating the supreme god above intelligence—but stops before reaching this goal. Again, in describing his supreme god as ineffable (*arrêtos*; *alêptos*; has no predicates, is neither *poios* nor *apoios*: ch. 4, 10),

[1] Cf. *Enn.* VI 5 [23] 1.

[2] As paradigmatic cause of natural genera: *fr.* 30 Heinze; Seneca, *Ep.* 58, 19.

[3] *Enn.* V 7 [18].

he is closer to Plotinus' One than to Aristotle's intelligence. Certainly Plotinus (rather than Plato) would subscribe to his thesis that the supreme god should not even be called good, as this would imply that he participates in goodness (ch. 10). But, with complete ease, Albinus describes this ineffable god as intelligizing himself and his intelligibles, which intelligizing is idea. Plotinus' 'the intelligibles are not external to intelligence'[1] is here all but anticipated.

When it comes to the problem of incarnation and reincarnation (including transmigration into bodies of beasts), we find no trace of Aristotle's *entelechy* doctrine. Souls become incarnate uniting themselves with the pliable nature of the embryo (ch. 25). But why incarnation at all? Albinus offers us a choice among several reasons. Some are particularly remarkable. The incarnation is the result either of divine will, or of licentiousness, or of love of body (*ibid.*).[2] We cannot blame a Platonist for not being willing to make up his mind which of these kinds of reasons to accept. For, as we have seen, it is Plato himself who offers us this choice. And, as to the range of incarnation, Albinus sides with Platonists who assume that reincarnation includes beasts.

Two more points should be mentioned. Not only does Albinus take over the whole Aristotelian syllogistic, but he explicitly credits Plato with the doctrine of the ten categories (see below, p. 68). This, of course, means that he has no objections to Aristotle in this respect.

Furthermore, he fully accepts the formula which we shall find in Eudorus (see below, p. 82), according to which it is the goal of the philosopher to become assimilated to God (in this context, too, he distinguishes a celestial from a hypercelestial god, the latter being above perfection [ch. 28; *Isag.* ch. 6]).

Plutarch, as we have seen, insisted that the cosmogonic processes presented in Plato's *Timaeus* should be understood in temporal terms: the cosmos originated in time. And, furthermore, he saw the source of evil in an evil soul, whereas matter, with regard to good and evil, is

[1] *Enn.* v 5 [32].

[2] One more possibility mentioned by Albinus: the souls become incarnate ἀριθμοὺς μενούσας. Neither Freudenthal's (*op. cit.*) emendation (*arithmous isarithmous menousas*) nor Dörrie's (H. Dörrie, 'Kontroversen um die Seelenwanderung im kaiserzeitlichen Platonismus', *Hermes*, LXXXV [1957], pp. 414–35, esp. pp. 418 f., 422) interpretation ('souls remain as numbers') is satisfactory. Perhaps ἀριθμοὺς μὲν οὔσας—they survive because they are numbers.

neutral—or even, to a certain extent, on the side of the good in that it longs to be 'informed'. Entirely different is the attitude of Albinus. He joins the first-generation students (Xenocrates, Crantor) of Plato in asserting that Plato's meaning is that the cosmos has no temporal origin, and he gives two formulas to explain Plato's 'it has come to be'. It means either 'it has always been in the process of becoming' or 'it depends on some higher principle for its cause' (ch. 14). This pattern (dependence on a cause) is applied by Plotinus to explain in what sense matter is eternal and yet *genêton*.[1]

As to the 'ethical' character of matter, Albinus expresses no opinion. But he stresses that matter is entirely without qualities, being neither corporeal *nor* incorporeal (ch. 8). With this Plotinus agrees.[2]

We said that Albinus freely incorporates all of Aristotle's logic into Plato's system (chs. 4–6). He feels justified in doing so, by pointing out that in several dialogues Plato actually uses all figures of the syllogism, and that in the *Parmenides* we find the ten categories (ch. 6). And Albinus treats all of these topics under the designation of dialectic (ch. 3). Dialectic itself is a kind of discipline preliminary to the three other disciplines which are the subdivisions of theoretical philosophy (theology, physics, mathematics—in this characteristic order). In other words, Albinus testifies to this situation: what we should call logic is treated as an organon preceding philosophical disciplines proper; and this logic is, despite its name of dialectic, what we today should call formal logic. Albinus is not aware that Platonic dialectic could be interpreted as 'contentual' logic, i.e. a logic in some way mirroring the structure of reality rather than being a summary of rules of the art of thinking. However, there are distinct traces of the difference between dialectic and formal logic preserved in Albinus. Dialectic, he says in a different context, is concerned with the divine and changeless (*bebaion*) and is therefore superior to mathematics (ch. 7). By implication, it is, of course, also superior to syllogistic and to formal logic in general. This distinction will be recognized by Plotinus—dialectic will be elevated above (formal) logic.[3]

We mentioned that Albinus enumerates the three parts of theoretical philosophy in the characteristic order of theology, physics, and mathe-

[1] *Enn.* II 4 [12] 4.

[2] E.g. *Enn.* II 4 [12] 5.

[3] *Enn.* I 3 [20].

matics (ch. 7). But when it comes to a somewhat more detailed description of these three, Albinus changes the order to that of theology, mathematics, and physics. Mathematics becomes intermediate (*ibid.*). We are immediately reminded both of the Aristotelian presentation of Plato's philosophy and of the Posidonian equation of souls and mathematicals. But if Albinus in any way stands in the tradition of this equation, then he must in some way connect mathematicals with what in Plato's philosophy is considered the most outstanding quality of the soul—that of motion (whether in the sense of self-motion or in that of being the source of all motion). And this is, indeed, what we find (ch. 7). It is the task of mathematics, says Albinus, to investigate motion and locomotion. As Aristotle, on the whole, asserts that mathematicals are characterized precisely by their changelessness, we of course have a reinterpretation of mathematicals, making possible their being equated with the soul. In other words, the transition from Aristotle's tripartition (ideas, mathematicals, physicals) to that of Plotinus (intelligibles, soul, physicals) has become even easier. Not only has the soul become mathematicized; mathematicals have become 'psychicized'.

An additional point of interest to establish the relation between Albinus and Plotinus is as follows.

Having introduced the difference between 'the father', 'celestial intelligence', and the cosmic soul Albinus says that the father implants intelligence in the soul, and then (the 'then' taken in a non-temporal sense) turns the soul towards himself, so that the soul now can contemplate the intelligibles and fill itself with ideas and forms (ch. 10). One feels reminded of the principle of *epistrophê* in Plotinus—the (non-temporal) event which constitutes every hypostasis.[1]

A special section of the practical part of philosophy is the doctrine concerning perfections (virtues). Albinus clings to the Platonic perfections (replacing *sophia* by *phronêsis* [ch. 29] and also otherwise using concepts of ethics of the Stoa); but he introduces the concept of a scale of perfections. Perfections can be 'natural' (*euphyiai*) or higher; and one of the differences between these two kinds is that the former do not

[1] *Enn.* v 2 [11] 1, 10, with Harder's commentary *ad loc.*

necessarily follow each other, whereas the latter do (chs. 29–30).[1] We find a similar doctrine in Plotinus.[2]

Similar in some respects to Albinus' presentation of Plato is that of Apuleius in his *De dogmate Platonis*.[3] While there are traces in Albinus preparing us for the triad soul–intellect–god, there is more than a trace of this in Apuleius. After having introduced the triad god–ideas–matter (I 5), he discusses another, viz. *deus primus*, *mens formaeque*, *anima* (I 6). Here we seem to have the Plotinian triad. For as the middle member of his triad Apuleius designates *mens formaeque*; and this sounds as if the forms, i.e. ideas or intelligibles, were strictly coordinated with

[1] Albinus rejects any intellectualistic interpretation of πάθη, some of which he defends as ἥμερα and natural, whereas he condemns others as unnatural. Thus, he disagrees with the Old Stoa on important points (he disagrees with the Peripatos in insisting that inner perfection suffices for happiness: ch. 27). But ἀντακολουθία τῶν ἀρετῶν is a Stoic term, though prepared by Plato's *Protagoras* 348C–360E.

[2] *Enn.* I 2 [19] 7.

[3] Since T. Sinko, *De Apulei et Albini doctrinae Platonicae adumbratione* (1905), the writings of these two are supposed to reflect the doctrines of Gaius, who, as we heard, was read in the school of Plotinus. On the other hand, though, the conclusion of Freudenthal (*op. cit.*) that the author of the *Didaskalikos* is Albinus rather than some Alcinous to whom our manuscripts attribute it, is accepted by most, but not all, scholars. The most recent attempt to return it to Alcinous (who is supposed to be the Stoic mentioned by Philostratus), we find in M. Giusta, ''Ἀλβίνου Ἐπιτομή ο Ἀλκινόου Διδασκαλικός?', *Atti della Accademia delle Scienze di Torino, Classe di Scienze morali...*, XCV (1960/1), pp. 167–94. Giusta is unfamiliar with E. Orth, 'Les œuvres d'Albinos le Platonicien', *L'Antiquité Classique*, XVI (1947), pp. 113 f. Orth, on the basis of a passage in Ephraem the Syrian in which Albinus is credited with having written a work Ὅτι αἱ ποιότητες ἀσώματοι and the fact that *Didaskalikos*, ch. 11 is precisely devoted to proving this, inferred that the *Didaskalikos* is indeed the work of Albinus and even that the work preserved under this title as a writing by Galen (vol. 19 Kühn) is his. However, as long as nobody denies that the *Didaskalikos* and the *De dogmate Platonis* are pre-Plotinian, we need not take sides in this controversy, nor commit ourselves unconditionally to the thesis of Sinko. In particular, no attempt will be made to reconstruct the doctrine of Gaius. Only one detail will be mentioned. K. Praechter tried to prove that Gaius, in this respect reminding us of the author of the anonymous commentary to the *Theaetetus* (H. Diels and W. Schubart, *Anonymer Kommentar zu Platons Theaetet* [1905], pp. xxiv–xxxvii; 5, 24 – 7, 20, pp. 5–7), denied the Stoic assertion that οἰκείωσις and self-preservation can be made the basis of both individual and social ethics and tried to prove that only the 'becoming godlike' can serve as such. If he or any other Platonists asserted this, we should have before us a complete repudiation of Antiochus. However, we should also notice that there seems to be a flaw in Praechter's use of Apuleius' *De dogm.* II 2, when he takes it to express the concept of οἰκείωσις and its grades, not realizing that we have before us a translation of Plato's *9th Letter*, 358A. (K. Praechter, 'zum Platoniker Gaios', Hermes, LI (1916), pp. 510–29).

...et illum quidem qui natura imbutus est ad sequendum bonum, non modo [sibi intimatum] ⟨sibimet ipsi natum⟩ putat sed omnibus etiam hominibus, nec pari aut simili modo verum [etiam unumquemque acceptum] ⟨civitati unumquemque assertum⟩ esse, dehinc proximis et mox ceteris qui familiari usu vel notitia iunguntur.	ἀλλὰ κἀκεῖνο δεῖ σε ἐνθυμεῖσθαι, ὅτι ἕκαστος ἡμῶν οὐχ αὑτῷ μόνον γέγονεν, ἀλλὰ τῆς γενέσεως ἡμῶν τὸ μέν τι ἡ πατρὶς μερίζεται, τὸ δέ τι οἱ γεννήσαντες, τὸ δὲ οἱ λοιποὶ φίλοι.

The genuineness of Apuleius' *De dogm.* is not above suspicion, but this is immaterial in the present context, as long as there is no reason to suspect that the writing is pre-Plotinian.

the second principle rather than the first. Indeed, the formula sounds as if Apuleius had anticipated the formula of Plotinus that ideas (forms) do not exist outside the intellect. And in that Apuleius designates the first of the three principles as the first god, he suggests the term second god for the intellect.

Moreover, Apuleius designates these three principles as being subdivisions of the realm of the intelligible. This is the standard pattern of Plotinus, who starts from the Platonic dualism *intelligibilia–sensibilia* but divides the former into his three supreme principles.[1]

As far as the problem of the interpretation of the 'it has come to be' is concerned, Apuleius somewhat unexpectedly asserts that we can find in Plato both doctrines, viz. that the cosmos is eternal, and that it has come to be. But, says Apuleius, the latter doctrine means only that the cosmos consists of non-eternal elements (I 8). In contradiction of this, Apuleius goes on to assert that the cosmos is imperishable because God will not permit it to perish, which, of course, would imply that the cosmos had a temporal origin. The whole passage once more shows that there was very much disagreement among Platonists with regard to this problem.[2] But what interests us mainly is that here we find another device to explain the phrase 'has come into being' in such a way that the cosmogonic process appears as atemporal.

De dogmate Platonis (chs. 6–20) contains Apuleius' demonology. To explain the nature of demons Apuleius quotes from the exoteric Aristotle (*fr.* 19 Rose), to whom he attributes the doctrine that demons live in the air—not in the air as we know it and in which birds live, but in the pure air. This is a doctrine strangely similar to, and at the same time differing from, that propounded in *De gen. anim.*[3] In Apuleius and in *De gen.* we find the same argument: if three elements are inhabited by living beings, viz. plants, fish, 'footed' animals (including birds), it is impossible to assume that the fourth should be void of any. But *De gen.* assigns fire, not air, to this fourth kind of living beings, the other three elements having already been taken. However, as we have seen, it is 'pure' lunar fire, different from the one we know. Apuleius

[1] Cf. P. Merlan, *Monopsychism, Mysticism, Metaconsciousness* (1963), pp. 69 f.

[2] On Albinus' own hesitations see Zeller, *Phil.* III/1 (⁵1923), p. 844. On his student Galen see above, p. 48 n. 1.

[3] III 11, 761 b 14–23 (see p. 34 n. 1 above).

distributes the living beings in a different way—obviously water to fish, earth to 'footed' animals, fire to fireflies and similar animals;[1] he, therefore, is left with air only—and now he distinguishes two kinds of air almost in the same way in which Aristotle distinguished two kinds of fire. But what about ether? According to Aristotle, it is the habitat of stars.[2] Now, it is true that Aristotle never says of his lunar animals that they are demons (cf. p. 34 n. 1 above); but it is difficult to escape the conclusion that that is what he meant, and Apuleius probably interpreted him in this sense.

Otherwise, the demonology of Apuleius is similar to that of Xenocrates. There are three classes of demons: permanently discarnates, souls of deceased, the soul in us. And the demon of Socrates belonged to the first kind. In this context, Aristotle is once more quoted with the assertion that everybody can 'see' his demon (guardian spirit).[3] Apuleius obviously refuses to recognize as evil demons the first kind of demons who accompany man, after he has died, to his place of judgement, to participate in the trial. In all these respects he is very close to the demonology of Plotinus.

The theology of Apuleius makes demons indispensable. For according to him the supreme god and all the other gods are absolutely transcendental, and there is no possibility of any contact between them and man. Thus, our prayers actually go to the demons. It deserves mention that, in describing the supreme and ineffable god, Apuleius says of him that he is free not only from *nexus patiendi* (which would simply be Platonic doctrine) but also from *nexus gerendi*.[4] This is almost Numenius' first inactive god who, therefore, must be distinguished from the artificer. It does not seem that in this respect the god of *De dogm. Platonis* bears any similitude to the supreme god of the *De deo Socr.* On the other hand, this supreme inactive god has nothing to do with Aristotle's changeless changer, for Apuleius very strongly stresses that

[1] It should not be forgotten that Aristotle, in the same *De gen. anim.* II 3, 737a 1—cf. *De gen. et corr.* II 3, 330b 29—and in *Meteor.* IV 4, 382a 7, denied that any animal could live in fire, whereas in *Hist. anim.* V 19, 552b 10–15, he says the opposite.

[2] In Apuleius, of the visible gods (*fr.* 23 Rose); see *De deo Socratis*, ch. 2.

[3] It should not be forgotten that Apuleius asserts that he was the first one who translated δαίμων into Latin by rendering it *genius*, when it signifies the soul of man, and by *Lar*, *Lemur*, *Larva*, and *Manes*, when it signifies the souls of the deceased ones (*De deo Socr.* ch. 15).

[4] *De deo Socr.* ch. 3.

all gods are exempt from both pain and pleasure, whether they are the supreme god, the invisible gods, or the visible ones, viz. the stars, whereas Aristotle's god enjoys uninterrupted *hêdonê*. With this doctrine of Apuleius, Plotinus agrees.[1]

D. *Atticus*

Albinus and Apuleius represent an almost complete synthesis of Plato with Aristotle. Atticus (see above, p. 64) represents the other extreme. He vigorously objects to Platonists who find Aristotelian doctrines helpful in teaching Platonism. Thus, Atticus is opposed not only to any kind of eclecticism or syncretism. He objects even to what in later Platonism will become standard, viz. treating Aristotle's philosophy as a kind of introduction to Plato. For, as Atticus sees it, Aristotle's doctrines are both opposed to those of Plato and false.

Drawing from Eusebius, we are going to present some aspects of Atticus' doctrines.[2] Central to the philosophy of Plato, according to him, is Plato's 'psychology'. On Plato's doctrine concerning the nature and particularly the immortality of the soul hinge his ethics and his epistemology (doctrine of anamnesis). As far as the world soul is concerned, it 'presides' over the universe.

To none of these doctrines does Aristotle's philosophy have anything to contribute. First of all, his doctrine of the soul (obviously Atticus alludes to the doctrine of *entelechy*)[3] deprives the soul of its substantial and incorporeal character. As a result, Aristotle even denies that thinking, willing, remembering, are soul's 'movements'. According to him, they are the activities of man, whereas the soul remains unmoved. Dicaearchus only drew the correct conclusions from this when he did away with the soul as an independent entity.[4]

[1] *Enn.* v 6 [24] 6. If the so-called Third Book of *De dogmate Platonis* (Περὶ ἑρμηνείας) is by Apuleius, it would prove that he, no less than Albinus, felt entitled to present Aristotle's logic as Platonic.

[2] As the collection of Atticus' fragments by J. Baudry (1931) seems hard to obtain, they will be quoted directly from the sources: Eusebius, *Praeparatio Evangelica*, XI 1–2 (*PG* 21. 845–7); XV 4–9; 11–13 (*PG* 21. 1303–32; 1335–42) and Proclus, *In Tim.* (see index *s.v.*).

[3] Eusebius interrupts his excerpts from Atticus to insert (XV 10) an excerpt from Plotinus (more will presently be said on this), and (XV 11) from Porphyry's writing, *Against Boethos*. I assume that the excerpt from Porphyry is limited to the first three sections of XV 11, and that the words τὰ μὲν οὖν ἄλλα resume the excerpts from Atticus. It is not in the style of Porphyry to say that it is *shameful* to define the soul as *entelechy*, whereas it is entirely in the style of Atticus.

[4] *PE* XV 9.

Of course, as Aristotle virtually denies the existence of the soul, it would be vain to see in him an ally of Plato's doctrine of immortality.

And, with the doctrine of immortality gone, one of the mainstays of ethics is gone.

As far as the world soul is concerned, Plato teaches that it 'rules' everything. In other words, he identifies *physis* and *psychê*, so that in him the expressions *kata physin* and *kata pronoian* mean one and the same thing. Entirely different is the doctrine of Aristotle. According to him, the realm of celestial bodies is ruled by *heimarmenê*, the sublunar realm by *physis*, the human realm by *phronêsis*, *pronoia*, and *psychê*. But if these three are ruled by three different principles, what becomes of the unity of the universe?

True, Aristotle derives all *kinêsis* from one principle. But he denies that this principle is the soul, precisely the opposite of what Plato asserted. What right has Aristotle to say that nature does nothing in vain, if he denies that nature is simply soul?

Some may assert that, though Aristotle denies that the soul is immortal, he grants immortality to the *nous*, and in this respect he proves himself an ally to the Platonists. But, counters Atticus, Aristotle leaves the nature of the *nous* entirely unexplained. Nor does he explain whence the *nous*, or whither. In any case, he disagrees with Plato, who denied that *nous* can exist independently from the soul.

In the same manner Atticus criticizes Aristotle's 'theology'. It is, as a matter of fact, worse than the theology of Epicurus. Epicurus realized that, if the gods shared the world with men, they could not help exercising providence over their affairs. Therefore, Epicurus exiled the gods to the *intermundia*. But what kind of god are the gods of Aristotle who, though connected in some way with the cosmos, pay no attention whatsoever to it? His doctrine is what many find those of Epicurus to be—atheism in disguise.

No immortality of the soul, an absentee god, no universal *pronoia*—small wonder that the ethical doctrines of Aristotle are entirely erroneous. He does not recognize, as does Plato (!), that perfection suffices for happiness, but says that luck must add its indispensable share. Whereas Plato's 'he who is most just is also the happiest' lifts the soul to the divine, no such effect can be expected from Aristotle's moral doctrines. His three ethics have something puny and vulgar in their thoughts about perfection.

For a moment let us interrupt our report from Eusebius on Atticus. It is remarkable that, after having presented Atticus' objection to Aristotle's psychology, Eusebius continues by excerpting Plotinus.[1] It is obvious that Eusebius correctly assessed the similarity of the attitudes of Atticus and Plotinus. A further similarity consists in Atticus' insistence that it is not man who thinks, wills, etc., but the soul itself. The problem is of great importance in connexion with the problem of immortality. For if it is not the soul that thinks, etc., what happens to all these activities after the soul has become separated from the body? Plotinus is particularly interested in the problem of memory.[2] And he decides that memory must be an activity of the soul; that, therefore, in some way the soul remembers even after death. Quite obviously there is no place for memory in Aristotle's theory of the *nous*. We have already mentioned this problem (above, p. 45). It is plainly a live issue in the second century.

And, of course, Plotinus agrees with Atticus as regards the autarky of inner perfection for happiness.[3]

The disagreement of Atticus with the Aristotelian ethics and theology continues in the field of physics. He rejects Aristotle's notion of ether (the way Aristotle describes its properties one would expect him to say that it is a bodyless body).[4] To it Aristotle transferred qualities which Plato had attributed to the incorporeal (eternity, divinity), but this is, of course, impossible.[5]

In this respect also, Plotinus agrees with Atticus.[6]

Furthermore, whereas Plato attributes to the celestial bodies generic

[1] *Enn.* IV 7 [2] 8, 1–50.

[2] *Enn.* IV 3–4 [27–8].

[3] *Enn.* I 4 [46] 4, 23.

[4] Cf. p. 41 n. 3.

[5] A writing now generally considered to be by Ps.-Justin, despite Photius, *cod.* 125, Ἀνατροπὴ δογμάτων τινῶν Ἀριστοτελικῶν, contains a sober and scholarly criticism of Aristotle's doctrine of the ether. As this writing was under the title *Justinus*, *Eversio falsorum dogmatum*... (1552) translated by a person no less than William Postel, it must have exercised considerable influence. We see to what extent the concept was controversial (*PG* 6. 1489–1564, esp. 1539). See below, p. 111–13. A survey of authors dealing with the concept of ether can be found in E. Sachs, *Die fünf platonischen Körper* (1917), pp. 15–22, 60–9; cf. also G. Luck, *Der Akademiker Antiochos* (1953), p. 40; P. Moraux, 'quinta essentia', *RE*, XXIV/1 (1963).

[6] *Enn.* II 2 [14].

immutability only (they 'emit' exhalations and 'receive' an equal amount instead), Aristotle attributes individual immutability to them.[1] Finally, whereas Plato distinguishes between involuntary and voluntary movements of the stars and particularly attributes to them their circular movement as caused by their souls, Aristotle tries to explain circular movement by qualities of the ether.[2]

Probably the best known of Atticus' philosophical opinions is his insistence that, for everybody who knows Greek, it should be obvious that Plato attributed a temporal origin to the universe. Atticus blames his co-Platonists for having been unduly impressed by Aristotle's criticism, as the result of which they tried to prove that Plato did not, as Aristotle had asserted, believe in a temporal origin of the cosmos, but only presented a timeless relation under the guise of a story, *didaskalias charin*. Of course, Aristotle's criticism presupposed that if the cosmos originated in time, it would also dissolve—and this was, he felt, impious nonsense. Atticus, therefore, denies the premise: not everything that has come into being in time will also perish. And it is entirely appropriate to say that the cosmos will not perish because such is the artificer's will.

Thus much for Eusebius. The other source of our knowledge of the doctrines of Atticus is Proclus' commentary on the *Timaeus*. Proclus not only confirms what Eusebius tells of Atticus' interpretation, he also adds many interesting details.

How does Atticus explain the origin of the cosmos?

As he sees it, the artificer faces a pre-existing matter, kept in a condition of permanent chaotic motion due to the activity of an 'irregular', i.e. evil, soul. In other words, an *atheos hylê* and an *anylos theos* face each other. But the artificer succeeds in imposing forms (ideas) on matter and intelligence (*nous*) on the evil soul. The latter thus becomes *psychê logikê*. As the pre-cosmic matter was in motion, this means that time existed before the creation of the cosmos.

This doctrine of the coevality is also used by Atticus to explain the famous phrase, interpreted by Plotinus so many times and in so many ways, that the artificer formed the soul out of the 'divisible' and the 'indivisible'. The latter is the divine intelligence, the former the evil soul.

[1] Cf. *Enn.* II I [40] I–2.

[2] *PE* XV 7; 8; cf. *Enn.* II I [40] 3.

The artificer himself Atticus identifies with the good (goodness). And, as he presents it, the artificer is permanently contemplating the ideas, in accordance with which he created the cosmos. He specifically states (contradicting Antiochus?) that he is outside the realm of the intelligibles.[1]

One detail deserves special mention. According to Atticus, there are two mixing bowls used by the artificer when he fashions the soul. Proclus is surprised by this interpretation. Otherwise, he says, Atticus remains close to the text. But where did he get the second mixing bowl?[2]

Now obviously, much of Atticus' interpretation is unacceptable to Plotinus. The cosmos did not originate in time. Aristotle misinterpreted Plato. But it is all the more remarkable that we find traces of the two-bowls interpretation in Plotinus.[3] It is difficult to escape the conclusion that in his early writing Plotinus was influenced by an interpretation peculiar to Atticus.

Now, if there are two mixing bowls, what is mixed in each of them? We probably should expect the world soul and the individual souls. But this is not what Atticus says. What is mixed in the first bowl is the *auto psychê*. It seems that Atticus distinguished what we call the psychical from the world soul and individual souls, considering the world soul, in comparison with the psychical, to be an individual soul. And, indeed, there are frequent traces of such a doctrine in Plotinus:[4] all souls stem from the same soul from which the world soul stems.

Different as is Albinus' and Apuleius' Plato from that of Atticus, there is one thing which they have in common: their Plato is not the Plato as Aristotle presented him. With the exception of the insertion of mathematics between theology and physics which, albeit hesitatingly, Albinus professes, and the attendant identification of mathematicals with the soul, we find no trace, in any of the three, of the Two-opposite-principles doctrine, nor of the derivation of successive spheres of being from them. And even these exceptions are expressed very weakly. If we were right in assuming that Antiochus had not much use for these doctrines of Aristotle's Plato, we could say that in this respect

[1] Ideas: Proclus, *In Tim.* I 305, 6; 366, 9; 391, 7; 394, 6; 431, 14 Diehl.

[2] *In Tim.* vol. III, pp. 246–7 Diehl.

[3] See *Enn.* IV 8 [6] 4, 35–9, whereas there is only one mixing bowl in IV 3 [27] 7, 10.

[4] E.g. *Enn.* IV 3 [27] 8, 2–3.

Albinus and Apuleius are closer to his Plato than was perhaps Eudorus. As for Plotinus, one could say that he is much more aware of the Two-opposite-principles doctrine, and, as we said, tries to incorporate it into his system. The importance of the horizontal tripartition for him is obvious, particularly after Posidonius' explicit equation soul = mathematicals. Indeed, Plotinus, against Aristotle, defends the existence of idea-numbers,[1] thus, to a certain extent, anticipating the attitude of a Syrianus, or Proclus.

Where is the place of Plotinus in the controversy regarding the compatibility of Aristotle with Plato? With some simplification, we could say: Plotinus sees Aristotle as belonging to the same chain to which he himself belongs—Pherecydes, Pythagoras, Empedocles, Heraclitus, Plato.[2] But essentially what he mainly takes over from Aristotle is his noetics. This is not little. The structure of the second hypostasis is built on it. But still it is a limited debt. Even as far as noetics is concerned, he blames Aristotle for seeing in intelligence the highest principle, for introducing a plurality of changeless changers into the realm of the intelligibles, etc.[3] In very many respects he either rejects Aristotle's doctrines entirely (so his *entelechy* concept) or assigns to them a rather subordinate place (so his logic which he considers much inferior to Plato's dialectic; so his doctrine of categories which he considers to be valid only for the sensible world).

E. *Other Platonists of the second century A.D. Summary*

To the second century A.D., in all likelihood, belongs Severus,[4] who is in our context of interest because he is another representative of the tendency to identify the soul with a mathematical.[5] He interprets the indivisible and the divisible of the *Timaeus* as geometrical point and extension,[6] thus replacing Xenocrates' 'arithmetical' definition of the soul by a 'geometrical'. In the latter he was preceded by Speusippus

[1] *Enn.* VI 6 [34]. [2] *Enn.* V I [10] 8. [3] *Enn.* V I [10] 9.

[4] On him, see K. Praechter, 'Severos', *RE*, II A/2 (1923).

[5] As is the source of Diog. Laert. III 67: according to Plato, the soul has an *arithmetical* principle, the body a *geometrical.* But Diogenes continues by defining the soul as ἰδέα τοῦ πάντῃ διεστῶτος πνεύματος. The last word is clearly a gloss—and the whole definition an excerpt from a source different from that of the preceding sentence.

[6] Iambl. in Stob. *Ecl.* I, vol. I, p. 364, 2 Wachsmuth; Procl. *In Tim.* vol. II 152, 27; 153, 21 Diehl.

(see above, p. 18), and either followed or preceded by one of the sources of Diogenes Laertius III 67 (see p. 78 n. 5). Remarkable is his doctrine that, though the cosmos had no temporal origin, it still is periodically destroyed and renewed[1]—in other words, Severus tried to mediate between the Aristotelian and the early Platonist interpretation of the *Timaeus* by utilizing the *Politicus* (see above, p. 26).[2] Plotinus accepts the idea of periodical destruction in his discussion of ideas of individuals.[3]

In some other context Severus objected to the doctrine according to which the human soul consists of a perishable and an imperishable part. This, he said, would deprive it of immortality.[4] We cannot be sure how he reconciled his objection with the explicit statement in the *Timaeus*; but we know that Plotinus also found it difficult to explain what actually of the soul survives.[5]

Finally, it seems that Severus tried to establish his own version of categories by assuming that there was only one supreme category, that of 'something', under which are the categories of 'being' and 'becoming'.[6] Stoic influence is obvious, but also the intention to overcome the Two-opposite-principles doctrine and to connect the doctrine of categories with ontology rather than treat it as a purely formal discipline.

This attempt to reformulate Aristotle's doctrine of categories reminds us to what extent it was a centre of controversies. We shall later speak of critics of Aristotle like Andronicus and Eudorus; Nicostratus[7] belongs among them also. He denied precisely what Severus assumed, viz. that the realms of the intelligible and the sensible could be subsumed under one genre. Plotinus continues with this anti-Aristotelian attitude, but, led by Porphyry, most Platonists decided to accept Aristotle's doctrine of categories and make it ancillary to the study of Plato. For Plotinus the Severus version of monism is, of course, unacceptable;[8] his own position agrees with that of Nicostratus.

[1] Procl. *In Tim.* vol. I 289, 7; II 95, 27 Diehl.

[2] Also otherwise he accepted Aristotle's interpretation of Plato: Syrian. *In Met.* 84, 23 Kroll.

[3] *Enn.* V 7 [18].

[4] Euseb. *PE* XIII 17.

[5] *Enn.* I 1 [53] 12; but cf. IV 7 [2] 13–14.

[6] Procl. *In Tim.* I 227, 15 Diehl.

[7] Simpl. *In Cat.* 1, 19; 73, 15; 76, 14 Kalbfleisch; K. Praechter, 'Nikostratos der Platoniker', *Hermes*, LVII (1922), pp. 481–517.

[8] *Enn.* VI 1 [42] 1–2; cf. II 6 [17].

Other Platonists of the first two centuries A.D. represent somewhat special cases. Theo of Smyrna (first century A.D.) is known to us mainly as a mathematician.[1] But we find in him the distinction of a higher from a lower One and learn also that to distinguish the two, the terms one and monad were used, by each of which some designated the higher One, others the lower.[2] In this context Theo quotes the *Philebus* (15 A) and identifies the higher One with the determined and the limit, whereas the lower Ones are supposed to be innumerably many.[3] It seems that for this distinction he was indebted to Moderatus (see below).[4]

The Platonism of Celsus (second century A.D.) is entirely in the service of his anti-Jewish and anti-Christian polemics. His concept of God is, on the whole, very similar to that of Albinus. But much more clearly than Albinus, he elevates the supreme god above intelligence, plainly anticipating Plotinus.[5] He differs from Albinus in describing matter as the source of evil;[6] and he operates with the concept of national demons. He is the first Platonist to turn sharply against Christianity; and at least one wing of Platonists, to which Plotinus also belongs, will follow him. His argument for polytheism (true piety worships the divine in its fulness of plurality: *Contra Celsum* VIII 66) recurs in Plotinus.[7]

[1] Theo compared the successive five steps in the study of Plato (mathematical disciplines; logic, politics [i.e. obviously ethics], physics; study of ideas; ability to instruct others; becoming godlike) to five steps of initiation into a mystery religion (purification; τελετῆς παράδοσις / ἐποπτεία / τέλος τῆς ἐποπτείας / εὐδαιμονία). There is a faint resemblance between these five steps and an equal number suggested for the study of Plato in Albinus' *Isagoge* (ch. 6). One wonders whether these divisions are not ultimately rooted in the desire to bring some kind of order into the works of Plato superior to the biographical one of Dercyllides and Thrasyllus (see Albinus, *Isagoge*, ch. 4), matching the systematic order of Andronicus' edition of Aristotle. We know that Andronicus grouped the several *pragmateiai* according to topics (Porphyry, *Life of Plotinus*, ch. 24). On the comparison of philosophy with mysteries see P. Boyancé, 'Sur les mystères d'Éleusis', *Revue des Études grecques*, LXXV (1962), pp. 460–73.

[2] *Expos.* pp. 19, 12 – 21, 19 Hiller.

[3] *Ibid.* pp. 21 f, 18 f. Hiller.

[4] On Theo's use of Peripatetic and Pythagorean doctrines, see Zeller, *Phil.* III/1 (⁵1923), pp. 840 f.; III/2 (⁵1923), p. 228.

[5] His adversary Origen agrees. He says: Νοῦν τοίνυν, ἢ ἐπέκεινα νοῦ καὶ οὐσίας, λέγοντες εἶναι ἁπλοῦν, καὶ ἀόρατον, καὶ ἀσώματον τὸν τῶν ὅλων θεόν... (*Contra Celsum* VII 38), while Celsus has said: ὅπερ ἐν τοῖς ὁρατοῖς ἥλιος...τοῦτο ἐν τοῖς νοητοῖς ἐκεῖνος, ὅσπερ οὔτε νοῦς, οὔτε νόησις, οὔτ' ἐπιστήμη, ἀλλὰ νῷ τε τοῦ νοεῖν αἴτιος...καὶ αὐτῇ οὐσίᾳ τοῦ εἶναι· πάντων ἐπέκεινα ὤν, ἀρρήτῳ τινὶ δυνάμει νοητός (VII 45); and οὐδὲ οὐσίας μετέχει ὁ θεός (VI 64). It should have become obvious by now that the elevation of the supreme god over intelligence and the attendant doctrine that he is accessible only through some suprarational act has become rather generally accepted by the time of Plotinus. On Celsus see P. Merlan, 'Celsus', *RAC* (1954); C. Andresen, 'Celsus', *RGG* (1957).

[6] Origen, *Contra Celsum*. IV 65.

[7] *Enn.* II 9 [33] 9.

Another special case is that of Maximus of Tyre (*c.* A.D. 180), certainly much more of a rhetor than a philosopher, and, therefore, a good standard to measure which philosophic ideas have become common knowledge. One of his orations bears the title 'God according to Plato', but to a surprising extent in describing this God (he is so elevated that secondary gods and demons are indispensable) he makes full use of Aristotle's noetics, including even such technical terms as active and potential intelligence and not forgetting to mention that the former acts unintermittently.[1] In justifying evil (the cause of which is matter, but also *psychês exousia*), he stresses, among other things, that it was necessary if good was to be produced,[2] an argument we also find in the Stoa[3] and in Plotinus.[4]

We said that the Two-opposite-principles doctrine seems to have been abandoned by Platonists later than the Old Academy. But the Platonists did not abandon it forever. It does not seem that Antiochus was interested in it, but Eudorus of Alexandria (*c.* 25 B.C.) was.[5] Discussing Aristotle's sentence attributing to Plato the doctrine that the One 'causes' ideas, these ideas 'causing' everything else,[6] Eudorus corrects (or, as seems more likely, perverts) the texts so that it becomes: The One is the 'cause' of everything, including even matter, as the initiated ones (those in the know) know.[7] And he distinguishes a first from a second One.[8] Both, the derivation of matter from the One and the distinction of a double One, pave the way for Plotinus' monism. Thus, in Eudorus Platonism once more begins to merge with Pythagoreanism.[9] It is, furthermore, characteristic that he not only commented upon the *Timaeus* (perhaps even wrote a commentary on it),[10] but also wrote on Aristotelian writings.[11] This does not mean that he followed Aristotle, for he criticized his doctrine of the categories.[12]

[1] *Or.* XVII 8.
[2] *Or.* XLI 4.
[3] *SVF* II 1169.
[4] *Enn.* III 3 [48] 7, 2.
[5] On him, see H. Dörrie, 'Der Platoniker Eudorus von Alexandria', *Hermes*, LXXIX (1944), pp. 25–39. However, we cannot be sure that he was a student of Antiochus.
[6] *Met.* A 6, 988a10–11.
[7] Alex. *In Met.* 59, 1 Hayd.
[8] Simpl. *In Phys.* 181, 10 Diels.
[9] On the influence of the Stoa on him see M. Pohlenz, *Die Stoa* (²1959, 1955), I, p. 357.
[10] Plutarch, *De an. pr.* 3, 1013B; 16, 1019E; 1020C. In it he tried to reconcile the literal and the 'didactic' interpretation of the 'has become': Zeller, *Phil.* III/1 (⁵1923), p. 612 n. 1.
[11] Alex. *In Met.* 59, 7 Hayd.; Simpl. *In Cat.* 159, 32 Kalbfleisch.
[12] Simpl. *In Phys.* 187, 10 Diels; cf. K. Praechter, 'Nikostratos der Platoniker', *Hermes*, LVII (1922), pp. 481–517, esp. p. 510.

The influence of Andronicus (see below, p. 114) seems to have begun early.

In one more way Eudorus is of importance in a history of Neoplatonism. In his survey of ethical systems,[1] he attributed to Plato the doctrine that the goal of philosophy is to become godlike[2] and this formula was adopted by virtually all Platonists, including Plotinus.[3]

Other Platonists representing ideas similar to those of Albinus are: the anonymous author of a commentary on the *Theaetetus*[4] (he objects to the doctrine of the Stoa according to which individual and social ethics can be derived from the principle of *oikeiôsis* and defends instead the *homoiôsis theôi* formula), and Diogenes Laertius III 41 (no trace of the Two-opposite-principles doctrine, while in III 74 we find the division of beings into relatives and irrelatives).

Thus, by the end of the second century A.D. we have a variety of Platonisms. Outstanding among them are:

(1) The Platonism of Aristotle and the Old Academy (stress on Two opposite principles and the horizontal tripartition of being [ideas; mathematicals = soul; physicals]; attempts to overcome the dualism, particularly by elevating a higher One which has no opposite above a lower which has; identification of the middle of the three parts with either the soul or mathematicals). After its disappearance from the Academy, it was perhaps represented only by Eudorus.

(2) The syncretistic system of Antiochus which combines the doctrines of Plato, as they appear in his dialogues and which have little to do with the first variety of Platonism, with the doctrines of the Stoa and, perhaps, some doctrines of Aristotle.

(3) The syncretistic system represented by Albinus and Apuleius, based on the doctrines of Plato's dialogues combined with the doctrines of *Aristoteles esotericus*, mainly his logic and noetics.[5]

[1] Stob. *Ecl.* II 7, vol. II, pp. 42, 7–57, 12 Wachsmuth; cf. Zeller, *Phil.* III/1 (⁵1923), p. 634 n. 3.

[2] Cf. *Theaetetus* 176B.

[3] *Enn.* I 2 [19]. Cf. Harder *ad loc.* According to Theiler (*op. cit.* p. 53), the formula originated with Antiochus. But this is hard to accept, as Antiochus derived ethics from the principle of living according to nature.

[4] Ed. by H. Diels and W. Schubart, *Anonymer Kommentar zu Platons Theätet* (1905).

[5] On Stoic influence on Plutarch, Albinus, Apuleius, and Atticus see M. Pohlenz, *Die Stoa* (²1959, 1955), I, pp. 358 f., 362.

(4) The non-syncretistic system of Plato, derived mainly from his dialogues, of which Atticus and, to a certain extent, Plutarch are the representatives. 'Non-syncretistic' in this case means that neither *wants* to reconcile Platonism either with Aristotle or with the Stoa.[1]

If we now, with regard to (3) and (4), ask which of the works of Plato or which parts of them form the basis of their image of him, we can answer that the political and the aporematic aspects of these dialogues have largely been relegated to the background. We shall, therefore, not be surprised to see that according to the index of Bréhier, Plotinus quotes only these works by Plato: *Timaeus*, *Parmenides*, *Phaedrus*, *Symposium*, *Republic* (and mainly x), *Sophist*, *Philebus*, *Phaedo*, *Alcibiades I*, *Letters*, *Nomoi*, *Hippias ma.*, *Politicus*, *Epinomis* (roughly in order of decreased frequency of quotations),[2] while Schwyzer adds *Cratylus* and *Critias*.

As to (1), it can, in general, be said that whereas the horizontal tripartition is of prime importance for Plotinus, his attempts to retain the identification of the soul with a mathematical or to approximate mathematicals and intelligence, or, within his system, to find an appropriate place for the Indefinite Dyad lead to ambiguous and unsatisfactory statements. The soul is sometimes designated as a number;[3] so is intelligence;[4] the whole sphere of intelligence as Indefinite Dyad, or containing indefiniteness;[5] and also to matter, be it intelligible or the lower, the same concept is applied.[6]

[1] Cf. Ueberweg–Praechter, *Grundriss*, §70; R. E. Witt, *Albinus and the History of Middle Platonism* (1937), esp. ch. IX.

[2] Cf. also H.-R. Schwyzer, 'Plotinos', *RE*, XXI/1 (1951), col. 551.

[3] V 1 [10] 5; VI 5 [23] 9.

[4] V 1 [10] 5.

[5] *Enn.* V 4 [7] 2.

[6] *Enn.* II 4 [12] 11, 34 under the designation 'the great-and-small', which is only another expression for the Indefinite Dyad.

CHAPTER 5

THE PYTHAGOREANS[1]

A. *Pseudepigrapha*

We know no Platonist later than the Old Academy and earlier than Eudorus who would have been interested in the Two-opposite-principles doctrine and the attendant horizontal stratification as attributed to Plato by Aristotle. Plutarch, who quotes Eudorus in a different context, knows the doctrine but makes very little of it. However, this does not mean that the doctrine was, before Eudorus, forgotten altogether. It rather seems that, while it lost its home in the Academy (or was relegated to some corner there), it was fully appropriated by the authors of post-Platonic Pythagorean writings.[2] However, they often equate the two principles with Aristotle's form and matter, or with the active and passive principles of the Stoa.[3] Syncretism makes its full appearance.

For our purpose it is best to distinguish three classes of these writings.[4] The first consists of pseudepigrapha. Two names are of particular interest in this group: that of Ps.-Archytas and that of Ps.-Brontinus (assuming the passage by the latter as quoted first by Syrianus, and the

[1] As a motto to this section could serve the words: *On ne relègue pas indûment les pythagoriciens sans enrichir indûment Platon* (P. Boyancé, 'Le dieu cosmique', *Revue des Études grecques*, LXIV [1951], pp. 300–13, esp. p. 303). For Plato we could substitute Plotinus. But, of course, the question of how much in later Pythagoreanism is Platonic, or how much in Plato and the Old Academy is genuinely Pythagorean, is irrelevant for the problem at hand. For a survey of the various answers, see W. Burkert, *Weisheit und Wissenschaft* (1962), pp. 1–9, cf. p. 73.

[2] I speak of Pythagorean writings rather than of Pythagoreans in order to evade the problem whether these writings were forgeries (perhaps simply literary fiction not pretending to be more than that) or actually written by Pythagoreans and *bona fide* attributed by them to famous members of the school. Of the former opinion is W. Burkert, 'Hellenistische Pseudopythagorica', *Philologus*, CV (1961), pp. 16–43, 226–46; of the latter H. Thesleff, *An Introduction to the Pythagorean Writings of the Hellenistic Period* (1961). For our purpose this problem is irrelevant as long as we can be reasonably sure that these writings originated in the time before Plotinus and were taken to be genuine.

[3] On Peripatetic and Stoic doctrines in Pythagorean writings see M. Pohlenz, *Die Stoa* ([2]1959, 1955), II, p. 188.

[4] Paralleled by Aetius I 3, 8 and I 7, 18 (Diels, *Dox.* pp. 280, 302). In the latter passage the Indefinite Dyad is identified with evil, as it is in Ps.-Galen, *Hist. phil.* 35 (Diels, *Dox.* p. 618); in Ps.-Plutarch, *De vita Homeri* 145, vol. VII, p. 416 Bernardakis; in Plutarch, *De Is. et Os.* 48, 570F, etc. Cf. C. Baeumker, *Das Problem der Materie in der griechischen Philosophie* (1890), p. 401, notes 3 and 5.

passage by the former as quoted by Joh. Stobaeus to belong to the pre-Plotinian period).[1]

Speaking of Brontinus, Syrianus assures us that the Pythagoreans were familiar with the doctrine that there is a principle higher than the two opposite principles. To prove it he quotes Philolaus as having said that God brought forth limit and the limitless; and he says that Archaenetus (there is hardly any reason to change this to Archytas) spoke of a cause prior to a cause and that Brontinus said of this cause that it is above intelligence and being (*ousia*), surpassing it in power and dignity.[2]

And somewhat later: The One and that which is good (goodness) are, according to Plato, above being (*ousia*); and the same is asserted by Brontinus and all members of the Pythagorean school.[3]

On the same Brontinus we read in Ps.-Alexander that he taught the essence of that which is good to be the One.[4] This is hardly anything but a repetition of the famous clause in which, according to Aristoxenus, Plato's *akroasis* on that which is good culminated (see above, p. 23).

And Stobaeus preserved for us a Ps.-Archytean passage of interest in our context. First Ps.-Archytas introduces as two opposite principles matter, which he also calls *ousia*, and form (*morphê*). He proceeds to state that there must be, then, a third principle which is self-moved and will bring the two together, so that we have three principles. This third principle must be not merely intelligence, but something superior to intelligence—and it is obvious that that which is superior to intelligence is precisely what we call God.[5]

It is difficult to imagine a more syncretistic passage in so small a compass. The two principles of form and matter are Aristotelian; to call the latter *ousia* is Stoic; to teach that form and matter must be brought together by another principle is Aristotelian again; to call this third principle self-moved is Platonic; to call it above intelligence is Platonic (and proto-Plotinian)—unless we say that it is also Aristotelian,

[1] I assume that all doctrines here attributed to Philolaus, Archytas, Archaenetus, Brontinus, and Callicratidas (see below) appeared in pseudepigrapha. But it would make no difference for our purpose if some had been expressed in genuine Pythagorean writings.

[2] *In Met.* 165, 33 – 166, 6 Kroll.

[3] *In Met.* 183, 1–3 Kroll. On these and related passages, see Zeller, *Phil.* 1/1 (^{6}1919), pp. 467–74; Zeller–Mondolfo (^{2}1950), pp. 460–7.

[4] *In Met.* 821, 39 Hayd.

[5] *Ecl.* I 41, vol. 1, 278, 18 – 281, 3 Wachsmuth.

because in *On Prayer* Aristotle says that God is either intelligence or something above intelligence,[1] and because, in the *Eudemian Ethics*, he says that there is only one thing which is superior to knowledge and intelligence, viz. God.[2]

Assuming that Syrianus, Ps.-Alexander (or his source, and it cannot be ruled out that it was the genuine Alexander), and Stobaeus quoted pseudepigrapha which existed before Plotinus, we can, therefore, say that in a number of these pseudepigrapha the Two-opposite-principles doctrine was stated as being Pythagorean;[3] furthermore, that in a number of such writings the attempt was made to overcome the dualism of this doctrine; finally, that in a number of these writings the principle transcending the opposites was described in terms somewhat similar to those used by Plotinus to describe his One, including the assertion that it transcends even intelligence. It can also be said that what Aristotle explicitly attributed to pre-Platonic Pythagoreans, viz. the principles of limit and the unlimited, were in these writings simply equated with Plato's One, and the Indefinite Dyad, despite the fact that, according to Aristotle, the latter was the innovation of Plato.[4] Once Aristotle said that Plato took over some of his fundamental doctrines from the Pythagoreans, this obviously was used as an excuse to attribute anything said by Plato to them. And as Plato decided to present the most famous of his dialogues as a work by Timaeus—whom everybody took to mean the Pythagorean Timaeus of Locri, though Plato never calls his spokesman a Pythagorean—it is possible, even *bona fide*, simply to equate Plato with Pythagoreanism, particularly with regard to the Two-opposite-principles doctrine.

One more pseudepigraphon deserves attention: Ps.-Callicratidas. Again, in a passage preserved by Stobaeus, we find the doctrine of the Two opposite principles restated with this interesting variant that they are related by Ps.-Callicratidas to the categories of the irrelative and the relative.[5] We are familiar with this combination from Hermodorus.[6]

[1] *Fr.* 49 Rose.

[2] Θ 2, 1248a27–9.

[3] Also Speusippus' 'pythagorizing' played its role here.

[4] *Met.* A 6, 987b25–7.

[5] *Flor.* 70, 101, vol. IV, 534, 10 — 536, 5 Hense.

[6] The Aristotelian doctrine of ten categories has also been claimed for Ps.-Archytas (cf. Zeller, *Phil.* III/2 [⁵1923], pp. 119 n. 1, 144 n. 2), but in him there is nothing of the combination of ontology with categories, nor any reduction to only two (see above, p. 37).

B. *Anonymi Photii, Alexandri, Sexti, etc.*

So much for the pseudepigrapha. A second group of Pythagorean writings is represented to us by three complexes: the anonymus Photii, the anonymus (or anonymi) of Alexander Polyhistor, and the anonymus (or anonymi) of Sextus Empiricus. All three present Pythagorean doctrines; but whether they base their presentation on pseudepigrapha or some other source remains unknown to us.

We begin with the anonymus Photii.[1] In him not only do we find the doctrine of the Two opposite principles—not only their monistic interpretation, elevating the monad to the rank of a supreme principle. We also find in him the principle of derivation, including the derivation of the sensible (*sôma*) from the intelligible. It is a peculiar variant of the derivation theory in two respects. First, it derives geometricals, i.e. neither numbers nor simply mathematicals, from the monad; secondly, it neither includes the soul among the products of derivation nor identifies it with the geometrical (or the mathematical or numbers). But clearly, it distinguishes the geometrical three-dimensionality from the three-dimensionality of what it calls a body.[2]

With regard to the pseudepigrapha we could be reasonably sure that they are pre-Plotinian. But how about the anonymus Photii?

The problem is highly controversial. Immisch identified the anonymus with Agatharchides, the 'reader' of Heraclides Lembus. That would place him in the second century B.C. This, plus the fact that Heraclides Lembus was already familiar with pseudo-Pythagorica, would prove that what is usually called Neopythagoreanism started

[1] *Bibl. cod.* 249.

[2] *Loc. cit. PG.* 103, 1579–88, esp. 1580 f. The anonymus equates Aristotle's changeless changers with Plato's ideas. He furthermore credits both with the doctrine of the immortality of the soul, admitting, however, that some deny that Aristotle believed in it. Why, then, does the anonymus attribute it to him? The text gives no answer; but there are obviously two possibilities. Either the anonymus simply attributed to the soul what Aristotle attributed to intelligence alone; or he was referring to some writing of the *Aristoteles exotericus*. And, indeed, it is somewhat difficult to assume that he had no knowledge of this other Aristotle. For the anonymus not only counts Plato as ninth in the succession of Pythagoras but also Aristotle as the tenth. Now, if the anonymus had been thinking of Aristotle's theory of the immortality of the intelligence, he must have known his *De anima*. But in the *De anima* Aristotle so clearly is anti-Pythagorean, so greatly ridicules the Pythagorean doctrine of the soul (and transmigration), that to make him a Pythagorean the anonymus must have known writings by Aristotle in which he professed doctrines of the soul compatible with the doctrine of its immortality (and perhaps even of transmigration) and incompatible with *De anima*.

much earlier than is usually assumed. However, Immisch was contradicted by Praechter, who seems to be inclined to place him in the post-Plotinian age.[1]

Now, whether the anonymus is identical with Agatharchides does not concern us here. What is of importance is only to decide whether we should place him after Plotinus (if Praechter meant to say this). And it seems that in this respect Praechter's arguments are not over-strong. But if the anonymus Photii is pre-Plotinian, it is certainly remarkable to what extent pre-Plotinian Pythagoreanism simply annexed Plato and Aristotle.

From the anonymus Photii we pass to the anonymus of Alexander Polyhistor.[2] Again we are not interested in the problem of how much of his report on the Pythagoreans can be traced to a pre-Stoic source—what is incontestable is that it belongs to the pre-Plotinian era, as Alexander Polyhistor lived in the first century B.C.

He interprets the Two-opposite-principles doctrine monistically and also assumes, as a matter of course, the derivation of sensibles from mathematicals. Remarkable is his admixture of Stoic materialism (e.g. the principles are equated with power and matter; furthermore, the soul is a particle of ether and as immortal as ether). How this can be reconciled with the doctrine that only the reasonable part of the soul (*phrenes*) survives remains unclear.

Much of what we could find in the anonymus Alexandri we can also find in the anonymi of Sextus Empiricus.[3] Sextus presents Pythagorean doctrines in three places.[4] The first of these is but a shorter version of the third; the second contains little pertinent to our present investiga-

[1] O. Immisch, *Agatharchidea* (*SB der Heidelberger Ak. d. Wiss., philos.-hist. Kl.*, Jahrgang 1919, 7. Abh., 1919); K. Praechter in Ueberweg–Praechter, *Grundriss*, pp. 518* and 157*. On additional evidence in favour of Immisch, see W. Burkert, *Weisheit und Wissenschaft* (1962), p. 49.

[2] Diog. Laert. VIII 1. Cf. Zeller, *Phil.* III/2 (^{5}1923), pp. 103–8. There is a considerable amount of literature on him, but, as it deals mainly with the problem how much of it can be considered pre-Platonic (genuinely Pythagorean), it does not concern us here.

[3] On the Sextus passages see Zeller, *Phil.* I/1 (^{6}1919), pp. 465, 471; III/2 (^{5}1923), pp. 148 f.; P. Merlan, 'Beiträge zur Geschichte der antiken Platonismus I.', *Philologus*, LXXXIX (1934), pp. 35–53, esp. pp. 37–44; P. Wilpert, *Zwei platonische Frühschriften über die Ideenlehre* (1949), pp. 125–48 and 168–94 (with review by W. Jaeger, *Gnomon*, XXIII [1951], pp. 246–52, esp. pp. 250 f., repr. in *Scripta minora* [1960], II, pp. 419–28, esp. pp. 424–6); W. Burkert, *Weisheit und Wissenschaft* (1962), p. 48; G. Vlastos, *Gnomon*, XXXV (1963), pp. 644–8.

[4] *PH* III 152–7; *Adv. math.* VII 94–109, and X 249–84. Whether and to what extent their source is Posidonius need not be discussed here. Cf. W. Burkert, *Weisheit und Wissenschaft* (1962), pp. 48–50.

tion; thus, we concentrate on the third. Here we learn that there are two schools of Pythagoreans, one reducing everything to two opposite principles, the One and the Indefinite Dyad, the other asserting that everything is reducible to the One, whose 'flow' engenders everything else (obviously including the Indefinite Dyad). But what the two schools have in common is their conviction that the sensible must be derived from the intelligible (incorporeal) and that within the intelligible (incorporeal) ideas do not represent the highest kind because each idea is a unit and can be combined with other ideas. Therefore, we must assume that above ideas are numbers, and it is through participation in these numbers that ideas are one or two, etc. We feel reminded of Plotinus' proof that numbers must precede that which can be numbered.[1]

Now, though Sextus clearly opposes one school as dualistic to the other as monistic, still the dualistic school is not so far removed from monism either. For it credits Pythagoras with having said that the monad is a principle which in some way by reduplicating itself (in modern terms we could probably say: by self-reflection) creates the Indefinite Dyad (it can be seen how reduplication engenders the Dyad, but it remains unclear why this Dyad should be Indefinite). Despite this, however, the school remains dualistic in that it proves the presence of the Two opposite principles in everything by its doctrines of categories in a manner strictly paralleling Hermodorus, the *Divisiones Aristoteleae*, and Ps.-Callicratidas. All existents are divided into irrelatives, existents having an opposite, and relatives. The genus of opposites is the equal and the unequal; the genus of the relatives is excess and defect; the unequal, excess, and defect belong under the Indefinite Dyad. The irrelatives and the equals belong under the One.

Again, sensibles are, as a matter of course, derived from geometricals. As we already know, this idea can be traced to the Old Academy and even to Plato himself (see above, p. 19).

It is worth noting that in the Pythagorean pseudepigrapha and anonyma we find a wide variety of doctrines concerning the soul, which *prima facie* seem incompatible. The soul is designated as number (or another mathematical entity), as consisting of ether and immortal, as having three parts, one of which is immortal (either Plato's immortal

[1] *Enn.* VI 6 [34] 9.

part or Aristotle's intelligence), as being some kind of harmony, as consisting of *pneuma*. Sometimes we find the doctrine of reincarnation (not too frequently[1] and, as we have seen, Ps.-Timaeus Locrus denied any kind of immortality to the soul), sometimes simply the doctrine of immortality, and sometimes we find the soul equated with a demon. We find it necessary to explain the contradictions, e.g. by assuming that the term 'soul' has several different meanings,[2] but it does not seem that in antiquity the problem of Pythagorean consistency was ever raised.[3] Plato[4] seems to be one of very few who are certain that the doctrine of the soul as harmony is incompatible with any belief in its immortality. Plotinus rejects any theory which would make the soul material (either ethereal or pneumatic), but he tentatively suggests that after death the soul inhabits its spherical body, so that it is never entirely disembodied.[5]

C. *Moderatus and Nicomachus*

The third class of Pythagorean writings (neither pseudepigrapha nor anonymous) consists of works by Moderatus of Gades;[6] Nicomachus of Gerasa (active *c.* A.D. 140–50); and Numenius of Apamea (second century A.D.). Their Pythagoreanism differs from that represented by the two other classes.[7]

Moderatus poses a particularly difficult problem.

First of all, he represents a new type of Pythagoreanism which we could call aggressive. He is not satisfied, as the anonymus Photii was, to see in Plato and Aristotle simply Pythagoreans. He asserts that these two

[1] The doctrine is attributed to Pythagoras, e.g. by Ps.-Plutarch (*Placita* IV 7, 1 [Diels, *Dox.* p. 392], and *De Vita Homeri* 125, vol. VII, p. 399 Bernardakis). Cf. W. Burkert, *Weisheit und Wissenschaft* (1962), p. 101.

[2] See W. K. C. Guthrie, *A History of Greek Philosophy*, I (1962), pp. 306–19.

[3] Ecphantus is credited with having been the first to identify numbers with bodies, and Ps.-Theano seems to protest against this materialism by insisting that Pythagoras did not say that everything consists of numbers but only that everything is constituted according to number. Cf. Zeller, *Phil.* III/2 (51923), pp. 152–5; Stob. *Ecl.* I 10, vol. I, p. 127, 16–18; pp. 125, 19 – 126, 5 Wachsmuth.

[4] *Phaedo* 86B.

[5] *Enn.* IV 4 [28] 5. One of the most remarkable passages concerning the journey of the soul through the celestial spheres, and its elongation resulting therefrom, we find in Aristides Quintilianus, *De musica* II 17, pp. 63, 8 – 64, 5 Jahn, p. 86, 24 – 88, 6 Winnington-Ingram. On the controversial question whether this writing is pre- or post-Plotinian, cf. A. J. Festugière, 'L'Âme et la Musique d'après Aristide Quintilien', *Transactions and Proceedings of the American Philological Association*, LXXXV (1954), pp. 55–78. Cf. p. 122 n. 3.

[6] First century A.D.; he is mentioned by Plutarch, *Qu. conv.* VIII 7, 727B.

[7] On this difference and the reason for it, see esp. W. Burkert, 'Hellenistische Pseudopythagorica', *Philologus*, CV (1961), pp. 16–43, 226–46, esp. p. 235.

(along with Speusippus, Xenocrates, and Aristoxenus) stole all important doctrines from the Pythagoreans and gave them out as theirs. They quoted some Pythagorean doctrines (thus hiding their theft), but what they quoted as Pythagorean were only things which were superficial and easily comprehended. By so doing, they exposed Pythagoreans to ridicule. This is one explanation of the fact that Pythagoreanism became extinct; among additional reasons is the one that the authors of allegedly Pythagorean writings were not Pythagoreans themselves.[1]

Moderatus thus feels entitled to claim everything said by Plato, Aristotle, Speusippus, etc. for Pythagoras and his 'genuine' pupils.[2]

Much more important, however, is another passage containing doctrines of Moderatus. It is quoted by Simplicius, who, however, in turn has it only from Porphyry. As a result, he quotes Moderatus in such a way that we cannot be quite sure where the quotation from him stops and words of Porphyry begin. It is, therefore, imperative to present the whole passage.

It seems the first among the Greeks who had such an opinion concerning matter were the Pythagoreans and after them Plato, as indeed Moderatus tells us. For he, in accordance with the Pythagoreans, declares of the first One that it is above being and any entity; of the second One (that which truly is and is an intelligible) he says that it is the ideas; and of the third One (that which is psychical) that it participates in the One and the ideas; of the last nature (which is that of the sensibles) derived from it that it does not even participate but rather receives its order as a reflection of the others, matter in them being a shadow cast by the primary non-being existing in quantity and having descended still further and being derived from it.

And in the second book of *Matter* Porphyry, citing from Moderatus, has also written that the Unitary Logos—as Plato somewhere says—intending to produce from himself the origin of beings, by self-privation left room to quantity, depriving it of all his ratios and ideas. He called this quantity, shapeless, undifferentiated, and formless, but receptible of shape, form, differentiation, quality, etc. It is this quantity, he says, to which Plato

[1] Porphyry, *Vita Pyth.* 53, p. 46 Nauck².

[2] It seems that Iamblichus took this quite literally. Of his work in ten parts devoted to an exposition of Pythagoreanism only four have survived. Of these we single out his *Protrepticus* and *De communi mathematica scientia* (omitting the *Life of Pythagoras* and the *Arithmetical Theology*). Now, it is highly remarkable that in these two works which profess to present Pythagorean doctrines we find passages taken without further ado from Plato and Aristotle (and from other authors of whom we never think as being Pythagoreans). If Iamblichus accepted the theory of Moderatus, he could do so *bona fide*.

apparently applies various predicates, speaking of the 'all-receiver', of that which is bare of species, 'the invisible' and 'the least capable of participating in the intelligible' and 'barely seizable by pseudo-reasoning' and everything similar to such predicates. This quantity, he says, and this species, viz. thought of in the sense of being privation of the Unitary Logos which contains in himself all ratios of beings, are paradigms of the matter of bodies, which itself, he says, was called quantity by Pythagoreans and Plato, not in the sense of quantity as an idea, but in the sense of privation, paralysis, dispersion, and severance and because of its deviating from that which is—for which reason matter seems to be evil, as it flees that which is good.

And this matter is caught by it and is not permitted to overstep its boundaries, as dispersion receives the ratio of ideal magnitude and is bounded by it, and as severance is by numerical distinction rendered eidetic.

Thus, according to this exposition matter is nothing else but deviation of sensible species from intelligible ones, as the former turn away from there and are borne down towards non-being.[1]

[1] Simplicius, *In Phys.* 230, 34 – 231, 27 Diels:
Ταύτην δὲ περὶ τῆς ὕλης τὴν ὑπόνοιαν ἐοίκασιν ἐσχηκέναι πρῶτοι
35 μὲν τῶν Ἑλλήνων οἱ Πυθαγόρειοι, μετὰ δ' ἐκείνους ὁ Πλάτων, ὡς καὶ
Μοδέρατος ἱστορεῖ. οὗτος γὰρ κατὰ τοὺς Πυθαγορείους τὸ μὲν πρῶτον ἓν
ὑπὲρ τὸ εἶναι καὶ πᾶσαν οὐσίαν ἀποφαίνεται, τὸ δὲ δεύτερον ἕν, ὅπερ ἐστὶ
p. 231 τὸ ὄντως ὂν καὶ νοητόν, τὰ εἴδη φησὶν εἶναι, τὸ δὲ τρίτον, ὅπερ ἐστὶ τὸ
ψυχικόν, μετέχειν τοῦ ἑνὸς καὶ τῶν εἰδῶν, τὴν δὲ ἀπὸ τούτου τελευταίαν
φύσιν τὴν τῶν αἰσθητῶν οὖσαν μηδὲ μετέχειν, ἀλλὰ κατ' ἔμφασιν ἐκεί-
νων κεκοσμῆσθαι, τῆς ἐν αὐτοῖς ὕλης τοῦ μὴ ὄντος πρώτως ἐν τῷ ποσῷ
5 ὄντος οὔσης σκίασμα καὶ ἔτι μᾶλλον ὑποβεβηκυίας καὶ ἀπὸ τούτου. καὶ
ταῦτα δὲ ὁ Πορφύριος ἐν τῷ δευτέρῳ Περὶ ὕλης τὰ τοῦ Μοδεράτου παρα-
τιθέμενος γέγραφεν ὅτι βουληθεὶς ὁ ἑνιαῖος λόγος, ὥς πού φησιν ὁ Πλάτων,
τὴν γένεσιν ἀφ' ἑαυτοῦ τῶν ὄντων συστήσασθαι, κατὰ στέρησιν αὑτοῦ
ἐχώρησε τὴν ποσότητα πάντων αὐτὴν στερήσας τῶν αὑτοῦ λόγων καὶ εἰ-
10 δῶν. τοῦτο δὲ ποσότητα ἐκάλεσεν ἄμορφον καὶ ἀδιαίρετον καὶ ἀσχημά-
τιστον, ἐπιδεχομένην μέντοι μορφὴν σχῆμα διαίρεσιν ποιότητα πᾶν τὸ
τοιοῦτον. ἐπὶ ταύτης ἔοικε, φησί, τῆς ποσότητος ὁ Πλάτων τὰ πλείω ὀνό-
ματα κατηγορῆσαι "πανδεχῆ" καὶ ἀνείδεον λέγων καὶ "ἀόρατον" καὶ "ἀπο-
ρώτατα τοῦ νοητοῦ μετειληφέναι" αὐτὴν καὶ "λογισμῷ νόθῳ μόλις ληπτήν"
15 καὶ πᾶν τὸ τούτοις ἐμφερές. αὕτη δὲ ἡ ποσότης, φησί, καὶ τοῦτο τὸ
εἶδος τὸ κατὰ στέρησιν τοῦ ἑνιαίου λόγου νοούμενον τοῦ πάντας τοὺς λό-
γους τῶν ὄντων ἐν ἑαυτῷ περιειληφότος παραδείγματά ἐστι τῆς τῶν σω-
μάτων ὕλης, ἣν καὶ αὐτὴν ποσὸν καὶ τοὺς Πυθαγορείους καὶ τὸν Πλάτωνα
καλεῖν ἔλεγεν, οὐ τὸ ὡς εἶδος ποσόν, ἀλλὰ τὸ κατὰ στέρησιν καὶ παρά-
20 λυσιν καὶ ἔκτασιν καὶ διασπασμὸν καὶ διὰ τὴν ἀπὸ τοῦ ὄντος παράλλαξιν,
δι' ἃ καὶ κακὸν δοκεῖ ἡ ὕλη ὡς τὸ ἀγαθὸν ἀποφεύγουσα. καὶ κατα-
λαμβάνεται ὑπ' αὐτοῦ καὶ ἐξελθεῖν τῶν ὅρων οὐ συγχωρεῖται, τῆς μὲν
ἐκτάσεως τὸν τοῦ εἰδητικοῦ μεγέθους λόγον ἐπιδεχομένης καὶ τούτῳ ὁριζο-
μένης, τοῦ δὲ διασπασμοῦ τῇ ἀριθμητικῇ διακρίσει εἰδοποιουμένου. ἔστιν
25 οὖν ἡ ὕλη κατὰ τοῦτον τὸν λόγον οὐδὲν ἄλλο ἢ ἡ τῶν αἰσθητῶν εἰδῶν
πρὸς τὰ νοητὰ παράλλαξις παρατραπέντων ἐκεῖθεν καὶ πρὸς τὸ μὴ ὂν ὑπο-
φερομένων.

Let us, first of all, interpret the passage,[1] assuming that it, as a whole, is from Moderatus. Moderatus would then attribute to Plato, the Pythagorean, these doctrines: There is a first, a second, and a third One. The first One is beyond all being and *ousia*. The second, i.e. that which is actually being and intelligible, equals ideas. The third One, viz. the psychical, participates in the first One and in the ideas. These three are followed by that which is sensible. And this realm of the sensible does not participate in the One or the ideas, but comes to exist as cosmos in that the One and the ideas are reflected in the matter of the sensibles. But whence this matter of the sensibles? It is something like a shadow of the first non-being which appears in quantity.

It is obvious what it would mean if this passage belonged in its totality to Moderatus. What we have before us is what has always been considered the very backbone of the Plotinian system. Three intelligible hypostases, the One above being, the intelligible (ideas) *sensu strictiori* or the realm of being, and the soul; matter which catches the reflection of the intelligible *sensu latiori*, as a result of which the realm of the sensible comes into existence; a double matter, viz. a lower which is a shadow of the higher—what remains for Plotinus?

It is, therefore, not surprising that Zeller should have objected and originally asserted (later to change his mind—but only in part) that the whole passage is by Porphyry and that Porphyry simply read Plotinian doctrines into Moderatus—more precisely, into Moderatus' presentation of Plato. Porphyry did it, says Zeller, basing his own interpretation of Plato on the *2nd Letter* and on *Nomoi* VI 509B.[2]

But the case for Moderatus was taken up by Dodds.[3] The most interesting of his arguments is connected with his assertion that the whole passage is an interpretation of Plato's *Parmenides*, which finds what will later be called five hypostases in five hypotheses of its second part (*hen* in 137D–142A; *to hen hen kai polla* in 145A; *to hen oute hen oute polla* in 157A; *ta alla* in 157B; *mê esti to hen* in 160B), with the One, intelligence (or the intelligible), soul, the sensible, matter.

This would make the debt of Plotinus to Moderatus even greater.

[1] Translated with commentary in A. J. Festugière, *La Révélation d'Hermès Trismégiste* (1954) IV, pp. 22 f. and 38 f.

[2] Zeller, *Phil.* III/2 ([5]1923), pp. 130 f.

[3] E. R. Dodds, 'The *Parmenides* of Plato and the Origin of the Neoplatonic "One"', *Classical Quarterly*, XXII (1928), pp. 129–42, esp. pp. 136–9.

For it is generally assumed that Plotinus was the first to interpret the *Parmenides* ontologically. And it would make the debt of other post-Plotinian Platonists to Moderatus considerable, for the explicit co-ordination of the five hypotheses of the *Parmenides* with the five hypostases of Plotinus in explicit form is found only in Plutarch of Athens.[1]

At the same time it cannot be asserted that the doctrines of Moderatus are identical with those of Plotinus. The obvious difference is in what can be called the derivation of 'higher' matter from the One. Moderatus has a very peculiar theory: by contracting, the One releases, if we may say so, sheer quantity, and it is this sheer quantity which is the Indeterminate Dyad.

Is Dodds right? Is all this Moderatus? Or is it rather Porphyry?

One argument seems decisive. The concept of a self-contracting deity is known to Numenius;[2] he attributes it to Pythagoreans who, he asserts, misunderstood the Two-opposite-principles doctrine (Numenius speaks of the [*unica*] *singularitas recedens a natura sua et in duitatis habitum migrans*).[3] It cannot, therefore, be the property of Porphyry. And, instead of assuming that Porphyry read into Moderatus partly doctrines of Plotinus, partly doctrines of Numenius, it seems simpler to assume that, indeed, the whole passage as quoted above belongs to Moderatus.[4]

Iamblichus preserved another doctrine of Moderatus. He counts him among those who identify the psychical with the mathematical. Specifically, his doctrine is that the soul is a number (or an entity: the text permits both interpretations) containing proportions. This seems to mean that the soul 'is' in some way the number four which contains the basic ratios constitutive of the octave (2:1), the fifth (3:2), and the fourth (4:3). Such an interpretation would explain why Iamblichus counts Moderatus also among those who apply to the soul the concept of harmony.[5] We have seen how important the identification of the soul with mathematicals is (see above, p. 62).

[1] R. Beutler, 'Plutarchos von Athen', *RE*, XXI/1 (1951), col. 970–5.

[2] In Calcidius, ch. 295; *test.* 30 Leemans.

[3] See, e.g., the apparatus in: *Timaeus a Calcidio translatus*..., ed. J. H. Waszink (1962), p. 297 and p. ciii, note; A. J. Festugière, *La Révélation d'Hermès Trismégiste* (1954) IV, pp. 37 f.

[4] W. Capelle, 'Moderatus', in *RE*, XV/2 (1932), seems to have had no knowledge of the paper by Dodds.

[5] Iambl. in Stob. *Ecl.* I 32–43, vol. I, 362, 24 – 385, 10 Wachsmuth. On this passage, see P. Merlan, 'Überflüssige Textänderungen', *Philologische Wochenschrift*, LVI (1936), p. 912; Idem, 'Die Hermetische Pyramide und Sextus', *Museum Helveticum*, VIII (1951), pp. 100–5. It is trans-

Two more aspects of the doctrines of Moderatus will be mentioned. As we have noticed, he, with many others,[1] distinguishes a first from a second One;[2] and he refers to the supreme One as the reason why the universe is animated by one spirit (breath), why all its parts are in 'sympathy' with each other, and why in the universe stability is preserved.[3] Here we have the doctrine of the One combined with Stoicism and its concept of the One. The importance of this combination for Plotinus will be discussed later (see p. 127).

Nicomachus is known to us primarily as the author of an *Introduction to Arithmetic* and of the *Arithmetical Theology*. The latter[4] is an extraordinary example of 'theologizing' concepts—in this case, numbers. Each number is identified with a number of deities, Greek and non-Greek; it is a strange kind of reconciling polytheism with mathematics. It is hardly possible to decide in which direction to read the equations: does Nicomachus intend to say that what is actually meant when people speak of divinities is numbers, or does he, on the contrary, teach the mathematician that he, whether he knows it or not, speaks of deities when speaking of numbers? In any case—we suddenly have before us a peculiar approach to polytheism. In Plotinus the divinization of numbers plays no conspicuous role; but it will be particularly Proclus (he thought of himself as Nicomachus' avatar), who will fully adopt the principle of Nicomachus.

Having identified numbers with gods, Nicomachus explains that they, i.e. the number-gods, are the causes of the being of beings. We feel reminded of Plotinus, who places the (ideal) numbers between being and beings,[5] and also of Proclus, who repeatedly stresses that the ideal numbers are universal causes.[6]

lated with a commentary in A. J. Festugière, *La Révélation d'Hermès Trismégiste* (1953) III, pp. 177–248. The fact that the soul 'contains' all the ratios fundamental to music would explain the therapeutic effects of the music on the soul: it helps to re-establish harmonies which have become disturbed.

[1] Cf. A. J. Festugière, *La Révélation d'Hermès Trismégiste* (1954) IV, pp. 23 f.

[2] Stob. *Ecl.* I, 8, vol. I, p. 21, 8–16 Wachsmuth.

[3] Porphyry, *Vita Pyth.* 49, p. 44 Nauck².

[4] Excerpts in Photius, *Bibl. cod.* 187.

[5] *Enn.* VI 6 [34].

[6] It is perhaps worth mentioning that the nature of the number-gods, as Nicomachus describes them, becomes entirely ambiguous. The One is male–female, thus, in some way, matter; the Dyad is 'daring' (*tolma*), but, in some way, also good. It does not seem that this aspect of Nicomachus' doctrines was of any importance to Plotinus. [On *tolma* in Plotinus see Part III, ch. 15, pp. 242–3.]

Secondly, in his *Introduction to Arithmetic*, Nicomachus speaks of numbers as pre-existing in the mind of God—in other words, he appropriates a doctrine which obviously originated in the Academy (ideas as God's thoughts). He can do it *bona fide* inasmuch as Plato himself and some of his pupils identified ideas and numbers. However, regardless of this ambiguity, he suggests a monistic interpretation of the Two-opposite-principles theory.[1]

D. *Numenius*

Plotinus was accused (obviously by Athenian Platonists) of plagiarizing Numenius; and Trypho, a Stoic and Platonist, notified Amelius of this. Thereupon Amelius wrote a little book (which he dedicated to Porphyry) on the difference between the doctrines of the two. This story told by Porphyry[2] cannot fail to arouse our curiosity. What were the doctrines of Numenius which we can still ascertain?[3]

We know something about his work on the difference between Plato and his disciples down to the time of Antiochus.[4] Numenius accuses them of having become untrue to their master, though Speusippus, Xenocrates, and Polemo, not being sceptics, preserved some of the Platonic heritage. As Numenius does not exclude Antiochus from this accusation (his philosophy, he says, contains a number of doctrines entirely foreign to Plato), he by implication warns us against attaching too much importance to Antiochus as a fountainhead of Neoplatonism. On the other hand, he obviously shares Antiochus' opinion that Zeno derived his philosophy from Xenocrates and Polemo. But he denies that Aristotle's philosophy has anything to do with Plato.

Numenius' own Plato is simply a Pythagorean—Socrates, by the way, another. Plato, he says, is, of course, not greater than Pythagoras but he is his equal. And Plato represents the medium between the loftiness of Pythagoras and the homeliness of Socrates.

[1] I 4. 6, Cf. Zeller, *Phil.* III/2 (⁴1903), pp. 135–41; M. L. D'Ooge, F. E. Robbins, L. C. Karpinski, *Nicomachus of Gerasa. Introduction to Mathematics* (Ann Arbor, 1938), esp. pp. 95 f. on the Stoic elements in Nicomachus' philosophy (cf. p. 98, 110); R. Henry, *Photius, Bibliothèque*, vol. III (1962).

[2] *Life of Plotinus* 17.

[3] The subsequent quotations are from E. A. Leeman's *Studie over den wijsgeer Numenius van Apamea* (1937). On Numenius, see R. Beutler, *RE*, Suppl. VII (1940); the introduction (pp. xxxviii–lxxxii) and the apparatus to Calcidius' *Timaeus* in the edition by J. H. Waszink (1962).

[4] *Fr.* 1–8 L.

So much for the general trend of his history of the Academy. Now, some details.

Plato was not the first philosopher whose doctrines students interpreted in many different ways, thus starting different schools. The same happened to Socrates; Aristippus, Antisthenes, the Megarians, the Eretrians—they all understood him in their own way. Why? Because Socrates assumed the existence of three gods and spoke of each in terms appropriate to each. But his students did not see this and thought that his doctrines were inconsistent.

Where did Numenius find Socrates teaching that there were three gods? It is usual to see in such a doctrine one of the most characteristic doctrines of Numenius himself. We shall see a little later that this, in all likelihood, is an erroneous opinion; but even if it were not, we should try to ascertain the basis on which Numenius attributed it to him. Now, Plato's *2nd Letter* contains two most striking passages. One already mentioned (above, p. 30) indeed teaches something which very easily could be called the doctrine of three gods. The other contains Plato's declaration that on certain things (and there can hardly be any doubt: he considers them to be of central importance) he has never written anything. And now the text: *ta de nyn legomena* belong to Socrates.

Nobody who reads the text will doubt that these words should be translated 'what now are said to be (or: pass for) Plato's writings are in fact writings by Socrates'. But quite obviously, Numenius took these words to be the beginning of a new paragraph and to refer to the whole preceding part of the letter. Thus, according to Plato as Numenius read him, the doctrine of the three gods belonged to Socrates.[1]

Let us stop our exposition of Numenius here and try to relate what we, by now, know of him, to Plotinus.

Undoubtedly Plotinus must have been in sympathy with interpreting Plato as a dogmatist. For Plato, the aporematic, he has no use whatsoever, and so he has no use for Socrates as he appears in the aporematic dialogues. He celebrated the birthdays of both Socrates and Plato, but, in all likelihood, he indeed either became convinced by Numenius or came to conclusions similar to his that Socrates was a Pythagorean. In

[1] See P. Merlan, 'Drei Anmerkungen zu Numenios', *Philologus*, CVI (1962), pp. 137–45, esp. p. 138.

any case, he quoted the trinitarian passage of the *2nd Letter* to prove that his own doctrine of the three hypostases was already taught by Plato (see above, p. 97). In other words, he used the *2nd Letter* very much like Numenius. Eusebius, who preserved for us the Numenius passage concerning Socrates, quoted it in connexion with the passage in which Plotinus refers to it. He obviously noticed the similar use of it by the two. Furthermore, Plotinus quotes Pythagoras as one of those who preceded him with the theory of three hypostases, thus plainly accepting his own filiation from him.

One detail of Numenius' history of the Academy deserves particular mention. He refers to Cephisodorus' criticism of Aristotle and ridicules it, because it treats Aristotle as professing the theory of ideas. Cephisodorus, Numenius says, simply did not know Aristotle.

We here have almost a duplicate of Plutarch's criticism of Colotes. What kind of ignoramus, Plutarch wonders,[1] was Colotes, who treated Aristotle as an adherent of the idea theory? Did he not know that in a number of his writings Aristotle objected to it?

In all likelihood, Jaeger and Bignone are right when they say that Plutarch and Numenius were mistaken in considering Colotes and Cephisodorus as entirely misinformed, and see in the passages in question a clear proof that in some of his writings Aristotle did profess the idea theory.[2] But, on the other hand, the passages also prove that even for Plutarch, who knew Aristotelian writings which we no longer possess, with regard to the idea theory the true Aristotle was the Aristotle of the *esoterica*, rather than of the *exoterica*. And Numenius seems to be completely unaware of any but the esoteric Aristotle. For Plotinus the same seems to hold; solely the *Eudemus*[3] seems once or twice to be quoted.[4] Only Iamblichus will again use the other Aristotle.

Another work by Numenius from which we have substantial excerpts is entitled *On the Good*.[5] In its first book Numenius declared that he is going to use for his topic Plato and Pythagoras, but that he will also bring in doctrines of famous nations which agree with Plato, especially

[1] *Adv. Col.* 14, 1115 A–C.

[2] W. Jaeger, *Aristoteles* (^{2}1955), pp. 436 f.; E. Bignone, *L'Aristotele perduto e la formazione filosofica di Epicuro* (1936), I, pp. 58–65; II, pp. 107 f. (see above, p. 59).

[3] *Fr.* 9 Ross.

[4] *Enn.* III 6 [26] 4; IV 7 [2] 84.

[5] *Fr.* 9–29 L.

those of Brahmans, Jews, Magi, and Egyptians.[1] This is the classic passage quoted by scholars who see in Numenius a representative of 'orientalism'. And Numenius' 'orientalism' is often taken to be a precursor of that of Plotinus. Therefore, we must discuss the passage at some length.

Why did Numenius have such a favourable opinion of these 'nations'? From a passage preserved by Origen[2] it would appear that it was because they believed in an incorporeal god. In addition, when he comes to speak of Moses,[3] he refers to him as a prophet and presents him as a magician greater than his rivals Iannes[4] and Iambres (though they succeeded in matching some of his minor miracles), because his prayers were more powerful than theirs (probably we here have the magic interpretation of prayers, as we find it in Plotinus).[5]

Does this prove much of an orientalizing or Judaizing tendency, if by this we mean recognition of superiority or derivation from the Orient? Hardly. There is not the slightest hint that he considered 'barbaric', particularly Jewish, wisdom as *superior* to that of Plato or as Plato's *source*. His attitude towards the Orient can best be compared with that of Plutarch, who liked to refer to Persian and Egyptian religions,[6] or of Diogenes Laertius. The latter, as is known, insisted on the autochthonous character of Greek philosophy, but he did not deny the existence of 'barbaric' wisdom.[7] Numenius might have been just a shade more favourable to the Orient. But after all, Aristotle already paid high tribute to the Egyptian priests who gave us the first example of contemplative life,[8] and unhesitatingly quoted Magi along with Empedocles and Anaxagoras (see above, p. 36 n. 6). It does not seem that Numenius' 'orientalism' went much further than that of Aristotle (or of Eudoxus; see above, p. 36).

But there is, of course, the famous phrase of Numenius saying that Plato was just a Moses talking Greek.[9] When we remember that Celsus, roughly a contemporary of Numenius, considered Moses nothing but a rebellious deceiver, and that Porphyry was entirely hostile to him, this

[1] *Fr.* 9a L. [2] *Fr.* 9b L. [3] *Fr.* 18; 19L.
[4] As such he is known also to Apuleius, *De magia* 90.
[5] *Enn.* II 9 [33] 14; IV 4 [28] 26; 38.
[6] *De def. or.* 10, 415A; 36, 429F; *De Is. et Os.* 46–7, 369E–370C.
[7] *Prooemium* 1–3. [8] *Met.* A 1, 981b23–5. [9] *Fr.* 10L.

is high praise indeed. When we now ask which aspect of Plato's philosophy Numenius had in mind when he compared him to Moses, it is perhaps a fair guess that it was only the way in which Plato, in connexion with introducing the artificer, used the terms *to on aei* on one side and the phrase reading in the Septuagint 'I am he who is' on the other. This still would be high praise for Moses—but limited to one detail. The other passage praised by Numenius is Gen. i. 2 ('And the Spirit of God moved upon the face of the waters') which he takes to mean that water contains divine spirit. And it is entirely possible that he referred to other Old Testament passages in a complimentary manner; but we do not find any proof that he recognized their doctrines as superior to Greek philosophy. If he, in one passage, referred to Jesus with sympathy,[1] this would not constitute such a proof either.

When we now pass to the core of the work, we shall find few additional traces of orientalism.

The main doctrines are these: There is a supreme god who can also be called goodness (*tagathon*), first intelligence, incorporeality, that One[2] which is, or being (*on* or *ousia*). He lives in the *aiôn* which can also be characterized as a *nunc stans*. This first god is the idea (in the Platonic sense of the word) of the second god who can also be referred to as second intelligence or as artificer, and is good by participating in goodness. Instead of speaking of a third god, we should rather say that the second god is a double one.[3] He is partly engaged in contemplating the first, or the intelligibles, partly he is creating and, looking to ideas to guide him, administering the visible cosmos. In the latter capacity he is in danger of devoting too much attention to the matter out of which he fashions the cosmos, and to its affairs. The main difference between the first and the second god is that the former is entirely at leisure; in other words, the cosmos is not his work; it is that of the second god, the artificer. The two gods preside over the realms of being and becoming, respectively. Therefore, it can be said of the first god that he has mounted being, or that he is the principle of being.

The similarities and the differences between Numenius and Plotinus are immediately visible. We see why some would say that Plotinus

[1] *Fr.* 19L.

[2] Calc. 294–7.

[3] But he might also have said that if we consider the world, product of the second deity, another god, then we have three gods.

plagiarized Numenius, whereas others with good reason would deny this. The distinction of a first god from the artificer who is called intelligence is the point of greatest similarity. Sometimes Numenius approaches the notion that this first god is above being, and again we feel close to Plotinus. But when Numenius describes his first god as intelligence, Plotinus must have considered it the same error which Aristotle had committed. Furthermore, what Numenius presents as a danger for the second god, viz. becoming too much involved with the administration of the cosmos, would, according to Plotinus, be a danger only to the third hypostasis (and even here only for those souls who administer mortal bodies.[1] On the other hand, Numenius often speaks of the second god as if he, in the capacity of an artificer, were the world soul (or at least closely associated with it). To this Plotinus would consent; and it is possible that those who accused Plotinus of plagiarism would simply say that while Plotinus distinguished neatly between intelligence and soul, Numenius saw intelligence and soul simply as two aspects of the second god. Moreover, we must not overlook the fact that Plotinus is not quite consistent when he speaks of the artificer: mostly he identifies him with the second hypostasis,[2] but sometimes with part of the third.[3] As is well known, Porphyry adopted this latter point of view.[4] Thus, similarities and differences between Numenius and Plotinus are almost in balance.

In the same work Numenius also described how the first god can be known.[5] To achieve this one must do what one does to espy, from a watch-tower, a little boat between waves. One exerts one's eyes—and then all at once one sees it. This is the way: to detach oneself from everything sensible and try to associate oneself 'alone with the alone'. Then one will see the first god in his gracious immobility. It is not an easy way. The best preparation is vigorously to pursue mathematics and so to excogitate what that which is, is.

The passage strongly reminds us of Plotinus' description of the flight of the 'alone to the alone'.[6] However, one wonders whether Numenius has in mind anything like a mystical ecstasy. The study of

[1] IV 8 [6] 4; cf. I 8 [51] 14.
[2] *Enn.* IV 4 [28] 10.
[3] *Enn.* III 9 [13] 1; IV 3 [27] 6.
[4] Procl. *In Tim.* I, 306; 322, 1; 431, 1 Diehl.
[5] *Fr.* 11 L.
[6] *Enn.* VI 9 [9] 11: cf. I 6 [1] 7, 9; 9, 24.

mathematics as preparation for the vision of goodness—this is not Plotinus' way.

The greatest dissimilarity, however, can be seen when we compare the ideas of the two on the relation between matter (referred to by Numenius as Dyad just as he refers to God as Monad [*singularitas*]) and what each of the two considers to be above matter, i.e. intelligence, according to Numenius; the soul, according to Plotinus. Numenius assumes some kind of influence of matter on intelligence (it splits intelligence into two because of the dyadic nature of matter). But it is out of the question for Plotinus that the lower could influence the higher. And with this difference is connected another: according to Numenius, the higher acts utilizing the lower, e.g. intelligence utilizes sensation. This again would be unacceptable to Plotinus.

Equally unacceptable for him would be Numenius' assumption of an evil cosmic soul associated with matter or the interpretation of matter as coeval with God (except in the sense that all hypostases are coeval). According to Plotinus, matter, and not the soul, is the source (or the element) of evil.

Another doctrine which we find in Numenius is the doctrine of undiminished giving.[1] This is a doctrine of central importance in the system of Plotinus.[2] It establishes what can be called dynamic pantheism (see below, p. 131): the higher is present in the lower only by its effects, not by its substance. And by exercising these effects the higher suffers no diminution. Numenius' illustrations are classic: the torch lighting another does not lose anything of its own light nor is the teacher's learning diminished when he imparts it to his pupil.[3]

In speaking of God, Numenius, among others, refers to him as *to agathon hoti estin hen*.[4] For this doctrine Numenius quotes Plato. Which passage does he have in mind? Quite obviously the same which Aristoxenus reported, viz. the concluding (or culminating) passage from Plato's *akroasis On the Good* (cf. p. 23).[5] If Plotinus was not familiar with this Platonic passage from any other source, he could have

[1] *Fr.* 23 L.

[2] See, e.g., v 1 [10] 3; v 1 9 [9] 9; vi 3 [44] 3.

[3] Cf. Plotinus, vi 5 [23] 32; iv 9 [8].

[4] *Fr.* 28 L.

[5] On the different interpretations of this passage, see e.g. K. Gaiser, *Platons ungeschriebene Lehre* (1963), pp. 452 f.

read it in Numenius and thus become confirmed in his opinion that Plato spoke of his supreme god as One.[1]

We tried to minimize Numenius' orientalism.[2] But there seems to be one doctrine which some scholars consider conclusively to prove it. Numenius spoke not only of two cosmic souls (the good virtually identical with the second god) but of two souls in man.[3] This, many scholars feel, is definitely non-Greek.[4] The only Greek author before the time of Numenius to suggest such a doctrine is Xenophon—and he has a Persian to profess it. Let us admit the possibility that here an argument can be made in favour of 'orientalists'. In Plotinus an evil soul is an impossibility; but he comes as close as possible to splitting man's soul into a higher and a lower soul.[5] Sometimes he even seems to assume that the lower soul is acquired by the higher on its downward journey,[6] much as he otherwise objects to any 'spatializing' of the soul. In Numenius this doctrine appears as acquisition of *pneuma* from the planets at the time of the soul's descent,[7] and this could be another 'oriental' doctrine.

To sum up: if by orientalism we mean knowledge of or sympathy for oriental wisdom, Numenius was an 'orientalist'. If, however, we mean by it being influenced by oriental doctrines to such an extent as to try to incorporate them into Greek philosophy or interpret Greek philosophy in the light of these oriental doctrines, then there are only a few traces of orientalism in either Numenius or Plotinus.

Numenius professes the doctrine of incarnation and reincarnation. He considers incarnation an evil and the result of some guilt. We are already familiar with the controversy between 'optimists' and 'pessimists' in this respect and know how Plotinus tried to solve the diffi-

[1] On this, see P. Merlan, 'Drei Anmerkungen zu Numenios', *Philologus*, CVI (1962), pp. 137–45, esp. pp. 143–5.

[2] By so doing we contradicted, e.g., H. C. Puech, 'Numénius d'Apamée et les théologies orientales au second siècle', *Mélanges Bidez*, II (1934), pp. 746–78.

[3] *Fr.* 36L.

[4] This is particularly the opinion of E. R. Dodds, 'Numenius and Ammonius', *Les Sources de Plotin, Entretiens*, V (1960), pp. 3–32, with discussion on pp. 33–61. In this he differs especially from P. Boyancé, 'Les deux démons personnels dans l'antiquité gréco-latine', *Revue de Philologie*, LXI (1935), pp. 189–202, who sees in the doctrine of two souls simply a variant of the undoubtedly Greek doctrine of two guardian spirits, one good, one evil.

[5] *Enn.* VI 7 [38] 5, thus not simply assuming higher and lower parts of one soul. However, we must not forget that this splitting of the soul is the result of a difficulty immanent in the system of Plotinus—to reconcile the elevated status of the soul with its presence in, or influence on, matter.

[6] *Enn.* IV 3 [27] 25; 27; 31; 32; III 5 [50] 3; 4.

[7] *Fr.* 47L.

culty. The soul has not really descended. When in us, it continues its 'higher' life, though we are not conscious of it. One could say: the intransigently pessimistic interpretation of the descent of the soul by Numenius was unacceptable to the optimistic strand in Plotinus and thus might have been a challenge to him to devise a theory to refute the former's pessimism.

The soul (probably every soul) Numenius also called a number, the factors of which were the One and the Indefinite Dyad—a doctrine obviously accepted also by Plotinus.[1]

Finally, if we can rely on Iamblichus,[2] Numenius enunciated the principle *en pasin...panta, oikeiôs mentoi kata autôn ousian en hekastois* (*omnia in omnibus sed secundum modum recipientis*)—a principle which, in a certain way, summarizes the whole emanative system of Plotinus and his followers.

Thus, while there was no plagiarism, similarity is obvious and influence possible.

What did Porphyry himself think of the plagiarism reproach? It seems that he admits the similarity between Numenius and Plotinus and only denies that this should be explained by plagiarism. Porphyry paraphrases part of Longinus' judgement thus: 'As far as the doctrines of Numenius are concerned, Longinus does not say that Plotinus passed them off as his own and honoured them,[3] but that he chose on his own to expound Pythagorean doctrines...'[4,5,6]

[1] VI 5 [23] 9.

[2] *Fr.* 33 L.

[3] I use this word in the way it is used in the phrase 'to honour a cheque'. We could also translate: 'and heralded them'.

[4] ...τὰ Νουμηνίου δὲ οὐχ ὅτι ὑποβάλλεσθαι καὶ τὰ ἐκείνου πρεσβεύειν (for πρεσβεύειν in this sense, see Eus. *PE* XI 17, *fr.* 20 L.) δόγματα, ἀλλὰ τὰ τῶν Πυθαγορείων αὐτοῦ...ἑλομένου μετιέναι δόγματα (*Life*, 21). In other words: the similarity between Numenius and Plotinus is to be explained by the fact that both are Pythagoreans. Once Plotinus seems to be quoting Numenius: III 5 [50] 6, 18

[5] Little remains to be said on Numenius' pupil, Cronius. Harpocration, student of Atticus, after agreeing with Cronius, followed Numenius' doctrine of the double god (Proclus, *In Tim.* I. 304, 22 Diehl). Like Numenius, he interpreted incarnation 'pessimistically' (Iambl. in Stob. *Ecl.* I 49, vol. I, pp. 375, 378 Wachsmuth) and extended it to beasts (Aen. Gaza, *Theophrastus*, p. 16 Barth, 12, 6 Colonna).

[6] A special problem is posed by the question whether Numenius was influenced by the *Chaldean Oracles* (more or less the *communis opinio* until recently) or whether the contrary is the case. Whichever it is, it is remarkable that we find in these *Oracles* a doctrine similar to that of the identity of intelligence with intelligibles—no intelligence without an intelligible, no intelligible without intelligence (*fr.* 11 Kroll) and the distinction between a First and a Second Intelligence. But, as Plotinus seems never to have used the *Oracles* and the question of priority of Numenius

Other aspects of anonymous and pseudonymous Pythagoreanism have been investigated by Bickel and Bömer.[1] Their theses amount to saying that these Pythagoreans were the first to interpret ideas as thoughts (instead of objects of thoughts), so that the realm of the immaterial becomes the realm of intelligence. Furthermore, according to them, already in Pythagoreanism we find a reception of Stoic ideas preceding the syncretism of Antiochus; thus, Stoic ideas in Plotinus could have come to him from Pythagoreans rather than from Posidonius. The first thesis is dubious; the second, in all likelihood, correct.

So far, we have dealt with Pythagoreanism as if it were strictly a philosophic school.[2] But quite obviously—either at times, or always—it was something in addition, a religious community and a way of life.[3] However, it does not seem that this aspect of Pythagoreanism interested or influenced Plotinus[4] (just as their arithmology or arithmo-theology did not attract him, whereas it attracted, e.g., Speusippus, Philo of Alexandria, and Iamblichus); he treats it just as a school of philosophy.[5]

Thus we can say: on the whole post-Academic Pythagoreanism exhibits two main aspects. It preserves the Two-opposite-principles doctrine

has not been established beyond doubt, this brief notice must suffice. Cf. H. Lewy, *Chaldean Oracles and Theurgy* (1956); E. R. Dodds, 'New Light on the "Chaldean Oracles"', *Harvard Theological Review*, LIV (1961), pp. 263–73.

[1] See particularly: E. Bickel, 'Neupythagoreische Kosmologie bei den Römern', *Philologus*, LXXIX (1924), pp. 355–69; F. Bömer, *Der lateinische Neuplatonismus und Neupythagoreismus und Claudianus Mamertus in Sprache und Philosophie* (1936), esp. p. 117.

[2] We omitted such doctrines as the atemporal origin of the cosmos, sometimes attributed to Pythagoras himself, as were many other Platonic doctrines.

[3] Zeller, *Phil.* III/2 (⁵1923), distinguished the two aspects of Pythagoreanism and while he was ready to admit the uninterrupted survival of Pythagoreanism as a religion, he denied its continuity as a school of philosophy. W. Burkert, *Weisheit und Wissenschaft* (1962), asserted the discontinuity in both respects; J. Carcopino, *La Basilique pythagoricienne de la Porte Majeure* (³1927), esp. p. 161 n. 1, and *De Pythagore aux Apôtres* (1956), the continuity in both respects. H. Thesleff, *An Introduction to the Pythagorean Writings of the Hellenistic Period* (1961), suggests philosophic discontinuity (on an overlooked passage in Plutarch having a bearing on this problem, see P. Merlan in *Mind*, LXXII [1963], pp. 303 f.). This duality (philosophy and religion) is well illustrated by a passage in Plutarch (*Qu. conv.* VIII 7, 727B). Here Lucius, introduced to the reader as a student of Moderatus, reports that Tyrrhenians still observe the Pythagorean taboos, but obviously refuses to explain their meaning to Plutarch. Cf. H. Dörrie, 'Pythagoreer', *RE*, XXIV/1 (1963), col. 268–70.

[4] For this reason we did not deal with Apollonius of Tyana. On his 'indianism' see Philostratus, *Vita Apollonii* VI 11; VIII 7; VI 15. Cf. Porphyry, *Life* 3.

[5] This is *a fortiori* true of the Platonism of the second and third centuries. H. Dörrie, 'Die Frage nach dem Transzendenten im Mittelplatonismus', *Les Sources de Plotin, Entretiens*, V (1960), pp. 191–223, seems to exaggerate its religious character.

from oblivion,[1] and it shows to what extent the derivation of all reality from non-sensible principles was a live philosophic option. But it also shows the permanent tension between a monistic and a dualistic interpretation of these principles, this tension often resolved by the assumption of a transcendental One beyond an inferior One.[2] In the persons of Nicomachus, Moderatus, and Numenius it claims all of Plato's philosophy for Pythagoreanism; and many doctrines of the two just mentioned are sometimes indistinguishable from doctrines of Plotinus. It incorporates Peripatetic and Stoic doctrines, thus preparing Plotinus' syncretism.[3]

[1] Cf. Zeller, *Phil.* III/2 (⁵1923), pp. 369 f.

[2] Retained by Plotinus, *Enn.* V I [10] 5. Cf. A. J. Festugière, *La Révélation d'Hermès Trismégiste* (1954) IV, pp. 18–25; 30 f.

[3] The political interests of Pythagoreanism produced a comparatively large number of pseudepigrapha (the best known: Charondas, Ecphantos, Diotogenes, Sthenidas, Zaleucus) devoted to problems of kingship, etc. Post-Plotinian Platonists, e.g. Iamblichus and Sopatrus, participate (Stob. *Flor.* XLVI = *Ecl.* IV 5, 51 – 60, 62, vol. II, pp. 212–19 Hense) by their writings and actions in political life. It is worth noticing that, according to A. Delatte, *La Constitution des États-Unis et les Pythagoriciens* (1948), their political doctrines were rooted in the Two-opposite-principles doctrine. As to Plotinus, whatever his involvement with political affairs in his private life (when Gordianus was slain, Plotinus had to flee his camp—which proves that he was considered a political figure; and courtiers of Gallienus would hardly have bothered to thwart his attempt to found a city unless they were of the opinion that the plan had some political purpose; cf. Porphyry, *Life* 3; 12), there is no trace of political interest in his writings; on the other hand, the political interest of Longinus is obvious.

CHAPTER 6

THE PERIPATOS

A. *The Peripatetic School from Theophrastus to Andronicus and Boethus*

The development of the Peripatos down to the time of Strato exhibits two main aspects. First, philosophic-speculative interest is largely replaced by interest in all kinds of special and empirical knowledge, this knowledge no longer to serve as foundation for something higher, but terminal. Secondly, to the extent that philosophic interest is preserved at all, it often finds its satisfaction in non-theological, naturalistic, or even materialistic doctrines.[1] For us only the latter aspect is important, as Plotinus' interest in empirical sciences is minimal.

Clearchus still seems to have refused to follow Aristotle's denial of the substantial character of the soul and presented him in a dialogue as having become convinced by what we should today call a telepathic experiment, that the soul can leave its body and return to it.[2] He, then, would represent Aristotle's original Platonism.

As to Theophrastus, his so-called metaphysical fragment[3] clearly proves that he retained Aristotle's speculative and theological interests. There is particularly no trace that he ever envisioned first philosophy to be anything but theology. The whole fragment is, from our point of view, remarkable mainly for three reasons. First, it shows to what extent Theophrastus connected the problems of Aristotle's *Metaphysics* with problems of the Two-opposite-principles system, including the

[1] Cf. Zeller, *Phil.* II/2 (⁴1921), pp. 805 f.; K. O. Brink, 'Peripatos', *RE*, Suppl. VII (1940), esp. col. 914–23; 926–49; F. Wehrli, *Die Schule des Aristoteles* (1959) X, pp. 96–128.

[2] *Fr.* 7 Wehrli. It cannot be excluded, however, that Clearchus' dialogue belongs to the period when Aristotle himself still professed the substantial nature of the soul; thus it would not express Clearchus' opposition to his master. Whatever the case, nothing indicates that he ever changed his 'Platonism'.

[3] W. D. Ross and F. H. Fobes, *Theophrastus. Metaphysics* (1929). Cf. P. Merlan, 'Aristotle's Unmoved Movers', *Traditio*, IV (1946), pp. 1–30, esp. pp. 29 f.; Idem, *From Platonism to Neoplatonism* (²1963), pp. 186–8; 208 f.; W. Theiler, 'Die Entstehung der Metaphysik des Aristoteles mit einem Anhang über Theophrasts Metaphysik', *Museum Helveticum*, XV (1958), pp. 55–105.

derivation of everything from these principles and including the relation between these principles and evil.[1] Secondly, it shows to what extent Theophrastus takes for granted that fundamentally all reality is divided into the spheres of the intelligible and the sensible, the former either including, or consisting of, mathematicals.[2] Thirdly, it shows to what extent Theophrastus takes it for granted that knowledge of first principles will be of a particular type, non-discursive and described best as a kind of touching, so that one can be ignorant of these principles but not mistaken about them (26). This, as is known, is the doctrine of Aristotle.[3] It is perhaps one of the most puzzling aspects of his system as it seems to assign a very particular kind of knowledge to the supreme principles which we at the same time could designate as divine. It is certainly characteristic that Plotinus in describing the ecstatic union with the One used precisely the same terms[4] which we find in Aristotle and Theophrastus. On the whole one could say that the fragment represents something like a blend of Aristotelianism and Platonism.

With Aristotle, Theophrastus tries to deflate the importance of mathematicals; but in one passage (30) he considers the possibility of replacing the concept of a transcendental deity by that of nature—he, in other words, prepares us for the immanentism of the Stoa or the naturalism of Strato.[5] But after all, even Aristotle himself sometimes speaks of nature as if it were identical with god.[6]

It has already been mentioned that Theophrastus raised several doubts with regard to Aristotle's celestial theology (e.g. its assumption of a plurality of unmoved movers: 4; 7); Plotinus was obviously inspired by them in his own criticism of Aristotle.[7]

So much about the metaphysical fragment. In dealing with psychology Theophrastus seems to have faced difficulties like those of Aristotle. In any case, he denied that all changes in man's mental life were simply somatic. He admitted it for desire and anger, but theoreti-

[1] 5–8; 11–13; 18; 32–3.

[2] 1; 3; 8; 13; 22; 25; 34; cf. *fr.* 27 Wimmer.

[3] In *Met.* Θ 10, 1051b24.

[4] *Thigein, thixis*: *Enn.* V 3 [49] 10, 42; VI 9 [9] 4, 27.

[5] Cf. E. Grumach, *Physis und Agathon* (1932), p. 49 n. 64; O. Regenbogen, 'Theophrastos', *RE*, Suppl. VII (1940), col. 1393; 1395; 1496; 1547 f.

[6] From the phrase 'god and nature do nothing in vain' (*De caelo* I 4, 271a35) a very short step seems to lead to the identification of god with nature. Cf. Zeller, *Phil.* II/2 (⁴1921), pp. 387 f.; 422–7; 803; F. Solmsen, *Aristotle's System of the Physical World* (1960), pp. 97–102; 272; 448 f.

[7] *Enn.* V 1 [10] 9.

cal activities took place, according to him, in the soul itself.[1] As for intelligence,[2] he asked how errors[3] and forgetting could happen to it and why its activity in man is not uninterrupted and without beginning (*euthys* and *aei*), though it must have been joined to us from the beginning of our existence. He seems to indicate that these 'defects' could best be explained by the fact that adventitious intelligence is involved (*dia tên mixin*) with the body or with the passive intelligence. The true meaning of this explanation might have been that all these conditions were actually conditions of the body[4]—just as Aristotle had explained that conditions like presbyopy are not conditions of intelligence and that if intelligence could receive a new somatic organ, it would again see well.[5] In facing the problem of whether the processes of intelligizing and of sensing imply the passibility of intelligence and the soul he distinguished the two processes by saying that the origin of the former is within (the objects of intelligizing being identical with the acts of which they are the object), whereas sensations originate from without. Thus, intelligizing would not really be a passion, as nothing can be affected by itself.[6]

Theophrastus also tries to reconcile the impassibility of intelligence with the concept that its activity is caused by intelligibles, which seems to imply that they affect and thus change intelligence. He does it by making use of the Aristotelian distinction between two kinds of change, only one resulting in alteration (destruction), whereas the other brings about perfection (preservation) of the subject of change.[7] It is this second kind of change which takes place when intelligence is acted upon by intelligibles.[8] In other words, the concept of passibility can be applied to intelligence only in a very peculiar way. Indeed, it is even

[1] *Fr.* 53 Wimmer; Simpl. *In Phys.* 964, 31 – 965, 5 Diels; cf. Arist. *De an.* I 4, 408b24–9.

[2] Cf. E. Barbotin, *La Théorie aristotélicienne de l'intellect d'après Théophraste* (1954).

[3] Cf. Arist. *De an.* III 10, 433a26: *nous...pas orthos.* Plotinus asserts that even the soul is infallible; error occurs only in the composite of soul and body (*Enn.* I I [53] 9).

[4] *Fr.* 53 Wimmer; but cf. Arist. *Eth. Nic.* X 2, 1173b10.

[5] *De an.* I 4, 408b18.

[6] *Fr.* 53B Wimmer plus Themistius, *De an.* 107, 30 – 109, 3 Heinze.

[7] *De an.* II 5, 417b2; III 5, 429b22–31; 7, 431a5; cf. *De an.* I 3, 407a33; *Phys.* VII 3, 247a28; 247b7.

[8] Themist. *De an.* 107, 30 Heinze and Prisc. *Metaphr.* 28, 21–3 Bywater = *Fr.* IV Hicks.

doubtful whether the change taking place in the organ of sensation is really an alteration.[1]

To a certain extent all these problems are rooted in, or lead to, the question: is it the body, is it the soul, or is it the composite of both which experiences affections, intelligizes, etc.?[2] And this question is permanent both in Platonism and in the Peripatos.[3] Plotinus discusses it at length.[4] And he also discusses all the other problems mentioned before. He is unwilling to admit that the process of sensing implies the passibility of the soul, which he expresses by saying that sensation is *energeia* rather than *pathos*. He is actually on the verge of asserting that sensation originates in the soul. This is *a fortiori* true of intelligizing, for intelligence is always stimulated *ap' autou* and not *ap' ekeinou*.[5]

As far as religion is concerned, Theophrastus, at times at least, seems to have been more 'pious' than his master.[6] He not only insisted that belief in the existence of gods was common to all men; he also pointed out that one well-known exception, the citizens of Akrothôoi, were, for their atheism, punished by the gods who destroyed them altogether by an earthquake.[7] Theophrastus is here writing entirely in the style of Heraclides (see above, p. 41). This is surprising in view of the fact that he also gave a naturalistic explanation of earthquakes,[8] entirely in the spirit of his master[9] and of Strato. One would like to know whether he participated in the discussions concerning the earthquake of Helice and Bura. Aristotle attributed it to natural causes; Heraclides saw in it a punitive action of the gods. With whom did Theophrastus side? We cannot decide; but the fact that the question can legitimately be asked proves the co-presence of supernaturalistic and naturalistic tendencies in Theophrastus—and perhaps in his master, too. In any case, we are

[1] *De sens.* 31; cf. 2; 49. Theophrastus also discussed other difficulties of the concept of active (acting) and passive intelligence, but it does not seem that his ideas in this respect left any traces in Plotinus. Cf. E. Barbotin, *op. cit.*; O. Regenbogen, *op. cit.* col. 1398.

[2] Cf. Aristotle, *De an.* I 4, 408a30; *Phys.* VII 3, 246b24–247b1.

[3] Cf. also Ps.(?)-Plutarch, *De lib. et aegr.*, which deals with the same problem (see above, p. 109). But the writing is perhaps post-Plotinian: see M. Pohlenz, *Die Stoa* (²1959, 1955), II, p. 175, but also K. Ziegler, 'Plutarchos', *RE*, XXI/1 (1951), col. 751.

[4] *Enn.* I 1 [53]; V 3 [49]—but cf. above, p. 46.

[5] *Enn.* IV 6 [41] 2.

[6] Cf. Zeller, *Phil.* II/2 (⁴1921), pp. 828; 866, somewhat contradicted by p. 867; Regenbogen, *op. cit.* p. 1557.

[7] Porphyry, *De abst.* II 7 f.; Simplicius, *In Epict. Ench.* p. 95 Dübner.

[8] Seneca, *Qu. nat.* VI 13, 1.

[9] *Meteor.* II 7–8, 365a14–369a9.

not surprised to find that Porphyry made extensive use of his *On Piety*. But, on the other hand, we should not be surprised, either, that a strand of naturalism or even materialism appears in several of Theophrastus' fragments.[1] At times at least, he equated god with *pneuma* (*fr.* 14 Wimmer; see above, p. 40 n. 9); and after what we said about the concept of *pneuma* in Aristotle (especially about its closeness to another materialistic or semi-materialistic concept of the divine, viz. that of ether),[2] it is difficult not to suspect that Theophrastus also tried sometimes to give a naturalistic interpretation of the divine—not under the influence of the Stoa and its concept of *pneuma*, but rather continuing along some lines present in Aristotle.

Significant in this context is the brief mention of Iamblichus[3] that Theophrastus sometimes (*en eniois*) joined Aristotle in calling the soul *endelecheia*, obviously because of its ethereal nature.[4]

The simplest explanation of these materialistic tendencies is that he (and other Peripatetics: see below) simply developed some aspects of the doctrines of their master. An alternative explanation would be that they misunderstood him.[5]

In comparison with the Platonism of Clearchus and the (temporary or partial) Platonism of Theophrastus,[6] Dicaearchus, Aristoxenus (and Strato) represent a different kind of Aristotelianism. In psychology all three are materialists. The soul is not even an entelechy; it is simply the result of the body.[7] In Strato the naturalistic and materialistic tendencies of the Peripatos culminate. One of the strongest arguments

[1] Cf. Zeller, *Phil.* III/2 (⁴1921), pp. 850 f.

[2] The existence of which Theophrastus also asserted: *fr.* 35 Wimmer. He was criticized for having identified god sometimes with intelligence, sometimes with *caelum*, sometimes with celestial bodies (Cic. *De nat. d.* I 35) or with *pneuma* (Clemens, *Protr.* 5, 44). Zeller, *Phil.* II/2 (⁴1921), p. 827, defends him, but his defence is based on the assumption that there was no trace of materialism in Aristotle's own theology.

[3] Stob. *Ecl.* I 49, 32, vol. I, p. 367 Wachsmuth.

[4] Not ἐντελέχεια as corrected by Wachsmuth. Cf. P. Merlan, *Gnomon*, XVI (1941), p. 34 n. 3; A. J. Festugière, *La Révélation d'Hermès Trismégiste* (1953) III, p. 188 n. 6, and above, p. 40.

[5] See, e.g., P. Moraux, 'quinta essentia', *RE*, XXIV/I (1963), col. 1206; 1229 f.

[6] And also with Eudemus, whose concept of first philosophy seems to have been similar to that of Theophrastus (*fr.* 32; 34 Wehrli; cf. P. Merlan, *From Platonism to Neoplatonism* [²1960], pp. 208 f.). It is perhaps worth mentioning that Eudemus referred to the Pythagorean doctrine of eternal recurrence (*fr.* 88 Wehrli) which Plotinus at least tentatively accepted (*Enn.* V 7 [18] 1, 12; 2, 20).

[7] Dicaearchus, *fr.* 7–12 Wehrli; Aristoxenus, *fr.* 118–21 Wehrli. On the germs of such a theory in Aristotle, see Zeller, *Phil.* II/2 (⁴1921), p. 489 n. 2. On the problem of reconcilability of the soul as harmony and its immortality, see Zeller–Mondolfo I/2 (1938 = 1950), pp. 560–3.

proving the radical difference between sensibles and intelligibles was, for both Plato and Aristotle, that thinking (intelligizing, whether intuitive or discursive) is entirely different from sensing. But Strato denied any essential difference between the two—even thinking is body-bound.[1] This, of course, implies the denial of any kind of immortality. As to the cosmos, he denied that it had life and saw it ruled entirely by blind corporeal forces (qualities).[2]

Aristoxenus is also important in the history of the Peripatos in that he —his opposition to the non-empirical Pythagorean musical theory notwithstanding—tried to achieve a kind of synthesis between the Peripatos and Pythagoreanism. Not only did he assert that Plato's and Aristotle's ethics were essentially Pythagorean; he, in constructing his own ethical system,[3] attributed its key concept—freedom from passions as man's supreme goal—to Pythagoreans. And obviously he interpreted Pythagoreans as materialists, at least in their psychology. Plato's Pythagoreans, represented by Simmias and Cebes, were converted by Socrates to the belief in a substantial and immortal soul; Aristoxenus' ones were not.

It should perhaps be added that neither Aristoxenus, nor Dicaearchus, nor Strato denied the possibility of mantic. But they might have interpreted it naturalistically.[4] However, Aristoxenus' Pythagoreans attributed luck and ill luck to demonic inspiration;[5] Dicaearchus attributed to the soul participation in something divine.[6] It is difficult to see how this can be reconciled with his theory that the soul is only the harmony of the body (see Wehrli's commentary *ad loc.*); we have a strange blend of naturalism with supernaturalism.

Critolaus too seems to have belonged to the materialists of the Peripatos. Soul and intelligence, according to him, consist of ether,[7] and he referred to the soul as *endelecheia*.[8] At the same time he identified

[1] *Fr.* 74; 107–31 Wehrli.

[2] Strato rejected the concept of ether (*fr.* 84 Wehrli). One wonders whether it could have been because he found the ether too little of a body—whereas others might have rejected it for just the opposite reason (see above on Atticus).

[3] *Fr.* 35–41 Wehrli.

[4] See esp. Aristoxenus, *fr.* 13–16 Wehrli, with his commentary.

[5] *Fr.* 41 Wehrli.

[6] *Fr.* 13 Wehrli.

[7] *Fr.* 17–18 Wehrli.

[8] *Fr.* 15 Wehrli.

the Pythagorean with the Peripatetic philosophy.[1] It could be that *On the All* by Ps.-Ocellus reflects this tendency of Critolaus (just as does Ovid's *Metam.* xv). Not only does Ps.-Ocellus teach the eternity of the cosmos in Aristotle's fashion; he even tacitly quotes *De gen. et corr.* But, on the other hand, he teaches transmigration and therefore vegetarianism. In this synthesis (or, as we could perhaps better say, juxtaposition) of Pythagoreanism and Aristotelianism the pro-Pythagorean tendencies of Aristoxenus would culminate.[2]

A student of Critolaus, Diodorus of Tyre, seems to have accepted his materialism,[3] but he still distinguished a reasonable from a non-reasonable aspect of the soul[4] and with Theophrastus differentiated between *pathê* in the true sense of the word (implying alteration) and *pathê* in the reasonable part of the soul, to which this term could be applied only by analogy. Thus Diodorus is fully aware of the difficulty resulting from separating the soul (or part of it) from the realm of the changeable, while having it in some way participate in activities implying changeability.

If Antisthenes of Rhodes was the author of Ps.-Aristotle's *Magicus*,[5] he would represent the survival of orientalizing tendencies (the Orient either as a source of, or as preliminary to, or simply parallel with, Greek philosophy) in the Peripatos.[6]

Further notice is deserved by Xenarchus, because he rejected the notion of ether.[7]

[1] *Ibid.*

[2] On Critolaus and Ps.-Ocellus, see the edition of *On Nature* by R. Harder (1926) with W. Theiler's review in *Gnomon*, II (1926), pp. 595–7, esp. pp. 595 f. and R. Beutler, 'Ocellus', *RE*, XVII/2 (1937); Zeller, *Phil.* III/2 (⁴1903), pp. 147 f.; 149–51. On his theory that eternity of the cosmos means eternity of species see Plotinus, II 1 [40] 1 with Bréhier's *notice*.

[3] Stob. *Ecl.* I 1, vol. I, p. 35, 5 Wachsmuth; Tertullian, *De an.* 5.

[4] PS.(?)-Plutarch, *De lib. et aegr.* 6, p. 44, 12 Pohlenz–Ziegler, if we here, with Zeller, read 'Diodorus' instead of 'Diodotus' or assume with him that Diodotus is simply another form for Diodorus.

[5] *Fr.* 32–6 Rose.

[6] Cf. W. Spoerri, *Späthellenistische Berichte über Welt, Kultur und Götter* (1959), pp. 64–9.

On Diodorus of Tyre and Antisthenes of Rhodes, see Zeller, *Phil.* II/2 (⁴1921), pp. 933; 84 n. 1; furthermore, *FgrH*, 508. However, on Aristotle's *fr.* 34 Rose, see W. Jaeger, *Aristoteles* (²1955), p. 136 n. 1. It is worth mentioning that Diodorus had some sympathy for Epicureanism, just as did Antiochus, Seneca and Porphyry. The urge to eclecticism is obvious. Diodorus particularly agreed with the concept of *vacuitas doloris* as aspect of the supreme good.

[7] On him see P. Duhem, *Le Système du monde* II (1914), pp. 61–6; IV (1916), p. 134; P. Merlan, 'Plotinus Enn. 2. 2', *Transactions of the American Philological Association*, LXXIV (1943), pp. 179–91; S. Sambursky, *The Physical World of Late Antiquity* (1962), pp. 122–32.

Among the later Peripatetics mention should be made of Cratippus. He explained (natural) mantic (i.e. mantic in dreams and ecstasy) by assuming that man's soul consists of two parts, one corresponding to Aristotle's entelechy, the other to Aristotle's *thyrathen nous*—and it is this latter part which, in sleep and ecstasy, becomes almost separated from the body and, therefore, capable of prophecy.[1] Here we have the germ of many medieval theories which explain prophecy by the active (agent) intelligence, and it is worth while to notice that a Peripatetic who remained true to the Aristotle *semi-platonizans* is responsible for this. It is not surprising to hear that he changed from the Academy to the Peripatos.[2]

Andronicus[3] gave, as is known, a new turn to the Peripatos. By his edition of Aristotle's *esoterica*, he started the process in which the *exoterica* slowly disappeared (therefore, it is reasonable to assume that his edition of Aristotle's works did not include the *exoterica*). In fact, Plotinus seems largely unfamiliar with them (see above, p. 98). Furthermore, Andronicus is the first Peripatetic to write a commentary on Aristotle's *Categories* (not on the so-called *Post-praedicamenta*, which he considered spurious), and to arrange the works of Aristotle in the order logic–ethics–physics plus metaphysics (thus, roughly, the tripartition going back to Xenocrates and Aristotle: see above, p. 64), so as to suggest that the study of Aristotle should begin with his logical writings, specifically with his categories which he listed as the first of his logical treatises. This implied a polemic with the Stoic doctrine of categories. Plotinus devoted to the doctrine of categories what amounts to 12 per cent of his written work; he must have considered the doctrine of categories of major importance for his system—contrary to what

[1] Cicero, *De div.* I 5; 70; Tert. *De an.* 46. K. Reinhardt (*Kosmos und Sympathie* [1926], p. 200 n. 1) denied that the phrase *animus hominum quadam ex parte extrinsecus tractus et haustus* in Cicero, as quoted above, corresponds to Aristotle's νοῦς θύραθεν. His denial is hard to accept, particularly if we do not overlook that, in spite of *Parva nat.* 2, 463 b 12–22, in his *Eudemian Ethics* (Θ 2, 1248 a 24 ff.) Aristotle himself explained prophetic dreams by the unhampered activity of the intelligence (here designated as θεῖον). But it cannot be ruled out that Cratippus at the same time was thinking in Stoic categories, according to which our intelligence would be an offshoot of the cosmic logos equal to intelligence. Cf. Zeller, *Phil.* III/1 (⁵1923), p. 650 n. 3; M. Pohlenz, *Die Stoa* (²1959, 1955), I, p. 256.

[2] *Index acd. Herc.* pp. 111 f. Mekler.

[3] On him see M. Plezia, *De Andronici Rhodii studiis aristotelicis* (1946), important also for Nicostratus, Albinus, and others. On Plotinus' praise of Andronicus: Boethius, *Liber de divisione* (*PL* 64.875.)

most modern interpretations of Plotinus implicitly assume. Indeed, he is one of the major sources of our knowledge of the Stoic doctrine of categories.[1] Some of Plotinus' objections are identical with those of Nicostratus (see above, p. 79).[2]

Andronicus, in interpreting Aristotle's categories, feels free to criticize or to correct them. This is also the attitude of Plotinus;[3] only Porphyry will concentrate on defending them from any criticism. In fact, Andronicus seems to have combined the Aristotelian categories with their Academic version, i.e. the division of existents into irrelatives and relatives.[4] But in psychology Andronicus joins the materialists in the Peripatos by declaring the soul (perhaps only its unreasonable part) to be the product of the body.[5] Xenocrates' definition of the soul he took to mean that the soul *causes* the ratios in which the somatic elements are mixed;[6] whether he agreed on this with Xenocrates remains unclear. In any case, he represents a mixture of Academic and Peripatetic doctrines.[7]

Boethus continues the work of Andronicus in writing commentaries on Aristotle's *esoterica* (to him we are indebted for fragments from Speusippus on categories; obviously to him too the Old Academy was of importance); he also denied the immortality of the soul.[8] According to Syrianus,[9] he identified Plato's ideas with Aristotle's *genika*. In discussing time, he asked whether it would exist even if there were no soul to count.[10] He thus reminds us of the two persistent tendencies in treating time: one according to which time is essentially the product of the soul, the other according to which it is essentially substance. The former point of view is that of Plotinus: the soul is unable to seize the content of intelligence in one indivisible act; it must, therefore, review its aspects one by one. In so doing, it engenders time and subsequently

[1] *Enn.* VI 1 [42] 25–30.

[2] See M. Pohlenz, *Die Stoa* (²1959, 1955), II, pp. 124 f.; 64; 875f.; 143 (on Athenodorus and Cornutus as critics of Aristotle's categories).

[3] *Enn.* VI 1 [42] 2–24.

[4] Simpl. *In Cat.* 63, 22 Kalbfleisch; cf. Zeller, *Phil.* III/1 (⁵1923), p. 645 n. 1; above, p. 37.

[5] Galen, *Quod animi mor.* 4, vol. IV, p. 782 Kühn.

[6] Themistius, *De an.* 32, 22 Heinze.

[7] On the source of Plutarch, *De virtute morali*, see above, p. 60 n. 1.

[8] For which he was criticized by Porphyry: Eus. *PE* XI 28. 1; XIV 10. 3.

[9] *In Met.* 106, 5 Kroll.

[10] Them. *Phys.* 160, 26; 163, 6 Schenkl; Simpl. *In Phys.* 159, 18; 766, 18 Diels; cf. Arist. *Phys.* V 14, 233a16 with Zeller, *Phil.* II/2 (⁴1921), pp. 402 f.

produces the sensible as temporal.[1] The latter point of view is, in Neoplatonism, represented by Iamblichus.[2] Both points of view obviously precede Neoplatonism.[3]

B. *Aristocles and Alexander Aphrodisias*

Aristocles (second half of the second century)[4] is the first Peripatetic whose writings permit us with certainty to assess the attitude of the Peripatos towards Plato in the post-Christian era. Somewhat unexpectedly, not only does he speak of Plato with great admiration,[5] but he calls his school Peripatos,[6] thus denying, so it seems, any essential difference between it and the Academy. Perhaps he even wrote a commentary on Plato's *Timaeus*.[7] Whether or not this was done under the influence of Antiochus (so Heiland, p. 35), in any case we see that the synthesis of Platonism and Aristotelianism is not entirely peculiar to Platonists and Neoplatonists.

In his favourable opinion of Plato, Aristocles includes Socrates.[8] Again it is striking that he sees in him the first representative of the idea theory; somehow he must have persuaded himself that even with regard to the idea theory no true difference between Plato and Aristotle exists. Furthermore, he seems to be in sympathy with the view attributed by him to Plato, viz. that to know man one must first know God.[9] This clearly refers to *Alcibiades I* (133 C). As some scholars are inclined to see in high esteem for this dialogue one of the hallmarks of Neoplatonism, Aristocles would in this respect belong among its precursors. At the same time we should not forget that many pre-Plotinian Platonists started their cursus of Plato with the reading of the *Alcibiades*.[10]

[1] *Enn.* III 7 [45].

[2] Cf. A. Levi, 'Il concetto del tempo nella filosofia dell'età romana', *Rivista critica di storia della filosofia*, VII (1952), pp. 173–200. One of the strongest expressions of the subjectivity of time: Alexander Aphrodisias, according to whom man is ποιητής of time (Themistius, *De an.* 120, 17 Heinze).

[3] On Boethus' polemic against the intellectualism of the Stoa see M. Pohlenz, *Die Stoa* (²1959, 1955), II, pp. 174 f.

[4] On him see: H. Heiland, *Aristoclis Messenii reliquiae* (1925); P. Moraux, *Alexandre d'Aphrodise* (1942), pp. 143–9; Fernanda Trabucco, 'Il problema del "de philosophia" di Aristocle di Messene e la sua dottrina', *Acme*, XI (1958), pp. 97–150.

[5] *Fr.* 1 Heiland.

[6] *Fr.* 2 Heiland.

[7] *Vestigium* V Heiland.

[8] *Fr.* 1 Heiland.

[9] *Ibid.*

[10] Albinus, *Isag.* ch. 5; the source of al-Fārābī's presentation of Plato. Cf. F. Rosenthal and R. Walzer (ed., tr.), *Alfarabius De Platonis philosophia* (1943); M. Mahdi (tr.), *Al-farabi's Philosophy of Plato and Aristotle* (1962), p. 54.

Aristocles criticizes sceptics, relativists, and sensualists, basing both his presentation and his criticisms on Plato. But though he insists that only the *logos* is the divine in us, he stresses that *logos* needs sensation, which itself is a kind of knowledge. This reconciliation of *logos* and *sensus* seems to have been undertaken already by Speusippus, who introduced the concept of *epistêmonikê aisthêsis*;[1] in the era of Aristocles it seems to underlie the assertion of Numenius (see above, p. 102) that there is something like use of the lower mental faculties by the higher ones. Here, of course, the way of Plotinus parts from those of Aristocles and Numenius.

It seems that Aristocles, to a certain extent, also combined Aristotelianism with Stoicism. In interpreting Aristotle's doctrine of the acting (active) intelligence, Aristocles assumes that this active intelligence is omnipresent but manifests itself in different ways *secundum modum recipientis*. Man is organized in such a manner that in him active intelligence manifests itself as power of intelligizing. This organization is simply a peculiar corporeal 'mixture' and, according to Aristocles, it is this mixture which Aristotle designates as passible (potential) intelligence. In reporting this view his pupil Alexander Aphrodisias characterizes it as Stoic in that it assumes the presence of the divine in everything, including that which is vile.[2]

It is likely that Alexander[3] developed his own interpretation of Aristotle's noetics against the background of that by Aristocles. He, as is known, unhesitatingly identified the intelligence of *Met.* Λ with that of *De anima* III, and in this he was followed by Plotinus. In interpreting the activity of intelligence he based his discussion on the radical difference between two kinds of intelligibles (cf. above, p. 65), one immanent, the other transcendent.[4] True, he insisted that only the singular existed in the proper sense of the word and thus treated the transcendent intelligibles as individuals (and, with Aristotle, rejected ideas, precisely because he took them to be universals), but by assuming two kinds of reality, sensible and intelligible, he returned to the kind of Aristotelianism which Strato had abandoned.

[1] *Fr.* 29 Lang. This resembles Strato's position: *fr.* 112 Wehrli.

[2] *Vestigium* IV Heiland.

[3] He deserves, but still has not received, a full monographic treatment.

[4] See, e.g., *De an.* 87, 5–32 Bruns.

To the two kinds of intelligibles belong two kinds of cognition. Intelligibles embedded in matter (i.e. Aristotle's forms) exist *qua* such only in the act of intelligence which lifts them from their matrix.[1] In other words, they exist *qua* intelligibles only in and through the act of intelligizing them.[2] It is completely different with the transcendent intelligibles. Here some kind of direct intuition takes place. But it is a peculiar kind of intuition in that these intelligibles have no existence apart from their being intelligized.[3] Whereas in the case of embodied intelligibles the identity of act and object takes place only in the moment of the actual act, such an identity is a permanent condition of transcendent intelligibles. They are 'known' permanently. Of course, the intelligence which knows them is not the human intelligence—if by 'human' we understand something which is part of man. Rather, it is the intelligence which enters man or his soul from without. And the activity of this 'divine' intelligence is incessant and eternal *a parte ante* and *a parte post*.[4]

As far as cognition of immanent intelligibles is concerned, the first step towards such a cognition is sensation. The next step, preceded by 'imagining' the object,[5] is to detach (to abstract) the intelligible from its matrix. Now, as far as cognition of transcendent intelligibles by the super-human (divine, extrinsic) intelligence is concerned, there is no difficulty in assuming that this extrinsic intelligence has a kind of cognition peculiar to it, perhaps a kind of touching. But after this extrinsic intelligence has in some way become united with the rest of the human soul, in what way does man (or his soul, or his intelligence) now intelligize the transcendent intelligibles? Alexander's answer is not altogether clear. It seems that in some way the human intelligence is capable of being assimilated to or identified with the extrinsic intelligence, and in this condition it is able to intelligize what the extrinsic intelligence has always intelligized. In what way this assimilation or transformation takes place remains unclear in Alexander. But he comes very close to saying that in the moment of assimilation the human intelligence is 'divinized'.[6]

[1] *De an.* 87, 24–88, 3. [2] *Ibid.* 90, 2–9; 84, 19–21. [3] *Ibid.* 90, 11–13.
[4] *Ibid.* 90, 11–14; 19–20. [5] *Ibid.* 83, 2–3.
[6] *Ibid.* 59, 21–2; 91, 5–6. We cannot discuss here the theory of P. Moraux, *Alexandre d'Aphrodise* (1942), according to which the section of Alexander's *De anima* which bears the title

It is obvious that in the sharp distinction between the two kinds of intelligibles, the identification of the extrinsic intelligence with god (the divine), the doctrine that in the moment of assimilation the human intelligence becomes divine, Alexander is very close to the Aristotle *platonizans* or *semi-platonizans*. There is no trace in Alexander proving that he rejected Aristotle's astral theology; nor is there any proof that he considered theology to be co-ordinated with or subordinated to another branch of theoretical philosophy whose object, designated as *on hêi on*, would differ from the divine. As far as theology and noetics are concerned, in comparison with Strato, Alexander is not a naturalist or materialist. And while a number of Peripatetics were attracted to equating the soul (or even intelligence) with ether, Alexander managed to reconcile the three aspects of Aristotle's kinetics by asserting that both ether and celestial souls have their share of responsibility for the motion of celestial bodies and that, with them, soul is their nature.[1]

With much greater clarity than Aristotle, Alexander distinguished between passive and active intelligence, calling the former hylic and making it definitely part of the human soul, which for him meant at the same time that its activity is bound to the body and therefore mortal. Thus, the doctrine of the embodied forms and of the hylic intelligence represents Alexander's naturalism (or materialism), whereas the doctrine of the adventitious intelligence and unembodied intelligibles represents his supernaturalism.

In his own way Alexander also asserted the absentee character of the divine (or the supreme deity). While professing the existence of providence, he at the same time insisted that this providence is exercised not *modo directo*, as if God would personally take care of the universe, but *modo obliquo*: while entirely turned towards himself, God by his mere

'Intelligence' (Περὶ νοῦ) is not by Alexander. As even Moraux admits a number of resemblances between this section and the rest of *De anima*, we limit ourselves to the points common to both (unicity and transcendence of the active intelligence, its identity with the divine, man's immortality consisting in the immortality of active intelligence with which human intelligence can in some moments become identical). In any case, there is no trace of a post-Plotinian origin of that section.

[1] See P. Merlan, 'Ein Simplikios-Zitat bei Pseudo-Alexandros und ein Plotinos-Zitat bei Simplikios', *Rheinisches Museum*, LXXXIV (1935), pp. 154–60; idem, *Philologische Wochenschrift*, LVIII (1938), pp. 65–9; idem, 'Plotinus Enn. 2. 2', *Transactions of the American Philological Association*, LXXIV (1943), pp. 179–91.

existence 'governs' the universe.[1] In many respects we are reminded of the discussion in *Enn.* III 2 and III 3.[2]

All these doctrines must have been significant for Plotinus. In fact, when he insisted that celestial bodies are animated, he felt that he had to refute Aristotle's objection that a soul which moves a body would be burdened by such a task and thus could not be considered as living a life of bliss. His defence was essentially to the effect that the celestial bodies offer no resistance to the soul because of their superior nature.[3] This is simply an adaptation of Alexander's theory that the ethereal body and the soul co-operate in causing motion of the celestial bodies. While rejecting ether, Plotinus transposed Alexander's related views.[4]

But probably no other piece of Alexander's noetics proved to be more attractive to Plotinus than his strong restatement of Aristotle's theory[5] that as far as incorporeals (transcendent intelligibles) are concerned, there is no difference between them and the act of intelligizing them. The whole doctrine reappears in Plotinus under the heading that intelligibles (ideas) have no subsistence outside intelligence.[6]

Alexander took over the nominalistic tendencies of Aristotle and rejected, therefore, ideas which he took to be universals, as we said. It seems that Plotinus never thought of ideas as being universals. If we remember that, according to him, the second hypostasis (sphere of intelligence) contains not only ideas but also individual souls and

[1] *Qu. nat.* II 21, pp. 66, 17; 70, 24 Bruns.

[2] Cf. P. Thillet, 'Un traité inconnu d'Alexandre d'Aphrodise sur la Providence dans une version inédite', *Actes du Premier Congrès International de Philosophie Médiévale: L'Homme et son Destin* (Louvain, Paris, 1960), pp. 313–24.

[3] Arist. *De an.* I 3, 407b1–12; *De caelo* II 1, 284a13–284b6; Plotinus, *Enn.* IV 8 [6] 2.

[4] On the connexion of this theory with those of Xenarchus (who denied the existence of ether) and Herminus (who attributed the celestial motion to the soul rather than the Unmoved Mover) on one hand, and with Plotinus, *Enneads* II 2 [14], on the other, see P. Merlan, 'Plotinus Enneads 2. 2', *Transactions of the American Philological Association*, LXXIV (1943), pp. 179–91.

[5] *De an.* III 4, 430a2; III 7, 431a1–2; *Met.* Λ 7, 1074b38.

[6] Cf. A. Armstrong, 'The Background of the Doctrine "That the Intelligibles are not Outside the Intellect"', *Les Sources de Plotin, Entretiens*, V (1960), pp. 391–413, esp. pp. 405–13; P. Merlan, *Monopsychism, Mysticism, Metaconsciousness* (1963), p. 9. That the doctrine of the identity of intelligence, act of intelligizing, and object of intelligizing was of great importance also to Philo of Alexandria has been argued by H. A. Wolfson, *Philo* (^{2}1948), I, pp. 229 f., 249 f. Attempts to attribute it to Xenocrates: R. E. Witt, *Albinus and the History of Middle Platonism* (Cambridge, 1937), p. 71; H. J. Krämer, *Der Ursprung der Geistmetaphysik* (1964), esp. pp. 120–4, mainly on the basis of his *fr.* 15; 16 Heinze and the interpretation by H. A. Wolfson, *Religious Philosophy* (1961), pp. 27–68, cannot here be discussed.

individual substances,[1] it is difficult to escape the conclusion that Plotinus conceived of ideas as individuals. And indeed, he could hardly do otherwise, considering that he professed the doctrine that there were ideas of individuals (see above, p. 55). What else could these ideas be but individuals themselves?

Of course, some of Aristotle's or Alexander's nominalism is otherwise unacceptable to Plotinus. He restates the principles of what we, by a modern term, call conceptual realism on the occasion of discussing the problem whether numbers have substantial existence.[2] Not only does he answer in the affirmative, but on this occasion he affirms the same of 'One' and 'being'—precisely the concepts the substantiality of which Aristotle denied at length.[3]

Unacceptable to Plotinus is, of course, that aspect of Alexander's psychology in which he deals with the soul in terms of entelechy and, therefore, denies its immortality. But, as we have seen, Alexander more than made up for his strictly immanentistic theory of the soul (including the hylic intelligence) by his transcendentalistic theory of active intelligence.

Concerning other doctrines discussed by both Plotinus and Alexander let us mention that Alexander defends the existence of two matters, one in the realm of the divine, the other in that of the sensible,[4] thus anticipating the doctrine of Plotinus[5] discussed above (p. 27). And he also professes the doctrine of the *antakolouthia* of perfections.[6] Of lesser importance for Plotinus is Alexander's discussion of the *krasis di' holou* problem,[7] and of the theories of vision.[8]

[1] Cf. A. Armstrong, *The Architecture of the Intelligible Universe in the Philosophy of Plotinus* (1940), pp. 79 f. Some scholars are inclined to derive this doctrine of Plotinus from the Stoic concept of ἰδίως ποιόν, but this seems to be doubtful.

[2] *Enn.* VI 6 [34] 12–14.

[3] *Met.* I 2, 1053b 9–1054a 19. We should not forget that in the *Categories* (the authenticity of their first part was not denied in antiquity) the semi-substantial existence of non-individuals (secondary substances) is admitted (cf. Zeller, *Phil.* II/2 [[4]1921], p. 68), and that in a number of passages in *Met.* Aristotle speaks like an adherent of the Two-opposite-principles doctrine, thus admitting the substantial character of entities like One, Indefinite Dyad, etc. (cf. P. Merlan, *From Platonism to Neoplatonism* [[2]1960], pp. 183 f.). For the opposite point of view, in addition to the passage in *Met.* I quoted above, see *Met.* N 1, 1087b 33–1088a 3; K 2, 1060a 36–1060b 17; cf. Zeller, *Phil.* II/2 ([4]1921), p. 302. I cannot discuss here C. Rutten, *Les Catégories du monde sensible dans les 'Ennéades' de Plotin* (1961).

[4] *Qu. nat.* I 15, pp. 26 f. Bruns.

[5] *Enn.* II 4 [12].

[6] *Qu. nat.* IV 22, pp. 142 f. Bruns; cf. *Enn.* I 2 [19] 7.

[7] *De mixt.* 216, 14 Bruns (cf. *Enn.* II 7 [37] 2).

[8] *De an.* 130 Bruns and *Enn.* II 8 [57]. Cf. H.-R. Schwyzer, 'Plotinos', *RE*, XXI/1 (1951), col. 574; P. Merlan, 'Plotinus Enn. 2. 2', *Transactions of the American Philological Association*, LXXIV (1943), pp. 179–91. Schwyzer also lists: *Enn.* III 1 ~ Alex. *De fato*; *Enn.* II 7 ~ *Qu. nat.* II 12.

On the whole it seems not unfair to say: despite his nominalism, despite the fact that he considers it necessary to prove the divinity of the cosmos against Plato, despite his rejection of ideas, despite his interpretation of the soul as entelechy and, therefore, as mortal, in Alexander's noetics we see Platonism staging its comeback within the Peripatos. However, the more Platonic the Peripatos becomes, the more it loses its *raison d'être.*[1] Furthermore, the most original aspect of the post-Stratonian Peripatos was inaugurated by Andronicus when he started writing formal commentaries on Aristotle's *esoterica.* But with Porphyry the study of Aristotle and the writing of commentaries on his *esoterica* became part and parcel of Platonism; thus there was little left for the Peripatos to do. Its history reads like a story of vacillations between materialism (which was much better represented by Epicureanism and Stoicism) and Platonism (or at least semi-Platonism). Therefore, in the long run, Platonism turned out to be the only school essentially impermeable to naturalism or materialism and able to absorb most of Aristotle's philosophy.[2] This was facilitated by the facts that so much of Aristotle's *esoterica* was metaphysically neutral,[3] and that so much of his philosophy retained a Platonic flavour.[4]

[1] This is essentially the perspective in O. Hamelin, *La Théorie de l'intellect d'après Aristote et ses commentateurs* (1953).

[2] Unless we consider the assumption of an elongation of the soul and of its astral body regaining spherical shape (cf. Dante's *cente sperule* in *Paradiso* XXII 23) as concessions to materialism (*Enn.* III 6 [17] 5; IV 3 [27] 15, 17; IV 4 [28] 5). Cf. p. 90 n. 5; Ueberweg–Praechter, *Grundriss* (^{12}1926), p. 629 n. (with reference to Plato, *Nomoi* X 899 A); E. R. Dodds, *Proclus, The Elements of Theology* (^{2}1963), App. II.

[3] According to Porphyry, the writings of Plotinus implicitly contain Peripatetic doctrines and are full of Aristotle's *Metaphysics* (*Life* 14).

[4] My interpretation of Alexander Aphrodisias differs from that accepted by Zeller and also by Ueberweg–Praechter. Justification seems indispensable. Zeller *charges* Aristotle with teaching a mystical unity of the human intelligence with the divine intelligence—i.e. he assumes that by intelligence in *De an.* Aristotle means strictly an actual part of the human soul (or of man), which then, of course, could not be identical with god or divine intelligence, and he *credits* Alexander with separating the two (and thus eliminating Aristotle's 'mysticism'—Zeller probably means 'obscurity'). Divine intelligence (god) simply *acts* on human intelligence (the latter being in all its aspects, i.e. as νοῦς δυνάμει, νοῦς ἐπίκτητος, νοῦς καθ' ἕξιν, bound to the body) and has its seat in the heart. At the same time, Zeller assumes that the result of the action of the divine intelligence is twofold: the development of the νοῦς δυνάμει into the νοῦς ἐπίκτητος (καθ' ἕξιν) and the intelligizing of the divine intelligence. And whereas Aristotle said only of one part of the human soul that it is mortal (Zeller again assumes that in *De an.* intelligence is considered actually *part* of the soul), Alexander asserts the mortality of the whole soul, including the νοῦς δυνάμει or ἐπίκτητος or καθ' ἕξιν. All this Zeller takes to mean that Alexander was much more naturalistic than Aristotle, and that he, in respect of his noetic, was as close to Strato as he was in other respects.

But if a philosopher asserts that human (passive, hylic) intelligence could not exercise its function without divine (active) intelligence acting on it or on its objects, can he be considered a naturalist? If a philosopher asserts that there exist unembodied intelligibles which can be known by some immediate intelligizing, i.e. not by abstracting them from a sensible in which they are embodied, can he be considered a naturalist?

When Zeller asked the question concerning the objects of non-discursive (immediate) intelligizing, he said it would be legitimate to infer from Aristotle's philosophy that divinity belongs among them. This, said Zeller, would, of course, bring us back to Plato's ideas (though they would be known not in the life beyond but in the present one). And this, in turn, would simply be the result of the fact that Aristotle never quite overcame Plato's hypostasizing of concepts. If we grant all this to Zeller, is it not obvious that Alexander indeed revived what Zeller himself considered to be the residue of Platonism in Aristotle? This can be seen even from Zeller himself if one compares *Phil.* III/1 (⁵1923), pp. 824–7; II/2 (⁴1921), pp. 572–5, and p. 196.

CHAPTER 7

THE STOA

A. *General*

The significance of some doctrines of Posidonius and of Seneca for the development of Neoplatonism has been indicated. But these doctrines concern only details, and the problem remains to what extent Stoicism at large contributed to Neoplatonism.

The Stoic system can be interpreted in two ways. We see in it either a 'mundanization' and a materialization of the divine, or, on the contrary, a divinization and spiritualization of matter. Nothing exhibits this ambiguity better than the relation between determinism (*heimarmenê*) and providence (*pronoia*) in the Stoic system. Strict determinism seems to leave no place for providence in any genuine sense of the word. But the Stoa tried to identify the two.[1] The same ambiguity is exhibited in one of the central concepts of the Stoa, the spermatic ratio (pattern). The adjective has materialistic connotations, the noun spiritualistic ones.[2] The strict immanentism of the Stoa can be taken to assert either the divine character of the cosmos or the strictly mundane character of the divine.

Like all monistic and deterministic systems which at the same time

[1] Some of the high points of the pre-Plotinian discussion concerning the relation between πρόνοια and εἱμαρμένη: the Platonist author (Numenius) who is the common source of Ps.-Plutarch, *De fato*, of Calcidius' *Timaeus* 142–90 = 203–32; cf. the apparatus in the edition by J. H. Waszink, *Timaeus a Calcidio translatus* (1962), of Nemesius, *De nat. hom.* 34–44, and of Alexander Aphrodisias, *De fato*. The two positions most frequently met are either the identification of the two or the subordination of the latter to the former. The second alternative is that of Plotinus (*Enn.* III 1–3); the first is that of the Stoa, and he finds it too rigidly deterministic (*Enn.* III 1 [3] 4, 7–8), as does also Alexander Aphrodisias. By distinguishing the two, the ἐφ' ἡμῖν is preserved. Cf. M. Pohlenz, *Die Stoa* ([2]1959, 1955), I, pp. 356 f. Cleanthes subordinated providence to *heimarmenê*. Cf. A. Gercke, 'Eine platonische Quelle des Neuplatonismus', *Rheinisches Museum*, XII (1886), pp. 266–91; H. v. Arnim, 'Kleanthes', *RE*, XI/I (1921), col. 567.

[2] Small wonder that non-materialistic philosophers also availed themselves of this concept (cf. O. Becker, *Plotin und das Problem der geistigen Aneignung* [1940], p. 93; the discussion in *Les Sources de Plotin, Entretiens*, V [1960], pp. 97–100 [Puech, Dodds, Henry, Schwyzer, Theiler participating]; A. H. Armstrong, *The Architecture of the Intelligible Universe in the Philosophy of Plotinus* [1940], p. 105). When Plotinus uses the term, he does not mean, as does the Stoa, germinative forces inherent in matter, but 'patterns' imposed on it from without (M. Pohlenz, *Die Stoa* [[2]1959, 1955], I, p. 392). Often Plotinus uses the term for ideas when present in the soul.

profess some kind of prescriptive ethics, Stoicism must try to find some place for freedom of the will (mostly, the formula will be accepted that we are free, because we can do whatever we want, but determined, because we must want what we want),[1] some meaningful discrimination between good and evil, some possibility of distinguishing between 'is' and 'ought'. Whether any of this can be done is doubtful. On the whole, every kind of monism must end in the assertion either that this is the best of all possible worlds, or the worst—in other words, it will be unable to explain the existence either of evil or of good. Stoicism is optimistic monism and, therefore, committed, in fact, to the denial of evil in any true sense of the word.

Finally, Stoicism speaks the language of materialistic monism. Though it may be dubious whether we, despite Diog. Laert. VII 135, where *sôma* is defined as *trichêi diastaton*, unhesitatingly should apply our concept of matter (something tangible, filling space, and resisting penetration) to the Stoic concept of *hylê* (surprisingly, it turns out that we may do justice to this concept if we apply to it our concept of field; immediately the highly paradoxical notion of a *krasis di' holou* makes sense),[2] antiquity sees in Stoicism a clear case of materialism leaving no place for any spiritual principles. As materialists, they are criticized by Plotinus for their doctrines of the soul[3] and god.[4]

Another contradiction inherent in the Stoic system is revealed in its attitude towards mantic. The Stoa insists on its veracity and at the same time tries to explain it in a 'natural' way.

Like Epicureanism, the Stoa subordinates theoretical philosophy to ethics. Its ethics culminates in the demand to become self-sufficient, i.e. to liberate oneself of everything that is external. This self-sufficiency guarantees happiness. Just as being dependent for happiness on circumstances over which we have no control is the sign of a fool, so the wise man knows that happiness depends upon himself alone.

The Stoa developed its own doctrine of categories. Because of its monistic character (*on* or *ti* as the supreme category), for Plotinus it was as unacceptable as that of Aristotle.[5]

[1] *Enn.* III 2 [47] 10.

[2] S. Sambursky, *Physics of the Stoics* (1959), p. 7. Plotinus justifies the concept (*Enn.* II 7 [37] 2), whereas Alexander Aphrodisias (*De mixt.* 216, 14 Bruns) rejects it.

[3] *Enn.* IV 7 [2] 4.

[4] *Enn.* II 4 [12] 1.

[5] *Enn.* VI 1 [42] 25–30.

B. *Posidonius*

Now, with Posidonius[1] (partly even with Panaetius) the Stoa opened itself to Platonic influence. Not only did Posidonius (like Panaetius) admire Plato[2] and comment on some of his dialogues, particularly on the *Timaeus*,[3] perhaps also on the *Phaedrus*,[4] though hardly in the form of formal commentaries. He also stressed his concordance with Pythagoras.[5] His main deviation from Stoic psychology consisted in what amounted to a denial of the unity of the soul and in the Platonizing assertion that it essentially contained a reasonable and unreasonable faculty,[6] so that emotions (*pathê*) would not simply be results of erroneous opinions concerning good and evil.[7] Thus, Stoic monism was in some respects on the verge of turning into dualism.[8]

At the same time it is possible that Posidonius distinguished two kinds of *pathê*, one, indeed, having its origin in somatic qualities, the other originating in the opinions, and that Plotinus[9] accepted this distinction.[10]

For this and other reasons, Posidonius was presented by Jaeger as the first Neoplatonist.[11] According to him, Posidonius, by placing the *Timaeus* in the centre of his interpretation of Plato, completely—and for centuries—changed the meaning of Platonism. In addition, in his philosophy of nature he managed to combine the Platonist with the Aristotelian approach, the synthesis of these two being one of the hallmarks of Neoplatonism.

[1] On him, in general, see M. Pohlenz, *Die Stoa* (²1959, 1955), esp. I, pp. 224–30, and K. Reinhardt, 'Poseidonios', *RE*, XXII/1 (1953). In Reinhardt's article (col. 799; 801) and in H.-R. Schwyzer, 'Plotinos', *RE*, XXI/1 (1951), col. 578 f., a number of Plotinian passages are mentioned for which the influence of Posidonius might be claimed. Many philosophic fragments of Posidonius can be found in C. J. de Vogel, *Greek Philosophy* (1959), III, nos. 1176–96; in German translation in M. Pohlenz, *Die Stoa und Stoiker* (1950).

[2] Galen, *Hipp. et Plato* IV 7, vol. 5, p. 421 Kühn; cf. V 6, vol. 5, p. 470 Kühn.

[3] Sext. Emp. *Adv. math.* VII 93; Plutarch, *De procr. an.* 22, 1023 B; Theo Sm. *Expos.* p. 103, 18 Hiller.

[4] Hermias, *In Phaedr.* p. 102, 13 Couvreur.

[5] Galen, *ibid.* IV 7, vol. 5, p. 425 Kühn; V 6, vol. 5, p. 478 Kühn.

[6] The latter subdivided into *thymos* and *epithymia*, these two in turn depending on the quality of the body; cf. Plotinus, IV 4 [28] 28.

[7] Galen, *ibid.* IV 3, p. 377; 5, 397; 7, 416; V 1, 429 f.; 5, 464 f.; 6, 473 Kühn.

[8] W. Jaeger, *Nemesius of Emesa* (1914), pp. 24 f.; G. Stahl, 'Die "Naturales Quaestiones" Senecas', *Hermes*, XCII (1964), pp. 425–54

[9] III 6 [26] 4; IV 4 [28] 28.

[10] Cf. W. Theiler, *Die Vorbereitung des Neuplatonismus* (1930), pp. 86–90. He quotes Marcus Aurelius, V 26 and Galen, *Hipp. et Plato* V 2, vol. 5, p. 442 Kühn.

[11] *Op. cit.*

To the extent that Jaeger's construction was based on the assumption that Posidonius wrote a commentary on the *Timaeus*, it has been weakened by the doubts Reinhardt cast on the existence of such a commentary. And it is also controversial whether the doctrine of the circular change of the elements into each other, contributing to the bond uniting the universe, attributed to Posidonius by Jaeger, was actually professed by him. Thus, for the time being it does not seem possible to assess the influence of Posidonius on Platonism, in general, with precision.

To what extent did Posidonius influence Plotinus himself? It is difficult to give an answer, as the reconstruction of many aspects of the Posidonian system is still under discussion (particularly controversial is the question what kind of immortality he admitted).[1] The most obvious case of such an influence seems to be provided by the concept of sympathy, which, as Theiler sees it, was taken over by Plotinus[2] from Posidonius.[3] But, as Zeller[4] judiciously observed, what the Stoa and Posidonius mean by this concept differs from what it means in Plotinus. In the Stoa it means that the universe is one coherent physical whole;[5] in Plotinus it means not only this but mainly that every part of the universe is immediately (by distant action) aware of what happens in another, which explains what we today should call occult phenomena. How great, then, is the similarity between the two concepts of sympathy?

Another similarity is provided by a doctrine attributed to Posidonius[6] that disembodied souls communicate with each other without any physical medium (a doctrine used, it seems, by Posidonius to explain mantic in some of its aspects), which doctrine is also professed by Plotinus.[7] But it is possible that Plotinus was familiar with this doctrine from Plutarch[8]—or from Plutarch's source, which could have been, e.g., Xenocrates.

[1] Cf. M. Pohlenz, *Die Stoa* (^{2}1959, 1955), I, p. 229; II, p. 141; C. J. de Vogel, *Greek Philosophy* (1959), III, nos. 959, 1192–5.

[2] *Enn.* IV 4 [28].

[3] W. Theiler, *Die Vorbereitung des Neuplatonismus* (1930), pp. 72; 112. But we must not forget that Moderatus already made use of the concept of sympathy (above, p. 95).

[4] *Phil.* III/1 (^{5}1923), p. 172, 2; III/2 (^{5}1923), p. 686.

[5] See, e.g., Cicero, *De nat. d.* II 19; Sext. Emp. *Adv. math.* VII 98.

[6] Mainly on the strength of the assumption that the source of Plutarch's *De genio* 20, 588B–589E is Posidonius; see K. Reinhardt, *Posidonius* (1927), p. 464.

[7] *Enn.* IV 3 [27] 18.

[8] *De def. or.* 37, 431C.

A somewhat similar case is presented by the problem of totality *vs.* isolation. It is entirely likely that Posidonius strongly stressed that everything continues to live as long as it has not become isolated from the whole to which it belongs, this whole being permeated by one all-comprehensive life (illustrating this thought by pointing at minerals which have the power of regeneration as long as they continue to be connected with the animated, divine earth, whereas the twig dies when it becomes separated from the tree). It is not impossible that this is the basis of Plotinus' tentative assertion that the soul of the plant resides in the earth (though he might have derived this theory from Antiochus—see above, p. 57). But it is unlikely that Plotinus 'transposed' Posidonius' thought by applying it to the 'defection' of the soul from the totality of the realm of the intelligible to which it belongs and from which it should not have defected.[1] Nor is it likely that Plotinus transposed other categories used by Posidonius to express the organic unity of the sensible cosmos (one all-permeating life force) to the intelligible cosmos.[2] On the other hand, Plotinus' grades of unity[3] may have been derived from Posidonius.[4]

Finally, Plotinus might have been influenced to a certain extent by Posidonius' theory of sensations, particularly of vision. The latter adopted the principle 'like through like'[5] and combined it with the theory that air is the medium necessary for vision. Plotinus[6] accepted that principle but objected to the theory and replaced it by the concept of action-at-a-distance made possible by 'sympathy' (again used in not quite the same way in which it was used in the Stoa). But it is probable that the background of Plotinus' theory of vision is the discussion in Alexander Aphrodisias' *De anima*.[7]

[1] Cf. W. Theiler, *Die Vorbereitung des Neuplatonismus* (1930), pp. 94; 114; 117; 123–5; see esp. Plotinus, *Enn.* IV 4 [28] 27 with Theiler's commentary and *Enn.* VI 7 [38] 11. But it should not be forgotten that Aristotle seems to attribute life even to the inorganic (*De caelo* II 12, 292a20; *De gen. anim.* IV 10, 778a2; *Meteor.* II 2, 355b4–356a33), nor that Plato (*Tim.* 30D) described the universe as one living being. Theiler (*ibid.* p. 91) asserts that Plotinus was 'reminded' of this Platonic passage by Posidonius; it is not easy to see why such an intermediary was necessary.

[2] Esp. in *Enn.* VI 5 [23] and IV 7 [2] 15.

[3] *Enn.* V 9 [5] 5, 25.

[4] In Sext. Emp. *Adv. math.* VII 107.

[5] Sext. Emp. *Adv. math.* VII 93; cf. Plato, *Rep.* VI 508B.

[6] *Enn.* IV 5 [29]; I 6 [1] 9.

[7] Pp. 42–9, 127–47 Bruns. Cf. W. Jaeger, *Nemesius of Emesa* (1914), pp. 27–53; Theiler's commentary *ad Enn.* IV 5 [29].

Thus, the influence of Posidonius on Platonism in general and on Plotinus in particular remains rather elusive. What is certain is that by his equation of mathematicals with the soul he paved the way to reconciling Aristotle's account of Plato's philosophy as assuming three spheres of reality: ideas, mathematicals, sensibles with their own triad: intelligence = ideas, soul, sensibles (cf. above, p. 62).[1]

C. *Later Stoics: Stoicism and Plotinus: the writing 'On the World'*

In Seneca, Epictetus, and M. Aurelius the Platonizing of the Stoa continues. Time and again they express attitudes strongly reminiscent of those of Plato's *Phaedo*. Indeed, some passages in these authors praising the condition of the soul relieved from the fetters of the body have an almost Plotinian ring.[2] Marcus Aurelius distinguishes not only the body from the soul but intelligence from the soul.[3] If the myth in Plutarch's *De facie*[4] is inspired by Posidonius,[5] then it was already he in whom this characteristic triad (certainly closer to Aristotle than to the Old Stoa) could be found.[6] For Plotinus the sharp distinction between soul and intelligence is, of course, of prime importance. But again, he could have derived it directly from Aristotle.

It is obvious which Stoic doctrines must have been unacceptable to Plotinus. His monism is spiritualistic; the materialism of the Stoa, particularly when applied to God, to the soul, or to epistemology (sensation as a kind of seal, *typôsis*), he rejected entirely. Moreover, in spite of his monism, Plotinus acknowledged the existence of evil and sees matter as its principle;[7] therefore, he cannot, without qualification, accept Stoic optimism (and the doctrine of neutrality of matter), though when confronting a fully pessimistic system like that represen-

[1] Cf. E. v. Ivánka, 'Die neuplatonische Synthese', *Scholastik*, XX–XXIV (1949), pp. 30–8, and W. Theiler, 'Plotin zwischen Plato und Stoa', *Les Sources de Plotin*, *Entretiens*, V (1960), pp. 65–86 (with subsequent discussion); R. E. Witt, 'Plotinus and Posidonius', *Classical Quarterly*, XXIV (1930), pp. 198–207.

[2] Sen. *Ep.* 65, 66; 102. 22; Epictetus, *Diss.* I 9. 10; M. Aur. X 1.

[3] III 16; cf. XII 3.

[4] 28, 943 A–945 A (see above, pp. 61).

[5] See H. Cherniss in the Loeb edition (1957) of *De facie*, pp. 18 n. b; 23–6; 147 n. c; 219 n. f; 221 n. b.

[6] Cf. Zeller, *Phil.* III/2 (⁴1903), pp. 258–61; but cf. W. Jaeger, *Nemesios von Emesa* (1914), p. 97; M. Pohlenz, *Die Stoa* (²1959, 1955), I, pp. 230–3 and, not quite consistent with it, *ibid.* p. 343.

[7] *Enn.* IV 7 [2]; IV 6 [41]; cf. I 8 [51] 7; IV 3 [27] 9; III 2 [47] 5; II 3 [52] 18; III 3 [48] 7.

ted by the Gnosis, he at times sounds as optimistic as any Stoic and makes full use of their theodicy.[1] This is particularly striking in one of his last essays (I 8, chronologically his 51st), which must have been written when the shades of death were on him.

As far as ethics is concerned, Plotinus must, of course, have been in sympathy with Stoic indifference to everything external; thus, he, differing from both the Academy and the Peripatos, recommends Stoic apathy[2] and, as we have seen, believes that perfection suffices to make its possessor happy. But what the Stoic considers to be man's ultimate goal, viz. independence and inner freedom, is, for Plotinus, only preliminary to the complete union with the supreme deity—be it in this life in mystical ecstasy, be it in the future, when the soul will return to its original home.[3]

As we have seen, the Stoa tries to reconcile determinism with freedom of the will. But, on the whole, antiquity assumed that Stoics are determinists (though even in the formula that freedom essentially consists in consent to the decrees of fate there is a trace of liberty preserved in that it is assumed that it is in our power to give or to refuse one's consent, just as obviously opinions as to what is good or evil are in our power; otherwise there would be no point in trying to change men from fools into sages). Therefore, Plotinus defends[4] the freedom of the will against them (just as did Epicurus; however, Plotinus treats Epicureanism as determinism and at the same time ridicules their concept of *parenklisis*, though recognizing that they try to preserve the *par' hêmin*). His own solution is that a soul is free which acts in accordance with reason.[5]

[1] *Enn.* II 3 [52] 18, 1–8; III 2 and III 3 [47–8] with Theiler's introductory note. and C. Schmidt, *Plotins Stellung zum Gnostizismus* (1901), esp. pp. 74–81

[2] *Enn.* I 4 [46] 8. Cf. Zeller, *Phil.* III/2 (⁵1923), pp. 610–19. He also agrees with the Stoa as to the permissibility of suicide (*Enn.* I 9 [16] with the commentary by R. Harder; *Enn.* I 4 [46] 7; II 9 [33] 8) for sufficient reasons.

[3] Stoic perfections Plotinus would probably accord the status of cathartic perfections (*Enn.* I 2 [19] 5)—a concept obviously related to Plato's *Phaedo* 68B–69E and *Soph.* 230D. Though he relegates them to an inferior rank, he defends them when he faces Gnostic anomianism (*Enn.* II 9 [33] 15).

[4] III 1 [3] 4; 5. On the similarity of some of his arguments to those of Oenomaus of Gadara, Bardesanes, and Origen the Christian (Eusebius, *PE* VI 6–7; 10; 11) see Bréhier's *notice* to III 1 [3].

[5] I 8 [51] 5; III 1 [3] 7, 9 f.; III 2 [47] 10; VI 8 [39] 3, 7. Cf. Zeller, *Phil.* III/2 (⁵1923), pp. 640–2.

But as the Stoa is, on the whole, an expression of 'cosmic' religiousness, a philosophic religion or a religious philosophy which incorporated virtually all popular religious beliefs and, by allegorico-physical explanations, managed to combine its monism with polytheism, it was a precursor of Neoplatonism in that the latter too wanted to be as much a religion as a philosophy. Finally, disregarding the difference between substantial and dynamic pantheism, the assertion that the divine is in some way omnipresent must have had a strong appeal to Plotinus. Iamblichus summed up the similarity between Stoa and Neoplatonism by saying: both systems believe in the identity of the cosmic soul with the soul in us.[1] To this, however, must be added that whereas the Stoa conceived the relation between the cosmic and the human soul as one of a whole to its part, the doctrine of Plotinus is much more subtle: all souls are one.[2] Yet even this doctrine is to a certain extent anticipated by Marcus Aurelius.[3] Both in the Stoa and in Plotinus the essential identity of the cosmic (= divine) and the human soul is used to explain how knowledge of the divine is possible.[4] Thus, some aspects even of the Old Stoa exhibit a certain affinity with some of Plotinus' doctrines.

Whereas Posidonius, Epictetus, and Marcus Aurelius combined Platonism with their Stoicism, the writing *On the World*[5] represents a peculiar blend of Heraclitean, Stoic, and Peripatetic philosophy, in which blend, however, the Peripatetic point of view predominates.[6] The transcendence of God (who, however, preserves cosmic harmony)[7] is strongly stressed,[8] but at the same time it is conceded (to the Stoa) that God is present in the cosmos, but only by his powers, which means that its pantheism of substance is replaced by dynamic pantheism: *panta*

[1] Stob. *Ecl.* I 37, vol. I, p. 372 Wachsmuth.

[2] *Enn.* IV 9 [8].

[3] XII 30.

[4] Sext. Emp. *Adv. math.* VII 93; Plotinus, *Enn.* III 8 [30] 9; VI 3 [44] 4.

[5] Before Proclus (*In Tim.* III, p. 272, 21 Diehl), nobody doubted that it was written by Aristotle. On it see A.-J. Festugière, *La Révélation d'Hermès Trismégiste* (1949), II, pp. 460–518; H. Strohm, 'Studien zur Schrift von der Welt', *Museum Helveticum*, IX (1952), pp. 137–75 (strongly stressing the Platonic elements); but cf. M. Pohlenz, *Die Stoa* (²1959, 1955), II, p. 244.

[6] It teaches the existence of ether (ch. 2, 392a5); it assumes the indestructibility of the cosmos (ch. 4, 396a27; ch. 5, 397a14–15; b5); it sharply distinguishes the sublunar from the celestial sphere (ch. 6, 397b30–3; 400a5–6; 21–35).

[7] In this respect it was preceded by Boethus: Diog. Laert. VII 48.

[8] 6, 397b24.

theôn pleia is true when it refers to *theia dynamis*, false if it refers to *theia ousia*.[1] Thus Stoicism is transposed into another key, so that it, in some respects, anticipates the system of Plotinus (particularly in that it preserves the divine transcendence), just as, in this respect, does Philo of Alexandria. But we should not forget that Plotinus does not accept the category of the presence of being (i.e. intelligence) in everything by its power only.[2]

D. *General conclusion*

To the extent that Plotinus' philosophy is treated from the point of view of its doctrinal content, rather than as a record of his personal experiences, it should have become evident from the preceding lines that it has deep roots in Greek philosophy. The space allocated to the several schools indicates their respective relevance for Plotinus. But it must not be overlooked that our knowledge of Greek philosophy, particularly in the period immediately preceding Plotinus, is fragmentary and that a complete knowledge of it would perhaps substantially modify our picture.

[1] 6, 397b16; the same doctrine we find in Ps.-Onatos (Stob. *Ecl.* I 92, vol. I, p. 48, 5 – 50, 10 Wachsmuth; cf. M. Pohlenz, 'Philon von Alexandrien', *Nachr. d. Ak. d. Wiss. in Göttingen, Phil.-hist. Kl.* [1942], p. 485 n. 2).

[2] VI 4 [22] 3; 9.

PART II

PHILO AND THE BEGINNINGS OF CHRISTIAN THOUGHT

BY HENRY CHADWICK

ABBREVIATIONS

PHILO

Abr.	*De Abrahamo*
Aet.	*De aeternitate mundi*
Agr.	*De agricultura*
Alex.	*Alexander (de animalibus)*
Cher.	*De Cherubim*
Conf.	*De confusione linguarum*
Congr.	*De congressu eruditionis gratia*
Decal.	*De decalogo*
Det.	*Quod deterius potiori insidiari soleat*
Ebr.	*De ebrietate*
Flacc.	*In Flaccum*
Fuga	*De fuga et inventione*
Gig.	*De gigantibus*
Heres	*Quis rerum divinarum heres sit*
Hyp.	*Hypothetica*
Immut.	*Quod Deus sit immutabilis*
Jos.	*De Josepho*
Leg. Alleg.	*Legum Allegoriae*
Leg. ad Gaium	*Legatio ad Gaium*
Migr.	*De migratione Abrahae*
Mut.	*De mutatione nominum*
Opif.	*De opificio mundi*
Plant.	*De plantatione*
Post. C.	*De posteritate Caini*
Praem.	*De praemiis et poenis*
Prob.	*Quod omnis probus liber sit*
Prov.	*De providentia*
Qu. Ex.	*Quaestiones in Exodum*
Qu. Gen.	*Quaestiones in Genesim*
Sacr.	*De sacrificiis Abelis et Caini*
Sobr.	*De sobrietate*
Som.	*De somniis*
Spec. Leg.	*De specialibus legibus*
Virt.	*De virtutibus*
V. contempl.	*De vita contemplativa*
V. Mos.	*De vita Mosis*

JUSTIN MARTYR	
Apol.	*Apologiae*
Dial.	*Dialogus cum Tryphone*

CLEMENT OF ALEXANDRIA	
Ecl. Proph.	*Eclogae propheticae*
Paed.	*Paedagogus*
Protr.	*Protrepticus*
Quis dives	*Quis dives salvetur?*
Str.	*Stromateis*

ORIGEN	
Comm. in Cant. Cantic.	*Commentarium in Canticum Canticorum*
Comm. in Joh.	*Commentarium in Evangelium Johannis*
Comm. in Matt.	*Commentarium in Evangelium Matthaei*
Comm. in Matt. ser.	*Commentariorum in Evangelium Matthaei series*
Comm. in Rom.	*Commentarium in Epistulam ad Romanos*
Exh. mart.	*Exhortatio ad martyrium*
Hom. in Cant. Cantic.	*Homiliae in Canticum Canticorum*
Hom. in Gen.	*Homiliae in Genesim*
Hom. in Exod.	*Homiliae in Exodum*
Hom. in Ezech.	*Homiliae in Ezechielem*
Hom. in Jerem.	*Homiliae in Hieremiam*
Hom. in Lev.	*Homiliae in Leviticum*
Hom. in Luc.	*Homiliae in Evangelium Lucae*
Hom. in Num.	*Homiliae in Numeros*
Hom. in Ps.	*Homiliae in Psalmos*
Orat.	*De oratione*
Princ.	*De principiis*
Sel. in Ps.	*Selecta in Psalmos*

CHAPTER 8

PHILO

The history of Christian philosophy begins not with a Christian but with a Jew, Philo of Alexandria, elder contemporary of St Paul. He was born probably about 25 B.C. and was dead by A.D. 50. Unyielding in meticulous observance of the Mosaic law as the infallibly revealed will of God not only for the chosen people but also for Gentile proselytes (for whose edification some of his writing is directed), Philo is also fully hellenized, presenting a very Greek face to the world. Hebrew he knew imperfectly if at all. His Bible is the Greek Old Testament, in which the Pentateuch towers in authority above the rest; and his belief that the Septuagint translation was divinely inspired[1] relieved him of any need or responsibility to refer to the original text.

Judaism had come into violent conflict with 'Hellenism' at the time of the Maccabean struggle which saved Israel from the destruction of its distinctiveness. Monotheistic Jews could never accept a syncretism which identified Yahweh with Zeus. Yet neither could they turn their back on Hellenism and devote themselves to their private pieties in a mood of nationalistic particularism. For Judaism was a missionary religion, and the ancient prophetic vision of Israel's call to be a light to lighten the Gentiles precluded isolationism, even if this had been a practical possibility, which it was not. The Jews were dispersed through the Mediterranean world. Their language and culture became Greek through and through, and well-to-do Jewish parents (like Philo's) provided their sons with a liberal education under Greek tutors.[2] A liberal education raised inevitable questions and opened fresh horizons. The monotheistic Jew might smile at crude Greek myths; but were the narratives of the Pentateuch wholly beyond critical irony? If one dismissed as childish legends the flood of Deucalion or the Aloadae piling

[1] *V. Mos.* II 40. In some treatises certain manuscripts show a divergent biblical text. Either this is a late aberrant recension of the Septuagint (influenced by Aquila?) or an early independent Targum.

[2] No doubt it reflects Philo's own experience when he credits Moses with Greek tutors (*V. Mos.* I 23); cf. *Alex.* 73.

Pelion on Ossa to reach heaven, what should one say about Noah or the Tower of Babel?[1] Allegorical interpretation, as long practised by exegetes of Homer and systematized by the Stoics especially on the basis of the etymologies of proper names, offered a way of liberation and modernization. Treated as symbol Genesis became not an ancient and in places slightly crude legend, but a strictly contemporary myth about the human condition and man's quest for salvation, a quarry not of remote history and geography but of highly relevant philosophical and moral truth. Before Philo's time a succession of Alexandrian Jews had built up a tradition of such interpretation, applying etymological exegesis to the names of the patriarchs, etc. Philo often makes acknowledgements to his anonymous predecessors, whose work he incorporates, sometimes (it appears) as almost unmodified blocks of matter, much as he also transcribes parts of Greek philosophical tracts.[2] This occasional appropriation of half-assimilated material inevitably diminishes Philo's reputation as an independent thinker, though it proportionately enhances his value to the historian. But it is wrong to exaggerate this phenomenon as if Philo were nothing but an uncritical compiler of pre-existing material and his mind a mere junk-shop. Philo always uses such material for a purpose; and although a clear and consistent system is not to be extracted from his writings, there at least emerges a coherent pattern of attitudes, a religious and philosophical climate which, judged from a historian's standpoint, is of far-reaching importance and influence.

Philo's work is an elaborate synthesis, or at least a correlation, of biblical revealed religion and Greek philosophy, mainly cast in the form of an allegorical commentary on Genesis: Moses used the outward form of myth, historical narrative and ceremonial law to express an inward, spiritual meaning which is wholly in line with the best Greek theology, science and ethics. It is axiomatic that nothing unworthy of God can be intended by the inspired text.[3] God is immutable and does

[1] *Conf.* 2 ff. (Similarly, Abydenus and Alexander Polyhistor in Eusebius, *P.E.* IX 14 and 17; Celsus in Origen, *Contra Celsum* IV 21.) Noah is Deucalion (*Praem.* 23).

[2] *Ebr.* 170 ff. incorporates the tropes of the sceptic Aenesidemus to enforce the frailty of reason and man's need for revelation; *Plant.* 142–77 uses a tract on drunkenness; etc. See H. von Arnim, *Quellenstudien zu Philo* (1888). W. Bousset, *Jüdisch-christlicher Schulbetrieb in Alexandria und Rom* (1915), overstates the case, but it is truth that he is exaggerating. Philo's familiarity with exercises in current philosophical debate appears especially in the group, *De providentia*, *De animalibus*, and *Quod omnis probus liber*; all have strong religious concerns but few references to Judaism.

[3] *Det.* 13.

not change his mind as Genesis might suggest.[1] His 'anger' and threats are not an emotional reaction but remedial and educative like the pain inflicted by physicians and schoolmasters, so that (as Plato argued in the *Gorgias*) it is a misfortune not to be punished by God.[2] Although man occupies a place of great dignity in the creation, God's providence is universal and the cosmos does not exist simply for the sake of mankind: God makes man to contribute his part to the whole.[3] God's activity is not seen in miraculous acts of interference with the natural order but precisely in the orderliness and uniformity of nature itself.[4] The heavens declare the glory of God.

Philo presupposes that the Greek sages are indebted to the Pentateuch for their wisdom.[5] In any event, he implies, it is one God who, directly or indirectly, is the source of the Mosaic law and of the truths of Greek philosophy; for the human mind is akin to God, being made in the image of the divine Logos or Reason, and therefore has some capacity for the reception and discovery of truth about realities beyond time and space. It is in the focus upon the transcendent world that religion and the best Greek philosophy coincide. Accordingly Philo's interest lies in Greek theology and ethics. His mind, it should be added, is in no sense a narrow one; various autobiographical passages show that, bookish as he is, he is no withdrawn rabbi cutting himself off from Alexandrian social life. He attends dinner-parties and theatres, he watches wrestlers and chariot-racing.[6] His explicitly philosophical writings other than his biblical expositions show easy and complete

[1] So the tract *Quod Deus sit immutabilis* (the second part of a single treatise of which *De gigantibus* is the first).

[2] *Immut.* 52; 54; 64–5; *Som.* I 236; *Leg. Alleg.* III 174; *Det.* 144 ff.; *Conf.* 165 f.; *Qu. Gen.* I 73.

[3] *Som.* II 115–16. On man's dignity Philo often repeats the traditional commonplaces that man is erect to look up to heaven (*Det.* 85; *Plant.* 17; *Abr.* 59; *Opif.* 54—from Plato, *Timaeus* 90 A), and that man is a microcosm (*Post. C.* 58; *Plant.* 28; *Heres* 155; *Prov.* I 40; etc.).

[4] *Mut.* 135; cf. the argument from the immutability of the cosmos to that of God, *Som.* II 220; *Aet.* 39–44. Portents like the dividing of the Red Sea or the fire rained on Sodom are not more miraculous than nature itself, all alike being the Creator's work: *V. Mos.* I 212; II 267. A fragment of *Qu. Gen.* (II pp. 217 f. Marcus) explains that the fire destroying Sodom proves *all* weather conditions to be caused not by sun and stars but by the power and free choice of the Father. In the *Life of Moses*, however, the supernatural is enhanced, or interpreted in such terms (visions and dreams, cf. *Som.* I 1) as a Greek would understand. Cf. G. Delling, *Wiss. Zeits. Halle*, 1957, 713–40.

[5] *Aet.* 18; *Prob.* 57; *Spec. Leg.* IV 61; *Leg. Alleg.* I 108; *Heres* 214; etc.

[6] Dinners: *Leg. Alleg.* III 155 f.; *Fuga* 28 f.; *Spec. Leg.* IV 74 f. Theatres: *Prob.* 141. Pancratiasts: *Prob.* 26. Racing: frag. *ap.* Eus. *P.E.* VIII 14. 58.

familiarity with the literary and scientific commonplaces of the age.[1] Nevertheless it is only on the theological and ethical side that he becomes seriously engaged with philosophy. This does not mean that, like the polymath Posidonius or Cicero, Philo is a philosopher with interests that happen to lie in the religious field. It is rather that his faith determines the nature of the questions he puts to the philosophical tradition of Hellenism. And although Philo is as deeply hellenized as a loyal Jew could conceivably be, he ultimately shares the Maccabean spirit of resistance to the totalitarian claims of Hellenistic culture. The spirit of his tract 'On the Contemplative Life' is an attack on the Greek moral tradition. Revealed religion is more than philosophy.

According to Posidonius the subjects studied by the young as their 'general education' (*encyclia*), i.e. grammar, rhetoric, dialectic, geometry, arithmetic, music and astronomy, though neither philosophy in themselves nor productive of moral virtue, are nevertheless an essential preparation. They have the status of a 'servant', just as earlier primary education prepares the mind for general education.[2] Philo takes this idea one stage further: the studies of general education prepare the mind for philosophy which in turn prepares the mind for the yet higher wisdom of revealed theology,[3] which the mind cannot grasp without the help of inspired prophecy.[4] With this qualification Philo's devotion to the study of philosophy is absolute.

The God whom Philo worships is the God of Abraham, Isaac and Jacob, a personal God who loves and judges his erring creatures; no local or tribal deity whose responsibilities are limited to Israel[5] but the one God of all the earth who has chosen Israel for a special destiny

[1] See the clichés collected by A.-J. Festugière, *La Révélation d'Hermès Trismégiste*, II (1949), pp. 519 ff.

[2] Seneca, *Ep.* 88. 20 ff.

[3] See *Som.* I 205; *Leg. Alleg.* III 244 f.; and the tract *De congressu eruditionis gratia* allegorizing Abraham's marriage to Hagar and Sarah as symbolic of the ministerial role of philosophy in relation to theology. (It is an adaptation of current allegorization of the *Odyssey*, according to which Penelope's suitors, successful with her maidservants, are those who pursue the *encyclia* but advance no further: cf. Diog. Laert. II 79; Plutarch, *Educ. Puer.* 10, 7D; Stobaeus III 4. 109; *Gnomol. Vaticanum* 166 ed. Sternbach; ascribed to Aristotle by Olympiodorus, Cramer, *Anecd. Paris.* IV 411.) For Philo's views on education see F. H. Colson in *JTS*, XVIII (1917), pp. 151–62, and references collected by J. W. Earp in the Loeb *Philo*, X 317; 345 f.

[4] *V. Mos.* II 6; *Sacr.* 64; *Immut.* 92 f.; *Ebr.* 120; *Fuga* 168 f.

[5] *Spec. Leg.* I 97: while pagan priests offer prayer only for their own people, the Jewish high priest offers for all men and for the natural order (cf. I 168; II 163; *Leg. ad Gaium* 278; 290; *Abr.* 98; *V. Mos.* I 149). His care is for the whole creation, not merely for his own race.

among the other races of mankind; a God whose thoughts are higher than our thoughts, and upon whose creative will the world and every creature are in continued dependence. This high ethical monotheism Philo fuses with the transcendentalist theology of Platonism. Strictly speaking, Philo is uncommitted to any single set of philosophical principles. He is an eclectic, and although he has swallowed a great deal of Plato he is not uncritical. For the most part, however, his eclecticism is not his personal construction. Before him philosophers had found it possible to reconcile the vitalistic cosmos of the Stoics with the transcendentalist world-view of the Platonists. His Jewish monotheism made especially congenial to him both the Stoic conception of the immanent divine power pervading the world as a vital force and the transcendent, supra-cosmic God of Plato. So he takes for granted the broad Platonic picture of this sensible world as an uneven reflection of the intelligible order; and he also looks beyond Plato to Pythagoras, the mystique of whose name had been steadily growing during the previous century. Pythagoreanism was particularly liked by Philo for its cryptic symbolism, its allegorical interpretations of poetic myth, its gnomic morality, its advocacy of self-discipline as a preparation for immortality, and above all its speculations about the mysterious significance of numbers, notably the number seven which played so important a role in sabbatarian Judaism.[1] Philo was no dabbler in the occult (as some Neopythagoreans were). But to represent Judaism as resembling an esoteric and slightly exotic philosophical tradition of pre-Platonic origin was skilful apologetic to the contemporary Hellenistic world.

Accordingly, Philo sets out to unite the personalist language of much of the Bible with the more impersonal and abstract terminology of the Platonists and Pythagoreans. God is the One or Monad, the ultimate ground of being beyond all multiplicity.[2] In speaking of him as the Monad, however, we must be on our guard against the implication that he is the first in a series of numbers. It is therefore also necessary to affirm that he is 'beyond the Monad'.[3] He is immutable, infinite, self-

[1] Philo's numerology is studied by K. Staehle, *Die Zahlenmystik bei Philon* (1931). Philo's adoption of so much Pythagoreanism suggests it was less unpopular than Seneca says (*Nat. Qu.* VII 32. 2, 'turbae invidiosa'), at least in high Alexandrian society.

[2] *Leg. Alleg.* III 48; *Immut.* 11 f.; *Heres* 187; *Spec. Leg.* II 176; *Qu. Gen.* I 15; *Praem.* 162; etc.

[3] *Leg. Alleg.* II 3; *Praem.* 40. Cf. *V. Contempl.* 2; *Opif.* 8; *Qu. Ex.* II 37; 68.

sufficient, not needing the world.[1] No creaturely language is adequate to express the being of the transcendent Creator.[2] He wills pure goodness,[3] and this cause of the creation is the divine bounty, an ungrudging overflow of benevolent giving[4] in which the Giver remains unaffected and undiminished, like a torch from which other torches are lit, like the sun in giving out sunlight, like a spring of water.[5] He created the cosmos out of non-being (*ek mê ontôn*),[6] ordering formless and chaotic matter,[7] stamping upon it the pattern of order and rationality, his Logos.[8] In the process of creation all the available matter was used. The world is unique; there is no infinite number of worlds.[9] The material world is not eternal, but created and dependent.[10] In agreement with Plato (*Timaeus* 41 A) Moses teaches that the world is created even though, by God's will, it may also be imperishable.[11] It mirrors the eternal, intelligible realm of Ideas which are God's thoughts.[12]

Philo is the earliest witness to the doctrine that the Ideas are God's thoughts. The notion, which is certainly earlier than Philo, that the Ideas are analogous to a human designer's plans, could naturally arise from a fusion of Platonism either with the Stoic doctrine of seminal principles (*logoi spermatikoi*) in nature or with the Aristotelian conception of the divine self-thinking mind.[13] Philo also has a developed notion of the great chain of being: the cosmos is a continuum of grades of

[1] Immutable, *Cher.* 19; *Qu. Gen.* I 93; *Som.* II 220; infinite, *Leg. Alleg.* III 206; *Fuga* 8; *Heres* 229; incomprehensible, *Spec. Leg.* I 32; *Qu. Ex.* p. 258 Marcus (p. 72 Harris); *Leg. Alleg.* I 91; *Mut.* 8 (we cannot even know ourselves, still less the world soul); nameless, *Heres* 170; *Mut.* 11 ff., 29; *Som.* I 27; 230; *Abr.* 51; *V. Mos.* I 76, cf. II 115 (on tetragrammaton); self-sufficient, *Migr.* 27; 46; 183; *Qu. Gen.* IV 188 (though needing nothing, God rejoices in his world); etc.

[2] *Leg. Alleg.* III 206; *Post. C.* 16; 168.

[3] *Leg. Alleg.* I 5; *Abr.* 268; *Spec. Leg.* IV 187.

[4] *Leg. Alleg.* III 68; *Opif.* 21 f.

[5] *Gig.* 24–7 (torches, spring); *Qu. Gen.* II 40 (sunlight). Similarly *Plant.* 89; 91; *Spec. Leg.* I 47; *Qu. Ex.* II 68.

[6] *Leg. Alleg.* III 10; *Heres* 36; *Fuga* 46; *V. Mos.* II 267.

[7] *Qu. Gen.* I 64; *Plant.* 3; *Som.* I 241; *Prov.* I 22; *Opif.* 22. In *Som.* I 76 God is 'not only δημιουργός but also κτίστης', which may imply that God created the pre-existent matter (as in the Greek fragment from *Prov. ap.* Eus. *P.E.* VII 21, and also apparently *Prov.* I 7 in the Armenian version).

[8] *Som.* II 45; *Mut.* 135.

[9] *Opif.* 171; *Aet.* 21; *Det.* 154 (citing *Timaeus* 32C); *Plant.* 5 ff. Cf. *Prov. ap.* Eus. *P.E.* VII 21.

[10] *Opif.* 7 f.; 170 f.; *Conf.* 114; *Som.* II 283; *Plant.* 50; *Aet.* 150.

[11] *Decal.* 58. *Aet.* 18 ff. argues that Plato followed Moses; cf. *Heres* 246.

[12] *Opif.* 17; 20; *Conf.* 63, cf. 73; 172; *Spec. Leg.* I 47–8; 329; *Cher.* 49.

[13] For the Ideas as God's thoughts see esp. Seneca, *Ep.* 58. 18 f.; 65. 7. Discussion by A. N. M. Rich in *Mnemosyne*, ser. 4, VII (1953), pp. 123–33; A. H. Armstrong in *Entretiens Hardt*, V (1960), pp. 393 ff.

being, filled out to the maximum possible plenitude,[1] the diversity of which is held together by the immanent power of the Logos.[2] This doctrine anticipates not only Plotinus but also the Christological terminology of St Paul in Colossians i, a passage for which Philonic texts provide numerous analogies.[3] Perhaps the closest analogy to Philo's picture of the world is found in the pseudo-Aristotelian tract *De mundo*, where God is both above the world and a vital force pervading it,[4] tranquil yet ceaselessly active,[5] reigning like the Great King of Persia whose local administration is done through subordinate satraps,[6] maintaining the world in one stay by means of a balance of power between the conflicting elements so that the cosmos is a harmony of opposites.[7] Philo, however, has given more thought to the problem of how the supreme, transcendent God is related to this lower world. The clue he finds in the doctrine of the Logos.

The Logos is 'the idea of ideas',[8] the first-begotten Son of the uncreated Father and 'second God',[9] the pattern and mediator of the creation,[10] the archetype of human reason,[11] and 'the man of God'.[12] (Philo interprets Gen. ii. 4 ff. of the creation of earthly man, and Gen. i. 26 of the heavenly Adam, the two accounts corresponding to the Platonic sensible and intelligible worlds.[13] As the archetype of the human

[1] *Opif.* 141 ff. (like magnetic chain); *Immut.* 35 (like relay race); *Plant.* 6; *Det.* 154; *Heres* 156 (perfect fulness); *Qu. Ex.* II 68 (no gap in the continuum); *Cher.* 109 (all nature interconnected in harmony). On cosmic sympathy see esp. *Migr.* 178–80, admitting 'sympathy' but denying that God is either the cosmos or the world-soul and that the stars cause earthly events. Several texts accept the Aristotelian view (generally rejected by Stoic exponents of cosmic sympathy) that the soul is of aether as a fifth *ousia* beside the four elements earth, air, fire and water: *Abr.* 162; *Qu. Gen.* III 6; 10; IV 8; *Qu. Ex.* II 73; 85. *Heres* 283 hesitates on this point.

[2] *Fuga* 112; *Heres* 188 (like glue); *Plant.* 9–10; *Qu. Ex.* II 89 f.; 118.

[3] H. Chadwick in *New Test. Stud.* I (1955), p. 273; for Ephesians, *ZNW*, LI (1960), pp. 150 f. For a study of the affinity between Philo and Colossians see H. Hegermann, *Die Vorstellung vom Schöpfungsmittler im hellenistischen Judentum und Urchristentum* (1961).

[4] *Leg. Alleg.* II 4, God pervades all (cf. *De mundo* 6, 397b17 ff.).

[5] *Post. C.* 28 f.; *Cher.* 86 f. (cf. *De mundo* 6, 397b23 f.).

[6] *Decal.* 61 (admittedly to make a different point); *Agric.* 51; cf. *De mundo* 6, 398a10 ff. This illustration is a regular cliché in later writers. The comparison of God to a puppet-showman pulling strings (*Opif.* 117) occurs in *De mundo* 6, 398b16 ff.

[7] *Heres* 130 ff.; *Qu. Gen.* III 5; *Cher.* 110–12; cf. *De mundo* 5, 396a33 ff. Both writers cite Heraclitus. E. R. Goodenough, *Yale Classical Stud.* III (1932), pp. 117–64, suggested a Neopythagorean source.

[8] *Migr.* 103; *Qu. Ex.* II 124.

[9] *Post. C.* 63; *V. Mos.* II 134; *Conf.* 63. 'Second God': *fr. ap.* Eus. *P.E.* VII 13. 1.

[10] *Conf.* 63; *Leg. Alleg.* III 96; *Immut.* 57.

[11] *Heres* 230 ff.; *Leg. Alleg.* I 31 ff.; etc.

[12] *Conf.* 41; 62; 146.

[13] *Leg. Alleg.* I 31, etc.

mind, the Logos is the heavenly Adam.) The Logos is God immanent, the vital power holding together the hierarchy of being, who as God's viceroy[1] mediates revelation to the created order so that he stands midway on the frontier between creator and creature.[2] Like the manna he is God's heavenly food to man,[3] and the high priest who intercedes with God for frail mortals.[4] The supreme God is too remote to have direct contact with this world, and it was the Logos who appeared, e.g., at the burning bush.[5] The Logos dwelt especially in Moses, who was thereby virtually deified.[6] By those less than fully enlightened the Logos is taken to be God, though in reality he is God's image.[7]

Philo's statements about the Logos were to have a notable future when adapted to the uses of Christian doctrine. But if the future of the notion is clear, its pre-Philonic history is obscure, and it has long been disputed whether the decisive impetus behind the conception comes from Greek or from Jewish influences. 'The word of God' by which the heavens were made according to Ps. xxxiii. 6 and the personified Wisdom of Proverbs viii are certainly not far away. Speculations about angels and archangels in post-exilic Judaism may well have helped on the formulation of the idea; Philo is very ready to describe the Logos as 'archangel'.[8] Moreover, except for the tract *De opificio mundi*, which falls outside the allegorical commentary on Genesis, Philo is reticent about the Logos in his apologetic writings intended for a Gentile public; in some passages he regards the doctrine of the Logos and of God's 'powers' mediating between God and the world as mysterious and in some degree esoteric.[9] From the way in which Philo's allegories assume that the conception will be readily understood by his readers, as also from St John i, it may safely be assumed that the Logos notion already enjoyed a measure of currency in hellenistic Judaism even before Philo.

[1] *Agr.* 51.

[2] *Heres* 205 f.; *Som.* II 188; *Qu. Ex.* II 68.

[3] *Leg. Alleg.* III 175; *Det.* 118; *Heres* 79; *Fuga* 137 f.

[4] *Migr.* 102; *Som.* I 215; II 183.

[5] *Som.* I 69 (where the plural *logoi* is used, as also elsewhere on occasion); *V. Mos.* I 66; *Som.* I 231 f.; *Fuga* 141; *Mut.* 134.

[6] *Sacr.* 8; *Mut.* 128; *Som.* II 189; *Prob.* 43; *Det.* 161 ff.; *V. Mos.* I 158; II 288. Some of Philo's language in these passages strikingly anticipates Christology.

[7] *Leg. Alleg.* III 207; *Qu. Gen.* III 34; *Fuga* 212; *Som.* I 238; *Migr.* 174 f.; *Qu. Ex.* II 67.

[8] *Conf.* 146; *Heres* 205; etc.

[9] For the doctrine of God and his powers as esoteric see *Sacr.* 60; 131–2; *Abr.* 122; *Fuga* 85–95; *Cher.* 48; *Qu. Gen.* IV 8.

On the other hand, the actual function of the Logos in Philo's thought points to the conclusion that the impetus is coming not so much from the Jewish side as from that of late Platonist philosophy, where the remote transcendent God requires a second, metaphysically inferior aspect of himself to face towards the lower world. Accordingly, Philo's Logos is not merely an essential clue to the Christian development but also a stage on the way towards the Middle Platonist and Neoplatonist speculations about two or three levels of being in God. It is, however, not more than a stage, and it is a warning against exaggeration that Philo betrays no special interest either in the *Parmenides* or in the passages from the Platonic epistles which were to play so substantial a role in giving authority to the Neoplatonic Triad.

There is another respect in which Philo's language looks forward to the language of his successors. To the contemplative soul, he says, God appears like a triad consisting of himself with his two chief powers, creative goodness and kingly power, which are symbolized by the Cherubim.[1]

Between the Creator and his creatures a great gulf is fixed.[2] To be fallen is inherent in being created, so that sin is 'congenital' in even the best men.[3] But Philo does not only interpret the human problem as one of finitude. He also sees pride, the lust to become equal to God, as the root of sin.[4] In more Platonic fashion he can also accept the myth in the *Phaedrus* about the fall of souls which lose their wings, a fall which results from 'satiety' with the divine goodness.[5] Some souls descend to bodies, others less far to serve as ministering angels, whom pagans call *daimones*.[6] In any event, God is not responsible for evil;[7] he can only be the cause of good. But the plural of Gen. i. 26 ('let us make man') shows that in creating man God was assisted by subordinate powers who, as Plato had taught in the *Timaeus* (41), made the mortal part of

[1] *Cher.* 26–8; *Sacr.* 69; *Qu. Gen.* I 57; II 16; 51; 75; III 39; 42; IV 2; 4; 87; *Qu. Ex.* II 62; 64 ff.; *Mut.* 28; *Som.* I 162 f.; *V. Mos.* II 99; *Spec. Leg.* I 307.

[2] *Sacr.* 92; *Opif.* 151; *Ebr.* 111; etc.

[3] *V. Mos.* II 147; *Spec. Leg.* I 252; *Jos.* 144.

[4] *Leg. Alleg.* I 49; *Cher.* 58–64. (The antithesis to Philippians ii. 6 is noteworthy.) By his fall Adam lost immortality: *Opif.* 167; *Qu. Gen.* I 55; *Virt.* 205.

[5] *Heres* 240; *Qu. Ex.* II 40. But heavenly natures are fixed and never experience satiety: *Qu. Gen.* IV 87.

[6] *Gig.* 12. Cf. *Plant.* 14; *Som.* I 141 (angels = heroes).

[7] *Agr.* 128–9. On Philo's gnostic affinities cf. *Bull. J. Ryl. Libr.*, March 1966.

man. The fact that inferior angels shared in the creation explains the existence of evil.[1] In this doctrine Philo's words foreshadow the Gnostics; but he has nothing to say about the use of ritual or of special ascetic prescriptions in order to placate evil powers in the cosmos. Some of the raw material of Gnosticism can be found in Philo. He is not, except in the vaguest sense, himself a Gnostic.

Nevertheless the tendency to dualism becomes very marked when Philo comes to expound his ethic, for which the antithesis of spirit and matter is fundamental. The 'coats of skins' that clothed Adam and Eve after their Fall mean bodies.[2] The soul dwells in the body as in a tomb[3] and carries it about as a corpse.[4] God gives this world to use, not to possess.[5] In a few places Philo writes with approval of the Aristotelian recognition that the good can include external and physical things, not merely the moral good of the soul.[6] But in other passages he takes the more austere Stoic view (also common among Platonists) that the only good is the good of the soul, the only value is moral value.[7] This doctrine is set within a Platonic framework: if we are to rise to the eternal world of mind we must suppress all responsiveness to the pull of the sensible world. When the senses are awake, the mind sleeps, and *vice versa*.[8] So in general Philo's ethic inclines towards a world-denying asceticism.[9] He disapproves of spectacular mortification or actual maltreatment of the body.[10] He does not think the rich should give away all their wealth; they ought rather to accept the high responsibility to use it for good and charitable purposes.[11] But his personal ideal is a frugal life of strict self-control. One must first learn the way of virtue in practical dealings with one's fellow-men before withdrawing to the higher contemplative life.[12] Sharing God's gifts with others

[1] *Opif.* 175; *Conf.* 179; *Abr.* 143; *Fuga* 68 ff.; esp. *Qu. Ex.* I 23 (good and evil powers enter every soul at birth, and the entire cosmos is created by these conflicting agents); *Qu. Ex.* II 33.

[2] *Qu. Gen.* I 53; IV I. Cf. *Leg. Alleg.* III 69; *Post. C.* 137; Porphyry, *Abst.* I 31.

[3] *Leg. Alleg.* I 108; *Qu. Gen.* II 69.

[4] *Leg. Alleg.* III 69–74; *Qu. Gen.* I 93; IV 77; *Agr.* 25.

[5] *Cher.* 119; *Spec. Leg.* I 295.

[6] *Sobr.* 6; *Heres* 285 ff.; *Qu. Gen.* III 16.

[7] *Fuga* 148; *Immut.* 6–8; *Virt.* 147; *Mut.* 32 ff.; *Som.* II 9.

[8] *Leg. Alleg.* II 30.

[9] Many passages show how highly Philo prized virginity, e.g. *Post. C.* 135; *Fuga* 50; *V. Mos.* II 68. But procreation is a participation in God's creativity: *Decal.* 107; *Spec. Leg.* II 2; 225. The main source for Philo's sex ethic is *Spec. Leg.* III.

[10] *Det.* 19 f.

[11] *Fuga* 28 f.

[12] *Spec. Leg.* II 20 ff.; *Mut.* 32; *Fuga* 38.

is that 'assimilation to God' held forth as the ideal in Plato's *Theaetetus*.[1]

The religious quest is for a true inwardness to which externals are irrelevant. Here some of Philo's language anticipates some early Christian polemic against Judaism. God, he writes, does not inhabit a house made with hands. The only worthy temple is a pure soul. Ritual without inner devotion is valueless. Circumcision must be that of the heart.[2] Such language moves towards a spirituality running out into an individualistic pietism. On the other side, his unbending loyalty to Judaism leads him to stern condemnation of Jews more hellenized and more liberal than himself—liberals who, because they understood the symbolic meaning of the Mosaic precepts, concluded that they were dispensed from any literal observance.[3] He believes the temple at Jerusalem will endure as long as the cosmos,[4] and has fervent hopes for the future of Judaism as a universal religion.[5] Nevertheless, in his apologia for Judaism the supreme place is occupied not by the central worship at Zion but by the Essenes in Palestine and the Therapeutae in Egypt, monastic communities devoted to asceticism, contemplation and a withdrawn, quasi-Neopythagorean life.[6]

During the span of this life the soul is here as a pilgrim and sojourner, like Abraham as he migrated from the astral religion of Ur to the true religion of the promised land, or like the Israelites wandering in the wilderness.[7] But the attitude is more than detachment. In the course of spiritual self-discipline the soul comes increasingly to realize that the body is a major obstacle to perfection. 'When the mind soars up and is initiated into the Lord's mysteries, it judges the body to be evil and

[1] *Theaet.* 176A–B. Cf. *Spec. Leg.* IV 188; *Virt.* 168; *Fuga* 63; *Qu. Gen.* IV 188; *Opif.* 144; 151.

[2] *Sobr.* 63; *V. Mosis* II 107–8; *Plant.* 107 ff.; 126; *Immut.* 8; *Det.* 20–1; *Spec. Leg.* I 305; *Qu. Ex.* II 51; *Praem.* 123.

[3] *Migr.* 88 ff. Cf. *Flacc.* 50 (where a negative must be inserted with Colson) on the pain caused to loyal Jews by over-liberal Jews compromising with paganism. On the temptation to compromise, cf. *Jos.* 254. *Spec. Leg.* I 315 ff. forbids compromise with pagan cult even in mixed marriages where a Jewish partner would be under pressure to make concessions.

[4] *Spec. Leg.* I 76.

[5] *Praem.* 163 ff. (comparison of this passage with St Paul's Romans xi is highly instructive).

[6] Essenes: *Prob.* 75 ff., and *Hypothetica* (an apology resembling Josephus, *c. Apionem*) *ap.* Eus. *P.E.* VIII 11. Therapeutae: *Vita Contemplativa*, *passim.* These texts may be balanced by the *Leg. ad Gaium* and *Spec. Leg.* I 68 ff. where the central place of the Jerusalem temple is stressed.

[7] *Heres* 82; *Qu. Gen.* III 10; IV 74; 178.

hostile.'[1] The soul has descended to the bondage of the flesh, like Israel enslaved in Egypt, and must seek its Exodus.[2] The way of salvation is by faith like that of Abraham,[3] a moral decision of the will to restrain the unreasoning lusts of the flesh and to advance beyond an Aristotelian 'moderation' to complete absence of passion (*apatheia*).[4]

The goal is the vision of God,[5] a mystical experience which Philo, in a notable anticipation of St Paul, describes as 'seeing and being seen', as 'drawing near to God who has drawn the mind to himself'.[6] In this vision the mind is at rest,[7] delighting in joy at the contemplation of God's immutable being (*to on*) in wordless mental prayer that has passed beyond all petitions.[8] Because God is transcendent, however, his dazzling light is blinding to the soul's vision.[9] While we may say (with the *Phaedrus*, 247c) that God is knowable only by the mind, we must also say that in himself he is unknowable.[10] Of God we can say nothing positive. We can know that he is, but not what he is.[11] His existence we can grasp.[12] The beginning of the knowledge of God is the contemplation of the world. The mind rises from the sensible world to the invisible immaterial order of God, whose existence, deduced from the design and rationality of nature, is attested by the universal consent of all races, Greeks and barbarians alike.[13] Considered simply on philosophical grounds, it is the superiority of monotheism over Gentile polytheism that the Bible places God above and beyond this world, whereas polytheism is a corrupt worship of the creature.[14] Where it rises above the level of crude idolatry, Egyptian animal cult, and morally repulsive

[1] *Leg. Alleg.* III 71.

[2] For Egypt as a symbol of the body and the passions see the references collected by J. W. Earp in the Loeb *Philo*, x, p. 303.

[3] *Migr.* 44; *Abr.* 268–73.

[4] *Leg. Alleg.* III 129–34; 143–4; *Qu. Gen.* IV 178; *Plant.* 98.

[5] *Immut.* 142 ff.; *Migr.* 39; etc.

[6] *Som.* II 226; *Plant.* 64. Cf. I Cor. viii. 3; xiii. 12; Gal. iv. 9; Phil. iii. 12.

[7] *Post. C.* 28; *Som.* II 228; *Fuga* 174; *Immut.* 12.

[8] *Gig.* 52; *Fuga* 91–2; *Heres* 15.

[9] *Opif.* 71; *Abr.* 74–6; *Immut.* 78; etc. (from Plato, *Republic* VII, 515–16).

[10] *Spec. Leg.* I 20; *Qu. Gen.* IV 26; *Mut.* 7; *Immut.* 62; *Qu. Ex.* II 45.

[11] *Leg. Alleg.* III 206. For *via eminentiae* cf. *Leg. ad Gaium* 5; *Qu. Gen.* II 54.

[12] For the atheist argument that God is an invention of authorities to make people behave properly out of fear, cf. *Spec. Leg.* I 330; II 283 ff.; *Leg. Alleg.* III 30 f.; *Praem.* 40; *Prov.* II 45 f.

[13] *Leg. Alleg.* III 97 f.; *Som.* I 203–4; 207–8; *Spec. Leg.* I 32–5; *Praem.* 40 ff. (design); *Spec. Leg.* II 165 (consent).

[14] *Ebr.* 109; *Som.* II 70; *Qu. Gen.* III 1; *Congr.* 133 f.; etc.

practices,[1] it nevertheless ends in a pantheistic deification of the elements of this world or of the stars;[2] even though worship of the heavenly bodies is much better than the cult of material objects, it still fails to rise beyond the creation to God himself.[3] Nevertheless, inferential reasoning cannot pass beyond God's existence. His essence is beyond the grasp of mind. The *via eminentiae* yields ground at the last to the *via negativa*. So, if God is to be known, it is because he makes himself known by grace when he grants revelation in accordance with the capacities of the recipients[4]—capacities which may greatly vary, so that different conceptions of God may be held by different people according to their stage of spiritual development.[5] There is a maturation in theological comprehension.

To affirm the possibility of revelation and grace is to affirm freedom in God,[6] and to be aware that to many God has not manifested himself. Yet this must offer no discouragement, for the serious quest for God is itself sufficient reward and produces noble fruits.[7] Ultimately, however, the highest knowledge of God is attained not by inferential reasoning but by intuition.[8]

The problem which leads Philo to despair of the powers of human reasoning is clear. The *via negativa* leaves him with a ground of being of which it is impossible to make any further affirmation than that it is the ground of being. The One has no other function to perform. For Philo the attainment of this knowledge is analogous to the geometrical definition of a point as having position without magnitude;[9] the negation is indispensable to the definition. Even though, according to the Platonic ontology which Philo takes for granted, being is an evaluative concept and the ground of being must lie at the summit of value, nevertheless Philo needs to assert more than this of God if he is to take his Bible seriously. He is therefore bound to conclude that the positive content of the doctrine of God is derived from revelation.

[1] *Spec. Leg.* III 40 f.; *Mut.* 205. For Egyptian cults, cf. esp. *Decal.* 76 ff., and the identification of Apis with the golden calf (*Ebr.* 95; *V. Mos.* II 161 f.).

[2] *Decal.* 53.

[3] *Congr.* 51; *Decal.* 66.

[4] *Spec. Leg.* I 41 ff.

[5] *Mut.* 19 ff.; cf. *Abr.* 119 ff. (three grades of apprehension).

[6] *Abr.* 80.

[7] *Leg. Alleg.* III 47; *Spec. Leg.* I 40; *Post. C.* 21; *Det.* 89.

[8] *Post. C.* 167; *Leg. Alleg.* III 97–9; *Praem.* 40–6; *Leg. ad Gaium* 5–6.

[9] *Decal.* 26; cf. *Opif.* 49; 98. God has no position: *Leg. Alleg.* I 43 f.

Grace is accordingly a subject on which Philo has much to say. In certain respects Philo's analysis of the psychology of faith anticipates St Paul's depth of insight. So far as our evidence goes, his thinking on this subject has the distinction of being a pioneer attempt to plumb one of the profoundest of all problems of religious thought, namely, the paradox that in the last resort moralism is unable to achieve its end. As Philo puts it, as the soul toils upward in its search of perfection, it ultimately comes to discover that it must cease from toil and acknowledge that every virtue is achieved only by the gift of God.[1] 'When Abraham most knew himself, at this point did he most despair of himself, that he might attain to an exact knowledge of him who truly is. And this is the fact of the matter: the man who has wholly comprehended himself utterly despairs of himself through having first discovered the absolute nothingness of created being. It is the man who has despaired of himself who comes to know him who is.'[2] So a true self-knowledge is an awareness of creaturely dependence before God. Were it otherwise, the strenuous moral striving to suppress the passions would end in complacency and self-congratulation.[3] So at the very climax of the long ascent of mental and moral discipline there stands a gift of grace which quite transcends it.

The theme of grace is closely bound up with the question of Philo's 'mysticism'. In many passages Philo speaks of 'ecstasy' as a being beside oneself, a state of 'sober intoxication',[4] a possession by a holy frenzy[5] in which the inspired saint is moved to corybantic excitement and discovers intense joy and inward repose. It is an experience symbolized, for example, by the narrative in Exodus of Moses' entrance 'into

[1] *Leg. Alleg.* III 136.

[2] *Som.* I 60.

[3] *Leg. Alleg.* III 136–7; cf. II 93; *Sacr.* 56; *Post. C.* 42; 175. On 'Know thyself' cf. *Spec. Leg.* I 263 ff.; 293; *Qu. Gen.* IV 114.

[4] *Opif.* 71; *Leg. Alleg.* III 82; *Ebr.* 147 ff.; *Fuga* 166; *Praem.* 122; *V. Contempl.* 85; *Prob.* 13 f.; *Qu. Gen.* II 68; *Qu. Ex.* II 15; cf. *Som.* II 249 (the Logos is cup-bearer of God, master of the feast, and is the draught that he pours) with St John ii. 1 ff. Plutarch, *Qu. Rom.* 112, taken with *Anth. Pal.* IX 752 (Cleopatra's ring apparently inscribed with the formula) and Philostratus, *V. Apoll. Tyan.* II 37 (bacchants of sobriety), suggests that the oxymoron may be a pre-Philonic coinage of Dionysiac origin with a metaphorical currency in Neopythagorean circles. A pre-Philonic origin is denied by H. Lewy, *Sobria Ebrietas* (1929). But I think the casual use of the phrase in *Fuga* 32 (cf. *V. Mos.* I 187) merely to enforce the lesson of temperance at the dinner-table tells against him.

[5] *Plant.* 39; *Ebr.* 145 ff. (with language analogous to the Pentecost narrative of Acts ii, as in *Decal.* 33. 46; *Heres* 68–70 and esp. 249 ff.

the darkness where God was',[1] or by the ritual of the high priest entering into the holy of holies.[2] His descriptions of this extraordinary condition of the soul have an emotional warmth. The soul, he says, is 'on fire',[3] stirred and goaded to ecstasy, dancing and possessed so that it seems drunk to the onlooker.[4]

In some of the passages where this lyrical language is used it is clear that one motive behind Philo's statements is to vindicate the inspiration of the Old Testament prophets.[5] He must defend the claim that in the sacred writings of the Bible, above all in Moses, there is a revelation of truth about God lying beyond the capacities of the natural unaided reason. For this purpose he found a language ready to hand in some of Plato's dialogues. Plato, who on the one side set the greatest value on logical clarity and intellectual precision, on the other side looked with great respect on the oracular. In Platonism ecstatic rapture is not an alien intrusion upon the deliverances of reason and logic, but in some sense that which underlies all; for the apprehension of the eternal ideas, which are the foundation of everything, comes by a memory of what the soul apprehended in direct vision before coming into the body. This direct vision is something that the soul may hope to regain. In the *Phaedrus* Plato uses ecstatic, corybantic language about the soul's frenzy as it is caught up in the contemplation of the eternal ideas.[6] In both the *Phaedrus* and the *Ion* he compares the inspiration of poets with that of oracles and seers and with the frenzy of the Corybantes. 'God takes away the mind of these men and uses them as ministers.'[7]

For Philo it is congruous with his favourite theme of the nothingness of man before God that he can regard inspiration as given in a trance where the prophet's mind is displaced by the divine Spirit.[8] So Moses' call to be a prophet is described as a second birth, implying a radical transformation of his personality.[9] According to this view, God is everything and the prophet's mind is merely an instrument on which the

[1] *Post. C.* 14; *Gig.* 54; *Mut.* 7; *V. Mos.* I 158.

[2] *Leg. Alleg.* III 125 f.

[3] *Leg. Alleg.* I 84; *Ebr.* 147.

[4] *Ebr.* 146, etc.

[5] *Heres* 69; *Migr.* 84; *Qu. Gen.* III 9.

[6] *Phaedrus* 244E; 245E.

[7] *Ion* 533D ff., esp. 534C. Cf. *Meno* 99C–D; *Timaeus* 71E.

[8] *Heres* 249 ff. explains that this displacement is the meaning of *ekstasis*. Cf. *Mut.* 139; *Qu. Gen.* IV 196; *Spec. Leg.* I 65; IV 49. When filled with grace the soul 'goes outside itself': *Leg. Alleg.* I 82; III 43 f.; *Heres* 68.

[9] *Qu. Ex.* II 46 (with the Greek fragment, Harris, pp. 60 f. = Marcus, p. 251).

Spirit plays,[1] in a state of pure passivity. On the other hand, Philo insists with special emphasis that this gift is bestowed exclusively upon those who have attained to the summit of holiness by training and discipline.[2] The normal Greek estimate of the character of oracular mediums was not high. Plato himself remarks that the priestesses of Delphi and Dodona do not say anything worth hearing except when they are vehicles of divine utterance.[3] For Philo, however, the holiness of the prophet is indispensable. He does not think that this grace of inspiration is magic.

Because Philo has an apologetic interest in the authentication of the biblical writings as inspired documents, and because much of his language echoes the terminology used by Plato about the inspiration of poets and oracles and about the frenzy of the soul as it soars to the contemplation of the ideas, it is not easy confidently to interpret his 'mystical' passages. Do they directly reflect Philo's personal experience? Or are they no more than literary reminiscence and clever apologetic? Interpreters have differed widely.

There may be some analogy in Philo's frequent use of the language of mystery initiations. Such mystery language is frequent in Philo, and might be taken to presuppose a literal mystery cult practised by very hellenized Jews. But this inference is not necessary,[4] since it is probably only an emphatic use of a long-established metaphor, widely current among philosophers at least since Plato's *Symposium* (a dialogue deeply influential on Philo) and expressive of a sense of privilege at admission to knowledge not granted to every man. The Jew in Philo is well aware of this privilege; and the metaphor, which the philosophic convention had long liberated from its specifically cultic association, was eminently suitable to the kind of hellenized Judaism that Philo sought to present to the would-be proselyte, and especially appropriate for a commentator who regarded the Pentateuch as an inspired cryptogram written to

[1] *Heres* 266. This metaphor is a platitudinous commonplace of Greek theories of inspiration.

[2] *Qu. Ex.* II 51 (purity a precondition of the vision of God); *Fuga* 117 (the Logos's presence in the soul precludes sin).

[3] *Phaedrus* 244B.

[4] For the opposite view see E. R. Goodenough, *By Light, Light* (1935), criticized by A. D. Nock in *Gnomon*, XIII (1937), pp. 156–65. Goodenough restates his case in *Quantulacumque, Studies presented to Kirsopp Lake* (1937), pp. 227–42, and in his *Jewish Symbols in the Greco-Roman Period* (11 vols., 1953–64), on which see Nock in *Gnomon*, XXVII (1955), pp. 558–72; XXIX (1957), pp. 524–33; XXXII (1960), pp. 728–36.

conceal truth from the unworthy and to stimulate the intelligent student to penetrate beneath the veil of the letter to the spiritual meaning. If Philo's mystery language does not require the hypothesis of an external rite to explain it, yet the *erôs* terminology of Plato's *Symposium* enabled him to describe an experience that, despite the conventionality of its expression, may nevertheless have been inward and personal.

In a few passages Philo appeals directly to his own experience. In *De Cherub.* 27, after mentioning cosmological interpretations of the Cherubim and the flaming sword (evidently taken from his exegetical predecessors), he goes on to a still higher meaning suggested, he declares, by an inner voice within his soul 'which is often possessed and divines matters beyond its knowledge'. In *Legum Allegoriae* II 85 he remarks that retirement to solitude is not necessarily a way to concentration; the fact that sometimes he has achieved a collected mind in the middle of a crowd shows that the concentration of the soul on spiritual realities is a gift of God and is not attained by physical isolation, even though it is true that the senses are a constant distraction to spiritual perception. In *De migratione Abrahae* 34 f. the words of God to Jacob, 'I will be with thee' (Gen. xxxi. 3), suggest to Philo reflections on the grace of God which showers blessings upon the soul quite independent of human toil, so liberating the soul from the poverty of its own unaided efforts. Philo proceeds to illustrate this from his own experience as a commentator and student. 'On innumerable occasions' he has found his mind a blank when he has sat down to write, even though his mind has clearly comprehended the task before him, and he has been compelled to abandon the attempt at composition. But 'sometimes' he has begun quite empty and then has suddenly become full, ideas falling like a shower of rain so that 'I have been in a state of corybantic frenzy, losing consciousness of everything, of the place, of anyone else present, of myself, of words spoken, of lines written'.

On a minimizing interpretation[1] such passages are merely using conventional terminology derived from the *Phaedrus* and the *Ion* to describe an experience frequently endured by academic minds: concentration is not always possible even when external conditions seem ideal, and insight is more than a matter of sitting down at a table to

[1] E.g. W. Völker, *Fortschritt und Vollendung bei Philo* (1938), pp. 260 ff.

write. But when such passages are taken together with Philo's many affirmations about the gift of grace and the 'yearning' of souls that long with an intense *erôs* for the true Being of God,[1] it seems clear that Philo is talking about a specifically religious experience which had for him an altogether dynamic quality.

Whether it is correct to describe Philo as a mystic depends entirely on what exactly one means by 'mystic'. It is clear beyond doubt that much of his language is closely akin to that which mystics since his time have used, especially in his repeated emphasis that salvation, though requiring of man everything in his power and a rigorous renunciation of the phenomenal world of the senses, is not something that can be achieved simply by an extension and enlargement of the innate resources of the soul but is only found in a losing of the self in something higher. There are many respects in which Philo looks like a blueprint for Plotinus, Gregory of Nyssa and Dionysius the Areopagite. It is important to notice, however, that because Philo is a monotheist with a biblical theology, his mystical language is not in the direction of total abstraction but is qualified by a personalist emphasis. There is no monism in him, no implication that the soul and God are ultimately identical and that the only genuine reality is this identity. That man is made in the image of God, possessing rationality and freedom,[2] confers upon him the capacity for knowing God and loving him. But Philo is continually stressing the gulf between Creator and creature, even though it is true that the Creator is the ground of man's being, the One beyond all the multiplicity of the created order. Philo does not speak of an undifferentiated identity of the soul with the One, but of an 'unbroken union with God in love'[3] which is 'deification'.[4]

The complexities of Philo make a just estimate of his work hard to achieve. The modern reader is exasperated by the repetitiousness and the verbose rhetorical style. Moreover, being conditioned to regard

[1] On *erôs* in Philo see Goodenough, *Jewish Symbols*, VIII, pp. 12–15.

[2] The human soul is a fragment broken off the divine soul (*apospasma*): *Det.* 90; *Leg. Alleg.* III 161; *Plant.* 19 ff.; *Mut.* 223; *Som.* I 34.

[3] *Post. C.* 12. The theme of the soul as God's bride appears especially in *Cher.* 42–53, a passage exploiting mystery terms, reminiscent both of the *Symposium* and of Ephesians v.

[4] *Qu. Ex.* p. 72 Harris = p. 258 Marcus (a fragment preserved in the *Sacra Parallela*): to see God human nature must first become God (θεὸν γενέσθαι). Cf. also *Qu. Ex.* II 29; 40, and the references at p. 144 n. 6 above.

allegories as nothing but a clever sophistical device for evading difficulties and rationalizing superstition, he necessarily meets a substantial barrier at the start when studying a writer who sincerely believed that the Pentateuch was intended by its author to be interpreted allegorically. Patience can quickly become exhausted when epic and moving stories in Genesis are transformed by exegetical alchemy into a string of colourless humanitarian platitudes. Even the most sympathetic critic whose question to Philo is strictly limited to his place within the inner development of Greek philosophy is bound to come to the conclusion that *qua* philosopher he is a well informed but not an original mind who has taken many bits and pieces out of other men's systems. Yet it is certainly wrong to think of Philo as a Jewish apologist with an interest in philosophy simply and solely because it offered devices for making Judaism intellectually respectable. It is true enough that Philo is an apologist for Judaism and that his writings contain much direct and indirect argument to vindicate the truth of his religious faith and his convictions about the mission of Israel in the world at large. Although, because of this apologetic interest, one does not learn very much from his writings about Jewish ideas which have no Greek analogy whatever,[1] it is the fact that Philo is using philosophy (and at times criticizing it) as a loyal Jew which often gives his work a greater degree of coherence than may appear at first sight. But if his religion quietly determines the eclectic character of his philosophy, his philosophy is in turn profoundly influencing his faith and its expression, and his full-blooded allegorism means that he is free to allow this influence to take effect. In short, philosophy, and especially Platonic philosophy, matters to Philo for more than superficial reasons of apologetic expediency. Philo is not trying to pretend to a veneer of hellenization; he is hellenized to the core of his being. To him theology is much more than dressing up Moses to look like Plato. Platonism was for him true in all its essential structure, and the fact that the cosmogony of the *Timaeus*

[1] Some distinctively Jewish concerns emerge especially in Philo's ethics: e.g. the distinction between voluntary and involuntary sins, *Opif.* 128; *Immut.* 128 f.; etc.; propitiation, *Som.* I 91; II 292; etc.; philanthropy, *Decal.* 41; *Agr.* 90; *Spec. Leg.* I 294; *Fuga* 28 f. Disapproval of paederasty, fornication, marital intercourse without the intention of begetting children, and abortion (*Spec. Leg.* III 34 ff.; 72; 117; cf. *Jos.* 43) is characteristic but not distinctive of Judaism. The Greek influence on Philo's ethics tends to make him more rather than less austere.

could so easily be reconciled with Genesis served not only to demonstrate the rationality of Moses but also to enhance the authority of the *Timaeus*. (In this respect Philo's work may be regarded as a stage on the way to the Hermetic tractates which express in the form of divine revelation a content derived from the commonplaces of popular philosophy.) Jerome and several Greek Fathers quote a Greek saying, 'Either Plato philonizes or Philo platonizes'.[1] Philo could not help platonizing. He needed Plato to expound his own faith. It is pre-eminently the uniting of the biblical faith with the religious side of Platonism, especially with its mystical language about ecstasy and its transcendentalist doctrine of God, that makes Philo a figure of seminal importance.

Except for some substantial borrowings in the pages of Josephus, the history of Philo's influence lies in Christianity, not in Judaism. The catastrophes of the two Jewish revolts did not, of course, kill hellenistic Judaism stone-dead. It is as good as certain that there long continued to be hellenized Jews who read Philo and said the kind of things that he had said.[2] Although the Septuagint came under the ban of rabbinic condemnation, it was only ousted slowly; it was being used in the synagogues in Asia Minor during the second century.[3] As late as the sixth century there was sharp controversy within the Jewish community between those who insisted that in the synagogue liturgy the Old Testament be read exclusively in Hebrew and those hellenized Jews who wanted it read in Greek—a dispute which occasioned an amazing law of Justinian (*Novel* 146) regulating synagogue worship. But apart from the Dura synagogue and some inscriptions, few significant monuments of Greek Judaism survive from this later period. The Judaism which established itself as normative was that of the rabbis. Philo stands closer to the second- and third-century Christians than to the Judaism of the Talmud, and is much less 'rabbinic' than St Paul. The points of

[1] Jerome, *De vir. inl.* 11; Isidore of Pelusium, *Ep.* III 81; etc.

[2] *Disiecta membra* of the literature and liturgy of hellenistic Judaism survive as incorporated in some Christian sources, e.g. an apology against paganism in *Clem. Hom.* IV–VI; liturgical prayers in *Apost. Const.* VII 33–8 (discussed by Bousset, *Götting. Nachr.* 1915, pp. 435 ff.). That Jewish proselytism continued is evident from the edict of Septimius Severus forbidding it early in the third century, and from the strong language which John Chrysostom found necessary to deter his congregation at Antioch from succumbing to synagogue influences.

[3] Justin, *Dial.* 72. 3; Tosephta, *Meg.* II 5; IV 13.

affinity between Philo and later rabbinic traditions turn out to be even less numerous than might be expected,[1] and if later Jewish writings mention him, which is not certain, it is in terms of bitter disapproval.[2] Nothing of his work was known to the medieval Jewish philosophers. By contrast his work was of great importance for the early Christians. It goes without saying that the differences are substantial and not less striking than the similarities.[3] But there can be no question that the affinities are of the first importance. The quantity of surviving manuscripts (including several papyrus fragments) shows how much he was read; in the fourth and early fifth centuries parts of his work were translated into Latin and Armenian, and the debt of Ambrose is particularly large. Philo's pages contain exegetical ideas that constantly seem like anticipations of St Paul, St John, and the author of the Epistle to the Hebrews (perhaps Apollos?). The philosophical side of Philo was taken up, after a surprising relative neglect in the second-century apologists, by Clement and Origen. We may see some symbolic recognition of the Christian debt to Philo in the legend quoted by Eusebius that when Philo went on his visit to Rome he met St Peter.[4]

[1] S. Sandmel, *Philo's Place in Judaism* (1956), argues that Philo had no close knowledge of rabbinic traditions. Minor correspondences are noted by P. Borgen, *Bread from Heaven* (1965).

[2] That there are two possible allusions has been shown by L. Finkelstein, *Journ. Bibl. Lit.* LIII (1934), pp. 142–9.

[3] Philo's eschatology is wholly expressed in terms of a Platonic immortality of the soul. (Transmigration: *Plant.* 14; *Gig.* 7 ff.; *Som.* I 138. Anamnesis: *Leg. Alleg.* III 91 f.; *Praem.* 9; *V. Contempl.* 78. The Ideas as the home of departed saints: *Heres* 280; *Gig.* 61.) Although he retains high hopes for a glorious future for Israel (esp. *Praem.* 163 ff.), there is no explicit and unambiguous hope of a Messiah. See the judicious discussion in H. A. Wolfson, *Philo* (1947), II, pp. 395 ff. On hell cf. *Congr.* 57; *Qu. Gen.* II 60; *Praem.* 152; *Mut.* 129; *P. Oxy.* 1356.

[4] Eus. *HE* II 17. 1. Ps.-Prochorus (fifth century?) introduces Philo to St John (*Acta Iohannis*, 110–12 Zahn).

CHAPTER 9

THE BEGINNING OF CHRISTIAN PHILOSOPHY: JUSTIN: THE GNOSTICS

Christian philosophy does not strictly begin with the New Testament, but even at this early stage it is easy to discern statements and propositions that implicitly and indirectly point towards certain metaphysical positions. The origins of Christian philosophy are therefore more than a matter of discovering passing echoes of Greek ideas within the New Testament writings, for example the Platonic and Philonic overtones of the Epistle to the Hebrews. The prologue of St John's Gospel, with its identification of the Logos as the light lightening every man with the Logos made flesh in Christ, initially provokes the expectation of an indirect apologia to the Greek world; but the remainder of the Gospel is more concerned with other questions that are oddly nearer to Kierkegaard than to Plato, who cannot be said to be more than a remote influence in the background of the evangelist's thought. In St Paul there are some occasional Platonizing hints, especially in the discussion with the Corinthians about immortality in II Cor. iii–v. The indictment of pagan cult as a worship of the creature in place of the Creator in Romans i is qualified by a recognition that 'that which may be known of God' may be grasped by the natural reason through the contemplation of the world. In Romans ii St Paul freely draws on Stoic notions of conscience and natural law, and writes nobly of self-sufficiency and natural goodness in Philippians iv. But it is a common mistake to see early Christian ethics as a mere assimilation of current Stoic ideals and to take Tertullian's *Seneca saepe noster* as a simple account of the phenomena. On closer examination the differences come to look more substantial than the likenesses.[1] For example, Seneca's prayer is an acquiescence to impersonal fate. His commendation of heroic suicide stands in striking contrast with Philippians i. His freedom is self-sufficiency, where St Paul's 'freedom' is redemption from the bondage

[1] See J. N. Sevenster, *Paul and Seneca* (Leiden, 1961).

of sin and a transference from a relation to God as guilty defendant to Judge into a family relationship of filial love. Seneca's pessimistic descriptions of human depravity surpass anything in St Paul, but for the apostle a sombre judgement on man is only a correlate of his intense consciousness of God's holiness and grace. Romans viii was not written by a pessimist. Where Seneca's ideals of universal brotherhood tend to pass into vague benevolence, St Paul thinks rather of concrete and costly acts of charity motivated by gratitude for the love of God manifest in the self-giving humility of Christ. These antitheses may warn us against over-simplified identifications even at the points where the similarity is at its maximum. Apart from any individual contacts in detail, however, the basic framework of New Testament thought is different from that in Platonism and Stoicism. The God of the New Testament is the Creator, 'the living God' of the prophets, who has inaugurated his 'kingdom' or rule on earth by the coming of his Anointed king and prophet, the 'Messiah' or Christ, calling out of this world a holy community to prepare for the final consummation. Revelation consists in divine acts within history, and is moving towards an end which is the full realization of the Creator's will and his final triumph over evil. Because of this framework the Christians possessed a 'rectilinear' concept of the Church in time as moving towards a goal under divine providence, a concept that stands in contrast to the cyclic conceptions of cosmic destiny professed by Platonists and Stoics.[1] Because of their belief in a supreme providence caring for all mankind, history became for them not just a local or national affair but concerned with the world as a whole. Even though the Old Testament occupied a unique place within the scheme, this particularity served a universal purpose, foreshadowed by the Hebrew prophets and now to be realized in the world mission of the Church to all peoples irrespective of race, class or education. This Christian Gospel presupposes a pattern of ideas about the plan of God in the Creation, a beneficent divine purpose frustrated by human pride and cupidity but in process of being brought to true fulfilment through a message of divine salvation, overcoming the gulf between man and God caused by the transitoriness of finitude and the resistance of sin.

[1] J. Barr, *Biblical Words for Time*, pp. 137 ff., warns against the generalization that all biblical thought about history is 'rectilinear' and all Greek thought cyclic.

Even though for individual elements in this pattern one may find anticipations and approximations both on the Greek and on the Hebraic side, yet its essential spirit is distinctively Christian, and determines more than anything else the character of Christian philosophy as that gradually emerges in the age of the Church Fathers.

The first serious beginnings of Christian philosophy appear in Justin Martyr in the middle years of the second century. We have from his pen an Apology addressed to the emperor Antoninus Pius, a so-called Second Apology which is a supplement to the first Apology issued in Rome at a time of persecution, and the long Dialogue with Trypho the Jew, transmitted incomplete but of great importance for Justin's theology. The Acts of his martyrdom (*c.* 162–8) also survive. He was born near Samaria and moved to Ephesus where he attended the classes of a succession of different philosophical teachers. As he describes it in the retrospect of the Dialogue,[1] it was primarily a religious need that impelled him. He began with a Stoic tutor, but the man was unable to satisfy his search, and he passed on to a Peripatetic; but he soon discredited himself as a guide to truth by showing an unphilosophical anxiety about his fee. Next came a Pythagorean, but he insisted that before Justin could comprehend theology he must undergo a preliminary discipline of music, astronomy and geometry by which his mind could be weaned from sensible phenomena and accustomed to think of immaterial realities.[2] So Justin went to a Platonist. With him he was content and made excellent progress in his personal quest, especially as the end of this philosophy is 'the vision of God'. But one day when meditating in solitude near the seashore he met an old man who undermined his confidence in Platonism (partly with Aristotelian arguments)[3] and proceeded to tell him of the inspired prophets of scripture. Justin was converted. In the Dialogue his conversion is the end of an intellectual inquiry; but from the Apologies it also appears that he was deeply impressed by the courage and integrity of the

[1] Justin, *Dial.* 2.

[2] Justin may have been fortified in his opinion that these studies were not indispensable by Plato, *Philebus* 55–6. Cf. *Protagoras* 318E; *Corpus Hermeticum. Asclepius* 13. The opinion of Justin's Pythagorean tutor is paralleled in Philo (*Congr.* 12 ff.), the Middle Platonists Albinus (*Isag.* 7) and Taurus (Gellius, *N.A.* I 9), and Clement (*Str.* VI 90).

[3] R. M. Grant, 'Aristotle and the Conversion of Justin', *JTS*, n.s. VII (1956), pp. 246–8.

Christian martyrs;[1] and perhaps there is a certain 'literary' element in the account in the Dialogue where the *mise-en-scène* has occasional Platonic overtones. The manner in which he describes his conversion has the repeated implication that the decision to become a Christian was not a clean break with his past and that there is much continuity between Platonism and Christianity. Justin is convinced that with a few necessary qualifications and corrections Plato and Christ can be happily reconciled; for, according to both the Bible and Plato, God is transcendent, beyond this material world of time and space, nameless, incorporeal, impassible and immutable.[2] Both Genesis and the *Timaeus* teach that the cosmos is created and dependent on the divine will (Justin does not insist on creation *ex nihilo*).[3] Plato also speaks rightly of the soul's kinship to God and of free will.[4] But Plato erred in his belief that the soul possesses immortality by its inherent nature rather than as God's gift, and in his acceptance of the cyclic doctrine of transmigration.[5] Nevertheless, he perceived that the cults and myths of paganism are false, and showed an awareness of the need for divine revelation in the famous declaration that 'it is hard to find the Maker of the universe and unsafe to declare him when found'.[6]

Justin's programme is clear. It is an absolute rejection of polytheistic myth and cult combined with a positive welcome towards the best elements in the Greek philosophical tradition. Of the harmony of Christianity with these elements Justin writes with unclouded optimism. Like Philo he is an eclectic, not in the sense of wanting to reconcile everyone and everything merely for its own sake, but in the sense that his acceptance of the biblical revelation provides him with a criterion of judgement for assessing what is true or false in the philosophers. So he declares that the Platonists are right about the transcendence of God but wrong about the doctrine of the soul's immortality and transmigration. The Stoics are right in their noble ethical principles, but grossly wrong in their fatalism and pantheism, and in their materialistic doc-

[1] Justin, *Apol.* II 12, 1.

[2] Justin, *Dial.* 5. 4; 127. 2; *Apol.* I 9–10; 13; 61; 63; II 6; 12.

[3] *Dial.* 5 rejects the exegesis of *Timaeus* 41 advanced by some Platonists that the cosmos is uncreated. Cf. *Apol.* I 10 and 59 (unformed matter), esp. 20 on the agreement of Christianity and Platonism about creation, and 60 on the *Timaeus* copying Genesis.

[4] *Dial.* 4. 2; *Apol.* I 44.

[5] *Dial.* 4–5.

[6] *Timaeus* 28C in *Apol.* II 10.

trine that the soul and even God himself are very tenuous spirit, not incorporeal.[1] Justin rejects the cosmic religion of his age as sharply as he rejects the pessimism of the Gnostics. He thereby points forward significantly to the Christian evaluation of the natural order as being not in itself divine but rather a sacramental ladder to the Creator. Justin's critique of Stoicism is in no way different from that which may be found in many contemporary Platonists. But his rejection of the innate immortality of the soul and of the doctrine of transmigration is determined by his entirely correct insight that the notion, with its implications of a possibly infinite series of lives for each individual and of the meaninglessness of existence, does not easily fit into the Christian conception of God and his relation to the world in creation and redemption.

Justin explains his positive appreciation of Greek philosophy partly by the conventional thesis that the Greek philosophers had studied the Old Testament, but chiefly by his doctrine of the divine Logos. The Word and Wisdom of God, who is Christ, is also the Reason inherent in all things and especially in the rational creation. All who have thought and acted rationally and rightly have participated in Christ the universal Logos.[2] Socrates and Abraham are alike Christians before Christ,[3] a striking conception by which Justin becomes the pioneer of the scheme of world-history which regards Christianity as the keystone of an arch formed by Hebrew and Greek civilizations blending. It is an explicit theology of history which gives Justin's approach to his pagan readers a powerful impetus.

In the Second Apology Justin develops an individual modification of the Stoic conception of *spermatikoi logoi* in nature, seminal principles which cause generation, and of God as the *spermatikos logos* of the world.[4] Philo had described the divine Logos as the *spermatikos logos*.[5] Justin uses the idea not to explain organic birth and growth but to assert that each rational being shares in the universal Logos, of which he has a piece like a seed sown by the divine Sower. By this idea he explains the disagreements of the philosophers in the investigation of the one truth: each has had only a part of the truth, while Christ is the

[1] *Apol.* II 7–8.
[2] *Apol.* II 10; 13.
[3] *Apol.* I 46.
[4] *Apol.* II 13.
[5] Philo, *Heres* 119.

whole of which they have had only fragments. Despite the naïvety with which Justin expresses himself, the underlying idea is not unimportant: Justin is striving to formulate a belief in the unity of all knowledge with faith in God as the linchpin and interpreter of the whole.

The Logos doctrine does not matter to Justin only as an apologetic concept, i.e. only as a helpful and useful idea which enables him to stretch out a hand of reconciliation to his intellectual opponents. It is essential to the structure of his own theology. In the Dialogue with Trypho Justin's argument turns upon the Platonic notion of God as too transcendent and remote to have direct dealings with this world. Accordingly the God who appeared to Moses at the burning bush and to the patriarchs in the Old Testament theophanies is affirmed to be the Son-Logos.[1] Justin brings together the biblical distinction of Father and Son with the Platonic distinction between God in himself and God as related to the world. 'Father' means God transcendent, 'Son' means God immanent. The consequences of this incorporation of Platonic thought within Justin's Trinitarian doctrine made for acute difficulties in the Arian controversy, but the pursuit of this theme belongs to the history of theology rather than that of philosophy. It is noteworthy, however, that Justin also finds an allusion to the Christian Trinity in the cryptic sentence of the second Platonic epistle: 'All things are round the King of All, and are for his sake, and of all good things he is the cause. And the second is about the second things, and the third about the third things.'[2] Justin's remark is the earliest evidence that this opaque utterance was being discussed in the Platonic schools in the century before Plotinus, for whom the sentence referred to his three fundamental hypostases.

Justin plays so considerable a part in establishing the Logos doctrine within the citadel of orthodox theology that it almost comes as a shock to discover that neither Philo nor St John's Gospel can be said to have done anything important to mould the essential structure of his thought. On balance it is more probable than not that Justin knew St John's Gospel, though he gives no verbatim citation; but Johannine theology

[1] Justin, *Dial.* 55 ff.; 126–8; *Apol.* I 63.

[2] *Apol.* I 60, citing Plato (?), *Ep.* II, 312E. Cf. Numenius in Eus. *P.E.* IX 18; Athenagoras, *Leg.* 23; Hippolytus, *Ref.* VI 37. 5; Clement, *Str.* V 103; Origen, *Contra Celsum* VI 18.

left him almost untouched. Justin represents a more popular Christianity, centred on morality, on the divine acts in history in the life, death and resurrection of Christ, and on the eschatological expectation of judgement to come. Distinctively Johannine themes are in general too subtle for his mind. His relation to Philo is no less problematical. As a person and as a writer he is altogether less sophisticated than Philo. The Dialogue and the First Apology are both dominated by the argument from prophecy, and his mind is full of typological correspondences between the Old and New Testaments. Justin justifies his rejection of literalism by pointing to oddities, contradictions, superfluities and silences in the text. Yet there is nothing seriously resembling Philonic allegory.[1] There are many apologetic motifs shared by both men, for example, that the philosophers owed their wisdom to the Bible and that their disagreements invalidate their claim to final truth; but these conventional commonplaces do not argue dependence on Justin's part. In a few respects the approximation is genuinely close. Justin has an extended development of the thesis that the Old Testament theophanies such as the burning bush are manifestations of the Logos, not of the supreme Father. He rejects all anthropomorphism in the doctrine of God and insists, like Philo, on God's namelessness.[2] He explains the coming forth of the Logos from God by the analogy that Philo has used to explain the principle of undiminished giving, of one torch being lit from another;[3] but he rejects as inadequate the analogy of sun and sunlight because this does not sufficiently safeguard the otherness of the Logos who is 'another God, other not in will but in number' (in a passage which may be polemic against hellenized Judaism).[4] These analogies, however, are again commonplaces of the age; and although

[1] E.g. the radical difference in exegesis of the defeat of the Amalekites (Philo, *V. Mos.* I 217; Justin, *Dial.* 90), the tower of Babel (Philo, *Conf.* 162; Justin, *Dial.* 102), or the curse of Ham (Philo, *Qu. Gen.* II 65–70; Justin, *Dial.* 139). In interpreting Gen. i. 27 ('Let us make man') Trypho rejects as heretical the view that the human body is the work of angels; Philo approximates to this view in *Qu. Ex.* II 33, cf. *Conf.* 179, *Fuga* 68 ff., etc. The case for Justin's dependence on Philo's exegesis is well stated by C. Siegfried, *Philo von Alexandria als Ausleger des alten Testaments* (1875), pp. 332–40, and in very vulnerable form by P. Heinisch, *Der Einfluss Philos auf die älteste christliche Exegese* (1907), pp. 36–9. Against it, cf. W. A. Shotwell, *The Biblical Exegesis of Justin* (1965).

[2] Justin, *Apol.* I 61; 63; II 6; 12.

[3] *Dial.* 61. 2.

[4] *Dial.* 128. 4. Irenaeus (*Adv. haer.* II 13) disapproves all analogies to explain the relation of Son and Father. For the Logos as 'another' or 'second' God cf. Philo in Eus. *P.E.* VII 13. 1–2.

there are a number of correspondences between Philo and Justin in minor details the comparison is in the main a long catalogue of dissimilarity. One notable difference is the attitude to pagan polytheism. Philo dismisses it as superstition, allowing that worship of the sun, moon and stars is at least a higher form of religion than materialistic idolatry, but seeing the essence of paganism as worship of the creature in place of the Creator.[1] Philo seldom writes about evil powers. For Justin, however, the pagan gods are actively malevolent demons, as immoral as Homeric myths portray them, sworn to enmity against God, out to dominate and to deceive humanity by counterfeit revelations, lying miracles, and parodies of the Gospel (an argument which is Justin's answer to relativizing arguments from comparative religion).[2] In the contemporary Platonists and Pythagoreans of Justin's time, there is a marked increase of interest in evil, or at least inferior, *daimones*.[3] In some degree Justin reflects this. But the devils are also important for him because the redemptive achievement of Christ consists in deliverance from their power and from the iron hand of 'necessity'.[4] In short, Justin is expressing the intensity of what the experience of salvation has meant to him. Perhaps the most striking difference (especially in view of Justin's professed quest for the vision of God) is the absence of any mystical language resembling Philo's. The attitude to philosophy is also different: Justin had received no education in music, geometry and astronomy, on the value of which Philo has much to say. On the other hand, Philo's use of the Stoic conception of *spermatikos logos* is quite other than Justin's. If Justin read Philo, he was not deeply influenced.

Justin's ethics are mainly a straightforward exposition of the Sermon on the Mount. The Christian ethic is in full accord with natural law.[5] Justin knows that the Christian doctrine of divine judgement hereafter (which he defends on the two grounds that it is like Stoic eschatology

[1] See p. 148 n. 14; p. 149 nn. 1, 2, 3. For the worship of heavenly bodies as allowed to heathen in accordance with Deut. iv. 19 see Justin, *Dial.* 55. 1, as later Clement, *Strom.* VI 110; Origen, *In Joh.* II 3.

[2] *Ap.* I 5 and II 5 are fundamental. Cf. H. Wey, *Die Funktionen der bösen Geister bei den griechischen Apologeten des zweiten Jahrhunderts* (Winterthur, 1957).

[3] Plutarch, *Dion* 2; *Def. Orac.* 14 ff.; *Daem. Socr.* 22 ff.; Porphyry, *Abst.* II 37–43 (perhaps from the pagan Origen, as H. Lewy suggested); Celsus in Orig. *Contra Celsum* VIII 55; Cornelius Labeo in Augustine, *Civ. Dei* VIII 13.

[4] *Dial.* 45; 88; 100. Baptism delivers from 'necessity': *Apol.* I 61.

[5] *Apol.* I 13 ff.; 27–8. Philo claims this for the Mosaic law (*Abr.* 6; *V. Mos.* II 52).

and that it produces excellent behaviour and good citizens) is vulnerable to the philosophical charge that it looks like frightening people into church and that in any event mercenary motives preclude that higher pursuit of virtue for its own sake which alone makes the pursuit itself virtuous.[1] But he regards the divine vindication of the right and the good, like the assertion of human responsibility, as essential to morality and to faith in providence.

Justin's basic presupposition is a highly optimistic confidence in human reasoning. If the barriers of prejudice and misinformation are removed, the truth of divine revelation in Christ will shine in its own light. In this confidence Justin and his fellow-apologists stand in contrast to the contemporary Gnostics.

Gnosticism is a dark form of the religious syncretism of the Hellenistic age, combining many diverse religious elements within a generally dualistic system to provide a rationale for a morality usually ascetic, though sometimes going to the opposite extreme. Gnosticism is obsessed with evil and consists essentially in a radical rejection of this world as being at best a disastrous accident and at worst a malevolent plot. In its lower forms astrology, magic and rites to placate hostile cosmic powers are very prominent. But in its higher forms, whether in the pagan gnosis of the Hermetic tracts or in the Christian Gnostic Valentine, there are strong philosophical ingredients drawn from a pessimistic interpretation of Platonism. The appeal of Gnosticism lay in its claim to reconcile a religion of redemption with a philosophic mysticism. Plotinus found this kind of theosophy prevalent even within his own circle of disciples, and wrote his impassioned tract 'Against the Gnostics' to repel it as a distorted caricature of Plato which could lay no reasonable claim to the allegiance of a Greek rationalist.[2] Admittedly Neoplatonists like Porphyry and Julian were aligned with the Gnostics against the Christians in rejecting the notion that the supreme God can himself be the Creator of this material world. But to the Christians Gnosticism was unacceptable for reasons often closely analogous to those set out by Plotinus. It was impossible to reconcile

[1] *Apol.* II 9; I 20; 44.

[2] For Plotinus and Gnosticism see Part III, ch. 12, pp. 205–7 and ch. 15, pp. 243–5.

with Christianity a radical pessimism about the created order. For this further involved a rejection of the Old Testament and the consequent disintegration of the central Christian pattern of creation and revelation within history. It also meant an assertion that the natural reason of man is completely impotent, and that religion must be pure revelation saving only the eternally predestined elect and dismissing the rest as beyond the possibility of redemption because without any original derivation from God's creative being.

Gnosticism had powerful attractions in the second century, notably for Christians of moderate or mediocre education who were troubled by the more sub-Christian parts of the Old Testament and repelled by the crudity of uninstructed believers. The insistence of the second, Christological article of the creed on the historical facts of the Gospel is a deposit of the resulting controversy. Reaction to Gnosticism led simple believers to make strident denials that baptismal faith required any supplementation and correction by higher and more philosophic knowledge, and the mood received forcible and eloquent expression from Tertullian when he denounced philosophy as the mother of heresy. Hippolytus constructed a refutation of the heretical sects on the preposterous presupposition that each one derived its ideas from some ancient Greek philosopher. The thesis as Hippolytus states it must have seemed to sensible readers at the time almost as implausible as it does today. The truth underlying the charge is simply that some of the basic propositions of the Gnostics came from their pessimistic view of Platonism. The man who developed at once a positive view of philosophy and a negative critique of Gnosticism was Clement of Alexandria.

CHAPTER 10

CLEMENT OF ALEXANDRIA

Clement was born probably of pagan parents about the middle of the second century and died probably before 215. He sat at the feet of a succession of Christian teachers, of whom the last was the Alexandrian Pantaenus, a Stoic philosopher converted to Christianity (according to the report of Eusebius). In the Alexandrian church of the second century a cleavage had arisen between the simple believers, whose fear of Gnosticism had made them the more tenacious of unreflecting 'orthodoxy' (the term itself is beginning to become current at this time),[1] and the educated Christians among whom tendencies towards Gnosticism were powerful if only because the most intelligent Christians at Alexandria had been Gnostics. Pantaenus was distinguished, according to Clement, by the fact that he intelligently expounded Scripture in a way that did not depart from the apostolic doctrine.[2] It appears that this was a little unusual. Clement understands his task as a continuation of this demonstration that authentic Christianity is not obscurantism and that there is a proper place within the Church for a positive appreciation of the human values of Greek literature and philosophy. Clement's argument is therefore directed simultaneously against the Gnostics, against the obscurantists in the Church, and against cultured despisers of the faith who were representing it as hostile to civilization and culture generally. He builds on Justin's thesis that while polytheism is to be rejected absolutely, the values in the best Greek literature and philosophy find not merely toleration but their actual fulfilment in Christianity. This thesis he combines with a Philonic view of the relation of reason and revelation.

Clement reproduces, often in Philo's words, the thesis of *De congressu eruditionis gratia* that philosophy prepares the soul for revealed

[1] Clement (*Str.* I 45. 6) writes of 'the so-called orthodox', who, 'like beasts which work from fear, do good works without knowing what they are doing'. Earlier Justin (*Dial.* 80. 5) describes Christians who believe in the coming millennium as ὀρθογνώμονες κατὰ πάντα. All the presuppositions of the concept of 'orthodoxy' are explicit in Irenaeus.

[2] *Str.* I 11.

theology just as music, geometry, and astronomy train the mind for philosophy by enabling it to conceive of abstractions independent of a concrete spatial form and by elevating the mind above the earth.[1] Clement, however, is much more interested than Philo in logic, not as a mere hair-splitting game for sophists, but as an indispensable mental skill for the theologian.[2] The eighth book of the 'Miscellanies' (*Stromateis*), which consists wholly of preliminary notes on topics discussed in the first seven books and may have been put together from Clement's papers after his death, plentifully illustrates the importance that he attaches to logical inquiries, especially in discussing epistemology and the nature of religious assent and in rebutting scepticism about the very possibility of knowledge. He shows that it is possible to see the act of faith either as analogous to a working hypothesis subsequently verified by moral experience or as assent to authority which, since the authority concerned is divine love, has no irrational element in it and has no grovelling servility.[3] Against unsophisticated believers who distrust such questions he once observes that the devil cannot have invented logic, as some of the obscurantists believe, since in the Temptation in the wilderness the Lord outmanœuvred the devil by an ambiguity which he failed to detect.[4]

Faith and knowledge, Clement repeatedly affirms, are not incompatible but mutually necessary.[5] Against Gnostic disparagement of faith Clement upholds vigorously the sufficiency of faith for salvation. The baptismal confession is not to be despised.[6] But educated and mature Christians will seek to achieve a higher understanding than that of the catechism, and this more advanced theology necessarily employs philosophy.[7] One must be on one's guard against the possible infiltration of pagan ideas incompatible with a true faith, but there is no escape from philosophical arguments, not only to refute heresy and to defend the faith against outside attack, but even to expound central matters of Christian doctrine.

[1] *Str.* I 30–2; VI 80 ff.; 90.
[2] *Str.* VI 81. 4 (citing *Republic* 534E); 156. 2.
[3] *Str.* II 7 f.; 27; V 85; VI 77–8; *Paed.* I 12 ff.; 83; 87 (not servility).
[4] *Str.* I 44.
[5] *Str.* V 1. 3.
[6] *Paed.* I 25–6. Note the polemical insistence on 'simplicity' as a mark of the children of God in *Paed.* I *passim.*
[7] *Str.* I. 35; VI 165; etc.

Clement meets every assertion of illiberalism and narrowness by standing on the doctrine of Creation. All truth and goodness are of God, wherever they may be found. Christ is the uniting principle of all the separate fragments of knowledge.[1] God who gave the Old Testament as a tutor to bring the Jews to Christ gave the Greeks philosophy for the same purpose. The Old Testament and Greek philosophy are two tributaries of one great river.[2]

Clement has two chief theories of the origin of philosophy. First there is his thesis that the Greeks plagiarized Moses and the prophets. Unlike Justin he gives this a polemical edge, perhaps with the motive of allaying the anxieties of simple believers. But the practical effect is to impart an aura of biblical authority to many Platonic propositions. Secondly, Clement affirms that the positive value of philosophy for theology is a simple corollary of the capacity for reason and insight implanted in man by the Creator. The image of God of Gen. i. 26 f. is the divine Logos who is the archetype of the human mind.[3] Clement quietly assumes Philo's position that the two accounts of creation in Genesis describe the making of the intelligible and sensible worlds.[4] Likewise, he attacks those who imagine that the divine image in man means something physical.[5]

Clement never mentions Justin Martyr (he warmly commends Justin's pupil Tatian and transcribes part of his chronological calculations to demonstrate the antiquity of Moses).[6] But his account of the value of the best elements in Greek philosophy is closely reminiscent of Justin, and he makes his own version of Justin's idiosyncratic notion of the 'spermatic logos' sowing a seed of truth in all rational beings. In more sophisticated language Clement repeats Justin's affirmation that in Christ there is the full truth only partially present in the individual schools of philosophy.[7] Clement's eclecticism is not, of course, a wholly independent construction any more than Justin's. It is largely derived from that of contemporary Middle Platonism which, as Clement explicitly remarks, had already fused Plato with much Stoic ethics and

[1] *Str.* I 58–9.
[2] *Str.* I 28–9; VI 67; 117.
[3] *Protr.* 98.
[4] *Str.* V 94.
[5] *Str.* II 74–7; VI 114. 4–5.
[6] *Str.* I 101. (In *Str.* III 81 he attacks Tatian's encratite heresy.)
[7] *Str.* I 37.

Aristotelian logic.[1] He has the conventional complaints against Aristotle that he disallows providence in the sublunary sphere, and against the Stoics that their principles are materialist, pantheist and determinist.[2] But much use is made of Aristotelian logic in Clement's discussion of the nature of assent, and on the ethical side he owes a large debt to the Stoics. The philosopher for whom he consistently reserves the highest praise is Plato. Even here he has his critical reservations. He rejects the Platonic notion that the stars are ensouled with divine souls that cause their orderly motion. In Clement's view the heavenly bodies primarily exist to indicate the passage of time; in so far as they control things on earth it is in obedience to their Creator, not with any independence.[3]

On the question of the creation Clement firmly rejects the idea that the world is eternal or that it is created in time.[4] He does not deny the existence of a qualityless matter as raw material and (like Philo and Justin) speaks with an ambiguous voice on creation *ex nihilo*. God creates the world of matter which, because formless, is initially in a state of relative non-being (μὴ ὄν), and this is the doctrine of both Genesis and the *Timaeus*.[5] Clement is content that this formula sufficiently safeguards the transcendence of God and the contingency of the created cosmos. It does not imply that matter is an ultimate principle coeternal with God. Beyond this Clement is reticent. His announced intention of discussing cosmogony was not fulfilled.[6] It is enough to say that nothing exists in being which is not caused by God, and that there is no part of his creation which falls outside his care.[7] Once he declares that 'God was God before becoming Creator', i.e. that the world is not necessary to God.[8]

In his doctrine of the soul Clement goes as far to meet the Platonists as possible. He freely accepts the Platonic doctrine that the soul has three parts, and that virtue consists in their harmony[9] (though this does not exclude both Stoic and Aristotelian language about virtue in other contexts). He fully accepts the soul's independence of the body as

[1] *Str.* II 22 ff.; 100–1; V 95–7; VI 5. 1; 27. 3.

[2] *Protr.* 66; *Str.* V 89–90.

[3] *Str.* VI 148; cf. *Protr.* 63; 102.

[4] *Str.* VI 142; 145.

[5] *Str.* V 89; 92.

[6] *Str.* III 13; 21; IV 2; V 140; VI 4; *Quis dives* 26.

[7] *Paed.* I 62.

[8] *Paed.* I 88; cf. *Str.* V 141.

[9] *Paed.* III 1. 3; *Str.* IV 18. 1.

proved by the soul's wanderings in dreams[1] and says that death breaks the chain binding the soul to the body.[2] Nevertheless he has many hesitations about the idea that the soul has fallen from heaven to become imprisoned in earthly matter. Although it is possible to find this idea in Clement,[3] it seemed to him so dangerously like Gnosticism that he formally denies that the soul is sent down to this world as a punishment.[4] He is able to show that the Gnostic interpretation of Plato is one-sided to the point of distortion;[5] but he has to admit that there is much in Plato with marked affinities to the Gnostic world-view,[6] and therefore tends to react against both, affirming that immortality is not an inherent and natural possession of the soul but a gift of salvation in Christ.[7] The soul is not a portion of God,[8] but is created by God's goodness and as such is the proper object of divine love.[9] But this love is not automatic, as the heretics assume. It is one of the fundamental grounds for complaint against the Gnostics that their doctrine of the divine spark in the elect obliterates the gulf between Creator and creature.[10]

Clement's judgement on the problem of transmigration is obscure since his promised discussion never materializes.[11] Photius accuses Clement of teaching metempsychosis and several other heresies in his 'Outlines' (*Hypotyposes*), perhaps rightly, though nothing could be more orthodox on this point than the extant Latin version of Cassiodorus.[12] But at least in the *Stromateis* Clement is less favourable. He remarks that if a Christian happens to be a vegetarian, it will not be on the Pythagorean principle which depends on belief in transmigration into animals.[13] He unambiguously rejects the deterministic Stoic notion of identical world-cycles punctuated by fiery conflagrations at immense intervals of time. Like Justin, he suggests that the Stoic cosmic conflagrations arose from a misunderstanding of what the Bible says about the purifying fire of the judgement of God.[14]

Determinism in any form Clement cannot abide. For him it plays

[1] *Paed.* II 82.
[2] *Str.* IV 12.
[3] *Quis dives* 33; 36; *Str.* VII 9. 3.
[4] *Str.* IV 167. 4; cf. III 93. 3; *Ecl. Pr.* 17.
[5] *Str.* IV 18. 1; III 12 ff.
[6] *Str.* III 12; 17–21.
[7] *Protr.* 120.
[8] *Str.* V 88.
[9] *Paed.* I 17.
[10] *Str.* II 74; 77.
[11] *Str.* IV 85. 3.
[12] See Stählin's edition, III, pp. 202–3.
[13] *Str.* VII 32. 8.
[14] *Str.* V 9; cf. Justin, *Apol.* I 20; II 7.

into the hands of the Gnostics and strikes at the root of the moral life. Virtue is directly dependent on free will; what is done by an automaton is neither virtuous nor vicious, neither praiseworthy nor blameworthy.[1] We are not marionettes.[2]

Clement's account of the Christian ethic is deliberately expressed in a form that coincides very nearly with the austere Stoic criterion of the wise man for whom nothing external, nothing other than virtue itself, is indispensable to happiness.[3] He rejects the Stoic view that mercy is a weak passion to be eradicated and that suicide can be heroic and right.[4] But the Stoic ideal of 'life according to nature' is congenial to the Christian doctrine that the proper pattern for man's existence is a correspondence to the end intended by his Creator and that sin is to fail to correspond to this intention. It was therefore the easier for Clement to welcome the current identification of 'life according to nature' with the Platonic definition of the highest good as 'assimilation to God as far as possible'.

Clement is sensitive to the criticism that in some degree the New Testament holds out heavenly rewards for virtue and threatens punishment for unrepented sin. But he defends rewards after death not only as good Platonic doctrine[5] but also as pedagogic: it is a necessary accommodation for inferior capacities, but the more advanced Christian is motivated by love of God and the good, not by fear of hell or hope of heaven.[6] This ethical issue is especially prominent throughout Clement's long discussion of martyrdom in *Strom.* IV. Often the martyrs were simple folk, and they needed to be warned against provoking the authorities (for Christianity does not allow suicide),[7] against praying for divine retaliation against their persecutors hereafter—instead of praying for their conversion and realizing that he who is now their enemy may become their brother[8]—, and against making the achievement of a heavenly crown their motive, rather than integrity and love to God.[9] Against pagan critics who regard martyrs as cranks, the Christian can point to the example of Socrates and many other instances of stoical

[1] *Str.* II 26; etc.
[2] *Str.* II 11, cf. IV 79; VIII 39.
[3] This theme is developed in *Str.* VII.
[4] *Str.* IV 38; VI 75.
[5] *Str.* IV 44. 2.
[6] *Str.* VI 98–9.
[7] *Str.* IV 13 ff.; 71; 76 f.
[8] *Str.* IV 77; VII 84.
[9] *Str.* VI 14; 29, 46; 75.

endurance in face of tyranny.[1] In any event, fear, hope and ambition are very low rungs on the ladder of spiritual advance. For beginners they may be needed, but they are left behind in the progress of the spiritual life.[2]

Underlying all discussion of fear as a defensible motive for right action the ultimate question for Clement is that of the proper place of the concept of law and justice, an issue especially raised by the Gnostics who, in rejecting this world, rejected also the God of the Old Testament as the Creator of it and therewith jettisoned the very notion of a moral law altogether.[3] They appealed to the letters of St Paul[4] to justify the proposition that the exclusive ethical principle must be love, and that this excludes any idea of fear or external restraint. In more than one sect the practical consequences of this antinomian principle took a grossly erotic form which appears to have been in part a deliberate rejection of the conventions of society as a corrupt and corrupting force. Clement reports that, perverting the language of Plato's *Symposium*, they even defended their idealization of sexual ecstasy by asserting it to be a sacred act of holy communion and a way to God. Antinomianism has here ended in a mere *religion de la chair*.[5]

Clement's reply is in effect that we accept life from our Maker with gratitude, and have to receive it on his terms if we are to attain the end for which we are intended by him. The affirmation that we are to use rather than to possess the world does not imply any dualism. And the primacy of love does not exclude restraints and rules. 'He who goes to the limit of what is lawful will quickly pass over into what is unlawful.'[6] The content of love is determined by the example of the divine Word whose compassion for humanity brought him to be born and to suffer death.[7] The Christian's calling is to love the Creator in his creatures.[8]

As a moralist Clement is concerned with all manner of questions of daily life, entirely in the style of the Stoic diatribe with its favourite

[1] *Str.* IV 80, and 56 ff.

[2] *Str.* I 171 ff.; II 32; VII 67.

[3] *Str.* II 34; III 76 ff.; IV 134.

[4] *Str.* III 27–32; cf. II 117–18. The tendency is illustrated in some of the Gnostic sects described by Epiphanius, and in *Clem. Hom.* V 10–19.

[5] As in *Anth. Palat.* V.

[6] *Paed.* II 14. For rules cf. I 101–3.

[7] *Quis dives* 37.

[8] *Str.* VI 71. 5.

themes: should one marry and beget children?[1] should one drink wine and eat rich food?[2] should women study philosophy?[3] should a rich man give away his wealth?[4] Clement treats these questions as the liberal Stoic Musonius Rufus had treated them a century earlier. He is utterly opposed to the rigid puritanism which condemned marriage as incompatible with the spiritual life and regarded teetotalism not as a matter of individual conscience and decision but as imposed upon all Christians. The rejection of wine is ruled out by the Lord's institution of the eucharist and his example of Cana. The rejection of marriage may be right in individual cases, but not as a general rule, for some of the apostles (among whom Clement surprisingly includes St Paul)[5] were married. Marriage and wine are among the good gifts of the Creator, to be gratefully accepted and rightly used. Again, a wealthy man is not necessarily instructed by the Gospel to divest himself of responsibility and give all his money away: it is not possession but use that is crucial. So Clement expounds the episode of Jesus and the rich young ruler. At first sight Clement's exposition looks a compromiser's attempt to wriggle out of the exacting standard of the legislator, but more careful scrutiny shows that Clement sees the point that the Gospel ethic is not an imposition of legal obligations but a statement of God's highest purpose for those who with heart and soul desire to serve him. The wealthy converts of Alexandria who followed Clement's directions would have bound themselves by a strenuous standard of charity and self-discipline, and might even have thought it less trouble to give everything away. Clement, apparently liberal and easy-going, always ends as an advocate of severe frugality and a passionate opponent of luxury. His sex ethic not only condemns homosexual practices, abortion, and marital intercourse merely for self-indulgence,[6] but also the eroticism of society in general.[7] In all his discussion Clement is free of fanaticism (even if he sometimes discovers justifications for his views which are comic in their absurdity). There is no recoil from sexuality. Parenthood, he writes, is co-operation with the Creator;[8] and (according to some passages) it is wrong to regard celibacy as inherently more

[1] *Str.* II 137 ff.; *Protr.* 113.
[2] *Paed.* II 1 ff. (wine, 19 ff.).
[3] *Str.* IV 59 ff.; cf. *Paed.* I 10 f.
[4] *Paed.* III 34 ff.; *Quis dives.*
[5] *Str.* III 52–3.
[6] *Paed.* III 44; 87; 96; II 87; 92; 107.
[7] *Paed.* III 31 ff.
[8] *Paed.* II 83, cf. *Str.* III 66.

spiritual than the married state.[1] Clement allows no divorce or re-marriage after divorce. He tolerates a second marriage after the death of a former spouse.[2]

The ground on which Clement's ethic is constructed is the doctrine of Creation. This excludes both the fanatical other-worldliness of the ascetic Gnostics and the materialism and hedonism of pagan society. He sees the Christian way as a *via media* between the two.

Clement loves to write of the natural knowledge of God found in all men.[3] There is no known race that has not the idea of God.[4] It was breathed into Adam at the creation.[5] The beneficence of God is universal and has no beginning at some special point in history—as if he had first begun to be interested in nations other than the Hebrews only after the coming of Christ.[6] There was primitive monotheism among the earliest races of men long before religion was corrupted into demonic polytheism.[7] Philosophy was given to Greeks, as the Law was given to the Jews, as a check on sin, to undermine bad religion by the acids of scepticism and to prepare men for the Gospel.[8] Finally the enfeebling of the soul of man called for divine intervention.[9] The incarnation, to which pagan Platonists like Celsus were objecting on the ground that it is incompatible with the universality of providence, is only an extension of the principle that God's providential care can also extend to the particular. The incarnation is a special case of divine immanence.[10]

We are not to think, like the Gnostics, that the incarnation was not a real taking of human flesh or an optical illusion, though Clement admits that Christ ate and drank, not because he really needed to do so, but to forestall the heretics.[11] He also insists that in the Passion there was no inner conflict.[12] Christ was without sin and suffered not for himself but for us.[13] Nor, on the other hand, are we to think that Christ was so good a man that he was 'adopted' as Son of God.[14] He is the eternal Logos who has descended from heaven, the flawless image of the Father, both

[1] *Str.* III 105; VII 70. (But in *Str.* IV 147–9 virginity is better.)
[2] *Str.* III 82; 145–6.
[3] *Protr.* 25 f.; *Str.* V 87 f.; etc.
[4] *Str.* V 133.
[5] *Paed.* I 7–8; *Str.* V 87; 94.
[6] *Str.* V 133–4; 141.
[7] *Str.* I 68; 71; VI 57. 3.
[8] *Str.* VI 156. 4.
[9] *Str.* V 7.
[10] *Str.* I 52; V 6; VI 12; VII 8.
[11] *Str.* VI 71; cf. III 91; 102; Valentine in III 59, 3.
[12] *Str.* III 69.
[13] *Str.* IV 81 ff. (against Basilides).
[14] *Paed.* I 25.

God and man,[1] mediating between the Creator and the creatures,[2] the high priest who is not ashamed to call us brethren.[3] He took our passible flesh and trained it up to impassibility.[4] The incarnation was an incognito, only penetrated by those to whom God's grace revealed it.[5]

Clement does not solve the problem of the reconciliation of the divinity of Christ and monotheism. He is writing at a period when he has virtually complete liberty to speculate in almost any direction, and his vocabulary is obviously experimental. He writes of the Son as an 'energy' of the Father.[6] He is ministerial.[7] He is the Father's will,[8] standing at the head[9] of the hierarchy of being, for which Clement uses the old Platonic image of a chain of rings held together by a magnet, that is, by the Holy Spirit.[10] But Clement (like Irenaeus) dislikes the idea that the Son is the *logos prophorikos*, the reason of God as expressed in contrast with the reason latent within the Father, just because it makes the coming forth of the Son like a Gnostic emanation;[11] and several passages speak of the unity of the Father and the Son. According to Photius, Clement distinguishes the Logos within God from the inferior Son-Logos who is a power of God coming down to become a *Nous* among the hearts of men.[12] The correctness of this report has been denied, and there is nothing in Clement's writings to provide a parallel. But such notions appear elsewhere in other theologians (mainly heretical), and perhaps Clement toyed with them also. Speculation of this sort could go with his emphatic affirmations about the remote transcendence of God, and with his acceptance from Philo and Justin of the axiom that the Logos is the divine power immanent in this world because the Father can have no direct contact with it.

The ground of redemption is creation.[13] Yet we may not say that redemption is wholly predictable and to be expected because of the natural relation and affinity between man and God. The paradox of God's mercy and love forbids that. It is in fact the greatest proof of the

[1] *Paed.* I 4; 7; *Str.* V 40.
[2] *Str.* III 68; VI 54; 146; VII 2; 4.
[3] *Protr.* 120; *Paed.* I 89; *Str.* II 134; V 39.
[4] *Str.* VII 6–7.
[5] *Str.* VI 132.
[6] *Str.* VII 7.
[7] *Paed.* I 4; III 2 (*diakonos*).
[8] *Paed.* III 98.
[9] *Str.* VII 2.
[10] *Str.* VII 9 (the image from Plato, *Ion* 533 D–E, as in Philo, *Opif.* 141); cf. *Str.* VI 148. 4–6.
[11] *Str.* V 6. 3; cf. Irenaeus, *Adv. haer.* II 13. 2 (p. 281 Harvey).
[12] Photius, *cod.* 109, discussed by R. P. Casey in *JTS*, XXV (1924), pp. 43–56.
[13] *Paed.* I 7–8.

goodness of God that he cares for us who are estranged by nature from him.[1] Grace is never automatic, but establishes a free personal relationship.[2] This stress on the paradoxical quality of grace and the freedom of man saves Clement from making redemption a naturalistic process moving on to an inevitable end. God's way is persuasion, never force.[3] Providence does not prevent evil from occurring, but seeks to overrule it for an ultimately good end.[4] The incarnation is the central moment in the unfolding plan of God for the education and restoration of frail, erring humanity, lost in the sin that results from neglect, weakness and ignorance and is perpetuated by society through upbringing and environment.[5] There is no inherited sinfulness transmitted from Adam and Eve through the reproductive process; and to think there is, means for Clement a surrender to the dualistic Gnostic view of the body and of sexuality.[6] The body is not evil, and to affirm that it is is incompatible with the incarnation.[7] Nevertheless, to be created is to be involved in φθορά, the finitude and transitoriness of existence outside of God,[8] and the body is an obstacle to the soul's clarity of vision.[9]

The Christian life is to be an implacable fight with the passions, and a steady abstraction from the things of sense, rising beyond Aristotelian moderation to a Stoic passionlessness, *apatheia*.[10] In this life we may expect few to attain holiness of this order. But in the life to come God's discerning (not devouring) fire will purify our polluted souls in the baptism by fire.[11] Divine punishment is educative and remedial.[12] At the end of the purging process we may hope to be fit to be near the Lord in the final restoration or *apocatastasis*.[13] At this summit of perfection the 'true gnostic' will have a love for God which is indefectible.[14] There is no word in Clement of the possibility of satiety. The true gnostic has an infinite advance into the mystery of the knowledge of God. If we could suppose that the true gnostic could be faced with a choice between the

[1] *Str.* II 73–5.

[2] *Str.* VII 42. On virtue as God-given see V 83; but Clement's standpoint is emphatically synergistic.

[3] *Paed.* I 9, etc.

[4] *Str.* IV 86 f.

[5] *Str.* VI 96; VII 16; 19; 101.

[6] *Str.* III 65; 100.

[7] *Str.* III 103.

[8] *Str.* III 63.

[9] *Str.* I 94; VI 46; VII 40; 68; etc.

[10] *Str.* VI 74; 105; 111.

[11] *Str.* VII 34; *Protr.* 53; *Paed.* III 44; *Ecl. Proph.* 25, 4; *Quis dives* 42.

[12] *Str.* VI 154; VII 102–3; *Ecl. Proph.* 38. 2 ff.; etc.

[13] *Str.* VII 56.

[14] *Str.* VI 75; 78; VII 46.

knowledge of God and everlasting salvation (which are in truth identical), he would unhesitatingly choose the former. He prefers dynamic advance to static possession.[1]

The final objective is 'the vision of God' or 'deification' or union with him, an experience which (as for Philo) is symbolized by the Mosaic high priest's entrance into the holy of holies or by Moses in the darkness of Sinai.[2] But this beatific vision and blessed union lie beyond the span of this life. Meanwhile we can strive to grasp what may be known of God by dialectic, so far as this is a rational problem. Apart from revelation, however, this knowledge of God can have no positive content.

Pagan critics were accustomed to scorn the Christians for thinking of God in anthropomorphic terms. Clement goes to great lengths to affirm the equivocal character of all the logical statements. God is incomprehensible by the mind and inexpressible in words. He is nameless. All human language about him is relative and symbolic. His essence we cannot know. Indeed the supreme Father is not an object of our knowledge at all, our limit being the Son, who is the Alpha and Omega. Because of the limits of religious knowledge, God can be known only by revelation and grace. Yet he remains indefinable in himself. Clement's language about the *via negativa* goes as far as anyone could go towards the apotheosis of the alpha privative. The supreme Father is the ground of being, but has no other function. The Son is the Mind of the Father, the circle of which the Father is the centre. The idea of God is wholly abstract, like the way in which the mathematical idea of a point is reached.[3] Clement's language in the passages where he writes as a forerunner of the Areopagite is obviously indebted to Philo, as well as to contemporary Platonists. It does not prevent him from writing elsewhere of God as love, goodness, and righteousness,[4] and does not dissolve his conviction that the Creator is guiding the cosmos by a providential plan towards a certain end.

It will need no emphasis that Clement has learnt many things from

[1] *Str.* VI 136, a passage plagiarized in a famous aphorism of Lessing.

[2] *Str.* V 39–40; VI 68; for Moses, II 6; V 78.

[3] *Str.* II 6; V 71, 81–2; VI 166. Cf. *Paed.* I 71 (God beyond the Monad); *Str.* II 72 f. (all human language about God symbolic).

[4] *Paed.* I 7–8; *Str.* IV 100; 113; V 13; *Quis dives* 37. Cf. the polemic against Marcion in *Paed.* I 62 ff.; 88; *Str.* VI 109; VII 15.

Philo. Both in the *Paedagogus* and in the *Stromateis* the borrowings and echoes are numerous. He assumes Philo's methods for expounding the Bible as symbolist allegory and extends them to the New Testament. He takes over Philo's argument that philosophy stands to theology as grammar and the *encyclia* to philosophy. Many of his statements about the Logos and his endeavour to fuse the biblical doctrine of God with the *via negativa* of late Platonism also owe an obvious debt to the same source. But there are interesting differences, of which the most striking is manifestly the immense content given to Clement's doctrine of God as active love by his faith in Christ. Moreover, Clement's most serious questions are different from Philo's. Where they agree, they are both writing as thinkers of the biblical, Judaeo-Christian tradition facing the Greek world, confronting the same general problems of apologetic in a broadly similar way. But there are questions being met by the Christian society of 200 which are absent from the Hellenistic synagogue of two centuries earlier. Clement belongs to a rapidly expanding community with its own growing pains, troubled by moral issues raised by the persecutions (illustrated by Clement's discussion of the meaning of martyrdom), and losing something of its intensity and depth as it seeks to fulfil the universality of its mission, with the consequence that it must reconsider its own function as a school for sinners rather than a society of saints. These very delicate problems underlie Clement's cautious remarks about repentance for sin after baptism,[1] as well as his general understanding of the Christian society as a school, a *didaskaleion*[2] with preliminary education in this life and further education in the next. Above all, however, the fight against the dualism and determinism of the Gnostics impels him to take his stand on the doctrine of the goodness of the divine Creation and to develop a strongly libertarian ethic on the basis of a voluntarist psychology. That Clement's achievement has many weaknesses and inconsistencies is evident. It is important not to claim too much for him. Nevertheless, there is no early Christian writer before Augustine who writes as well as he about the grammar of assent and the nature of faith or about the Christian attitude to the natural order.

Clement sought to make the Church safe for philosophy and the

[1] *Paed.* I 4; *Str.* II 26–7; 56 f.; 60 ff.; IV 154; VI 97. Cf. Philo's discussions of voluntary and involuntary sins (above, p. 155 n. 1).

[2] *Paed.* III 98.

acceptance of classical literature. But of Clement one could say what Plotinus said of Longinus, that he is more a man of letters than a philosopher.[1] And he only indicates in modest hints of deliberate and exasperating obscurity how he would set about constructing a synthesis of Christianity and philosophy. Justin had quietly taken it for granted that the best elements in Greek philosophy fitted into Christianity without any conflict whatsoever. He did not propose in any degree to modify either the form or the content of catechetical instruction to meet the philosophers half-way, and in his eschatology there is no dilution or mitigation of his usual candour. In Clement the primitive eschatology has been radically transmuted, not least because his theology is deeply influenced by St John and the Epistle to the Ephesians. He has therefore a more open path than Justin in advancing a synthesis of Christianity and Platonism. The question raised by Clement and above all by Origen is whether the marriage of Christianity with Plato must necessarily end in an absorption of a drastically modified Christianity within an essentially hellenic system or whether it is possible without pain and distress to fit certain selected elements from the philosophers into a broadly Christian pattern of thought. In the second and third centuries no one would have dreamt of claiming mutual independence and autonomy for either party. Christianity and contemporary Platonism were too closely akin (as Justin rightly saw) to achieve a distant neutrality and respectful coexistence. They had either to love or to hate. In Celsus, Porphyry, and later Julian we see the sharp pagan reaction of abhorrence and recoil. But their attempt to maintain the religious tradition of the old classical world is in practice an ambivalent apologetic in which all three antagonists of Christianity can only make out their case by substantial concessions to their Christian opponents. Augustine's observation (*ep.* 118) that the late Platonists moved either into Christianity or down to theurgy and magic is more unkind than untrue. On the other side of the line stand Clement, Origen and later Augustine, uniting Christianity with late Platonism and constructing thereby a speculative type of religious thought, the impressive power of which is writ large in the subsequent history of Western theology and philosophy.

[1] Porphyry, *Life of Plotinus* 14.

CHAPTER 11

ORIGEN

Origen was born about 184–5 at Alexandria, probably of Christian parents (Porphyry and Eusebius contradict one another on this point). When he was nearly seventeen his father was martyred in the persecution of Severus in 202/3, and the event left a deep mark on Origen's mind. He always writes with an impassioned sense of belonging to a church called to fearless martyrdom and resistance to all compromise with the world which ever threatens it at least as much by the infiltration of merely nominal belief as by external attack and persecution. With this attitude there goes a strongly world-denying strain of personal detachment and ascetic self-discipline, symbolized in the story, told by Eusebius from hearsay and possibly true, that in the zeal of youth Origen took literally Matt. xix. 12 and castrated himself.[1] He lived on the minimum of food and sleep, and took seriously the gospel counsel of poverty.[2]

For a time he studied Greek philosophy in the lecture room of Ammonius Saccas, with whom Plotinus was later to study for eleven years. Ammonius is a mysterious figure.[3] All we know of him probably comes directly or indirectly from Porphyry who describes in his life of Plotinus how Ammonius' esoteric teaching fired Plotinus with a (typically Neopythagorean) desire to investigate the antique wisdom of Persian and Indian sages. But it is a forlorn and foolish undertaking to attempt a reconstruction of Ammonius' metaphysical doctrines by looking for synoptic elements common to Origen and Plotinus. It is impossible to determine what, if anything, Origen really drew from Ammonius. What is certain is that Origen possessed an exhaustive comprehension of the debates of the Greek schools and that to his contemporaries he stood out as an intellectual prodigy. Until 231 Origen worked at Alexandria, though often travelling about on visits elsewhere. But his relations with his bishop were strained and eventually

[1] Eus. *HE* VI 8; Porphyry's account in VI 19.

[2] Eus. *HE* VI 3. 8 ff.; cf. Origen, *Hom. in Gen.* XVI 5.

[3] For a fuller discussion of Ammonius see Part III, ch. 12, pp. 196–200.

came to breaking point, so that he had to migrate to Palestinian Caesarea. He died at Tyre about 254.

Origen's work resembles Philo more closely than Clement's, mainly because, except for the two great works *De principiis* and *Contra Celsum*, its form is almost entirely a series of massive commentaries and expository sermons on the Bible. He bases himself on the principles of allegorical interpretation by which Philo had been able to discover in the Pentateuch the doctrines of Greek ethics or natural science. But Origen's evident debt to Philo must not be used to put Origen into a Philonic strait-jacket with the effect of obliterating the important differences between them. The ethical, psychological and scientific exegesis of Philo is now being combined with the typological exegesis of Justin and Irenaeus, seeking in the Old Testament for specific foreshadowings of Christian doctrine in a way that is a natural and easy extension of the argument from prophecy common in the canonical gospels and going back to the earliest Christian generation.[1] Besides the literal and historical meaning (sometimes, but not usually, Origen denies that there is one) and the moral interpretation akin to Philo's, Origen seeks a spiritual meaning that refers to Christ's redemption and a 'mystical' sense that concerns the ascent of the individual soul to union with God and to perfection. In some places Origen tries to schematize his exegesis by boldly arguing from an analogy with St Paul's trichotomy of man's body, soul, and spirit;[2] but in practice he may at times give four or even only two concurrent interpretations.[3] What is impossible is that the text should only have a literal meaning. Much in the Old Testament when interpreted literally and not spiritually is unworthy of God, and this is in itself a sufficient refutation of Judaism.[4] It is blasphemy to ascribe to God human weaknesses like wrath or changes of mind.[5]

Two differences between Origen and Philo are noteworthy in the matter of Scripture. First, controversy with rabbis and differences of

[1] See C. H. Dodd, *According to the Scriptures* (1952), a masterly study; cf. the interesting but speculative book of B. Lindars, *New Testament Apologetic* (1961).

[2] *Princ.* IV 2. 4; *Hom. in Lev.* V 1 and 5; *Hom. in Num.* IX 7.

[3] See H. de Lubac, *Histoire et Esprit* (1950), *Exégèse Médiévale* I i (1959), pp. 198 ff.; J. Daniélou, *Sacramentum Futuri* (1949).

[4] E.g. *Comm. in Rom.* VI 12; *Hom. in Gen.* VI 3; *Hom. in Lev.* X 1.

[5] Cf. *Contra Celsum* IV 72; *Hom. in Jerem.* XVIII 6.

opinion within the Church have made Origen hesitant about the authority and inspiration of the Septuagint. Unlike Philo and Justin he never alludes to the propagandist legends about the inspired unanimity of the translators, and, though he feels committed to maintaining the majority view of the Greek churches about the accepted status of the Septuagint, he implies that the Hebrew original is of more certain authority. He accordingly took the trouble to learn Hebrew. Secondly, he provides some positive argument for regarding the Bible as the work of the Holy Spirit, notably in *De principiis* IV, where his crowning point is the power of the Scriptures, as demonstrated by the mission of the Church throughout the world, to set souls on fire with faith and to transform moral life.

In Origen's attitude to philosophy there is not much, when it comes to detail, that we have not already found in Philo, Justin or Clement. Against the Gnostic exponents of total depravity Origen retorts that 'a totally depraved being could not be censured, only pitied as a poor unfortunate', and insists that in all men some elements of the divine image remain. The Logos lights every man coming into the world; all beings that are rational partake of the true light.[1] The Gospel brings to actuality what in unbelievers is present potentially.[2] The preacher need not hesitate to claim for a Christian possession all that seems sound and good in Hellenic culture. Origen is unmoved by the pagan accusation that he is borrowing Greek tools to rationalize a barbarian superstition.[3]

Philosophy is a valuable preparatory discipline for revealed theology. 'Human wisdom is a means of education for the soul, divine wisdom being the ultimate end.' Philosophy is not indispensable for receiving the truth of God's revelation.[4] If it were, Christ would not have chosen fishermen.[5] To the two (hardly compatible) pagan charges that the Christians are quite uneducated and that Christian teaching is no different from that of Plato and the Stoics, Origen answers that the proportions of educated and uneducated in the Church represent a fair cross-section of society as a whole, and that, while the study of philosophy is confined to an educated élite, the Christians have brought an acceptance of moral truth to classes of society where philosophy has

[1] *Comm. in Joh.* XX 28; *Hom. in Jerem.* XIV 10.
[2] *Comm. in Rom.* VIII 2.
[3] *Hom. in Gen.* XIII 3.
[4] *Contra Celsum* III 58; VI 13–14.
[5] *Contra Celsum* I 62.

never penetrated.[1] If philosophy is not indispensable, yet it is a valuable tool for understanding the meaning and underlying principles of revelation.[2] In the propositions of the baptismal creed the apostles laid down authoritatively and in language adapted to simple folk what is necessary in Christian belief. The grounds for their statements they left for others to investigate.[3] The Bible does not discourage the pursuit of philosophy.[4] Logic is of great utility in defending Christianity, though the greatest arguments establishing the truth of the Gospel are not natural but the supernatural guarantees of miracle, fulfilled prophecy and the miraculous expansion of the Church in face of powerful prejudice and governmental opposition.[5] To his pupil Gregory (later to become the apostle of Pontus) Origen writes that the Christian may use philosophy as the Hebrews spoiled the Egyptians of their jewels at the Exodus.[6]

In much of this we are frequently reminded of Justin or Clement. But the accent and tone are different. Origen is so much more detached. The reader of Clement is sometimes inclined to suspect him of being so over-anxious to rebut the scornful charge that Christians are uneducated that he indulges in name-dropping. The *Contra Celsum* is wholly without trace of any inferiority complex and is an attack as much as it is a defence. Origen is not one of those apologists who derived encouragement from similarities to Christian ideas in Plato or Chrysippus.[7] He is completely free of the notion that there is a mystique of authority attaching to the great classical philosophers, and is without the least desire to claim the protection of their name for any statement. Nothing for Origen is true because Plato said it, though he thinks that Plato, being a clever man, said many things that are true. What Origen claims is not an affinity with this or that philosophy, but the right to think and reason from a Christian standpoint.[8]

[1] *Contra Celsum* I 9 f.; III 44 ff.; VI I ff.

[2] *Contra Celsum* VI 14.

[3] *Princ.* I, praef. 3.

[4] *Contra Celsum* VI 7 quotes texts from the Wisdom literature; note the discussion of I Cor. i in I 13 and III 47 f.

[5] *Contra Celsum* I 2. See Gregory Thaumaturgus' account of Origen's educational method in *Paneg.* VII 100 ff.

[6] *Philocalia* 13. Cf. *Hom. in Gen.* XIII 3 (Isaac's servants may dig wells on Philistine land).

[7] For the plagiarism thesis cf. *Contra Celsum* IV 39 (the garden of Zeus of *Symp.* 203 from Genesis ii–iii): did Plato hit on it by chance? or did he meet exegetes of Genesis when in Egypt?

[8] *Contra Celsum* VII 46; 49 (disowning captious criticism); *Hom. in Ex.* XI 6. Justin (*Dial.* 6. I) and Clement (*Str.* VI 66) state the principle.

In the *Contra Celsum* and elsewhere he is occasionally prickly to the point of rudeness towards the classical tradition. This is partly to be explained by the inward psychological effort that a man wholly trained within a metaphysical tradition must make in order to achieve detachment, and partly by the fact that pagan Platonists like Celsus were denying the right of Christians to think at all. The Platonism of Celsus, Porphyry, and, for that matter, Plotinus is in its feeling and temper a scholasticism bound by authority and regarding innovation and originality as synonymous with error. They would not have understood an attitude such as that expressed by Origen when he writes that 'philosophy and the Word of God are not always at loggerheads, neither are they always in harmony. For philosophy is neither in all things contrary to God's law nor is it in all respects consonant.' Origen proceeds in this passage to list some of the points of agreement and disagreement. 'Many philosophers say there is one God who created the world; some have added that God both made and rules all things by his Logos. Again, in ethics and in their account of the natural world they almost all agree with us. But they disagree when they assert that matter is coeternal with God, when they deny that providence extends below the moon, when they imagine that the power of the stars determines our lives or that the world will never come to an end.'[1]

Like Justin and Clement, Origen attacks the Stoics for their materialism, pantheism and deterministic doctrine of world-cycles.[2] He distinguishes the Christian doctrine of God's providential care from the Stoic idea of God as a material immanent force.[3] The Stoic doctrine of natural law and of 'universal notions' of God and conscience he accepts without the least demur.[4] Every man has an innate awareness of right and wrong.[5] The Sermon on the Mount accords with what natural consent acknowledges to be the ideal pattern in human relations.[6] The Mosaic law spiritually interpreted is the natural law, as Philo said, and both are identified with Christian morality.[7] For Origen there is no

[1] *Hom. in Gen.* XVI 3; cf. *Princ.* I 3. 1; *Contra Celsum* VI 8; 47 (Plato teaches that the Creator is Son of God).

[2] *Contra Celsum* IV 67–8; V 20; *Princ.* II 3. 4.

[3] *Contra Celsum* VI 71.

[4] E.g. *Comm. in Joh.* I 37; XIII 41; *Contra Celsum* III 40; VIII 52.

[5] *Hom. in Luc.* 35 (p. 196 Rauer²).

[6] *Comm. in Rom.* III 7; cf. *Contra Celsum* I 4 f.

[7] *Comm. in Rom.* VI 8; cf. Philo, *Opif.* 3.

distinctively Christian ethic, but rather moral attitudes that are characteristically Christian, above all the recognition that the divine love and righteousness are the ground of this morality. The dormant soul is awakened to this realization by the Gospel.[1] Everyone acknowledges that a truly spiritual religion involves a rejection of polytheistic idolatry, even if he does not act upon that knowledge.[2] The soul of man has an intuitive longing for God; and Origen will not believe that this yearning can have been implanted in man's heart unless it is capable of being satisfied. Just as each faculty of our senses is related to a specific category of objects, so our *nous* is the correlate of God.[3]

Nevertheless, natural religion and natural morality are not enough. There is salvation only in Christ, and good works done before justification are of no avail.[4] The soul of man is so weakened and distracted that it cannot be redeemed apart from the power and grace of God in Christ.[5] The severity of Origen's judgement on 'the good pagan' is, of course, much qualified by his denial that this life is the only chance a man has.

Origen is aware that the Christian estimate of man is in one aspect less exalted than the more aristocratic view of the Stoics with their doctrine of the wise man unmoved by disaster without or passion within, presupposing an innate strength and nobility of soul that is distinguishable from the Christian judgement that, though intended for high things, the soul is frail, bound by the fetters not so much of the body as of sin, and in need of help. Origen occasionally mentions the Stoic moral paradoxes, but with characteristic coolness does not say that he wholeheartedly approves, only that at some more suitable time he might discuss the extent to which these pagan principles accord with Christianity.[6] On the other hand, he makes generous use of the Stoic theodicy. The problem of evil greatly exercised the ingenuity of the Stoic philosophers in their conflict with Sceptics and Academics, and Chrysippus had created an arsenal of argument which Origen exploits. In Christianity the problem of evil was a no less serious question than it was for the Stoics in the time of Carneades. The Gnostics had thrown

[1] *Comm. in Rom.* VIII 2.

[2] *Contra Celsum* III 40.

[3] *Exh. Mart.* 47; *Princ.* II 11. 4; *Sel. in Ps.* (XI, 424 Lommatzsch); cf. *Comm. in Cant. Cantic.* I (p. 91 Baehrens).

[4] *Comm. in Rom.* III 9 (Tura papyrus, p. 166 Scherer); *Hom. in Num.* I 2; XI 7.

[5] *Contra Celsum* IV 19; *Hom. in Ps. 36*, IV 1; *Hom. in Ps. 37*, I 4 (XII, 205; 253 Lommatzsch).

[6] E.g. *Comm. in Joh.* II 16.

it into the forefront of the discussion, and had answered the problem by teaching, on the basis of some Platonic support, that evil inhered in matter. This solution was not open to Clement and Origen.[1] Neither, on the other hand, could the Christians happily use the Neoplatonist theodicy that evil is a privation of good. Biblical language about the devil,[2] if not personal experience, ensured that Christian theology must recognize evil to be a positive force, a *depravatio* rather than only a *deprivatio*. Moreover, the Christian belief in a historical revelation having the incarnation at its climax inevitably seemed to link the Christian interest with the Stoic defence of providential care not merely of the cosmos in general but of man in particular. A large part of the second and third books of Origen's *De principiis* is dominated by these questions in the form in which the Gnostics put them, and in the *Contra Celsum* Origen significantly turns for Stoic help in replying to Celsus' Platonizing argument that providence cares for the cosmos as a whole rather than for particularities and has no more concern for mankind than for dolphins.[3] Likewise Origen makes common cause with the Stoa in accepting the argument from design.[4] He sees difficulties in Scripture as analogous to those encountered in nature—of which he wisely observes that only a fool would try to find an explanation of every single detail.[5]

Origen's attitude towards Platonism is more complicated. He sets an immediate distance between himself and Plato by sharp accusations that Plato was a pagan who, despite the high insights of dialogues such as the *Republic* and the *Phaedo*, failed to break with polytheism.[6] It is significant that the complaint is directed not against Plato's metaphysics but against his behaviour. Origen simply assumes as axiomatic the Platonic conception of the intelligible world with the sensible world as a reflection of it. For Origen the idea is fundamental to his view of revelation. Both the Bible and the Incarnation exemplify the principle that God uses earthly symbols to help us to rise to the spiritual reality that

[1] *Contra Celsum* IV 66 (decisively rejecting the view that evil inheres in matter); cf. VI 53 (we do not make God responsible for evil by saying he made matter).

[2] To Celsus' remark that 'it is not easy for one who has not studied philosophy to know the origin of evils' Origen replies that it is only possible to begin if one knows (from the Bible) about the devil (IV 65). Celsus finds the idea of Satan impossible (VI 42).

[3] *Contra Celsum* IV 74 ff.

[4] *Contra Celsum* VIII 52; *Princ.* IV 1. 7; *Exh. Mart.* 4.

[5] *Princ.* IV 1. 7; II 9. 4.

[6] *Contra Celsum* III 47; VI 3–4; VII 42; 44.

they veil.[1] Furthermore, Origen's doctrine of God unreservedly accepts the traditional Platonic definitions that God is immutable, impassible, beyond time and space, without shape or colour, not needing the world, though creating it by his goodness.[2] He assumes the truth of the late Platonic axiom that, in the hierarchy of being, what is produced must be inferior to that which produces it, an assumption which involved him in difficulties in expounding the doctrine of the Trinity,[3] though his Trinitarian and Christological statements are in fact vastly more 'orthodox' than his later reputation would suggest. Platonic language about the eternity of the cosmos provided him with terminology to express the eternal generation of the Son-Logos from the Father.[4] He echoes Philo's declaration that the Logos stands midway, as high priest and mediator, between the Creator and the created natures.[5] The Logos is the 'idea of ideas'.[6] And so on.

Nevertheless, there are certain points where Origen has substantial disagreements. He rejects the doctrine of the *Timaeus* that the Creator God made souls but delegated the making of bodies to inferior powers.[7] He will not admit that the cosmos is divine or that the stars are gods (though he believes the stars probably have souls).[8] He unambiguously teaches creation *ex nihilo*: creation is not out of relative but out of absolute non-being. 'I cannot understand how so many eminent men have imagined matter to be uncreated.'[9] Origen also rejects the view that this material world will never come to an end. Plato's doctrine

[1] *Contra Celsum* VI 68.

[2] Immutable: *Contra Celsum* VI 62; *Orat.* XXIV 2; *Comm. in Joh.* II 17; VI 38. Impassible: *Contra Celsum* IV 72 (of wrath); *Hom. in Num.* XVI 3; XXIII 2; *Princ.* II 4. 4; etc. *Hom. in Ezech.* VI 6 accepts passibility in the sense of love and mercy. Transcendent: *Contra Celsum* VI 64 f. (*via negativa* qualified by *via eminentiae*); cf. VII 42 f. Needing nothing: *Hom. in Gen.* VIII 10, etc. Creative goodness: *Princ.* I 4. 3; *Comm. in Joh.* VI 38; cf. *Princ.* I 5. 3 (only the Trinity is good essentially; all else has goodness but can lose it).

[3] See, for example, *Comm. in Joh.* XIII 25. (For contacts at this point between the thought of Origen and that of Plotinus see Part III, ch. 12, p. 199.)

[4] *Princ.* IV 4. 1 ff.

[5] *Princ.* II 6. 1; *Contra Celsum* III 34.

[6] *Contra Celsum* VI 64.

[7] *Contra Celsum* IV 54. (*Princ.* I 8. 2 attacks a Gnostic variant of this.)

[8] *Contra Celsum* V 6–13, disowning not only Plato but Anaxagoras' notion that the stars are masses of hot metal. Origen thinks the stars spiritual beings who have fallen but a little way, are imprisoned in the stars and compelled to regulate earthly weather. He justifies prayer for fine weather on the hypothesis that the sun has free will. (It is fair to add that he regarded all this as speculative.)

[9] *Princ.* II 1. 4; *Comm. in Gen. ap.* Eus. *P.E.* VII 20; etc.

that, although the cosmos is created and so in principle corruptible, yet by God's will it will never in fact be destroyed, holds good in Origen's view not of the sensible world, but of the higher world, the heavenly realm of discarnate spirits, saints and angels, which should not be called the realm of ideas lest anyone suppose that it exists only in our minds as a metaphysical hypothesis.[1] All this marks a considerable modification of the Platonic scheme. Nevertheless, Origen was convinced that much of Platonism is true. In one of his earliest works, the *Stromateis* (extant only in sparse fragments), he even attempted to express the fundamental ideas of Christianity wholly in Platonic language. Neither the theory of Ideas nor the doctrine of Anamnesis plays much part in the structure of Origen's thought, though there are places where he assumes these conceptions. The main problem lay in the nature and origin of the soul.

Origen teaches that souls are not unbegotten and eternal,[2] but created by God, who from overflowing goodness created rational, incorporeal beings. But they neglected to love God, being overcome by 'satiety', and fell, some only a short distance, becoming angels, some a very long way, becoming devils, and some of a middle class, becoming human beings. The material world was not, as the Gnostics declared, an accidental consequence of the Fall, but was made by the goodness of God—not, however, with the intention that anyone should be too comfortable in it, but with the intention of educating humanity by the insecurity and transitoriness of existence to return to God. So in the divine plan some souls are sent down into bodies because of their failures, while others may ascend into bodies because they are showing improvement.

Origen's mythological picture of the hierarchy of being as a diversity resulting from free choices (a conception with which the Neoplatonists could not come to terms) is explicable against the Gnostic background. Origen's anxiety is to defend God from the charge of injustice and arbitrariness. In the doctrine of the soul he was faced by a choice between three possible doctrines: (*a*) the Creationist view that God creates each soul for each individual as conceived and born; (*b*) the

[1] *Princ.* II 3. 6.

[2] *Princ.* I 3. 3. The following résumé is mainly based on the *De principiis*.

Traducianist view that the soul is derived, like the body, from the parents; (*c*) the Platonic Pre-existence theory, according to which immortal and pre-existent souls temporarily reside in the body. Creationism seemed to involve God in endless fuss; Traducianism seemed to endanger the transcendence of the soul in relation to the body by making it something corporeal. Pre-existence had the merit of making a theodicy possible which answered the Gnostics' complaint against the justice and goodness of the Creator. But the final result was a mythological theory of the creation which bore at least a superficial resemblance to the theory it was intended to refute; and orthodox churchmen were disturbed by a doctrine apparently more Platonic than biblical and strongly suggesting the corollary of transmigration. On several occasions Origen disclaims the myth of transmigration as false.[1] Yet his own system presupposes a picture of the soul's course which is strikingly similar. Probably the right solution of this problem is to be found in Origen's insistence on freedom rather than destiny as the key to the universe. In other words, he objected to the fatalistic principles underlying the doctrine of transmigration; he did not object to the idea if its foundations rested on the goodness and justice of God assigning souls to bodies in strict accordance with their merits on the basis of free choices. Because God is good, the process of redemption, which is not confined to this life on earth and does not only include the human race but angels also, will go on and on until God has won back all souls to himself, including even the devil himself who retains freedom and rationality and must therefore have still the power to respond to the wonder of divine mercy. Because freedom is essential to the very constitution of rational beings, universal restoration cannot be asserted to be a predictable end in the sense that the cosmos is moving towards it by an irresistible evolution. But only a belief in total depravity so drastic as to make redemption an act of omnipotent power rather than gracious love can justify the denial of universalist hope. God never abandons anyone. The fire of his judgement is purifying and his punishment is always remedial, even if it may be extremely severe. And because freedom is eternal, even at the summit of the process when all

[1] *Contra Celsum* V 29; *Comm. in Matt.* XIII 1 (the fullest discussion); etc. Nothing can be based on Koetschau's hypothetical reconstruction of *Princ.* I 8. 4.

have been restored, it is possible (Origen speculates) that there may be another Fall, so that a series of unending cycles stretches out before the mind.

Origen is not an easy figure to assess. Other, later theologians soon came to look with misgiving upon his devaluation of history as the sphere of divine revelation. Yet his principles of allegorical exposition lived on to become an accepted tradition in medieval commentaries on Scripture. Though his doctrine of the pre-existence of souls (necessary to his theodicy) had occasional later advocates, it seemed too dangerously reminiscent of transmigration to be widely acceptable to the orthodox tradition. His universalism seemed to make redemption almost a natural cosmic process and to eliminate the element of freedom from divine grace and from human responsibility. Despite all his critics and the stormy controversy of the sixth century, culminating in Justinian's condemnation of some of the more extravagant speculations attributed to him by the Origenist monks of Palestine, much in his essential theological position became permanently at home within the Greek orthodox tradition in the revised and restated form given to it by the Cappadocian fathers, especially by Gregory of Nyssa. Widely divergent estimates of him were passed in his lifetime and throughout the patristic and medieval periods. These divergences will no doubt continue so long as there remains debate on the tenability of Christian Platonism.

PART III

PLOTINUS

BY A. H. ARMSTRONG

CHAPTER 12

LIFE: PLOTINUS AND THE RELIGION AND SUPERSTITION OF HIS TIME

Plotinus begins a new period in the history of Greek philosophy, but his achievement cannot be described as either a revival or a revolution. As Part I has shown, Platonism in the second and early third centuries A.D. was very much alive, and by no means merely stereotyped and superficial: and the thought of Plotinus in many ways continues along lines laid down by his predecessors. But he was an original philosophical genius, the only philosopher in the history of later Greek thought who can be ranked with Plato and Aristotle, and was impelled by a personal mystical experience of a kind and quality unique in Greek philosophical religion. So the result of his critical rethinking of the long and complex tradition which he inherited was a really original philosophy with far greater coherence and vitality than Middle Platonism, and one which had a wide and deep influence on later European thought.

We have only one reliable source of information about the life of Plotinus. It is the *Life* of his master which Porphyry, his disciple and editor, wrote in the year 301, more than thirty years after he had parted from Plotinus, and prefixed to his edition, the *Enneads*. This is generally recognized as a work of quite unusual quality, with no parallel among ancient philosophical or literary biographies, and giving a great deal of authentic information.[1] It tells us, however, very little about the early life of Plotinus for the simple reason that Plotinus himself told his disciples next to nothing.[2] We can, however, be reasonably certain of the year of his birth. We know that he died at the end of the second

[1] Very little has been written about the *Life*. The best edition is that of R. Harder, posthumously published as part of the new edition, with Greek text and notes, of his German translation of Plotinus. (*Plotins Schriften. Neubearbeitung mit griechischem Lesetext und Anmerkungen.* Band Vc: Anhang. Zum Druck besorgt von W. Marg. Felix Meiner Verlag, Hamburg, 1958.) An article on the *Life* by Harder appears in his *Kleine Schriften* (C. H. Beck, München, 1960; pp. 275–95). The dating of the work here given follows Harder: see his note, *op. cit.* pp. 119–20.

[2] *Life*, ch. 1.

year of Claudius II, i.e. in 270, and, as his disciple and doctor Eustochius told Porphyry, that he was then 66 years old, which makes his birth-date 204–5 (day and month are unknown: Plotinus would never allow his birthday to be celebrated).[1] We cannot really be certain where he came from. It has been generally assumed since the fourth century that his country of origin was Egypt: and Eunapius gives his birthplace as Lyco (i.e. probably Lycopolis in Upper Egypt, the modern Assiut). But if this information is authentic, it is curious that Porphyry did not have it, and it cannot be taken as certain. There is nothing else in the very short life by Eunapius, or in the notice in the *Suda* (that in Pseudo-Eudocia is a sixteenth-century falsification), which gives any reason to suppose that Eunapius or the Byzantines had access to any good source of information other than Porphyry's *Life*. The general belief in the Egyptian origin of Plotinus may be based on nothing more than the fact that he studied in Alexandria.[2] Nor do we know anything about his family or race. His name sounds Latin, and may possibly be taken to suggest some original connexion of his family with the household of Trajan's wife Plotina; but this shows nothing about his race. One thing, however, is certain from the internal evidence of his writings, and that is that his education and intellectual background were entirely Greek. (There is no evidence anywhere that he understood any other language: the passage in the *Enneads* (v 8 [31] 6), which has sometimes been quoted to show that he could read hieroglyphics, shows in fact precisely the opposite, as Bréhier, Schwyzer and others have noted—even if it really refers to hieroglyphics exclusively, or at all, which is doubtful.)[3]

In 232, in the 28th year of his life, Plotinus went to Alexandria to study philosophy; he found no teacher there to satisfy him till, at the end of 232 or the beginning of 233, someone took him to Ammonius. When he heard him, Porphyry tells us, he said 'This is the man I was looking for',[4] and his teaching satisfied him so completely that he remained with his master for eleven years. About the teaching of

[1] *Life*, ch. 2. On the chronology of the *Life* see the careful discussion by H.-R. Schwyzer in his article 'Plotinos' in *RE*, xxi, col. 472–4.

[2] Schwyzer, *art. cit.* col. 476–7.

[3] Cf. the careful discussion of this passage in E. de Keyser, *La Signification de l'Art dans les Ennéades de Plotin* (Louvain, 1955), pp. 60–3.

[4] *Life*, ch. 3.

Ammonius very little is known, though a great deal has been written by modern scholars. The most fantastically improbable hypothesis yet put forward is that of Elorduy,[1] that he was the author of the pseudo-Dionysian writings, a suggestion which, as later sections of this History[2] show clearly, stands the whole history of philosophy and theology in the next three centuries on its head and makes all discernible currents of influence flow backwards. Others have seen in him an Indian, perhaps even a Buddhist monk,[3] or a somewhat unorthodox Christian theologian.[4] But the very small amount of evidence which we have about him is certainly not sufficient to support these remarkable suggestions, and provides all too little ground even for the soberer attempts at the reconstruction of Ammonius' thought which have been made, and will continue to be made, by scholars who are rightly convinced that a master who could give such satisfaction to Plotinus must have been a philosopher of unusual quality who is likely to have contributed a good deal to the development of Plotinian Neoplatonism.

The information which we have about Ammonius which there is no reason at all to doubt is as follows. He wrote nothing, or nothing of any importance[5]—a discouraging start for our investigations. He held that the soul was immaterial[6] and that Plato and Aristotle were in fundamental agreement[7]—perfectly normal and commonplace views for a Platonist of his period. To this very short list we could till recently have confidently added two further items; that he was brought up a Christian and became a convert to paganism, and that he was the

[1] *¿Es Ammonio Sakkas el Pseudo-Areopagita?* (Estudios Eclesiásticos, 18 [Madrid, 1944]), pp. 501–57.

[2] Parts IV and VI.

[3] E. Seeberg, 'Ammonius Sakkas', in *Zeitschrift für Kirchengeschichte*, LXI (1942), pp. 136–70; Benz, 'Indische Einflüsse auf die früh-christliche Theologie', in *Akad. d. Wissenschaften u. d. Literatur* (Mainz), *Abhandl. d. Geistes- u. Sozialwissenschaftlichen Klasse* (1951), no. 3, pp. 171 ff.

[4] H. Langerbeck, 'The Philosophy of Ammonius Saccas', in *JHS*, LXXVII, Part I (1957), pp. 67–74.

[5] Longinus, quoted by Porphyry, *Life*, ch. 20. Longinus admits that some of the philosophers in his 'non-writing' group, which includes Ammonius, wrote occasional minor treatises, but he does not mention any such work by Ammonius.

[6] Nemesius, *On the Nature of Man*, ch. 2.

[7] Hierocles in Photius, *Bibl. cod.* 251: cf. *cod.* 214. On the question whether further *reliable* information about Ammonius is to be found in Nemesius and Hierocles see H.-R. Schwyzer in his article 'Plotinos' in *RE*, XXI, col. 477–81, and E. R. Dodds, 'Numenius and Ammonius', IV, in *Entretiens Hardt*, V (*Les Sources de Plotin*), Vandœuvres, Genève, 1960. These, with the articles by H. Dörrie and H. Crouzel to be cited, are the best modern surveys of the evidence about Ammonius.

teacher of the Christian as well as of the pagan Origen.[1] But since Dörrie's brilliant and penetrating examination of the difficulties which are, as is generally admitted, raised by the conflicting evidence of Porphyry in Eusebius and Eusebius himself,[2] it is no longer possible to be quite so certain. There *may* have been a Christian Ammonius, master of the Christian Origen, who was a different person from the pagan Ammonius who taught the pagan Origen and Plotinus: though on the whole the probabilities seem in favour of the simpler hypothesis, that it was the same Ammonius who taught both Origens and Plotinus and that, though Porphyry and Eusebius both made mistakes, their mistakes were not as far-reaching as Dörrie supposes (this is the view of Dodds).

At this point it is desirable to say something about the pagan Origen (the Christian Origen is treated at length elsewhere in this History).[3] He is mentioned three times in Porphyry's *Life*,[4] in terms which should make it clear to the discerning reader that he was a different person from his Christian namesake, of whom Porphyry so heartily disapproved,[5] and that Plotinus and the scholarly Platonist Longinus[6] regarded him with considerable respect. He is also mentioned a number of times by Proclus, and occasionally by other later writers.[7] The passages in which he is mentioned, however, tell us little about his thought, and it seems likely that he was not a very original or important thinker. But one thing that we do know about him is that, unlike Plotinus, he did not make the first principle of reality the One beyond intellect and being: his first principle is the supreme intellect and primary being.[8] This is not, of course, particularly original or surprising.

[1] Porphyry in Eusebius, *HE* VI 19.

[2] *Hermes*, LXXXIII (1955), pp. 439–78. Dörrie's conclusions have been criticized by Dodds (*art. cit.*) and by H. Crouzel in *Bulletin de Littérature Ecclésiastique*, I (Toulouse, 1958), pp. 3–7.

[3] Part II, ch. 11, pp. 182–92.

[4] Chs. 3, 14 and 20 (in the preface of Longinus).

[5] Porphyry in Eusebius, *loc. cit.* There are other serious obstacles of chronology, etc., against identifying the two, for which see ch. II of the work of K.-O. Weber cited in note 7 below.

[6] For Longinus see below, Part IV, ch. 18, pp. 283–4.

[7] The passages are collected by K.-O. Weber in his *Origenes der Neuplatoniker* (Zetemata, 27 [Beck, München, 1962]). In his commentary Weber deals excellently with the biographical problems, but goes far beyond the reliable evidence in dealing with the thought of Origen and Ammonius.

[8] Proclus, *In Platonis Theologiam* 2. 4, pp. 89 f. Portus (*fr.* 7 Weber). The treatise mentioned by Porphyry (*Life*, ch. 3.33) *That the King is the only Maker* (ὅτι μόνος ποιητὴς ὁ βασιλεύς) may possibly have been a defence of the position that the supreme principle of reality is identical with the Intellect-Demiurge.

Origen simply kept to the traditional Middle Platonist position from which Plotinus departed. But it is interesting, though hardly helpful to any attempt to reconstruct the thought of Ammonius, to find two of his pupils taking such different lines. That Ammonius believed that Plato and Aristotle were in agreement suggests that he is more likely to have agreed with Origen than with Plotinus. If you hold that the doctrine of the One beyond being and intellect is Platonic, it is very difficult indeed to believe also that the theologies of Plato and Aristotle are essentially the same, and Plotinus was very well aware that this was one of the great points of difference which separated his Platonism from the thought of Aristotle and the Peripatetics. But we find that the Christian Origen (also, probably, as we have seen, a pupil of Ammonius), though his teaching about God's transcendent unity does not go beyond that of the Middle Platonists or his Christian predecessor Clement of Alexandria,[1] speculated about the distinction between the Father and the Son in a way rather like some aspects of Plotinus' thought about the distinction between the absolutely unlimited and undetermined One and the determinate being of Intellect:[2] we do not however find in him that absolute denial that 'being' and 'intellect' are terms which can properly be used of the first principle which is the distinguishing mark of the thought of Plotinus.[3]

All this, though it does not tell us very much about the personal views of Ammonius, does suggest that the question of the transcendence and unity of the first principle, with all its implications, was much discussed in this circle, and that it was in these discussions that Plotinus found the starting-point for the development of his thought which led him to his own distinctive doctrine. Even if, on our evidence, it seems likely that the position of Ammonius himself was nearer to those of the two Origens than to that of Plotinus, we should remember that Plotinus never seems to have thought that he was departing in any important way from the thought of his master. Perhaps the most original feature of the teaching of Ammonius, and what attracted Plotinus to him in the first place, may have been that, instead of expounding a cut-and-dried

[1] Cf. *De Principiis* I 1. 6, where God is both monad and mind.

[2] *Contra Celsum* VI 64; cf. VII 38 and *Comm. Joh.* I 39. 291–2.

[3] For the 'telescoping' of the hypostases in fourth-century Neoplatonism, which was in some ways a return to the immediately pre-Plotinian position, see below, Part IV, ch. 18 B, pp. 287–93.

dogmatic system, Ammonius showed some sense of how difficult philosophy was, encouraged discussion and left some questions open, even at the cost of vagueness, indecision, and, sometimes, inconsistency. In chapters 13 and 14 of the *Life* Porphyry describes Plotinus' method of teaching, stressing his willingness to allow discussion, his patience with objections, and his refusal to take over any philosophical doctrine just as he found it; then he remarks, rather cryptically, that he brought 'the mind of Ammonius' to bear in the discussions.[1] Was perhaps the distinctive thing about the mind of Ammonius that it was a comparatively open mind?

At the end of eleven years Plotinus left Ammonius, according to Porphyry because he wished to learn something of the philosophy of the Persians and Indians. With this intention he joined the expedition of Gordian III against the Persians. When Gordian was murdered in Mesopotamia and Philip proclaimed emperor he escaped with difficulty to Antioch and afterwards went to Rome; he was, when he arrived there, forty years old.[2] Too much significance should not be read into this adventurous interlude in an otherwise unexciting life. The reason given by Porphyry why Plotinus wanted to visit the East may perfectly well be the true one. There would be nothing surprising in a Greek philosopher having a respect for Oriental wisdom and wanting to know more about it. And a number of philosophers before Plotinus had been interested in Persian thought in particular.[3] (Harder is probably right in not attaching too much importance to Porphyry's mention of Indians, and in supposing that Plotinus never expected to get to India, but only to meet more and better educated Indians in Persia than he could find in Alexandria.) But there is no real reason to suppose that Plotinus already knew anything much about Persian or Indian thought, and as things turned out the expedition cannot have added anything to his knowledge. As we shall see, his thought is entirely explainable as a personal development of Greek philosophy, without any need to postulate Oriental influences. It would be hard indeed to find any real point of contact between his philosophy and the orthodox Zoroastrian-

[1] Chs. 14, 15–16. Cf. Harder's note *ad loc.*

[2] *Life*, ch. 3.

[3] Cf. Harder's note on the passage of Porphyry's *Life* just cited, and the comparatively well informed and by no means uncritical account of Persian theology given by Plutarch in *De Iside et Osiride*, chs. 46–7 (369D–370C).

ism of the Sassanids, or any other form of ancient Persian thought known to us. And even if there are resemblances to some forms of Indian thought,[1] these are probably better accounted for by independent reflection on similar religious or metaphysical experiences than by any sort of influence or borrowing.

Harder's suggestion, in his note on the relevant passage just cited, that the fact that Plotinus went on the expedition shows that he was already in relations with senatorial circles close to Gordian III has something to be said for it, though the evidence is slight. Porphyry's phrase about his joining the expedition[2] tells us nothing about the capacity in which he joined it; it is likely enough that he was a very insignificant hanger-on indeed with no definable rank or function: and the danger from which he escaped with difficulty to Antioch need not have been more than the general insecurity to be expected in a camp where the soldiers had just murdered their emperor; there is no necessity to assume a direct threat to his life because he had been a close associate of Gordian and his friends. But the fact that he went to Rome, not at that time a particularly suitable place for studying or teaching philosophy, requires some explanation. And the simplest explanation would be that he was already in touch with someone (or some people) with influence, connexions and property at Rome sufficient to offer him at least a chance of living the life he had chosen, with a reasonable hope of security and peace (there would be no real need to fear trouble from Philip, who observed the proprieties in the matter of Gordian's deification, treated his family with respect, and remained on good terms with the Senate). But this must remain very uncertain. We cannot of course argue back from the state of affairs which Porphyry found when he came to Rome in 263 (see below). Plotinus had had plenty of time in nineteen years to become well known and make distinguished friends.

[1] This is a question which can only be profitably discussed by someone who has an equal mastery of both traditions, based on a solid and scholarly knowledge of the Greek of the *Enneads* and the Sanskrit of the Upaniṣads. The present writer, whose knowledge of Indian thought is scrappy and superficial in the extreme and based entirely on translations, does not qualify. But R. C. Zaehner's account of the thought of the Muṇḍaka and Svetàsvatara Upaniṣads in his *At Sundry Times* (London, 1958), pp. 107–16, shows some striking similarities with the thought of Plotinus, and a comparison between them by someone properly equipped by nature and training to understand both might be very fruitful.

[2] δοὺς ἑαυτὸν τῷ στρατοπέδῳ συνεισῄει (*Life*, ch. 3, 18–19).

It was at Rome that Plotinus began to teach philosophy and, after ten years, to write.[1] This is the period of his life which we know best from Porphyry: though we should remember that Porphyry was with him only for six years nearly at the end of his life. The picture he gives us is of Plotinus firmly established, with his circle of friends and disciples already formed, and his method of teaching fully developed. If there were any early struggles, insecurities and uncertainties we know nothing about them. It is an attractive picture, and includes some details which are helpful to our understanding of the philosophy of Plotinus. First of all we find that this most other-worldly of philosophers, this Platonist who ignored the whole social and political side of Plato's philosophy, not only lived in considerable style in the aristocratic world of Rome but gave a great deal of extremely practical, businesslike and entirely disinterested service to his friends and neighbours. He certainly always preached withdrawal from the world, and perhaps attempted to organize it on a fairly large scale for his circle. The most striking instance of his influence which Porphyry gives[2] is that of the senator Rogatianus, who gave up his property, refused to accept the praetorship when the lictors were waiting to escort him on his first ceremonial progress from his house, and thereafter lived the ascetic life of a sort of dignified philosophical mendicant—which, Porphyry remarks, cured his gout. And the most satisfactory explanation of the unsuccessful attempt to found a 'Platonopolis' in Campania[3] is Harder's,[4] that what was being proposed was a sort of pagan monastery to which Plotinus and his friends and pupils, many of whom were senators and their wives, would withdraw from the life of Rome; and that the real reason why the Emperor Gallienus stopped the project was his polite hostility to the Senate. But Plotinus certainly believed that it was the duty of a good and wise man living in the world to give to others not only spiritual guidance but whatever practical and material help his enlightened judgement told him they required, and he gave such help generously. He acted as arbitrator, Porphyry tells

[1] *Life*, ch. 4. [2] *Life*, ch. 7. [3] *Life*, ch. 12.

[4] See the essay, already referred to, published in his *Kleine Schriften*, and the discussion in *Entretiens Hardt*, v, pp. 320–2. Harder's remarks on the probable real attitude of Gallienus to Plotinus are worthy of attention: Plotinus was not, as he has sometimes been represented to have been, a court philosopher or imperial spiritual director.

us,[1] in disputes, and, unlike most people who engage in that thankless activity, never made an enemy. He was often appointed by his aristocratic friends as legal guardian and trustee for their children, and carried out his duties most conscientiously. 'His house', Porphyry tells us, 'was full of boys and girls'[2] (it must therefore have been a large one, and kept up in some style; Plotinus, however austere his personal life may have been, was no beggar-philosopher of the Cynic type). And he looked after both their education and their property in the most thorough and businesslike manner. He seems to have taken the view that if, when they grew up, they turned to philosophy, they would of course give up their property like Rogatianus, but that until they came of age and made this decision for themselves, he had to fulfil the obligations of a *tutor* under Roman law with scrupulous exactitude. This close connexion of giving up property with turning to philosophy throws a good deal of light on the way in which later Greek philosophers thought of the philosophic life, and explains why it seemed natural to some educated Christians in the next century to speak of the early monks as 'Christian philosophers'.

Plotinus was always at the disposal of his friends if they were in any kind of trouble or difficulty, minor or serious, from losing a necklace to a persistent impulse to suicide. Porphyry says[3] that when he himself was meditating suicide Plotinus suddenly came to him, told him that this was not a rational decision but due to too much black bile, and ordered him to go away for a complete change. Porphyry obeyed and went to Sicily, and this (whether Plotinus intended it so or not) was the end of their connexion, for Plotinus died soon after. Like other great contemplatives, he seems to have had the gift of keeping his inner life untroubled by these many outward activities. He could deal with Porphyry's suicidal tendencies, or Chione's lost necklace, or Potamon's lessons, without any break in his contemplation: this, as we shall see, is relevant to his psychological doctrines.

What Porphyry has to tell us about the circle at Rome, and the gossip about the Master which circulated in it, throws a little light on some questions important for understanding the relationship of his thought to the ideas of his time, those of his attitude to pagan religion,

[1] *Life*, ch. 9. [2] *Loc. cit.* [3] *Life*, ch. 11.

Gnosticism, and magic. The episode in the *Life*[1] which, rightly interpreted in its context, helps us to understand the attitude to the pagan religion of his time which is indicated casually and incidentally in the *Enneads* is that of the famous answer to Amelius. Amelius Gentilianus, from Etruria, was the senior member of the school, the oldest and closest associate of Plotinus and an indefatigable and long-winded expositor and defender of his teachings. He became *philothutes* (rather licentiously translated by the present writer 'ritualistic') and attended the sacrifices at all the temples on the appropriate occasions. One day he asked Plotinus to go with him; but he replied 'It is for them to come to me, not me to them'. Whatever this 'exalted utterance' may have meant[2] (and it is possible that his devoted disciples took it rather too seriously), it makes clear that Plotinus did not find the external observances of religion of any great interest or importance. And this is certainly the impression conveyed by reading the *Enneads*. Religion for Plotinus is individual, not social; it is a solitary journey of the mind to God in which external rites and ceremonies can be of little or no help. But the Amelius story, and the *Enneads*, also show us that this indifference was only indifference, not hostility. Plotinus did not go to the temples himself, but there is no evidence that he objected to Amelius going. Amelius, after all, *was* the senior member of the school, and everything which is said about him in the *Life* shows that Plotinus esteemed him highly precisely as a philosopher: the worst he can have thought of his ritualism is that it was an amiable weakness which in no way disqualified Amelius for philosophy.[3] And in the *Enneads* his use of illustrations taken from the beliefs and practices of popular religion[4] certainly does not suggest any hostility, though it equally does not suggest any enthusiasm or interest. External ceremonies, whether of the public cult or the mystery-religions, can provide solemn and not unworthy images for the inner experiences of true, philosophical, religion: but that is all.

[1] *Life*, ch. 10.

[2] For some suggested explanations see my article 'Was Plotinus A Magician?', *Phronesis*, I, I (Nov. 1955), pp. 77–9.

[3] Porphyry may well have judged Amelius more harshly if, as seems quite likely, the allusions in *De abstinentia* II, chs. 35 and 40 to philosophers who share in and encourage the beliefs and practices of popular religion are to Amelius and others like him in the Plotinian circle. It is possible that this whole passage (chs. 34–43) may throw some light on the reasons which led Plotinus to stay away from sacrifices, but we cannot be certain how far it represents the master's own opinions.

[4] Cf. IV 3 [27] 11; V I [10] 6; VI 9 [8] 11.

There was, however, one kind of religion current in his own time, and in his own circle, which Plotinus really hated and this was Gnosticism. There is a passionate intensity of feeling about some passages of the treatise *Against the Gnostics*[1] which is fiercer than the sharpest of his school-polemic against Stoic materialism or Epicurean denial of providence, or even his indignation with the blasphemous silliness of some of the beliefs of the astrologers. The reason for this intense hostility is apparent from ch. 10 of the treatise and ch. 16 of the *Life*. In ch. 10 Plotinus speaks of 'some of our friends who happened upon this way of thinking before they became our friends, and though I do not know how they manage it, continue in it'. And Porphyry tells us in the *Life* 'There were in his time many Christians, among them some who were sectarians influenced by the ancient philosophy...',[2] and goes on to describe the 'revelations' they produced in a way which makes it clear that they were Gnostics: he then describes the regular campaign of polemic directed against them by Plotinus, Amelius and himself, in the course of which he demonstrated that the revelation attributed by the Gnostics to Zoroaster was a late forgery, probably by the same sort of arguments which he later used in dealing with the Old Testament in his great attack on the Christians. From this evidence it is clear that Plotinus regarded the Gnostics as the deadliest enemies of everything he stood for, and that he found them so dangerous because they were attacking from within: there were men in his own circle who were Gnostics, men close enough to him for him to call them 'friends' in spite of their opinions. There may even have been a time when he still thought that it might be possible to come to a friendly understanding with these Gnostics. There are certainly to be found in the *Enneads* ideas which appear to have some affinity with Gnosticism.[3] Plotinus may only gradually have become aware of the dangers into which this side of his thought might lead him and of the irreconcilable differences between his interpretation of Platonism and any sort of Gnosticism. But there is no doubt that Plotinus eventually came to think of Gnosti-

[1] II 9 [33].

[2] γεγόνασι δὲ κατ' αὐτὸν τῶν Χριστιανῶν πολλοὶ μὲν καὶ ἄλλοι, αἱρετικοὶ δὲ ἐκ τῆς παλαιᾶς φιλοσοφίας ἀνηγμένοι... (ch. 16, 1–2). For the translation see the discussion in *Entretiens Hardt*, V, pp. 175–6. αἱρετικοί does not, of course, mean heretics or sectaries from the point of view of orthodox Christianity, but people who gave their own peculiar interpretation to 'the ancient philosophy'.

[3] See below, ch. 15, pp. 243–5.

cism as a poisonous influence within his circle, corrupting the minds and lives of its members, which, if it was not checked, would dissolve their true Hellenic philosophy into an amorphous mess of barbarian nonsense and immorality. His protest against the Gnostics is made at once on grounds of tradition, of reason and of morality. There is and can be for him no possible conflict between the traditional authority he recognizes, that above all of Plato, and reason. The Dialogues of Plato are not for him inspired scripture or divine revelation to which his reason must submit, nor does it ever occur to him that he might be a better reasoner than Plato, and so in a position to criticize him and correct him, as he criticizes and corrects Aristotle. Plato is, quite simply, always perfectly rational and right—provided, that is, that one understands him rightly, that is, as Plotinus understands him. An important reason for Plato's authority was, of course, his antiquity. Plotinus, like other men of his time, believed that the more ancient a doctrine was the more profoundly true it was likely to be: and Plato was for a Platonist the supreme ancient sage, and the faithful interpreter of any true wisdom there might be more ancient than himself—though the appeal to 'Orphic' and 'Pythagorean' wisdom plays a much smaller part in the *Enneads* than it does in Iamblichus and his successors, there is no doubt that Plotinus recognized its traditional authority. The revelations of the Gnostics had to be shown to be recent forgeries, because they claimed the authority of sages, like Zoroaster, whom everyone admitted to be more ancient than Plato. They were using a spurious ancient wisdom to commend their modern perversion, corruption and fantastic inflation of the true ancient wisdom. And their motives in doing this seemed to Plotinus to be an immoral and irrational arrogance and impatience. Their 'revelations' fed their delusions of grandeur and made them think themselves superior not only to the sages of the Hellenic tradition but to the visible universe and the divine power which made it and the astral divinities which ruled it: why the Gnostic contempt for the visible world was so profoundly shocking to a Platonist will be discussed later. And because they thought of themselves as a privileged caste of beings in a special relationship to the divinity they believed that they could take a short and easy way, by their secret knowledge and techniques, back to their rightful place in the spiritual world, and need not follow the long hard road of the practice of virtue and the exercise of intelligence which true philosophy showed to be the only way to God. These were the reasons why Gnosticism seemed so dangerous to Plotinus and why he fought it so strenuously.

Plotinus strongly disapproved of the Gnostic use of magic;[1] but there are two stories in the *Life* and some passages in the *Enneads* which have led some scholars to believe that he was not above practising it himself when the occasion required.[2] The two stories come in ch. 10 of the *Life*. Both refer to periods long before Porphyry came to Rome and joined Plotinus: they are therefore told at second or third hand, and may well have been improved in the telling. But there is nothing intrinsically improbable about them, and they cannot be rejected as fiction or gossip. After all, Plotinus himself may have told them to Porphyry; in the case of the first, this seems likely. This first story is about Plotinus' only (according to Porphyry) personal enemy, Olympius of Alexandria, who had been for a short time a pupil of Ammonius (it is therefore quite likely, though by no means certain, that this episode took place at Alexandria, not at Rome). He tried to practise star-magic against Plotinus, and (on the most probable interpretation of Porphyry's obscure and ambiguous phrasing) succeeded so far that Plotinus had a particularly severe attack of the colic to which he was subject, which he attributed to the machinations of Olympius (how seriously he meant this cannot be quite certain). But Olympius felt his magic bouncing back on him, so he said, from the superior soul-power of Plotinus, and stopped his operations because he found himself in danger of suffering himself rather than injuring his rival. This story certainly shows that Olympius and Plotinus, like everybody else in the third century, believed in magic. But it does not seem to contain any clear evidence that Plotinus on this occasion practised magic: if he did so, it was only in self-defence, but the suggestion seems rather to be that Plotinus was so highly charged with soul-power that he naturally

[1] II 9 [33] 14.

[2] A good deal has been written on this subject: see E. R. Dodds, Appendix II to *The Greeks and the Irrational* (Berkeley, California and C.U.P. 1951); P. Merlan, 'Plotinus and Magic', *Isis*, XLIV (Dec. 1953), pp. 341–8; A. H. Armstrong, 'Was Plotinus a Magician?', *Phronesis*, I, I, pp. 73–9 (these articles might be described as speeches for the prosecution and the defence of Plotinus on the charge of practising magic); R. Harder, in the essay already cited and his notes to the relevant passages of the *Life*.

radiated occult influences which made him a dangerous subject for magical attack. And there is nothing in Plotinus' theory of magic as expounded in the *Enneads* to contradict this interpretation of what happened. There are a number of references in the *Enneads* to magic which make it clear that Plotinus believed that it really worked. The longest and most careful discussion is at the end of the second treatise *On the Problems of the Soul*,[1] where Plotinus gives his views on the limits of magical action on good and wise men and on the gods. From this it is clear that Plotinus believed that only the body and the lower, irrational soul which is intimately related to the body could be affected by magic, and that magical injury there, even if it was enough to kill the body, was unimportant; there is no suggestion that the good and wise man should take counter-action on this level. But if the magical disturbance in this lower part should be of a kind which might affect the rational soul (as a love-spell might) he will use 'counter-spells' to do away with it: there seems at least a strong possibility that the word Plotinus uses here[2] is used in a metaphorical sense, as ἐπῳδή (spell) is used elsewhere in the *Enneads*, following Plato in the *Charmides*,[3] of philosophical exhortation. As for the gods, only the astral gods come at all within the sphere of magic, and even their bodies cannot be really affected by it: all the magician can do is to manipulate the effluences coming from sun, moon or stars without the deities themselves knowing anything about it.

This last point is worth bearing in mind when we consider the next story, that of the 'séance in the Iseum', fully and illuminatingly discussed by Dodds in his appendix to *The Greeks and the Irrational*. Plotinus was persuaded to attend a conjuration of his guardian spirit in the temple of Isis in Rome. (There is no evidence to show in what frame of mind he went, or how interested he was in the proceedings.) To everyone's admiration a god appeared instead of a spirit: but owing to a technical hitch (the choking of a pair of apotropaic fowl) it was impossible to ask it any questions. Porphyry appears to connect the writing of the treatise *On our Allotted Guardian Spirit*[4] with this episode. If this is so, a careful reading of the treatise will show that

[1] IV 4 [28] 40–4.
[2] ἀντεπᾴδων, ch. 43, 8.
[3] 156–7.
[4] III 4 [15].

Plotinus is unlikely to have been very thrilled or exalted by what happened (or appeared to happen). According to it our own decision whether to live by the higher or lower in us determines the rank of our guardian spirit by determining whether we are animal, man, spirit or god in each of our successive lives; for the guardian spirit is always on the next higher level of the hierarchy of being above that which our personality at its highest reaches. So the guardian spirit of the perfectly good and wise man (σπουδαῖος), who lives on the level of Intellect, is the One or Good itself, and therefore far beyond the reach of any conjuration.[1] There are men who have an astral god, the highest being which is in any way within the sphere of magic, for their guardian spirit: but they are the lowest rank of good men, of those, that is, who go to the upper world and not to the place of punishment (the whole treatise is an interpretation of Plato's teaching about guardian spirits, and especially of the myth in the *Republic*). The higher ranks of good men belong outside the visible world altogether, and are therefore beyond the guardianship of astral gods.[2] The appearance, therefore, in the Iseum of a god of this inferior rank would have been at best a certificate of spiritual respectability, indicating that he was on the right road, but with a long way to go before becoming a *spoudaios*. And of course, if at the time of the séance he already held his later, fully developed theory of magic, he would not have believed that it was the real god which appeared, but only an image produced by magic art from its effluence. We are justified, then, on the evidence in concluding with Dodds that Plotinus was neither a magician nor a theurgist. He admitted the reality of the powers of magicians and astrologers as far as his theory of the workings of the physical universe required him to: but he had no personal desire to exercise such powers and when the occult practitioners went beyond the limits of reason and reverence and made exaggerated claims, or blasphemous statements, imputing evil to the astral gods, he attacked them sharply.[3]

We have discussed Plotinus' attitude to the pagan religion of his time, to Gnosticism and to magic, but have said nothing of his views about orthodox Christianity: and there is, in fact, nothing to say. If

[1] Ch. 6, 1–5. [2] Ch. 6, 18–37.

[3] Cf., besides II 9 [33] 14 already cited, *Life*, ch. 15 and II 3 [52] 1–6 (against the astrologers).

we assume, as seems most likely, that Origen the Platonist pupil of Ammonius mentioned in the *Life* was a different person from Origen the Christian,[1] then there is no evidence that Plotinus ever had any contact or conversation with orthodox Christians. Nor does he anywhere in the *Enneads* specifically mention or attack orthodox Christian doctrines (as distinct from doctrines or attitudes of mind common to both Gnostics and orthodox). It seems likely, therefore, that Plotinus never really came close to orthodox Christianity, either as friend or as enemy. In view of the great influence which his philosophy later exercised on Christian thought, it is interesting to speculate what his own attitude to it might have been: but we cannot safely say more than that even if he had known it well he would probably have disliked it. The question of what likenesses and differences there are between his thought and the Christian thought of his own or later periods is quite a different, and a very interesting, one which will be touched on here and there in this Part; and the question of his influence on later Christian (and Moslem) thinkers will be repeatedly discussed elsewhere in this History.

[1] See *Life*, chs. 3, 14 and 20.

CHAPTER 13

TEACHING AND WRITING

The part of Porphyry's description of Plotinus at Rome which is most interesting to a historian of philosophy is of course his account of his master's method of teaching and writing, of his knowledge and use of previous philosophers and his relations with the philosophers of his own time. About all this Porphyry tells us a good deal which is helpful to our understanding of the *Enneads*. The lectures of Plotinus were not the formal, carefully arranged, set speeches developing a theme along lines fixed by established tradition which were customary in the philosophical schools of his time. The procedure in his school was informal, some said disorderly.[1] Plotinus was a systematic and dogmatic philosopher, who had no doubt that he knew the right answers to the great philosophical questions which he treated: but he was not the sort of systematizer and dogmatist who cannot tolerate queries, objections and interruptions. He had a Socratic belief in the value of discussion, and once a discussion had started in his school it had to go on to the end, till the difficulties raised had been properly solved, however long it took. A story which Porphyry tells gives an excellent idea of the spirit in which Plotinus met queries and objections. A man called Thaumasius came into the school one day when Plotinus was arguing with Porphyry about the relationship between soul and body (the argument lasted three days) and demanded a set lecture suitable for writing down; he could not, he said, stand Porphyry's questions and answers. But Plotinus said 'If we do not solve the difficulties which Porphyry raises in his questions we shall be able to say absolutely nothing suitable for writing down'.[2] And we can find traces of discussions of this kind in many treatises of the *Enneads* (not, that is, actual reports or summaries of the discussions which took place, but passages of argument which look as if they were inspired not simply by Plotinus' reading but by his memory of objections actually raised by members of the school). But, though Plotinus was always ready to stop for discussion,

[1] *Life*, ch. 3.

[2] *Life*, ch. 13.

it is also clear from Porphyry's account that he was capable of sustained exposition and of speaking in a way which impressed his audience and conveyed to them something of his own philosophical passion: and this again is confirmed by his written works, which contain much continuous, strongly knit exposition and many passages of impressive eloquence which have moved and excited readers of every generation from that of St Augustine to our own, and sometimes even stimulated them to grapple with the tough expositions and close, obscure arguments which fill the greater part of the *Enneads*. But the eloquence of Plotinus is not the artificial, self-conscious, over-literary sort common in his age; it is simple and direct, springing from his passionate concentration on the matter in hand.

What Porphyry has to say about his master's knowledge and use of previous philosophers has been confirmed and amplified by recent studies of the *Enneads*, and is extremely helpful to our understanding of how Plotinus worked out his own philosophy. He tells us[1] 'In the meetings of the school he had the commentaries read, it might be of Severus or Cronius or Numenius or Gaius or Atticus, and among the Peripatetics of Aspasius and Alexander and Adrastus and any others which came to hand'. The starting-point (Porphyry makes clear that it was only a starting-point) of a Plotinian lecture or discussion was the study of one of the Platonic or Aristotelian commentators and expositors of the century or so before he began his philosophical career. Again and again as we read the *Enneads* we find him critically considering the opinions of his predecessors, or reproducing some piece of school discussion or polemic as a starting-point for his own reflections; this is very well brought out in the volume 'Les Sources de Plotin' (*Entretiens Hardt*, v) already referred to. His use of the great Peripatetic commentator Alexander of Aphrodisias is particularly interesting in its constructively critical handling of a version of Aristotelian thought which he obviously found attractive and often true up to a point, though inadequate, and in the way in which he brings Aristotle himself into the discussion and corrects Alexander by him, as he sometimes corrects the Platonists by Plato.[2] Plotinus knew the works of Aristotle well, and

[1] *Life*, ch. 14.

[2] See in particular P. Henry's paper 'Une Comparaison chez Aristote, Alexandre et Plotin', and the discussion, in *Entretiens Hardt*, v, pp. 429–49.

frequently refers to them (Porphyry notes his frequent use of the *Metaphysics*,[1] but he also knew the *De anima*, the logical works, the *Nicomachean Ethics*, etc.), and was deeply influenced by Aristotelian ideas, as will appear at several points later, though his attitude towards them always remains independent and critical. The same is true of Stoicism. Porphyry speaks of the presence in his works of 'unobserved Stoic and Peripatetic doctrines';[2] and, besides a great deal of traditional Platonist polemic against Stoicism, there are many passages in the *Enneads* which show considerable Stoic influence, though the Stoicism is not as a rule left raw or unmodified;[3] of this again we shall have examples later. As for other philosophers, he neither liked nor understood the Epicureans any better than most of his predecessors and contemporaries did, and his references to them are confined to a few stock polemical observations; and the Presocratics provide him only with a few doxographic tags, interpreted in accordance with his own ideas.

The supreme authority for Plotinus, and the only philosopher whom he regards as beyond criticism, is of course Plato. But his way of using the works of his master is somewhat disconcerting to the modern Platonic scholar. As Theiler excellently puts it, the Plato of Plotinus is a very restricted Plato, a 'Plato dimidiatus', a Plato without politics.[4] As we have seen, the other-worldliness of Plotinus did not lead him to neglect his duties to society. No ancient philosopher has a better record of disinterested service to his fellow-men. But it did lead him to preach withdrawal from public life and to take little or no interest in the political side of Plato's thought. And his use even of the non-political parts of Plato's writings is highly selective.[5] Practically nothing is taken from the early, 'Socratic' dialogues. The *Republic* is often referred to, but the references are nearly all to a few passages (the Cave, the Idea of the Good, the concluding myth). *Theaetetus* 176 A–B (the flight from evil) is referred to again and again; there are a fair number of references

[1] *Life*, ch. 14, 6–8. [2] *Ibid.* 5–6.

[3] See W. Theiler's 'Plotin zwischen Plato und Stoa' in *Entretiens Hardt*, v, pp. 65–103.

[4] Theiler, *art. cit.* p. 67. [For some evidence of serious study of Plato's political writings by late Greek philosophers see the account of the political thought of al-Fārābī, Part VIII, ch. 40 C, pp. 658–61.]

[5] There are good detailed surveys of the quotations from Plato in H.-R. Schwyzer, *art. cit.* col. 551–2 and W. Theiler, *art. cit.* pp. 68–71. The identification of the passage which Plotinus has in mind is often by no means easy, because of his inexact ways of citation or allusion.

to isolated passages of the *Sophist*, *Parmenides* and *Philebus*; *Alcibiades I*, the *Greater Hippias*, *Politicus*, *Cratylus* and *Laws* and perhaps *Epinomis* are used occasionally; the passage about the three principles in the *2nd Letter* 312E is several times given as authority for Plotinus' doctrine of the Three Hypostases. The dialogues which Plotinus used most frequently and extensively are the *Phaedo*, *Phaedrus*, *Symposium* and *Timaeus*. These, with *Republic* VI and VII, are the real sources of his Platonism. But he uses even these selectively, and a great deal in them is never referred to or considered at all. There are, here and there in the *Enneads*, some acute discussions of difficulties or apparent (for Plotinus they must be only apparent) inconsistencies in Plato, notably of the differing accounts he gives of the reasons for the soul's descent into this world and its relationship to body.[1] But usually his Platonic quotations or references are simply brought in to provide authority for his own views or a starting-point for his own speculations: and the meaning he gives them is either very much his own or derived from his Middle-Platonist or Neopythagorean predecessors (whose interpretations may of course in some cases be traced back to the Old Academy). He uses texts from Plato, in fact, rather as Christian preachers or scholastic theologians use texts from the Bible, and not as a scholar would use them (his use of Aristotle is considerably more scholarly because he does not feel any particular reverence for him). This does not mean that the Platonism of Plotinus has nothing to do with the Platonism of Plato: one can only arrive at that conclusion by neglecting a great deal of Plato and misunderstanding a great deal of Plotinus. But the resemblances and differences will be better seen when we are considering Plotinus' thought in detail.

Before going on to consider the writings of Plotinus, something must be said about the end of his life and the breaking up of his circle. The painful and unpleasant illness from which he suffered in his last years and which eventually killed him is described by Porphyry[2] so imprecisely that H. Opperman has identified it as *Elephantiasis graeca*

[1] IV 8 [6] and I 1 [53] 12.

[2] *Life*, ch. 2. The account given by Porphyry, with that of Firmicus Maternus (*Mathesis* I 7. 14 ff.), which probably depends on Porphyry, is discussed by H. Opperman in *Plotins Leben* (Orient u. Antike, 7 [Heidelberg, 1929]); P. Henry, *Plotin et l'Occident* (Louvain, 1934), pp. 25 ff.; P. Gillet, *Plotin au point de vue médical et psychologique* (Paris, 1934); H.-R. Schwyzer, *art. cit.* col. 474–6.

(a form of leprosy) and P. Gillet as tuberculosis. It led him to give up teaching and withdraw from the society of his friends, who were avoiding meeting him out of disgust for his condition; he went to the estate of one of his oldest friends, Zethus, in Campania, where he died alone except for his faithful doctor Eustochius. Porphyry, on the authority of Eustochius, records his last words, but unfortunately text and interpretation are doubtful.[1] He probably said either 'Try to bring back the god in you to the divine in the All', or 'I am trying to bring back the divine in us to the divine in the All'. When he died his circle had already broken up. Porphyry had gone to Sicily some time before, because of the nervous crisis already mentioned, and Amelius was in Syria. It had never been a formally organized philosophical school; its existence depended entirely on Plotinus himself; and on his retirement and death it dissolved without any possibility of re-forming. This is a fact of some importance for the history of philosophy. Plotinus was not the founder of Neoplatonism in the sense that he founded a school with a continuous tradition based on his teaching. The survival of his authentic thought has depended entirely on the literary and editorial activity of Porphyry. He stood apart from the philosophers of his time (who are as obscure to us as Plotinus would have been without Porphyry). The most notable of them, Longinus, spoke of him with respect but disagreed with him profoundly.[2] The Neoplatonism of Iamblichus was in many ways a fresh start, which helps to account for the fact that those very authority-minded people the later Neoplatonists never regarded Plotinus as an authority of the first rank, with whom it was not proper to disagree. The influence of Plotinus on later philosophy was very great, but he did not dominate the thought of his time or entirely determine the later development of Platonism.

Plotinus, as has already been mentioned, did not begin to write till he had been ten years in Rome. There has been much discussion about the reason given by Porphyry why he delayed so long. Porphyry says[3] 'Erennius, Origen and Plotinus had made an agreement not to disclose any of the doctrines of Ammonius which had been made clear to them in his lectures. Plotinus kept the agreement and, though he held con-

[1] See P. Henry, 'La Dernière Parole de Plotin', *Studi classici e orientali*, II (Pisa, 1953), pp. 113–20 and Harder's note in his edition of the *Life*.

[2] *Life*, chs. 19–20.

[3] *Life*, ch. 3, 25–30.

ferences with people who came to him, maintained silence about the doctrines of Ammonius. Erennius was the first to break the agreement, and Origen followed his lead....' The best explanation of this is that given by Harder in his long note on the passage in his edition of the *Life*. He rejects, for good reasons, the idea that there is any implication here of anything like the obligation of secrecy imposed on those initiated into a mystery. The agreement not to publish refers, he thinks, to a common stock of ideas worked out by discussion between Ammonius and his three pupils and set down in written notes which represented their joint work, in which it was not possible to distinguish the parts belonging to each individual, and which the three pupils therefore agreed should not be published by any one of them as his own work, or even (apparently) incorporated in his own writings. As Harder points out, an agreement of this kind would be impossible to keep for very long, and Porphyry thought that all that was needed to save his master from any discredit was to make clear that he was not the first to break it; which, as Harder says, would have been no excuse if anything like a mystery-secret had been involved.

Once Plotinus had begun to write he continued to do so to the end of his life, but his writings were not intended for general circulation; they were meant for a few of his close friends, and disciples, and it was not easy to get hold of copies.[1] Porphyry carefully collected everything that this master wrote and eventually, in 301,[2] in his 68th year, over thirty years after the death of Plotinus, published his great collected edition. This was not the first edition of the writings of Plotinus. There was an earlier one by his friend and doctor Eustochius, of which we know from an ancient note which appears in some manuscripts of the *Enneads* at the end of ch. 29 of the second treatise *On the Problems of the Soul*.[3] This tells us that Plotinus' book on the soul was differently divided in the two editions, the break between the second and third parts coming in that of Eustochius at the point where the note appears. Henry and Schwyzer believe that the quotations in Eusebius, *Praeparatio Evangelica* XV 10 and 22, come from this edition and not from the *Enneads*, but their belief, though supported by some evidence, has

[1] *Life*, ch. 4.
[2] See Harder's note on *Life*, ch. 23, 13.
[3] IV 4 [28].

not found general acceptance among Plotinian scholars.[1] If it is well founded (and the present writer is inclined to think that it is), these fragments in Eusebius provide a valuable check on Porphyry's editorial methods, and go a long way to confirm that what he gives us in the *Enneads* is substantially what Plotinus wrote, without significant additions or alterations. But even if it is not, and Eusebius was quoting from Porphyry's edition, there seems no reason to suppose that Porphyry did not do his work as editor conscientiously and accurately. Almost all Plotinian scholars nowadays would agree that in the words of the *Enneads* we have what Plotinus wrote, and that Porphyry did no more than correct the spelling, etc., of his master's carelessly written and unrevised manuscripts.[2] In the division and arrangement of the treatises, however, he allowed himself to take some most unfortunate liberties in order to force Plotinus' writings into the artificial scheme he had devised, of six sets of nine treatises ('Enneads'), grouped roughly according to subject-matter.[3] It was of no great importance that he divided a number of longer treatises into several parts which appear consecutively in the right order in his edition (III 2–3, IV 3–5, VI 1–3, VI 4–5), or that he collected a number of short detached notes into something that looks on casual inspection more or less like a treatise (III 9). What was a good deal more serious was that he broke up one of Plotinus' longest and most impressive works into four separate parts, placed out of order and without apparent connexion in three Enneads (III 8, V 8, V 5, II 9).[4] One of the advantages of following the chronological order of the treatises, which is given by Porphyry in the *Life*,[5] instead of the Ennead arrangement, as is done by Harder and a few others, is that it is possible to read this work as a coherent whole: and Harder's demonstration, on grounds quite independent of Porphyry's chronological list, that it is a whole, with the parts arranged in that order, provides impressive confirmation of the accuracy of the list: we can be reasonably sure, at least about the treatises written after Porphyry came to Rome, that Plotinus did write them in the order in which Porphyry

[1] See the prefaces to Henry–Schwyzer, *Plotini Opera*, I, pp. ix–x and II, pp. ix–x.

[2] Cf. the vivid but, as Harder points out, rather uninformative account of Plotinus' way of writing in *Life*, ch. 8.

[3] See *Life*, chs. 24–6 for Porphyry's own account of his editorial proceedings.

[4] See R. Harder, 'Eine neue Schrift Plotins', in *Kleine Schriften*, pp. 303–13.

[5] Chs. 4–6.

says he did. We should have, therefore, an unusually solid basis on which to erect a theory of the development of Plotinus' thought, if only we could discover any evidence in his works that such a development took place during the period when he was writing them. But in fact all attempts to find evidence for a real development have (in the present writer's opinion at least) ended in failure. Plotinus is continually re-stating and clarifying his ideas, returning again and again to the same points and adding new touches of precision, but there is no evidence that he changed his mind about any question of real importance during his writing period (there are perhaps one or two points where we can see him making up his mind finally after an earlier indecision). And this is not surprising when we remember that he only began to write after ten years' teaching, at the age of fifty, so that his writings all belong to the last sixteen years of his life. Any real development in his thought is likely to have been completed by then, and we have no sufficient means of knowing how it went.[1]

It should be obvious from what has been said that the titles of the treatises in Porphyry's edition cannot have been given them by Plotinus: and in fact Porphyry says explicitly that Plotinus gave them no titles:[2] the twenty-one which Porphyry found in circulation when he came to Rome bear, he says, the titles which became current in the school. He is probably himself responsible for the titles of most of the later treatises. There is some variation, in some cases, between the titles in Porphyry's own two lists, and between the lists and the titles borne by some treatises in the MSS of the *Enneads*; and in one or two cases other titles are known. Of the commentaries and summaries or tables of contents which Porphyry says in the last chapter of the *Life* that he prepared for his edition, no trace has survived, except perhaps for an Arabic version of part of the table of contents for IV 4 [28].[3]

Plotinus, Porphyry tells us,[4] thought out so thoroughly beforehand

[1] In spite of its obvious advantages, the chronological order has not been generally adopted by Plotinian scholars, because of the difficulties which it causes over citation: the form of reference used in the notes to this History, which is that agreed on by the Plotinian scholars who met at Vandœuvres in 1957, provides a satisfactory compromise. In it the Ennead and treatise reference is immediately followed by the number in Porphyry's chronological order, e.g. VI 9 [9].

[2] *Life*, ch. 4, 16.

[3] On Porphyry's commentaries, etc., see H.-R. Schwyzer, *art. cit.* col. 508–10: for the Arabic version of the κεφάλαια see Henry–Schwyzer, II, pp. 62–127 and preface, pp. xxvii–xxviii.

[4] *Life*, ch. 8.

the question on which he was writing, and kept his mind fixed on it with such intensity, that he wrote 'as if he was copying out of a book', and could go straight on with his writing after an interruption, just as if he had not had to break it off: and he never read through again what he had written, because of his bad eyesight. This does something to account for the extraordinarily direct and personal quality of the style of his treatises. Plotinus wrote very much as he lectured, and intended his writings for the people to whom he lectured. He did not, as Thaumasius would no doubt have liked him to, write up his treatises for the cultured public according to the accepted conventions of late Greek literary rhetoric. Some of his writings have the appearance of being intended for a wider audience than others. The work on the Categories (VI 1–3 [42–4]), for instance, or the treatises *On Potency and Act* (II 5 [25]) and *On Substance and Quality* (II 6 [17]) can only have been intended for his closest collaborators, the real working members of his circle. But even those which look as if they were meant for a wider circle of readers, like the great work which Porphyry so cruelly quartered, were not meant for readers outside the group of Plotinus' friends, admirers, and regular hearers. Nor is it possible to make a hard and fast distinction of style or manner between different groups of treatises. All contain passages of argument of more than Aristotelian toughness and dryness; and most, including some of the toughest and driest, contain passages of exalted and moving eloquence.

That Plotinus wrote very much as he lectured does not mean that we have in any of the treatises reports of actual lectures or school discussions; nor does it mean that he wrote bad Greek. His writings are addressed to readers, not to hearers. The arguments, the objections and the answers to them may well in some cases have been inspired by school discussions (though we can find origins for many of them in Plotinus' reading), but they are never transcripts of the proceedings in the school. As for his Greek, the judgement with which H.-R. Schwyzer concludes his admirably precise, detailed and sensitive examination of Plotinus' language and style[1] seems true and well founded. Schwyzer says[2]

The judgement that Plotinus writes bad Greek...is only correct if one considers the rules of school grammars as alone authoritative. Plotinus writes an

[1] *Art. cit.* col. 512–30.

[2] Col. 530, 41–66.

individualistic, but never deliberately obscure Greek. The serious difficulties for understanding do not lie in an unclear manner of expression, but in the abstractness of the thought. In spite of many freedoms, Plotinus' language conforms to the laws of Greek grammar, and is not at all the stammering utterance of a mystic. It is rather an ever renewed, intelligent struggle to express the inexpressible, in which all the stylistic resources of the Greek language are employed. These, however, never become an end in themselves, but are brought in only to clarify the processes of philosophical thought. Plotinus is convinced that the majesty of the world which transcends our senses, and still more the goodness of the One, can never be expressed in words: but if anyone ever could find adequate words for that world, Plotinus has succeeded in doing so.

One particular stylistic means which Plotinus used deserves some special study. This is his use of images taken from the sense-world to describe the realities of the intelligible world. Plotinus inherited and developed the traditional polemics of the Platonic and Peripatetic schools against the Stoic way of thinking about God and the soul as supremely refined and subtle forms of body, and in consequence has a very clear conception of the meaning and implications of immateriality; he brings out those implications, as we shall see, in ways which are important for his thought. But no philosopher has ever used images from the sense-world to express intelligible reality with more originality and force. His language is full of vivid, concrete expressions taken from sense-experience to describe the activity and interaction of immaterial beings, not only the traditional metaphors of sight and light, or growth and flow, but expressions of violent contact and vigorous bodily movement, pushing, striking, breaking, throwing, running, leaping.[1] And he has more elaborately presented images of extraordinary imaginative power. One of the most striking of these is the image of the material universe floating in soul like a net in the sea: 'It is like a net in the waters, immersed in life, but unable to make its own that in which it is. The sea is already spread out, and the net spreads with it, as far as it can.'[2] (A comparison with the tight tidy mathematical structure of soul in which the Demiurge wraps up the universe in the *Timaeus* tells us a good deal about the differences between the mind of Plotinus and that

[1] A large number of these are collected by Schwyzer, *art. cit.* col. 526–7.

[2] IV 3 [27] 9, 38–41.

of Plato.) Another is this image (carefully stated to be inadequate because it is looking at it 'from outside') for the unity-in-diversity of Intellect: 'One might compare it to a living sphere of varied colour and pattern, or something all faces, shining with living faces.'[1] This seems to take us right outside the range of the classical Hellenic imagination into the sort of imaginative world inhabited by the great artists of India. The use of these vivid sense-images is not, as we shall see more clearly later, inconsistent with Plotinus' philosophical assumptions: after all, everything in the sense-world is for him an image of the intelligible; and his sense of the inadequacy of all language in speaking of these higher realities would prevent him from regarding any abstract 'philosophical' term as completely satisfactory by itself, from thinking that when he had used the term 'Being' or 'Intellect' he had said all that needed to be or could be said, even about that second reality which he is prepared to call 'Being' and 'Intellect'. When he comes to the primary reality, the One, of course, he is completely certain that no kind of language, 'philosophical' and abstract or 'poetic' and concrete, is in the least adequate or satisfactory. And he keeps his images under very firm control, sometimes criticizing and refining them in a very unusual way. The most interesting and important example is the passage where he takes the traditional image of radiating light, and by correcting it gets rid of the idea of emanation or radiation altogether, and leaves the reader with an extremely vivid picture of spiritual omnipresence.[2] But there are other passages (e.g. the one just quoted about the 'living faces') where he points out some particular inadequacy of the image he is using and encourages the reader's mind to go beyond it: his images are always intended to keep the mind moving, not to arrest it in a false contemplation of a fantasy and a static satisfaction with the ultimately unsatisfying. By his use of images he is able to convey something (not, in his own view, nearly enough) of his intense and immediate sense of the life, strength, splendour and solidity of spiritual reality. It is this, perhaps more than anything else, which gives his writings their peculiar power and attractiveness.

[1] VI 7 [38] 15, 24–6.

[2] VI 4 [22] 7, 23–40; cf. the discussion of this passage in *Entretiens Hardt*, V, pp. 337–8.

CHAPTER 14

MAN AND REALITY

Perhaps as good a starting-point as any for a consideration of the rich, complex and difficult thought of Plotinus is to see what he himself thought that he was really trying to do, what the aim was which he constantly pursued in all his thinking, teaching and writing. As he summed it up himself on his deathbed (whichever version of his last words we accept),[1] it was to bring back the divine in man to the divine in the All. This is an ambiguous enough statement, which can be interpreted in a variety of ways, beginning with the crudest Stoic pantheism. But if we come to understand as precisely as possible what Plotinus meant by it, we shall be well on the way to understanding his philosophy as a whole. Man for Plotinus is in some sense divine, and the object of the philosophic life is to understand this divinity and restore its proper relationship (never, as we shall see, completely lost) with the divine All and, in that All, to come to union with its transcendent source, the One or Good. We must, of course, in studying Plotinus, beware from the beginning of the confusion that can so easily arise if we neglect the wide and vague meaning of *theos* and *theios* in Greek and understand his statements about divinity in terms of the Judaeo-Christian tradition, which, in its normal way of speaking, reserves 'God' and 'Divine' for the transcendent creative cause of all things, and only uses them of created beings rarely, and generally with carefully expressed qualifications (e.g. 'divine by participation'). The pagan Platonic tradition, on the whole, tends to use *theos* and its derivatives in almost exactly the opposite way. They are rarely used of the transcendent source of being, and only when the context makes it perfectly clear what is meant: but they are normally used of a variety of beings of different ranks within the universe (down to and including man's true self) which depend wholly for their existence on the supreme principle.[2]

[1] See ch. 13, p. 215.

[2] Plotinus sometimes makes use of the traditional distinction between *theos* and *daemon*, though he does not take it very seriously. The rigid and elaborate theological classifications of later Neoplatonism are foreign to his way of thinking.

The object, then, of philosophy according to Plotinus is to attain to our true end, union with the Good, in the divine All, by waking to a knowledge of our true self and its place in reality. He always makes it clear that we cannot truly know ourselves except in our context; we must know our place in and relationship to the whole which, in a sense, we are. The divine All, the world of real being, and its source, the Good, are always there and always present to us, and the impulse to return to the source is given in the very being of all derived existence. But we have to choose and make the effort to turn and concentrate ourselves upwards, towards that good the desire of which is constitutive of our very being, in order that we may become that which we always are. This sounds highly paradoxical, and the most careful study of the *Enneads* never completely resolves the paradox: but if we are to understand Plotinus at all we must make some attempt to see what it means. First we must remember that the universe according to Plotinus, the total order and structure of reality, is static and eternal. Even the physical universe is eternal and unchanging as a whole, and only in its lower parts are there cycles of change as individuals come into being and perish: and in the world of immaterial being all the individual parts are everlasting, without beginning and without end. 'Static' certainly does not mean 'lifeless'. No philosopher has ever asserted so strongly, and pictured so vividly, the unity of being and life, as Plotinus. The intelligible world, the highest level of being, is for him a world 'boiling with life'.[1] But the highest life is a life of intense, inturned, self-contained contemplative activity, of which the life of movement, change, production and action on the physical level is only a very faint and far-off image, changing (though without ever producing anything really new) because of its very imperfection. It is against this background of thought that we must try to understand Plotinus' conception of man. Man for him is a being on the lowest divine level, that of soul, which extends from the lower edge of the intelligible, down through the sense-world (it should always be remembered that these inevitable spatial metaphors, which Plotinus himself uses freely, are for him only metaphors: the intelligible world is not above the stars; it is not in space at all). He is a being of considerable complexity, and Plotinus is very

[1] VI 7 [38] 12, 23.

much concerned to locate the 'we' (ἡμεῖς), that is, our true self, within that complexity, to determine which among the many functions, activities and interests of our soul on its various levels are really proper to man. The question 'Who (or what) are we?' recurs several times in the *Enneads*, and a reading of the difficult late treatise which Porphyry put at the beginning of the First Ennead, with the title *What is the Living Being and What is Man?*,[1] will show with what care and precision he tried to find the answer. In this treatise and elsewhere[2] the answer he gives is that man is double.[3] Our true self, the 'man within', is our higher soul which exists eternally close to and continually illumined by Intellect. This does not sin or suffer and remains essentially free and unhampered in its rational and intellectual activities by the turbulence of the body and its world, into which the higher soul does not 'come down'. What enters the lower world is only an irradiation from the higher soul, an image or expression of it on the lower level, which joins with the bodily organism to form the 'joint entity', the 'composite'; it is this 'other man' or lower self which sins and suffers and is ignorant and emotionally disturbed, and in general is the subject of what most people regard as ordinary human experience. This is a clear-cut and comprehensible conception of man, with a pedigree which can be traced back to the sharp separation of immortal and mortal soul in the *Timaeus*[4] and of the intellect as true self from the moral personality in the *Nicomachean Ethics*.[5] But it leaves out of account a great deal which occurs elsewhere in the *Enneads*, and in particular it makes almost incomprehensible that passionate concern for the philosophical salvation of the soul, for its 'purification', 'separation' and reversion to its proper place and state which Plotinus, rightly, finds in Plato and which is, as we have seen, the driving force behind his own philosophical activity. On this 'double personality' view nothing needs to be done, or can be done, about the higher self; and the disciplining and ordering of the lower self, though a necessary duty, does not seem to be a very interesting or important task for the philosopher: even in our

[1] I I [53].

[2] E.g. VI 4 [22] 14.

[3] But in I I [53] II Plotinus speaks of the 'middle' (τὸ μέσον) of the soul, which we can direct either upwards or downwards: this shows how easily he can pass from the view of man as double to the view of man as triple discussed below (p. 225).

[4] 69 C–D.

[5] 1177b–1178a.

final withdrawal from this world there is no essential change. The higher self is not really more 'separate' than it was before; it merely ceases to irradiate and govern the lower individual (it still shares in the universal government of universal soul). But there is another more precise analysis of man to be found in the *Enneads* which adds an important element and by doing so makes Plotinus' philosophical activity a good deal more consistent and comprehensible. In this account man is not double but triple. In the treatise *Against the Gnostics* he says 'One part of our soul is always directed to the intelligible realities, one to the things of this world, and one is in the middle between these: for since the soul is one nature in many powers, sometimes the whole of it is carried along with the best of itself and of real being, sometimes the worse part is dragged down and drags the middle with it; for it is not lawful for it to drag down the whole'.[1] And in the late treatise *On the Knowing Hypostases* he identifies this middle part clearly with the discursive reason, and states definitely that it is the 'we', our true self. 'It is we who reason, and think the thoughts in discursive reasoning ourselves: for this is "we": the activities of the intellect come from above, just as those of sense-perception do from below: we are the principal part of the soul, which is the middle between two powers, a worse and a better, the worse being that of sense-perception, the better that of intellect.'[2] We should notice in the first of these passages the insistence of Plotinus that the soul is a unity in all its powers and on all its levels; this is an important part of his thought, and makes it easier to see how he could allow himself a good deal of variation in his analyses of soul in different contexts and from different points of view: they are variant partial descriptions of an extremely complex unity. He, at least, would not have regarded the three-part analysis as inconsistent with the account of man as double. And if we accept the former as representing his real

[1] II 9 [33] 2, 4–10 ψυχῆς δὲ ἡμῶν τὸ μὲν ἀεὶ πρὸς ἐκείνοις, τὸ δὲ πρὸς ταῦτα ἔχειν, τὸ δ' ἐν μέσῳ τούτων· φύσεως γὰρ οὔσης μιᾶς ἐν δυνάμεσι πλείοσιν ὁτὲ μὲν τὴν πᾶσαν συμφέρεσθαι τῷ ἀρίστῳ αὑτῆς καὶ τοῦ ὄντος, ὁτὲ δὲ τὸ χεῖρον αὑτῆς καθελκυσθὲν συνεφελκύσασθαι τὸ μέσον· τὸ γὰρ πᾶν αὑτῆς οὐκ ἦν θέμις καθελκύσαι; cf. I 1 [53] 11.

[2] V 3 [49] 3, 34–9 ἢ αὐτοὶ μὲν οἱ λογιζόμενοι καὶ νοοῦμεν τὰ ἐν τῇ διανοίᾳ νοήματα αὐτοί· τοῦτο γὰρ ἡμεῖς. τὰ δὲ τοῦ νοῦ ἐνεργήματα ἄνωθεν οὕτως, ὡς τὰ ἐκ τῆς αἰσθήσεως κάτωθεν, τοῦτο ὄντες τὸ κύριον τῆς ψυχῆς, μέσον δυνάμεως διττῆς, χείρονος καὶ βελτίονος, χείρονος μὲν τῆς αἰσθήσεως, βελτίονος δὲ τοῦ νοῦ. It is characteristic of this treatise that the transcendence of Intellect is stressed. We are illumined by Intellect and can operate on its level: but we are not strictly speaking Intellect, and to be illumined and raised by it means a certain transcendence of self.

thought we shall find it easier to make sense of what he has to say about the philosophic life, because it does provide a real foundation in man's nature for the possibility of choosing to live on different levels which is taken for granted throughout most of the *Enneads*. The limits of choice for Plotinian man, even on this account of him, remain narrow. He cannot spoil or corrupt or in any way essentially change his nature. Plotinus always maintains that immaterial being on any level is impassible; though it becomes clear from the early chapters of his treatise *On the Impassibility of Beings without Body*[1] that the opposing view which he is particularly concerned to refute is that of the Stoics, according to which the soul is a material substance subject to physical impressions, contaminations and modifications, and consequently the kind of impassibility which he is primarily trying to establish is that which seems to be inseparably connected with the notion of incorporeality (for Plotinus an Aristotelian form would be just as impassible in this sense as a Platonic soul). But in his account of soul he carries his assertion of impassibility well beyond the point necessary to disassociate himself from Stoic materialism. It does not seem that he thought that our true rational self could ever sin or suffer: it is even doubtful whether he thought it could be genuinely ignorant.[2] It cannot come down to the level of the body or be completely involved in its life. What it can do is to direct its attention upwards or downwards; to concentrate downwards on the petty individual concerns of this world, of its body and the body-bound lower soul concerned with growth, nutrition and sensations, or upwards, using the illumination of Intellect which is always available to it, to expand to universality in the eternal world of truth and real being, from which it can be raised to union with the Good: or it can be divided and fluctuate between the two. On this direction of attention our whole way of living depends: and it is the function of philosophy to turn us and direct us rightly, upwards.

It should be noted that for Plotinus this right direction of attention, this activity of the soul on its proper, intellectual, level, is not necessarily conscious. The philosopher need not be aware all the time that

[1] III 6 [26].

[2] [For the Christian rejection of this conception of man see Part v (Augustine), ch. 22, pp. 359–69 and Part vi (The Greek Christian Tradition), chs. 28 and 3c, pp. 426–7 and p. 485.]

his true self is living on the level of Intellect. Consciousness, in the sense of self-awareness, registering that '*I* am doing something' or 'Something is happening to *me*', is for Plotinus an epiphenomenon, a secondary, and not particularly desirable, effect of our proper activity. He is perfectly prepared to admit that consciousness in this sense depends on the faculties of our body–soul complex. If these are damaged or disturbed, as by drugs, or suspended, as in sleep, there is no consciousness, but the fundamental activity, and so the fundamental well-being, of our higher self continues undisturbed. Plotinus points out that even on the level of ordinary experience many of our activities go better if we are not conscious of ourselves acting: he gives the examples of reading, and of acting courageously.[1] You will not get on very fast or well with reading the *Enneads* if you keep on stopping to think 'Here am I reading the *Enneads*'—and almost inevitably adding 'How intelligent I am!' And the man performing an act of heroism is not likely to think at the time 'I am being heroic', and will be less heroic if he does.

Plotinus often describes this turning and concentration of attention upwards as 'waking': and waking ourselves up from our dream-like obsession with the needs and desires of our lower self in the world of the senses is for him a difficult process requiring vigorous intellectual and moral self-discipline. The moral side of the process is very much stressed. Some modern Christian writers are in the habit of talking about 'Greek' or 'Platonic intellectualism' in a way which suggests that they think that only Christians (or Jews and Christians) believe that religion and morality are closely connected, and that Plotinus and other Greek religious philosophers did not regard the practice of virtue and the attainment of the highest possible degree of moral perfection as indispensable for contemplation of and union with God. This of course is very far from the truth. Plotinus makes his own position perfectly clear in the passage where he speaks most explicitly about the attainment of mystical union. 'We learn about it [the Good] by comparisons and negations and knowledge of the things which proceed from it and intellectual progress by ascending degrees; but we advance towards it by purifications and virtues and adornings of the soul and by gaining a foothold in the world of Intellect and settling ourselves firmly

[1] I 4 [46] 9–10.

there and feasting on its contents'.[1] Here moral progress is closely linked with the attainment of the intuitive, contemplative knowledge which is the last stage before the final vision and union. It sets us on the way to the Good, but the rational-discursive thinking which is what we generally understand by intellectual activity only teaches us about it. Plotinus, however, does not usually make the sharp separation between discursive reasoning and the practice of the virtues which his language suggests here. It would be anachronistic and wrong to consider his thought, or that of any other late Greek philosopher, in terms of that disassociation of moral and intellectual concerns characteristic of our own way of thinking, which would lead us to consider it absurd and impertinent, for instance, to inquire closely into the degree of moral virtue possessed by a candidate for a Chair of philosophy and to require him, if he was even to be put on the short list, to be free from envy and ambition and indifferent to such worldly considerations as the salary scale. Plotinus, like most Greek philosophers, thought that a philosopher ought to be an extremely good as well as an extremely intelligent man, and did not believe that true intelligence was possible without virtue, or true virtue without intelligence.

The moral teaching of Plotinus is, as has often been remarked, strongly influenced by Stoicism. But he firmly adapts Stoicism, where necessary, to the requirements of his own distinctive form of the Platonic conception of man. Plotinus vigorously supports the Stoics against the Peripatetics on the much-debated question whether external goods are necessary to well-being. This is the main theme of his treatise *On Well-Being*.[2] But by adapting the Stoic teaching to his own conception of man he is enabled to avoid some of its paradoxical consequences. For him the well-being of man's true self is what really matters, and this cannot be harmed by any external sufferings or losses, however great, or helped by acquiring even the most generally coveted of external goods. He preaches magnificently on this text, quite in the tone of a Stoic diatribe. But because he sees man as a complex being he can easily maintain the main position, that external goods are not

[1] VI 7 [38] 36, 6–10 διδάσκουσι μὲν οὖν ἀναλογίαι τε καὶ ἀφαιρέσεις καὶ γνώσεις τῶν ἐξ αὐτοῦ καὶ ἀναβασμοί τινες, πορεύουσι δὲ καθάρσεις πρὸς αὐτὸ καὶ ἀρεταὶ καὶ κοσμήσεις καὶ τοῦ νοητοῦ ἐπιβάσεις καὶ ἐπ' αὐτοῦ ἱδρύσεις καὶ τῶν ἐκεῖ ἑστιάσεις, ...

[2] Περὶ εὐδαιμονίας, I 4 [46].

necessary for true well-being, without denying that their presence or absence can really affect our lower self. This 'other man', the body–soul complex, can be distressed and suffer pain. Plotinus, like Cicero, finds the claim of the Epicureans and Stoics that the wise man can positively enjoy being slowly roasted in the bull of Phalaris merely silly: their belief in the unity of man's soul makes such a claim mere rhetoric. For him the true self maintains its contemplation of the Good, and so its happiness, unbroken in the midst of the torture, but the lower self, which can suffer, really does suffer.[1]

Plotinus keeps the Stoic ideal of freedom from irrational affections and passions (ἀπάθεια) but because of his different conception of man it means something very different for him. There is no question of eradicating or destroying the emotions and affections of the lower self. *Apatheia* means freeing the true, rational self from distractions and illusions originating in the lower self, and so enabling it to live its proper life undisturbed. This can only be done if the lower, body–soul complex, the 'beast' or the 'child' in us, is kept under strict discipline and control. But neither the *Enneads* nor Porphyry's *Life* suggest that the spirit in which Plotinus undertook this disciplining and training of our lower nature was one of anxious negation and repression. There was nothing of the sin-obsessed schoolmaster about him. His attitude is rather one of austere detached tolerance for what after all is an image or reflection of our true self, and good on its own lowest level. We must provide for the real needs of our body (as distinct from the imaginary ones provoked by its disordered desires and the fantasies of lust, covetousness and ambition that arise from them): and we must not neglect the duties which arise for us from our presence with the body and its world. We have seen already how conscientiously Plotinus himself discharged his social duties,[2] and he recognizes the civic or social virtues[3] as true virtues, which play their part on their own level in making us godlike, though they are of lower rank than the virtues which are purifications.[4] The virtues on both levels are the usual Greek cardinal virtues, prudence, justice, fortitude and temperance, to give

[1] I 4. 13, 7–12: cf. Cicero, *Tusculans* II 17; Usener, *Epicurea* 601; *SVF* III 586.

[2] Above, ch. 12, pp. 202–3.

[3] πολιτικαὶ ἀρεταί. For his teaching about these see particularly I 2 [19] 1–3.

[4] καθάρσεις. For these see the same treatise, chs. 3–7.

them their conventional names, and Plotinus has nothing new or particularly interesting to say about them on the 'civic' level. On the 'purificatory' level these virtues are simply different ways of looking at that detachment from bodily illusions, concerns and desires and freedom in living man's true divine life which, we have already seen, it is the philosopher's first concern to attain. Plotinus always insists that the philosopher can reach this purity, separation and freedom in this life without physical separation from the body. Death is to be welcomed by the philosopher, because the earthly body is a burden and a source of distractions. (This is true only of the earthly body: as we shall see, there are other material bodies in the universe which are not impediments to the life of the soul.) But the philosopher can live out his philosophical life to the full and reach its goal, the vision of and union with the Good, in this world and with his body. (There seems to be no suggestion in Plotinus that the vision of the Good after death is intrinsically different from or superior to that attainable in this life, or that the soul when it is out of the cycle of reincarnation has greater purity or capacity of vision than when it is in it, though it is free from distraction by memories of its bodily lives, which may persist to some extent between incarnations:[1] it is, after all, only the lower soul that can really be affected by incarnation.) Death, therefore, though it is to be welcomed, is not an event of the first importance, and is not to be sought before the proper time. The teaching of Plotinus on suicide does not differ as much as has sometimes been said from that of the Stoics. He allows it, but only in extreme cases and for very grave reasons.[2]

The teaching of Plotinus about the human, earthly body is very much influenced by the *Phaedo*: but when he considers what the philosopher's attitude should be to the material universe as a whole and its order and beauty the predominant Platonic influence is that of the *Timaeus*. In so far as it is a world of forms, a structured, patterned unity in extreme diversity, it is a good world, the work of the good power of soul. It is true that for him the forms in matter are ghostly and sterile, not truly real but only the remotest reflections of the true realities in the world of Intellect: and the matter of the sublunary world,

[1] Cf. IV 3 [27] 27 ff. for memory in disembodied souls.

[2] See I 9 [19] with Harder's introductory note in his second edition (1*b*, 546–7); I 4 [46] 7–8.

at least, because it is absolute negativity and unreality, is the principle of evil.[1] But Plotinus is so concerned to stress the absolute unreality of matter that he makes it very clear that everything observable in the material universe, including its spatiality and corporeality—everything, that is, except its necessary imperfection—is form, not matter, and all activity in it is the activity of soul; and form and soul as such are good. This view of the material universe as last and lowest in the order of goodness, unity and reality, but the image and reflection of what is higher, leaves room for a good deal of variation of attitude. When Plotinus has to defend the divine powers which made this world against charges that they have made it very badly, and are responsible for a great deal of avoidable evil, he stresses the necessary reasons for its imperfection, matter, the low status of its forms, and the relative inferiority of the soul which is directly responsible for its making:[2] he maintains, in a genuinely Platonic way, that it is neither a perfect world nor a wholly bad world, but the best world which divinity could produce in the difficult conditions of this lowest level. But, when he is considering the material universe as a whole, it is its relative beauty and excellence which he stresses rather than the evil in it. Even when he is straining all his resources to demonstrate that matter is absolute evil, he remembers sometimes to remind his readers that the material universe is, none the less, good. So he ends his treatise *On What Are and Whence Come Evils*, which is entirely devoted to showing that matter is the principle of evil, with the words 'Because of the power and nature of the good, the bad is not only bad; for it appears necessarily bound in a sort of beautiful chains, as some prisoners are bound with gold; and so it is hidden by them, in order that, though it exists, it may not be seen by the gods, and that men may be able not always to look at the bad, but, even when they do look at it, may be in company with images of beauty to help their recollection'.[3] It is when he is arguing with the Gnostics that Plotinus most vigorously asserts the goodness and beauty of the material universe and of the divine power which made it.[4] He passionately maintains, against their melodramatic dualism, the true Platonic

[1] The hierarchy of forms, and Plotinus' strange conception of matter, will be further discussed in the next chapter.

[2] II 3 [52] 17; III 8 [30] 4–5.

[3] I 8 [51] 15, 23–8.

[4] II 9 [33] 8, 16–18.

doctrine that this world is 'a clear and noble image of the intelligible gods',[1] and insists that no one who despises and hates its beauty can really know and love the beauty of the intelligible world. In this anti-Gnostic polemic, besides the general Platonic assertion of the goodness of the sense-world, there is another element, also originating from Plato. Plotinus fully accepted the 'cosmic religion' of post-Platonic philosophers, though it was not of the first importance in his religious thought or life. The heavenly bodies are for him divine, and he regards it as blasphemy when the Gnostics deny their divinity and assert that the elect are superior to the stars in spiritual dignity (a view which of course they share with orthodox Christians). Because of his belief that the divinity of the cosmos as a whole is particularly manifested in its upper part, where universal Soul works unhampered and the divine heavenly bodies move in their everlasting circuits, he will not admit any evil at all in the regions above the moon. Rather illogically, in view of his own doctrine that the matter in bodies (as distinct from intelligible matter) is the principle of evil, he maintains that there is no evil or imperfection at all in the bodies of the star-gods. Not only are they everlasting and incorruptible, but they are completely dominated by soul and in no way hinder its working, as earthly bodies do.[2] There is a good deal of resemblance between the contrast of earthly with heavenly bodies made by the Neoplatonists and the contrast of 'natural' with 'spiritual', post-resurrection, bodies made by Christians, as Augustine remarks.[3]

It is by the *kosmos* of the cosmos, its beauty and order, that we are to know its divinity and be led to the contemplation of the intelligible. And Plotinus, unlike Plato, puts the beauty of art on a level with the beauty of nature as a way to the intelligible beauty. The ideas of Plotinus about the beauty of works of art have received a good deal of attention,[4] and their practical influence on artistic production has, perhaps, sometimes been rather exaggerated (though there is still room here for a

[1] ἄγαλμα ἐναργὲς καὶ καλὸν τῶν νοητῶν θεῶν: II 9 [33] 8, 15–16—an adaptation of *Timaeus* 37C, 6–7.

[2] II 9. 8, 35–6, cf. II 1 [40] 4, 6–13, and cf. below, ch. 16A, p. 257.

[3] *City of God* X 29; XXII 26.

[4] Two good recent books on the subject are *La Signification de l'Art dans les Ennéades de Plotin* by Eugénie de Keyser (Louvain, Publications Universitaires, 1955) and *Il Problema dell'Arte e della Bellezza in Plotino* by Fiammetta Bourbon di Petrella (Florence, Le Monnier, 1956).

good deal of research, and it might be possible to produce more solid evidence than has yet been brought forward for a real influence of the ideas of Plotinus on the minds of European artists at certain periods). It is of course important always to remember that aesthetics in Plotinus cannot and should not be separated from the rest of his philosophy: this is as true of him as of Plato or most other ancient philosophers. He is only interested in the beauty of art, or of nature, as a help in our ascent to the intelligible beauty and beyond it to its source, the Good. The contemplation of the beauty perceived by the senses is for him a good starting-point for that lifting and wakening of the soul and direction of its attention to the higher world with which we are concerned in this chapter. But it is only a starting-point, and in one superb passage he shows himself well aware that the disturbing love of beauty can, at least temporarily, conflict with the deeper and more universal, but less exciting, love of the Good, and draw the mind away from its goal instead of towards it. 'The Good is gentle and kindly and gracious and present to anyone when he wishes. Beauty brings wonder and shock and pleasure mingled with pain, and even draws those who do not know what is happening away from the Good, as the beloved draws a child away from its father: for Beauty is younger. But the Good is older, not in time but in truth, and has the prior power; for it has all power.'[1]

Plotinus does once speak of the inferiority of human skill and its products, 'toys of little worth', in comparison with the activity of divine soul in making the material universe.[2] But this is part of his depreciation of planned, rational (in the ordinary human sense) activity as inferior to the divine creative spontaneity which works without planning or apparatus. Plato's view of the artist as a copyist of sense-objects, at two removes from the truth, has left traces here and there in the *Enneads*, but Plotinus' considered view is that, however inferior the procedures of human art may be to those of divine, its products are, like the products of divine making, images of forms in the intelligible world to which the artist's mind, like all human minds, has direct access. And he will even go so far as to say that, in some cases, art can improve on nature. 'But if anyone despises the arts because they produce their

[1] v 5 [32] 12, 33–9: the whole chapter should be read.
[2] iv 3 [27] 10, 17–19: cf. for depreciation of art *Life*, ch. 1 (the episode of the portrait).

works by imitating nature, we must tell him, first, that natural things are imitations too: and then he must know that the arts do not simply imitate what they see: they go back to the rational formative principles from which nature derives: and also that they do a great deal by themselves: since they possess beauty they make up what is defective in things. Phidias did not make his Zeus from any model perceived by the senses; he understood what Zeus would look like if he wanted to make himself visible to us.'[1]

It is in so far as it reflects the living organic unity and wholeness of the intelligible form that the work of art is beautiful. Plotinus rejects the Stoic view that beauty consists of good proportions combined with appropriate colour[2] as altogether too superficial. Beauty is the domination of matter by form, which shows itself in a sort of organic unity, which a simple thing can have as well as a complex whole of parts.[3] In a complex thing, of course, good proportions are essential to unity. But not only the beauty which form gives to works of nature and art in the world of the senses, but even the beauty of the forms themselves in the intelligible world, would for Plotinus be ineffective and unable to stir the soul to love, and so not really beautiful at all in the (for a Platonist) all-important sense of lovely and lovable, if it was without the life which has its source beyond the world of forms in the Good, the life which is the radiance of the Good giving colour and grace to beauty. It is this which even here below makes beauty which is real, with power to draw and move us. 'So here below too, beauty, that which is really lovely, is what illuminates good proportions rather than the good proportions themselves. For why is there more light of beauty on a living face, and only a trace of it on a dead one, even if its flesh and its proportions are not yet wasted away? And are not statues more beautiful if they are more lifelike, even if others are better proportioned; and is not an ugly living man more beautiful than a beautiful statue?'[4]

The intellectual side of the process of wakening and liberating the self

[1] v 8 [31] 1, 34–40. The 'Phidias commonplace', which implies that at least some art has an origin higher than the sense-world, goes back to the first century B.C. It first appears in Cicero, *Orator* II 8–9, and again in Dio Chrysostom, XII 71 and Philostratus, *Life of Apollonius* VI 19. 2. Its ultimate source is clearly Greek, but there is not sufficient evidence to determine who originated it, or what precisely it originally meant (if it meant anything precisely).

[2] Cf. Cicero, *Tusculans* IV 31.

[3] I 6 [1] 1–2.

[4] VI 7 [38] 22, 24–31.

is of course for Plotinus at least as important as moral discipline and the right appreciation and use of the beauties of nature and art. But Plotinus never goes into any very precise details about it, and has not much that is original to say about philosophical method. In his short treatise *On Dialectic*[1] he is content to summarize Plato's statements about *dialektikê* and to distinguish it sharply from Aristotelian logic, which he dismisses rather hastily as an inferior preparatory discipline which the dialectician has the right to judge and use or ignore as his superior wisdom dictates. Dialectic for him is the way in which the mind lays immediate hold on intelligible truth; its operations are determined by the structure of the intelligible world and it comes into play naturally when the mind reaches the level of Intellect. As for the method to be employed in bringing the mind to that level, he is content to give a summary of the teaching of the *Symposium* and *Republic*, giving a respectful endorsement in passing of Plato's view on the importance of mathematics as a means for training the philosopher, though he does not elsewhere show much interest in the subject. His summary dismissal here of logic does not mean that he was ill informed about it or uninterested in it. He is capable of some penetrating and important criticisms of Aristotelian doctrines[2] when he is arguing for what he considers to be the true Platonic doctrine of the 'categories of the intelligible world', which will be considered in the next chapter.

[1] I 3 [20].
[2] Cf. A. C. Lloyd, 'Neoplatonic Logic and Aristotelian Logic', in *Phronesis*, I, I, pp. 58–72 and 2, pp. 146–60.

CHAPTER 15

THE ONE AND INTELLECT

It is now time to attempt a fairly systematic and detailed description of the universe in which, according to Plotinus, we find ourselves when we are wakened, recalled to our true self, and liberated into a genuine universality of experience by the kind of moral and intellectual self-discipline sketched in the last chapter. The thought of his Middle-Platonist and Neopythagorean predecessors, described in Part I, formed the basis of the metaphysical speculations of Plotinus, but he worked over the pre-existing material available to him with such critical penetration and careful attention to his own mental experience that the resulting system was in many ways original, and far more coherent and attractive than anything to be found in Middle Platonism. This originality is particularly obvious in the account which Plotinus gives of the first principle transcending being from which all reality springs, the One or Good. There had already appeared in his predecessors, in a variety of more or less confused forms, the idea that the supreme principle of reality was beyond all determination or description. But Plotinus was the first to work out a coherent doctrine of the One or Good clearly distinguished from and transcending its first product, the divine Intellect (Νοῦς) which is also real being in the Platonic sense, i.e. the World of Forms.[1] In elaborating this doctrine it seems that, as so often happened, he was helped to clarify his mind by a critical consideration of Peripatetic thought about the simplicity of the divine intellect. This was a point on which the great Aristotelian commentator Alexander of Aphrodisias, whose work Plotinus knew well, had insisted strongly.[2] And Plotinus, in the treatise which contains his final reflections on the Peripatetic doctrine of a simple self-thinking intellect as first principle,[3] is quite prepared to admit that divine intellect is

[1] At this point there seems to be some contact between the thought of Plotinus and the speculations of his older contemporary, the Christian Origen (probably also a pupil of Ammonius), about the relationship of the Father and the Son; see *Contra Celsum* VI 64; cf. VII 38 and *Comm. Joh.* I 39, 291–2: and above, ch. 12, p. 199.

[2] Cf. *Mantissa* 109, 38 – 110, 3 Bruns.

[3] V 3 [49]. Cf. V 6 [24].

simple in a sense which would have satisfied the Peripatetics. Even soul for him is single and simple when compared with the multiplicity of body. But it seemed to him that our thought about intellect, if it was to have any content at all, must be a thought of something thinking about something, and thus involve a certain duality: and that this remained true even of intuitive self-thinking intellect (Νοῦς, that is, in the proper later Platonic and Peripatetic sense) whose object was itself immediately apprehended without any seeking or movement 'outside' itself; even here the duality of subject and object could be detected. And Plotinus' conviction that the first principle must be beyond all determination or limitation, and therefore free from even the minimum duality implied in intellection, which would bring a sort of internal limitation through distinction, made him quite certain that it could not be an intellect, even one of divine simplicity which possesses all being in its single apprehension of itself. He was not only willing, but anxious, to maintain further that this placing of the first principle, the One, so absolutely beyond even the highest conceivable sort of limitation or determination meant that it was not a being; for this he claimed the authority of the famous text about the Idea of the Good in the *Republic* and of a curious Neopythagorean exegesis of the *Parmenides*.[1] A being for Plotinus is always limited by form or essence.[2] An absolutely formless being is impossible, and perfect or absolute being is the unified whole of all forms which is the divine Intellect: therefore that which is beyond the limitation of form is beyond being. This doctrine of the One beyond being again distinguishes Plotinus sharply from those of his immediate predecessors who stood closest to him in some ways, the school of Numenius, for whom the first principle was both supreme intellect and absolute being.[3]

It is this absolute absence of limitation and determination, seen primarily as the absence of duality, making analytic description impossible, which Plotinus intends to convey by his use of the name 'One', which he inherited from his Neopythagorean predecessors. He regards it as inadequate, like all names for the first principle, but preferable to others because it has this power of lifting our minds beyond limitation.

[1] See Part I, ch. 5, pp. 93–4.

[2] V 5 [32] 6.

[3] Numenius, *fr.* 25; 26 Leemans.

But he has another preferred name for it, the Good (which he also admits to be inadequate). This name, consecrated by Plato's use of it, has the purpose of reminding us that the undetermined, unlimited first principle is not a mere negation, but something supremely positive, so positive that it is both the cause of the existence of the whole universe of formed being and the goal to which all things in it aspire. The universe of Plotinus is conceived entirely in the classical Hellenic manner, the manner of Plato and Aristotle, up to the level of divine Intellect, in that, up to that level, the more formed and definite a thing is, the better and the more real it is. The beings of the world of Intellect, the Forms, are definite in character (a Form can hardly be conceived as formless) and finite in number, and they are the best of beings and the only real beings. Beyond Intellect lies the total indetermination of the One or Good, which is the source, as we shall see, of a certain indeterminate vitality underlying the formed and defined world of Intellect itself. But this creative indeterminacy or infinity which produces all the forms and beings which can exist cannot be thought of, and Plotinus certainly does not intend us to think of it, as an unconscious, shapeless nothing-in-particular. Plotinus associates being too closely with form, limit and determination to admit the way of speaking which P. Hadot has traced back to Porphyry, in which the One, the first principle, is pure and absolute being, in which the first existent, Intellect, participates:[1] though no one who seriously reads the *Enneads* can be in any doubt that the Good is for Plotinus the supreme reality. But as regards his other great negation, the denial of intellect or thinking to the first principle, Plotinus does take some precautions to make sure that this is not misunderstood in a way which would really make the One something less than intellect. Sometimes he says that it has a special kind of transcendent thinking of its own, more immediate even than that of Intellect, with no duality of subject and object.[2] Elsewhere he suggests that it may be something like a pure thought without object, superior to

[1] P. Hadot, 'Fragments d'un Commentaire de Porphyre sur le Parménide', *Revue des Études Grecques*, LXXIV, nos. 351–3 (juillet–décembre 1961), pp. 410–38. Porphyry, here, as Hadot points out, stands very close to the position of Numenius. E. R. Dodds suggests tentatively the reading (οἶον) τὸ...αὐτοεῖναι in III 8 [30] 10, 31, but the context seems to me to make it improbable (cf. his 'Notes on Plotinus Ennead III, viii' in *Studi Italiani di Filologia Classica*, XXVII–XXVIII (1956), p. 112).

[2] V 4 [7] 2; cf. VI 8 [39] 16.

the self-thinking of Intellect, a sort of 'Form of thinking' (though he does not use precisely this expression).[1] The whole purpose of the critical purification of our minds by negation which Plotinus requires of us if we are to pass beyond Intellect to the first principle of reality is to reveal to us the eternal source of being, intellect, good and unity as we know them at their highest, which is more than they are because it is their source and free from their limitations. It is an essential part of this process of purification by negation that what is denied of the One should be strongly affirmed, as unchangeably true, of that which immediately proceeds from it, Being or Intellect. It is the shock of this coupled affirmation and negation which drives us beyond the highest intelligible perfection, prevents us from settling down comfortably in the universe in which our perfected minds discover themselves, and pushes us on to an obscure awareness of something greater and better than any possible thought can contain. If all this still seems excessively odd, perhaps we should remember that for Plotinus the critical purification of the mind is inseparably linked with moral and religious purification; you cannot have one without the other. Plotinian purification cannot be effectively thought through (except perhaps in the second-rate and second-hand manner proper to historians of philosophy) without being lived through: though it is also true that, in distinction from other less intellectualist mystics, Plotinus does not believe that you can live through it without thinking through it. His intellectualism can, certainly, easily be exaggerated or misstated. It should be clear from what has already been said that what lies beyond thought cannot be reached in the conclusion of a process of philosophical thinking. The mind has to be purged of its philosophy to find the Good. The supreme achievement of the intellect is to leave itself behind. But for Plotinus there is no way of passing beyond intellect other than through intellect. We cannot leave our philosophical minds behind till we have used them to the full. There is, in his way of thinking, no alternative route to God for non-philosophers.

The way in which the second hypostasis, Intellect, proceeds from the One has often been misunderstood as the result of a too loose and indiscriminate use of the term 'emanation'. Plotinus is certainly fond of

[1] VI 9 [9] 6, 52–5; cf. VI 7 [38] 37.

describing the production of Intellect from the One, or of Soul from Intellect, in terms of the radiation of light from the sun or of heat from fire (he also occasionally uses other metaphors of the same sort, the diffusion of cold from snow or of perfume from something scented): and it seems probable that the origin of this way of speaking is to be found in a late Stoic doctrine of the emanation of the *hêgemonikon*, the ruling intellectual principle in man, conceived in the usual Stoic way as a material *pneuma*, a 'fiery intelligent breath', from the sun, its source, which, as in Plotinus, remains unchanged and undiminished by this giving out.[1] But Plotinus is not content simply to use this traditional analogy and leave it at that—he is always, as was remarked at the end of the second chapter of this Part,[2] an acute critic of his own images. Even when he does use it without explicit correction or supplementation, it would be a radical misunderstanding of his thought to suppose that he intends to say that this 'emanation' is automatic and necessary in a sense which excludes freedom and spontaneity or makes it inferior to a consciously intended creative act. It is certainly true that, whether he is using emanation-imagery or not, he always insists that Intellect proceeds from the One (and Soul from Intellect) without the production in any way affecting the source. There is no deliberate action on the part of the One, and no willing or planning or choice or care for what is produced. We should remember at this point that, as we saw in the last chapter,[3] conscious awareness, in the sense of thinking about what one is doing (and so being in a position to choose between alternative courses of conduct), is for Plotinus characteristic of rather a low level even of human activity. His ideal man always does the right thing immediately and spontaneously, without having to think about it. And when it comes to divine action, Plotinus is more conscious than either Plato or most Jewish and Christian theologians of the disadvantages of analogies drawn from human artists or craftsmen, with the picture which they are liable to convey, unless used with great caution, of a rather limited, anxious and arbitrary deity choosing what to create and making elaborate (and sometimes rather ineffective) plans to ensure that it turns out as he wishes. He prefers to take his analogies for divine

[1] On this cf. my article '"Emanation" in Plotinus' in *Mind*, XLVI, N.S. no. 181, pp. 61–6.
[2] Ch. 13, pp. 220–1. [3] Pp. 226–7.

action even on its lowest level, that of Soul, from the spontaneous, unwilled, unthinking processes of nature (which is for him, as we shall see, divine soul operating at its lowest level). But though this production or giving-out is necessary in the sense that it cannot be conceived as not happening, or as happening otherwise, it is also entirely spontaneous: there is no room for any binding or constraint, internal or external, in the thought of Plotinus about the One. The One is not bound by necessity; it establishes it. Its production is simply the overflow of its superabundant life, the consequence of its unbounded perfection. A perfection which is not creative, which does not produce or give out, is for Plotinus a contradictory and obviously untenable conception.[1]

When Plotinus tries to give a more precise account of how Intellect proceeds from the One than the emanation-images can furnish, he does so in terms which owe a good deal to Aristotelian psychology. He distinguishes two 'moments' in its timeless generation: the first in which an unformed potentiality, an indeterminate vitality, a 'sight not yet seeing', proceeds from the One, and the second in which it turns back upon the One in contemplation and so is informed and filled with content and becomes Intellect and Being.[2] He sometimes speaks of this indeterminate substratum of Intellect in Aristotelian language as 'intelligible matter' (as in the passage just referred to) and sometimes in Platonic and Neopythagorean terms as the 'indefinite dyad'.[3] The forming and giving of a real and definite content to this indeterminate vitality is the result of Intellect's turning back upon the One in contemplation; but this does not mean that Intellect takes the form of the One and simply 'becomes what it thinks' in the Aristotelian manner. It cannot, for the One has no form or forms to give it. It is beyond all form, and Intellect can only reach its unformed and unbounded simplicity by rising above itself, leaving its proper nature behind. What happens, according to Plotinus, in Intellect's normal contemplation of the One is that, though it directs itself towards the absolute unity of its source, it cannot receive it as it is, but 'breaks it up' or 'makes it many', and so, by the power of the One, constitutes itself as a unity-in-multiplicity, the World of Forms which, though it is as unified as any-

[1] Cf. V 1 [10] 6; V 2 [11] 1; V 4 [7] 1. [2] Cf. II 4 [12] 5.
[3] Cf. V 1. 5.

thing except the One can be, is many as well as one, a rich and complex whole of parts.[1]

At this point we must pay some attention to an important feature of the thought of Plotinus which has sometimes been unjustifiably neglected (though it should not be over-emphasized). This is the idea which appears in a few passages, that the original giving-out of the indeterminate vitality, the 'indefinite dyad' which is the basis of Intellect, from the One, and the giving-out of Soul from Intellect which is the next stage in the 'unfolding' of derived being and depends upon the first, are acts of illegitimate self-assertion (τόλμα). All existence, in this way of looking at it, depends on a kind of radical original sin, a wish for separation and independence, of which Plotinus says explicitly in one passage that it would have been better if it had never been.[2] It seems difficult to reconcile this idea with the account given in the passages referred to in the last paragraph of the relationship between Intellect and the One. In the first set of passages we have an unformed desire, the overflow of the spontaneous creativity of the One, which is directed back to its source, and by returning upon it receives its form and content. In the others we have a desire directed away from the One, a desire which produces separation and otherness. Plotinus never explicitly tries to harmonize these two ways of thinking. But perhaps if we look at the probable origin of the idea of *tolma* as accounting for the first separation from the One, we can see a way in which they might be harmonized without being unfaithful to his thought. Plotinus seems to have taken it from the Neopythagoreans, who called the dyad *tolma* 'because it was the first to separate itself from the monad'.[3] Now for both Plotinus[4] and the Neopythagoreans the dyad is, not multiplicity, but the principle which makes multiplicity and number possible.[5] Multiplicity means otherness from the One, and whatever is other than the One must in some sense be multiple. And, as we have seen, the dyad is for Plotinus the indefinite desire which is the basis of Intellect.

[1] Cf. V 3 [49] 11; VI 7 [38] 15. For a possible analogy here with the thought of Philo see my *Architecture of the Intelligible Universe*, pp. 68–71.

[2] III 8 [30] 8, 32–6; cf. VI 9 [9] 5, 29 and for Soul V 1 [10] 1, 3–5; III 7 [45] 11.

[3] According to Anatolius (the Aristotelian professor at Alexandria who became bishop of Laodicea about 268: cf. Eusebius, *HE* VII 32. 6), quoted by Iamblichus in *Theologoumena Arithmeticae* 7, 19 and 9, 6 De Falco.

[4] V 4. 2.

[5] For the history of the indefinite dyad cf. Part I, *passim*.

So perhaps we can distinguish two sides to this original unformed desire. There is the desire for separate existence, the desire to *be* at all: this Plotinus in some moods, when he is concentrating on the transcendent excellence of the One, regards as regrettable because it is a desire for something less than the Good. But the desire to exist must also be a desire directed towards the Good, because it is the return upon the Good in desiring contemplation which makes Intellect exist as what it is, real being possessed of all the goodness and unity which anything that is not the One, which has any multiplicity in it at all, can receive. It is a desire to be as close as possible to the One, as good and unified as possible, while remaining other than it. So it is both a principle of separation and a principle of internal unity, of the maximum reception of the One compatible with separate existence. And if the One is to produce at all (on Plotinus' assumptions) it must produce something which is other than and inferior to itself by being in some sense multiple, that is, Intellect whose base is the 'dyadic' will to otherness, the *tolma* which is cause of its multiplicity. So in a way the One is ultimately responsible for the *tolma*, the will to separateness which is necessary if there is to be anything other than it at all, by the very fact that it produces something other. And it is because this 'dyadic' will to separateness which is principle of multiplicity is there, and must be there if Intellect is to remain distinct from the One, that Intellect, as long as it remains itself, can only receive the One in multiplicity. This, at least, seems a Plotinian way of looking at the problem, though it does not represent anything which is explicitly said in the *Enneads*.

In some Gnostic systems there appears the idea of *tolma*, of an act of illegitimate boldness or rashness which results in the formation of the material world. But the connexion between the *tolma* of the Gnostics and that of Plotinus is not at all close; the differences are so considerable that it is not at all likely that the thought of Plotinus was influenced at this point by Gnosticism. In the system of Valentinus[1] the Pleroma, the total unity-in-diversity of Aeons, spiritual beings produced by successive emanation from the Father, which corresponds very inexactly with the world of Intellect in Plotinus, was fully constituted before there was any question of any sort of *tolma*. Then the youngest Aeon,

[1] Cf. for what follows Irenaeus, *Adv. Haer.* I 2. 2 ff.

Sophia, was filled with a rash passion to attain to the transcendent and incomprehensible Father, and share the direct contemplation of the first Aeon (*Nous* in the Valentinian system), and would have been totally dissolved in the Father if the principle of limit, *Horos*, had not firmly checked her and returned her to her place. From the emotional disturbance produced in her by her abortive attempt the maker of the material world, and the material world itself, eventually resulted. In this story the *tolma* of *Sophia* is almost the exact opposite of the *tolma* of Intellect in Plotinus. It is a desire for that union with the first principle which in the system of Plotinus is the legitimate and necessary aspiration of all derived beings. In the possibly older system of the 'Barbelo-Gnostics'[1] the aberrant Aeon *Sophia-Prounikos* makes a rash excursion into the lower regions (the result of which is, as usual, the maker of this world of ours), because the higher powers have thoughtlessly forgotten to provide it with a consort (all the other Aeons are neatly coupled, as in Valentinianism). This has no real resemblance even to the self-assertion which constitutes Soul as a separate being in Plotinus: and, as we have seen, the *tolma* of Soul depends on the *tolma* of Intellect. And in no Gnostic system is the Pleroma, the higher spiritual world, the result of *tolma*. There is always in the Gnostic systems a break in the middle of the procession of all things from the first principle, a radical disorder and discontinuity between the spiritual world and the ignorant and inferior power which makes the material world. This is something which Plotinus cannot tolerate, any more than he can tolerate the introduction of passions, emotions, changes and adventures into the spiritual world which is again a general characteristic of Gnosticism. His *tolma*, the will to separate existence, does not break the even, inevitable flow, without change or passion, of eternal reality from the One; it is the necessary condition for its taking place. But when we have said this we must admit that there is a vague general resemblance between the outlines of the upper part of the Gnostic spiritual universe and of that of Plotinus. In both we have the absolutely transcendent and unknowable first principle, from whom proceeds the highest reality, which is complete in itself and perfect and

[1] Cf. Irenaeus, I 29.4, and the comparison of this text with that of the 'Apocryphon of John' in F. M. M. Sagnard, *La Gnose Valentinienne et le témoignage de S. Irénée* (Paris, 1947), pp. 444–5.

is a unity-in-diversity. It is when we come down to the level of creative Soul in Plotinus and the fallen or aberrant Aeon and her child the world-maker and ruler in Gnosticism that the divergence becomes too great for any talk of resemblance. It is easy to attribute the resemblances higher up to Platonic and Neopythagorean influences on Gnosticism, which there undoubtedly were. But the thought of Plotinus about both the absolute transcendence of the One and the living unity-in-diversity of Intellect differs very much, especially in tone and emphasis, from that of earlier Platonists and Pythagoreans, and the possibility of some Gnostic influence at these points cannot be absolutely ruled out.

The most strikingly original features of the account which Plotinus gives of his second hypostasis, Intellect, are the stress which he lays on its vitality and activity and the way in which he describes its unity-in-diversity and the relationship in it of parts to whole in terms of the interpenetration of a community of living minds. These two characteristics of Intellect are obviously closely connected in his mind, and nothing like them appears, as far as we know, in the speculations of his Middle-Platonist predecessors for whom the Platonic Forms were 'thoughts of God'.[1] It is in describing them that he uses the largest number of those vivid images drawn from sense-experience which were mentioned at the end of the second chapter of this Part, and his language when speaking of them sometimes rises to an intensity of imaginative power which compels us at least to believe that he is describing some sort of personal experience of intellectual vision. Here, for instance, is a passage[2] in which he speaks of the unity-in-diversity of Intellect:

Everything is clear, altogether and to its inmost part, to everything, for light is transparent to light. Each, There, has everything in itself and sees all things in every other, for all are everywhere and each and every one is all, and the glory is unbounded; for each of them is great, because even the small is great: the sun There is all the stars, and each star is the sun and all the others.

And here is another[3] in which he speaks of the life of the intelligible world in its unity.

...in that world There where there is no poverty or impotence, but everything is filled full of life, boiling with life. Things there flow in a way from a

[1] See Part I, ch. 4 A, pp. 54–5.
[2] V 8 [31] 4, 5–10.
[3] VI 7 [38] 12, 22–30.

single source, not like one particular breath or warmth, but as if there were a single quality containing in itself and preserving all qualities, sweet taste and smell and the quality of wine with all other flavours, visions of colours and all that touch perceives, all too that hearing hears, all tunes and every rhythm.

Plotinus is always concerned to keep being, life and thought very closely linked in his descriptions of Intellect, to show it as a single reality which is at once the only perfectly real being, the fulness of life, and the perfection of intuitive thought which is identical with its object. He makes it clear that there can be no real separation of the three even in those one or two passages of the *Enneads* where he gives a certain priority to being,[1] which may have provided a starting-point for the sharp separation of being, life and intellect as three separate hypostases arranged in descending order which we find in the later Neoplatonists.[2] In view of these passages we cannot assert quite positively that life for Plotinus is more important than the other two aspects of Intellect. But it is certainly true, as we have seen, that Intellect for him originates from the Good as life. Being and thought are the self-determination and self-limitation of this life in its return to the Good, and are always living being and living thought.[3] The World of Forms, the universe of real being, is a kind of spontaneous patterning of the flow of this inexhaustible life out from and back to the Good: and it seems to be this endless vitality which prevents Intellect from ever getting bored or 'fed up' with its eternal contemplation, which makes it eternally fresh, interesting and delightful. Plotinus speaks of Intellect in relation to the Good as 'always desiring and always attaining its desire',[4] and this is surely to be connected with what he says about the immanent contemplation of the World of Forms (which is contemplation of the Good as Intellect can receive it, in multiplicity),

[1] The most important is VI 6 [34] 8; cf. for the relationship of being to thought V 9 [5] 8, where Plotinus is careful to insist that this priority does not mean any sort of separation.

[2] See next Part, pp. 299–300.

[3] See P. Hadot's paper 'Être, Vie, Pensée chez Plotin et avant Plotin', in *Entretiens Hardt*, V, pp. 107–41 (with the discussion pp. 142–57), which is an admirable account of the whole of this aspect of the thought of Plotinus.

[4] ἐφιέμενος ἀεὶ καὶ ἀεὶ τυγχάνων: III 8 [30] 11, 23–4. (Cf. for the development of this idea by Gregory of Nyssa and Maximus Part VI (The Greek Christian Tradition), chs. 29 C, pp. 455–6 and 32 E, pp. 501–2.)

in a passage which brings out well the unity for him of thought and life.

There is a lack of satisfaction There in the sense that fulness does not cause contempt for that which has produced it: for that which sees goes on seeing still more, and, perceiving its own infinity and that of what it sees, follows its own nature. There is no weariness of life There, since it is pure; for how should that which lives the best life grow weary? This life is wisdom, wisdom not acquired by reasonings, but always all present, without any failing which would make it need to be searched for.[1]

It is probably right to see some influence of Stoic dynamic vitalism in Plotinus' insistence on life.[2] But Plotinus himself, of course, thought that here as elsewhere he was expounding the authentic thought of Plato, and he was able to express his doctrine to his own satisfaction in Platonic terms by the remarkable use which he makes of the 'very important kinds' of *Sophist* 254–5 as 'categories of the intelligible world'. These 'primary kinds',[3] Being, Motion, Rest, Sameness and Otherness, are not for him genera or categories in any ordinary sense. They are, rather, different ways of looking at one single reality, and the process by which he discovers them in the intelligible world has been well described by Bréhier,[4] using an expression of Leibniz, as 'a reflective analysis which brings to light different aspects of the same whole'.[5] So, when we concentrate our attention on its reality we see Being in it; when we attend to its life and activity of thought we see Motion; when we turn back to its eternal changelessness we see Rest; when we concentrate on its diversity we see Otherness; when we recognize that in all its diversity it is still a unity we see Sameness. In this way, by an exegesis no more arbitrary than is usual for him, he is able to find support in the text of Plato for a view of the World of Forms as a world of boundless life expressing itself in an intense activity of contemplative thought, very different from the world of statuesque immobility which appears in Plato's descriptions.

[1] v 8 [31] 4, 31–7.

[2] Cf. Hadot, *art. cit.* p. 140: but cf. also P. Henry's introduction to MacKenna's translation of the *Enneads* (3rd ed. Faber, 1962), pp. xlix–l, for the radical differences here between Plotinus and Stoicism, which, as always, he transposes and transforms to suit his own thought.

[3] γένη πρῶτα: vi 2 [43] 9, 1.

[4] *Notice* to vi 1. 2 and 3 [42–4] in his edition, p. 37.

[5] For this 'reflective analysis' see vi 2. 6–8: cf. also v 1 [10] 4.

The difference from Plato becomes still more striking when we turn to consider the relationship of part and whole in the intelligible world. Plotinus carries his insistence on the unity of being, life and thought to the point of making each one of the Forms in that world a living mind.[1] This enables him to find an original solution to the problem of how, in all its diversity, Intellect remains a unity. He does so in terms of Aristotelian psychology; the mind is what it thinks.[2] Therefore, since each part of Intellect or the intelligible world (we must always remember that these are names for two aspects of one entity) is itself an eternally actual and active intellect, it thinks and so is the whole.[3] What makes it this or that particular intellect seems to be that one element in the complex whole 'stands out' in it:[4] this is the idea of 'naming by predominance', which was well established in the Platonic tradition long before Plotinus.[5] This same interpretation of part and whole applies also, as we shall see, on the level of Soul, and is of great importance for human destiny. We can choose whether to stay shut up in our particularism or to think and be the All, and everything depends on this choice.

At this point in Plotinus' thought we are obviously very far indeed from the vitalist corporealism of the Stoics. His real universe of interpenetrating minds is not simply the organic universe of Posidonius transposed to a higher level of being. It is a highly original conception based on ideas derived from Plato and Aristotle. We can see well here one of the most important and interesting characteristics of Plotinus' thought, the way in which he saw more clearly than any of his predecessors that separation and distinctness, as we usually conceive them, are essentially bound up with matter, space and time.[6] Difference of essence in the immaterial world does not exclude, and in fact demands, copresence and interpenetrability of the different entities, so that they can be at once really one and really different.

The rich and complex content of Plotinus' intelligible world includes

[1] VI 7 [38] 9; cf. V 9 [5] 8.

[2] Cf. *De anima* III 4, 429b–430a.

[3] Cf. besides the passages already referred to (V 8. 4 and VI 7. 9) VI 5 [23] 6; 7; 12.

[4] V 8. 4, 10–11 ἐξέχει δ' ἐν ἑκάστῳ ἄλλο, ἐμφαίνει δὲ καὶ πάντα: but in VI 7. 9 he gives a rather different account in which each intellect is the individual 'in act' and the whole 'potentially' which is difficult to reconcile with his general view of Intellect as always wholly and eternally in act: he says in the same passage that the particular thing is where the particular intellect 'stops' in its outgoing, which seems to be an application of the τόλμα idea.

[5] Hadot, *art. cit.* pp. 126 ff. and discussion pp. 143–5.

[6] Cf. e.g. VI 4 [22] 4.

Forms, not only of every possible kind of thing, but of individuals.[1] The question of whether there were Ideas of individuals was already being discussed in the second century A.D., but most Platonists then rejected them.[2] Plotinus is the first Platonist whom we know to have accepted them, and the reasons he gives for doing so show an appreciation of the value of individuality, of the differing beauties of particular things, and especially of human personality, which is not characteristic of the thought of Plato and Aristotle; some Stoic influence is possible here. Plotinus, however, will not allow his acceptance of Forms of individuals to lead him to introduce actual numerical infinity into the intelligible world (as Amelius was prepared to do).[3] He escapes the necessity of doing so by accepting the Stoic doctrine of world-periods, endlessly repeating cycles in each of which the individuals are formally or essentially the same as in all the others. This means that the only infinity he has to assert in the intelligible world is, not numerical infinity of Forms, but an undivided infinity of productive power, and this he is not only willing but anxious to do.[4] The World of Intellect for him is finite, limited and determined in its structure or pattern, but infinite in its life and power.

[1] V 7 [18]; IV 3 [27] 5. Plotinus is not, however, always consistent on this: cf. the rather casual acceptance of the more usual Platonic doctrine in V 9 [5] 12, 3 and VI 2 [43] 22, 11–13.

[2] Cf. Albinus, *Didaskalikos*, ch. 9.

[3] Cf. Syrianus, *In Metaph.* 147, 1 ff.

[4] This is the main question discussed in V 7 [18].

CHAPTER 16

FROM INTELLECT TO MATTER: THE RETURN TO THE ONE

A. *Soul and the material world*

Soul is, of Plotinus' three hypostases, the most wide-ranging and various in its activities. At the top of its range it lives on the highest level, in the world of Intellect, and with Intellect can rise in self-transcendence to union with the One. At the bottom, it is responsible for the formation of bodies in the visible world. But, however widely Soul may range, Plotinus never allows the distinction between it and Intellect to disappear (though it may in some passages become a little blurred), and he preserves its distinctive Platonic function of being the intermediary between the worlds of intellect and sense-perception, the immediate cause of the latter, and the representative in it of the former. Its proper and most characteristic activity is discursive thinking, reasoning from premises to conclusions; but it possesses the whole range of lower forms of consciousness, with the external activities appropriate to them; and it can and should, and, it seems, while it remains universal always does, rise above its reasoning to share Intellect's life of immediate intuitive thought. The initiative in this self-transcendence, as always in Plotinus, comes from above. It is Intellect which, by illuminating Soul, raises it to its own level.[1] The relationship between the three hypostases in Plotinus is one of hierarchical distinction in unity. They are not cut off from each other. The One and Intellect are always present to Soul and acting on it, and this eternal presence and action is the most important thing which we (who are Soul) discover in philosophical reflection.

The way in which Soul proceeds from Intellect and is informed by returning upon it in contemplation is closely parallel to the way in

[1] This doctrine of the illumination of Soul by Intellect is particularly stressed in the late treatise v 3 [49]. But it does not now seem to me to be inconsistent with what is said about the relationship of Soul and Intellect in iv 3 [27] 5 and 12, or with Plotinus' account of his personal experience in iv 8 [6] 1, though the emphases are different in different places.

which Intellect proceeds from the One, though Soul remains closer and more intimately related to Intellect because Intellect has not the unique transcendence and total otherness of the One. And, as in Intellect's proceeding from the One, so in Soul's proceeding from Intellect, there is an element of *tolma*, of illegitimate self-assertion and desire to be independent and live a life of its own.[1] The particular form which the *tolma* of Soul takes is for Plotinus the origin of time. It is a desire for a life different from that of Intellect. The life of Intellect is a life at rest in eternity, a life of thought in eternal, immediate and simultaneous possession of all possible objects. So the only way of being different which is left for Soul is to pass from eternal life to a life in which, instead of all things being present at once, one thing comes after another, and there is a succession, a continuous series, of thoughts and actions. Soul's *tolma* is in fact a sort of restlessness, a desire of movement for movement's sake, a desire not to have all things at once so that it can pass from one to another. This restless life of continuous succession, passing on to one thing after another, is, Plotinus says, time. Time is 'the life of the soul in a movement of passage from one way of living to another'.[2] This is for him the only satisfactory explanation of Plato's description of it as 'a moving image of eternity'.[3] It is the best possible image on its own level, though immeasurably inferior to its original because it is more diffuse and divided, less of a unity. He makes a significant comparison to the growth-principle in a seed which 'unfolding itself, advances, as it thinks, to largeness, but does away with the largeness by division and, instead of keeping its unity in itself, squanders it outside itself and so goes forward to a weaker extension:'[4] from which we can see that Plotinus' scale of values is the exact reverse of that of most modern men conditioned by evolutionary conceptions, who think very much like his seed-*logos*. The material universe comes into being in this soul-time, and all its movements are subject to and dependent on soul-time. A good deal of the treatise *On Time and Eternity*[5] which we have been citing is taken up with acute criticism of the Peripatetic definition of time as the number or measure of motion. According to Plotinus time is not the measure of motion (which is necessarily in time) but we use

[1] V I [10] I, 3–5; III 7 [45] II, 15–20.
[2] III 7. II, 43–5.
[3] *Timaeus* 37D 5.
[4] III 7. II, 23–7.
[5] III 7.

the intervals between the regular recurrences which we observe in the movements of the heavens, sunrise and sunset, etc., to measure the passage of time.

In the continuous movement, without beginning or end, of its life which is time Soul everlastingly forms, orders and governs the material universe, which is itself without beginning or end in time (though spatially finite, as it was for all post-Platonic philosophers except the Epicureans). Plotinus follows older Platonic tradition in calling Intellect 'the true demiurge and maker' of the universe:[1] but it is so only in so far as it provides Soul with the *logoi* which direct its making and produce the embodied forms of the things it makes. Soul is always the immediate maker, operating directly on the material universe with what it receives from Intellect. Plotinus makes much use at this point in his system of the term *logos* in a special sense. A *logos* in this sense (he uses the word, of course, also in the other senses usual in Greek philosophical writing) is an active formative principle (not a static and lifeless pattern) which is the expression or image, on a lower level of being, of a principle which belongs to a higher level. Soul is the *logos* of Intellect and the forms in it are *logoi* of those in the intelligible world. In the late treatises *On Providence*[2] he speaks of the *logos* of the whole universe in a way which has misled some interpreters into seeing it as a distinct hypostasis, a complete departure from the scheme of three, and only three, hypostases on which he insists so strongly elsewhere. But Bréhier[3] is almost certainly right in understanding *logos* here not as a distinct hypostasis but as a way of speaking of the living formative and directive pattern, derived from Intellect through Soul in the usual way, which keeps the material universe in the best possible order and brings it into a unity which, though far inferior, is the best possible image in the sharply divided world of space and time of the unity of Intellect; this it does by bringing the opposing forces whose existence space-time separation makes inevitable into a Heraclitean harmony of contrasts and tensions.

Soul orders and governs the material universe 'not from outside like

[1] V 9 [5] 3, 26; cf. II 3 [52] 18, 15.

[2] III 2 [47] and 3 [48]: as often in Porphyry's edition, these are divisions of a single work of Plotinus.

[3] In his *Notice* to III 2 and 3, vol. III of his edition, pp. 17–23.

a doctor, but from inside like nature'.[1] This does not mean that Soul is immanent in the universe in the sense of being contained or confined by it. Plotinus, when he uses spatial metaphors to describe the relationship of the two, prefers to say that body is in soul rather than soul in body, as in his great image of body floating in soul like a net in the sea.[2] It means that Soul does not work on the universe from outside, making plans to deal with it on the basis of an external knowledge of it. There is no thinking things out or planning, no willing or choosing this or that, in its government of the world.[3] The universal order springs from Soul spontaneously, as a tree grows. The laws of nature are not laid down in advance and then applied, but are the immediate undesigned result of Soul's contemplation of the higher order of Intellect, of which they are a reflection (somewhat distorted by the reflecting medium) rather than a laboriously painted picture. At this point in the system the principle, which applies throughout, that all action is dependent on contemplation becomes particularly important.[4] Soul springs from Intellect as the spontaneous result of Intellect's contemplation of the One, and its own production of and action upon body is the spontaneous result of its return in contemplation to Intellect. (There is the same tension at this point in Plotinus' thought between the contemplation-production idea and the *tolma*-idea which we have already discussed when considering the production of Intellect from the One.) This applies at all levels, even the lowest, of Soul's action as a universal principle in the world of body, space and time. It applies too to human action when man is living at his highest level; his right action springs spontaneously from his higher self's unbroken contemplation. On lower levels, human action still derives from and is directed to contemplation; but, when men's contemplative powers are too weak for them to arrive directly at the vision which they desire, they try to satisfy themselves by action, doing and making things which are images of the object they seek, the good which

[1] A summary of IV 4 [28] 11, 1–7.

[2] IV 3 [27] 9, 36–42.

[3] This is very different from Plato's way of thinking about the divine formation and government of the universe. The change seems to be due very largely to the influence of Aristotle: see J. Pépin, *Théologie cosmique et théologie chrétienne* (Paris, Presses Universitaires de France, 1964), pp. 502–4.

[4] For this see particularly the treatise *On Contemplation* III 8 [30], though the doctrine is often alluded to elsewhere in the *Enneads*.

they wish to have in their soul, and may eventually lead them back to it by a roundabout route.[1]

Below the higher soul, which is in direct touch with Intellect and is the intermediary between the intelligible and material worlds, lies its image or impression[2] or *logos*, the immanent principle of form, life and growth which Plotinus calls 'Nature'. He does not think of this as a distinct hypostasis but rather as universal Soul operating on its lowest level, on which it is entirely concerned with body. His concept of *logos* enables him to bring all the varied activities traditionally attributed to Soul into a unity by representing it as a single living and formative force which operates on different levels and in different ways by producing progressively dimmer images or reflections of itself charged with a diminishing amount of its power. But in fact the relationship of Nature to higher Soul is described in terms not very different from those in which Plotinus describes the relationship of Soul to Intellect (though there is no question of *tolma* at this level). As Soul returns upon Intellect in contemplation, and consequently produces, so Nature returns in contemplation upon higher Soul. But at this lowest level its contemplation is the weakest of all possible contemplations, unconscious and dreamlike,[3] and the production which is its spontaneous and inevitable result is the production of the last and lowest things which have in them any shadow of reality, the forms in body. These are dead, that is, incapable of producing further forms, because of the weakness of the contemplation which produces them. They stand at the end of the process of going out from the One, at the third remove from their ultimate archetypes in Intellect, being *logoi* of the *logoi* in Nature itself which are *logoi* of those in Soul. They make up the ghost-world (for so Plotinus sees the material universe in comparison with the intelligible) in which Nature operates as the principle of unity and wholeness which prevents this world from falling apart into the anarchy of complete separation because it is itself a single life, the last manifestation of universal soul which cannot, like individual souls, fall into space-time separateness. It is thus both separate from body and bound to body because wholly concerned with it. The material world is its reason for existing. It is the part of Soul which has the function of giving life and

[1] III 8. 4, 31–47 and 6, 1–10. [2] IV 4 [28] 13. [3] III 8. 4.

reality to body by making it determinate. But it does not form a single reality with body but retains the essential separateness of all Platonic soul.

At the highest level, where Soul is assimilated to Intellect, the relationship of parts to whole in it is the same as that which we have already seen to exist between part and whole in the intelligible world.[1] Individual souls retain their individuality at this highest level.[2] But they are one with universal soul and themselves universal in that they are not confined by any spatial barriers or limits and the whole is present in every part.[3] Even at this level, however, the unity of parts and whole is less perfect than that of the Forms in Intellect: and because it is the nature of Soul also to operate on the lower levels of the world of space and time, some individual souls at any rate have a tendency to a greater degree of separation and isolation. This tendency leads them to embodiment and the bringing into being of that lower self (a *logos* of their true selves) which we have already discussed.[4] Plotinus firmly resolves the contradiction which appears in Plato's thought between the ideas of embodiment as a fall of the soul and as a good and necessary fulfilment of its function to care for body, by maintaining that it is both. It is in accordance with the universal order, which requires that everything down to the lowest level should be ensouled, that souls descend, and appropriate bodies and lower selves are prepared for them. But they want to descend, and are capable of descending, only because they have already a weakness, a tendency to the lower, which seems to be a development of the original *tolma* which carried Soul outside Intellect.[5] They descend necessarily and in accordance with universal law because they are the sort of beings which want to descend, and this wanting is already a falling away from the highest. But the descent, as we have seen, is never complete. The higher self always remains above, and we can when we are in the body choose whether to live on its level and expand to its universality or to sink ourselves as far as we can into the isolated separateness of the material world, where things are external to and cut off from each other (and consequently clash and hurt each other),

[1] Ch. 15, p. 248.
[2] IV 3 [27] 5.
[3] IV 3 [27] 8; V I [10] 2; VI 4 [22] 14.
[4] Ch. 14, pp. 224–6.
[5] IV 8 [6] 5; IV 3 [27] 12–18 (the fullest discussion of the problem).

and busy ourselves with the petty concerns of our particular body.[1] The sin of the soul which is too much bound to and concerned with body is for Plotinus self-isolation and blind narrow egoism rather than self-pollution. It is this sin which is automatically atoned for in the next world and in this by the punishments in Hades and reincarnations in human or animal form which Plotinus accepts from Plato and understands quite literally: they are the working out of universal law which takes each soul at the end of one life on earth to the place for which it is then best fitted (though the higher self remains throughout unchanged and unaffected).

At the very end of the descent from the One lies the utter negativity and darkness of matter,[2] the absolute limit, one might say, for Plotinus in both the metaphysical and the colloquial sense. Plotinus is not a metaphysical dualist. Matter is produced by the principles which come before it, and so, ultimately, by the One.[3] The eternal creative process must necessarily, he thinks, bring into being everything which can have any kind of existence, however shadowy. The Good can only stop communicating itself when it reaches the level where there cannot be even a ghost of goodness. The descending stages of this process are marked by progressive degrees of otherness from the One and Good, that is, by a steadily increasing lack of unity and goodness and so of reality. And the descent can only have a stop when it reaches its logical end at the point of absolute otherness from the Good, where there can be no longer any unity, goodness or reality at all, at the baffling quasi-existence of matter, in which the last and lowest forms, the forms of bodies, are present like reflections in an invisible and formless mirror, as Plotinus puts it in a passage which brings out to the full the strangeness of his conception.[4] These forms of bodies do not, as in Aristotle, unite with matter to form a single reality. Matter in the sense-world for Plotinus is not a potentiality which can be actualized. It is the passive receptacle of forms, a sort of medium in which they are present which remains totally unchanged and unaffected by them. It can never be

[1] Cf. VI 4 [22] 14–16.

[2] ὕλη. In 'Plotinus on Matter and Evil' (*Phronesis*, VI 2 [1961], pp. 154–66), J. M. Rist has convincingly refuted H. C. Puech's suggestion that Plotinus tended to abandon his view of matter as evil after his break with the Gnostics, and shown the general consistency of his doctrine. I accept his interpretation of a number of passages, notably IV 8. 6.

[3] I 8 [51] 7; II 3 [52] 17; III 4 [15] 1.

[4] III 6 [26] 13.

given any positive quality or brought any nearer to reality and goodness, but remains always total negativity and otherness, absolute privation.[1] This is the great difference between the matter of the sense-world and the matter of the intelligible world, which is a real potentiality eternally actualized and informed. Because of this utter negativity, this total lack of reality and goodness, the matter of the sense-world is for Plotinus absolute evil, and, paradoxically in view of his insistence on its absolute powerlessness and inability to affect or be affected by form, the principle of evil.[2] This absolute negation, this dark void, seems to be able somehow to infect the things which enter it with its darkness and emptiness, to impart a defect to them which makes them less real and good than they ought to be. Another minor paradox in Plotinus' account of the matter of the sense-world is that its evil effects stop at the moon. Plotinus rejects Aristotle's doctrine of the 'quintessence'[3] and holds the Platonist view that the heavenly bodies are made of fire, though fire of a much better quality than that in the sublunary world.[4] (Their light for him is not a bodily thing, but their incorporeal activity, a doctrine which had great influence on medieval thought.)[5] But he insists that there is no evil in their bodies, which are perfectly conformed to and mastered by soul although they are material.[6]

To end this section, we should consider very briefly Plotinus' account of how souls know this material world into which they descend. Our higher knowledge, the knowledge of the Forms in Intellect, owes nothing to the body or its senses: it comes to soul directly 'from within', by virtue of its contact and kinship with Intellect. The most the senses can do here is to provide us with remote images of intelligible reality which may help us to recollect ourselves and turn our attention 'inwards' and 'upwards' towards it. But our knowledge of the intelligible world does not derive in any way from our sense-perception of its images. And it is this higher knowledge which provides our discursive reason with the principles which it should use in making judgements on our sense-experience and regulating our life in the body. But

[1] Plotinus rejects Aristotle's distinction between ὕλη and στέρησις. Matter for him *is* privation (II 4 [12] 14–16).

[2] For this see particularly the two treatises, one early and one late, which deal particularly with matter, II 4 [12] and I 8 [51], though the doctrine occurs throughout the *Enneads*.

[3] II I [40] 2.

[4] II I. 4–5.

[5] II I. 7; IV 5 [29] 6–7.

[6] II I. 4–5; II 9 [33] 8.

of course Plotinus admits that we are not only aware of our own bodies and what happens to them, their states and modifications, but also receive information, reliable as far as it goes, through our sense-organs about the material world outside our bodies. In all his discussions of our bodily experiences in his great work *On the Problems of the Soul* and elsewhere,[1] there are two points which he is particularly concerned to make clear. One is that sense-perceptions, feelings and physical desires are not purely corporeal, not simply material impressions on or modifications of a body, but result from the conjunction of body and soul. A body which was not ensouled could have no perceptions, feelings of pleasure or pain, or desires. The other is that soul, even in its lowest phase, is never passive to or affected by body; there is no real interaction between them, still less do they combine to form a single reality which perceives, feels and desires as a unified whole: the living thing, the composite of soul and body, is for Plotinus, so to speak, a structure built in layers, separate but in contact. He distinguishes clearly in his account of both sense-perception and feeling between the physical event, the impression on the sense-organ or the change in the body, the awareness of this by the perceptive power of the soul,[2] and the formation of a mental image by the image-making faculty,[3] which can keep its images and is so the seat of memory. The transition from lower to higher Soul takes place at the image level (each has a separate imaging faculty and so a separate memory):[4] and the power of making judgements and decisions on the information received belongs to the higher soul (i.e. our reasoning part). This can be distracted or bemused by the confusion of images presented to it from below: but it always retains its independent power of selection, judgement and decision according to the principles which it receives from Intellect, with which at the highest level it is always in contact.

B. *The return: the religion of Plotinus*

We have already[5] considered how the soul re-establishes itself on its own highest level in the world of Intellect. It remains to say something about how it rises from this to the union with the One which is the goal

[1] Cf. especially IV 3 [27] 22–32; IV 4 [28] 17–25; IV 6 [41]; III 6 [26] 1–5.

[2] αἴσθησις.

[3] φαντασία (the Aristotelian term).

[4] IV 3 [27] 31.

[5] Ch. 14.

of all Plotinus' philosophical effort. Discussion of this has been deferred to this point because what Plotinus has to say about the final union cannot be understood at all without some knowledge of what he means by the One and how all things derive from and depend upon it. We are bound to misunderstand his mysticism if we know nothing of his metaphysics. But before we go on to this, it will be as well to recapitulate the earlier stages briefly, and look at them from a rather different point of view. The philosophy of Plotinus is also a religion; and it will help our understanding of it if we try to see how it differs from other kinds of religion with which we may be more familiar.

We have seen how the soul reaches its proper level in Intellect by a vigorous combination of intellectual and moral effort and training, helped at least in the earlier stages by the contemplation of visible beauty (this perhaps can never be altogether dispensed with in this life, for our recollection of intelligible beauty is always needing to be quickened again). We have observed that it is a mistake to ignore the moral component in this training and effort. We certainly pass beyond virtue in our ascent. The Good is above virtue, as he is above everything: and on the level of Intellect the virtues exist archetypally but there is no virtuous action because there is no action at all. The life and activity of the intelligible world is all contemplation. But, for Plotinus, to pass beyond virtue does not mean any repudiation of virtue or any denial of the continued obligation of virtuous conduct on the level on which it is possible. Plotinus is no antinomian Gnostic. There is no break in his system between the higher world of spiritual liberty and the lower world of moral law. The perfectly good and wise man, the sage, only passes beyond virtue to reach the source of virtue, the Good who makes good actions good. And, just because he has reached the Good, his actions on the lower level where virtue and vice are possible, on which his soul must continue to operate as long as it is in this world, must be morally better, not worse, than before.

The mystical religion, then, of Plotinus does not differ from other religions in any absence of moral seriousness. The ethical demands which it makes are exceedingly high. Its most striking differences lie in the absence of any recommendations of any practices of the sort which we commonly regard as religious. There is no place in it for rites or sacraments: nor are there any methods of prayer or meditation or devices for concentrating and liberating the mind such as are used by both theistic (Christian and Moslem) and non-theistic (Vedāntin and Buddhist) mystics. The probable reasons for these differences are worth investigating. There can be no place, or at least no important place,[1] for rites or sacraments in the religion of Plotinus, first because of his beliefs about the nature of man. Man is for him, as we have seen,[2] not an integrated unity of body and soul as in the Judaeo-Christian tradition, but a being whose true self exists on a purely intellectual or spiritual level; only a *logos* of it descends into this lower world of body, and body and lower self can contribute nothing to the spiritual life of the higher self. The Good cannot act on our true self through our body: this would be for Plotinus a complete inversion of the real order of things. Another reason is that there is no room in the system of Plotinus for any special saving action of God which might require a special rite or the symbolic communication of a special revelation to bring it to bear on our souls. In giving us being the Good gives us all we need for our salvation in his eternal, inevitable outpouring,[3] because he gives us a dynamic being directed back to him.

The other great difference, the absence of any methods of prayer or techniques of meditation,[4] can be accounted for quite simply by the fact that, for Plotinus, the whole of Platonic philosophy as he understood it is a method of prayer in the large traditional sense of 'lifting up the heart and mind to God'. Philosophical discussion and reflection are not, for Plotinus, simply means for solving intellectual problems (though they are, and must be, that). They are also 'charms' (ἐπῳδαί) for the deliverance of the soul.[5] By continual repetition and reflective elucidation of the great truths of philosophy we bring our soul not just to see things as they really are, but to live in contemplation on the highest level of reality from which, and only from which, it can be raised to union.

Plotinus says comparatively little about this final union. He insists that only those who have shared his experience of it can really under-

[1] As we have seen in discussing the story of the 'answer to Amelius' (ch. 12, p. 204), Plotinus probably did not positively object to a philosopher using external religious observances if he found that they helped him.

[2] Ch. 14, pp. 224–6.

[3] Cf. ch. 15, pp. 239–41.

[4] Plotinus discusses prayer in the *Enneads* as a magical activity, cf. IV 4 [28] 26 and 40–2: but cf. also V 1 [10] 6, 9–11.

[5] V 3 [49] 17.

stand what it is, and when he speaks of it he does so with reserve and in highly figurative and symbolic language.[1] No summary can give any adequate idea of the quality and force of these passages in the *Enneads*, but there are one or two points in what he says which it will be helpful to our understanding of his mystical experience to discuss. The mystical union is, as we have seen, the climax of a long process of self-preparation, which Plotinus describes as an ascent which is also a turning inwards to the ultimate depth of the self, and as a stripping, purification and unification.[2] But the final contact or vision (Plotinus uses both ways of speaking) is not something which we can attain when we choose by our own effort. We have to wait for the One to 'appear', to make us aware of his eternal presence to our souls.[3] It would be going too far to see in this anything like the Christian doctrine of grace, in which union with God is only possible by his free gift of himself. But it does seem to indicate that the One is not simply identical with our true self, so that the mystical experience would simply be the end of the process of rediscovery of what we really are, nor yet a mere passive object of our search, lying at our disposal for us to find when we are ready and able to do so. We can reach the same conclusions by a different route if we examine what Plotinus has to say about the part played by love (ἔρως) in the mystical union. Plotinus only once calls the One himself *erôs*,[4] in a passage which needs to be used with some caution, since he has shortly before warned his readers that, for the sake of persuading the opponents with whom he is arguing, he is using language loosely and incorrectly, in that he is applying terms to the One which can be taken to imply some sort of duality.[5] It should certainly not be taken to imply that the One has any sort of love or care for what proceeds from him, which Plotinus explicitly denies.[6] But it none the less remains true that *erôs* is not for Plotinus a wildly unsuitable and totally misleading name for the

[1] Some of the most important passages in which he speaks of the mystical union are I 6 [1] 9; V 3 [49] 17; VI 7 [38] 34–6; VI 8 [39] 15; VI 9 [9] 11; cf. also V 5 [32] 12 for the perpetual, normally unobserved, presence of the Good to the soul on which the possibility of the mystical union is founded.

[2] The figurative language which Plotinus uses has been brilliantly analysed by Paul Henry in his introduction to the third edition of MacKenna's translation of the *Enneads* (London, 1962), section VII, *Structure and Vocabulary of the Mystical Experience*, pp. lxiv–lxx, where the resemblances and differences between Plotinus and Christian mystics are illuminatingly discussed.

[3] V 3 [49] 17, 28–32; V 5 [32] 8.

[4] VI 8. 15, 1.

[5] VI 8. 13, 1–5.

[6] V 5. 12, 41–9.

One (as Intellect would be). The One is the cause and giver of the love by which we love him,[1] a love which, as in Plato's *Symposium*, does not disappear when it attains its object but persists in the final union.[2] We can only be united with him because we are perfectly conformed to him and made like him; and we are made like him precisely as loving. The mystical union with the One is union in a love which he originates in us and by which we are brought to resemble him as closely as possible. This central importance of *erôs* becomes particularly clear in the passage where Plotinus most completely integrates his mysticism with his metaphysics.[3] Here he says

Intellect has one power for thinking, by which it looks at its own contents, and one by which it sees that which is above it by a kind of intuitive reception, by which it first simply saw and afterwards, as it saw, acquired intellect and is one. The first is the contemplation of Intellect in its right mind, the second is Intellect in love. When it goes out of its mind, being drunk with the nectar, it falls in love and is simplified into a happy fulness; and drunkenness like this is better for it than sobriety. But is its vision partial, now of one thing and now of another? No; the course of the exposition presents these states as [successive] happenings, but Intellect always has thought and always has this state which is not thought but looking at him in a different way. In seeing him it possesses the things which it produces and is conscious at the same time of their production and their presence within it. Seeing them is what is called thinking, but it sees him at the same time by the power which makes it able to think.[4]

Plotinus goes on to make it clear that the individual soul attains to the mystical union by sharing in the 'drunken' state, the loving self-transcendence of Intellect (in which, as always, the initiative comes from the One). It is, he says, 'carried out by the very surge of the wave of Intellect and lifted high by its swell, and suddenly sees without knowing how'.[5]

Intellect, then, is eternally and unchangingly in two simultaneous states, one 'sober' and one 'drunk', one knowing and one loving. It eternally pursues its proper activity of knowing while it is eternally raised above itself in the union of love. And its power of love seems to be identical with that unbounded life as which it first came forth from

[1] VI 7. 22 and 31.
[2] I 6. 7, 14–19; cf. III 5 [50] 4, 23–5.
[3] VI 7. 35.
[4] Lines 19–33.
[5] Ch. 36, 17–19.

the One.[1] The soul of the individual mystic in its ascent to the mystical union is raised first to one and then to the other of these states. Its contact, vision or union in love with the One is identical with Intellect's contact, vision or union. Now it should be clear, even without this passage, to any reader of the *Enneads* that Intellect never discovers itself to be an illusion or loses its identity in the One, which remains eternally other than it and all things. There is no room in the thought of Plotinus for the idea that all things other than the One are an illusion, or for any change or disappearance of any of the levels of being below the One. And this passage alone should make it clear that he was not content to keep his mysticism and his metaphysics in separate compartments, but found, and wished to show, that his mystical experience was in accordance with philosophy. We seem bound, therefore, to draw the conclusion that the mysticism of Plotinus is not 'monistic' but 'theistic', using these rather vague terms in the reasonably precise sense given them by R. C. Zaehner in his classification of different types of mysticism.[2] It is, that is to say, a mysticism in which the soul seeks to attain a union with the Absolute of which the best earthly analogy is the union of lovers, not a mysticism in which the soul seeks to realize itself as the Absolute. This is a conclusion of some importance for historians of religion. It means that, however great the differences may be between Plotinus and later theistic mystics who show signs of his influence (and there are great differences, mainly due to the absence from the thought of Plotinus of the idea that God loves men, and of any conception of sin, grace and redemption in the Christian sense), we cannot assume *a priori* that any Christian or Moslem mystic whose thought and language are directly or indirectly influenced by Plotinus is either grossly misrepresenting and distorting Plotinian mysticism or being faithless to his own religious tradition.

[1] Ch. 15, pp. 241 and 246.

[2] See his *Mysticism Sacred and Profane* (Oxford, 1957), especially chs. VIII and IX, 'Monism *versus* Theism' and 'Theism *versus* Monism'.

Connecting Note

PLOTINUS, AMELIUS AND PORPHYRY

In order to complete our account of the thought of Plotinus and his circle, and to provide a connecting link to the next Part, in which the later Neoplatonists are treated, it will be worth while here to discuss what little we know about the thought of Amelius, the senior member of the school and Plotinus' close friend and associate in teaching, and also to say a little about the relationship of Porphyry's thought to that of his master. Porphyry, whose importance for the later development of Neoplatonism was, as far as we can tell, much greater than that of Amelius, is dealt with at length in the next Part. But it is interesting to compare his way of understanding, or misunderstanding, the teaching of his master with that of Amelius, and by doing so we may be able to see some possibilities in the thought of Plotinus of development in different directions which it has not been possible to bring out clearly in the inevitably summary and dogmatic account of it given in this Part.

Amelius Gentilianus, from Etruria, appears in the *Life of Plotinus* as a pious, long-winded and rather pompous person. But Porphyry tells us nothing about any distinctive philosophical views which he held, and the disjointed information about him which we find in later sources gives a curiously incoherent picture. The points on which he is said to have differed from Plotinus are three. He held that all soul was numerically one but was temporarily pluralized by its 'states' or 'relations' and 'arrangements'.[1] This may possibly have been due to the influence of Numenius, whose works he copied out and learnt by heart.[2] It has points of contact with the monistic development of one side of the thought of Plotinus by Porphyry which is fully discussed in the next Part.[3] But Amelius seems to show none of that sense of the permanent reality and value of the individual which we have seen in Plotinus himself,[4] and which was one of the forces which held him back from

[1] σχέσεσι καὶ καταтάξεσιν: Iamblichus, *On the Soul*, in Stobaeus, *Ecl.* I 41. 38 (376 Wachsmuth); cf. Proclus, *In Tim.* II 213, 9–214, 4; A.-J. Festugière, *La Révélation d'Hermès Trismégiste*, III, Appendice I.

[2] *Life*, ch. 3, 44–6. For the view of Numenius that the soul after death was united indistinguishably with its principles cf. Iamblichus in Stobaeus, *Ecl.* I 41. 67 (458 Wachsmuth).

[3] Part IV, ch. 18 B, pp. 287–93.

[4] Above, ch. 15, pp. 248–9.

ever becoming a consistent monist. It is therefore surprising to find him and his school maintaining not only, like Plotinus, that there were Forms of individuals, but that there was an infinite number of them which could not be reproduced in the finite cosmos, even in infinite time.[1] This belief in an infinite number of Forms seems oddly inconsistent with belief in the numerical unity of soul. It is just possible that if we had the text of Amelius we should find that his real thought was something like that of the medieval scholastics, St Bonaventure and St Thomas, according to which, though there is an infinite number of Ideas, they are all one thing, the single and simple divine essence; their multiplicity is a relative multiplicity with respect to the *ideata*, the infinite variety of things which are or could be created in their likeness. This would be consistent with the way in which Amelius thought of the one soul as pluralized by its 'relations' and 'arrangements', that is, presumably, by the multiplicity of functions which it performs in relation to the various bodies which it animates and orders on the different levels of the cosmos.[2] But this is pure speculation, going far beyond the available evidence, and inspired by nothing more than a feeling that this lumbering devout philosopher of whom Plotinus thought so highly cannot really have been as muddle-headed as the evidence makes him appear.

The third point on which Amelius differed from Plotinus is not inconsistent with the first two, though it is not closely connected with them. This is his splitting of Intellect into three, that which is, that which has, and that which sees.[3] Here we find Amelius taking the opposite direction to Porphyry's monistic interpretation of Plotinus, with its 'telescoping' of the hypostases, and thinking in a way which points forward to Iamblichus and post-Iamblichean Neoplatonism.[4] It is interesting to find that something like this tripartition was actually discussed in the school of Plotinus, and that Plotinus himself was apparently at one time prepared to entertain it as a possibility, though

[1] Syrianus, *In Metaph.* 147, 1 ff. For the doctrine of Plotinus, who held that the number of individual Forms was finite, see above, ch. 15, p. 249.

[2] The account (referred to above) which Proclus gives of the way in which Amelius interpreted the composition of the World-Soul in the *Timaeus* suggests a view something like this.

[3] τὸν ὄντα, τὸν ἔχοντα, τὸν ὁρῶντα: Proclus, *In Tim.* I 306, 2–3.

[4] Theodore of Asine was directly influenced by this tripartition of Amelius according to Proclus, *In Tim.* I 309, 14–15.

he later very firmly rejected it, when it was put forward, not by the good Amelius, but by the hated Gnostics.[1] In the odd little collection of notes on various questions which Porphyry assembled to make up the number of treatises for his third Ennead,[2] the first and longest is concerned with the exegesis of the *Timaeus*, the question at issue being that so much discussed by the Platonists of the precise relationship of the Demiurge to the Forms (this is also the context in which the views of Amelius as reported by Proclus appear). Here Plotinus discusses the possibility of a bipartition or tripartition of Intellect, and finds no objection to a view very like the distinction of Amelius between the 'possessing' and the 'seeing' intellect,[3] the same which he decisively rejects in the treatise *Against the Gnostics*. It would be dangerous to base too much on an isolated note of this kind: and Plotinus cannot be said to have committed himself decisively in it to a dividing up of Intellect. All that we can safely say is that he did not come to his considered opinion, that the complex unity of Intellect and World of Forms must be maintained at all costs, without some discussion and consideration of alternative possibilities. The doctrine of Intellect is, as we have seen,[4] one of the most distinctive and original features of the philosophy of Plotinus, and it was obviously important to him to maintain the unity of this reality which was at once world and mind, in which being, thought and life were one. But there were obviously different ways of dealing with the traditional data which he, Amelius and the later Neoplatonists accepted, and all his efforts could not succeed in closing, even for his close friend and associate, the way which led on to the complicated intellectual hierarchy of Proclus.

Porphyry, as far as we can tell, remained closer to the thought of his master and was more consistent than Amelius. In so far as he differed from Plotinus it was, as A. C. Lloyd shows in the next Part, by virtually abandoning the real distinction between Intellect and Soul, on which Plotinus sometimes insists very strongly; though, as Lloyd says, there are other passages where he talks in a way which suggests that there is little if any real difference between them. Plotinus does, however, always seem to have considered it important, from some points of view

[1] See II 9 [33] 1, 25 ff.

[2] III 9 [13].

[3] III 9. 1, 15 ff.

[4] Above, ch. 15, pp. 245–8.

at least, to assert a certain transcendence of Intellect over Soul: and in his last and fullest treatment of the relationship between the two, in his treatise *On the Knowing Hypostases*,[1] he is concerned to stress and sharpen this transcendence rather than to abolish it; so that it seems unlikely that he would have approved of Porphyry's tendency to monism here. If Porphyry was really, as Hadot thinks, the author of the fragments of a commentary on the *Parmenides* discussed below,[2] then he carried his monistic tendency a good deal further, and departed more radically from the thought of Plotinus than what we have of the works which are certainly his would suggest. To blur the distinction between Intellect and the One, to reduce the sharpness of the transition from determinate being to the undetermined beyond being, is a more radical revision of Plotinus than to abolish the frontier between Intellect and Soul. The three hypostases in Plotinus are not, so to speak, evenly spaced. The distance and difference between the One and Intellect is normally far greater than that between Intellect and Soul. Yet there are places in the *Enneads* where the One and Intellect are drawn closer together (notably in the treatise *On the reason why Being is everywhere all present, one and the same*).[3] And we cannot say that the line of thought followed by the commentator (whether Porphyry or a near-contemporary) has no starting-point in the thought of Plotinus, any more than we can deny the Plotinian origins of Porphyry's way of thinking about Intellect and Soul. It obviously mattered very much to Plotinus that there were three hypostases, neither more nor less. But he does not seem to have been able to pass on his conviction of the importance of this even to his closest associates.

If we can draw any sort of general conclusion from this survey of the differences between Amelius and Porphyry and their master, it is perhaps that the doctrine of Intellect was both the weak point and the growing point of Plotinian Neoplatonism; and this seems to be confirmed by what happened in the next few centuries. The account which Plotinus gave of the complex reality which he situated between the transcendent source of being and the region of Soul which encompasses all the modes and levels of our normal living and thinking, in

[1] v 3 [49] 2–10.
[2] Part iv, ch. 18 b, pp. 291–2.
[3] vi 4 and 5 [22 and 23].

spite of the intellectual and imaginative power of his descriptions of it, was not acceptable as it stood to any of his successors. But it influenced the thought of all of them in many and various ways, and a good deal of the rest of this History is concerned with the different adaptations and developments of it, or of parts of it, which were made by thinkers of differing philosophical outlooks and religious traditions. Not only the intellectual hierarchies of the later Neoplatonists but, for instance, the Trinitarian theology of Marius Victorinus and the ideas of the Greek Christian theologians about the divine powers and energies and the angelic world, though in some ways they have moved very far from Plotinus, still show the influence of this majestic centre-piece of his speculation.

PART IV

THE LATER NEOPLATONISTS

BY A. C. LLOYD

ABBREVIATIONS

PORPHYRY

De abst.	*De abstinentia*
In Cat.	*In Categorias* (see *Commentaria in Aristotelem graeca*)
Sent.	*Sententiae ad intelligibilia ducentes*

PROCLUS

El. theol.	*Elements of theology*
In Alcib.	*Commentary on the First Alcibiades of Plato*
In Parm.	*Commentarius in Parmenidem*
In Remp.	*In Platonis Rempublicam commentarii*
In Tim.	*In Platonis Timaeum commentarii*

DAMASCIUS

Dub.	*Dubitationes et solutiones de primis principiis*
Vit. Is.	*Vita Isidori*

CHAPTER 17

INTRODUCTION TO LATER NEOPLATONISM

The philosophers who are the subject of this Part make a sufficiently identifiable group. On the scale of this history all are adherents of Plotinus' version of Platonism although in some cases this may have to be argued and certainly the system was developed in directions which would not all have been approved by Plotinus. The survey runs from Porphyry, who was born in about the year when Plotinus started studying at Alexandria, to the last professors in Alexandria and Greece who were not concerned primarily to apply philosophy to Christian theology—that is from the middle of the third century A.D. to about the end of the sixth.

It is as well to have signposts even if they turn out, as signposts sometimes do, to need a little correcting. A century and a half from Plotinus' death (270) to the middle of Constantine's reign will be dominated by the figures of Porphyry and the Syrian Iamblichus (died 326). Pupils of Iamblichus continued to teach in Syria; but there is almost no trace of their contribution to philosophy; they probably made none. We therefore move to Athens where his influence was also very strong. The School at Athens had a continuous history from Plato, but we know nothing of its philosophy for some time before the great century of Athenian Neoplatonism. This begins with a man called Plutarch towards the end of the fourth century but consists substantially of the trio Syrianus, Proclus and Damascius; in fact their teaching seems sufficiently static for it to be examined only as it appears in Proclus, at least four of whose major works have survived. It ceased when Justinian closed the School in 529; but it made an unexpected reappearance, for the philosophy behind the Aristotelian commentaries of Simplicius in the 530's is that of Proclus.

Porphyry, Iamblichus, the Athenians throughout the fifth century—the fourth stage is the Platonic School at Alexandria. It is cloaked in obscurity from the time Plotinus was there till about 400; and its heyday coincides with that of Athenian Neoplatonism, though in fact it carried on, increasingly eclipsed by Byzantine theology. The man who dominates it is Ammonius the son of Hermias, whose lectures on Plato and Aristotle are virtually repeated by two more generations of professors.

Schools of philosophy in the sense of characteristic points of view will not appear quite so neatly distinguished and distributed as is customary in a textbook. The approach which has seemed better (but is perhaps the same method with less pretensions to science), is at each stage to select innovations on two principles: to select what is likely either to be of philosophical interest in some currently accepted sense of philosophy or to make characteristic features of Neoplatonism philosophically more intelligible. Porphyry will be seen to point to the monistic tendency in Plotinus. Iamblichus will have seemed—as he seemed to Praechter in an article which has been something of a turning-point in Neoplatonic history—to be the second founder, the Chrysippus of the school:[1] but while Praechter was emphasizing (and surely exaggerating) his contributions to method, it will be Iamblichus' building of the logical structure of Neoplatonic metaphysics in its final Greek form that will be noticed here. Everyone agrees in finding this final form in Proclus. The Alexandrians seem tacitly to have accepted it, though this is not the view of Praechter who, as we shall see, believed in an Alexandrian Platonism that went back to a simpler system of the Middle Academy. Their importance, however, is in the exposition of Aristotle.

Of the surviving Neoplatonic literature far the greatest part is commentary. Except for Proclus' *Timaeus*, which is indispensable to the historian, the most important are the commentaries on Aristotle to be found in the Berlin *Commentaria in Aristotelem graeca*.[2] But the lists of known works by our authors, which are best found in Zeller or (under their authors) in the *Real-Eycyclopädie*, show what an overwhelming proportion of the literature is lost. And one possible question can only be given a disappointing answer: there is no work of our period which

[1] K. Praechter, 'Richtungen und Schulen im Neuplatonismus', *Genethliakon C. Robert* (Berlin, 1910).

[2] References will be by page and line number to this edition (*C.A.G.*).

could be recommended with any confidence as an introduction to Neoplatonism.

Throughout the period Neoplatonism presents a number of constant features. Some of them reflect pressure from the outside as much as any internal development of Plato's or Plotinus' doctrines. The political setting is always the Roman Empire, whether the capital is in Rome or Byzantium. Even the barbarian invaders were at pains to reproduce the imperial and municipal forms of government; and so far from obliterating academic life they often encouraged it. Not that the Neoplatonists show that awareness of being citizens of a state which is familiar in earlier philosophy from the Sophists to Aristotle. The social or political virtues are low in the official Neoplatonic scale. Porphyry follows Plotinus in a positive quietism; he cites as an ideal the famous description in Plato's *Theaetetus* of the unworldly nature of philosophers.[1] Neither he nor his successors had anything substantial to say that we know of on the political writings of Plato or of Aristotle; and we have to wait for the Arabs for a revival of political philosophy.[2]

True, it is possible to see their metaphysics, the hierarchies of strata which they find in reality and the intermediate levels which they interpose, as an ideology of the imperial chain of command. (Leibniz's monadology has been similarly related to the seventeenth-century princes and the balance of power.) That was not the origin of the system: but there are signs that its continuance and even lack of radical development owed something to its mirroring a political structure which its proponents only theoretically despised—the literal squalor of much of the life under it was outside their field of vision.

However, it is the place of the Platonic philosophy (as of course it was called) as an institution whose influence is more direct. During most of our period there were chairs of philosophy at Athens, Alexandria and Constantinople, and the last two were filled and paid for by the municipalities with occasional intervention by the emperor. At least at Athens and Constantinople there seem often to have been two chairs, one for a Platonist and one for an Aristotelian. But how regularly one does not know; and it seems clear that some of the subject-matter of

[1] Plato, *Theaet.* 173C–174A; Porphyry, *De abst.* I 36. In the later Empire professors were often employed in diplomacy. [2] [On this see Part VIII (Early Islamic Philosophy), ch. 40 C, pp. 657–61.]

Neoplatonic philosophy is dictated by the need to provide a teaching curriculum which would not so much rival the Aristotelian as take its absent place. Because it was normally accepted that the disagreement between Aristotle and Plato was unreal or only verbal, the lectures of Aristotle himself could be read and accompanied by suitable exegesis. Their systematic character gives them obvious advantages over Plato's Dialogues when philosophy is a 'subject' in which students take notes.

This supposed agreement of the two authorities must not be played down. It had been commonplace for a long time; and Porphyry was only one among several to write a book to demonstrate it. Broadly speaking, Aristotle's denial of an existence apart from matter to motion, numbers, qualities and so on is believed to apply only to a level of reality below that of the 'intelligible' world. A very simple division of the branches of philosophy follows: one goes to Plato for metaphysics or 'first philosophy', to Aristotle for the remaining and subordinate branches. But clearly this is too simple in practice, for among other Dialogues the *Republic* and *Timaeus* contribute to psychology and ethics and the *Timaeus* to physics. This was recognized in the Schools; and we find Iamblichus concerned to classify the Platonic Dialogues and deduce the correct order of reading them. Book Λ too was regarded not unnaturally as correcting false impressions which might be gained from other books of Aristotle's *Metaphysics*. It is perhaps surprising that the work which has been so popular in modern times, the *Nicomachean Ethics*, was largely ignored. The position of physics is rather peculiar. The importance of the *Timaeus* had a long history behind it; at the same time it represents the subject in which the Neoplatonists borrowed possibly the most from Stoicism; and again Aristotle's *Physics* was to hand and welcomed because it was systematic. For the most part Aristotle's system seems to have been accepted without serious demur—the fact that the exceptional criticisms are what interest a modern scientific reader must not obscure the fact that they are exceptional. But adjustments were made to both sides in attempts to bring, for example, Aristotelian matter into line with Plato's Receptacle. In questionable but unquestioned juxtaposition with all this, one is liable to find a vague theory of sympathies and antipathies which owes as much to occult or Hermetic beliefs as to Stoicism. Unlike Aristotelianism,

Neoplatonism encourages of itself a contempt for the empirical study of nature; and while this may be divorced from the philosophy of nature, one would not expect to find Neoplatonists at their best or their most interesting in this philosophy. With few exceptions they are not.

The renewed impact of Aristotle on Platonic philosophy after Plotinus is in psychology and logic if only because these were studied in Aristotle and early in the curriculum. In formal logic Neoplatonists neither desired nor achieved any originality although they often achieved a clarity of exposition. But Aristotle's logic had never been purely formal; and they came to grips with the problems of classifying terms and the ways in which one can be predicated of another and of deciding what divisions and relationships these implied among real things. These are difficulties which were bound, as their author had intended, to present themselves acutely to any Platonist who read the *Categories* and *Topics*; and the Neoplatonist commentators found more, which they retorted on Aristotle.

The chief characteristics which distinguish Neoplatonism from other schools of philosophy are already apparent, and most would say more attractively apparent, in Plotinus; the additions and qualifications which his successors made can be studied when we deal with these writers individually and in order. But, for the theory of the active and passive intellect in Aristotle's psychology and the theory of logic, they went, as it were, behind Plotinus and were drawing much more on second-century material. The first theory, which is not integrally Neoplatonic, cannot be considered here. The logical theory is best treated continuously, not writer by writer. It is essential to a philosophical understanding of the Neoplatonic metaphysical system. As with Spinoza—or with Bishop Berkeley—so with Plato or Plotinus it is possible to find oneself deeply sympathetic or antipathetic to the system: but unless the pattern of relations between the concepts used has been discovered and found logically coherent or incoherent it is not philosophy which is sought but edification; and the fact ought to be considered whenever the dryness and scholasticism of a Proclus is contrasted with the richness or profundity of Plotinus. Aristotle's logic, that is to say the content of the *Organon*, determined the structure of relations which made up the structure of the Aristotelian metaphysical system;

and it is this logic which Porphyry and his successors tried to interpret in such a way that it would determine the structure of their system.

Neoplatonism grew up not only as an academic institution of the Empire but as a spiritual movement in an age of religions. This is a development which had begun long before Plotinus, and the character of it is sufficiently familiar. Theology had always belonged to Greek philosophy, both nominally and in fact. What is new is the attitude of academic philosophers to religion. From having viewed religion with varying degrees of respect as morally valuable, Platonists came to accept it as aspiring to the same end as philosophy. To describe the change in anthropological terms—it was no longer merely the myth which was regarded as philosophically relevant but the ritual. What matters here is the effect which this new attitude has on the philosophy itself.

The religious practices which interested the philosophers can all be brought under their own term, 'theurgy'. They were intended finally to make men gods; and the modern attempt to distinguish theurgy objectively from magic is not very satisfactory.[1] For the philosophers this final achievement appears sometimes as the mystical union with the One and always as release from the bonds of fate. The theurgic practices to which the Neoplatonists, under the influence of Iamblichus, were particularly attached were the so-called Chaldaean rites. Indeed the name 'theurgist' (according to a suggestion of Bidez) had been invented to fit a certain Julianus who in the reign of Marcus Aurelius had written down a large number of hexameter verses purporting to be a divinely inspired account of the Chaldaean system—gods, archangels, angels, daemons and many other powers together with their manifestations in the visible world—and known as the Chaldaean Oracles. If so, the appellation was intended 'to go one better than the "theologian" and remind people that the theurgist does not limit himself to talking about the gods but knows how to act'.[2]

The environment in which Neoplatonists of the fourth century grew

[1] For the etymology of the term see H. Lewy, *Chaldaean Oracles and Theurgy* (Cairo, 1956), pp. 461–6; ἱερατική, the 'hieratic art', is a synonym. For practices see Porphyry, *Ad Anebonem*, ed. A. R. Sodano (Naples, 1958); E. R. Dodds, 'Theurgy and its Relation to Neoplatonism', *J. Roman Stud.* XXXVII (1947), pp. 55–69; reprinted as Appendix II of *The Greeks and the Irrational* (Berkeley, Cal. and Cambridge, 1951), pp. 283–311.

[2] J. Bidez, *La vie de l'Empereur Julien* (Paris, 1930), p. 369 n. 8.

up, and to which indeed they contributed, is illustrated by the dramatic career of Sosipatra, who became the wife of a distinguished rhetorician-philosopher in the Neoplatonizing circles associated with the Emperor Julian's apostasy. Her history is told in Eunapius' *Lives of the Sophists* (pp. 466–70). At the age of five this lady was entrusted by her parents to two old men who came to work on the estate near Ephesus and astounded its owner by the size of the vintage they extracted from it. When later they brought the girl back, she had the clairvoyance of one in contact with the gods, and they confessed that they were initiates of the so-called Chaldaean wisdom and then left with her the robes in which she had herself been initiated as well as certain books which she was to keep sealed in her chest. In fact they were daemons (or at least heroes) in disguise, for they told her that they were on their way to the Western Ocean but that they would come back. Just before she married Eustathius she informed him in public that he would die before her and go to a suitable resting-place but one inferior to hers: 'Your orbit will be that of the moon, and you will serve as a philosopher only five years more—so your phantom tells me—but you will have a prosperous and smooth passage through the sublunar sphere. I meant to tell you my fate...' Here she broke off, only to exclaim, 'But my god prevents me!'

After her bereavement (five years later) she retired to Pergamum, where her skill as a philosopher and expositor made her house as popular with students as the lecture room of Iamblichus' most respected pupil, Aedesius. One of her lectures—the casual information is interesting—was on the descent of the soul and the question what part of it is subject to punishment and what part is immortal. Unfortunately a relative of hers called Philometor admired her person as well as her eloquence—and Sosipatra was disgusted to find that she was equally in love with him. Another pupil of Aedesius was sent for and told that if he was a godfearing man he must do something about it. The magical means by which Philometor had cast his spell were discovered through theurgic science, and defeated by more powerful magic, and Sosipatra was cured. The name of Aedesius' pupil was Maximus, from whom Julian learnt theurgy. And we may perhaps explain this digression by adding that he wrote a commentary on Aristotle's *Categories*.[1]

[1] Simplicius, *In Cat.* I 13–15 Kalbfleisch (*C.A.G.* VIII).

Various religious or magical practices of the 'Chaldaeans' were firmly believed in by distinguished philosophers at least until the sixth century. But there were controversies about their relation to the dialectical ascent of reason, which of course the Platonic tradition claimed as the way to salvation and apotheosis, and about the comparative merit of the two ways. Porphyry and Plotinus, a later writer pointed out, put philosophy first, Iamblichus, Syrianus and Proclus theurgy.[1] Some of the Alexandrians probably did not believe in theurgy at all. It is these controversies, together with the rationalizations which accompanied them, that make the whole business impinge on the history of philosophy. It is pointless for the historian to call these beliefs and rituals superstitions. In such a context superstition usually means other people's religion. Julianus had credited himself—as men of the age would readily have credited him—with supernatural powers: but we do not know what circumstances he claimed for the inspiration of his Oracles. It is likely that, so far from being a modern discovery, his authorship or publication of them was quite well known to one of their most passionate admirers, Proclus.[2] Their content, the Chaldaean theology, is best left until we consider Iamblichus. As for the interpreting and eliciting of meanings from sacred writings, there is nothing to choose between, say, Egyptians, Christians and Neoplatonists. It was of course an old practice which had been put to wider uses than theology by Stoics and Pythagoreans. Indeed Porphyry could reprove the ingratitude of an Origen who, a Christian in his life but a thorough Greek in his theology (he says), had learnt from the Stoics how to interpret the Jewish scriptures figuratively.[3] The degree to which the philosophers wanted to treat theurgy as symbol or in other ways rationalize it varied from one to another. There were certainly two religious practices which official Christianity came to defend with commonplaces of Neoplatonic teaching: prayer (justified by Pseudo-Dionysius) and the cult of images (justified against the Iconoclasts by John Damascene).[4]

It is well known that the hostility of Neoplatonists to Christianity

[1] Olympiodorus, *In Phaed.* 123, 3–5 Norvin.

[2] See L. G. Westerink, *Mnemosyne*, ser. 3, x (1942), pp. 276–8.

[3] Eusebius, *Hist. eccl.* vi 19. 7–8.

[4] [See Part vi (The Greek Christian Tradition), ch. 30, pp. 457–72 (Pseudo-Dionysius), and ch. 33, pp. 506–17 (The Philosophy of Icons).]

was partly political. Their policy after the conversion of Constantine of restoring traditional cults—not always the Hellenic cults—was clearly connected with the belief, which was quite normal in an educated pagan Greek, that different pantheons and different sacred writings were just so many ways of naming the rulers of the cosmos and of describing man's relation to them. But there was nothing to prevent them, as there was to prevent Christians, from believing that religious dogma duly interpreted and philosophical reasoning coincided. Syrianus and his successors at Athens were not so much making gods out of abstractions as turning traditional gods into abstractions. Nor in theory did they confuse the two sources of truth. We shall see Iamblichus drawing attention to the distinction when he reads Porphyry. In any case, since Plato had appealed to tradition and invented myths of his own, not only philosophers but professors of literature were accustomed to dividing and subdividing 'mythological' and 'dialectical' demonstration.

Many of the features which we have been considering could be described by a quality often attributed to the philosophy of the later Roman and Byzantine empires. It is scholastic. This is no accident, for it has more historical continuity with medieval philosophy than with that of classical Greece. Like the Schoolmen, the Neoplatonists have their authorities. These are Plato and Aristotle[1] and, from a different point of view, the inspired writings, chiefly the Chaldaean Oracles and Orphic hymns, both of which are freely quoted as 'the gods' as well as 'the theologians' or 'the theurgists'. Incidentally, although not one of them could have written as he did without Plotinus his successors take remarkably little notice of him. The Neoplatonists can be said, too, to write often in the interests of a theology, even though in theory there is no part of this theological philosophy which they would not have expected to defend on philosophical grounds. It is the grounds, not the motives, with which we shall be concerned.

It is because they possess authorities that their method, too, is scholastic. The natural way, though it is not their only way, of expounding their philosophy is by commentary on a text. This makes naturally for hair-splitting, for jargon, for repetition and restraint on

[1] [On the attitude of Plotinus to Plato and Aristotle see the preceding Part (III, Plotinus), chs. 12 and 13, pp. 206 and 212–14.]

imaginativeness. But much of that is compensated for by the equally scholastic habit of expecting conclusions to be argued, if possible demonstrated deductively, but at least in such a manner that the train of thought is explicit or readily made so.

Lastly, like any Aristotelian system theirs is built on technical concepts, most of which are of course familiar from Plotinus. It is a necessary truth that technical terms must be at least partially explicable in everyday terms. But unlike Plato the later Neoplatonists do much too little of this kind of explaining. How far it can be done is something which can legitimately be asked when we have looked at what they have to say. Certainly the modern reader finds himself, as it were, thrown into mid stream. But the Neoplatonists were aware of this danger. They would have retorted that in their curriculum the beginner learnt to swim when he read Aristotle—not to mention ethics, whose syllabus we know little about. In fact Porphyry's *Isagoge* and his elementary commentary on the *Categories* are admirable introductions to the concepts of Aristotelian logic. Why then, when we come to commentaries on the works which first bring us into contact with specifically Neoplatonic philosophy, the *De anima* and the *Metaphysics* (let alone the Platonic Dialogues, which were read later), do we find that the specifically Neoplatonic concepts are so largely taken for granted? The short answer to this paradox is that they did not think their hypostases and processions and living thoughts anything like so foreign to Aristotle and therefore so unclear as we do. More particularly it may be suggested that what they took for granted was a Neoplatonizing interpretation of Aristotelian doctrine about intellect. This had certainly been made before Plotinus, and possibly by the most respected Peripatetic commentator, Alexander of Aphrodisias, a fact which would explain a good deal of the Neoplatonists' complacency. It can be seen in the little tract *De intellectu* which has come down under Alexander's name.

There is always an internal development of philosophical ideas which depends only very indirectly on external conditions, and which is the chief business of the history of philosophy. In this, too, certain constant features appear after the death of Plotinus. The most noticeable is the tendency to multiply the links in the chain of being by the insertion of further hypostases between Plotinus' three and by division of hypostases into further triads. It is justified always in the same way that is familiar from Plato's use of 'intermediates': reality is continuous, 'nature makes no leaps'. These philosophers, it has often been said, were at pains to keep God and man as far apart as possible: but they often stress the opposite, and there is no paradox in this, for to double the rungs of a ladder is from one point of view to increase the separation of the highest rung from the lowest but it also makes it easier to reach one from the other. Similarly, the reason why there are daemons and heroes between gods and disembodied souls is not merely to ensure the harmony of the universe but to make theurgy and contact between gods and men possible.[1] The grounds given for distinctions which are of greater philosophical interest must be examined in their place. For although they often occur as inferences from Plato's text, it was thought that, as Proclus said when he interposed Eternity between the One and Intellect, 'the things *are* distinct in this way' and were mistakenly 'confounded' by Plotinus.[2] On the other hand the doubling of every essence into one participated in and one imparticipable—a doctrine universally accepted from Iamblichus onwards—is not only required by Neoplatonic logic but can be found implied in the *Enneads*.

[1] Iamblichus, *De myst.* I 5 and 8. Julian says that being a mean (μεσότης) can be defined 'not as being equidistant from opposite extremes...but as the kind of thing Empedocles called harmony' (*Or.* IV 138D).

[2] *In Tim.* III 12, 8–11 Diehl.

CHAPTER 18

PORPHYRY AND IAMBLICHUS

A. *Porphyry's philosophical career*

Most of the features of Neoplatonism that we have been sketching are evident in the work of Porphyry. So it will avoid repetition to give him more attention than might otherwise have seemed due to him. Porphyry was born in about 232, the year when Plotinus started to study philosophy at Alexandria. His parents were well-to-do Syrians, and he spent most of his boyhood, so far as we know, in the busy Phoenician city of Tyre. Even if he did not travel he had ample opportunity there to make the far from superficial acquaintance with the mystery cults and magical practices of the Middle East and beyond which his writings were to show.[1] He probably knew several languages by the time he came to the West; he continued to read widely; and it was not a conventional compliment that Simplicius paid when he called him the most learned of philosophers. Three later stages of his career have left their mark on his philosophy, his attendance at Longinus' lectures, his friendship with Plotinus and a period away from Plotinus in Sicily.

Like other young foreigners of means but a little older than most, it would seem, Porphyry continued his education at Athens. Here the dominant influence was that of Longinus (who died in 272). The old-fashioned taste of the famous critic no doubt had some part in the clarity of Porphyry's style which was soon contrasted with Plotinus' indirectness.[2] But this 'living library and walking museum', as Eunapius called him, lectured on philosophy too;[3] and we have the testimony of both to their friendship.[4] It is fairly clear that Porphyry accepted his version of Platonism before being persuaded from it by Plotinus. Longinus had learnt this from his contact with Ammonius Saccas and the pagan Origen at Alexandria. He wanted to make the Ideas thoughts, but thoughts which were really distinct though not separable from the

[1] For the long list of his writings see J. Bidez, *Vie de Porphyre* (Ghent–Leipzig, 1913); R. Beutler, *RE*, XXII/1 (1953), col. 278–301.

[2] Eunapius, *Vit. soph.* 456 *ad fin.*

[3] *Ibid.*

[4] See Porphyry, *Life of Plotinus* 19 and 20.

mind or, as one may say, from acts of thinking. This at once brought him into disagreement with Plotinus, for whom the acts and objects of thought were identical. In fact his position was intermediate between Plotinus and the extreme realism which seems to be maintained in Plato's Dialogues and which makes the Ideas independent of mind or God's mind. He tried to explain it by pointing to the analogous status of propositions and terms—the immaterial meanings or significata of expressions and sentences—in Stoic theory.[1] Both facts are characteristic of Middle Platonism, represented for instance by Albinus. It would not be surprising if he had also refused to accept the decisively Neoplatonic doctrine of a One above Mind; Origen had not accepted it.[2]

When he went to Rome in 263 Porphyry defended the independence of the mind's objects against a fellow pupil and Plotinus himself, but gave way.[3] During six years' stay he profited also from private and sometimes prolonged discussions with Plotinus. Then came an attack of such acute depression that he was thinking of suicide. Plotinus sensibly persuaded him to travel, and he settled for several years in Sicily. He was there when Plotinus died in 270, and it is likely that he returned to take over the School at Rome only several years afterwards. He was an old man when he married a widow called Marcella. (A journey abroad meant a temporary parting from her and so occasioned the rather stylized, indeterminately Neoplatonizing *consolatio* addressed to her.)[4] It is to these later years, too, that the edition of Plotinus' works and his biography belong.[5] Otherwise we know nothing about this time. His death must be placed somewhere between 301 and 306.

The Sicilian period is more interesting to us for Porphyry's own philosophy. During this period he worked on those problems of Aristotelian logic which have already been mentioned (but will be dealt with separately) and wrote at least one book specifically comparing Platonism and Aristotelianism.[6] The work which brought him fame and odium beyond the Schools, the lengthy polemic *Against the*

[1] Syrianus, *In Met.* 105, 25–6 Kroll (*C.A.G.* VI 1).

[2] *Fr.* 7 Weber (Proclus, *Theol. plat.* 90, 1–14 Portus).

[3] *Life of Plotinus* 18. Cf. Plot. V 5 [30], *That the intelligibles are not outside the intellect* (*mind*).

[4] *Ad Marcellam*, ed. A. Nauck in *Porphyrii philosophi platonici opuscula selecta* (Leipzig [Teubner], 1886).

[5] [On these see the preceding Part (III, Plotinus), chs. 12 and 13, pp. 195 and 216–18.]

[6] Elias, *In Isag.* p. 39, 4–19 Busse (*C.A.G.* XVIII 1). Nothing of it has survived.

Christians, was also composed in Sicily;[1] but this does not seem to have been particularly philosophical. His attitude to pagan religion and theurgy was very different. But the common assumption that one can find in it a progress from superstitious acceptance (before he met Plotinus) to philosophical rationalization is apt to beg the question of chronology and certainly underestimates the degree to which Porphyry withheld commitment in it as a philosopher.[2] He denied that the practice of theurgic rites could achieve complete salvation;[3] but he was able to justify theosophy as an allegorical version of the philosophical truth. An Epicurean had accused Plato of abandoning demonstrable truth for falsehood in the guise of poetic myth. Porphyry's reply was to quote 'Nature loves to hide herself' and so claim that in a way myth is natural. Indeed, he added, it is suitable for all human beings because they must think in images.[4] But the more one reads him and compares him with his successors the more one gains the impression of a man who is interested in religion rather than religious. And this probably explains much of Iamblichus' irritation with him.

Plato made Timaeus begin his cosmogony by invoking the gods. This provided every commentator with a conventional occasion for his set piece on the subject of prayer. Porphyry in his logical and scholarly way divided people into classes according to their acceptance or non-acceptance of prayer, which in turn furnished the principle for dividing beliefs about the gods. He pointed out that a good man ought to pray to the gods because his prayer would be a contact of like with like, and went on to show that the wisest men of all races have prayed, Brahmans, Magi and the rest.[5] Iamblichus found this commonplace—as it was. He complained that Porphyry's commentary was off the point: the passage in Plato had not been concerned with atheists, 'nor with people who hold conflicting beliefs about the works of piety, but with people who possess the power of being saved by the saviours of all

[1] Eusebius, *Hist. eccl.* IV 19. 2.

[2] Cf. *Letter to Anebo*, *ap.* Iamblichus, *De myst.* III 18; 145, 4–7 Parthey, and IX 8; 282, 6 ff. (16–17 and 28, 1–8 Sodano); *Ad Gaur.* VI 1; Iamblichus, *ibid.* 90, 7–8; 147, 15–16; 150, 3 Parthey. Eusebius, *Praep. ev.* IV 7. 2 (I 77 Mras), from the proem to the *Philosophy from Oracles* (pp. 109–10 Wolff), suggests that what has survived of this work is misleading.

[3] Augustine, *De civ. dei* X 29 and 27.

[4] Proclus, *In Remp.* II 105, 23–5; 107, 5–7 and 14–23.

[5] Proclus, *In Tim.* I 207, 23–209, 1 Diehl. [For the views of Plotinus on prayer see Part III, ch. 16 B, p. 260.]

things'; and he went on to speak of the power and 'surpassing hope' of prayer before explaining the, so to say, metaphysical machinery of it.[1] The difference speaks for itself.

Except for exposition of Aristotle's logic, only one work of Porphyry's written in academic style for an academic or student audience has survived. This is the *Sententiae ad intelligibilia ducentes*; even this is incomplete, and we do not know how incomplete.[2] It is composed very largely of paraphrases of the *Enneads* arranged in paragraphs or 'propositions' whose exact order may here and there be doubted. In fact it is a textbook of Plotinian Neoplatonism, although the belief that it provides an easy introduction to the *Enneads* is unlikely to survive the experiment. One may infer from Porphyry's own account that he did not regard his own philosophy as differing much from Plotinus'. The inference is confirmed by what we know of his lost works from later writers. From these scraps of information and from the *Sententiae* it is possible to see his contribution to the theory of the three hypostases as twofold. In the first place he established it, that is, established it against the conservative Platonism of the Middle Academy which he had learnt from Longinus. But secondly this was not a matter of mere repetition or even perhaps of emphasis but of interpretation: he selected and expounded one version of the theory where others were possible, and the fact that this may well be thought to have been Plotinus' intended version must not allow us to forget that it was only one of the possibilities.

The first task consisted in demonstrating two decisively Neoplatonic theses, the independence and priority of the One and the identity of Intellect (or Mind: νοῦς) and its objects. In fact he made a weaker version of the latter, the *inseparability* of intellect and its objects, part of an argument for the priority of the One, or unity. Unity is logically prior to plurality, and Intellect forms a plurality because its thoughts are many and these are within it. That intellect is introspective in this way is shown by contrasting it with the faculties of sensation and imagination (including memory) whose being or substance is 'in something else' and therefore destroys itself by 'reverting to itself' in the hope of knowing itself. We can make good sense of Porphyry's point when we

[1] Proclus, *In Tim.* I 209, 1 ff.

[2] Ἀφορμαὶ πρὸς τὰ νοητά, ed. B. Mommert (Leipzig [Teubner], 1907).

see it as the claim that these faculties are neither viable nor comprehensible without their bodily concomitants. But his contrasting of intellect is a *petitio*. To give a meaning, too, to thoughts which are '*in*' the intellect but not identical with it is probably impossible, since it would have to be more than the 'inseparability' which we found in Origen's and perhaps Longinus' view; for that would not, it would seem, entail that intellect itself possessed the plurality possessed by its thoughts, any more than extension itself possesses colour. But very likely Porphyry himself thought that the distinction could not be made, for he went on to argue that, because the object of intellect's thinking is itself, intellect will be both thinking and thought of, so that the object of thought is identical with the thinking; it cannot be one part of intellect, i.e. thought, which is thinking of another part, since there can be nothing unthinking in thought. This last piece of Platonism (of the 'beauty is beautiful' kind) comes from the *Parmenides*;[1] but the whole argument is taking for granted *Metaphysics* Λ, ch. 9, in which Aristotle argued that intellect would have to think of its own thinking if it was to be an actuality, not a potentiality. This characteristic combination of Plato and Aristotle was already to be found in the *Enneads*, but only more succinctly or by allusion.[2] Although in the text as we have it Porphyry's exposition is not altogether successful, he has consciously tried to sustain a full-length demonstration of the two theses which divided his earlier Platonism from that of Plotinus.[3]

B. *The monistic tendency of Porphyry*

He gave much thought to the relations between the three hypostases, and it is here that we find his second contribution, the distinctive version of the theory that he chose. Plotinus was dogmatic that there were neither more nor less than three hypostases above matter (whose reality was illusory); and this dogmatism has little meaning unless those hypostases are stages of existence which exist in their own right even though they are not, except for the highest, independent; they must not be mere appearances of the One. But the opposite is also suggested, for he seems often to care little whether it is Intellect or Soul which he is

[1] 132 C 9–11.
[2] V 9 [5] 5; cf. V I [10] 4, 15–16; 3 [49] 13, 14–16; II 9 [33] I.
[3] *Sententiae*, nos. XLI, XLIII, XLIV Mommert.

talking about. This, as it were, telescoping of the hypostases is prominent in Porphyry. Of course the whole theory of emanation can be described as an effort to combine both points of view: but Porphyry emphasized the monistic tendency because he was prepared to pay the price, a certain belief in the reality of the individual person, which Plotinus, possibly preferring the price of consistency, was not.

Iamblichus mentions that Plotinus, Amelius and Porphyry all distinguished only doubtfully or vaguely between Intellect and Soul.[1] They agreed in denying that the soul 'in itself', or essentially, was divided into parts.[2] But Porphyry went quite beyond Plotinus as well as Plato in preventing any real distinction between the two by claiming that soul could not be affected by anything.[3] Quite consistently he recognized only one kind of soul, the rational, which was possessed by men and brutes alike.[4] 'Everywhere and nowhere' is the formula which he constantly applied to each of the hypostases;[5] and certainly we find it in Plotinus expressing the monistic tendency of his system. Similarly the assumption that intellect is the real self had been commonplace for centuries. (It is the combination of these two doctrines which enables him to infer somewhat glibly that while he has departed on a journey his 'intelligible' self is still with his wife.[6]) But it is surprising, however logical, for anyone to take the further step of regarding the embodiment of soul as an illusion of thought.

In the *Sententiae* Porphyry seems to have used a characteristically Plotinian device in turning the subject of the dispersal of one universal soul in many particular or embodied souls into the subject of *our* personally 'reverting' to the All by our abandoning in thought whatever is logically particular. He is in fact quoting extensively from the rhetorical close of *Ennead* VI 5 [23] ('That reality is everywhere'). But either because he is following a different version from the one we possess

[1] *Ap.* Stob. I 365, 14–19 Wachsmuth.

[2] Porphyry *ap.* Stob. *loc. cit.* p. 354. [On Soul in Plotinus see Part III, ch. 14, pp. 224–6 (higher and lower self) and ch. 16 A, pp. 250–1 (Intellect and Soul) and pp. 255–6 (Universal Soul and individual souls).]

[3] Nemesius, *De nat. hom.* 140, 4 Matthaei (Migne, *PG* 40. 604 A). Contrast *Enneads* I 8 [51] 4, 4; III 1 [3] 10, 6; IV 4 [28] 17, 10; following Plat. *Phaedo* 65 A; *Phaedr.* 256 B.

[4] Nemesius, *op. cit.* 117, 4 (584 A Migne). In *De abst.* III 1 Porphyry calls it Pythagorean doctrine.

[5] *Sent.* no. XXXI Mommert; cf. Nemesius, 136, 3 ff. (597 B ff. Migne).

[6] *Ad Marcellam* 280, 22 Nauck.

or because he has deliberately altered it Porphyry has inserted a sentence of great philosophical significance. Once the undiminishable and inexhaustible nature of reality is grasped, he says, if you add to it something in the category of place or of relation this might seem to entail a diminution of it in proportion as it could have lacked that property: but you would not have diminished reality, the reversion would be in yourself, away from reality, because you had hidden the meaning of it behind a screen of imagery.[1] It is true that this is said directly about 'Being', and the immediate context of the paragraph may be open to question: but its applicability to the embodied soul, which is what is first to come in contact with place, is unmistakable. Porphyry's meaning depends on the Aristotelian doctrine that substance is prior to relation, which is an 'accidental' category; no statement of what a thing (if it is a substance) is in itself can contain a reference to a relational property. For a Platonist what a thing is in itself means what it is really, in the plain sense of 'really' that is contrasted with 'apparently'. Thirdly 'appearance' in this sense belongs primarily to the world of sense perception, and following the *Timaeus* most Platonists would have thought its application to thinking a metaphor only in grammar; they would have believed that the intellectual hesitancy or error which it connoted was caused by sense perception or more directly by the mental images consequent on sense perception. Thus to describe a soul in relation to a body—as, for example, Aristotle does in the whole of the *De anima* except when he is alluding to the 'separate intellect'—must be to describe, as we might say, *less* than the reality or soul as it really is, which must have been something independent of that relational property. It is then only a soul as it appears to be; but there are not two souls for us to think of, a real one and an apparent (but unreal) one: there are merely two ways of our thinking of the soul, on the one hand correctly, on the other hand inadequately, confusedly.

All this lies behind Porphyry's favourite, almost technical, term for the embodied soul: he calls it 'the related soul' or 'soul in a relation'.[2] At the same time he is willing to describe the relation of particular souls to the universal or world soul just as Plotinus does, that is, not as mere

[1] *Sent.* no. XL, § 1 Mommert. 'Diminish' is a Plotinian term (VI 7 [38] 33 and 41).

[2] κατὰ σχέσιν (*ap.* Nemesius, 136, 9 [600 B Migne] *ap.* Stob. I 354, 13). Cf. Proclus, *In Tim.* II 105, 22–5, apparently quoting Iamblichus).

appearances but as parts of a whole.[1] This may be inconsistent: but more probably he is presenting another aspect, which is less 'ultimate' —Neoplatonism is bound like Spinoza's to be a philosophy of *quatenus*. He and Iamblichus both accept the theosophical theory of elemental 'vehicles' for the lower activities of the soul; it is in terms of this theory and in a way which hardly matters philosophically that they differ about the survival of 'the non-rational soul'.[2]

In fact Porphyry's account of Soul, which he seemed to his successors to have confused with Intellect, followed from a universally accepted principle: the first term of any ordered series is the *real* representative of that series. This must apply not only to the particular intellect, which is what the rest of the soul that contains it *really is*, but similarly to intellect and soul considered universally or absolutely, and similarly even to universal and particular intellect; the last pair makes a series because any universal is treated as a whole which contains but is prior to its parts. Porphyry's offence was to have drawn the monistic consequence without putting equal weight on the emergent properties of the posterior terms in these series. Other Neoplatonists try to hold the producer and the product in balance: Porphyry could not forget that the relation between these two is not a symmetrical one. We should therefore expect the others to restore the independent character of soul but also to have consciously or unconsciously to concede a good deal of Porphyry's case. And it is what we find Iamblichus doing.

His position can be stated here quite shortly. It is in many ways a return to Plato. If Porphyry was right, he complained with some insight, 'the soul is impeccable'.[3] Secondly, it was absurd to suppose that there was only one kind of soul: there must be different kinds corresponding to different kinds of living creature.[4] In general, soul was that which was intermediate between the immaterial and the material. As a sober expositor of Plato, Porphyry had said exactly the same—

[1] *Sent.* no. XXXVII; cf. *On the faculties of the soul*, *ap.* Stob. I 354, 11–18; Proclus *In Tim.* I 77, 16 and 22.

[2] Porphyry, *Sent.* no. XXIX; Proclus, *In Tim.* III 234, 8 – 235, 9; cf. Simplicius, *In Cat.* 374, 24 ff. The question does, however, affect the value of theurgy.

[3] Proclus, *In Tim.* III 334.

[4] *On the soul*, *ap.* Stob. I 372, 15–20; Nemesius, *De nat. hom.* 117, 5–8 Matthaei (584A Migne); cf. Julian, *Or.* VI 182D.

but as Iamblichus rightly suspected, not of the pure soul.[1] Iamblichus wanted soul to be a genuine third thing which 'both proceeds *integrally* in its descent into nature and remains unmixed'.[2] But he still said that its essential activities were 'divine transports' and 'those thoughts which are free from matter and bring us in contact with the gods'.[3] Iamblichus developed his view in a commentary on the *De anima*; and Porphyry's venture was never openly repeated.

In the *Sententiae*, or what has survived of it, there is no corresponding treatment of Intellect as a mere appearance of the One. To find these hypostases telescoped in that way we should have to go to an anonymous fragment, or rather fragments, which expound the first two hypostases as they appear in the *Parmenides*.[4] The One which is (or Intellect) is no longer the One, but according to its 'idea' (as its name shows) it still *is* the One; at the same time the 'idea' in which it participates must be the idea of being; but this, we learn, does not itself have a form or a name or substance (being) because it does not belong to anything, and it turns out to be the first hypostasis itself, which can only be known by the way of negation.[5] The whole fragment presents a very simple scheme with none of the more complicated subdivisions or intermediate hypostases which we find after Iamblichus.[6] It is interesting to find such a clear case of an intermediate term, 'the idea as it were of being' (the author is diffident about 'idea'), which functions by *uniting* the extremes—as when we see that $A = B$ and $B = C$. But we have no parallel for exactly this intermediate.[7] Porphyry also went against Plotinus in putting something between Intellect and the One and gave the same ground for doing so: but it was eternity, not being.[8]

[1] Cf. Proclus, *In Tim.* II 105.

[2] Simplicius, *In De an.* 6, 12–16, and frequently. A number of relevant passages and all Stobaeus' extracts from *On the soul* are translated in A.-J. Festugière, O.P., *La révélation d'Hermès Trismégiste*, III (Paris, 1953), App. I.

[3] *On the soul*, *ap.* Stob. I 371, 17–22.

[4] For text and notes see W. Kroll, 'Ein neuplatonischer Parmenides-commentar in einem Turiner Palimpsest', *Rhein. Mus.* XLVII (1892), 599–627.

[5] See particularly folios XII–XIV Kroll. [For a Christian adaptation of this by Marius Victorinus see the next Part (V), ch. 20, pp. 333–7.]

[6] It does divide the One which is into existence, life and intelligence (folio XIV): but this is Plotinian (e.g. VI 7 [38] 36, 12).

[7] But Julian, *Or.* IV 132D is suggestive (τὸν πάντων βασιλέα εἴτε τὸ ἐπέκεινα τοῦ νοῦ καλεῖν αὐτὸν θέμις, εἴτε ἰδέαν τῶν ὄντων...εἴτε ἕν).

[8] *Sent.* no. XLIV; cf. Proclus, *Plat. theol.* p. 27 Portus.

But in the same spirit as the *Sententiae* the fragment argues that what we attribute to the One belongs not to it but to our thinking (III and IV Kroll). Like Porphyry its author has perhaps unconsciously selected the monistic version of Plotinus by emphasizing the way in which hypostases 'telescope' and, what is complementary to that, the subjectivism of his approach.[1]

Porphyry seems often to present a simpler doctrine than Plotinus; partly it is a matter of exposition and partly a matter of going back to second-century writers.[2] From Moderatus the Neopythagorean he learnt a doctrine about sensible matter that he claimed was also Plato's and that described it as 'a shadow of not-being in the category of quantity'.[3] If we abstract every determinate quantity—a foot, a metre and so on which are forms—from bodies, we are left with the indeterminate notion of what Locke called bulk. It cannot of course exist indeterminately like this, and should be called 'quantum' rather than 'quantity'. Quantity is what has a real existence as a determinate category and object of thought, according to Plotinus, and his prototype of matter is a product of the One. In Porphyry's account, the paradigm which bulk or sensible matter copies is not properly a form at all but 'the *logos* of the One'—i.e. the Model of the *Timaeus*—'which has deprived itself of all its forms', in short Aristotle's prime matter identified as the Receptacle. One might think that this would leave us with the indeterminate notion of quality: but as the paradigm of sensible or physical matter it is quantity, because, in Pythagorean and Platonic thought, to be physical is just to be extended (continuous quantity) and separate or countable (discontinuous quantity or number). One might now think that it was the property of being three-dimensional: this would make it a form, and goes to show how it eludes us as soon as we think of it in any positive terms. But that is as much as to say that, if there is anything which it must *be* positively, then to that extent matter cannot be matter. And this is why its prototype is not-being; for

[1] The fragment seems close to *Ennead* V 1 [10], especially 4 and 10–12. P. Hadot has argued (*R. des Études gr.* LXXIV [1961], pp. 410–38), on different grounds and in detail that its author is in fact Porphyry.

[2] But a suggestion of Proclus' (*In Tim.* I 77, 22–4) that Porphyry regularly depended on Numenius has more than once been abstracted from its context, which is only daemonology.

[3] What follows is based on an extract from Porphyry's book *On Matter* in Simplicius, *In Phys.* 231 Diels (*C.A.G.* IX).

matter is what has potentially any form, but unrestricted possibility coincides with nonentity; '*S* may be *P* or *Q*' is informative, but '*S* may be *P* or *Q* or *R* or ... *ad infinitum*' indicates no state of affairs.

So even the sensible world is telescoped with Soul and Intellect. What is thinkable or real is precisely what is not 'material'; it never left its place inside Soul and Intellect. The 'descent' of the forms into nature is an illusion of thought. Or rather it is a *failure* of thought. The seeing and touching which seem to bring us into contact with a sensible world are unenlightened forms of thinking. Since degrees of reality are also degrees of value ('the Good'), matter, says Porphyry, is thought evil, for it flees the good; but by the same reasoning, of course, nothing is wholly bad—in fact one should conclude, though Porphyry does not, that nothing can seem wholly bad and nothing be really bad at all. Matter comes about 'by a deviation from reality'; and Simplicius expressed the whole doctrine more accurately by defining it as the 'deviation' itself.

C. *Theory and practice according to Porphyry and Iamblichus*

By and large this theory of matter was accepted by all later Neoplatonists. Except for the details which have been mentioned it had been Plotinus'.[1] Theory can never be divorced from practice in Neoplatonism; and the moral applications which Porphyry made depart little from Plotinus. They can be summed up in three equivalent injunctions. First, it follows from the elements of his metaphysics that to pursue the good or, what is the same thing but paradoxical, for something to become what it essentially is, is for a product to 'revert' to its producer. For a human being, that is, for his soul, as all Platonists incorrigibly put it, this meant the self-awareness that was to accompany intellectual thought. Finally, this was equivalent to turning inwards instead of outwards, which, following the religious tradition and dualistic psychology of the *Phaedo* and the *Timaeus*, was described as release from the body or purification and in practice meant asceticism. By schematizing Plotinus' tract on the subject Porphyry produced a scale of virtues that became conventional in the Schools but added little to ethics beyond a

[1] [On Plotinus' theory of matter see Part III, ch. 16 A, pp. 256–7.]

jargon.[1] The soul or the intellect could achieve them by its own efforts.[2]

All this was already and was to remain Neoplatonic commonplace. It is quite wrong to see anything novel or non-Plotinian in assertions that 'the non-material can be where and how it chooses or wishes'[3] and the like. They are not noteworthy claims to recognition of 'the will'; they mean only that within the limits recognized in quite ordinary discourse the ways in which we behave are voluntary.[4]

Iamblichus dealt in the traditional way with the relation between freedom and necessity;[5] the causal starting-point of actions is in ourselves and independent of the cosmic motion, that is fate or natural laws, but when we act we *use* these laws. (This was good Aristotle, for events did not for him form a closed Laplacean net of cause and effect but always allowed unattached causal lines to attach themselves to the net.) But in this tradition the Stoic conception of freedom as the necessity of reason, which is providence, is never far away. It is this that Iamblichus had in mind when he called the intellectual life, which is the release from fate, the divine life.

The crown of virtue was to lose all qualities that were specifically human and to become God; God was unity or 'the One'; the highest activity of the intellect was a form of thinking which was supposed to be logically simple, like a feeling presumably—but like it only in this respect—in which there is no succession and no distinction of subject and predicate. It is hard to see then how it can be an intellectual activity at all. But this is not so much of a difficulty if one believes that Neoplatonic principles imply the degree of 'telescoping' which Porphyry seems to have supposed. For the hypostases are grades of activity; and it may have been the key to the understanding of the whole theory as he saw it, that the limit, the final term of intellectual activity, was sufficiently unlike the rest of the intellectual series to be called a different grade of activity. If so, this pure unity which thought, that is the

[1] A. Psychic: 1. civic, 2. purificatory; B. Intellectual: 3. contemplative, 4. paradigmatic. See *Sent.* no. XXXII; cf. *Enneads* I 2 [19]; Olympiodorus, *In Alc.* 4, 15 – 8, 14 Creuzer (pp. 7–9 Westerink); Marinus, *Vit. Procl.* 3–26.

[2] *Sent.* nos. VIII, XXVII.

[3] *Sent.* no. XXVII.

[4] Cf. *On free will*, *ap.* Stob. II 163–73 Wachsmuth. This essay was intended only to explain how the myth of Er leaves room for free will. It does so very sensibly.

[5] *Letter to Macedonius on fate*, *ap.* Stob. II 173–6.

intellect, *becomes* if it can surmount all internal distinction may have been for him the One above being or God, so that the self *qua* intellect would then be identical with God. This would not be the same thing as the exercise of even the highest intellectual virtue, the 'contemplative': Porphyry learnt from Plotinus that the mystical union was something which occurred when the person himself was passive.[1] One could be taught to look (dialectic and virtue) but not to see.

It would follow that philosophy, while not the goal of life, was the best means to it, and that the intellectual virtues were the highest. There is good evidence that Porphyry held both these beliefs. But it is just these that Iamblichus certainly denied. He said categorically that it is not knowledge that unites the initiates to the gods although it is a necessary condition;[2] and, what is directly to the point, he held that the religious activities of the initiates were more effective than those of philosophers and he made room for them at the top of the scale of virtues in a new class which he called 'theurgic'.[3] Can we find signs of a corresponding *absence* of 'telescoping' in his theory of hypostases?

Iamblichus was born in the middle of the third century, fifteen or twenty years after Porphyry and like Porphyry of rich Syrian parents. But next to nothing is known of his life. It is an open question whether or not he studied under Porphyry or only studied his books.[4] He himself taught philosophy for many years at Apamea in Syria, and died in about 326.[5] Eunapius depicts him as a religious-minded philosopher who believed himself occasionally clairvoyant and even by the gods' powers able to raise phantoms, but who showed also the same deprecatory attitude as Plotinus to credulous admirers. The picture is likely to be true. His 'divine inspiration' remained a cliché for centuries; and after Constantine's death his intellectual authority stayed fresh for a whole generation of rebels against the official Christianity that had 'moved the things which should not be moved'. The most famous of

[1] [On this see Part III, ch. 16B, pp. 260–3.]

[2] *De myst.* II 11. [Cf. and contrast the Christian view summarized (with references to fuller discussions) in Part VI (The Greek Christian Tradition), ch. 28, pp. 426–7.]

[3] Olympiodorus, *In Phaed.* 114, 22–2 Norvin; Marinus, *Vit. Procl.* 26.

[4] The identity of his previous teacher, Anatolius, is also disputed (literature in E. Zeller–R. Mondolfo, *Filosofia dei greci*, Parte III, vol. VI, ed. G. Martano [Florence, 1961], p. 2 n. 2) but has little bearing on his philosophy. Porphyry's undoubted pupils are mere names to us.

[5] J. Bidez, 'Le philosophe Jamblique et son école', *R. des Études gr.* XXXII (1919), pp. 29–40.

these, the Emperor Julian, often reproduces popularly intelligible pieces of the Neoplatonism that he had learnt from Iamblichus' own writings and through Iamblichus' pupil Aedesius.[1]

Iamblichus has been described as more committed to theurgy and magic than to philosophy.[2] Certainly it would be to misunderstand him to think of him merely as the father of the scholasticism which is associated with the Athenian School. He wrote a commentary (now lost) on the Chaldaean Oracles, which lies behind much of Proclus' occult theology, and an encyclopaedic work on Neopythagorean philosophy, including arithmetic, geometry, physics and astronomy but of which we possess only the *Life of Pythagoras*, the *Protrepticus* and some books concerned with the symbolism of numbers and of mathematics in general.[3] But his commentaries (also lost) on Plato and Aristotle were admired by scholars such as Simplicius. A careful reading even of the *De mysteriis* will not support the picture which has so often been drawn of Iamblichus replacing Plotinian rationalism by a superstitious acceptance of all the excesses of theurgists and mystagogues.[4] He criticized those who, like Plotinus, explained divination as the reading of signs which were founded on the 'sympathies' in nature; he recognized the practice but objected first that it was a purely human activity and secondly that it could logically yield only probability, not certainty; real foreknowledge resulted from the union of our intellect with a divine intellect.[5] He made the same kind of distinction in the case of prayer, sacrifices and astrology;[6] and he placed the highest value on activities which he called divine gifts but still described in terms of the Neoplatonic *philosophical* system. Like Porphyry he thought that they could also be described in terms of Chaldaean (and indeed Egyptian) theosophy. But his commentary on the prayer in the *Timaeus* showed us the warmth of his religious feeling; and to try to translate into philosophical terms (even Neoplatonic ones) the religious rites which were

[1] See particularly *Orations* IV–VII.

[2] Bidez, *loc. cit.*

[3] *Theologoumena arithmeticae*, ed. V. de Falco (Leipzig [Teubner], 1922); *De communi mathematica scientia*, ed. N. Festa (Leipzig [Teubner], 1891).

[4] C. Rasche, *De Iamblichi libro qui inscribitur de mysteriis auctore* (Diss. Münster, 1911), argued adequately for Iamblichus' authorship. See further S. Fronte, 'Sull'autenticità del "De mysteriis" di Giamblico', *Siculorum Gymnasium* (Catania), n.s. VII (1954), pp. 1–22.

[5] *De myst.* III 26–7; X 3.

[6] II 11; V 7–8, 10 *ad init.* and 15; IX 4–5.

means to the union of intellects would be silly and would contradict Iamblichus.

Iamblichus made the proper philosophical response to this situation. He tried to separate, as a matter of method, religious or 'theurgic' exposition from philosophical exposition. He reproved Porphyry for failing to treat 'theurgic questions theurgically and philosophical questions philosophically';[1] for Porphyry thought he could explain away salvation as knowledge and the 'personal daemon' as the intellect.[2] This illustrates the philosophical significance of later Neoplatonists' emphasis (which might seem lecture-room pedantry) on the 'aim' of a book. In this book he left it an open question whether 'divine' life meant the same as 'intellectual' life;[3] but elsewhere he systematically classified traditional gods as 'intellectual' and 'intelligible', and intended these terms to have their regular meaning. In Julian's *Hymn to King Helios* 'the sun' is a name of the first hypostasis, or Idea of the Good, then of the good in the second hypostasis as what confers value on thought (existence, beauty and the like), then of the good in the second hypostasis considered as acts instead of objects of thought ('intellectual' instead of 'intelligible') but both apparently identified with Mithras, and finally of the sun in the sky which was a visible god.[4] It is tempting to speculate that Iamblichus felt this kind of rationalization to apply no higher than the aetherial gods.[5] We do not know that he ever mentioned, as Plotinus did, a suprarational union with the 'one god': but Proclus who echoed him so faithfully did, and thought theurgy the means to it.

D. *The metaphysics of Iamblichus*

We know that he attributed a degree of independence to souls that he found uncertain in Plotinus and Porphyry. The division of the second hypostasis into Intellect *qua* intelligible (or Being) and *qua* intellectual (or Intelligence) seems also to have originated with Iamblichus. It follows logically enough from the implicit Neoplatonic principle that a fundamental distinction of thought implies a distinct link in the chain of

[1] *De myst.* I 2 *ad fin.* [2] *Ibid.* II 11; IX 8. [3] *Ibid.* III 3.

[4] *Or.* IV. For 'intelligible goodness' Neoplatonists drew on the properties of the 'mixture' in the *Philebus* (see 25 E–26 B; 64).

[5] See *De myst.* VIII 2–3; cf. Porphyry, *De abst.* II 34.

being; and thinking and its object are certainly distinct in thought. Plotinus had rightly decided that, if they were not mutually implicative, being was logically prior to thought; so thought will now be an emanation from being, to which ideally it reverts.[1] The order agrees with the fact that Soul comes next to it in descending by containing the Ideas as its thoughts.

More fundamental was his introduction of 'imparticipables' (ἀμέθεκτα, ἐξῃρημένα). But it is best understood in a wider setting. Neoplatonic metaphysics already rested on the relation of 'procession' which was the generation of the less unified from the more unified. One scale of unity or simplicity will be represented by the series 'indivisible', 'divisible' and 'divided'; and this corresponds to a series familiar in Proclus but certainly recognized by Iamblichus, that of a whole *before* (i.e. prior to) its parts, a whole *of* (i.e. contained by) parts and a whole *in* (i.e. in each of) its parts. In the descending scale of simplicity a lower term possesses, or rather reflects inadequately, the property of the one above it. This is the relation of 'participation', in which what is participated is a whole of parts but what is properly real ought to be the prior and indivisible but therefore unparticipated whole; the third term is the participant, the subject which contains the second, participated term as a property—or, more strictly, it is each of the individual instances of that property. Iamblichus claimed that every self-subsistent thing including the hypostases existed, as each kind of whole, first 'imparticipably', then as the participated form which (by the familiar divisive activity of 'infinity') 'proceeded from' that as its 'illumination'.[2] Any level ('order') of reality is thus connected to the one above it by containing as its highest or best feature a participated form which reflects the imparticipable substance that identifies the next higher order. There is, for example, the physical world which is the participating subject, the participated soul which is present in it, and in a higher order unparticipated Soul. Soul in turn contains participated intellect which has proceeded from, but does not participate in, the Intellect of the next hypostasis.[3]

[1] [On thought and being in Plotinus see Part III, ch. 15, pp. 246–7.]

[2] Proclus, *In Tim.* II 105, 16–28; 240; 313, 19–24; cf. I 426.

[3] But Iamblichus put an ineffable One before the imparticipable One (Damascius, *Dub.* chs. 43–4, 51) presumably to ensure logically that the unknown god should be unknown.

This apparent doubling of each substantial form had always been necessary if the absoluteness or independence of the Ideas was to be reconciled with the theory of participation, which required an *in re* form. Plotinus had implied it more than once;[1] and so had Porphyry by denying that there was participation in the intelligible world.[2] Porphyry had professed to find a hypercosmic as well as cosmic soul in the *Timaeus*: identifying the former with the imparticipable, Iamblichus claimed that it was this and not the cosmic or immanent soul which was Plato's 'intermediate substance'.[3] He was campaigning for a distinction between intellect and soul *as such*; and the point is significant because it shows how one of the functions or effects of introducing the imparticipables is to prevent the telescoping of one hypostasis in another. Or, if it does not prevent it, it hedges it with more qualifications, so that the monistic tendency of Plotinus and Porphyry is weakened.

As well as the procession of hypostases there was, as Iamblichus saw, procession within each hypostasis. Not only is imparticipable Soul a self-subsistent thing which generates an order below it, but the participant intellect which it contains, or at least the compound of the two, forms a recognizable and self-subsistent thing that must also proceed. The product or 'illumination' was the lower 'life' of intellect and identified with all those intellectual faculties which Aristotle had described as in some degree dependent on our bodies. Procession, which was a Pythagorean notion, was associated with triads; and Neoplatonic sources of inspiration—not only numerology but religious myth and philosophy—offered an embarrassing choice of triads. In the present context the most used was perhaps that of being or substance, life, and intelligence or thinking.[4] At other times the Pythagorean Limit, Unlimited (or Infinity) and Mixture of the *Philebus* seemed better to fit a particular group of concepts. But while the 'permanence (μονή)' of any first term was always contrasted with the 'procession (πρόοδος)' and comparatively inessential character of what it generated, generator and generated did not necessarily form a triad at all.

[1] E.g. *Enneads* II 3 [52] 17–18; V 9 [5] 3.
[2] Syrianus, *In Met.* 109, 13 Kroll; Proclus, *In Tim.* III 34, 1–2.
[3] Proclus, *In Tim.* II 105 and 240; cf. I 322, 1–3.
[4] Iamblichus *ap.* Proclus, *In Tim.* III 145, 8–11.

In theory, however, being, life and intelligence were there to be discovered as three aspects of anything whatever. This followed from the fact that they were among the genera or categories of being, as Plotinus had shown, so that they applied to anything to which the verb 'to be' could be attached. Plotinus' successors have seemed to some readers to be indulging in vain and unwarranted repetitions of triads: they might have retorted that when animal has been divided into male and female it is not arbitrary multiplication of pairs to go on to find bull and cow, dog and bitch, man and woman. How could these triads be justified philosophically? The basic one was the procession of a divisible whole from an indivisible whole; and it was taken for granted by Iamblichus and everyone else that this was to be understood in terms of Plato's Dialectic. The first term corresponded to identity (Plato's 'sameness') and the second to difference.[1] In the reverse direction thought moves from the complex to the simple, from particulars, which, if *per impossibile* they were mere particulars, would be infinite or numberless and coincide with Plato's 'not being' or Porphyry's matter, to species which are the Limit or Number of the *Philebus* and can (by no accident of language) coincide with an 'order' (τάξις) in Iamblichus;[2] finally from species to genus, which is not an Aristotelian genus but the first term or primary meaning that Aristotle said took the place of the universal and the essence in an ordered series.

When, first, procession and, secondly perhaps, triads are posited, as they almost certainly were by Iamblichus, at every level or order of Intellect and Soul, and, thirdly, these orders are seen to be held together and yet held apart by the relation of imparticipable to participated form, then we have the structure of Neoplatonic metaphysics as it remained for two centuries.[3] It had been discernible in Plotinus, and much of it had been emphasized by Porphyry, who showed (as we shall see) how to use Aristotelian logic in its service. We do not know that Iamblichus systematized it, but he pointed out—rather than added—certain features which made it look less monistic. This is not, although the opposite is commonly repeated, because the intermediate terms that he

[1] Iamblichus *ap.* Proclus, *In Tim.* II 215, 7–9.

[2] Cf. Plotinus VI 2 [43] 22; Proclus, *El. theol.* 64.

[3] See the diagram on p. 301. [For the survival of the triads in Greek Christian thought see Part VI *passim*.]

wanted, the imparticipables, made God more distant from the aspiring soul. It was philosophical monism that he made more difficult, a monism of Spinoza's or of Bradley's kind which relates appearance and reality to confused and clear thinking. Iamblichus allowed or seemed to allow rather more independence to the appearances. His system could not be described without the term 'self-subsistent', which was wider than 'substance' but narrower than 'appearance', 'image' and so on—even particular souls are self-subsistent according to Proclus.[1] But the notion is one which was absent or not prominent in Porphyry and was first systematized in the Athenian school.

THE BASIC STRUCTURE OF IAMBLICHUS' METAPHYSICS

Arrows represent procession or irradiation, > participation by

Imparticipable intellect
↓
{(Participated intellect > Imparticipable soul) = Participant Intellect} → Proceeding intellect
↓
{(Participated soul > body) = Participant soul} → Proceeding soul

NOTE: This omits the procession of Soul as a hypostasis from Intellect as a hypostasis, which is a complementary point of view representing what Plotinus (VI 2 [43] 22, 26–8) called the *external* activity of Intellect. Here the proceeding intellect is the *intellectus in habitu* and *possibilis* (Simplicius, *In De an.* 311, 29), the proceeding soul the non-rational soul.

[1] Cf. *Ad Maced.*, *ap.* Stob. II 174, 21–4; Proclus, *El. theol.* 189.

CHAPTER 19

ATHENIAN AND ALEXANDRIAN NEOPLATONISM

A. *Proclus and his predecessors*

With the death of Iamblichus it is to Athens that serious philosophical history must move. The Athenians learnt much from him, and the work of a younger contemporary of his, Theodorus of Asine, is probably to be seen as only reinforcing the lesson.[1] Plutarch of Athens undergoes the same influence, and in the hands of his pupils Syrianus and even Proclus the main themes of Neoplatonism do little else than become more systematized and more canonical. Plato, Iamblichus, Syrianus: that was the road to knowledge according to the last holder of the chair.[2]

When Proclus came to Athens, Plutarch held the chair but was too old to lecture (he died in 431 or 432). Later writers speak of him as though he were the first of the Neoplatonists of Athens. Much of the psychology which Proclus learnt from him privately is taken for granted by Simplicius and the Alexandrians. But its essential character was simply what Iamblichus had emphasized: Aristotle and Plato were not at loggerheads, the *De anima* represented sound psychology, the *Timaeus* and *Parmenides* the theology which would complete it. In a number of details, too, when he was not just repeating Alexander of Aphrodisias, Plutarch followed Iamblichus or a common source.[3] But the philosophically important fact is that he at least theoretically conceded that psychology as the study of a soul in a body can be pursued independently of metaphysics.

Plutarch seems to have been quite original in interpreting the

[1] Our knowledge comes mostly from Proclus, *In Tim.* His career and chronology are open to question: see K. Praechter, *RE*, V A, 2 (1934), col. 1833 for the conflicting evidence.

[2] Damascius in *Lex. Souda*, *s.v.* Συριανός. His teacher Isidorus had admired Iamblichus next after Plato (Damascius, *Vit. Is.* 1257B Migne [p. 23 Asmus]; 1257D [p. 24, 28 Asmus] adds Porphyry).

[3] Zeller's suggestion that Plutarch wrote the first commentary on *De an.* since Alexander has had unfortunate effects (e.g. on R. Beutler's article, *RE*, XXI, 1 (1951), col. 962–75). For a commentary by Iamblichus cf. Simplicius, *In De an.* 6, 16; 217, 27; 313, 2–3 and 18; Ps.-Philop. *In De an.* III 533, 26 Hayduck (*C.A.G.* XV).

Parmenides—a matter, as we know, crucial to Neoplatonists even if less interesting to us. Describing the history of its formal exegesis Proclus counts the turning-point as the recognition that the first five hypotheses deduce true conclusions from true premises and the remaining four are reductions to absurdity.[1] Plutarch, he says, did recognize this; and it enabled him to do what no one had done before, to say correctly what the last six hypotheses were about. After God, intellect and soul the fourth hypothesis (157 B–159 B) described the forms immanent in matter and the fifth (159 B–160 B) matter, all these requiring the existence of unity; hypothesis VI (160 B–163 B) described sensation, corresponding to relative not-being but shown to be impossible if that is all there can be, i.e. in the absence of unity; VII (163 B–164 B) described the absence of any kind of awareness—of the possibility of it, as we should say—which would be absolute not-being; VIII (164 B–165 E) showed the absurdity of there being only shadows and dreams, and IX (165 E–166 C) the absurdity of there not being even these. Hypotheses II, III, IV and V corresponded to the four segments of Plato's Divided Line.[2]

This scheme was accepted in the School. The seeming corrections which were made after Proclus showed only that it was accepted with understanding. For example, Damascius explained how the last four hypotheses really combined 'direct' or positive and 'indirect' or negative demonstration; for one of the chief points of the Dialogue was that Parmenides recognized only being and not-being (VII and IX) while Plato saw that the category of relation implied an intermediate kind of not-being (VI and VIII).[3] The Neoplatonists were more conscious of the links between the *Parmenides* and the *Sophist* than many modern scholars. It is a pity that their version of the first three hypotheses, which was both the most important to them and, because it drew on Aristotle, the most unhistorical, has eclipsed an intelligent and historically plausible interpretation of the remainder.

Proclus insists that the hidden doctrine of Plato had been expounded by Syrianus; and not enough has survived of Syrianus himself to suggest that he had not anticipated the innovations which Neoplatonists

[1] *In Parm.* VI 24 ff. (1055, 25 Cousin, 1864); cf. *Plat. theol.* 31, 28–41 Portus.

[2] *In Parm.* VI 27–30 (1058, 21 – 1061, 20 Cousin). Beutler's attributions (*art. cit.* 974–5) from Proclus *In Parm.* Bk I are speculation.

[3] See particularly *Dub.* 433 (II 289–91 Ruelle).

accepted from Proclus. Of the third principal figure at Athens, Damascius, enough has survived to show that he added nothing of particular philosophical interest. Nor do we know anything relevant about Syrianus' life beyond the fact that Proclus read systematically both Plato and Aristotle under him; the only date which can be fixed in it is the year 431 or 432 when he became head of the Platonic School. Of numerous commentaries which he wrote, only those on Aristotle, *Metaphysics*, Books Γ, E, M and N, are extant.[1] The last pair defend, as they would have to, Ideas and ideal numbers. The arguments rest only on Platonic or Neoplatonic principles, and reflect the Pythagorean influence which came from Iamblichus and Theodorus of Asine. The rather surprising feature—but no more than that—is the abusive language with which Aristotle is castigated, for the familiar compromise which limited these books of the *Metaphysics* to the 'lesser mysteries' and the explanation of the sensible world was accepted by Syrianus.

Proclus' career and even personality are much better known. Although Marinus' *Life* was written, like most Greek 'biographies', not to illustrate the man but a way of life, it was written very soon after his death and by a former pupil.[2] Even if we do not see in it the beatific life we shall recognize a typical career of a Neoplatonic professor. Proclus was born at Constantinople in 410 or shortly afterwards. But his parents, who were patricians from Lycia in south-west Asia Minor, sent him to school in their country and then to Alexandria to study literature and rhetoric. Instead of law, which was his father's profession, philosophy attracted him, so he attended lectures on mathematics and on Aristotle. The next stage was Athens. Here at the age of about twenty he read the *De anima* and the *Phaedo* under Plutarch, and after Plutarch's death covered 'systematically' with Syrianus 'all the works of Aristotle in logic, ethics, politics, physics and even theology' (Marinus is simply naming the standard order of study) and then 'the greater mysteries of Plato'. Syrianus offered to expound either Orphic or Chaldaean theology to Proclus and a fellow pupil: but, apparently because their choice did not agree and Syrianus died soon afterwards,

[1] Ed. W. Kroll, *C.A.G.* VI, 1 (1922).

[2] Ed. J. F. Boissonade (Leipzig, 1814); reprinted with Latin transl. in Diogenes Laertius, ed. G. Cobet (Paris [Didot], 1850); Engl. transl. in L. J. Rosán, *The Philosophy of Proclus* (New York, 1949).

Proclus had to learn these subjects from the writings of Porphyry, Iamblichus and Syrianus himself. It is not known when he took over the School, but he remained at its head till he died in 485. He never married and his only defects were a jealous nature and a short temper.

Proclus moved in important political circles, but like other leading Platonists he was a champion of pagan worship against imperial policy and found himself more than once in trouble. There is no doubt of his personal faith in religious practices. A vegetarian diet, prayers to the sun, the rites of a Chaldaean initiate, even the observance of Egyptian holy days were scrupulously practised. He is said to have got his practical knowledge of theurgy from a daughter of Plutarch, and according to his own claim he could conjure up luminous phantoms of Hecate. Nor is there any doubt that he put theurgy, as liberation of the soul, above philosophy.[1] But while his philosophy is full of abstract processions and reversions, philosophy was nothing for him if not itself a reversion, a return to the One, though achieving only an incomplete union. Its place can be seen in an almost fantastically elaborated metaphysical system: but although this system would not have been created had there not been a religion to justify, its validity does not depend and was not thought by Proclus to depend on the religion.

B. *The realist metaphysics of Proclus and Damascius*

Proclus believed that his metaphysics was the true though hidden meaning of Plato and that this like all Greek 'theology' derived from the secret doctrines of Pythagoreans and Orphics.[2] It can be studied in two works, the *Elements of theology* and the *Theology of Plato*, with help here and there from the commentaries on the *Parmenides*, *Timaeus* and *Alcibiades*. (The incompleteness of these commentaries is due to Proclus; and in the case of the commentaries on the *Republic* and *Cratylus* it would have been no loss to philosophy if a good deal less had been written—they are not, for instance, the place to look for Proclus' epistemology.) Discrepancies of doctrine between these works are probably trifling. Although Iamblichus is the most important figure behind this final development of Platonism, the *Elements*

[1] E.g. *Plat. theol.* 63, following Iamblichus, *De myst.* X 4–8.

[2] *Plat. theol.* 13 Portus; cf. Syrianus, *In Met.* 190, 35 Kroll (Plato the greatest of the Pythagoreans).

owes a greater and more direct debt than has been recognized to Porphyry's *Sententiae*. While confined to metaphysics it is a handbook of the same kind, but formally it takes a remarkable step beyond the *Sententiae*: it is not merely presented as a set of theorems, but each of these is proved and (at least in intention) so that the proofs depend only on preceding theorems. Its clear parallel is in fact Spinoza's *Ethics*. The book was responsible for a good deal of the Neoplatonic current in scholastic theology through its silent absorption by Pseudo-Dionysius[1] and the *Liber de causis*. Its contents are thoroughly abstract. Beginning with theorems (1–6) about unity and the One it expounds at length the formal relations of generator and generated (7–112) and then in turn the formal character of the participated One or 'henads' (113–58), of Being (159–65), of Intellect (166–83) and of Soul (184–211).

On Plato's theology is four times as long, but in spite of considerable obscurity in describing the triads within triads of the hypostases it has the advantage of starting at a slow pace in a recognizable country of Plato's Dialogues. In it we see theology or 'first philosophy' in Aristotle's sense made to coincide with theology in the ordinary sense, divine substances with gods. Proclus claims in the introduction that alongside the philosophy of the Ideas there is to be found in Plato a secret philosophy which Plotinus and his successors have helped to expound; but the present work will aim at literalness in preference to symbolism and proof in preference to assertion; if it is objected that there is a diversity of sources the answer is to lie in the unique authority of the *Parmenides*. Most of the work is in fact an account of the structure of reality which Proclus claimed to be intended by Parmenides' first two hypotheses. Book I describes the universal qualities of gods, II God in the strict sense or the One, III the intelligible gods or Being, IV the gods which are intelligible and intellectual, or Life (an intermediate order which is omitted in the *Elements*), and V the intellectual gods or Intelligence; VI deals less thoroughly with the hypercosmic gods or Soul, and the cosmic gods or Nature, and makes more use of the *Timaeus* than of the *Parmenides*.

The outlines of the scheme we have already seen in Iamblichus. If we have to decide which of the wealth of its characteristics to put in the

[1] [See Part VI, ch. 30 A, pp. 457–60.]

foreground, or which of the theorems stated in the *Elements*, we can perhaps do worse than to repeat the four reminders that Proclus offers his readers before he describes the uncreated gods. First, he says, the orders of these gods are as many as are shown in Parmenides' second hypothesis; secondly, every monad generates a co-ordinate number; thirdly, the nearer to the first monad the greater the generative power of anything; and fourthly, every participated cause is preceded by an unparticipated cause.[1] Quite consistently he took over from Syrianus a class of participated forms of the One which proceed from it and are present primarily in Intellect but also in each hypostasis below the One and all the processions of each hypostasis.[2] He called them 'henads'. The term 'monad', a literal synonym, was normally reserved for the defining term or 'leader' and so normally the 'imparticipable' of any order or series. Since the One was God—and indeed simplicity by entailing indestructibility had been a mark of divinity from the *Phaedo* onwards—these henads were the quality of being divine which necessarily was possessed by anything real; or rather, in accordance with Neoplatonic logic, there would be as many kinds of them as kinds of participant and, secondly, so far as they were self-subsistent they would be things and not qualities. With equal consistency, therefore, Proclus identified them with the traditional Hellenic gods. They exemplified *par excellence* the golden rule of Neoplatonic metaphysics, 'All things in everything, but appropriately'.[3] But on the same principle one god can be found by the interested reader functioning at more than one level as more than one henad.

Proclus' philosophy is marked by a more extreme realism than seems possible to most modern readers and which probably outdid any earlier Platonism. The problem how to distinguish a merely conceptual distinction from a real distinction—how to decide whether something non-empirical, say a class, a number or a sense datum, to give modern instances, is validly said to exist—this ontological problem may be considered quite factitious; it may be thought that, in the form of the so-called problem of universals, it was shown to be factitious by Aristotle's doctrine of categories, or alternatively that it did not occur to

[1] *Plat. theol.* 118–21 Portus.

[2] For Syrianus cf. *In Parm.* I 34; VI 36 (641, 3–9; 1066, 21 Cousin[2]). Hermias, *In Phaedr.* 84–7; 121, 19; 152 Couvreur.

[3] πάντα ἐν πᾶσιν, ἀλλ' οἰκείως.

him. Later it was not so much the quarrel between Aristotelians and Platonists which raised the theoretical question of a criterion for reality: it was the intervention of the Stoics. As materialists they had such a criterion, but they needed a whole class of objects of thought which were neither material nor non-existent but whose reality was just to be objects of thought. Much of this conceptualism, to give it a name, attached itself to orthodox Aristotelianism—indeed it has remained there since Alexander of Aphrodisias. No one was more conscious than Proclus that it was contrary to the spirit of Platonism. He criticized some earlier interpretations of the *Parmenides* precisely because they mistook distinctions of thought or abstractions for the real principles which they were rightly expecting to find. 'The principles do not get existence from concepts but from being. Where thought is sovereign, once the thought is removed the existence of what was conceived vanishes too. The principles are principles *per se* and not through our concepts.'[1] The word translated 'being' is a name of the first term of the triad, 'being, life (or power) and intelligence (or thought)' which is the three aspects of every existing thing.

The formal requirements of a 'principle' are conveniently put together by Damascius. It must not be deficient in any respect (the notion which comes from the *Sophist* and which we saw used by Porphyry); consequently it must not be in a subject (i.e. belong to an accidental category), nor (rather surprisingly) be an element or composed of elements, since elements require each other as well as the whole; finally it must revert to itself and consequently be separable.[2] Taken strictly they defined the One. All that is needed for a serviceable criterion of realities in the plural is to make each of the requirements *relative* instead of absolute. Soul for instance is 'deficient' in respect of Intellect, but only, as it were, *sub specie aeternitatis*: as Soul it already contains Intellect, in the same way as its reversion is its perfection as a soul even though it is also a return to the One. It may help to understand this relative independence to think of the scholastic and Cartesian notion of 'perfections' which have to be perfections in a *kind*. This is Proclus' theory of self-subsistence—'self-subsistent', 'self-sufficient',

[1] αἱ γὰρ ἀρχαὶ κατ' ἐπίνοιαν τὴν ὑπόστασιν οὐκ ἔχουσιν, ἀλλὰ καθ' ὕπαρξιν... (*In Parm.* VI 23 [1054, 27–31 Cousin²]).

[2] *Dub.* I, pp. 19–21 and 23 Ruelle.

'self-perfect' are the frequent and interchangeable terms which characterize his philosophical realism.[1] It is the theory, too, which explains how the henads are not merely qualities of divinity but gods. Does it entail a circular criterion? Probably, for what is self-subsistent determines what is a real order, but its self-subsistence has to be relative to some determined order. But this should perhaps be expected. The logical test of any claim to represent a metaphysical structure will have to be coherence.

There is, however, a special difficulty about henads. As an 'order' of reality they are unique in being by definition participated: how can they be self-subsistent if they are necessarily in subjects, dependent on their participants? If Proclus has an answer it can only be his doctrine of 'separable participation' in which, like soul in body, one term is not contained by the other.[2] This is a return to Porphyry's God that is everywhere and nowhere.[3] But he seems oddly unaware of the difficulty.

Because being real entails being one, everything self-subsistent possesses a henad which is appropriate to it. The gods must therefore be studied indirectly by studying the orders and orders within orders of reality. This is how a large part of the *Theology of Plato* is devoted to the various triads which make up the main triad of the second hypostasis. This main triad contains the gods of the intelligible order, the gods of the intellectual order (that is, the distinction of thinking from thought which had been made by Iamblichus) and between them (an innovation) the gods who are simultaneously intelligible and intellectual. Its terms are respectively the being or essence, the life or power, and the intelligence or thinking of the second hypostasis, Intellect in general, and correspond to its permanence, procession and reversion; and each one of these generates its own triad of being, life and intelligence, all representing, we might suppose, different concepts or categories, such as plurality, eternity, shape, but *perfect* ones and so, according to Proclus, self-subsistent things. Since the second order of the hypostasis must also participate in the first, and the third in the first and the second, Intellect should consist of 9 + 27 + 81 terms.[4] But the reader may have

[1] αὐθυπόστατος, αὐτάρκης, αὐτοτελής.

[2] *El. theol.* 81.

[3] Cf. 140, especially ll. 5–7 Dodds.

[4] Proclus does not pursue the subject as systematically as this; but details have been systematized by L. J. Rosán.

less patience than Proclus had gods; and we must ask instead what philosophical merit there is in all this. Is it just an historical curiosity?

The content of these triads is supposed for the most part, but not entirely, to rest on the text of Plato. In fact it involves the analysis of concepts and their relations to one another that has always been signified by philosophy. The task of Proclus's ontology was to show what things could be said to have *separate existence* and what is their *rational order*. The 'life' which the *Sophist* and the *Metaphysics* had attributed to divine intellect and which the Neoplatonists treated as power or activity is made intermediate between being and thinking, for the straightforward reason that whatever thinks must be alive but not conversely and whatever is alive must exist.[1] This relation of implication shows that there is similarity (a species of sameness and of unity) in the terms it relates, as well as dissimilarity; otherwise we should have only a truth-functional or material implication which does not hold between concepts. According to Proclus the middle term of a triad *ABC* joins dissimilars, for *A* is similar to *B* and *B* is similar to *C* but *A* is dissimilar to *C*.[2] Though not the only one, this is a valid concept of similarity, namely similarity as it presents itself to us, which is a non-transitive relation. It applies to the classing of colours or sounds, for example, and, analogously, to the recognizing of non-empirical connexions, in particular to the recognizing of implication—inferring, which belongs to thought, not implying, which belongs to its object and is transitive. Proclus reaches the structure of reality through the structure of thought. The form of the triad will thus be x, xy, y. Hence the order of things which are simultaneously intelligible and intellectual and connect these otherwise dissimilar aspects of *nous*.

Parmenides' second hypothesis showed that the concept of something real, that is of anything which is thought of as one and existing, entailed the concept of a whole consisting of parts (viz. unity and existence) and then the concept of an indefinite plurality (viz. the infinite regress of parts which are also wholes). It is easy to see—and far from certain that Plato did not see—that the concept of species can fall under that of the whole and of individuals under indefinite plurality. The whole of parts is the class concept of Proclus' intermediate order of the

[1] *El. theol.* 101.

[2] *Plat. theol.* 123 *fin.*–124 *in.*

intelligible–intellectual. As well as being the category which 'makes species' it is the one where number first appears. The generic notion on which number depends is plurality and in this sense it existed in the intelligible order, but only 'occultly' or 'as its cause', not as 'actual' number.[1] It also involves definiteness or 'limit'—which is the necessary condition of any specific idea; and Proclus followed the Pythagoreanizing *Philebus* in talking of 'number' where we might talk more generally of class—hence the form taken by the second of his reminders: 'every monad generates a co-ordinate number'.[2]

The concepts we find here and in the rest of the hypostases are not on the whole original but complete those which Plotinus had claimed as Plato's. Sometimes Proclus openly disagrees with the tradition. Time is not generated by soul, for just as soul is the image of intellect time is the image of eternity which (being participated by intellect) is prior to intellect.[3] And this illustrates quite well how their peculiar dependence on authority did not prevent Neoplatonists from being *philosophers*. For it is true that in the *Timaeus* time was put 'over' the world and its soul and that it was deified by the Chaldaean Oracles. Proclus adduces both facts.[4] But the *grounds* of his conclusion are the logical relations of the four concepts involved. In general, however, too much of the philosophical argument was traditional, so that it is either missing or present only allusively and with too much taken for granted in page after dry page of these earnest men. This has to be said.

When the One that is was seen as implying a whole of parts and this in turn an indefinite plurality one might have been puzzled that this did not place them in the reverse order of logical priority. The reason why, on the contrary, the second is regarded as 'procession' and 'descent' from the first is that in one sense thought demands the whole of parts—but thought which is not of the highest kind, in which the thought, as we know, was supposed to be logically simple. What reflection finds is inferior to what one might almost call single-mindedness, in the way that one reads better—the image is Plotinus'—when one is not con-

[1] κρυφίως, κατ' αἰτίαν not καθ' ὕπαρξιν. This systematic distinction became the Schoolmen's 'eminenter' and 'formaliter'.

[2] For the priority of number to species see *Plat. theol.* 226.

[3] *In Tim.* III 27, 18–24. [This is a criticism of Plotinus, for whose view of time see Part III, ch. 16 A, pp. 251–2.]

[4] *Ibid.* 3, 32 – 4, 6; 27, 8–12.

scious of reading.[1] The logical priority, too, is taken care of by Proclus, for he puts *wholeness* in the order above.

But it is reflection which shows that the higher terms are necessary conditions of the lower. And that is why Proclus called the lowest term of each procession thinking and at the same time said that it corresponded to reversion. Is it then we who revert to the One in our thinking, not those self-subsistent objects of our thought? It is the essence of Neoplatonism that no such simple or unqualified distinction can be made. When Proclus expounds Plato's two methods of describing the One, the analogical and the negative, he presents them as the reversion of the *things*.[2] But he has learnt too much from Iamblichus to have gone back to Porphyry's position. The ascent of the soul is a gathering of itself into a unity by the standard process of asceticism and dialectic; the unity which it becomes is its henad. This is new doctrine because the henad of soul is not intellect, but a participated One;[3] and the next stage, unification with the unparticipated One, is beyond the scope of intellectual virtue and accomplished by theurgy. Indeed it is the descent even to the terrestrial sphere of gods in the form of henads that brings about physical 'sympathies' and so makes theurgy possible.[4] 'All things pray except the First,' he was fond of quoting;[5] for prayer is a turning to God as the sunflower turns to the sun and the moonstone to the moon.[6] Concentration on the henad does not pass the intellect by since the soul which is to be unified contains a *participated* intellect which will have to be unified.[7] But it does indicate a relative autonomy of the soul as a self-subsistent thing, which can achieve salvation without 'telescoping' the hypostases. It is in fact a self: 'We', says Proclus,

[1] [On this see Part III, ch. 14, pp. 226–7.]

[2] *Plat. theol.* 93, 24–94 *fin.*

[3] Proclus and his successors often call it the summit (ἀκρότης, τὸ ἀκρότατον) or flower (ἄνθος) of the soul, copying a Chaldaean expression (Kroll, *De orac. Chald.* p. 11), 'flower of intellect'. Clearest description: *In Alcib.* 519 Cousin² (p. 114 Westerink). But confusingly 'summit' also denotes any first term.

[4] *El. theol.* 140; *In Remp.* II 232 ff. Cf. Iamblichus, *De myst.* I 15 and *ap.* Proclus, *In Tim.* I 209.

[5] From Theodorus of Asine, *In Tim.* I 213, 3; *On the Hieratic Art*, *Cat. MSS. alchimiques grecs*, ed. J. Bidez, VI, 147.

[6] *On the Hieratic Art*, p. 148 Bidez; cf. Damascius, *Vit. Isid.* 1296B–C Migne [p. 7 Asmus]; Olympiodorus, *In Alcib.* 18, 10 – 19, 4 Creuzer (p. 14 Westerink).

[7] Proclus may have avoided the difficulty that Soul ought to participate the One through the intermediate hypostasis only by allowing with Iamblichus that this did not apply to gods (*In Tim.* I 209).

'are not just intellect (or reason) but also thought, belief, attention, choice and before these faculties a substance, that which is one and many.'[1] A deification seems to be possible that is comparatively independent of the universe. The individual will not, as it were, have abolished the universe. He will, of course, have lost his self-identity: that is the aim.[2]

We can obtain fascinating if incoherent glimpses of the School of Athens when Proclus died from Damascius' biography of his teacher, Isidorus.[3] Isidorus was 'unwilling to worship images but preferred to approach directly the gods who are concealed within—not in temple sanctuaries but in the hidden depths of unknowing'.[4] Perhaps it was from him that Damascius learnt to emphasize the transcendence and ineffability of the One. This is prominent in the early part of the only philosophical work which we have from him, the so-called *Dubitationes et solutiones*.[5] But he was only saying lengthily what Proclus said in equally superlative language ('more ineffable than all silence') but more succinctly.[6] The whole book covers roughly the same ground as the *Theology of Plato* and is in the form of commentary on the *Parmenides*. It is not that Damascius was a negligible philosopher: but even if we examined his version of the later hypotheses, which Proclus never had time to reach, we should only be repeating what has been said in the case of his predecessors. He was the last of the official Platonic Succession. A year or two after the closing of the School in 529 he went with Simplicius and others to the court of King Chosroes of Persia.

[1] *Eclogae e Proclo De philos. Chald.* ed. A. Jahn (Halle, 1891), p. 4, 25–7 (quoted with other relevant texts in L. H. Grondijs, 'L'âme, le nous...', p. 131); *In Parm.* III 225 (957, 35 – 958, 4 Cousin[2]).

[2] *In Tim.* I 211, 24 – 212, 1.

[3] Preserved fragmentarily in Photius, *Bibliotheca*, *Cod.* 242 (*PG*, 1249–1305); and *Lex. Souda*; reconstructed and translated into German by R. Asmus (Leipzig, 1911).

[4] 1260 A–B Migne [26, 4–8 Asmus]. [Cf. the attitude of Plotinus to external religious observances, Part III, ch. 12, p. 204.]

[5] We have also a not very good student's notes of his lectures on the *Philebus* (ed. L. G. Westerink, *Damascius: Lectures on the Philebus wrongly attributed to Olympiodorus* [Amsterdam, 1959]).

[6] *Plat. theol.* 103–5, 109–10.

Correspondence between Triads in Athenian School

	(1)	(2)	(3)
A.	Being (ὄν, οὐσία)	Life (ζωή)	Intelligence (νοῦς)
B.	Existence (ὕπαρξις)	Power (δύναμις)	Intelligence (νοῦς—also = activity, ἐνέργεια)
C.	Permanence (μονή)	Procession (πρόοδος)	Reversion (ἐπιστροφή)
D.	Object of thought (νοητόν)	Object of thought and thought (νοητὸν καὶ νόησις, νοητὸν καὶ νοερόν)	Thought (νόησις, τὸ νοερόν —also = specification, εἰδοποίησις)
E.	Father (πατήρ)	Father and mother (πατὴρ καὶ μήτηρ)	Mother (μήτηρ)
F.	One which is (ἓν ὄν)	Whole of parts (ὅλον ἐκ μερῶν)	Indefinite plurality (ἄπειρον πλῆθος)
G.	Limit (πέρας)	Infinity (ἀπειρία)	Mixture (μικτόν)
H.	Symmetry (συμμετρία)	Truth (ἀλήθεια)	Beauty (κάλλος)

Note: The horizontal lines represent manifestations of every reality; but no two concepts in any column are necessarily identical; one is said, for example, to 'characterize' another. Cf. Proclus, *Plat. theol.* 174–80 Portus. A and B depend partly on Plato, *Soph.* 247 E, 249 A, F on *Parm.* 142 B–143 A, G on *Phileb.* 16 C ff., H on *Phileb.* 65 A. The list of triads is not complete.

C. *Neoplatonism at Alexandria*

In Alexandria we hear nothing of Neoplatonic philosophy till the fifth century. It was mostly imported from Athens. From the time of Syrianus it was common for philosophers to have lectured in both cities. An Alexandrian professor was married to a daughter of his; Isidorus had married the famous pagan martyr, Hypatia (d. 415), a mathematician who was also a professor of philosophy 'but inferior to Isidorus not only as a woman is to a man but as a geometer is to a philosopher', according to his biographer.[1] The Platonism that appears in Synesius, who was her pupil, is of a simple kind and is supposed to go back to the Middle Academy, perhaps through Porphyry.[2] But this was conventional in the *belles lettres* which he was writing. It must have been shortly afterwards that Hierocles was lecturing in Alexandria. He tells us himself that he had been a pupil of Plutarch (who died in 431 or 432); and he is the author of a surviving commentary on the Pythagorean Golden Verses and a partly surviving tract on providence, which cannot be said to have made at this stage a fresh contribution to philosophy. It is noticeable that although they refer regularly to processions, reversions, illuminations, orders and triads, they seem to

[1] Damascius, *Vit. Isid.* 1285 C Migne [97, 32–5 Asmus].

[2] *De prov.* I 9 (*Opuscula*, ed. Terzaghi, pp. 79 ff.; *PG* 66. 1225–8).

ignore anything higher than Intellect. This can perhaps be explained by classing him with the Neopythagoreans whose doctrines Iamblichus and Theodorus of Asine were trying to combine with those of Plotinus and Porphyry. Some close parallels with Proclus only indicate a common source in Iamblichus.

Hierocles could hardly have omitted the One because it was irrelevant. But when the simplicity and hard-headedness of the Alexandrians' Neoplatonism is contrasted with the elaboration and 'speculative' character of Athenian metaphysics, a simple but hard fact must be remembered. We have not got their metaphysics. Most of them accepted the principles that Aristotle was studied as a preliminary to Plato and that the *Alcibiades*, *Gorgias* and *Phaedo* were studied as preliminaries to the metaphysical Dialogues.[1] What has come down to us? Several people's lectures on Aristotle's logic and psychology, and on Plato one man's lectures—on the *Alcibiades*, *Gorgias* and *Phaedo*. And the 'henads above being' are in Olympiodorus' *Alcibiades* no less than they were in Proclus'. Conversely we have nothing (unless we count Simplicius) with which to compare their exposition of the *Organon* and *De anima* and the detachment that they brought to it. Against this fact we must set another, which has often been noticed. At Alexandria, more than in Greece, students and professors alike were often Christians. There would seem to be a sorry tale of compromise on both sides;[2] and while we can find only a few points of exposition which it affected, it may help to solve the problem of Alexandrian metaphysics. It may well be that the Platonists there were less inclined to choose between the details of one system and another. Content with the general principles of Neoplatonism they may have approached each text pragmatically: if the *Phaedrus* was to be expounded, there was a model in Syrianus; if the *Alcibiades*, in Proclus.[3] But by burying themselves in Aristotelian psychology and logic they could avoid the ideological stresses altogether. And for the most part they did—it is not just that texts have been lost: they did not write theologies of Plato or commentaries on the *Timaeus*.

[1] E.g. Elias, *In Cat.* 123, 7–11 Busse (*C.A.G.* XVIII) for Aristotle. For Plato see L. G. Westerink, *Anonymous Prolegomena to Platonic Philosophy*, Introduction, pp. xxxvii–xl.

[2] See Westerink, *loc. cit.* pp. x–xxv. [Also Part VI, ch. 31 B, pp. 477–8.]

[3] Hermias, *In Phaedr.* is nothing, or almost nothing, but Syrianus.

But it is doubtful whether we ought to accept Praechter's positive case for an Alexandrian Platonism which was orthodox in Ammonius' School (second half of the fifth century) and which was the non-Plotinian version of Origen and Longinus.[1] It rests on a misreading of the theological excursus in a commentary which Simplicius wrote on Epictetus' *Enchiridion*.[2] There the highest principle is not, as Praechter thought, the Demiurge, who is Intellect, but the One above Intellect;[3] and it is not called (even with qualifications) 'philanthropic', 'lord' and so on.[4] Nor does Asclepius' version of Ammonius bear out the case, particularly if we compare like with like by judging it against only the first half of Syrianus' commentary. But it would be out of place to do more here than suggest that this pre-Plotinian survival should defer its entry into the history books.

Willingness to depend on previous models, characteristic of Graeco-Roman culture, was carried to an extreme by the Alexandrian professors. For this reason it is pointless to pursue a chronological history with them. Their contribution to philosophy which lies in interpreting and assimilating Aristotle's psychology and logic should be looked at as a whole; and even then it will be seen to consist in selecting the best of their predecessors' work.

The dominant figure is Ammonius, the son of Hermias. He was Syrianus' son-in-law and heard lectures on Aristotle's logic from Proclus before being appointed to a chair in Alexandria. It follows that he was teaching in the second half of the fifth century; we know nothing more definite than that. He dominates the interpretation of Aristotle till Simplicius, and far more than a library catalogue may suggest. We have his commentaries on the elementary logic: but commentaries in Philoponus' name on the *Categories*, *Analytics*, *Physics*, *De generatione et corruptione*, *De anima*, and possibly *Meteorologica* are notes taken at Ammonius' lectures and written up with the addition of comments by Philoponus.[5] This was not concealed, but what was the master's and

[1] See K. Praechter *s.v.* 'Hierocles' and 'Simplicius' in *RE*.

[2] 95–101 Dübner (pp. 356–78 Schweighäuser).

[3] 100, 39 ff. Dübner (pp. 371 ff. Schweighäuser). The Ideas were regularly called δημιουργικοὶ λόγοι in this School. [On Intellect as the Demiurge in Plotinus see Part III, ch. 16 A, p. 252.]

[4] 101, 35–8 Dübner (p. 376 Schweighäuser).

[5] The Greek text of *In De an.* III is now credited to Stephanus of Alexandria (first half of seventh century).

what was the pupil's was not indicated. Ammonius' *Metaphysics* is partly incorporated in Asclepius. Interpretation which did not affect Neoplatonism—and so most of Simplicius' learned work—is irrelevant here. But one attempt made by Ammonius to harmonize Plato and Aristotle is worth mentioning because its historical effect may have outweighed its merits. He claimed that Aristotle meant the prime mover to be an efficient cause. His argument (if it is his) that *Physics* II 194b29–33 showed that the cause of change is efficient cause is plain silly, but his explanation of Aristotle's doctrine about God is interesting: efficient causes seem to work within time, while the first cause and its effect, the movement of the heavens, are both eternal.[1] Simplicius accepted this, but he could not allow the system to be subverted by Philoponus' suggestion that the supralunar world obeyed the same physical laws as the sublunar.[2]

Of Ammonius' pupils who became professional philosophers the Christian Monophysite Philoponus falls outside our scope except incidentally,[3] and Olympiodorus is known by 'ethical' commentaries on Plato which are not merely second-hand but philosophically negligible. Some commentaries on Aristotelian logic by Elias and David clearly depend on Olympiodorus. By this time we are into the middle of the sixth century. His more distinguished student, the Cilician Simplicius, undoubtedly acquired in Alexandria his knowledge of logic and perhaps his scholarly approach (which is not the same as an historical approach) to the text of Aristotle. But he studied also under Damascius, and the philosophy which he takes for granted, as well as his admiration of Iamblichus, is that of the Athenian School. Whether because he had been in that School when Justinian closed it in 529 or just from friendship with Damascius, he spent a year or two with him in Persia. His paganism then barred him from lecturing, and perhaps this enabled his Aristotelian commentaries (*Categories*, *Physics*, *De caelo*, *De anima*) to be the learned and polemical works that they are.

A proposition (XXVII) of Epictetus' handbook gave Simplicius the opportunity for a full statement of the Neoplatonic doctrine on evil.

[1] Simplicius, *In Phys.* 1360–3 Diels.

[2] *In De caelo*, 87–9 Heiberg (*C.A.G.* VII). See further S. Sambursky, *The Physical World of Late Antiquity* (London, 1962), ch. VI, although it exaggerates Philoponus' scientific merits.

[3] [For Philoponus see Part VI, ch. 31 B, pp. 477–82.]

'The nature and origin of evils' had been something of a required theme long before Plotinus' important essay (*Ennead* I 8 [51]), and it is impossible to say what was original with any particular writer. Simplicius' statement followed Proclus very closely but is definitive for all later Neoplatonists.[1] If we analyse it we find that it makes a theory by combining the following Platonic, Peripatetic and Stoic doctrines. (1) Form fails to master matter completely (*Timaeus*). (2) Matter has no qualities (*Timaeus* and Stoics). (3) Evil is only apparent inasmuch as in the context of the whole it is no longer evil (*Laws* VII and X, and Stoics). (4) The cause of evil is soul (*Laws* X). (5) It is never caused by God (*Republic* and *Timaeus*). (6) Privation is not a contrary like a co-ordinate species (Aristotle). (7) Final causes are forms and entelechies (Aristotle). (8) Failures are without goals because they are unintentional (Stoics).

What is new since Plotinus? It is explicit that matter is not the origin of evil; the false inference from (1) is prevented, as Porphyry had seen, by (2) and (3). Gone too is the alternative explanation of evil, that it is *logically* required to make sense of the notion of good. This suggestion had been made in the *Theaetetus* (176 A) and repeated sometimes by Stoics and Plotinus. Evil is now seen as necessary, but only indirectly so: matter and privation are necessary conditions of it, and these are necessary because everything flows from the One, including, and indeed first of all, indefiniteness. This is the meaning Simplicius gave to the Demiurge's famous statement that heaven would be imperfect if it did not contain mortal creatures, though in fact the requirement of logical necessity was probably the one Plato had in mind.[2] The agreed formula was that evil had a quasi-existence: it was a 'parahypostasis'. Nothing was wholly bad, but what was bad was brought about by the free choice of individuals. There was room neither in us for Plotinus' 'soul which always thinks' nor among the Principles for a Gnostic evil spirit. But the problem of evil in a theodicy was not unnoticed by the Neoplatonists. 'God is not responsible'—for evil. But he is responsible

[1] Simplicius, *In Enchirid.* 69–81 Dübner (pp. 162–87 Schweighäuser); Proclus, *De mal. subsist.* See further E. Schröder, *Plotins Abhandlung* ΠΟΘΕΝ ΤΑ ΚΑΚΑ (Diss. Rostock, 1915) (Borna–Leipzig, 1916), pp. 186–206. [For Plotinus' doctrine of matter as principle of evil see Part III, ch. 16 A, pp. 256–7.]

[2] Simplicius, *In Phys.* 249, 26 – 250, 5 Diels; Plato, *Tim.* 41 B.

for free will, which involves an 'aversion from the good'; only this, they said, is for the sake of greater good.

Free will was held to imply the contingency of propositions about the future. The basis for reconciling this with divine foreknowledge was laid by Iamblichus, who argued that the character of any object known was one thing, that of the knowing another.[1] The interest in logic later pointed to the distinctions made about necessity and possibility by Aristotle and Theophrastus. Thirdly the Athenian School examined time and eternity. All three elements are combined in Book v of the *Consolation of Philosophy* which represents the final solution of the Neo-platonists.[2] It is philosophically more sophisticated than Augustine's version. After distinguishing the grades of knowledge from those of its objects Boëthius argues that (1) God's eternity is of the extra-temporal kind which necessarily has an infinity of moving time (past and present) present to it; (2) therefore his *praevidentia* which is really *providentia* no more makes its objects necessary than our seeing what is going on makes what is going on necessary. (Ammonius had added that because the future will turn out one way or the other the gods necessarily know it.) (3) The necessity which does attach to events known by God is not simple ('All men are mortal') but conditional ('If you know that *A* is walking *A* is necessarily walking'); this kind is not the result of nature—*non propria facit natura sed condicionis necessitas*—so that who goes of his own accord, for instance, is not made to go by necessity, but while he is going he is necessarily going.

D. *The assimilation of Aristotle's logic*

Aristotle's logic particularly interested Ammonius' School, but they were drawing on a long tradition of assimilation. The Middle Academy had accepted the Aristotelian concepts, Plotinus had examined them dialectically and, as is well known, Porphyry restored them with qualifications but with a canonical position that they retained until

[1] *Ap.* Ammonius, *In De int.* 135, 14 Busse (*C.A.G.* IV 5); cf. Proclus, *De prov. et fato*, §§62–5 Boese (col. 193–5 Cousin [1864]; *In Parm.* III 224; 956, 30 ff.

[2] Cf. Ammonius, *In De int.* 135, 12 – 137, 11. But P. Courcelle's argument (*Les lettres grecques en occident*, nlle éd., Paris, 1948, pp. 288 ff.) that Boëthius (*c.* A.D. 480–525) studied in Alexandria is not cogent. [On this see Part VII (Western Christian Thought from Boëthius to Anselm), ch. 35, pp. 553–5.]

Boëthius could hand it unaltered to the Latin West.[1] It is the restoration and the qualifications which concern us; we have to explain how the metaphysically minded Neoplatonists ended with a logic which was more formal, autonomous or 'nominalist' than Aristotle's. The fact can be observed in Porphyry; and the modern belief that the paradox was due to Stoic influence rests on preconceived ideas rather than historical evidence.[2]

Aristotle's logic is a logic of terms. Its extra-logical foundations are the doctrines of categories and of predicables. The first classifies terms absolutely or, if not quite independently of propositions, independently of their truth. The predicables (in the *Topics*) are ways in which terms are predicated and dependent on the truth of propositions—quite acceptably for Aristotle since definition does not just relate concepts but describes nature; they are fundamental because they represent the formal relations of a classification by genus and species or the elements of Boolean algebra. But the two doctrines conflict at a non-logical or metaphysical level as can be seen in the case of the differentia. White, for example, can only be a quality but when it is a differentia it is predicated 'synonymously',[3] and this prevents it from being in subjects and therefore from being a quality.[4] Already felt in Aristotle's day, the difficulty was more noticed by the ancient commentators than it has been by the modern.[5] But the Neoplatonists saw in it a symptom of a graver malady.

How could any property belong to the substance of anything? According to the Aristotelians the differentia must come from outside the genus, but this would mean that the species was only half a substance, because it is the genus from which it gets its 'being'. (Aristotle's answer, that the species is not even divided as subject and predicate because it is form and appropriate matter, is in fact circular without an independent criterion of appropriateness.) The alternative, that the differentiae should fall under the genus, prevents the genus from being predicated unequivocally of its species and superordinate species. In

[1] The *Isagoge* was a regular part of the syllabus at Antioch by the 370's (Jerome *Ep.* L *ad init.*).

[2] See further A. C. Lloyd, 'Neoplatonic and Aristotelian logic', *Phronesis*, I (1955–6), pp. 58–72, 146–60; for a rather different view see C. Rutten, *Catégories du monde sensible dans les Ennéades de Plotin* (Paris 1961).

[3] κατὰ τὸν λόγον ὡς λόγον. See Aristotle, *Cat.* 3a33–4, and b9.

[4] *Ibid.* 2a30–1.

[5] Aristotle, *Top.* 128a20–9; cf. 122b16; Simplicius, *In Cat.* 48, 1–11. For Neoplatonists cf. *Phronesis*, *loc. cit.* 154.

fact such a series, 'in which there is a prior and a posterior' like the three kinds of soul or the numbers, does not have a generic universal at all, according to Aristotle;[1] an order of priority as we advance from species to genus, however, is just what Platonism did require. The dilemma was therefore either to save the logic at the cost of metaphysics—the substances—by accepting the Aristotelian genera or to save metaphysics at the cost of the logic. In fact both horns were sharper than that. Aristotelian logic 'telescoped' the genera and subaltern genera into the species, for it was a mere class algebra; on the other hand if the genus (being equivocal) could not be predicated of all that fell under it the Neoplatonic chain of being was meaningless.

The Neoplatonists found their solution in Aristotle himself. The first member of an ordered series was not predicated unequivocally of the successive members: but Aristotle recognized a class of terms which was not unequivocal but nevertheless not equivocal, namely those which were *ad unum* or *ab uno* by being dependent for their meanings on one which possessed it primarily or *par excellence*. Unity and being were both terms of this kind according to the *Metaphysics*.[2] Neoplatonists did not, so far as we know, simply say this of ordinary genera, but they were ready to whenever need arose;[3] and there are many signs of the species–genus relationship being replaced by the other; the clearest is the case where *procession or illumination* replaces *participation*—for that structural difference is the logical significance of the distinction between proceeding and participating.

In fact they accepted the two structures simultaneously, each possessing the appropriate kind of first term. A long quarrel over the actuality or potentiality of the differentiae in the genus was settled by Ammonius: the Platonists were referring to the genus which was 'prior to the many', the Aristotelians to the 'genus in the many'.[4] But the lecture-room question 'What is the subject-matter of logic?' had to have an answer which did not presuppose three kinds of whole to be discovered in the *Parmenides*. The categories, with which the subject

[1] *Met.* B 999a6 ff.; *Pol.* 1275a34–8; *De an.* 414b20–5.

[2] Γ 1, E 1, K 3.

[3] It was one of the meanings of 'genus' in the *Isagoge* (*ad init.*); and Ammonius significantly says that the terms of the relation involved are cause and effect (*In Isag.* 50, 7–9 Busse [*C.A.G.* IV 3]).

[4] Ammonius, *In Isag.* 104, 27 – 105, 13. See *Phronesis*, *loc. cit.* pp. 153–4.

was begun, were said to be neither words nor things, but words signifying things.[1] But what are primarily signified are mental concepts;[2] this point was used to meet objections which made the *Categories* either bad grammar or bad metaphysics; and it marked an advance beyond anything explicit in Aristotle of the conception of logic as an independent branch of philosophy.[3] So far from being Platonized it had fewer metaphysical commitments than Aristotle's. Despite the repetitions of historians, whoever made species a fifth predicable, it was not Porphyry, whose *Isagoge* aimed just to describe the terms (the 'quinque voces') necessary to the understanding of the *Categories*.[4]

It was a sign of the growing autonomy of the subject that Neoplatonists carried it well beyond the *Analytics* by examining hypothetical syllogisms; these had not been monopolized by the Stoa; and a classification of them has survived from Ammonius.[5] Even the Emperor Julian had taken part in a traditional dispute about the reduction of the second and third figures of categorical syllogisms to the first.[6] But the School made no fruitful discoveries of theorems in formal logic.

EPILOGUE

The philosophical characteristics of Neoplatonism

By the end of this pagan period of Neoplatonism it is easy to see how it completes one of the few undeniable 'dialectical' processes in the history of philosophy. The absorption of Aristotle transformed Platonism. But it is only when we have seen how Aristotle's logic was faced that it is possible to have some view of Neoplatonism in the round. The emphasis on the *ad unum* or *ab uno* concept by which he justified in *Metaphysics* E a universal science of being was fundamental. It would be exaggerating only a little to call Neoplatonism a protracted commentary on the Pythagoreanizing text there, 'Universal because first'

[1] φωναὶ σημαντικαὶ τῶν πραγμάτων, Porphyry, *In Cat.* 56, 34 ff. Busse (*C.A.G.* IV 1); *ap.* Simplicius, *In Cat.* 10, 21 – 11, 29. πράγματα has not its Stoic sense.

[2] νοήματα, Dexippus (pupil of Iamblichus), *In Cat.* I 3, pp. 6–10 Busse (*C.A.G.* IV 2).

[3] Cf. Simplicius, *In Cat.* 11, 33 David; *In Isag.* 120, 19 – 121, 2; 125, 7 – 126, 1 Busse.

[4] *Phronesis*, *loc. cit.* p. 156. For the significance of species as a predicable see H. W. B. Joseph, *Introduction to Logic*, 2nd ed. (Oxford, 1916), pp. 106–10.

[5] *In An pr.* 68 Wallies (*C.A.G.* IV 6).

[6] See Praechter, *s.v.* 'Maximus', *RE*, XIV, 2 (1930), 2567–8.

(1026a30). The paradox of Neoplatonism is the concept of emanation or procession, in which the cause produces its effect without containing it but is not a mere temporal antecedent because, on the contrary, reason can find the cause in the effect; and again, a concept which makes the cause logically simpler than the effect, the prior logically simpler than the posterior. An anthropomorphic notion of causing? Perhaps: but to their credit the Neoplatonists did not think this relevant. By developing Plotinus' philosophy as philosophy, his successors have made it possible for us not to resolve the paradox but to place it in relation to more familiar philosophical positions.

The fifth-century system represents above all rationalism in the sense that Descartes and Hegel are called rationalists. Degrees of reality coincided with degrees of simplicity because that made a real order coincide with a logical order; for to analyse a concept is to find the elements which are prior to it and which make it a complex by their presence. This rationalism necessarily makes relations internal relations, because the only truth it recognizes belongs to what Hume called relations of ideas. The golden rule of 'All things in everything, but appropriately' exemplified doubly a doctrine of internal relations. First, every substance had to be defined by referring to—and therefore as a thought by containing—all that it was not, in the way that Proclus found in the *Sophist* and Hegel in Proclus; secondly, the qualification 'appropriately' follows from the theory that a difference of relation or subject entails a difference in a quality possessed by the subject. It is illuminating to compare the way in which Leibniz applied the rule to what he too called monads. It may also help to compare the double structure of Aristotelian genera which obeyed formal logic and Platonic 'kinds' which did not with Hegel's 'concepts' and 'universals'.

This rationalism seems to have ebbed and flowed over the neighbouring position of monism. Once simplicity, unity, wholeness are marks of reality, parts of wholes and wholes which are only complexes can only have the status of appearances: such were the lower hypostases for Porphyry. And this at once suggests a further position, that of idealism. If there are illusions, what can they be but illusions of thought? But after Porphyry any idealist trend was resisted; Being was placed firmly above Thought (Intellect), where Plotinus had been thoroughly equivocal;

and with Iamblichus the priority of thought to thinking was schematized. There is, by the way, a good example here of the variety of dress in which philosophical problems can disguise themselves. Which place in which hypostasis was occupied by the Demiurge? The great quantity of ink spilt over this question looks at first sight to be a commentator's scholasticism run wild: in fact it conceals the problem of the relation of thought to its object.[1]

But there is a tendency which runs counter to all this and could be called romantic because it was anti-intellectual and because it imposed the language of poetry and religion on that of abstract philosophy. Even when Porphyry had rejected the Aristotelian view of God or the highest principle as thought and its object united, it was possible for him to suppose that the One above thought was *the unity* which was not thought but was attained in thought. But the next generation of Iamblichus and Theodorus ruled that out; it was one of the functions of the new term 'imparticipable' to do so. It is very difficult, though it has to be done in Neoplatonism, to call the 'single-mindedness' attributed to Intellect intellectual. But about the mystical union with the One there can be no question; it is not only ineffable, it is the negation of thought; more than that it is the negation of consciousness—Neoplatonists were quite clear about this. And this seems to belong to some Indian mysticism but to have no place in what counts as philosophy in Europe.[2]

But if the matter were as simple as that, the ascent to the One could logically be detached from the ascent to the unity of Intellect, the upward path of Dialectic. It is easy to see reasons why it ought to be; and there are two signs that it was thought so. It was not held to be within our control; and with Proclus the theory of henads may have allowed an independent path to God. But they universally held that the theoretic virtues were necessary preliminaries to the theurgic, and this objection is unanswerable. Nor do these merely reflect two quite unintegrated traditions. The division of unity into a unity which exists and of that into the kinds of existing unities and then the species of these represented successive applications of thought or reflection—or, generalized, the 'procession' of Intellect. From this point of view the

[1] As E. R. Dodds pointed out, Proclus, *Elements*..., pp. 285–7.

[2] [On the mystical union in Plotinus see Part III, ch. 16 (b), pp. 258–63: on Plotinus and Indian thought, ch. 12, pp. 200–1.]

reverse process represents successively *less* thought or reflection; we make fewer discriminations. So the One as non-thought will not be at the end of a different series from that of the unity of intellect.

The problem which remains is how the essential activity of thought should apparently lie in thinking less. It is the second paradox to emerge; and it is best to see the Neoplatonists' attempt to solve it as something which was quite peculiar to themselves and lay in their accepting two logical structures. 'Essential' thinking was thinking at its best rather than thinking most, just as the essential or definitive kind of soul was not *more* alive than its lower and mixed forms—in a plain sense, that might be said rather of these. Its objects were a series of 'ones' over 'manies'. But whatever these had been in the *Symposium*, the Neoplatonist has now distinguished them from the Aristotelian genera of species; each is a whole which is prior to its parts, the *unum* from which members of a series take a name by analogy, not a class which exists by being the disjunction or logical sum of sub-classes. Suppose animal is a genus, membership of which makes land, water and air animals animal: to try to think of animal without thinking of land, water and air animals is defective thinking. Suppose sunlight is light *par excellence* and by analogy to which other grades of light are counted as light: to try to think of sunlight without thinking of gas mantles and glow-worms is not defective thinking. The procession of thinking proceeds by one structure, the genera of Aristotle's logic; the reversion, though it has to pass through the genera as well, returns by the other kind of unity, which was the imparticipables. The structures are two points of view.

But each step, because perfect of its kind, was relatively real (Proclus' self-subsistence) and, because real, was also a thought; therefore at each step and not only at the summit there was involved some kind of simple awareness not divisible into the subject and predicate of a proposition. Indeed the idea of this non-discursive knowledge (which was not a disposition) is needed to make sense of 'the return' as a mental activity. Unfortunately it was so taken for granted in Greek epistemology that the group of philosophers that might have been expected to go some way towards explaining it did not.

PART V

MARIUS VICTORINUS AND AUGUSTINE

BY R. A. MARKUS

ABBREVIATIONS

MARIUS VICTORINUS

Ad Cand.	*Ad Candidum*
Adv. Ar.	*Adversus Arium*

(References to these, and to *Hymns* and *Candidi Epistola* I and II are to the Henry and Hadot edition (see bibliography); column numbers in *PL* 8 are added in brackets.)

Expl. in rhet.	*Explanationes in rhetoricam Ciceronis*
In Ephes.	*In epistolam Pauli ad Ephesios*
In Gal.	*In epistolam Pauli ad Galatas*
In Phil.	*In epistolam Pauli ad Philippenses*

AUGUSTINE

All references are given in the standard form of the text-division of the Benedictine edition, with variant text-divisions of modern critical editions noted where necessary. The volume and column numbers in *PL* are always added in brackets. Critical editions in *CC* and *CSEL* are noted in the following list where available.

Conf.	*Confessiones* (*CSEL* 33. 1)
C. Acad.	*Contra Academicos* (*CSEL* 63. 3)
C. Cresc.	*Contra Cresconium* (*CSEL* 52)
C. Faust.	*Contra Faustum Manichaeum* (*CSEL* 25. 1)
C. Jul.	*Contra Julianum*
C. litt. Pet.	*Contra litteras Petiliani* (*CSEL* 52)
De beata vita	(*CSEL* 63)
De cat. rud.	*De catechizandis rudibus*
De civ. Dei	*De civitate Dei* (*CC* 47–8)
De div. qu. LXXXIII	*De diversis quaestionibus* LXXXIII
De doctr. chr.	*De doctrina christiana* (*CC* 31)
De fide r.q.n.v.	*De fide rerum quae non videntur*
De Gen. ad litt.	*De Genesi ad litteram* (*CSEL* 28. 1)
De Gen. c. Man.	*De Genesi contra Manichaeos*
De imm. an.	*De immortalitate animae*
De lib. arb.	*De libero arbitrio*
De mag.	*De magistro* (*CSEL* 77)
De mor. eccl.	*De moribus ecclesiae catholicae et de moribus Manichaeorum*

De mus.	*De musica*
De ord.	*De ordine*
De praed. sanct.	*De praedestinatione sanctorum*
De quant. an.	*De quantitate animae*
De spir. et litt.	*De spiritu et littera* (*CSEL* 60)
De Trin.	*De Trinitate*
De urb. exc.	*Sermo de Urbis excidio*
De ut. cred.	*De utilitate credendi* (*CSEL* 25. 1)
De vera rel.	*De vera religione* (*CC* 31)
En. in Ps.	*Enarratio*[*nes*] *in Psalmos* (*CC* 38–40)
Ep., Epp.	*Epistola*[*e*] (*CSEL* 34, 44, 57, 58)
In Ep. Jo. Tr.	*In Ioannis epistulam ad Parthos tractatus*
In Jo. Ev. Tr.	*Tractatus in Evangelium Joannis* (*CC* 36)
Prop. Ep. Rom. Exp.	*Expositio quarumdam propositionum ex epistula ad Romanos*
Qu. in Hept.	*Quaestiones in Heptateuchum* (*CC* 33)
Retr.	*Retractationes* (*CSEL* 36)
Sermo	*Sermo*[*nes*]
Sol.	*Soliloquia*

CHAPTER 20

MARIUS VICTORINUS

A. *Life and writings*

What is known of Marius Victorinus' life is contained in the short notice given by St Jerome in his *De viris illustribus*[1] and in the better known remarks made by St Augustine in the course of the narrative of his own conversion.[2] African by birth and a rhetorician by profession, he taught in Rome under the Emperor Constantius. His fame as a rhetorician is attested not only by Augustine, but also by the statue which was erected to him in the Forum of Trajan in his lifetime, probably in the early fifties of the fourth century. An inscription of the late fourth century shows that it survived in Rome for at least two generations.[3] He had written grammatical, rhetorical and logical treatises, commentaries on Cicero and Aristotle. He had also translated 'books of the Platonists', as Augustine called them, and some of Aristotle's logical treatises and, very probably, Porphyry's *Isagoge*.[4] 'In extreme old age', as Jerome tells us, he became a Christian. This must have been soon after the erection of his statue in Rome, in the early or mid fifties, at any rate before 357 or 358, when the flow of his Christian theological writings begins.

Victorinus was closely associated with the senatorial aristocracy which became the last stronghold of Roman paganism. Augustine's celebrated narrative of Victorinus' conversion to Christianity allows us to glimpse something of the force of the social and cultural links which had held the distinguished rhetorician allied to the traditions of his class. To break them required the strength of mind which Augustine's story stresses and which served Augustine as a model for his own conversion. Augustine had already read Victorinus' translations of Neoplatonic literature when his Milanese friend, Simplicianus, who had known Victorinus well, told him the story of his conversion. Victorinus'

[1] *De vir. ill.* 101 (*PL* 23. 739). [2] *Conf.* VIII 2. 3–5 (*PL* 32. 749–51).
[3] Diehl, *Inscriptiones latinae christianae veteres* (Berlin, 1925), I, n. 104.
[4] Details in Henry and Hadot, I, p. 11. Surviving works are listed on p. 329.

greatest importance lies in the fact that he, more than anyone else, can claim to be the one great link between Greek philosophy and the Latin world in the fourth century. His literary output before his conversion strongly suggests that even as a pagan he wanted to provide the Latin West with new means of thought and expression. His theological works are a far-reaching attempt to use Neoplatonic philosophical concepts in Christian trinitarian theology.

Victorinus had become a Christian at a time of acute doctrinal conflict. The figure of St Athanasius divided the Church and the Empire; debate raged around his doctrine and his person for a generation. Victorinus' theological works are contributions to this debate. One of the many great merits of the superb edition of these works which we owe to Père Henry and M. Hadot is the new clarity with which it endows these obscure writings by relating them carefully, at every step, to the contemporary controversy between the years 355 and 363. With the theological controversy and with Victorinus' contribution to it we are not concerned.[1] His overriding purpose was to defend the Nicene doctrine of the consubstantiality of the Father and the Son, expressed in the formula which had become the rallying-point of Athanasian orthodoxy and the stumbling-block to opponents, that the Son is 'of one substance' (ὁμοούσιος) with the Father. The interest of Victorinus' defence of homoousian teaching, for the purposes of the present discussion, lies in his utilization of Neoplatonic ontological terms and concepts in the course of it. Victorinus' originality is the result of the tension between his concern to vindicate the equality and consubstantiality of the divine hypostases, and his use of a conceptual framework with a strong tendency to subordinate the hypostases to one another.[2] In order to make the ontology of Plotinus the foundation for homoousian trinitarian theology, the basic conceptions of that ontology had to undergo a considerable transformation in Victorinus' hands. In this Victorinus paved the way for a long tradition of Christian thinking. This transformation of Neoplatonic ontology is one of the two themes singled out for discussion in this chapter. The other is Victorinus' conception of the human soul and its threefold structure.

[1] Cf. Henry and Hadot, I, pp. 18–89 and II, *passim*.

[2] This is the argument of Gerhard Huber, *Das Sein und das Absolute* (Basel, 1955), pp. 93–116. I agree with its main outlines.

B. *Trinitarian ontology*

In his reply to the first letter of the Arian Candidus, Victorinus distinguishes four modalities of being.[1] This classification, deriving ultimately from Plato and incorporated into Neoplatonic scholasticism, distinguished between four levels of being and non-being. First, *ea quae vere sunt* (ὄντως ὄντα), the highest level, which is that of intelligible reality.[2] Second, *quae sunt* (ὄντα), the level to which the soul belongs. The soul is able to know the highest level of being, in virtue of the intellect (νοῦς) which enters the intelligent soul, as well as its own level, which it understands in virtue of its own nature.[3] Beneath these two levels are two grades conceivable only in terms of being, as its degradation. Third, *quae non vere non sunt* (μὴ ὄντως μὴ ὄντα), that is to say, the things which the mind knows in the material world, which in some manner participate in the nature of animated reality. They belong to *quae sunt* in virtue of their affinity with soul, to *quae non sunt* in virtue of their being material (ὕλη) and subject to changing qualities.[4] Fourth, *quae non sunt* (μὴ ὄντα)—inanimate matter.[5] Below this there is nothing, for *quae vere non sunt* have no name or being of any sort.[6] This enumeration is carried out from the point of view of the soul; the various levels of being are distinguished according to their relation to the soul and its awareness of them.[7]

God is not included in any of the four modalities of being; he is their cause and brings them into being, but is himself above all being, above 'what is really being', above all life and all knowledge; he is therefore non-being.[8] This non-being above being is known only by ignorance.[9] Victorinus refers to it as 'pre-being' (προόν).[10] This is the 'divine perfection, perfect in every way, full, absolute and above all perfections. This

[1] *Ad Cand.* 6. 1 – 11. 12 (1023a–1026c). On the sources and development of this doctrine, see F. W. Kohnke, 'Plato's conception of τὸ οὐκ ὄντως οὐκ ὄν', *Phronesis*, II (1957), pp. 32–40.

[2] *Ad Cand.* 7. 8–9 (1023b).

[3] *Ibid.* 8. 2–7 (1024a).

[4] *Ibid.* 9. 4–10. 6 (1024b–1025b).

[5] *Ibid.* 10. 7–37 (1025b–1026b).

[6] *Ibid.* 11. 1–12 (1026b–c); the kinds of non-being are discussed in *Ad Cand.* 4. 1 – 5. 16 (1022a–c).

[7] As noted in Henry and Hadot, p. 703. This appears particularly clearly in *Ad Cand.* 9, where sensation of the μὴ ὄντως μὴ ὄντα is described as 'simulacrum...intellecti et imitamentum intelligendi...' (9. 8–9, 1024c).

[8] *Ibid.* 13 (1027b).

[9] *Ibid.* 14. 1–5 (1027b–c).

[10] *Ibid.* 15. 2 (1028b); 2. 28 (1021a); 3. 7 (1021c).

is God, above mind, above truth, omnipotent power and therefore unlimited by any formal specification.'[1] It is the wholly transcendent One of Neoplatonic thought,[2] and the whole ontological scheme falls squarely within its tradition of 'negative theology'. The novelty in Victorinus' use of this scheme lies in the way he uses it to establish the consubstantiality of God's *Logos* with God.

'God', in this context, is the person of the Father. His Son is properly called Logos, the first existence, the first substance, wisdom, and so forth.[3] In terms of the relation between the Plotinian hypostases, the relation of Father to Son corresponds to the relation of the One to Intellect. But Victorinus repudiates the tendency implied by the Neoplatonic scheme to subordinate the second to the first hypostasis.

Whereas the Father is above Intellect, above truth and indeterminate,[4] Intellect and truth are determinate 'forms'. The Father is silence, rest and immobility; the procession of his power is a Word, movement and life. Essence, silence, rest are the Father; life, word, movement or action are the Son.[5] The Son is conceived as the 'form' of God. 'God is, as it were, something hidden...the Son is the form in which God is seen.'[6] The Son is thus the determination of God, he is being (ὄν), the first and perfect being.[7] But, as form, the Son is not external to the Father; as formless *esse* and formed being (ὄν) respectively, they are one substance, in which is shown forth what is hidden in the Father.[8] The Son is the Father's manifestation, wherein what is manifested and its manifestation are one 'subsistent substance'. Victorinus is using Neoplatonic conceptions to distinguish Father and Son: the Father is beyond all knowledge, the Son reveals him and manifests him. The Son 'forms' the Father's formless substance and thereby manifests him; 'manifestation is bringing forth from a state of latent darkness, and this bringing forth is a birth: it is the birth of a reality existing prior to its

[1] '...plena, absoluta, super omnes perfectiones, omnimodis est divina perfectio. Hic est deus, supra νοῦν, supra veritatem, omnipotens potentia et idcirco non forma' (*Adv. Ar.* III 7. 15–17, 1103c).

[2] *Adv. Ar.* I 49. 9–40 (1078b–d).

[3] *Ibid.* I 56. 15–20 (1083a).

[4] Cf. above, n. 1.

[5] *Ibid.* in the sequel to the passage quoted in n. 1. Its interest lies in the *rapprochement* between νοῦς and the Son made in this passage.

[6] *Adv. Ar.* I 53. 13–15 (1081c); cf. *In Gal.* II [4. 6] (1179a–b).

[7] *Ad Cand.* 2. 28–35 (1021a–b); 14. 23–7 (1028a–b).

[8] *Adv. Ar.* I 53. 9–13 (1081c); I 22. 28–37 (1056b).

coming forth'.[1] Together with their distinction, Victorinus is always insisting on their substantial unity: 'all being has its determination inseparable from itself, or rather the determination is itself substance, not because it is prior to that which is being, but because the determination defines that which is being. That which is being is the cause of the being of its determination....'[2] This distinction between *esse* and *species* is parallel to the distinction between *substantia* and *forma*.[3] In both types of language Victorinus asserts the consubstantiality of Father and Son, and at the same time their mutual relation.

This central concern to vindicate the consubstantiality of the hypostases, which Neoplatonic thought would separate and subordinate, leads Victorinus to take considerable liberties with the philosophical framework within which he works. To assert the substantial identity of something absolutely transcendent and something specified by form, of something wholly beyond knowledge with something which reveals it, constitutes a radical departure from the original philosophical framework within which these radical distinctions are drawn. It amounts to a fundamental change of view about the unknowability of the absolute, and indeed we find the 'negative theology' characteristic of the Neoplatonic framework receding into the background with Victorinus.[4] The substantial unification of the two hypostases closes the gulf between absolute transcendence and determinate being and therefore between unknowability and knowability. Victorinus is prepared to make statements about God which Plotinus could not have countenanced of the One. 'To remain orthodox as a theologian he was forced to achieve some degree of originality as a thinker.'[5] Victorinus telescopes into his conception of God what Neoplatonic ontology had separated among the hypostases, and emphasizes the features of one or other of the hypostases as it suits his purpose.

[1] *Ibid.* IV 15. 23–6 (1124b).

[2] 'Omne enim esse inseparabilem speciem habet, magis autem ipsa species ipsa substantia est, non quo prius sit ab eo quod est esse, species, sed quod definitum facit species illud quod est esse. Et enim quod est esse causa est speciei esse...' (*Adv. Ar.* I 19. 29–34).

[3] Cf. above, p. 334.

[4] On this topic cf. P. Henry, 'The *adversus Arium* of Marius Victorinus: the first systematic exposition of the doctrine of the Trinity', *JTS*, n.s. I (1950), pp. 42–55, especially pp. 48–9; also Huber, *op. cit.* pp. 95–7.

[5] Henry, *loc. cit.* p. 48. [For the closest approach within pagan Neoplatonism of the fourth century to the position of Marius Victorinus see the preceding Part (IV), ch. 18 (b), pp. 291–2.]

Transcendence in the order of knowledge is the correlative of transcendent being. To do away with the transcendence of the absolute in the order of knowledge involves a different conception of absolute being. The transcendent is itself drawn into the sphere of being, and although Victorinus refuses to speak of the Father as *on*, he is forced to concede that he has being (*esse*);[1] and this *esse* is in turn described in terms of a 'negative theology' which, in the Neoplatonic scheme, would be appropriate to the One.[2] *Esse* is removed from the realm of understanding (λόγος); it is thought of as something beyond rationality and thought, which is brought into the realm of rationality only when defined by a *logos*. The effects of telescoping the Neoplatonic hypostases are far-reaching: on the one hand absolute transcendence is brought into the realm of being; on the other, being as such is removed from the realm of rationality.[3]

Related to Victorinus' concentration in God of attributes which are found dispersed among the Neoplatonic hypostases is what Père Henry has called his 'concrete and dynamic outlook'.[4] One of the ways in which Victorinus defines the relation between Father and Son is that of potency to act, this being equivalent to the relation of hidden and manifest.[5] Just as hidden and manifest are consubstantial, so are potency and act. 'God is potency and the Logos is act, and each is both...the Father is Father because potency engenders act, and the act is the Son because it is act proceeding from potency.'[6] Through their consubstantiality, activity becomes the essential constitutive character of being. The second trinitarian hypostasis is 'a certain active paternal potency in movement, which constitutes itself to be in act rather than in potency'.[7] Thus the Father is the source of being, brimming over with life and potentiality, and his Word, the Son, is his creative activity whereby everything is brought into being.[8]

The duality of potency and act is further equivalent to that of being and its image: 'for all that proceeds into action is the image of what it is

[1] *Adv. Ar.* II 4. 2–34 (1091d–1092c); IV 19. 4–37 (1127a–d).

[2] *Ibid.* IV 19. 4–37 (1127a–d); cf. Huber's remarks, *op. cit.* pp. 114–15.

[3] A particularly fine passage which illustrates both these tendencies simultaneously is *Adv. Ar.* IV 23. 12–45 (1129c–1130a).

[4] *Loc. cit.* pp. 50–1.

[5] *Adv. Ar.* I 19. 23–4 (1052d); *Ad Cand.* 14. 11–13 (1028a).

[6] *Adv. Ar.* II 3. 34–9 (1091b).

[7] *Ad Cand.* 17. 2–4 (1029b–c).

[8] *Ibid.* 22. 10–19 (1031c); 25. 1–10 (1032b–c).

in potency'.[1] Substance and image imply one another mutually. They are correlatives, and the image is itself substantial. Father and Son are consubstantial in their image; the two are one image as they are one substance, the image being in potency in the Father, in act in the Son.[2] The importance of this further duality of substance and image will emerge in the next section of this chapter.

C. *Trinitarian psychology*

Victorinus had devoted some thought to the soul before becoming a Christian.[3] In his Christian writings his interest in it is both deepened and narrowed: he is now primarily concerned with the soul as the image of the Logos. Christ is the Logos and the image of God; the soul is not the Logos, but, being rational (λογικός), it participates in the nature of the Logos. It is not, therefore, the image of God, but, in the words of Genesis (i. 26), made *iuxta imaginem*.[4] Victorinus is careful to distinguish its being made in the image of God from its being made in his likeness: rationality belongs to the soul's nature, whereas likeness obtains between things in virtue of their respective qualities. Hence, to be made in the image of God concerns the soul substantially, to be made in his likeness concerns it in respect of its qualities.[5] The former is essential and cannot be lost, whereas the latter is accidental and may be lost and recovered.[6] The soul is primarily the image of the Logos; it is the image of the Trinity indirectly, in so far as the Logos itself mirrors the life of the whole Trinity. It is the 'image of an image'.[7]

In the divine Trinity the basic duality of Father and Son, which has been considered under various aspects in the previous section, produces a Trinity because the Logos is itself a duality. From the *esse* of the Father proceeds a single movement which is both life (*vivere*) and understanding (*intellegere*).[8] With the Trinitarian theology we are not concerned here; what is of interest is how the soul, image of the Logos,

[1] *Adv. Ar.* I 25. 32–3 (1059a).
[2] *Ibid.* I 20. 7–23 (1053c–d).
[3] *Expl. in rhet.* I 1 (Halm, p. 155); I 2 (Halm, pp. 160–1).
[4] *Adv. Ar.* I 20. 24–36 (1054a).
[5] *Ibid.* I 28. 7–12 (1056d); I 41. 9–19 (1071d–2a).
[6] *Ibid.* I 20. 37–65 (1054b–c).
[7] *Ibid.* I 63. 7–18 (1087c–d). On this, see the excellent analysis by P. Hadot, 'L'Image de la Trinité dans l'âme chez Victorinus et chez saint Augustin', *Studia Patristica*, VI [*Texte und Untersuchungen*, Bd. 81] (1962), 409–42, especially p. 411.
[8] E.g. *Adv. Ar.* III 2. 12–32 (1099b–d).

reflects this threefoldness in God. The structure of the soul as described by Victorinus reflects the trinity of *esse*, *vivere* and *intellegere* closely. Victorinus, again, begins with a duality: the soul, like matter, being a substance, must have a determinate form and image. Matter receives its determination through quantity, soul through its vital and intellectual potency.[1] Just as the Logos is the 'dynamic definition of the divine substance',[2] its movement, actuation and manifestation, so the soul is defined by its life and intelligence. In the soul, too, life and intelligence are a 'double potency, existing in a single movement'.[3] The trinity in the soul, as in God, is the result of a further duality in the Logos within the primary duality of Logos and *esse*.

The soul's self-defining movement, its life and understanding, is consubstantial with its being, and in this respect the trinitarian structure of the soul reflects that of God. In the soul, however, life and understanding can be, in a certain sense, 'alienated' from the soul's being. 'The soul with its *nous*, which it has from him who is *nous*, is the potency of intellectual life. It is not itself *nous*, but it becomes, so to speak, identified with *nous* in beholding *nous*: for here vision is the same as union. But turning away from *nous* and looking downwards, it drags itself and its own proper *nous* downwards, becoming only intelligent, having previously been both intelligent and intelligible.... Since the soul is a kind of Logos but not the Logos, being poised mid-way between spiritual and intelligible realities on the one hand and matter on the other, and able to turn with its own *nous* towards either, it becomes either divine or descends to the level of intelligence.'[4] Even in its fallen state the soul preserves a spark of its own *nous* which enables it, if it chooses, to return to its higher state.[5] In its fallen state the substance of the soul's activity retains its identity with its being, and hence remains in the image of the Logos. But the direction of its activity determines the

[1] *Adv. Ar.* I 32. 16–29 (1064d–1065a).

[2] The phrase is Hadot's, *loc. cit.* p. 414, whose exposition I follow here.

[3] *Adv. Ar.* I 32. 29–78 (1065a–d); cf. *ibid.* I 63. 24–7 (1088a).

[4] *Ibid.* I 61. 7–21 (1086b–c): 'Anima autem cum suo νῷ, ab eo qui νοῦς est, potentia vitae intellectualis est, non νοῦς est, ad νοῦν quidem respiciens quasi νοῦς est. Visio enim ibi unitio est. Vergens autem deorsum et aversa a νῷ, et se et suum νοῦν trahit deorsum, intellegens tantum effecta, non iam ut [et?] intellegens et intelligibile...Etenim cum quidam λόγος sit anima, non λόγος, cumque in medio spirituum et intelligibilium et τῆς ὕλης, proprio νῷ ad utraque conversa, aut divina fit aut incorporatur ad intellegentia.

[5] *Ibid.* I 61. 21–4 (1086c).

soul's character and its likeness or unlikeness to the Logos. In entering the realm of passion, change and corruption, the soul loses its primal likeness to God. It remains his image, however, and it can therefore return to its primal condition of likeness. Its likeness is recovered by returning to the contemplation of divine realities.[1]

Here in brief outline we have, some fifty years before Augustine, the 'psychological doctrine' of the Trinity,[2] that is to say, an account of it elaborated in the same terms as apply to the life of the soul. There is much in Saint Augustine's work that recalls Victorinus' treatment. Père Henry has rightly stressed the pioneering originality of Victorinus in this field.[3] But if the two writers share much of their central inspiration, there are nevertheless important differences between their respective trinitarian theories. Some of these have been studied by M. Hadot in an illuminating article.[4] He has drawn attention to important differences in their conceptions of generation (involving Augustine's use of the category of relation); to Augustine's preference for trinitarian schemes such as that of memory, intelligence and will, in which the three terms are consubstantial between them, rather than for schemes like that of Victorinus (being, life, understanding; Augustine: e.g. mind, knowledge, love), schemes in which the second and third terms are of the substance of the first, their substantiality being communicated to them by it. He has also noted that, whereas Victorinus' trinitarian theology is a theory of the procession of the second hypostasis from the divine being, Augustine in fact only discusses the image of this procession in the human soul. Behind this difference there seems to me to lie a deeper difference of approach and temper which deserves more emphasis than is given it by M. Hadot: Victorinus' trinitarian theology is essentially an essay in metaphysics, based on Neoplatonic ontology, though transforming this in the course of adapting it to the purpose in hand. His theology is scriptural in the second place only. Notwithstanding the considerable place occupied by scriptural discussions in his work, his system of trinitarian doctrine is the product of an independent

[1] Cf. *ibid.* I 32. 61–78 (1065 c–d), and the exposition by Hadot, *loc. cit.* pp. 415–21.

[2] Cf. Henry, *loc. cit.* (p. 335 n. 4 above), p. 54.

[3] Henry, *loc. cit. passim*; though he assumes too readily that Victorinus' influence is responsible for the similarities of doctrine.

[4] *Art. cit.* (p. 337 n. 7 above), especially pp. 424–42.

philosophical inquiry deductive, we might almost say, in nature. The scriptural testimony is adduced as a further and parallel approach leading to the same set of conclusions. It does not underlie the whole inquiry as its essential premise. On Augustine's trinitarian theology this is not the place to dwell.[1] To contrast it with Victorinus', it is sufficient to characterize it as at once more scriptural in its approach and less metaphysical in procedure. The 'psychological trinitarianism' of the second part of his treatise *De Trinitate* is a study not of the divine substance and persons, but of the human soul as an image of God. Its psychology is more tentative and more empirical; the theological application of the analogies more indirect and more agnostic. That it nevertheless springs from a similar philosophical background is beyond doubt, even though it is far from clear what immediate sources lay behind it. M. Hadot has provided strong reasons for thinking that they did not include Victorinus' anti-Arian treatises;[2] and in my view further study is only likely to confirm this judgement. Victorinus was certainly a pioneer; and through his translations of 'books of the Platonists' he provided Augustine with expressions of the philosophical outlook which they had in common. But it is Augustine who 'has determined for centuries the standard western doctrine of the Trinity'.[3]

[1] Cf. the remarks below, ch. 21, pp. 352–3.

[2] *Loc. cit.* pp. 432–42. Augustine may, however, have read commentaries on letters of St Paul by Victorinus.

[3] Henry, *loc. cit.* (p. 335 n. 4 above), p. 42.

CHAPTER 21

AUGUSTINE

BIOGRAPHICAL INTRODUCTION: CHRISTIANITY AND PHILOSOPHY

St Augustine's life spanned almost eighty years of a period during which the 'decline of the Roman Empire' passed through its most dramatic, if not its most decisive, phase. Born into the Christian Empire of Constantine's successors, his youth saw the brief pagan reaction under Julian the Apostate, followed by the return to Christianity and the ever closer linking of the Empire to Christianity under the Emperors Gratian and Theodosius I. During the latter part of his life Roman paganism, which had rallied its forces during the last decade of the fourth century, was rapidly becoming a relic of the past, though it remained a force to be reckoned with. He witnessed not only an important phase in the Christianization of the ancient world; he also lived through some of its gravest military and political upheavals: the military disaster of Adrianople (378), the division of the Empire after Theodosius, the irruption of Vandals, Sueves and other barbarians into the western provinces of the Empire (406), the increasing barbarization of the Roman armies and of the imperial court, the sacking of the City of Rome by the Visigoths (410). These are some of the landmarks. The Vandal invaders of his own North Africa had just reached his episcopal city of Hippo as he lay on his deathbed. In an important sense his life may be said to coincide with the transition from antiquity to the Middle Ages.

Augustine belonged to both worlds, in many ways, and not least intellectually. He received the kind of education which was typical of late antiquity, characterized by a predominantly literary or rhetorical outlook. It was strongly conservative in that its aim was to form the mind on the pattern of outstanding products of the past. In an age when the gap between this literary culture and popular speech was widening, the natural tendency of this kind of education was to produce a somewhat artificial form of 'polite' letters, a kind of learning which set little value on improvisation, liveliness or originality, and could, sometimes, consist of little more than arid stylistic exercises. Its store of philosophical learning was normally derived from compendia and excerpts from philosophical writers.

The traditional round of elementary and secondary studies—grammar, dialectic, rhetoric, music, geometry, astronomy and arithmetic—was generally held to be the necessary preparation for a philosopher. Sometimes, indeed, they succeeded in providing the stimulus for serious and sustained thought. Augustine's own intellectual pilgrimage began with a reading of Cicero's now lost *Hortensius*. He read this work at the age of eighteen. Recalling, in his forties, the impact it had made on his mind, Augustine describes the experience in terms of a 'conversion'. It had led him to break through the limits of the purely rhetorical conception of his education: he used the work not 'for the sharpening of his tongue', but followed its 'exhortation to philosophy'. It had given him a new purpose and a new concern, the pursuit of immortal wisdom. Looking back on the experience, Augustine could interpret this turning to philosophy as the beginning of his journey of return to God.[1]

His quest of wisdom led him through devious paths; it was not for another fifteen years that his intellectual restlessness finally brought him to the font, to the acceptance of the Christian faith. Before reaching its assurance, he entered on the career of a professional teacher of rhetoric, which he pursued first at Thagaste, his native city, then at Carthage, Rome and, finally, the imperial capital, Milan. Reflecting in his *Confessions* on this scintillating career of worldly success, he describes the tension in his mind between the lure of public reputation and the quest for wisdom on which he had been launched. During this time Manichaean teaching offered Augustine a temporary resting-place. Its teaching about two warring worlds, the good world of a perfect deity and the evil world of a primordial adversary, provided him with a mythological projection of the fierce tensions of his own make-up. The Manichaean 'elect' felt himself to belong by nature to the pure world of light, though temporarily caught up in the world of darkness. To realize the promise of deliverance held out to him and to satisfy his longing for it,

[1] *Conf.* III 4. 7 (*PL* 32. 685); cf. *De beata vita* I. 4 (*PL* 32. 961).

he had to repudiate the realm of the body as something foreign to him, to be cast aside. It is not difficult to understand why such a world-picture should appeal to Augustine's spiritual restlessness and longing, and his passionate, strongly emotional temperament. For some years Augustine remained an adherent of the sect, but its teaching could not afford him intellectual satisfaction, and he became gradually disillusioned with it. Much of his own later thinking is shaped by a concern to reject some of the basic Manichaean tenets.

The great turning-point in his life came with his appointment to the chair of rhetoric at Milan. He got the appointment through the influence of some of his Manichaean friends; but his new post brought him into contact with Ambrose, the bishop of Milan, and his circle of Christian intellectuals, who were above all instrumental in bringing about his final break with the Manichees. This was not Augustine's first encounter with Christianity: he had had ample opportunity to learn of its teaching from his devout mother, Monica. But it was in St Ambrose's preaching that he first encountered Christian teaching in an intellectually satisfying form. It soon gained the ascendancy in his mind. All that was left now was for Augustine to overcome his hesitation and reluctance. The agonizing conflict of desires which he records in Books VI–VIII of his *Confessions* was finally resolved with his conversion in 386 and baptism the following Easter.

In the circle of Ambrose, Simplicianus, Mallius Theodorus and others, Augustine came across a Christianity coloured by Neoplatonic interpretation. He does not appear to have felt any sharp need, at the time of his conversion, to disentangle the teaching of Christianity from that of the 'Platonists'. It was easy to pass from the atmosphere of Plotinus and Porphyry to that of St Paul and the Fourth Gospel, and Augustine had no sense of any radical transition. He was content to find in 'the books of the Platonists' the main doctrines of Christianity anticipated. There, in so many words, he had read of God and his Word, of the creation, of the divine light shining forth in the darkness, and so forth; it was only the belief in the incarnation of the Word, and the earthly life and death of Jesus, which he had not found anticipated in the works of the philosophers.[1] In later life Augustine came to see a wider gulf

[1] *Conf.* VII 9. 13–14 (*PL* 32. 740–1).

between Christianity and Platonism, but essentially Platonism remained in his eyes a preparation for the Gospel. His fundamental charge against its exponents is that the blindness of their pride and self-sufficiency has prevented them from accepting the way to salvation, Christ made man, crucified and risen.[1] In his *Confessions* he describes the new discovery brought him by a reading of the Scriptures (*after* his reading of the Neo-platonists). It was the difference between 'presumption and confession, between those who see the goal but do not see the way, and those who also see the way which leads us to that country of blessedness which we are made not only to know, but also to dwell in'.[2] Throughout, from his conversion to 'philosophy' at the age of eighteen to his conversion to Christianity some fifteen years later, and for the remainder of his life, Augustine conceived of 'philosophy' in a sense which would be odd to twentieth-century usage, but was generally shared by his contemporaries. He included under this heading everything that was of ultimate concern to man, everything relevant to the question: how is a man to attain his ultimate fulfilment, that is, 'blessedness' (*beatitudo*)?

This conception of philosophy as an all-embracing activity concerned with everything relevant to the realization of the ultimate purpose of human life is itself derived from antiquity. Augustine refers to Varro's now lost manual of philosophy, in which 288 different 'philosophies' had been distinguished precisely according to the kinds of answer it was possible to give to the question how the happy life is to be attained.[3] They were all assumed to agree on the purpose, and to differ among themselves only concerning the means by which this was to be attained. According to this usage, Christianity was clearly a 'philosophy'; and in the works written at the time of his conversion to Christianity and immediately following it, Augustine interpreted his conversion as the result of his quest for wisdom, and often speaks of having arrived 'in the haven of philosophy'.[4] 'Christianity' and 'true philosophy' are practically synonymous terms; and, indeed, Augustine later once defined Christianity simply as the one true philosophy.[5] He often

[1] Cf. *De civ. Dei* x 29 (*PL* 41. 307–9); *Epp.* 118. 17; 120. 6 (*PL* 33. 440; 455).

[2] *Conf.* vii 20. 26 (*PL* 32. 747).

[3] *De civ. Dei* xix 1. 2 (*PL* 41. 621–3).

[4] E.g. *De beata vita* 1. 1; 1. 5 (*PL* 32. 959; 961).

[5] *C. Julian.* iv 14. 72 (*PL* 44. 774).

defines 'philosophy', following the etymology, as the love of wisdom;[1] and wisdom has to do with the truth about the nature and the attainment of the supreme good,[2] that in which man finds his complete and ultimate fulfilment. Once he had come to accept Christian teaching as the way to salvation, it inevitably followed from these definitions that Christianity was the 'true philosophy'. The desire for happiness is common to philosophers and Christians;[3] but philosophers, 'even though endowed with great intelligence and plenty of time, and well-versed in profound learning, relying on human argumentation', only rarely reach the truth, and then not the whole truth; as often as not their inquiries lead them into falsehood—hence the variety of philosophic schools and their disagreements among themselves.[4] The Christian faith, however, is based not on human guesswork, but on the sacred scriptures, in which God commends his truth to his people: its authors are their 'philosophers, that is, their lovers of wisdom, they are their wise men, their theologians, their prophets, they are their teachers of righteousness and of holiness'.[5] The scriptures are the authoritative source of 'Christian philosophy'.

Notwithstanding, therefore, the conception of Christianity as the true philosophy, Augustine clearly recognizes a fundamental difference between the philosophy pursued by philosophers and the 'philosophy' adhered to by Christian believers. This difference is not one concerning only the contents of their respective teaching; it is also, and primarily, a difference in procedure: as he puts it in one of his earliest works, one proceeds by reasoning, the other from authority.[6] The key constituents of Christian belief are credal statements concerning historical occurrences and, as such, lie outside the realm of the abstract, general truths accessible to philosophical reflection. In a later work Augustine gives a very clear statement of this inaccessibility to philosophical reflection of the contingent, historical facts of Christian belief, such as the resurrection of Jesus Christ.[7] It appears, therefore, that although he was content to speak of Christianity as 'philosophy', he also used the term 'philosophy' in a narrower, technical, sense akin to that of modern usage.

[1] E.g. *De ord.* I 11. 32 (*PL* 32. 993); *De Trin.* XIV 1. 2 (*PL* 42. 1037).

[2] Cf. *De lib. arb.* II 9. 26 (*PL* 32. 1254).

[3] *Sermo* 150. 3. 4 (*PL* 38. 809).

[4] *De Trin.* XIII 7. 10 (*PL* 42. 1020–1); cf. *De civ. Dei* XVIII 41. 2 (*PL* 41. 601).

[5] *De civ. Dei* XVIII 41. 3 (*PL* 41. 602).

[6] *De ord.* II 5. 16 (*PL* 32. 1002).

[7] *De Trin.* IV 16. 21 (*PL* 42. 902); cf. *De vera rel.* 7. 13 (*PL* 34. 128).

How did Augustine consider philosophy in this narrower sense to be related to the true, 'Christian philosophy'? As we have already seen (see above, p. 343), he thought that the 'Platonists', whom he calls *praecipui gentium philosophi*,[1] had anticipated some aspects of Christian teaching, notably those which were not historical and contingent in character. Thus the scriptures warn not against philosophers as such, but against 'philosophers of this world'.[2] The fact remains, however, that no matter how close philosophers have got to Christianity, they can add nothing to its saving doctrine: the uninstructed, faithful believer, by clinging to the cross of Christ, can reach the heavenly home denied to the learned philosopher whose reasoning enables him to know it;[3] the ignorant Christian who knows nothing of philosophy knows all he needs to know in order to achieve happiness in cleaving to God.[4] Augustine is here following the Pauline teaching about the wisdom of the world which God has made foolishness, and the foolishness of preaching Christ crucified, through which it has pleased God to save the world.[5] To this Pauline doctrine Augustine adhered even in his earliest works, where—in a more uncritically intellectualist temper of mind—he confessed that he could not see how people who were content to rely on authority, and either could not or would not resort to the 'liberal arts', could possibly be called happy in this life.[6] In his *Confessions*[7] Augustine expresses gratitude for having encountered the 'books of the Platonists' before those of the scriptures: they had thus prepared him to accept the scriptures, whereas his fear is that had he encountered them in the reverse order, 'they [the books of the Platonists] might perhaps have swept me away from the solid ground of piety' or, alternatively, that he might have come to think of them as sufficient by themselves. Philosophy, it appears, has nothing to contribute to the believer, and might even constitute a danger to his faith.

But Augustine does not belong with that strong current of Christian

[1] *De Trin.* XIII 19. 24 (*PL* 42. 1034); this thought is central to *De civ. Dei* VIII.

[2] *De ord.* I 11. 32 (*PL* 32. 993); the undue *rapprochement* between Christianity and Platonism in this passage for which Augustine criticizes himself in *Retr.* I 3. 2 (*PL* 32. 588–9) is a different matter and does not affect his interpretation of the warning against philosophy; cf. *De civ. Dei* VIII 10. 1 (*PL* 41. 234), and below, p. 364.

[3] *De Trin.* IV 15. 20 (*PL* 42. 901–2).

[4] *De civ. Dei* VIII 10. 2 (*PL* 41. 235).

[5] I Cor. i. 18–25.

[6] *De ord.* II 9. 26 (*PL* 32. 1007).

[7] VII 20. 26 (*PL* 32. 746–7).

tradition which can find no place for philosophy in the mind of the Christian believer. In a classical image he sums up the attitude he recommends: as Israel had spoiled the Egyptians of their treasures and had taken them with them on their journey to the promised land, so philosophers who have spoken truly and in consonance with the Christian faith are not only not to be feared, but what they have to offer 'the Christian is to take from them in order to devote it to the just purpose of preaching the Gospel'.[1] The second book of his work *De doctrina christiana* is devoted to a discussion of the principles on which Christianity can adopt and utilize the culture of classical antiquity. Compared with the youthful enthusiasm for its achievements which is so marked a feature of his earliest dialogues, Augustine is much more reserved here. Philosophical thought, as well as the other branches of learning, are no longer to be pursued for their own sake. All the fields of knowledge and the arts are rigidly subordinated to the service of a purpose which lies beyond them, that of the Christian faith. On a superficial reading the programme of the *De doctrina christiana* seems almost inhumanly narrow, with its uncompromising exclusion of all that is not relevant to the study of the scriptures. The narrowing of outlook, however, seems to me to be illusory. M. Marrou has described[2] Augustine's achievement as a 'real liberation' from the fetters of the culture of his time. Whatever he owed to it—and it was a great deal—at a profounder level than any of his Christian predecessors, he has in reality broken with it. 'His attitude represents an effective and momentous realization of the decadence of the ancient world.... In spite of appearances, it is he, with his sombre asceticism, rather than the refined urbanity of a Symmachus or an Ausonius, that represents the lasting values of humanism at this time.'[3] There is certainly a kind of concentration noticeable in Augustine's interests beginning in the mid 390's. On returning to Africa after his baptism, Augustine first lived in a kind of monastic retirement with a group of like-minded, cultivated friends. Within a few years, however, he was made a priest of the church of Hippo, to assist its aged bishop Valerius; and soon Augustine succeeded him as bishop. The whole orientation of his intellectual life

[1] *De doctr. chr.* II 40. 60 (*PL* 34. 63).

[2] H. I. Marrou, *Saint Augustin et la fin de la culture antique* (Paris, 1938), pp. 352–6.

[3] *Ibid.* p. 353.

was modified in these years. All his energies and interests are now turned into pastoral channels; the needs of his own church of Hippo, and of the church of North Africa, of which he rapidly became one of the most distinguished and most influential figures, are uppermost in his mind. He has not ceased to be a scholar and thinker, but has become a scholar and thinker entirely at the service of his church and of his people. As his Christian faith penetrates his mind more deeply, all his learning and talents are brought into intimate relation with it. In putting the legacy of classical culture at the service of the Christian faith, Augustine did not only contribute much to shaping the minds of men of the Middle Ages; he also helped to keep some of the achievements of antiquity alive by using the materials, as it were, of a crumbling edifice for building anew, on different foundations.

The present chapters are in large part an attempt to discover how Augustine carried out the 'spoiling of the Egyptians', so far as the field of philosophy is concerned. Before we discuss how he utilized his inherited philosophical equipment in the service of his faith we must investigate a little more precisely what exactly he meant by *using* philosophy in this way; how, in other words, he thought philosophical reflection and faith to be related within the Christian mind.

What, then, is an act of faith, and what is its place within the intellectual life of a Christian? In one of his last works, *On the Predestination of the Saints*, Augustine defines 'believing', in a formula which became classical, as 'to think with assent'.[1] Thought is the necessary prerequisite of belief: however sudden and rapid the assent of belief, it is necessarily preceded by thinking; and the act of believing is itself an act of thinking, thinking of a special kind: 'not all thinking is believing, for people often think in order to withhold belief; but all believing is thinking'.[2] Augustine is insisting here that believing is part of the normal mental process of thinking and belongs inescapably to a context of thinking, and he defines it as a special kind of thought. Let us first examine what distinguishes believing from other kinds of thinking, before investigating how it is related to its context of thinking.

To believe means to give one's assent to what one has learnt.

[1] *De praed. sanct.* 2. 5 (*PL* 44. 963): 'credere nihil aliud est quam cum assensione cogitare'.
[2] *Ibid.*

Augustine is fond of contrasting 'believing' with 'seeing': the basic distinction within the contents of human knowledge which this distinction enshrines is the distinction between what we know through having learnt it from others and accepted on their testimony, and what we know through our own experience. 'Seeing', in this context, can of course mean either sight in the literal sense or, in the metaphorical sense of which Augustine is notoriously fond, applied to the mind's understanding. In either case, belief, in contrast with sight, is knowledge of a more rudimentary kind. The object remains obscure and distant to belief; its assent, though rational, is in a sense blind.[1] For this reason belief is inferior to understanding or to knowledge from direct experience, even though it may precede understanding in time.[2] It is nevertheless woven into the fabric of human existence; the life of the family and of society would crumble without it; believing on the authority of other people is a necessary condition of their functioning.[3] Belief is ubiquitous, but Augustine insists on the need to be discriminating in the choice of the authorities on which belief is based.[4] To give or to withhold assent is ultimately a matter of one's own free and responsible choice. In this sense it is an act of the will; but it is no more arbitrary than any other act of deliberate choice, made for good reasons.[5]

This description of belief is of quite general applicability, as appropriate, for instance, in the case of believing a historical narrative as it is in the case of Christian belief in Jesus Christ. Religious faith is in no way a special kind of knowledge, the work of a special mental faculty. Its difference from other kinds of belief lies not on the side of the believer, but on the side of the objects believed in, and in the kind of authority and evidence required for the respective beliefs. The religious faith of a Christian comes, like all belief, *ex auditu*;[6] it differs from other instances of belief in that the authority of the revelation which forms its

[1] *Ep.* 147. 2. 7 – 3. 8 (*PL* 33. 599–600); cf. *De fide r.q.n.v.* 1. 1–3 (*PL* 40. 171–3).

[2] *De ord.* II 9. 26 (*PL* 32. 1007); cf. *De mor. eccl.* I 2. 3 (*PL* 32. 1311–12).

[3] *De ut. cred.* 12. 26 (*PL* 42. 84); cf. *De fide r.q.n.v.* 2. 4 (*PL* 40. 173–4); *De Trin.* XV 12. 21 (*PL* 42. 1073–5).

[4] *De ord.* II 9. 27 (*PL* 32. 1007–8); cf. *De vera rel.* 25. 46 (*PL* 34. 142); *De ut. cred.* 9. 21 (*PL* 42. 79–80).

[5] *De spir. et litt.* 31. 54; 34. 60 (*PL* 44. 235; 240–1).

[6] Rom. x. 17, alluded to in *De Trin.* XIII 2. 5 (*PL* 42. 1016).

content is divine.[1] With its specific nature and sources we are not here further concerned.

Augustine frequently discusses the relation between belief and understanding. His succinct classification of *credibilia* in an early work provides a suitable starting-point.[2] He here divides objects capable of being believed (*credibilia*) into three classes: (1) those which can only be believed, never understood; (2) those where belief and understanding go together: to believe these is *ipso facto* to understand them; (3) those which must first be believed and may subsequently be understood. As examples of the first class, Augustine gives historical truths; of the second, mathematical and logical reasoning; of the third, truths about God which believers will one day understand if they live according to the commandments. There are difficulties about this classification. Minor obscurities apart, however, it seems clear that Augustine thought that to understand something necessarily implies believing it, but that the reverse is not necessarily true: we may believe something to be the case without understanding it, without, that is to say, having insight into the rational necessity of its truth. Such insight may either be impossible to obtain, as it is for instance in the case of the contingent truth of historical statements, or may be attained at a stage subsequent to their being first believed.[3] Statements about God, the truths of religious faith, belong to this class. They must first be believed, and they may subsequently become understood. It is, of course, axiomatic for Augustine that a clear vision and understanding of God cannot be had in this life, where we see 'as in a glass, darkly'; in speaking of understanding, what he has in mind above all is the vision of God vouchsafed to the pure in heart at the end of their journey in faith. Faith, we may summarize, is something incomplete for Augustine, something that by its nature points to something else and more complete: the vision of God face to face which is the reward of faith.

Faith is thus related to understanding in a twofold manner:

Some things must be understood before one can believe in God; nevertheless, the faith whereby one believes in him helps one to understand more. . . . Since

[1] *De civ. Dei.* XI 3 (*PL* 41. 318); cf. *De ord.* II 9. 27 (*PL* 32. 1007–8).
[2] *De div. qu. LXXXIII* 48 (*PL* 40. 31); cf. *Ep.* 147. 6–8 (*PL* 33. 599–600).
[3] *De mag.* 11. 37 (*PL* 32. 1216); cf. *Solil.* I 3. 8 (*PL* 32. 873).

faith comes from hearing, and hearing through the preaching of Christ, how could one possibly believe a preacher of the faith unless one at least understood his language, to say no more? But conversely, there are things which must first be believed in order to be understood: this is shown by the Prophet's statement 'Unless you believe, you shall not understand' [Isa. vii. 9].[1] The mind thus progresses in understanding what it believes....[2]

On the one hand, understanding serves as a preparation for faith; it interprets the meaning of the message, scrutinizes the authority of its bearers, and so on. On the other hand, faith is a preparation for understanding; and this is the relation on which Augustine prefers to dwell, and does so repeatedly, and not only in his later works. The full, final completion of what is begun in faith is beyond the limits of this earthly life. Nevertheless, even within the limits of the life on earth faith is only a beginning, a first step. Augustine always envisages the life of the faithful mind as growing and developing in understanding, even though the fulness of understanding cannot here be attained. The life of the mind is in no sense at an end once it has come to submit itself to the Christian faith. In a horticultural metaphor he depicts faith, having once germinated, requiring perpetual watering, nourishing and strengthening for its growth.[3] Since his conversion to Christianity, Augustine had regarded his Christian faith as an essential step on the way to truth; but from the beginning he thought of it as the firm, certain and authoritative foundation for further progress in understanding. He never lost the passion for a deeper penetration into the wisdom made accessible by faith, tenaciously guarded and accepted on authority; and the agency of this further penetration was to be reason, above all in the form of the insights offered by the 'Platonists'.[4] To stop short in one's intellectual development at the point of accepting the Christian faith seemed to Augustine to remain content with something less than fully human, something childish and immature: 'God cannot hate that in us in virtue of which he has created us more excellent than other animals. Let us then on no account make our belief a pretext for ceasing to welcome and to pursue reason: for we could not even believe, if we had not rational

[1] *nisi credideritis non intelligetis* in the version used by Augustine.

[2] *En. in Ps.* 118, *Sermo* 18. 3 (*PL* 37. 1552); cf. *Sermo* 43, 3. 4 and 7. 9 (*PL* 38. 255; 258).

[3] *Sermo.* 43. 6. 7 (*PL* 38. 257); cf. *De Trin.* XIV 1. 3 (*PL* 42. 1037).

[4] For a clear and early statement of this programme, see *C. Acad.* III 20. 43 (*PL* 32. 957).

souls.'[1] Faith then is the first step, and only the first step, on the way to truth; it is the condition of, but also the prelude to, understanding. Nothing is more characteristic of this point of view than Augustine's recurrent exhortation, 'Believe that you may understand.'[2] His correspondent Consentius had presented him with the dilemma: 'If the faith of the Church were the outcome of reasoning and discussion rather than of pious credulity, only philosophers and orators would qualify for blessedness; but since it has pleased God to choose the humble of this world to confound the strong, to save by the foolishness of the preaching those who believe, we should not so much seek reasons as follow the authority of the saints.' To this Augustine's reply was simply that the labour of rational inquiry is to be undertaken 'not in order to reject faith, but in order to understand by the light of reason what you already firmly hold by faith'.[3]

It is difficult not to read these passages insisting on faith as the gateway to truth—but only as the gateway, with a long road yet to follow—in the light of Augustine's own personal drama. His tortuous and agonized search for wisdom, his despair of finding it, the series of false trails and disillusion, followed by his discovery of the Christian faith as the answer to his gropings, and certainly his final experience of an intellectually deepened faith, embody in practice the theoretical itinerary. The method of his own theological writings also illustrates this conception of the relation between faith and understanding. This is perhaps clearest in the best planned of his greater theological works, the *De Trinitate*. This work is an attempt to gain insight into the mystery of the Trinity, a doctrine at the heart of the Christian faith, and one for which no other grounds than the authority of the Scriptures and of the Church can be assigned. In his work Augustine studies the meaning of the doctrine, seeks analogies and metaphors which may help to illuminate it, tries to clear up some of the logical and linguistic confusions which give rise to difficulties, and so forth. There is no attempt to go behind the doctrine to establish it on grounds independent of faith;

[1] *Ep.* 120. 3 (*PL* 33. 453); the whole letter is devoted to this subject.

[2] See above, p. 351 n. 1. Among the many occurrences of this theme the following may be noted: *De Trin.* VII 6. 12; IX 1. 1; XV 2. 2 (*PL* 42. 946; 961; 1057–8); *In Jo. Ev. Tr.* 40. 9; 29. 6 (*PL* 35. 1691; 1630–1); *C. Faust.* XII 46 (*PL* 42. 279).

[3] *Ep.* 120. 2 (*PL* 33. 452).

there is only the sustained attempt to penetrate deeper into its meaning, utilizing all the resources of his mind in the quest of understanding. The method and spirit of his investigation are well characterized by a statement at the beginning of its second part: 'The right direction for the search must start from faith...let us seek like men who shall find; and let us find like men who still must go on seeking.'[1] The quest for understanding does not end this side of the grave.

Modern usage would not, of course, treat this inquiry as a philosophical one, but would assign it to the discipline of theology. The distinction between the two disciplines did not exist in Augustine's world, and their realms are merged in his 'Christian philosophy'. Philosophical thinking enters into it, and does so precisely as one of the instruments, and one of the most important instruments, utilizable in the process of deepening the understanding of the faith. Augustine's theological procedure, with its heavy indebtedness to Greek, particularly to Neoplatonic, philosophical thought, is a concrete instance of the 'spoiling of the Egyptians': its techniques, conceptual structures and terminology are utilized, no longer pursued for their own sake, but rigidly subordinated to the service of an end beyond them: the understanding of the Christian faith in its totality. This is no more and no less than the working out in practice of the programme outlined in the *De doctrina christiana.*

[1] *De Trin.* IX I. I (*PL* 42. 961).

CHAPTER 22

AUGUSTINE

MAN: BODY AND SOUL

Augustine's views concerning the nature of man and of his place in the universe inevitably underwent profound transformations during his intellectual journey from Manichaean, through Neoplatonic, to Christian teaching. The three outlooks differ profoundly in their estimate of man. In Manichaean doctrine, man is a being torn in two, or two beings, just as the world itself is divided or thought of as two worlds, a world of darkness and a world of light. According to its cosmogonic myth, these are created by different creators, ruled by their own rulers, and are perpetually at war. Man is an episode in the inter-cosmic warfare: he is the product of an emission from the kingdom of light into that of darkness. The myth pictures him as the emissary of light devoured by the darkness, kept imprisoned by it and prevented from returning to his home. Man is object, stage and agent of this cosmic struggle. The cosmic forces are mobilized to prevent or to assist his return to his spiritual home; he is himself a composite of the two worlds which are at war within as well as around him; and he has some power to co-operate with the forces of darkness or to resist. In this last capacity man is not quite a passive spectator of the conflict: he is called to resist the entanglement with evil, to repudiate the body, its main agency. Rejection of and liberation from the body are therefore a vital part of the Manichaean doctrine of salvation: they belong to a realm essentially evil, and are foreign to man's inmost nature, serving as the prison of his real self.

Neoplatonic views on the nature of man, which this is not the place to describe, are far removed from Manichaean teaching in their insistence on the goodness of matter and of the human body.[1] The body has its place in a hierarchically ordered universe, and its purpose is to enable the work of intellect—rationality, order—to be expressed in the lower orders of the cosmos. Hence it is not an object of loathing and hatred,

[1] [For Neoplatonic views of the nature of man see Part III (Plotinus), ch. 14, pp. 222–35.]

though it is an obstacle to man's easy progress towards virtue and wisdom; and, above all, it has no part in man's final salvation. Hence the deep opposition of Neoplatonists to the Christian teaching concerning the resurrection of the body and the positive value set upon the body and the world of matter in Christian teaching. Notwithstanding this opposition, the attitudes of Christians to the material world, and to the body in particular, could in practice often be very close to those of Neoplatonist or even of dualistic Gnostic writers.

Augustine's views on man were worked out after his conversion to Christianity. His break with Manichaean teaching—despite the alleged survival of some Manichaean influences in his mind—seems to have been absolute. His sharp distrust of sensual delight, for example, the suspicion with which he treats church music,[1] far from being Manichaean in inspiration, contains no hint of revulsion from the world of the body but shows, on the contrary, a deep sensitiveness to beauty and a concern not to allow it to run away with reason and judgement. This concern is all of a piece with his moral theory on the use to be made of created things, which will be discussed later. The essentially ethical background of his practical attitude to the life of the body serves to bridge, to a large extent, the gulf between Augustine's Christian views and the Neoplatonic views on the body. The very positive valuation of the body by Christian teaching could always be tempered by a strong other-worldliness; and this allied it with the ethical protest, which Neoplatonism had in common with much of ancient philosophy, against all manner of worldliness of life, and its recommendation of detachment from what Aristotle called 'the things men quarrel about'. Long after his turning to Christianity, Augustine could feel he had much in common with the 'Platonists'.[2]

Augustine's reflection on this subject, beginning with the works written in the years immediately following his conversion, is permeated by a concern to stress the unity of man, body and soul. He never hesitates in his view that both are essential constituents of what we call man. The conviction appears in one of his earliest letters,[3] and is equally

[1] *Conf.* X 33. 49–50 (*PL* 32. 799–800).

[2] A concise statement of his views on Manichaean and Neoplatonic teaching on the body: *De civ. Dei* XIV 5 (*PL* 41. 408–9).

[3] *Ep.* 3. 4 (*PL* 33. 65).

characteristic of his later works. It appears in one of the ways in which he frequently defines man: 'man is a rational animal subject to death'[1]—a definition designed precisely to stress the need to allude to both body and soul in defining man. Notwithstanding this unwavering conviction, Augustine did have difficulty in embodying this conviction in the conceptual structure at his disposal. A passage from an early work is particularly revealing of these difficulties:[2]

Since it is almost universally agreed that we are made up of soul and body, and since for the purpose of our present discussion such agreement can be taken for granted, what we must ask now is what man really is: is he both these constituents, or is he body only, or soul only? For although soul and body are two things, and neither of them alone is called 'man' in the absence of the other (for a body is no man unless it is animated by a soul, nor is a soul a man without a body which it animates), it nevertheless happens that one or other of these is alone taken for and referred to as man. What, then, shall we say man is? Is he soul and body together, as a pair of horses or a composite beast like a centaur is one thing? Or shall we say that he is a body only, albeit a body used by a soul which rules it?—just as we call a clay lamp a 'light': we do not say that the clay vessel and the flame together make up a light; we call the lamp a light, but we do so on account of the flame. Or, finally, shall we call the soul alone man, and do so on account of the body which it rules?—just as we call a man a knight, not the man and his horse together, but we do so on account of the horse he rides. The solution of this problem is difficult—or, if it be easy to see, it nonetheless requires a lengthy explanation, and it is not necessary here and now to undertake the labour and delay.

Augustine prefaces this passage with a disclaimer to the effect that he is not concerned to give a formal definition of man here. The sequel to the passage makes it quite clear that what interests him in this discussion is the question 'what is the good for man?', and that the foregoing puzzle about the definition of man is subsidiary to this question; indeed, the answer to it does not really matter very much so long as it is clear that man's greatest good is not to be identified with the good of the body alone, but must consist either in the good of body and soul together or of the soul. It is a tentative passage, and the centre of Augustine's

[1] *De ord.* II 11. 31 (*PL* 32. 1009); also *De quant. an.* 25. 47 (*PL* 32. 1062); *De Trin.* XV 7. 11 (*PL* 42. 1065); *De civ. Dei* IX 13. 3; XIII 24. 2 (*PL* 41. 267; 399–400).

[2] *De mor. eccl.* I 4. 6 (*PL* 32. 1313); cf. *De civ. Dei* XIX 3 (*PL* 41. 625–7), where the source of the discussion appears.

interests lies elsewhere, in the sphere of ethics; it would be unwise to attach too much significance to it and to expect from it the decisive clue to his view of body and soul. Nevertheless, the passage does convey a suggestion of the kind of difficulties which Augustine found in his way when trying to give conceptual expression to his conviction of the substantial unity of man, composed of soul and body. The source of these difficulties was the framework of the Platonic concepts which he utilized. When, later in the same work, he returns to this question, he defines man in a traditional Platonic formula as 'a rational soul using a mortal and earthly body'.[1] For a reason Augustine does not state, man is now identified with his soul, though reference is made to the body. And indeed this reference to the body is incorporated in the definition of the soul given in another work dating from about the same time: it is 'a substance endowed with reason and fitted to rule a body'.[2] The soul by its nature points towards a body, and is not complete without it. Augustine is laying as much stress as he can on the unity of body and soul in man, though his adopted conceptual structure makes it difficult to speak of the substantial unity of man.

One of the most interesting features of Augustine's attempts to explain the union of body and soul in man, which the studies of Père Fortin and H. Dörrie[3] have brought to light, is that Augustine owed not only his difficulties but also his manner of solving them to the philosophical framework he adopted. His conception of the union of soul and body appears in passages in which he defends against philosophical objections the doctrine of the two natures united in the person of the Word made flesh. The argument, as it appears most clearly in his correspondence with Volusianus, is that there can be no *a priori* objections to this doctrine on philosophical grounds. For it is easier to conceive of the union of two spiritual substances than of a spiritual and a material substance; and yet the possibility is admitted of the latter's taking place in the union of soul and body in man.[4] Augustine is clearly alluding to a philosophical theory of the union of mind and body according to which

[1] *De mor. eccl.* I 27. 52 (*PL* 32. 1332); cf. *In Jo. Ev. Tr.* XIX 15 (*PL* 35. 1553): 'anima rationalis habens corpus'.
[2] *De quant. an.* 13. 22 (*PL* 32. 1048).
[3] E. L. Fortin, *Christianisme et culture philosophique au cinquième siècle* (Paris, 1959), H. Dörrie, *Porphyrios' 'Symmikta Zetemata'*... (München, 1959), and J. Pépin, 'Une nouvelle source de St Augustin...', *R. Ét. Anc.* 66 (1964), pp. 53–107.
[4] *Ep.* 137. 3. 11 (*PL* 33. 520).

these could come together in a 'union without confusion' (*unio inconfusa*, ἄμικτος, ἀσύγχυτος ἕνωσις). The theory was of Neoplatonic origin. It appears to go back to Ammonius Saccas, and was certainly held by Porphyry, with whom Augustine in fact appears to associate it by implication.[1] The Neoplatonic notion of a 'union without confusion' had been developed precisely to make it possible to maintain the possibility of the union of soul and body, a possibility denied by Stoic thought. The Stoics had distinguished mere 'juxtaposition' (παράθεσις) from 'mixing' (κρᾶσις) as alternative forms of union. The latter implied alteration in the character of the substances mixed, and their transformation into a new, third substance. Neither category of union, for obvious reasons, could accommodate the Neoplatonists' conception of the union of soul and body. The third mode of union added by them to the Stoic enumeration provided a suitable category of union for this purpose, and one of which Christian theologians were quick to see the value in their attempts to defend the union of divine and human natures in the person of Christ. Augustine, then, availed himself of a current philosophical theory for the purposes of Christological debate: he never seems to have doubted its adequacy for formulating the mode of union of soul and body in man.[2] He appears to have had something like the same notion in mind in another early, anti-Manichaean work when he drew a parallel between the manner in which water, when added to soil to make mud, holds it together and compacts it, and the union of soul and body: 'the soul forms the material of the body which it animates into a harmonious unity and secures and preserves its integrity'.[3] Augustine, to summarize, stressed the unity of soul and body in man as strongly as his inherited conceptual equipment allowed it to be stressed, certainly far more strongly than Plato himself had done. But he was also well aware that this union fell short of substantial unity; 'though united in one man, my flesh is another substance than my soul'.[4] The union has well been called 'hypostatic'; indeed, had Augustine been able to think of it as substantial, it would not have

[1] *De civ. Dei* x 29 (*PL* 41. 307–9). [For the use made of the theory of the ἀσύγχυτος ἕνωσις in the Christian East, see the next Part (vi, The Greek Christian Tradition), chs. 31 D and 32 E, pp. 489–91 and pp. 504–5.]

[2] *In Jo. Ev. Tr.* xix 15 (*PL* 35. 1553); cf. *Ep.* 137. 3. 11–12 (*PL* 33. 520–1); *De civ. Dei* x 29 (*PL* 41. 307–9).

[3] *De Gen. c. Man.* ii 7. 9 (*PL* 34. 201).

[4] *De Trin.* i 10. 20 (*PL* 42. 835).

served him as so useful an analogy for the purposes of Christological discussion.

We shall encounter some of the difficulties raised by this view when we come to discuss Augustine's theories of sense-perception. He was not apparently worried by these; and in any case the whole question was one of very subordinate importance in his eyes. What mattered far more to him were questions concerned with man's supreme good, and the great virtue of his picture of man was that it fitted into a clear scheme which laid all the stress on the good of the soul. The identification of man with his soul, even with the rider 'using a mortal body', is, for all its difficulties, in line with the deepest tendencies of Augustine's mind. It presents man as a being placed in a hierarchical order, an order which is repeated in the structure of his own being. The very definition of man involves reference to two entities, one subordinated to the other as ruled to ruler. Augustine likes to describe man as a kind of intermediary between the realms of spirit and of matter—a unique status symbolized by his erect bodily posture.[1]

Man is related to the hierarchy of the cosmos both above him and beneath him in multiple ways. He is not, of course, poised between the world of matter and of spirit as a third thing between them, but rather, having a share in both worlds, he is situated on their borderline. He is a being in whom the two worlds overlap. The human soul is the closest of all things in creation to God.[2] Close as it is, however, it is not divine, or of God's substance.[3] This apparently trite insistence of Augustine's has some importance. Manichaean doctrine had affirmed the human soul to be a fragment or spark of divine nature inserted into the inimical world of matter.[4] To assert such an identity of nature meant either to claim immutability for the human soul, or to subject God to change, both repugnant doctrines. There is a more profound reason, however, for Augustine's insistence on the mutability of the human soul, and the distance between it and the divine nature. The character-

[1] *De Gen. ad litt.* VI 12. 22 (*PL* 34. 348); cf. *De civ. Dei* IX 13. 3 (*PL* 41. 267); *In Jo. Ev. Tr* XX 11; XXIII 5 (*PL* 35. 1562; 1584–5).

[2] *De beata vita* I. 4 (*PL* 32. 961) (where Augustine refers to Ambrose and Theodorus of Milan); cf. *De Gen. ad litt.* X 24. 40 (*PL* 34. 426–7).

[3] *De quant. an.* 31. 63; 34. 77 (*PL* 32. 1070; 1077–8); cf. *De civ. Dei* XI 26 (*PL* 41. 339); *De Trin.* XIV 8. 11 (*PL* 42. 1044); *De Gen. ad litt.* VII, *passim*.

[4] *De Gen. c. Man.* II 8. 11 (*PL* 34. 202).

istics of immateriality, intelligence and immortality had been widely attached to the soul by Neoplatonic and other thinkers. These characters were thought of as endowing the soul with divinity; and in consequence some Christian thinkers had gone to great lengths to deny the spirituality of the soul, for to admit this would have been to condone the blasphemous claim for its divinity. This problem had not ceased to agitate Christian minds in Augustine's day, and indeed later in the fifth century. Following St Ambrose, Augustine chose the alternative of asserting the soul's immateriality and immortality, and qualifying this assertion by an uncompromising insistence on the mutability of the soul.[1] This qualification placed Augustine in a position to underline the cleavage between the type of view according to which man's real self was an eternal, intelligent soul, which could neither change nor suffer, sin or repent, and his own view, according to which the human soul shares the essential instability of all created being. He appears to take particular care to dissociate himself from the specifically Plotinian doctrine of the 'double personality': he states his own distinction between the 'interior man' and the 'exterior man' in terms such as would allow no room for mistaking his 'interior man' for the sinless, unchangeable and eternal 'man within' of Plotinus. This is the reason for his monotonous insistence that the interior man judges and understands in the light of 'incorporeal and eternal reasons', which, being unchanging, are above the human soul.[2] The soul itself is liable to all the vicissitudes of change and living, to sin and repentance, and is ever in need of God's grace. Man only has one self, which is the subject and the agent of his empirical career; there is not a recondite real self exempt and remote from the turmoils of life.

Negatively, Augustine defines the soul's relation to God as being different from him in nature. Positively, he formulates his view by reference to the teaching of Genesis that man was made by God to his own image and likeness. Here he departs from the dominant trend of patristic tradition, according to which man had retained the image of God at the time of the fall, but had lost his likeness to him. The restoration of this likeness was to be the end-product of the long process of

[1] E.g. *Ep.* 166. 2. 3–4 (*PL* 33. 721–2).

[2] *De Trin.* XII 1. 1 – 2. 2; XI 1. 1 (*PL* 42. 997–9; 983–5). [For the divinity of the 'man within' in Plotinus see Part III (Plotinus), ch. 14, pp. 222–6.]

man's divinization, wrought in man through Christ's saving work and by the operation of his grace.[1] Augustine's departure from this tradition appears to have been prompted by purely logical, linguistic considerations, not by disagreement with the theology of sin, grace and sanctification embodied in this tradition. An image, he thought, necessarily implies the presence of some likeness to its original, whereas a likeness may exist between two objects one of which is not the image of another, for instance two eggs. An image is a special kind of likeness, on his analysis,[2] whereas, on the view he rejected, an image could exist without likeness. Augustine therefore preferred to speak of both image and likeness of God surviving man's fall, though in a damaged and distorted state and in need of reformation. Augustine is here undertaking a piece of clarification and analysis, a typical instance of the purely rational techniques of philosophy being put at the service of the Christian faith to clarify its meaning.

It would take us too far into the realms of Augustinian theology to give more than the most summary account of what Augustine thought man's likeness to God consists in.[3] Man, he thought, is the image of God in respect of the highest part of his soul, the 'interior man' or intelligence, that is to say, in respect of what distinguishes man from beast: rationality, will, capacity to share in the divine life.[4] This is essential to man's nature, not a further gift bestowed on him;[5] no matter how deformed by sin, it always remains in him, its likeness to God being restored with baptism and perfected by daily renewal in charity.[6] His work *On the Trinity* is in large part an attempt to trace God's image in man specifically in his three-in-oneness.

To God, the human soul is related as his image and likeness; to the realities beneath it in the order of things, it is related principally in its ability to know them and to act on them and among them. To these themes we turn next.

[1] [On 'image' and 'likeness' in later Greek Christian thought see Part VI (The Greek Christian Tradition), ch. 29C, pp. 449–56 and ch. 32E, pp. 503–4.]

[2] *De div. qu. LXXXIII* 74 (*PL* 40. 85–6); *Qu. in Hept.* V 4 (*PL* 34. 749–50). On Augustine's analysis and its development, cf. my paper '"Imago" and "similitudo" in Augustine', *Rev. des études augustiniennes*, X (1964), pp. 125–43.

[3] *De Gen. ad litt.* III 20. 30; VI 12. 21–2 (*PL* 34. 292; 348); *De Trin.* XII 1. 1; XI 1. 1 (*PL* 42. 997–9; 983–5).

[4] *De Trin.* XIV 8. 11 (*PL* 42. 1044).

[5] *Ibid.* XIV 10. 13 (*PL* 42. 1047).

[6] *Ibid.* XIV 16. 22 – 17. 23 (*PL* 42. 1053–5).

CHAPTER 23

AUGUSTINE
REASON AND ILLUMINATION

Augustine likes to distinguish different grades in the range of knowledge of which the human mind is capable. We have already noted[1] one distinction, that between belief and understanding. Understanding, Augustine seems to suggest, is the distinctive work of human reason: it is the result of its application and pursuit.[2] When he is concerned to contrast understanding with belief, Augustine normally speaks of *intellectus*, *intelligere*, *intelligentia*; when he discusses the result in the mind of the work of reasoning, he speaks of *scientia*. Thus one of his definitions of *scientia* in effect almost identifies it with *intellectus*: in the course of a lengthy discussion of the distinctive character of human knowledge (*scientia*)[3] he likens the relationship between reason and knowledge to that between looking and seeing: knowledge is the success of the enterprise of reason.[4] Its chief characteristic is rational cogency; something is known when it is fully clear and transparent to the mind, and is, so to speak, seen by it.[5]

Before we examine the various mental processes involved in different kinds of knowledge, we must note a distinction which Augustine introduces within *scientia*: he defines wisdom (*sapientia*) as knowledge of a special kind. He calls it a 'contemplative knowledge',[6] and describes it as being concerned with eternal objects, whereas the remainder of *scientia*, to which he now confines the term in a narrower sense, is concerned with temporal things.[7] Knowledge and wisdom differ only in virtue of the difference in the objects concerned, and Augustine allows that their distinction is not radical: the words may indeed be used interchangeably.[8] Both knowledge and wisdom are the products of the same

[1] Cf. above, p. 349.
[2] *Sermo* 43. 2. 3 (*PL* 38. 255).
[3] *De quant. an.* 26. 49 – 30. 58 (*PL* 32. 1063–9).
[4] *Ibid.* 27. 53 (*PL* 32. 1065).
[5] *Ibid.* 30. 58 (*PL* 32. 1068–9).
[6] *De Trin.* XV 10. 17 (*PL* 42. 1069).
[7] *Ibid.* XII 14. 22; 15. 25 (*PL* 42. 1009–10; 1012).
[8] *Ibid.* XIII 19. 24; XIV 1. 3 (*PL* 42. 1034; 1037).

activity in the same mind, though Augustine makes a corresponding distinction between a 'higher reason' and a 'lower reason'. These again are distinguished only in virtue of their respective objects; they are man's rational mind, in the one case looked at in so far as it is concerned with the realm of eternal truth,[1] in the other in so far as it is concerned with 'corporeal things and temporal activity'.

These gradations in the mind and in its knowledge are the result of the hierarchical order of their objects; there is no real distinction between the respective mental processes involved in knowing them. This is not the case, however, with another distinction which Augustine also states in terms of the objects known: 'there are two classes of things known: one is of those which the mind perceives through the bodily senses, the other is of those which it perceives by itself.'[2] Here the distinction is between the mental processes involved, as indeed appears more clearly from parallels elsewhere.[3] We take the two kinds of knowledge, that which the mind obtains by itself and that which it obtains through sense, in turn.[4]

Augustine's earliest attempts to grapple with the philosophical problems of knowledge stem from a desire to vindicate the very possibility of human knowledge against the 'Academics', philosophers whom he understood to dispute all claims to certainty. This accounts for his search for items of indubitable truth, propositions which it is quite literally impossible to doubt.

This desire for unimpeachable certainty was satisfied by a number of arguments which terminate in such apparent certainties. The arguments are all of the type familiar in Descartes' *Cogito ergo sum*: in knowing anything one is immediately aware of being alive and—as Augustine formulates the argument on one occasion—this awareness includes the body;[5] in knowing anything—even if one is in error—one knows one is thinking.[6] The arguments occur in Augustine's earliest works, but survive as stock *loci* against the Academics in later writings.[7] Despite their

[1] *Ibid.* XII 3. 3 (*PL* 42. 999).
[2] *Ibid.* XV 12. 21 (*PL* 42. 1075).
[3] Cf. *Ep.* 13. 4 (*PL* 33. 78).
[4] I have treated these topics from a somewhat different point of view and sometimes a little more fully in chapter 5 of *Critical history of Western philosophy*, ed. D. J. O'Connor (New York, 1964).
[5] *De beata vita* 2. 7 (*PL* 32. 963).
[6] *Sol.* II 1. 1 (*PL* 32. 885); cf. *De lib. arb.* II 3. 7 (*PL* 32. 1243–4).
[7] *De Trin.* XV 12. 21 (*PL* 42. 1073–5); *De civ. Dei* XI 26 (*PL* 41. 339–40).

resemblance to Descartes' more famous argument, their purpose is slightly different: Augustine is simply seeking arguments sufficient to reply to absolute scepticism. These and similar examples of indubitable knowledge suffice for this purpose; but Augustine never plans to build up a structure of similarly indubitable knowledge on their basis. This would have been quite unnecessary, for he rejected the basic tenet that only indubitable knowledge is admissible as knowledge.[1]

In his attempt to define his position *vis-à-vis* Academic scepticism, Augustine found the Platonic tradition of great value. Hence his theory of knowledge, particularly of rational, non-sensuous knowledge, is cast in the moulds of Platonic thinking. Plato's teaching 'that there are two worlds, an intelligible world where truth itself dwells, and this sensible world which we perceive by sight and touch'[2] was very attractive to the recent convert faced with the need to come to terms with scepticism, and exercised a deep influence on him. Indeed, at this stage, he scarcely distinguished the teaching of Christianity from that of Plato and was very ready to read each into the other.[3] Reviewing his endorsement of this view of Plato's at the end of his life, Augustine criticizes himself for having identified the teaching of the Gospels and of Plato too uncritically. He now sees more clearly that what Plato meant was different from the other world which Christ hinted at when he said, 'My kingdom is not of this world' (John xviii. 36); he appreciates the eschatological bearing of Christ's words more clearly and is less ready to read Platonic overtones into them. But, nevertheless, he does not revise his endorsement of Plato's assertion of the existence of an intelligible world, by which he meant 'the eternal and unchanging reason whereby God made the world'.[4]

Augustine's interpretation of the Gospel became more eschatological in the course of the years, but Platonism, and particularly the Platonic theory of the intelligible world, continued to play a key part in his thought. He followed a tradition, already respectable in his day, of identifying Plato's intelligible world of forms with the divine mind containing the archetypal ideas of all its creatures, the creative Wisdom and Word (Logos) of God.[5] Augustine describes our knowledge of this

[1] Cf. *De Trin.* XV 12. 21–2 (*PL* 42. 1073–5).
[2] *C. Acad.* III 17. 37 (*PL* 32. 954).
[3] *De ord.* I 11. 32 (*PL* 32. 993).
[4] *Retr.* I 3. 2 (*PL* 32. 589).
[5] *Ibid.*; cf. *De div. q. LXXXIII.* 46 (*PL* 40. 29–31); *De civ. Dei* XI 10. 3 (*PL* 41. 327).

intelligible world as analogous to sight: 'Understanding is the same thing for the mind as seeing is for the bodily senses',[1] or 'reason is the mind's sight, whereby it perceives truth through itself, without the body's intervention'.[2] The analogy between seeing and understanding is one of Augustine's most cherished and most deeply held views. Some of his arguments even suggest that his belief in an intelligible world derives from this view. 'You will recall', he says to his interlocutor in one of his early dialogues,[3]

> what we said earlier about knowledge through the bodily senses. We noted that the objects of our senses, the things which we can all see and hear, colours and sounds which you and I see simultaneously, belong not to the nature of our eyes and ears, but are common to us precisely as the objects of our senses. Likewise, we must not say that the things which you and I both perceive mentally belong to the nature of our minds. For what the eyes of two persons perceive simultaneously cannot be identified with anything belonging to the eyes of either one or the other, but must be some third thing to which the sight of both is directed.

Augustine here had the propositions of mathematics and of logic primarily in mind, which constituted indubitable truths of the kind which he was concerned to oppose to the sceptical denial of the possibility of certain knowledge. Such propositions, he thought, possess a character of universality, necessity and immutability for which sense-experience can supply no warrant;[4] we hold them to be true notwithstanding any apparent exceptions which sense-experience may suggest. He concluded that such truths were known independently of sense-experience, and derived from experience of another range of objects, capable of being known with superior clarity and certainty independently of the bodily senses but through an analogous type of experience, intellectual 'sight'. He did not, however, regard the propositions of mathematics and of logic as by any means the sole, or even as the most important, class of truths which are known in this way. He assimilated the statements of moral and aesthetic value judgements, and indeed the whole realm of 'wisdom'—i.e. everything that philosophy is concerned with

[1] *De ord.* II 3. 10 (*PL* 32. 999). [2] *De imm. an.* 6. 10 (*PL* 32. 1026).

[3] *De lib. arb.* II 12. 33 (*PL* 32. 1259); cf. *De imm. an.* 6. 10 (*PL* 32. 1025–6); *De Trin.* XII 14. 23 (*PL* 42. 1010–11).

[4] *De lib. arb.* II 8. 21 (*PL* 32. 1251–2).

—to their status.[1] This inclusive realm of 'eternal truths' was easy to identify with the creative, archetypal ideas of the divine mind.

For Augustine, as for Plato, the contents of this intelligible world were known by the mind independently of sense-experience. Some passages in his early works suggest that he may have adopted, at least in part, the Platonic theory of 'reminiscence', according to which such knowledge formed part of the mind's equipment brought with it into this life from a pre-mundane existence in the world of eternal truths and in direct contact with them.[2] In later works he rejects this view. It is more credible, as he puts it one place, to account for the kind of knowledge displayed by Plato's slave-boy in the *Meno* by saying that 'the light of the eternal reason is present to them, in whatever measure they are able to receive it, in which they can see these unchanging truths; not because they once knew them and have forgotten them, as Plato and others have held'.[3] Knowledge of the eternal truths is not the result of the rediscovery of a residual deposit left in the mind from a previous existence, but is the work of continuous discovery by the mind, made in the intellectual light which is always present to it and is its means of contact with the world of intelligible reality.[4] Augustine also speaks of this divine illumination in the mind as the mind's participation in the Word of God, as God's interior presence to the mind, as Christ dwelling in the human soul and teaching it from within, and in other ways.

What exactly the content of the knowledge made accessible by this intellectual illumination was, is a question difficult to decide. Much of the debate which has taken place on this subject has been conducted in terms of concepts which Augustine would not have distinguished very carefully or explicitly. The text of his writings therefore often appears to give support to rival interpretations of his thought. We may rule out the view on which Augustine's theory would give the human mind direct access to the divine mind by illumination. This interpretation runs counter to everything else in Augustine's conception of man in

[1] *De lib. arb.* II 9. 25 – 10. 29 (*PL* 32. 1253–7); cf. *De vera rel.* 39. 73 (*PL* 34. 154–5).

[2] *Sol.* II 20. 35 (*PL* 32. 902–4); cf. *De quant. an.* 20. 34 (*PL* 32. 1054–5). I remain unconvinced by the arguments put forward by R. J. O'Connell in a number of recent articles, conveniently summarized in *Rev. des études augustiniennes*, XI (1965), pp. 372–5.

[3] *Retr.* I 4. 4; cf. *ibid.* I 8. 2 (*PL* 32. 590; 594); *De Trin.* XII 15. 24 (*PL* 42. 1011–12).

[4] *De Trin.* XII 15. 24 (*PL* 42. 1011–12).

relation to God in this life, and is also explicitly rejected.[1] The difficulty of deciding between two other views which have been proposed—(1) that illumination provides the concepts with which the mind works in its interpretation of sense-experience and (2) that it provides the mind with a yardstick by which to regulate its judgements—may be illustrated by means of some significant passages. In a passage of his mature work, *De Trinitate*,[2] he discusses how we make comparative value judgements. After enumerating a number of good things, he writes:

Among all these good things which I have listed, or any others that we care to think of, we should not be able to say that one was better than another when making a true judgement about them, unless there were imprinted upon us a concept of good itself (*nisi esset nobis impressa notio ipsius boni*), according to which we approve things and prefer some to others.

This terminology is identical with that of an early discussion, in which Augustine speaks of the mind possessing a *notio impressa* of blessedness and of wisdom.[3] This 'impressed notion' is clearly both a concept and a criterion of judgement—the two things merge into each other. Any radical distinction between illumination as a source of concepts and illumination as a rule of judgement lay far beyond Augustine's horizon. How closely the two functions were identified in his view appears from a passage in which he discusses how we know the human mind. We each experience our own mind directly, and each differs from all other minds; it is not from our experience of many minds and generalizing from their common characteristics that we arrive at a general idea of the mind, but 'we perceive the inviolable truth, whence we define perfectly, as far as we are able, not what this or that man's mind is like, but what it should be like in the light of the eternal truth' (*qualis esse sempiternis rationibus debeat*).[4] In the eternal truth the mind perceives 'the pattern which governs our being and our activities, whether in ourselves or in regard to external things, according to the rule of truth and right reason'.[5] Passages like this show how closely these discussions of rational knowledge are related to Augustine's ethical interests. When he speaks of the eternal truths as the standard and measure of human judgement, he is very often asserting more than

[1] *Ibid.* IV 15. 20 (*PL* 42. 901–2).

[2] VIII 3. 4 (*PL* 42. 949).

[3] *De lib. arb.* II 9. 26 (*PL* 32. 1254–5).

[4] *De Trin.* IX 6. 9 (*PL* 42. 966).

[5] *Ibid.* IX 7. 12 (*PL* 42. 967).

a theory of knowledge. Sometimes he is almost alluding to the final divine judgement on all human things, and represents human judgement under the light of the eternal truth as a kind of echo of, or participation in, the divine judgement on all human concerns.

Nevertheless, Augustine intended his theory of illumination to be a quite generally valid account of the process of rational knowledge. He does sometimes speak of illumination in terms which suggest a more special relation between the human mind and God: for instance when he says that we are rendered unfit to receive it by 'the impurity of sin',[1] or, as in the passages quoted above, where he almost seems to be suggesting that illumination by the divine light should enable a man to judge himself, his concerns and commitments as they would appear in God's sight. There is something very characteristically Augustinian in this way of using a general, philosophical notion and allowing it to acquire much less philosophical and much more scriptural overtones in certain contexts. One of the features which made Platonic formulae so attractive to him was their suitability to being exploited in this way. This is the case with the theory of illumination: fundamentally it is a statement in completely general terms of what Augustine considers the ultimate ground of the possibility of rational knowledge, that is to say, God's intimate presence to the human mind: God is in the mind as he is in everything, and his presence is the condition not only of its being, but of its functioning in the ways proper to its nature. But on this fundamental, metaphysical, presence of God Augustine is sometimes prepared to superimpose further, special modes of his presence, or absence. The theory of illumination is used to state not only the inescapably necessary requirements of any rational knowledge whatever, but also to describe special kinds of knowledge or wisdom such as a man might or might not have, the result of special grace, the reward of special virtue. One of the most interesting discussions of this question occurs in a passage in which Augustine deals with the accessibility of the eternal standards of conduct to the wicked.

God is wholly everywhere; whence it is that [the mind] lives and moves and has its being in him, and therefore it can remember him. Not that it remembers him because it knew him in Adam, or at any other time and place before

[1] *De Trin.* IV 2. 4 (*PL* 42. 889).

entering the life of its body, or at the time it was created and inserted into its body; it remembers none of these things, whichever of them really happened to it, they are all consigned to oblivion. It remembers him by turning towards the Lord, as to the light which in some fashion had reached it even while it had been turned away from him.

This is the reason why the wicked, too, can think of eternity and make correct judgements of approval and disapproval about human conduct. What are the rules according to which they judge, but the rules which show everyone how to live, even though they may not themselves live according to them? How do they know them? Certainly not in their own natures: for although undoubtedly it is by the mind that these things are seen, it is clear that their minds are changeable, whereas whoever perceives in his mind these rules as the standard of conduct also perceives them to be unchangeable. Again, it is not in any disposition (*habitu*) of their minds, since these rules are rules of righteousness whereas their minds are, *ex hypothesi*, unjust. Where then are these rules written, where is it the unjust can discover what is just, where do they see what they ought to have and lack? Where are the rules written but in the book of that light which we call truth? Here it is that all the rules of righteousness are inscribed and it is from here that they pass into the heart of the just man, not by bodily transfer, but as though leaving their imprint on him, just as the design of a seal is impressed in the wax without leaving the seal.[1]

The image of the seal impression recalls the 'impressed notion' by means of which the mind is able to make judgements.[2] But whereas there the 'impressed notion' was what enabled the mind to judge, here the 'impression' denotes more: it is the actual moral appropriation of the rule of conduct, already known, now entering man's moral character. Augustine's terminology fluctuates; but he does make it quite clear that he envisages more than one mode of the divine presence to the mind, more than one level at which the mind participates in the eternal truth. The possibility of presence on levels additional to the basic and universal level of God's presence to the mind is what accounts for the possibility of conversion, which, for Augustine, consists in 'turning towards the light which in some fashion had reached one even while one had been turned away from it'. God is always, radically, present to the mind, but in this turning towards him the mind makes itself present

[1] *Ibid.* XIV 15. 21 (*PL* 42. 1052).

[2] Cf. above, p. 367 nn. 213.

to him in an additional way, in free acknowledgement. Augustine also calls this turning of the mind to God 'remembering' God.

This conception of 'remembering' and of *memoria* (to stress the difference between this and 'memory' as commonly understood, the Latin term will be used here) is closely bound up with the theory of illumination. Augustine's conception of *memoria*, like his theory of the mind's illumination, is the direct consequence of his adoption of the essential core of the Platonic theory of knowledge. As we have seen,[1] he rejected Plato's mythological account of our knowledge of the intelligible world, the account cast in terms of reminiscence of a previous state of existence. Nevertheless, his theory of illumination, which accounts for such knowledge in terms of a continuous discovery rendered possible to the mind by the presence to it of the intelligible world in illumination, is really not so much an alternative to as a translation of the Platonic theory of reminiscence. What both accounts express in different terms is that rational knowledge enters the mind not from outside, but is, in some way, present to it: either as a relic of its previous contact with another world, or as the result of continuing contact with it which it enjoys in virtue of its nature. Augustine's *memoria* is, in the first place, his equivalent of Plato's *anamnēsis*; though, as we shall see, it is also more than this. Augustine's conception has two roots: the ordinary, common-sense conception of memory as the mind's ability to preserve and to recall past experience, and the Platonic conception as revised by him to free it from reference to the past. An early letter to his friend Nebridius, who had questioned him on the subject of memory, indicates his approach very clearly. He begins with the common-sense notion of memory, according to which we remember objects encountered in our past experience. In this sense, memory refers to the past, even if the objects remembered may still exist. He then goes on to include in the sphere of memory the knowledge which we learn by reasoning, such as that which Socrates elicited from the slave-boy in the *Meno*, an example which Augustine mentions here. But since this knowledge is not really derived from past experience, and not through the senses, so Augustine argues, it follows that *memoria* does not necessarily refer to the past and need not necessarily involve images derived from sense-experience.[2]

[1] Cf. above, p. 366.

[2] *Ep.* 7. 1. 1–2 (*PL* 33. 68).

Experience, Augustine held, leaves traces in the *memoria*, which he calls *species*. The mind can subsequently recall these by an act of deliberate attention,[1] or utilize them in constructive imagination.[2] From this point of view Augustine conceived *memoria* as a vast store-house in which experiences are stored in orderly fashion,[3] or as a stomach in which things are digested.[4] This image is less applicable to *memoria* considered in so far as it contains knowledge not derived from past experience. *Memoria* embraces 'the multitude of principles and laws of arithmetic and geometry, none of them derived from any sense-impression...; numbers, admittedly, have been perceived by the bodily senses in the objects counted: but the numbers *by* which we count are not the same numbers, nor are they their images, but more real'.[5] The *a priori* concepts, such as number, in terms of which the mind interprets the empirical world of its experience, are here included among the contents of *memoria*; and in the course of the long section devoted to *memoria* in his *Confessions*,[6] Augustine extends its scope step by step until it includes everything that the mind is capable of knowing or thinking about, whether it has previously encountered it in experience or not, whether it is actually thought about or not.[7] This is why the mind can be said to 'remember' objects such as God, the eternal truths, or the mind itself, none of which are 'remembered' from previous encounters, and all of which far transcend the limits of any past experience. In its simplest terms, *memoria* is the whole potential knowledge of an individual mind at any one time. 'Just as in regard to things past *memoria* is what enables them to be recalled and remembered, so in regard to the present we may properly call *memoria* that which the mind is to itself, its presence to itself whereby it may grasp itself in its own reflection'.[8]

Augustine explores this duality of the mind, the mind as knowing itself and the mind as being (actually or potentially) known to itself, in

[1] *De Trin.* XI 3. 6 (*PL* 42. 988–9). Sense-experience and the part played in it by *memoria* are discussed in ch. 24, pp. 376 ff., below.

[2] *Ibid.* XI 10. 17 (*PL* 42. 997–8).

[3] *Conf.* X 8. 12–15 (*PL* 32. 784–6).

[4] *De Trin.* XII 14. 23 (*PL* 42. 1011); cf. *Conf.* X 14. 21–2 (*PL* 32. 788–9).

[5] *Conf.* X 12. 19 (*PL* 32. 787).

[6] X 8. 12 – 27. 38 (*PL* 32. 784–95).

[7] Cf. *De Trin.* XV 21. 40 (*PL* 42. 1088).

[8] *Ibid.* XIV 11. 14 (*PL* 42. 1048): 'sic in re praesenti, quod sibi mens, memoria sine absurditate dicenda est, qua sibi praesto est ut sua cogitatione possit intelligi...'.

his *De Trinitate*. It also lies behind much of the section devoted to *memoria* in the *Confessions*, and indeed his inquiry into this mysterious power of the mind begins with an image expressive of this duality: '[*memoria*] is a power of my soul, and belongs to my nature; yet I myself cannot grasp all that I am. The mind is not large enough to contain itself.'[1] Self-knowledge is a task, and a task never fully to be achieved. Augustine discusses the process of actualizing this latent knowledge with a wealth of psychological subtlety on a number of occasions. In the *Confessions* he says[2] that learning those truths

> which do not come to us in images through the senses, but are known to us inwardly, without images as they really are, is, so to speak, to gather together things which the *memoria* already contained in a scattered and random way; and by holding them with our attention, to raise them from their previous scattered and submerged state to be within easy reach in the *memoria*, so that they are readily available when we are interested in them.

In the *De Trinitate*, where he touches on this question frequently, Augustine stresses even more sharply the formless, inchoate and merely potential character of the contents of *memoria*. Here he speaks of the process of creating actual knowledge from its contents as involving the mind's symbol-making activity, the creation of a *verbum* as the vehicle of meaning. It is beyond the scope of this chapter to follow Augustine's complex and subtle account of this process. It must suffice to observe here that although, in his view, the mind is in one sense always 'present to itself as a whole',[3] this presence is only made actual and concrete in individual acts of thinking, involving the creation of some symbolic vehicle of thought, a *verbum*. Augustine compares the mind with the eye in this respect: whereas the eye 'is never in its own field of vision (except, as we mentioned, when it sees itself in a mirror), this is not the case with the mind, which can place itself into its own field of vision by thinking'.[4] Outside the focal area of the individual act of thought in which the mind is reflexively aware of itself, it is only present to itself in the formless and potential way of *memoria*. The *verbum* in which the act of thinking formulates itself is at the same time the mind as known to

[1] *Conf.* x 8. 15 (*PL* 32. 785).

[2] x 11. 18 (*PL* 32. 787); I have paraphrased this difficult passage slightly.

[3] *De Trin.* x 4. 6 (*PL* 42. 976–7).

[4] *Ibid.* xiv 6. 8 (*PL* 42. 1041).

itself in the thought, the achieved piece of self-knowledge. The *Confessions* are indeed a large-scale exercise in creating such self-knowledge from the formless chaos of memory, an attempt to penetrate into what Augustine elsewhere calls 'the more obscure depths of the *memoria*'[1] by seeking to disclose to the mind's conscious gaze the truth lying latent and unsuspected within itself.

[1] *Ibid.* xv 21. 40 (*PL* 42. 1088): 'abstrusior profunditas memoriae'.

CHAPTER 24

AUGUSTINE
SENSE AND IMAGINATION

Sense-knowledge, as Augustine always insists, is, like all knowledge, a work of the soul, not of the bodily organs; it is a work 'of the soul by means of the body'.[1] All his more sustained discussions of this type of knowledge are attempts to make comprehensible the way in which the mind uses the bodily organs of sense in obtaining knowledge from sense-experience. His treatment of sensation (*sentire*) is therefore in line with his view of man as a soul using a body, and the analogy of the craftsman using his tools is the model on which it is constructed. Thus he begins the long discussion of this topic in his *De quantitate animae* with the following definition: 'sensation consists in the mind's awareness of the body's experience'.[2] A necessary condition of sensation, according to this definition, is the encounter between the bodily sense-organ and the object perceived; but sensation is more than this physical encounter on which it depends, and involves the mind's awareness. The definition assimilates sensation to the category of *passio*, or, more precisely, to an awareness by the mind of what the body 'suffers'. Augustine deals at length with the difficulties of treating sensation in these terms. What, he asks, do the eyes 'suffer' in seeing something? Evodius, his interlocutor in the dialogue, invokes the analogy of feeling pain and emotions: what the eyes suffer when seeing is sight itself, just as a sick man suffers sickness or a rejoicing man joy. The difficulties of assimilating sight to feeling in this way, as Augustine goes on to point out, come to light when we consider statements such as 'I can see you' or 'You can see me'. Statements such as these are commonly made, but it does not make sense

[1] *De Gen. ad litt.* III 5. 7 (*PL* 34. 282): 'sentire non est corporis sed animae per corpus'. Cf. *ibid.* XII 24. 51 (*PL* 34. 475); *De ord.* II 2. 6; 11. 30–4 (*PL* 32. 996; 1009–11); *De Trin.* XI 2. 2 (*PL* 42. 985–6).

[2] *Op. cit.* 23. 41 (*PL* 32. 1058): 'non latere animam quod patitur corpus'. The minor amendment added to this later in the same work (25. 48: *PL* 32. 1063) does not concern us here; it is intended to exclude from the scope of sensation knowledge which is inferred ultimately from sense-experience but is not directly disclosed in sensation.

to say 'I suffer you' or 'You suffer me', as this account of sensation would require us to say. For how can I be said to 'feel' or 'suffer' you, when you are over there and I am here? Feeling or 'suffering' requires the physical presence and contiguity of the object felt; if seeing is feeling, I should have to be where you are in order to see you, since one can only feel a thing in the place where it is. It ought, therefore, to follow that the eyes should be able to see only themselves, because there is nothing else in the place where they are. But this is manifestly absurd, for what the eyes see is clearly not themselves, their own states and modifications; nor is it the case that we infer from such an awareness of the modifications of the state of our sense-organs the existence and character of the objects which cause these modifications in them. As Augustine stresses, what we see is 'out there'.

These are the difficulties raised by this account of sensation, and Augustine states them with admirable perspicacity. He solves them by likening sight to using a stick held in the hand to explore a surface at some distance from the hand. The plausibility of the analogy depends on the physiological account of sight which Augustine appears to have accepted, according to which vision takes place in virtue of an emission from the eyes which impinges on the object.[1] Recourse to this analogy saves the account of sight Augustine gives here: 'Just as when I touch you with a stick, it is I that touch you, and I that feel that I am touching you, without myself being at the place where I am touching you; so when we say that I see you by means of sight, without being in the same place as the objects seen, this does not entail that it is not I myself who see.'[2] The theory of sight is, in fact, a special case of the theory of feeling and of touch, and this is made possible for Augustine by the conception of sight according to which sight involved the 'manipulation' by the eyes of an emission analogous to the manipulation of the stick by the hand.

Apart from the assimilation of all sensation to the case of touch and feeling, Augustine's account comes up against a second difficulty, which arises from the fact that to constitute a case of sensation, the physical

[1] *De quant. an.* 23. 43 (*PL* 32. 1060): 'emisso visu per oculos video'.

[2] *Ibid.* 23. 43 (*PL* 32. 1059–60). The whole discussion here summarized is to be found in the long section of the work 23. 41–4 (*PL* 32. 1058–60). Cf. *Ep.* 137. 5 (*PL* 33. 517–18).

encounter of sense-organ and object has, somehow, as Augustine saw and insisted, to be registered by the mind. But it is axiomatic, for Augustine, that body cannot act on spirit, and that no modification can therefore arise in the mind caused by the bodily sense-organs and their changing states. The reason for this is that body is below mind in the hierarchy of nature, and lower cannot act upon higher on the premises of Augustine's metaphysical scheme. Hence the mind's ability to register sensations is *quiddam mirabile*.[1] Augustine solves this difficulty by denying that this is a case of action by body on mind, and asserting that it is merely a special case of the mode in which the soul is present in its body. This presence is not one of 'spatial diffusion', for the soul is not present in parts distributed throughout different parts of the body, but is present in the whole body by what Augustine calls 'a kind of vital attention'.[2] The soul's ability to perceive pain in its body, to be generally aware of its states and to know what is going on within it is part of its vivifying presence to the body.[3] The soul animates its body by acting within it and 'using it', and Augustine apparently envisaged its awareness of bodily states as a kind of awareness by the mind of variations in the conditions of its operation.[4] This obscure explanation seems to have been forced on Augustine by the Platonic elements in his definition of man as a rational soul using a material body.[5] His two-substance theory of man led him to explain sense-perception as the concurrence of two processes, one in the body and the other—not caused by it, but connected with it (as instrument 'used' with its user)—in the soul.

A substantially similar description of sense-experience is given in somewhat different terms in the great commentary on Genesis of Augustine's maturity.[6] He begins this description by distinguishing three kinds of sight (*visio*), which he calls 'corporeal sight', 'spiritual sight' and 'intellectual sight'.[7] The first of these denotes seeing with the

[1] *De Gen. ad litt.* XII 16. 33 (*PL* 34. 467); for the statement of the difficulty, *ibid.* XII 16. 32–3 (*PL* 34. 466–7); cf. *De mus.* VI 4. 7 (*PL* 32. 1166). [For the Plotinian background of this see Part III (Plotinus), ch. 16 (a), pp. 257–8.]

[2] *Ep.* 166. 2. 4 (*PL* 33. 722): 'quadam vitali intentione'.

[3] *De Gen. ad litt.* III 16. 25 (*PL* 34. 290).

[4] *De mus.* VI 5. 9–10 (*PL* 32. 1168–9); cf. *De quant. an.* 33. 71 (*PL* 32. 1074); *De Gen. ad litt.* VII 19. 25 (*PL* 34. 364–5).

[5] Cf. above, p. 357.

[6] *De Gen. ad litt.* XII, *passim.* A parallel formulation appears in *De Trin.* IX 6. 11 (*PL* 42. 966–7). Cf. *Ep.* 120. 11; 162. 3–5 (*PL* 33. 457–8; 705–6).

[7] *De Gen. ad. litt.* XII 6. 15 – 7. 16 (*PL* 34. 458–9).

eyes, and offers no difficulties. It is the equivalent of the physical encounter between sense-organ and object of the account formulated in terms of *passio*, which has been considered above. As there, Augustine again insists that sensation cannot take place without awareness of it by the mind; I cannot be said to see unless I know that I see. The mental process which accompanies 'corporeal sight' is what Augustine calls 'spiritual sight', at any rate, when he wishes to draw attention to it in its own right, or when it occurs in the absence of corporeal seeing. This spiritual sight is not caused by bodily seeing, since matter cannot act on mind; indeed, it frequently takes place in the absence of the corporeal seeing which accompanies it in cases of ordinary visual awareness. This spontaneous, 'free-wheeling' process of spiritual sight is what happens in dreaming, visions, hallucination, or simply when we visualize remembered objects, or construct imaginary ones. So far as what goes on in the mind is concerned, there is no difference between ordinary seeing and imagining, dreaming, remembering, etc. The process in both cases is 'spiritual sight'; in both cases, what is before the mind is not physical objects themselves, but their likenesses.[1] What the mind 'sees', in both sorts of case, is of the same nature as itself;[2] it is an image created by the mind out of its own substance.[3]

What is the difference, on this view, between real sight and imagination, dreaming, etc.? How do we know when we 'see' something that it really is there and that we are not just dreaming or imagining it? The difference lies solely in the fact that in cases of genuine sight, the bodily process accompanies the process of 'spiritual sight', whereas in cases of imagination, etc., there is no such parallel process of bodily seeing taking place. In the first case, our bodily sense-organs are affected by the things we see, in the second they are not. To know that we are seeing and not imagining, it is necessary to be conscious of the bodily modification which accompanies our awareness. Thus, Augustine remarks, it is sometimes difficult to be certain—for instance, we take our dreams seriously and only realize that they were 'unreal' when we wake up.[4] In our waking, normal state, Augustine appears to think, we

[1] *Ibid.* XII 24. 50 (*PL* 34. 474).
[2] *Ibid.* XII 21. 44 (*PL* 34. 472).
[3] *Ibid.* XII 16. 33 (*PL* 34. 467); cf. *De Trin.* X 5. 7 (*PL* 42. 977).
[4] *De Gen. ad litt.* XII 2. 3–4; 19. 41 (*PL* 34. 455; 470).

are usually sufficiently conscious of being externally affected and we have no hesitation about being in *rapport* with physical objects in our experience. But this awareness may be suspended or prevented in a number of ways, such as by damage to the bodily receiving system, or by exclusive concentration of the attention on what goes on in the mind, or a withholding of attention from the body. This latter is what happens in deep sleep, or in ecstasy or any of the many kinds of 'abstraction' of mind from its actual physical surroundings and the body's *rapport* with them. In all such cases the mind contemplates its own images without attending to the accompanying bodily states; its 'spiritual sight' is, so to speak, free-wheeling.[1] Attention, and the way in which it is directed, withheld or immobilized, is the decisive factor which distinguishes seeing from imagining. Attention, in general, is the deliberate concentration of the mind on some part or parts of the whole field before it. In imagination the imagined object claims all the mind's attention and exhausts it, in sleep the effort of deliberate attention is suspended and leaves the mind free among the images which well up within it; whereas, in sensory awareness of which one is conscious as such, one is also aware of being subjected to outside agency concurrently with the 'spiritual sight' of the mind's images.[2] The will thus has a central part to play in Augustine's account of sensory awareness in virtue of the decisive role of attention. Attention is the deliberate direction of the mind's 'gaze' (*acies*), as Augustine often calls it, towards a particular portion of its field. It is an act of will whereby the mind turns either towards its own contents exclusively, as it does in remembering or in imagining, or includes within its field the bodily senses, thereby checking the free play of images in the mind and converting the experience into one of corporeal seeing.[3]

This account of sense-perception, to be found in the great commentary on Genesis, and in a less systematically detailed form in the *De Trinitate*, adds nothing to the solution of the central problem left by Augustine's earlier account. It makes it no clearer how the image seen in 'spiritual sight' can represent the object seen by the eyes, how it can be like it, or arise from it. Augustine is content to speak of the physical

[1] *De Gen. ad litt.* XII 12. 25 (*PL* 34. 463). [2] *De Trin.* XI 4. 7 (*PL* 42. 989–90).
[3] *Ibid.* XI 8. 15 – 9. 16 (*PL* 42. 995–7).

processes involved in sense-perception as conveying 'messages' to the mind, of 'corporeal sight' as the messenger to the superior 'spiritual sight';[1] or, alternatively, of the *species* in the one 'producing' or 'giving rise to' similar *species* in the other.[2] But his two-tier account of man, with the resultant duplication of physical and mental processes in perception, makes it difficult to understand how messages can be conveyed across a gulf so radical, or indeed what meaning can be ascribed to the vague language of one kind of *species* 'arising' from another.

The 'messages' conveyed from the bodily organism to 'spiritual sight' are also, Augustine says, conveyed to the rational mind or intelligence. The first message produces mental images; the second, conveyed to 'intellectual' sight, appears not to produce any new and different kind of image or likeness. Augustine describes it rather as reaching the highest kind of sight, as it were, in code form: it is only at this stage, in the intellect, that the images of the spirit are understood as signs pointing to other things, only here is their meaning sought and discovered.[3] The task of this third kind of 'sight' therefore appears to be to decode the images received by the second from the first. This appears to include interpreting, judging and correcting the messages received: it refers the images in the mind to external objects, or, alternatively, refuses so to refer them. Thus, for instance, it is its task to decide whether the image of the bent oar half-submerged in water is or is not to be referred to the actual object. The mind is not deceived in receiving misleading images, it is wrong only when it mistakenly judges on their strength that things are what they are not—that the oar is really bent when submerged. It is for the intellect to safeguard the mind against such deception.[4] Its nature and its work have already been considered in the previous chapter.

[1] *De Gen. ad litt.* XII 11. 22 (*PL* 34. 462). Cf. *Ep.* 147. 38 (*PL* 33. 613–14).

[2] *De Trin.* XI 9. 16 (*PL* 42. 996–7).

[3] *De Gen. ad litt.* XII 11. 22 (*PL* 34. 462).

[4] *Ibid.* XII 25. 52 (*PL* 34. 475–6); cf. *C. Acad.* III 11. 24–6 (*PL* 32. 946–8); *Ep.* 147. 41 (*PL* 33. 615).

CHAPTER 25

AUGUSTINE

HUMAN ACTION: WILL AND VIRTUE

The sources of Augustine's reflection on human conduct, as of much of his thought, are the teaching of the Scriptures and the Church, and of Greek, particularly of Neoplatonic, philosophy. Sometimes, as we have noted, these two are in tension; in the present case, however, they blend completely in his mind. Indeed, it was here that he was above all impressed with the convergence he detected between Platonic and Christian teaching. His readiness to adopt other aspects of Platonic modes of thought, for instance in his discussion of soul and body,[1] can in part be accounted for by this conviction of the similarity of their ethical bearings to those of Christian teaching. Tensions which can sometimes be detected between his Christian belief and his adopted philosophical concepts and language, tensions of the kind we have encountered, for instance, in his account of man as a soul using a body, are here totally absent.

Blessedness, as we have seen,[2] was, for Augustine, the aim of philosophy. The wisdom which philosophy strove to attain would fill and satisfy all the deepest human needs and longings. Augustine was very ready to read back into Plato his own interpretation of what this love of wisdom consists in: Plato, he says, identified the supreme good, in the enjoyment of which man finds blessedness, with God. 'And therefore he [Plato] thought that to be a philosopher is to be a lover of God.'[3] Affirmations of this kind pave the way for an almost wholesale adoption of Platonic notions, especially in the sphere of ethics. It was very easy to fit them into the traditional language of the Church, and indeed the cleavage which sometimes appears between the language of philosophical discussion and the language of popular preaching, devotion and catechetical instruction disappears almost totally when Augustine speaks about ethical subjects.

[1] See above, pp. 357–9.

[2] See above, pp. 344–5.

[3] *De civ. Dei* VIII 8 (*PL* 41. 233).

Blessedness is the complete satisfaction of human nature: 'The life of blessedness and repose for man consists in the harmonious rationality of all his activity.'[1] This definition emphasizes that not only are all human desires and impulses brought to rest in the state of blessedness; but that in addition, human nature being rational, this harmonious state of total satisfaction expresses a rational order. It is clear enough that happiness (blessedness) is incompatible with lacking what one wants; but the converse, Augustine notes, does not follow: it is not true that, if one has what one wants, one is therefore happy. Following Cicero, Augustine holds that 'to want what is not right is the supreme misery'.[2] Satisfaction of perverse and evil desires is not, in the end, real and lasting satisfaction of the kind that blessedness consists in. Hence the need for the qualification which Augustine adds in defining happiness: 'No one is happy unless he has all that he wants and wants nothing that is evil.'[3]

All men desire this state of happiness.[4] Indeed, this natural desire for blessedness is simply the logical consequence of the very notion of desire; for to have a desire for anything at all means that one desires the satisfaction of that desire, and to say that man has a natural desire for blessedness means that man has a multitude of desires, and desires their satisfaction. But it does not follow that all men will be blessed, for the achievement of this state depends on the righteousness or otherwise of desires, as well as on their eventual satisfaction.[5] And this depends on the way to blessedness being revealed to men by God in Christ, and the redemptive work of Christ was necessary as the source of the grace required to enable men to travel along the way revealed.[6] By means of this final assertion Augustine lifted the basically Platonic account of man's quest for blessedness on to a specifically Christian plane; and in being thus transposed, the account needed no radical revision to serve his purpose.

Human nature embraces a multitude of desires, impulses and drives—

[1] *De Gen. c. Man.* I 20. 31 (*PL* 34. 188): 'cum omnes motus eius rationi veritatique consentiunt'. Cf. *C. Acad.* I 2. 5 (*PL* 32. 908–9).

[2] *De beata vita* 2. 10 (*PL* 32. 964).

[3] *De Trin.* XIII 5. 8 (*PL* 42. 1020); on the whole question, *ibid.* 3. 6 – 9. 12 (*PL* 42. 1017–24); *De civ. Dei* VIII 8 (*PL* 41. 233); and *Ep.* 130. 10–11 (*PL* 33. 497–8).

[4] *De civ. Dei* X 1. 1 (*PL* 41. 277).

[5] *De lib. arb.* I 14. 30 (*PL* 32. 1237).

[6] *De Trin.* XIII 9. 12 (*PL* 42. 1023–4); cf. *De civ. Dei* X 29. 1–2 (*PL* 41. 307–9).

not all conscious, and certainly by no means all operative all the time. As Augustine knew only too well, there is a bewildering variety of them, and often they are in serious and sometimes agonizing conflict. They cannot all be satisfied—the satisfaction of one inevitably means the frustration of others. This tension in the human condition, Augustine thought, was the result of a disorder and loss of harmony incurred by man with the fall of Adam. But for this distortion in his nature, man would simply have to follow out his natural desires to their goal and in satisfying them reach blessedness. In his disordered state, however, the human task is complicated by the need to discern the right direction in the midst of the tension. Augustine's *Confessions* is, in one sense, the record of such a discovery and of the struggle to follow the way discovered. The restlessness of the human heart is its primary datum, expressed in the famous exclamation at the beginning of the work: 'Thou [O God] hast made us, and in making us turned us toward thyself; and our hearts are restless until they come to rest in thee.'[1] The longings and impulses are in reality our groping for the satisfaction which is to be had finally only in the state of blessedness, in the vision of God. Only in its attainment lies the satisfaction of man's restless seeking, the rest and peace for which Augustine concludes the *Confessions* with a moving prayer.[2]

The deep and dramatic inwardness of the struggle recorded in the *Confessions* is very much Augustine's own; the metaphysical picture in terms of which he records it is a commonplace of Greek philosophy. It is the picture of Plato's *Symposium* and of Aristotle's *Physics*, of man as part of a cosmic order in which each constituent is related to the rest in a system of permanent *rapport*, as fragments seeking completion in the whole, or, in Dante's image, seeking rest in their own proper havens on the 'great sea of being'. Each thing, in pursuing its own natural purposes, is thereby seeking its proper place in the hierarchical structure of interrelated things; and, achieving it, achieves its rest and satisfaction. Augustine refers collectively to the driving forces of human nature, the inclinations, desires and drives behind human action, by the name 'love' or 'loves'. He conceives them, in terms of this classical cosmology, as

[1] I 1. 1 (*PL* 32. 661); the middle phrase, *fecisti nos ad te*, is untranslatable.
[2] *Conf.* XIII 35. 50 – 37. 52 (*PL* 32. 867–8).

the dynamic forces inscribed in human nature, and likens them to physical weight.[1]

> Bodies tend by their weight to move towards the place proper to them. Weight pulls not only downwards, but to its proper place: fire tends upwards, stone downwards; moved by their weight, things seek their right place. . . . Out of their place, they are not at rest; they come to rest in being brought to their right place. My weight is my love: wherever I am carried, it is by it that I am carried.

'Love', therefore, in Augustine's vocabulary, stands for any of the diverse forces which 'carry' man in his activity in whatever direction he is moving. He uses the same imagery of weight to speak of the perverse love which seduces him from God[2] as he does of the love which moves man towards God, and sometimes contrasts the two as *cupiditas* (or *avaritia*) and *caritas* respectively.[3] He uses these contrasts in many contexts, some of which will engage our attention later. 'Love', in this terminology, may be bad or good; it is morally neutral.

The metaphor of 'weight' and the analogy with the falling stone need qualification, however, in their application to human action. Man is not the victim of his 'weight' in the way the stone is, in such a sense that given the conditions (removal of support, in the case of the stone) he would naturally and inevitably 'fall', that is to say, he does not necessarily seek to satisfy his desires and follow his impulses. In two respects man differs from this model: being very much more complex, there are many more desires of a diverse kind in him than the simple weight in the stone. But, even with this qualification, it does not follow that man necessarily and inevitably follows what we might describe as the resultant of all his impulses. He is able to select, if not without restriction among all, at least among some of them. Augustine describes this difference between inanimate and human behaviour by saying that whereas the stone's behaviour is 'natural' (or 'necessary'), man's is 'voluntary',[4] at least in part. The latter kind of behaviour is the range of ac-

[1] *Ibid.* XIII 9. 10 (*PL* 32. 848–9): 'pondus meum amor meus, eo feror quocumque feror'. Among the many parallels the following are noteworthy: *De Gen. ad litt.* II 1. 2; IV 3. 7–8; 18. 34 (*PL* 34. 263; 299; 309); *De civ. Dei* XI 28 (*PL* 41. 342).

[2] *Conf.* VII 17. 23 (*PL* 32. 744).

[3] *De Trin.* IX 8. 13 (*PL* 42. 967–8); cf. *De div. qu. LXXXIII* 35. 2 – 36. 1 (*PL* 40. 24–5); *De Gen. ad litt.* XI 15. 19–20 (*PL* 34. 436–7); *De civ. Dei* XI 28 (*PL* 41. 342).

[4] *De lib. arb.* III 1. 2 (*PL* 32. 1271–2); cf. *De Civ. Dei* XI 28; V 10 (*PL* 41. 341–2; 152): '. . . necessitas nostra illa dicenda est quae non est in nostra potestate. . .'.

tions for which a man can be held responsible, for which praise or blame is appropriate; whereas 'natural' action, so far as man is concerned, is more properly the name for things which go on in man or to which he is subjected rather than for what he does: the kind of activity or states of mind and feeling which are not in his control.[1] Only in man can these two kinds of action be distinguished. He is the only creature who is not at the mercy of all the forces acting upon him and within him in their totality. Augustine calls the capacity which sets man apart from beasts in this respect, whereby he is in command over at least some of his actions, his will. To say that man is endowed with free choice is no more than another way of saying the same thing.

Augustine did not think that this freedom of human action was incompatible with God's certain foreknowledge of all actions, of events and their outcome. While it is necessarily true that what God foresees will come about, it does not follow that what he foresees will come about by necessity, i.e. in a manner which excludes free choice. God is able to foresee acts of choice no less than actions performed under the compulsion of necessity.[2] The whole Augustinian theory of predestination, the cause of so much subsequent difficulty, hinges on this argument. That theory, and its correlative theology of grace and justification, are beyond the scope of this chapter.

Man alone is thus free, in the sense that, though foreseen by God, some at least of his actions are not subject to 'necessity', or, to use Augustine's alternative terminology, are not determined by 'nature'. Human behaviour is therefore shaped on different levels, both by forces which are 'natural' in the sense in which Augustine contrasts these with 'voluntary', such as feelings, desires, passions, unconscious drives and impulses; and free acts of choice. As we have seen, Augustine refers to all these by the blanket term 'love' or 'loves', and speaks of behaviour as determined by the particular sort of 'love' by which it happens to be motivated. This duality of the factors which shape human action endow the term 'love', when applied to man, with a peculiar complexity which it does not have in its other, non-human, applications. Here, 'love' stands both for the natural impulses, physical and emotional needs of

[1] *De lib. arb.* III 1. 1–3 (*PL* 32. 1269–72).

[2] *Ibid.* III. 2. 4 – 3. 8 (*PL* 32. 1272–5); cf. *De civ. Dei* V 9–10 (*PL* 41. 148–53).

man's nature, and for the deliberate and conscious choice whereby he selects from among these impulses and inclinations and freely moulds his behaviour in accordance with some of them, in opposition to others. In terms of the analogy between 'love' and 'weight', Augustine describes this peculiarity of human love as having a capacity, so to speak, of controlling its centre of gravity by choice. Thus he writes that when we are bidden not to covet, 'we are bidden nothing else than to abstain from unlawful desires; for the soul, as if it were by its own weight, is carried wherever it is carried by its love. So that what we are bidden is to take away from the weight of unlawful desire (*cupiditatis*) and to add to the weight of charity (*caritatis*), until the former vanish and the latter be perfected.'[1] This metaphor of transferring one's own weight or throwing in one's weight with one or other of the 'weights' pulling in different directions is a picturesque expression of the duality in human love. Love, in non-human creatures, is natural, given; in man alone has it this self-regulating character. Upon this duality, in virtue of which human love is both what regulates and what is regulated, Augustine bases his discussion of the morality of human action.

The subject of moral praise or blame is the will alone. The feelings, passions, emotions and so forth whereby it is moved are not, themselves, objects of moral assessment, except marginally, in so far as they are themselves capable of deliberate cultivation, or the result of failure to 'educate' them. At any particular moment, however, these are simply 'there', given, and what matters morally speaking is not what they are, but what a man decides to do: to yield to them, restrain them, encourage them, which to select to follow in action. Hence Augustine speaks of the will as love, regarded in its regulating, deciding aspect;[2] and in this aspect alone is love morally good or bad:[3] 'Both upright and perverse love are will; love as longing for its object is desire; as possessing and enjoying it, it is joy; seeking what is hurtful to it, it is fear; feeling its presence, it is pain. All these are evil if the love is evil, good if it be good.' Love, then, regarded in its regulative aspect, in which it is synonymous with 'will', can be praiseworthy or reprehensible: 'there is love whereby we love what ought not to be loved; and he who loves

[1] *Ep.* 157. 2. 9 (*PL* 33. 677).
[2] *De Trin.* XV 20. 38; 21. 41 (*PL* 42. 1087; 1089).
[3] *De civ. Dei* XIV 7. 2 (*PL* 41. 410).

what ought to be loved hates this [reprehensible] love in himself. Both loves may be present in a man, and this is for his good, so that the love whereby we live well should grow at the expense of that by which we live in evil fashion....'[1] In this conception of 'love of love' we can observe, perhaps at its clearest, Augustine's two-level theory of love used to discriminate between primary inclinations which ought to be endorsed in voluntary choice and those which ought to be resisted or restrained.

Virtue is 'the art of living well and righteously',[2] its object is 'the proper use of things which are also capable of abuse'.[3] But when Augustine defines in more personal terms what it consists in, he prefers to define its function and the order which is its result in terms of love:[4]

> Bodily loveliness, made by God, is nevertheless temporal, carnal, and a lesser good; it is wrongly loved if it is loved above God, the eternal, inward and lasting good. Just as the covetous man subordinates justice to his love of gold—through no fault in the gold but in himself—so it is with all things. They are all good in themselves, and capable of being loved either well or badly. They are loved well when the right order is kept, badly when this order is upset....Hence it seems to me that the briefest and truest definition of virtue is that it is the order of love.

This definition brings together two features of his reflection on virtue which can be traced to his early writings: the concern to explain virtue in terms of love,[5] and to describe the life of virtue in terms of order.[6] The definition of virtue as 'the order of love' (*ordo amoris*, or *dilectionis*) struck Augustine quite early as a neat and expressive formula in which these concerns would both be summed up. In the *De doctrina christiana*[7] he defines the righteous man as 'the man who values things at their true worth; he has ordered love, which prevents him from loving what is not to be loved, or not loving what is to be loved, from preferring what ought to be loved less, from loving equally what ought to be loved

[1] *De Trin.* XI 28 (*PL* 41. 342).

[2] *Ibid.* IV 21 (*PL* 41. 128).

[3] *De lib. arb.* II 19. 50 (*PL* 32. 1268); cf. *De quant. an.* 16. 27 (*PL* 32. 1050): '...virtus aequalitas quaedam...vitae, rationi undique consentiens'.

[4] *De civ. Dei* 22 (*PL* 41. 467).

[5] Cf. e.g. *De mor. eccl.* I 15. 25 (*PL* 32. 1322) and *Ep.* 155. 4. 13 (*PL* 33. 671–2).

[6] Cf. e.g. *De div. qu. LXXXIII* 31 (*PL* 40. 20–2).

[7] I 27. 28 (*PL* 34. 29): 'ille autem iuste et sancte vivit, qui rerum integer aestimator est; ipse est autem qui ordinatam dilectionen habet...'. Cf. *Ep.* 140. 2. 4 (*PL* 33. 163).

either less or more, or from loving either less or more what ought to be loved equally'. This definition brings us to the heart of the Augustinian universe. Man's self-regulative love is face to face with the hierarchically ordered cosmos; man's moral excellence is a matter of establishing a right order among his own inclinations in the value set upon things, and embodying these rightly ordered valuations in conduct.

Behind Augustine's ethics stands the classical world-picture of the ordered cosmic hierarchy, with its conviction that some things are more worthy of being loved than others, and that man's task is to conform himself to this order in his actions. This appears most clearly in those definitions which Augustine gives of virtue where he is following classical, especially Ciceronian, precedents, as, for instance, when defining virtue as 'the disposition of the mind whereby it agrees with the order of nature and of reason'.[1] The objective order of nature or of reason is the pattern to be embodied in man as agent. The pattern to which human action is required to conform is also called 'law' by Augustine, again, of course, following classical usage. From here, too, derives his distinction of what is just by nature (*natura*) and what is just by custom or of human institution (*consuetudine*).[2] As this distinction indicates, Augustine included within the realm of 'law' more than ordinances of promulgated, written law. He thought that behind human law stands an eternal law, to which we appeal when we criticize particular enactments of human laws. Unlike human law, this eternal law is necessarily just, and it is all-embracing, in that it covers the whole range of human action; unlike it, too, in that it is unchanging, whereas human laws can be and often are changed to suit the circumstances of time and place. In his earlier writings, Augustine thought that the changeable institutions of human law, though framed with the needs of particular societies at particular times in mind, ought also to be modelled, as far as possible, on the eternal law and should seek to embody its precepts.[3] In his later works this view receded into the background, as Augustine thought of human society less and less in terms of being modelled on an intelligible archetype, and more and more as a contrast

[1] *De div. qu.* LXXXIII. 31. 1 (*PL* 40. 20); cf. above, p. 386 n. 3.

[2] *Ibid.*

[3] *De lib. arb.* I 5. 11 – 8. 18 (*PL* 32. 1227–31).

with the eschatological society of the kingdom of God.[1] The distinction between human and divine law, however, remained a part of his vocabulary.[2]

Augustine's conception of society will engage our attention later; so far as the individual is concerned, it is clear that the relation between the unchanging, eternal standards of conduct and human ideas about it are an instance of the general relation between the eternal truths and the human mind. This appears very clearly in one of Augustine's earliest discussions of the question:[3] he here speaks of God's law, which,

> while always remaining in him fixed and unchanging, is, so to speak, transcribed into the souls of the wise, in such a manner that they know that their lives are the better and the more sublime in proportion to the degree of perfection of their contemplating it by their minds and their zeal in keeping it in their lives.

The language of this is almost identical with the language in which Augustine describes the mind's illumination by the light of the eternal truth.[4] As we have seen, even in contexts not specifically ethical, Augustine's theory of illumination often takes on distinctly moral overtones. His chief concern in adopting it appears to have been to buttress his moral theory; it is scarcely surprising that it is here that it really comes into its own. The eternal law is identical with the eternal truths taken in their normative, moral aspect: it is God's sovereign reason considered in its bearing on human behaviour. As man's reason is his participation in the divine mind, so his conscience is his participation in the eternal law; the deliverances of conscience are the unchanging law of God as present in the mind, 'an inward law, written on the heart itself'.[5] This human participation in the eternal law Augustine also refers to as 'natural law' and describes it as a function of human reason.[6] 'Reason assesses value by the light of the truth, subordinating

[1] This is convincingly argued by F. E. Cranz, 'The development of Augustine's ideas on society before the Donatist controversy', *Harvard Theol. Rev.* XLVII (1954), pp. 255–316. Cf. also B. Lohse, 'Augustins Wandlung in seiner Beurteilung des Staates', *Studia patristica*, VI (1962) [*Texte u. Untersuchungen*, Bd. 81], pp. 447–75.

[2] Cf. e.g. *De civ. Dei* XV 16. 2 (*PL* 41. 459).

[3] *De ord.* II 8. 25 (*PL* 32. 1006).

[4] Cf. above, pp. 366–9. Also *De lib. arb.* I 6. 15 (*PL* 32. 1229), where Augustine speaks of 'aeternae legis [notio] quae nobis impressa est'.

[5] *En. in Ps.* 57. 1 (*PL* 36. 674): 'lex intima, in ipso...corde conscripta'.

[6] *Ep.* 157. 3. 15 (*PL* 33. 681); cf. *En. in Ps.* 118, *sermo* 25. 4 (*PL* 37. 1574).

in a true judgement lesser [worth] to greater.'[1] The object of the eternal law, of which reason enables us to have an 'impressed notion', is that 'all things shall be perfectly ordered'.[2] Virtue, in Augustine's view, we might say, consists in realizing this order among the manifold impulses of human nature and in shaping human activity in accordance with it.[3]

We are thus brought back to Augustine's definition of virtue as 'ordered love'. The order envisaged here is the order of reason, or of the eternal law. Hence it is impossible to contrast love and law in Augustine's way of thinking; his celebrated 'Love, and do what you will'[4] is very far from being an endorsement of love as an elemental force which knows no discipline. Love is of its nature, in man, self-discipline; and law, far from being an external, imposed restriction on it, is inscribed in human nature in virtue of what is specifically distinctive of it, its rationality.

Having now examined the conception and definition of virtue, we must briefly sketch the content given it by Augustine. What kind of order did he think human love ought to embody, what things were to be loved, loved more or loved less?

Augustine's views, here again, were developed quite naturally in the context of classical notions as he encountered them in the pages especially of Varro and Cicero.[5] The Stoics' threefold scheme of classification of goods—the 'pleasant' (*delectabile*), the 'useful' (*utile*) and the 'right' (*honestum*)—had become something of a commonplace, and was repeated by pagan and Christian writers alike. Augustine adopted this classification, but it suited his purpose better to reduce its three classes to two. Such use of bi-polar schemata was very much in keeping with Augustine's predilections, and often, as in this case, with the deepest tendencies of his mind. The distinction between *utile* and *honestum* seemed to Augustine more fundamental, and he therefore adopted it as the basic classification of things held valuable.[6] This classification rests on the distinction between 'what is desired for its own sake [*honestum*],

[1] *De lib. arb.* III 5. 17 (*PL* 32. 1279): 'ratio aestimat luce veritatis, ut recto iudicio subdat minora maioribus'.

[2] *Ibid.* I 6. 15 (*PL* 32. 1229): 'ut omnia sint ordinatissima'.

[3] Cf. *ibid.* I 8. 18 (*PL* 32. 1231).

[4] *In Ep. Jo. Tr.* VII 8 (*PL* 35. 2033).

[5] R. Lorenz, 'Die Herkunft des augustinischen frui Deo', *Zeits. f. Kirchengeschichte*, LXIV (1952–3), pp. 34–60, has sketched the Stoic background of this doctrine, and concluded that Augustine's source for it was probably Varro.

[6] Cf. *De div. qu. LXXXIII* 30 (*PL* 40. 19–20).

and what is desired for the sake of something else [*utile*]', that is to say, as a means to an end. Augustine makes a parallel distinction between the two human attitudes corresponding to this distinction of valuables: 'we are said to enjoy (*frui*) things which satisfy our desire; we use (*utimur*) those which we refer to the acquisition of the things which satisfy our desires'.[1] The distinction between use and enjoyment (*uti–frui*) is the basis of Augustinian ethics. 'All human perversion, which we also call vice', Augustine goes on to say, 'consists in wanting to use things which are meant to be enjoyed, and to enjoy things which are meant to be used. And all order (*ordinatio*), which we also call virtue, consists in wanting to enjoy what is to be enjoyed and to use what is to be used. What is right is to be enjoyed, what is useful is to be used.'[2] In typically Platonic language Augustine concludes this discussion with the insistence that the sole object proper for man's enjoyment is 'intelligible beauty, which we call spiritual'; everything else is for use only, to be referred ultimately to this.

Augustine admired the ethics of the 'Platonists' because, he thought, they taught that human happiness is to be found in the enjoyment not of bodily goods, or even of the mind, but of God.[3] Augustine's ethical theory has important links with Plato, and with Middle and Neo-platonism; but the central place given to the 'enjoyment of God' (*frui Deo*, ἀπολαύειν θεοῦ) appears to be specifically Augustinian, although the notion had previously appeared in patristic thought.[4] It is one of the architectonic ideas of his work *De doctrina christiana*, where he defines *frui* and *uti* in terms of love:[5] 'To enjoy something is to possess it, loving it for its own sake; to use something is to refer the object which is taken into use to the obtaining of something that we love.' This dichotomy of things to be enjoyed and things to be used served Augustine as a basis on which to organize the subject-matter studied in this work; and this division became one of the standard architectonic principles of medieval theology. Why it appealed so strongly to

[1] *De div. qu. LXXXIII* 30 (*PL* 40. 19–20). [2] *Ibid.*; cf. *De lib. arb.* I 15. 33 (*PL* 32. 1239).

[3] *De civ. Dei* VIII. 8 (*PL* 41. 232–3); cf. *De mor. eccl.* I 3. 4 (*PL* 32. 1312).

[4] Cf. Lorenz, *art. cit.* above, p. 389 n. 5; generally, ἀπόλαυσις θεοῦ appears to have had specifically eschatological overtones in earlier patristic literature.

[5] I 4. 4: (*PL* 34. 20): 'frui enim est amore alicui rei inhaerere propter seipsam. Uti autem, quod in usum venerit ad id quod amas obtinendum referre'. Cf. *De Trin.* X 10. 13; 11. 17–18 (*PL* 42. 981; 982–4).

Augustine's mind appears most clearly from two paragraphs of this work.[1] 'The objects of enjoyment are those which make us blessed; those which are to be used are the things by which we are helped on our way to achieving blessedness'; although Augustine allows that in common speech the words can be used in a looser and less mutually exclusive sense,[2] 'enjoyment' is man's proper attitude to God and to his heavenly home, 'use' is his proper relation to everything else. Nothing but God can finally serve as a resting-place in which all man's longings are satisfied; to seek to 'enjoy' anything else is to be retarded in one's journey, mistaking, as it were, the road and the vehicles used for the destination. With the aid of this pair of concepts Augustine has constructed a morality for the pilgrim on the way to his heavenly *patria*.[3]

This does not, to Augustine's mind, imply that things 'used' are not to be loved; though he repudiates the converse, that things 'used' are all to be loved.[4] Creatures, in their right scale of priority and subordination, are perfectly proper objects of love. As we have seen, he identifies virtue with properly ordered love; and indeed he is on occasion prepared to identify it with charity.[5] Behind this identification lies the contrast he often draws between 'charity' and 'cupidity',[6] with its close relation to the contrast between *frui* and *uti*. The contrast is not between love of God and love of creatures, but between a rightly ordered love which embraces both God and creatures, and a perverse or disordered love by which creatures are loved inordinately, for their own sakes, without reference to God. Love by man of his fellow-men is a special case, the description of which appears to have given Augustine some difficulty in this framework. The logical conclusion of his dichotomy between things to be enjoyed and things to be used, rigidly pursued, would have led him to exclude fellow-men from the range of objects rightly loved for their own sake. But Augustine could not quite bring himself to accept the alternative, of saying that they are to be 'used' by man in the advancement of his own happiness. He accordingly supplemented his dichotomy by a third class, that of objects to be

[1] I 3. 3 – 4. 4 (*PL* 34. 20–1).
[2] Cf. *De civ. Dei* XI. 25 (*PL* 41. 339).
[3] Cf. *De Trin.* XI 6. 10 (*PL* 42. 992).
[4] *De doctr. chr.* I 23. 22 (*PL* 34. 27).
[5] *Ep.* 167. 4. 15 (*PL* 33. 739).
[6] Cf. above, p. 383 n. 3.

'enjoyed', but 'enjoyed in God'.[1] But he is generally content to speak only of the duality of *uti* and *frui*, of *cupiditas* and *caritas*; and the contrasts provide the pivot of a great deal of his thought on conduct, not only in his more academic writings, but also in his popular preaching. They also have an important place in his views on human society, which will be discussed in the last chapter of this Part.

To conclude the present chapter, it is instructive to single out as an example of Augustine's views concerning the attitude required of man to other things, the attitude he thought man should adopt to his own physical reality, the body, its needs, pleasures and their satisfaction. In one sense, the body with its life is simply one example of the things not to be loved for their own sake but to be referred to the enjoyment of higher goods. Once, Augustine went so far as to say that to love the body is 'to be estranged from oneself'.[2] Reviewing his work in old age, he took himself to task over this statement:[3]

What I said here is true only of the love whereby we so love an object that we think that to enjoy it would mean blessedness. For it is by no means to be estranged from oneself to love corporeal beauty for the praise of the Creator, with the knowledge that blessedness lies only in the enjoyment of the Creator himself.

This is entirely in line with his view on the attitude proper to things in general. His conception of 'estrangement', however, is a unique illustration of the manner in which perversion of the right order in love can also 'estrange us from our [heavenly] home'.[4] The point he appears to be making here is that habitual perversion of the right order in this respect threatens man's freedom to re-establish the right order in himself. The mind is closely identified with its thoughts: it gives to them 'something of its own substance'; as Augustine puts it in one place,[5] it becomes only too easily submerged among the objects of its continual occupation. But it is the essential prerogative of a rational nature to

[1] *De doctr. chr.* I 33. 36–7 (*PL* 34. 32–3); *De Trin.* IX 8. 13 (*PL* 42. 967–8). A fourfold scheme is adopted in *De doctr. chr.* I 23. 22 (*PL* 34. 27).

[2] *De Trin.* XI 5. 9 (*PL* 42. 991): 'id amare alienari est'.

[3] *Retr.* II 15. 2 (*PL* 32. 636). It is interesting that this is one of only three statements singled out by Augustine for criticism.

[4] *De doctr. chr.* I 4. 4 (*PL* 34. 21): 'alienaremur a patria'. On this theme, cf. my paper read at the Fourth International Conference on Patristic Studies, Oxford, 1963, '*Alienatio*: philosophy and eschatology in Augustine's intellectual development', *Studia patristica*, 9 [= *Texte und Untersuchungen*, 94] (Berlin, 1966).

[5] *De Trin.* X 5. 7 (*PL* 42. 977).

judge, and the mind is required to judge itself in respect of its implication with the objects of its daily concerns. Its judgement manifests a dimension of freedom which belongs to it in virtue of its rationality. This freedom gives it a power to resist the tendency to identify itself with the material images and thoughts which solicit its care and attention and threaten to engulf it. Judgement is the mind's return to itself from such 'estrangement' incurred by captivity to the sphere of its practical engagement, to the things to which, as Augustine graphically says, 'it is stuck by the glue of its attachments'.[1] The importance of man's attitude in this particular instance is that habitual perversion of the 'order of love' here threatens the mind's freedom to return to itself; it threatens it with a blindness to the standards of judgement and hence with a growing loss of its rational rule over itself and the atrophy of its powers of self-criticism.[2]

Of the four 'cardinal' virtues it is 'temperance' that specifically concerns man's attitude to bodily pleasure and desire. Following classical precedents, especially Cicero, Augustine defines this as the virtue by which reason rules, restrains and controls bodily desires.[3] Generally speaking, he simply takes over the classical enumeration and definitions of the four cardinal virtues, and shows little interest in developing his own thoughts on this subject. Where he does so, indeed, he is happy to allow them to merge into love of God; in their relation to this he is much more interested than in what is distinctive of each. Thus he defines all the cardinal virtues in terms of love of God in his *De moribus ecclesiae*;[4] his approach is typified by the definition here given of temperance as 'love giving itself entire to what it loves' (i.e. to God). Temperance secures the 'integrity' of the human composite, soul and body, by subduing the body to the rational order imposed by the mind, so that together they become an expression of rationality embodied. This must serve as an example of Augustine's treatment of the cardinal

[1] *Ibid.*: 'curae glutino inhaeserit'.

[2] Cf. *De Trin.* X 5. 7 – 8. 11 (*PL* 42. 977–80); *De vera rel.* 29. 52 – 31. 58 (*PL* 34. 145–8); *De lib. arb.* I 9. 19 (*PL* 32. 1231–2).

[3] Cf. e.g. *De div. qu. LXXXIII* 31. 1; 61. 4 (*PL* 40. 20; 51); *De civ. Dei* XIX 4. 3 (*PL* 41. 628–9); *De lib. arb.* I 13. 27 (*PL* 32. 1235–6).

[4] I 15. 25 (*PL* 32. 1322): 'amor integrum se praebens ei quod amatur'. Cf. *Conf.* X 29. 40 (*PL* 32. 796): 'per continentiam quippe colligimur et redigimur in unum...'. *Continentia*, as we learn from *De div. qu. LXXXIII* 31. 1 (*PL* 40. 21), is a 'part' of temperance.

virtues. It illustrates his relative lack of interest in them; they are part of the stock of classical ideas which forms his inheritance, and when he goes beyond the range of the classical discussions of them, his sole concern is to relate them to his own characteristic moral *leitmotivs*, especially to his conception of love. In this process their outlines become blurred, their individuality tends to be merged, because Augustine is interested in what they have in common as virtue rather than in what is specific to them each severally.[1] The keynote of his reflection on human morality is the notion of order, order conceived as a task to be accomplished amid the tensions and confusion of man's condition after the fall. In this central conception his classical, Platonic inheritance and his Christian faith blended at a very deep level. The tone is set in one of his very first works, significantly one devoted to the notion of order itself: 'order is that which, if we keep it in our lives, leads us to God';[2] it remained constant throughout all Augustine's writings, and echoes of the statement reach us in his mature works.

[1] Cf. the references in nn. 3 and 4 above, p. 393, where all the cardinal virtues are under discussion.

[2] *De ord.* I 9. 27 (*PL* 32. 990); cf. e.g. *De Trin.* XI 6. 10 (*PL* 42. 992); *De civ. Dei* XIX 12–15 (*PL* 41. 637–44).

CHAPTER 26

AUGUSTINE
GOD AND NATURE

The two chief—or even the sole—objects of interest to philosophy are God and the human soul. This was Augustine's view in his earliest works;[1] and, ironically, the furthest departure from this view, that which owes most to philosophical inspiration, occurs in his long commentary on the book of Genesis, written some fifteen or twenty years later. It is here that he gives freest rein to the discussion of questions concerning nature other than human or divine. Nevertheless, physical nature never assumed the central place in Augustine's interests which the world of man and God held in them. The problems which interested Augustine most in this field were those which were forced upon his attention by the scriptural teaching. We shall confine our attention to three of them: the order of nature as related to God, natural function and development in the physical world, and time, all arising for Augustine from the doctrine of creation.

Two related thoughts form the kernel of Augustine's reflection on the physical world. These are that God created the world of nature and has ordered it, in the words of the Book of Wisdom often quoted by Augustine, 'by measure and number and weight' (xi. 20); and that this order in the world allows man to see the world as God's handiwork. The orderliness in which God created the world was universal and all-pervasive, except for such disturbances as were set up in it by sin or its effects. But this universal order, Augustine thought, was only apparent to men partially. Their knowledge of the universe being limited, they are unable to see everything in its right place, and the place of many things in God's order may therefore be concealed from them. Furthermore, God's order is not always and not necessarily identical with our human conceptions of order, and his order may well, at times, appear to

[1] *De ord.* II 18. 47 (*PL* 32. 1017); cf. *Sol.* I 2. 7 (*PL* 32. 872).

us as disorder, in our own limited perspectives.[1] His purposes must always remain in large part dark and unknown to us. Even evil—the nature and origin of which we are not here concerned with—has its place in the design.

Even with such limitations on our appreciation of the universal order, the world, Augustine thought, proclaimed itself by means of its orderliness, variety, and beauty to be God's creature, and pointed to a transcendent beauty as its source.[2] Augustine sometimes spoke of 'traces' (*vestigia*) of God in created things, which enabled the mind to see the Creator behind them.[3] But none of the ways in which things testified to the presence and the activity of their Creator interested Augustine as the starting-point for arguments claiming to prove the existence of God. In such arguments he had little interest; his purpose in seeking testimony to God in the order and beauty of creatures is an essentially moral one. He usually goes on to draw the conclusion from such arguments that we must follow the right order and prefer the higher to the lower, the better to the worse, and so on, and, especially, prefer the Creator to his creatures.[4] A famous passage in the *Confessions*[5] underlines the moral purpose of such arguments. Augustine here speaks of interrogating things about God and receiving the reply from each in turn, 'We are not your God; seek higher...he made us'. Behind the superb rhetorical imagination of the passage lies a deep conviction of Augustine's, that things do indeed have to be put to the question before they will speak of God. In a similar passage in a sermon[6] he remarks on the 'dumbness' of creatures, their lack of voice for praising the Creator. But, he goes on, when we examine them and interrogate them by seeking out their beauty, we endow each creature with its voice: 'That which you have found in it is the voice of its confession, whereby you praise the Creator.' It is not things themselves that compel us to affirm a being on whom they depend; it is rather that the appropriate attitude whereby we respond to creatures leads us to

[1] *De civ. Dei* XII 4; XI 16 (*PL* 41. 351–2; 331); *De Gen. c. Man.* I 16. 26 (*PL* 34. 185–6); *Conf.* VII 14. 20 (*PL* 32. 744).

[2] *De civ. Dei* XI 4. 2 (*PL* 41. 319).

[3] E.g. *De Trin.* XII 5. 5; XI 1. 1 (*PL* 42. 1001; 983–5).

[4] E.g. *De Trin.* XV 4. 6 (*PL* 42. 1061); *Conf.* VII 17. 23 (*PL* 32. 744–5); *En. in Ps.* 26, II 12 (*PL* 36. 205–6).

[5] X 6. 9–10 (*PL* 32. 783).

[6] *En. in Ps.* 144. 13–14 (*PL* 37. 1877–9); cf. *Sermo* 241. 2. 2 (*PL* 38. 1134).

acknowledge their Creator as above them, and to praise him in his creatures. In the *Confessions*[1] he goes on to remark that things will not answer all interrogators equally: they will answer only those who have the power to judge. And subjection to things by inordinate love deprives men of the power to judge; they will only receive an answer, or only understand it, in so far as they can exercise their judgement in the light of the truth within them. The purpose of the argument is not to prove from the existence of order and beauty in nature the existence of a God who is responsible for them; but rather that since God has created all things we must learn to seek him behind them, to value them in their right order for his sake, and to refer them to the praise of the Creator rather than worship his handiwork. When Augustine does set out to produce an argument proving God's existence, as he does in an early work at considerable length,[2] the argument starts from an examination of the powers of the human mind. This examination leads Augustine to assert that the mind in its distinctive activity of judging is subject to standards which are independent of it and above it; and these are identified with the divine ideas, the eternal truth in the light of which the mind judges.

For all his insistence on man's ability to know God 'through the things that are made', Augustine was careful to safeguard God's transcendence. In one of his first writings he says 'God is known better by ignorance';[3] and he never ceases to stress the inaccessibility of God to human comprehension and the inadequacy of human language to speak truly about him.[4] God creates all the sensible and visible world in order to allow it to show him forth and to point towards him; but he does not himself appear in his own nature in it, remaining always above and beyond it as well as hidden in its mysterious innermost being.[5]

A special way in which God shows himself in nature is by means of miraculous events. The consideration of these brings us to a second problem raised for Augustine by the doctrine of creation, the problem which we may, speaking broadly, call the problem of nature. This is essentially the problem of distinguishing in natural processes and events

[1] Cf. above, p. 396 n. 5
[2] *De lib. arb.* II 3. 7 – 15. 39 (*PL* 32. 1243–62).
[3] *De ord.* II 16. 44 (*PL* 32. 1015): 'scitur melius nesciendo'.
[4] Cf. *De Trin.* V 1. 1–2; VII 4. 7; VIII 2. 3; XV 27. 50, etc. (*PL* 42. 911–12; 939–40; 948–9; 1096–7).
[5] *Ibid.* III 4. 10 (*PL* 42. 874).

between the divine activity present in everything that happens and the natural activity of each creature. It was forced on Augustine's attention in one form by the apparent contradiction between the scriptural doctrine that God created all things 'in the beginning', simultaneously, and the obvious fact that many things have come into being since and are still to come into being. Even the story of the work of the seven days in Genesis suggests a sequence of some kind in the work of creation. How is such a chronological unfolding of the act of creation to be reconciled with the belief in a divine creation of everything 'in the beginning'? And, furthermore, how can we speak of the natural development and generation of creatures which have come into being since, without either withdrawing them from the scope of God's creative work or depriving them of their own distinctive principles of development and functioning which we call their 'natures'?

The essentials of Augustine's answer are simple, and are based on the biological analogy with the development of a seed. God, he affirms, did create everything 'in the beginning', but allowed some of his creatures to remain latent, in a state of potentiality, waiting for the right time and the right environment for their actual appearance. He refers to things created in this condition as having been created 'potentially', 'seminally', 'invisibly', 'causally', and in other ways, and likens their coming into being to the germination of a seed and its development into the mature plant under the appropriate conditions.[1] Following Stoic precedents, he calls the equivalent of the seed from which the plant develops *rationes seminales* or *rationes causales*, and thinks of these as a kind of germinal existence of the fully actualized creatures, containing the principles of their subsequent development.[2]

Augustine did not postulate the existence of these 'seminal reasons' in order to make it possible to account for the emergence of novelty in the universe; nor, as has also been suggested, did he seek, by their means, to deny the very possibility of genuine novelty by asserting, in effect, that there can be nothing really new since everything is latently present from the beginning. Genuine novelty or its impossibility was not a topic that interested Augustine; he was more concerned to

[1] *De Gen. ad litt.* VI, *passim*, particularly 6. 9–11; 11. 18; V 4. 9 (*PL* 34. 342–3; 346; 324); cf. *De civ. Dei* XII 25 (*PL* 41. 374–5) [= XII 26 in *CC*]; *De Trin.* III 8. 13; 9. 16 (*PL* 42. 875; 877–8).

[2] *De Gen. ad litt.* V 7. 20 (*PL* 34. 328).

reconcile divergent implications of the scriptural account of creation, and his theory is primarily the by-product of scriptural exegesis. It is, in fact, another typical example of his concern to understand the scriptural belief with the aid of philosophical concepts. It served him well in this concern, since it enabled him to safeguard the natural, causal efficacy of things and the temporal unfolding of causal sequences, and to keep them, at the same time, within the scope of God's creative activity. A tree grown from a seedling, or the seedling grown from a seed, are creatures of God; so the creator of all invisible germinal principles is also the creator of all the visible things they give rise to.[1]

Though primarily exegetical in its purpose, the notion of 'seminal reasons' had far-reaching implications for Augustine's conception of nature. It suggested a conception of nature as a system of processes, subject to their own laws, of things interacting, functioning, and developing according to the primordial principles of their being. In one passage[2] Augustine relates the idea of a 'natural law' to that of 'seminal reasons':

All the normal course of nature is subject to its own natural laws. According to these all living creatures have their particular, determinate inclinations... and also the elements of non-living material things have their determinate qualities and forces, in virtue of which they function as they do and develop as they do, and not in some other way. From these primordial principles everything that comes about emerges in its own time in the due course of events, and having come to its end passes away, each according to its nature.

The theory of seminal reasons is here used to state a theory of natural law; and Augustine saw that this involved distinguishing a nexus of creaturely, natural causality from the creative causality of the 'first cause'. 'It is one thing', he writes,[3]

to build and to govern creatures from within and from the summit of the whole causal nexus—and only God, the creator, does this; it is another thing to apply externally forces and capacities bestowed by him in order to bring

[1] *De Trin.* III 8. 13 (*PL* 42. 875–6).

[2] *De Gen. ad litt.* IX 17. 32 (*PL* 34. 406), freely translated: 'omnis iste naturae usitatissimus cursus habet quasdam naturales leges suas, secundum quas et spiritus vitae, qui creatura est, habet quosdam appetitus suos determinatos quodammodo.... Et elementa mundi huius corporei habent definitam vim qualitatemque suam, quid unumquodque valeat, vel non valeat, quid de quo fieri possit vel non possit. Ex his velut primordiis rerum, omnia quae gignuntur, suo quoque tempore exortus processusque sumunt, finesque et decessiones sui cuiusque generis.'

[3] *De Trin.* III 9. 16 (*PL* 42. 877–8).

forth at such and such a time, or in such and such a shape, what has been created. For all things were created at the beginning, being primordially woven into the texture of the world; but they await the proper opportunity for their appearance. Like mothers heavy with their offspring, the world is heavy with the causes of things still to be; and they are created in the world by no one except by that supreme being in whom there is no birth and no death, no beginning and no end.

Augustine is feeling his way towards the later scholastic distinction between a 'first cause' and the whole order of 'second causes'. According to this, if an event or process is in accordance with the normal order of nature, it is 'caused' on two different levels: it can be explained in terms of natural laws, according to the relevant principles of physical, chemical, biological, etc., function; it can also be explained in terms of God's will and activity. The two explanations are on different levels, and the two kinds of 'cause' are causes in different senses. Augustine appears at times to have got very close to this view of nature as a complex of processes, things and events subject to their own laws and explicable in terms of their own make-up. But how far he was from really holding a view of nature on such lines appears from what he has to say about miracles.

In the sequel to the passage quoted above,[1] Augustine goes on to say that God has power over all his creatures in such a way as to enable him to produce results other than those which their natural operation would produce. Such abnormal occurrences in nature are 'miracles', and Augustine explains them as the result of God's operation alone, without the further causality of created causes; they are not, therefore, explicable in terms of natural law, but only in terms of God's hidden purposes. Here, Augustine is still maintaining a fundamental distinction between events and processes which are 'natural' and those which are not. But more often, in his writings, this difference tends to be blurred. Even in this same work, the conception of seminal reasons is sometimes[2] expressed in a way such as to suggest that normal and abnormal development are both 'natural' and potentially contained in the 'primordial causal principles' of things. There is no radical difference between the two kinds of happenings. The only difference lies in their relative frequency

[1] P. 399 n. 2.

[2] *De Gen. ad litt.* VI 14 25 (*PL* 34. 349).

of occurrence. Miraculous events are only 'against nature' in so far as our notion of nature is derived from what normally happens; they are not against nature from God's point of view, 'for to him that is nature which he has made'.[1] In general, Augustine thought, God preferred to keep to the accustomed order: 'He governs all the things he has created in such a manner that they are allowed to function and to behave in the ways proper to them.'[2] God is omnipotent not by arbitrary power (*potentia temeraria*) but by the power of wisdom (*sapientiae virtute*);[3] but Augustine did not think that a breach of the order of nature was more arbitrary than its observance. Both, ultimately, from God's unrestricted point of view, were 'natural'. We speak of miraculous events as being 'against nature' in ordinary speech; but they are not, Augustine writes; 'how could anything that happens according to God's will be against nature, since the will of the Creator *is* the nature of each created thing? Miracles are therefore not against nature, but against nature as known.'[4] The distinction between a natural order and a departure from it is here obliterated in the identification of all happenings as willed by God; and we are left with a conception of 'nature' as compatible with any possible happening, contrasted with a 'nature as known', a limited understanding, almost a human prejudice, based on experienced normality. As we have seen, Augustine was groping towards a genuine concept of nature; why he abandoned it is not difficult to see. The clues are scattered in the *De civitate Dei*: he wished to appeal to his pagan opponents' criterion of what was feasible and believable. His defence of the doctrine about bodily punishment after death in Book XXI is a clear example of the method of his argumentation; and his famous chapter on miracles[5] shows it clearly:

We need take no notice of those who deny that the invisible God works visible miracles; since he made the world, as they admit, and they cannot deny that it is visible. And any miracle worked in this world is less than this world itself, less than the heavens and the earth and all that is in them, and God made them all. Both he who made them, and the manner in which he

[1] *Ibid.* VI 13. 24 (*PL* 34. 349); cf. *De ord.* I 3. 8 (*PL* 32. 981–2).
[2] *De civ. Dei* VII 30 (*PL* 41. 220).
[3] *De Gen. ad litt.* IX 17. 32 (*PL* 34. 406).
[4] *De civ. Dei* XXI 8. 2 (*PL* 41. 721); cf. *C. Faust.* XXVI 3 (*PL* 42. 480–1).
[5] *De civ. Dei* X 12 (*PL* 41. 291).

made them, are mysterious and inconceivable to man. And although having grown accustomed to seeing these visible miracles of nature we no longer admire them, yet if we consider them wisely, they are greater than the rarest and strangest miracles. And man himself is a greater miracle than any miracle worked through men.

God's freedom to act in nature is triumphantly vindicated, but nature itself is dissolved in the freedom of the divine will.

The problem of time, and the relation between eternity and time, was another of the subjects in which Augustine's interests were aroused through his reflection on creation. The starting-point for his discussion was the Manichaean opposition to the Christian doctrine of creation. Augustine's account suggests that Manichaean polemic had seized on the apparent arbitrariness of the doctrine of creation. If God created the world, and created it out of nothing, why did he create it at the time he did and not sooner or later? and what was he doing before he created the world?[1] Augustine was not content to answer with the joke that he was getting hell ready for people who asked such questions, though he could not resist including it in his *Confessions*;[2] he tried to face the difficulty which such arguments spotlighted, namely the difficulties involved in speaking, as the Christian doctrine of creation had taught men to speak, of an absolute beginning.

The essentials of his answer consist in a rejection of the conception of time which suggested such objections. On that conception time was thought of as not fundamentally different from particular events or happenings; it has the same kind of substantiality as the things going on in time. The core of Augustine's answer to objections based on this picture was to repudiate the assumptions behind it and to draw attention to a categorical difference between time and the things that go on in time. To ask 'What happened before time?' is grammatically like asking 'What happened', for example, 'before the French Revolution?' One is apt to picture time to oneself in such a way that if we only go on far enough with the latter type of question, and ask a long enough string of questions, 'What happened before...?', one will arrive at a last member of this series, 'What happened before (the beginning of) time?'; and one will tend to see this question as being logically, and not only in

[1] *De Gen. c. Man.* I 2. 3 (*PL* 34. 174–5); *Conf.* XI 10. 12 (*PL* 32. 815).
[2] *Conf.* XI 12. 14 (*PL* 32. 815).

grammatical shape, homogeneous with the rest of the series. Augustine, however, denied the logical similarity, and pointed out that while it makes sense to ask what happened before any particular event or set of events, it does not make sense to ask what happened before the whole set of events in their totality; and this is what the Manichees were doing. For 'before' is a relation between happenings in time which requires two terms to relate; and there is *ex hypothesi* no event or set of events outside the total set of events between which the relation 'before' (or 'after') could hold.[1] The questions with which the Manichees had tried to show up the arbitrary absurdity of the doctrine of creation were, therefore, meaningless. Time, in Augustine's view, was a relation between temporal things, in virtue of which they could be said to be before or after one another. It came into being with temporal things, and it makes no sense to speak of time before there were temporal things. He rejected, in effect, his opponents' conception of time as substantial in the way that temporal things are substantial, and as capable of being spoken about in the same type of language as things and events.[2]

But Augustine did not stop in his reflection on time at this answer to the objections to the doctrine of creation. He appears to have had a deeper interest in this topic; and since in Neoplatonic thought a close connexion had been made between time and the soul,[3] Augustine could scarcely have failed to be stimulated to rethink this theme in terms of his own very different views on the soul.

In the *Confessions*, which contains his most sustained discussion of time, Augustine begins, as we have seen, by establishing that time is a relation between temporal things, that is to say, between things capable of being ordered in terms of the relations 'before' and 'after'. As such it is characteristic of all created things; to say that a thing is temporal is only another way of stating that it is created. All creatures are subject to becoming and passing away: future being and past being are inherent in their creaturely being; only God, who is not subject to time, is

[1] The argument summarized is in *Conf.* XI 10. 12 – 14. 17 (*PL* 32. 815–16); cf. *De civ. Dei* XI 5–6; XII 15. 2 (*PL* 41. 320–2; 364).

[2] *De Gen. ad litt.* V 5. 12 (*PL* 34. 325–6). In *De civ. Dei* XI 5 (*PL* 41. 320–1) Augustine indicates that the same kind of treatment could be extended to space.

[3] [On Plotinus' account of time as the 'life of the soul' see Part III (Plotinus), ch. 16 (a), pp. 251–2.]

eternally 'present'. But the past *is* no longer, it *was*; and the future *is* not yet, but *will be*. And the present, if it were lasting, would not be time but eternity. Its being as time depends on its perpetual passing away. What kind of reality, then, can we ascribe to time?[1] The present, which alone appears to have a claim to *being*, vanishes to a point without dimension at which the future becomes past; for any determinate duration can be divided into smaller units, some of which are past and some future. All we are left with is a point without dimension, the point at which the not-yet-real becomes the no-longer-real; and whatever reality it has cannot have any duration.[2] Nevertheless, we not only speak of long or short times, but we are aware of durations of time (*intervalla temporum*), we can compare them and even measure them. We measure time precisely in its passing, for we cannot measure what has been or what is not yet.[3] In our consciousness the past and the future have being of a sort, in so far as the past is remembered and the future foreseen or anticipated, and without this consciousness we should have no awareness of the length of any duration. This does not, however, mean that past and future are after all real. They are real only in so far as they are present to the mind, in memory and expectation: 'The present of things past is memory, the present of things present is sight (*contuitus*) and the present of things future is expectation.'[4] Whatever reality extended time or duration has, is in the mind and is a result of the mind's ability to unite in its present awareness both past and future. Hence Augustine's final definition of time, propounded with considerable hesitation: 'It seems to me that time is nothing else than extension (*distentio*); but extension of what I am not sure—perhaps of the mind itself.'[5]

In passing, Augustine examines attempts to define time in terms of movement.[6] He rejects the identification of movement, either the movement of heavenly bodies or that of anything else, with time. He notes that it is perfectly meaningful to speak of the sun changing its speed, i.e. moving a greater or lesser distance in a given time; we may even

[1] *Conf.* XI 14. 17 (*PL* 32. 815–16).
[2] *Ibid.* XI 15. 18–20 (*PL* 32. 816–17).
[3] *Ibid.* XI 16. 21; 21. 27 (*PL* 32. 817; 819–20).
[4] *Ibid.* XI 20. 26 (*PL* 32. 819).
[5] *Ibid.* XI 26. 33 (*PL* 32. 822).
[6] On their history, cf. J. F. Callahan, *Four Views of Time in Ancient Philosophy* (Cambridge, Mass., 1948).

imagine it standing still, as it did at Joshua's prayer while the Israelites were beating the Amalekites in battle—but time would not have 'stood still'. Hence the sun's movement certainly does not constitute time; nor does bodily movement in general, for even if all bodily motion were to cease, we could still be conscious of greater or lesser periods of rest in our awareness. We measure movement by time (as well as using regular motion to measure time): time and movement cannot, therefore, be identical.[1] And so Augustine is brought back to his psychological definition of time.

Some chapters of the *De civitate Dei*[2] throw into sharper relief the underlying reasons for Augustine's vehemence in repudiating the identification of time with the movement of the heavenly bodies. In these chapters he joins issue with the conception, common in Greek philosophy, of time as a circular movement. Events, according to this theory, succeed each other in the same order in an endless series of recurrent cycles. There was, of course, no room in such a picture of the temporal process for the unique significance with which Christianity endowed certain historical events; and Augustine shrank with horror from the absurdity and triviality to which it would condemn human life and history. Even in his early writings, Augustine appreciated the essentially historical nature of Christian belief, with its claim that God's revelation for the salvation of men consisted in a particular set of historical events;[3] and he had a deep sense of the unique, if impenetrably mysterious, significance imparted to each and every moment of time by God's all-embracing providence.[4] His views on human history in the concrete we shall examine in the next chapter.

[1] *Conf.* XI 23. 29 – 24. 31 (*PL* 32. 820–2); cf. *De Gen. c. Man.* I 14. 20–1 (*PL* 34. 183).

[2] XII 13; 17–20 (*PL* 41. 360–2; 366–72) [= XII 14; 18–21 in *CC*]. A possible reason for the topicality of this question has been suggested by J. Hubeaux, 'Saint Augustin et la crise cyclique', *Augustinus magister*, II (1954), pp. 943–50 and in 'Saint Augustin et la crise eschatologique de la fin du IVe siècle', *Bull. de la classe des lettres et des sciences morales et politiques*, 5e série, XL (1954), pp. 658–73.

[3] Cf. *De vera rel.* 7. 13 (*PL* 34. 128); cf. above, pp. 343–6.

[4] Cf. e.g. *Conf.* VII 15. 21 (*PL* 32. 744).

CHAPTER 27

AUGUSTINE
MAN IN HISTORY AND SOCIETY

We must begin an account of Augustine's views on human history with a distinction between 'sacred history' (*Heilsgeschichte*) and secular history. He does not often use such phrases, but the distinction is implicit in all his utterances. Sacred history is the history of God's revelatory action among men, contained in the books of the Old and New Testaments. It concerns the redemption of the human race wrought in the work of Jesus Christ, and the preparation for this in the history of the chosen race, Israel. In these actions God has revealed his purpose in history; and the Scriptures are their record, the authoritative and certain source for Christian belief.[1] The Scriptures, however, are not a mere formless historical record; the narrative they contain is shaped by the interpretative action of their authors, and would, indeed, be meaningless without this. Being inspired by the Holy Spirit, the significance with which the authors endow the events recorded is itself of divine origin. The scriptural history is therefore sacred in the double sense of containing a narrative of divine action and of telling the narrative in terms of divine providence, endowing its events with a significance within God's plan. Apart from the sacred history contained in the Scriptures, men have no revelation of God's plan, no indication of the significance of historical events in terms of God's purposes. Christians are in the same position as secular historians, except in regard to scriptural history.[2]

With Augustine's views on the Scriptures, their meaning and interpretation, their authority and inspiration, we are not here directly concerned. The implications of the distinction between scriptural and non-scriptural history, however, are far-reaching. Augustine's favour-

[1] *De civ. Dei* XVIII 40 (*PL* 41. 600); cf. also above, p. 405 n. 3.

[2] *Ibid.* XVIII 40 (*PL* 41. 599–600): the biblical record can only be used as a criterion for selecting among divergent secular histories where the latter overlap with scriptural history. On the theme of this paragraph as a whole, cf. my paper 'History, prophecy and inspiration', to be published in *Augustinus* [in honour of V. Capánaga].

ite periodization of world-history displays them clearly. Following an ancient Christian tradition, he frequently divides[1] the course of history into six periods, corresponding to the six days of creation; they are followed by the 'eternal Sabbath' when men shall cease from their labours in the rest of blessedness, which will be ushered in by the return of the Lord in glory. The 'seventh day', in Augustine's mature writings, is beyond history, its dawn is the end of history, and its substance the eschatological winding up of all history. Human history falls within the first 'six days', between the creation of the world and the last day. The first five periods together correspond to the time before the incarnation of Christ, and it suffices to note here that the divisions between them are marked by key points in the Old Testament history. The sixth age is the period we live in now, and stretches from the coming of Christ in the flesh to his return in glory. The landmarks in terms of which history is mapped out are wholly contained in the sacred history; hence for the period after Christ there are no more divisions; the rest of history is homogeneous, and as devoid of any pattern of religious significance as is all earlier history outside the biblical history. In asserting the homogenity of history in the period after Christ, Augustine was denying the chiliastic view (based on an interpretation of Rev. xx. 1–5) that there would be a period of a thousand years preceding the second coming of Christ during which he would reign on earth with his saints. Augustine rejected both the literal interpretation of the text 'One day is with the Lord as a thousand years, and a thousand years as one day' (II Pet. iii. 8)—the text which suggested the equivalence of the six days of creation with six historical epochs of a thousand years each—and the chiliastic suggestion that history could now, in this last epoch, be interpreted and predicted with the aid of biblical patterns.[2] Chiliasm, though it enjoyed a brief revival towards the end of the fourth century, was scarcely a living force in Augustine's day; but his *Auseinandersetzung* with its teaching contains some of his most forceful

[1] The most detailed version is in *De Gen. c. Man.* I 23. 35 – 24. 42 (*PL* 34. 190–3); cf. also *De cat. rud.* 22. 39 (*PL* 40. 338–9); *De div. qu. LXXXIII.* 58. 2 (*PL* 40. 43); *De Trin.* IV 4. 7 (*PL* 42. 892–3); *In Jo. Ev. Tr.* 9. 6 (*PL* 35. 1461); *De civ. Dei* XXII 30. 5 (*PL* 41. 804); *Sermo* 125. 4; 259. 2 (*PL* 38. 691–2; 1197–8). Cf. on this now the detailed study by A. Luneau, *L'histoire du salut chez les Pères de l'Église: la doctrine des âges du monde* (Paris, 1964), pp. 285–407.

[2] On chiliasm, cf. *De civ. Dei* XX 7; 9 (*PL* 41. 666–9; 672–5).

statements of the key themes of his thought on history: that only the framework of sacred history can enable us to interpret history in terms of a divine pattern, that in this framework the present epoch is all homogeneous and all equally ambiguous in terms of this pattern, and that its end is unpredictable.[1]

The force and significance of these themes become more starkly apparent in Augustine's views on the history of the Roman Empire, particularly in his own time. This is the context, too, in which he formulates some of his most distinctive views about human society and the organized state. To the examination of this group of themes we now turn.

The stimulus to Augustine's deepest reflection on God's working in human history, and on the place of the organized state in his providential plan, came in the form of the sacking of Rome by the Visigoths under Alaric in the summer of the year 410. His great work *De civitate Dei*, though written over the years 413–27, was a direct outcome of the sack, being conceived by its author as an answer to pagan controversialists who blamed the fall of the city in 410 on the state's adoption of Christianity and its desertion of the old gods, under whom the Empire had flourished.[2] Many of its key themes had been prepared in Augustine's mind over a long period; and two tendencies of particular importance for its argument had ripened in his mind by the time he came to write it. First, he had definitively abandoned all traces of millenarist thinking, and adopted a view of history during the period after Christ as entirely secular, in the sense of being incapable of treatment in accordance with the categories of the redemption-history. Secondly, he had moved away from his earlier views concerning the state, formulated under the impact of Platonic modes of thought, as a stage on the way to

[1] R. Schmidt, '"Aetates mundi." Die Weltalter als Gliederungsprinzip der Weltgeschichte', *Zeits f. Kirchengeschichte*, LXVII (1955–6), pp. 288–317, draws attention to the originality of Augustine's division. Cf. also J. Daniélou, 'La typologie millénariste de la semaine dans le christianisme primitif', *Vigiliae christianae*, II (1948), 1–16. In an important paper G. Folliet, 'La typologie du sabbat chez saint Augustin; son interprétation millénariste entre 388 et 400', *Rev. des études augustiniennes*, II (1956) [*Mémorial Gustave Bardy*, t. 2], pp. 371–90, has traced some markedly chiliastic elements in Augustine's earlier views on this subject, and his movement away from them, completed by the time he wrote the *Confessions* (400). My argument in the text corresponds to Augustine's later views.

[2] *Retr.* II 43. 1 (*PL* 32. 647–8); *De civ. Dei* I *Praef.*; I 1; II 2; IV 1–2; VI *Praef.*, etc. (*PL* 41. 13; 14–15; 48; 111–13; 173–5).

the eternal *patria* and related to it as its temporal reflection; he had become very much more reluctant to identify the eschatological purpose of history with the Platonic intelligible world. The state, which, for Augustine, inevitably meant the Roman Empire, had lost a great deal of the religious importance it had possessed in the earlier perspective.[1]

Augustine's mind had already moved far in this direction when the news of the fall of Rome reached Africa. Consternation and dismay were widespread, and quite out of proportion to the real political significance of the events. The pain and stupefaction of pagans, as expressed for instance by the poet Rutilius Namatianus, are easily accounted for. The myth of *Roma aeterna* had not only a respectable literary history, but also a life in the consciousness of Romans since Virgil's day; and never can it have acted more powerfully on men's imaginations than during the generation immediately preceding the Gothic sack. But to judge from the grief expressed by St Jerome writing in his distant monastic retreat in Palestine, or from the general state of feeling among Christians which some of Augustine's sermons[2] on the fall of the city allow us to infer, Christians were equally shocked and bewildered by the news. The reason for this state of mind must be sought in the current ideas about the Roman Empire and its place in the scheme of things.[3] Before Constantine granted the Church public recognition in 312, the Empire had often, though by no means always, been represented in the apocalyptic imagery of the Book of Revelation as the Beast to whom the Dragon had entrusted his world-wide authority, or as the harlot arrayed in purple and scarlet, seated upon the seven hills and drunk with the blood of the saints and the martyrs of Jesus. With the recognition of the Church in 312, however, a different type of view, though one which had also been held before, came into its own. One of the outstanding exponents of this was the Christian historian Eusebius, the publicist of the first Christian Emperor. In

[1] Cf. above, p. 388 and n. 1.

[2] Details in J. Fischer, *Die Völkerwanderung im Urteil der zeitgenössischen Schriftsteller Galliens unter Einbeziehung des heiligen Augustinus* (Heidelberg, 1947); and J. von Campenhausen, 'Augustin und der Fall von Rom', *Universitas*, II (1947), 257–68.

[3] On what follows, cf. my paper 'The Roman Empire in early Christian historiography', *Downside Review*, LXXXI, no. 265 (1963), pp. 340–54.

Constantine Eusebius had seen the realization of God's purposes in history; to him he refers many of the Old Testament prophecies which the Church had interpreted in a Messianic sense. The Empire, in his eyes, was God's chosen instrument for healing the division and disintegration inherent in man's condition as the result of Adam's sin. The one true Empire, in his view, was the political expression of the one true worship of one true God, and the Empire thus assumed an important place in God's plan for the redemption of men and was the continuation of the sacred history related in the Scriptures. On this view, as indeed on the diametrically opposed and intransigeantly anti-imperial views of apocalyptic writers, the fate of the Empire was bound up with the realization of divine purpose in history. Its fall would usher in the end of history. Views of this type became very common during the fourth century, indeed appear to have become generally current except in circles opposed to imperial orthodoxy. Some of its implications seem to have become deeply embedded in popular imagination; in the eyes of the Christian poet Prudentius, for instance, the progress and continued safety of the Christian Empire is the direct consequence of Rome being assumed into the unfolding of God's redemptive scheme. The news of the fall of Rome in 410 must have shattered this vision of history, threatened the faith that sustained it and precipitated a dismay out of all proportion to the scale of the physical catastrophe. The alternative to despair was either a facile optimism in face of the danger, minimizing the impact of the barbarian onslaught on the Empire, or a radical readjustment of thought about the place of Rome in the divine plan. The latter is Augustine's great achievement.

From this point of view Augustine's *De civitate Dei* amounts to a systematic rejection of the Eusebian picture of the Empire. Its argument is essentially that the working out of God's purposes does not stand or fall with the fate of Rome or, indeed, with the fate of any earthly society whatever. The apocalyptic prophecies are not to be referred directly to any particular historical catastrophe; they concern the final winding up of history at the end of time.[1] Augustine always insists that this is something we cannot predict, that the scriptural revelation is no guide to the remainder of history until the second

[1] *De civ. Dei* XX 11 (*PL* 41. 676–7).

coming of the Lord.[1] He resolutely holds aloof from both historical optimism and pessimism; as we have no clues to the course of the future in Scripture, we can neither affirm nor deny, 'only renounce the rash presumption of asserting anything'.[2] The Roman Empire is removed from the dimension of sacred history, being no longer regarded either as God's chosen instrument for the salvation of men or as a Satanic opposition power. It is simply an empirical, historical society with a chequered career, theologically neutral. This explains Augustine's curiously ambivalent attitude to Rome, which has given rise to a great deal of debate. In his anti-Roman polemic he tends to contrast Romans and Christians, to speak as a hostile outsider, almost reflecting the language of a persecuted Church. Nevertheless, he often appeals to Roman examples for the condemnation of what he saw as the corruption rife in his own day. In such passages the tone of authentic Roman pride is unmistakable in his writing.[3] His endorsement of the typical Roman values is unreserved, even though it is restricted: ultimately, in terms of the categories of salvation and damnation, all Roman and indeed all human achievement is unavailing. Thus he apostrophizes the 'praiseworthy nation of the Romans, the progeny of the Reguli, the Scaevolae, the Fabricii': 'If nature has given you any praiseworthy excellence, it is purged and perfected only through true piety; impiety consumes and destroys it.'[4] Of itself, the Empire is theologically neutral, the symbol of Rome has been deprived of religious meaning. To re-enter the dimensions of the ultimate divine judgement on history it is necessary to invoke the categories of sin and holiness; these are what determine the perfecting or the destruction of the purely secular values embodied in the state.

The state, as such, no longer has an eternal destiny. The vehicles of this are two societies to which Augustine refers in various ways, but most frequently as the 'city of God' and the 'earthly city' respectively. The pair of concepts had a long pre-history in Augustine's writings

[1] *Ibid.* XVIII 53. 1 (*PL* 41. 616–17); cf. *Ep.* 199 (*PL* 33. 904–25); *De div. qu. LXXXIII* 58. 2 (*PL* 40. 43); *De Gen. c. Man.* I 24. 42 (*PL* 34. 193).

[2] *De civ. Dei* XVIII 52. 2 (*PL* 41. 616).

[3] *Ibid.* II 29; V 15; 18 (*PL* 41. 77–8; 160; 162–5), *pace* F. G. Maier's otherwise excellent book, *Augustin und das antike Rom* (Stuttgart, 1956), which is hag-ridden by the necessity to rule out any trace of Roman 'patriotism' in Augustine.

[4] *De civ. Dei* II 29. 1 (*PL* 41. 77); cf. *Ep.* 138. 3. 17 (*PL* 33. 533).

before becoming the theme of his work *De civitate Dei*. The origins and development of his language,[1] and its precise correlations in Augustine's vocabulary with other terms such as 'church', 'kingdom of God', etc.[2] are beyond the scope of the present chapter. Augustine defines and distinguishes the two cities in various ways, more or less informally, and it is clear that these various ways are intended to be equivalent among themselves. Thus in the *De civitate Dei* we often find Augustine relating the two cities to predestination: he speaks, for instance, of two kinds of men (*genera hominum*), 'one of those who live according to man, the other such as live according to God; these we also call figuratively (*mystice*) two cities, that is, two societies of men, one of which is predestined to reign eternally with God, the other to undergo eternal torment with the devil'.[3] On other occasions he defines the two cities in terms of 'two loves', 'one holy, the other impure; one sociable, the other selfish (*alter socialis*, *alter privatus*)...'[4] or contrasts them as the cities of the proud and the humble respectively.[5] In whatever way Augustine describes them, he always makes it clear that *as societies* the two cities are eschatological realities. That is to say, they have no discernible reality as societies until they shall be separated at the final judgement. Here on earth, throughout all the ages of temporal history which Augustine often calls *saeculum*, 'the two cities are interwoven and mixed into one another (*perplexae...invicemque permixtae*), until they shall be separated at the last judgement'.[6] The ultimate categories of Augustine's vision of history are those of eternal destiny and of the divine judgement; all human enterprise is judged in the last resort in terms of the stark opposition of sin and holiness. The two cities are eschatological realities precisely because the distinction between them hinges on the divine judgement: the application of its simple categories

[1] The best account is by A. Lauras and H. Rondet, 'Le thème des deux cités dans l'œuvre de S. Augustin', in H. Rondet and others, *Études augustiniennes* (Paris, 1953), 97–160.

[2] For a summary of recent discussion, cf. Y. M. J. Congar, '"Civitas Dei" et "ecclesia" chez saint Augustin', *Rev. des études augustiniennes*, III (1957), pp. 1–14; and the decisive contribution to the debate by F. E. Cranz, '*De civitate Dei* XV 2 and Saint Augustine's idea of the Christian society', *Speculum*, XXV (1950), pp. 215–25, reprinted with Père Congar's paper, *loc. cit.* pp. 15–28.

[3] *De civ. Dei* XV 1. 1 (*PL* 41. 437).

[4] *De Gen. ad litt.* XI 15. 20 (*PL* 34. 437); cf. *De civ. Dei* XIV 28 (*PL* 41. 456).

[5] *De cat rud.* 19. 33 (*PL* 40. 334–5).

[6] *De civ. Dei* I 35 (*PL* 41. 46); *De Gen. ad litt.* XI 15. 20 (*PL* 34. 437); *De cat. rud.* 19. 31 (*PL* 40. 333–4).

to the complex fabric of empirical history is bound to be a matter of doubt and perplexity. Men, Augustine therefore insists, can have no knowledge of the careers of the two cities except in so far as God has in fact revealed their separate existence in history.[1] Hence the biblical narrative is the indispensable source of the greater part of Augustine's exposition of the careers of the two cities. Beyond the limits of biblical history all we know is that their careers continue and that they shall be made apparent at the end. They cannot be distinguished in their outward careers: sinners often prosper and saints suffer; the two cities differ not in an outwardly discernible way but in their inward response to their experience, in what they make of their fate: 'Both feel the same vicissitudes of fortune, good or bad; but they do so not with the same faith, nor the same hope, nor the same love—until they shall be separated in the last judgement.'[2]

Augustine does, of course, assimilate the Roman Empire to the 'earthly city', speaks of it as 'another Babylon',[3] and generally, especially in the polemical first five books of the *De civitate Dei*, assumes the identification of Rome with the earthly city. The reason for this is not far to seek: in her capacity as the idolatrous persecutor of the saints, the Empire clearly qualified for the position of representing the ungodly city in post-biblical history, in virtue of the biblical categories themselves. To its idolatry Augustine often adds the proud quest of glory and lust for power as a second count under which Roman history stands condemned. But Augustine makes it quite clear that notwithstanding this 'extrapolation' from the scriptural history of the two cities into the realm of empirical history, the case of Rome really forms no exception to his general principle of eschatological ambiguity. Worship of God in the true faith is, of course, a necessary condition of membership of the city of God: but significantly—in sharp contrast with Eusebius, for instance—Augustine does not treat the Christian Empire as radically different from its pagan predecessor. He sees no real break in Roman history with the advent of Constantine. The Christian Roman Empire is as ambiguously poised with regard to the two cities as any other

[1] *De civ. Dei* XIV 11. 1 (*PL* 41. 418).

[2] *Ibid.* XVIII 54. 2 (*PL* 41. 620); cf. *De cat. rud.* 19. 31 (*PL* 40. 333), where Augustine speaks of the two cities 'nunc permixtae corporibus, sed voluntatibus separatae, in die vero iudicii etiam corpore separandae'.

[3] *De civ. Dei* XVIII 22 (*PL* 41. 578).

society. We have already noted[1] that Roman virtue was for Augustine essentially something which required perfecting by true piety; he goes on, in the passage in which he apostrophizes a personified Rome, to invite Rome to enter the city of God, which some of her members, the Christian martyrs, have already entered. Nothing could show more clearly that Augustine is consistent in refusing to treat Rome as unambiguously monolithic in the dichotomy of the two cities. Although in this particular passage—in a context of anti-pagan polemic—true and false belief are in question, it scarcely needs stating that Christian faith is not, for Augustine, a passport to the city of God. During the present epoch, while the city of God is a pilgrim on earth, 'there are many who partake with her of the same sacraments and yet shall not partake with her in the eternal glory of the saints'.[2] Although Augustine sometimes identifies the Church with the city of God, just as he sometimes speaks of Rome as the terrestrial city, the identification depends on the fact that he distinguishes within the Church an *ecclesia peregrina* and an *ecclesia coelestis*, and is prepared to refer to both simply as the 'church', without always explicitly noting the distinction between the Church as she is now and as she will be.[3] His terminology fluctuates and has given rise to much debate; but his view emerges clearly of the two 'cities' as eschatological societies related to, but not to be identified with, the Christian Church as an empirical institution and the Roman state respectively.

The reason why no single, empirically defined society can be identified with either of the two cities is that ultimately the two cities are each defined by the wills, or loves, as Augustine also puts it, of the individuals composing them. 'Two loves have built the two cities; self-love and contempt of God the earthly city, love of God and contempt of self the heavenly. The first seeks to glory in itself, the second in God.'[4] In any empirical society the two loves are inevitably interwoven, since it must embrace within itself members with different ultimate loyalties. A society is only the sum of its members: 'What is Rome but the Romans?'[5]

[1] Cf. above, p. 411 n. 4.

[2] *De civ. Dei* I 35 (*PL* 41. 46).

[3] On this topic, which is beyond the scope of this chapter, cf. the articles referred to above p. 412 n. 2.

[4] *De civ. Dei* XIV 28 (*PL* 41. 436). The *uti–frui* scheme implicit behind this is made explicit in *De civ. Dei* XIX 14; 17 (*PL* 41. 642–3; 645–6); cf. below, p. 416.

[5] *Sermo* 81. 9 (*PL* 38. 505); cf. *De urb. exc.* 6 (*PL* 40. 721).

A society (*civitas*) is 'a multitude of men congregated together'.[1] Since the two loves which build the two cities are inevitably present in any given concourse of men, the two cities are both inevitably present, intertwined, in any particular historical society. No state, even that ruled by Christian emperors like Constantine or Theodosius, can be identified with the city of God; and the Christian Church as an organized institution, as Augustine stressed, especially in his anti-Donatist writings, is the threshing-floor on which Christ separates the wheat from the chaff, and inevitably contains both until the day of judgement.

Augustine's much-debated views on justice in the state follow from his premise that the city of God is the unique repository of perfect justice. 'Where there is not that justice according to which God alone rules by grace over a society which obeys him...',[2] there Augustine refuses to allow that we can speak of the requirements of real justice being met. Hence his rejection of the Ciceronian definition of the state (*res publica*). This hinged on the definition of a *populus* as 'a multitude joined together by one consent of law and their common good'.[3] Augustine poured a great deal of meaning into the *jus* here envisaged, and interpreted the word to imply the perfection of justice which exists only in the perfect society of the heavenly city. It followed that Rome, according to this definition, was no state, since its people failed to satisfy the conditions laid down in the Ciceronian definition. Augustine quotes Cicero's own identical argument, which used this definition to establish that Rome was a *res publica* only in name, having lost the substance through her vice.[4] This kind of rhetorical exploitation of the overtones of 'justice' served Augustine well (as it did Cicero) in polemical passages; it showed all actual societies to be 'dens of robbers' in greater or lesser degree;[5] but Augustine was quite prepared to speak of the Roman state, and adopted for this purpose a more positivistic definition, which did not require the possession of perfect justice.

[1] *Ep.* 155. 3. 9 (*PL* 33. 670); cf. *De civ. Dei* I 15. 1 (*PL* 41. 29): 'multitudo constat ex singulis'.

[2] *De civ. Dei* XIX 23. 5; cf. II 21. 4 (*PL* 41. 655; 68–9).

[3] *Ibid.* II 21. 2; XIX 21. 1 (*PL* 41. 67; 648): 'coetus [multitudinis] iuris consensu et utilitatis communione sociatus', quoted from *De Rep.* V; and *res publica* is *res populi.*

[4] *Ibid.* II 21. 3 (*PL* 41. 68).

[5] *Ibid.* IV 4 (*PL* 41. 115): 'remota itaque iustitia, quid sint regna nisi magna latrocinia?'

According to this definition, a people is 'a multitude of reasonable beings united by their agreement on the things they respect'.[1] This allows the claim of any society to be a *populus*, and its public organization to be a *res publica*, so long as there is some agreement on common purpose, whatever the ultimate purposes and loyalties of individual members may be. The character of a society, according to this definition, is determined by the choice of its members. The range of public purpose in the pursuit of which a society may be united will not, of course, include the ultimate loyalties of its members, the loyalty to God or to something else, which respectively define the two eschatological societies. The shared purposes lie in a restricted field which is of common concern to all, whether they are citizens of the heavenly or of the earthly city. Its limits Augustine never specifies; he only describes its range in the most general terms. They appear to be 'the goods appropriate to this life, that is, the temporal peace required for the sustenance and safety of this earthly life, and whatever is necessary for the defence or recovery of this peace...':[2] we might paraphrase, the sphere of economic necessities and of public order. This restricted field is the sphere of the state, and within it the aims of the two cities coincide; the difference between citizens of the two cities lies in their attitude to worldly goods: 'In the earthly city all use of temporal things is referred to the enjoyment of earthly peace; in the heavenly city it is referred to the enjoyment of eternal peace.'[3] The theory of the two cities at this point appears quite clearly as an application of the distinction between use and enjoyment on which much of Augustine's moral theory is based.[4] The morality of the pilgrim on his way to his heavenly home is the morality of the *peregrina civitas*, the heavenly city during its pilgrimage on earth; the morality of the earthly city is centred on narrow, temporal, material ends; its members are those who place ultimate value on the things which should be referred to the enjoyment on which the city of God sets its sights. Augustine conducts this discussion in terms of 'peace': this is a conception of universal scope, and capable of existing on many levels; it is the final purpose of all activity, the harmonious orderly

[1] *De civ. Dei.* XIX 24 (*PL* 41. 655): 'Populus est coetus multitudinis rationalis, rerum quas diligit concordi communione sociatus.' Cf. *Ep.* 138. 2. 10 (*PL* 33. 529).

[2] *De civ. Dei* XIX 13. 2 (*PL* 41. 641–2).

[3] *Ibid.* XIX 14 (*PL* 41. 642).

[4] Cf. above, pp. 390–2.

repose reached at the end of all striving and tension, not only of human but also of animate nature. Augustine defines it as 'the tranquillity of order', and describes it in its cosmic bearings,[1] and then states the relation between the two cities in terms of their respective attitudes to 'earthly peace'. The faithless, worldly city does not look beyond the requirements of earthly peace; these exhaust all its concerns, whereas the heavenly city, though its interests coincide with those of the earthly over this restricted sphere, sets its sight beyond it; it refuses to allow its concern for temporal peace to divert it from its true objective, the eternal peace with God. To that it will refer its concern for the institutions, its observance of the law and morality which belong to the temporal peace.[2]

In this theory of the two cities there is nothing to suggest any specific conception of the relation between Church and State. The general implications of this view, however, are clearly hostile to any close linking of the two institutions, and indeed part of Augustine's purpose appears to have been to question radically the theological premises of the view of history which led to so close a linking of the Christian Church to the Roman Empire during the fourth century. This is also the general tendency of passages in which Augustine exhorts his congregations 'to render unto Caesar' what is his due: he reminds them of the duty to obey legitimate civil authority, whose exercise is limited to temporal matters relating to earthly life.[3] More generally he uses Christ's command (in accordance with its original intention) to exhort his hearers to give themselves entirely to God, whose image they bear, just as they give Caesar his due.[4] But rulers, too, are subject to God's law, and are called to God's service; and indeed, especially during the Donatist controversy, Augustine came to lay some stress on their being called to serve God in their special way as rulers.[5] The views he came, in practice, to adopt in the course of the Donatist controversy[6] cut across the general

[1] *De civ. Dei* XIX 12–14 (*PL* 41. 637–43); the definition of universal peace quoted from 13. 1 (*PL* 41. 640). Cf. H. Fuchs, *Augustin und der antike Friedensgedanke* (*Neue philologische Untersuchungen*, 3, Berlin 1926).

[2] *De civ. Dei* XIX 17 (*PL* 41. 645–6).

[3] *Prop. Ep. Rom. Exp.* 72 (*PL* 35. 2083–4); cf. *En. in Ps.* 55. 2 (*PL* 36. 647).

[4] *Ep.* 127. 6 (*PL* 33. 486); cf. *En. in Ps.* 94. 2; 103, *Sermo* 4. 2 (*PL* 37. 1218; 1379); *In Jo. Ev. Tr.* 40. 9 (*PL* 35. 1691).

[5] *C. litt. Pet.* II 210–12 (*PL* 43. 330–2); *C. Cresc.* III 51. 56 (*PL* 43. 527).

[6] Details in G. G. Willis, *Saint Augustine and the Donatist Controversy* (London, 1950). The most penetrating discussion of Augustine's views on religious coercion is by P. R. L. Brown, 'St Augustine's attitude to religious coercion', *J. Rom. Stud.* LIV (1964), pp. 107–16

tendency of his theory to sever the close links between Empire and Church. After much misgiving and in response to pressure from his fellow bishops he endorsed the use of force and of imperial legislation against the schismatics; and views of this kind find a place even in the very differently orientated *De civitate Dei*, in the celebrated 'mirror for princes' and in his portrait of the Emperor Theodosius.[1] The Donatist controversy seems, in this respect, to have been the occasion of a reversal in the direction Augustine's mind had been taking; his own reluctance to accept the policy of *coge intrare*[2] is evidence of a tension between this and his general outlook. The relation between the two themes in Augustine's thought, and the movement of Augustine's mind in this respect, still need to be studied; their tension, despite Augustine's growing confidence and later lack of misgivings, appears never to have been fully resolved.

It was not only Augustine's repudiation of the prevailing estimate of the place held by the Roman Empire in God's providence that pointed in the direction of a limited, secular state; his reflection on human nature and society in their fallen state also pointed in the same direction. Society, Augustine held, was natural to man—man is essentially a social creature,[3] and the life of the saints in the heavenly city, once arrived at their final destination, is also social.[4] But whereas man is naturally social and was so both at his creation and will be in his blessed state, servitude and subordination of man to man do not belong to his nature. They are the consequence of the primal sin and characterize only the life of fallen man on earth.[5] The state, its apparatus of subjection of ruled to ruler, coercion and the whole machinery of government are, on this view, dispensations of divine providence appropriate to the fallen and sinful state of humanity, and their purpose is to check the results of sin, the disorder and lack of harmony into which Adam's sin plunged the human race. The state is not, as it would be if it were an ordinance of nature, an essential means towards the realization of human ends; rather,

[1] *De civ. Dei* V 24 and 26; cf. II 20 (*PL* 41. 170–1; 172–3; 65–6).

[2] *Ep.* 93 (*PL* 33. 321–47).

[3] *De civ. Dei* XII 21; 27 (*PL* 41. 372; 376 [= XII 22; 28 in *CC*]).

[4] *Ibid.* XIX 5 (*PL* 41. 631–2).

[5] *Ibid.* XIX 15 (*PL* 41. 643–4); cf. *En. in Ps.* 124. 7 (*PL* 36. 1653–4). Cf. on this my paper 'Two concepts of political authority: Augustine, *De civitate Dei* XIX 14–15 and some thirteenth century interpretations', *JTS*, n.s. XVI (1965), pp. 68–100.

t exists to secure the outward, social conditions for the individual's ·asier attainment of his legitimate objectives. Its sphere is that of the emporal necessities of the pilgrim on his way to the heavenly *patria*:[1] t does not prescribe the direction of his journey.

It would not be appropriate within the scope of this general exposi- ion to consider Augustine's views on practical aspects of life in society: he tasks of government and law, the institutions of property, slavery ınd freedom, and many others. The still unwritten full picture of his nind on these topics would have to take into account not only the undamental theological background of his thought—in itself changing ›ver the years in its emphases—but also the social and political situa- ion of Roman Africa in the early fifth century, and Augustine's hanging alignment and sympathies; and it would have to bring into ntimate and detailed relation these many-sided studies. Here it must uffice to draw attention to what appear to be the basic tensions which haped his practical attitudes. For centuries, his writings proved to be ın inexhaustible quarry in which men writing on the political questions gitating medieval—and later—Christendom could find support for the nost diverse views. The gulf between Augustine and the Middle Ages ies not so much in the difference between what he thought and how nedieval writers made use of his works; it is primarily a reflection of the imple fact that Augustine was one of the last of the great Christian vriters who still breathed the intellectual atmosphere of the Roman vorld. The civilization which to Gregory the Great was a distant nemory, was, to Augustine, a living reality. In one way or another, his ntellectual biography is the counterpart of the story of his *Confessions*: t is the story of his admiration for the values of classical culture and hought, his attempt to take their measure from the point of view of the Christian Gospel, and, in the end, to free himself from their spell. More han by anything else, he pointed to the Middle Ages by the programme aid down in his *De doctrina christiana*, and its practical realization: the onsecration of intellectual disciplines to the service of the Christian aith.

[1] *Ibid.* XIX 17 (*PL* 41. 645–6).

PART VI

THE GREEK CHRISTIAN PLATONIST TRADITION FROM THE CAPPADOCIANS TO MAXIMUS AND ERIUGENA

BY

I. P. SHELDON-WILLIAMS

ABBREVIATIONS

PSEUDO-DIONYSIUS

Cd	*Corpus dionysianum*
DN	*De divinis nominibus*
CH	*De caelesti hierarchia*
EH	*De ecclesiastica hierarchia*
MT	*De mystica theologia*
Epist.	*Epistolae* I–X

ST BASIL

Hex.	*Hom. in Hexaëmeron*
Adv. Eun.	*Adversus Eunomium*

ST GREGORY NAZIANZEN

Orat.	*Orationes*
Orat. theol.	*Orationes theologicae*

ST GREGORY OF NYSSA

C. Eun.	*Contra Eunomium*
Apol.	*Apologia in Hexaëmeron*
De an. et res.	*De anima et resurrectione*
De hom. opif.	*De hominis opificio*
In Eccles.	*In Ecclesiastem*
In cant. cant.	*In canticum canticorum*
In Hex.	*In Hexaëmeron*
Vit. Moys.	*Vita Moysis*
De Beat.	*De Beatitudinibus*
Vit. Macr.	*Vita Macrinae*
De inst. Christ.	*De instituto Christo*
De virg.	*De virginitate*
De orat. dom.	*De oratione dominica*

ST MAXIMUS THE CONFESSOR

I Ambig.	*Ambigua prima*
II Ambig.	*Ambigua secunda*
Quaest. ad Thalas.	*Quaestiones ad Thalassium*

ERIUGENA

De praed.	*De praedestinatione*
Annot. in Marc.	*Annotationes in Marcianum*
Comm. in Boet. Cons. Phil. III, 9	*Commentaria in Boethii 'De Consolatione Philosophiae'* III, 9
De imag.	*De imagine*
Expos.	*Expositiones super Ierarchiam Caelestem*
Hom.	*Hom. in prologum Evangelii Sancti Ioannis*
Comm. in Ioann.	*Commentaria in Ioannem*

CHAPTER 28

INTRODUCTION: GREEK CHRISTIAN PLATONISM

A Christian Platonist may be either a Platonist who requires to substantiate his speculations by a faith which transcends them, or a Christian who thinks of his faith, and desires to expound it, in terms intelligible to Platonists. St Augustine is the outstanding example of the former type,[1] with whom could perhaps be associated from among the Greeks the ps.-Dionysius and Johannes Philoponus if we knew more about their origins. But the thinkers who built up the Greek Christian Platonist tradition and kept it within the bounds of orthodoxy mostly belonged to the latter: the Alexandrians, the Cappadocians, possibly the ps.-Dionysius, certainly St Maximus Confessor. And it was by following in the footsteps of these, but particularly of St Gregory of Nyssa, the ps.-Dionysius and Maximus, that Johannes Scottus Eriugena introduced this form of Christian philosophy to the West.

Three attitudes towards pagan learning were possible for the Christian: uncompromising acceptance, which led to heretical Gnosticism; uncompromising rejection,[2] as shown by the early apologists and ascetics, favoured by the School of Antioch, and surviving into the Iconoclastic movement and into some forms of modern protestantism; and controlled acceptance, the attitude of the Alexandrians and of the writers discussed in this Part, which produced the Christian philosophy, or Christianism.[3] This attitude acknowledges that the current

[1] [For Augustine's views on the relationship between Platonic philosophy and Christianity, which are rather more complex than is suggested here, see the previous Part (v), ch. 21, pp. 343–6.]

[2] Cf. St Greg. Naz. *Orat.* XLIII 9 and 11 (*PG* 36. 503–5, 507–9) and below, p. 440.

[3] By Christianism is meant a philosophical system constructed upon Christian doctrine. While Christian theology interprets the doctrine, Christianism uses it as the basis for a rational account of the universe. It is thus analogous to the term Platonism in its extended sense of a philosophy constructed upon principles first enunciated by Plato. Christian Platonism, the subject of this Part, is a philosophy based on both sets of first principles where they are reconcilable. The earliest examples of Christianism, and indeed of Christian Platonism, are St John the Evangelist and St Paul. A Christian philosophy (though not necessarily synonymous with Christianism as defined here) is mentioned as early as the second century: cf. Melito *ap.* Eusebius, *Hist. eccles.* IV 26. 7: ἡ καθ' ἡμᾶς φιλοσοφία. For later examples see St Greg. Naz. *Orat.* XXVII 6 (*PG* 36. 19A) (10. 13 Mason), and below, p. 447.

philosophical systems contained elements of truth, a fact taken for granted by the Alexandrians and openly asserted, with particular reference to Platonism,[1] by the Cappadocians,[2] while rejecting what is evidently falsified by the Christian Revelation.

The most important rejections were the eternity of the cosmos, the divinity of the individual human soul,[3] and the belief that the soul is a substance distinct from the body from which it can and should escape as from something evil.

The eternity of the cosmos was accepted without question by the Greeks,[4] to whom the very notion of creation was alien. For them the great division lay not between God and his creatures, but between the intelligible world and the sensible. Consequently, God and the soul, being intelligibles and not sensibles, were species of the same genus,[5] and if the latter is found to be entangled in the sensible world, to which the body belongs, it has fallen from its proper place and must attempt to free itself from the one so as to return to the other, that is to say, it must abandon the body. This is unacceptable to Christianism[6] since it makes the doctrine of the Redemption meaningless. If the soul is itself a trammelled God, it does not need God to set it free. Aristotle was nearer the truth,[7] except that the indissoluble association of soul and body meant, for the Christian, not that the soul perished with the body but that the body is resurrected with the soul.[8]

This rehabilitation of the body implies a continuity of the sensible and intelligible worlds in face of a transcendent Creator; and this in turn affected the division of all human knowledge into *praxis* and *theôria*.[9] So long as the two worlds were held to exhaust the whole of being, theology could be regarded as the perfection of the theoretical sciences as ethics of the practical; but when being was seen to require a cause beyond itself, theology could no longer be included among the theoreti-

[1] St Greg. Naz. *Orat.* XXXI 5 (150. 3–4 Mason; *PG* 36. 137B) below, p. 440.

[2] St Basil, *Ad adolescentes de legendis libris gentilium* (*PG* 31. 564), ed. F. Boulenger (Paris, 1935); St Greg. Naz. *Orat.* IV 100; XI 1; XLIII 11; St Greg. Nyss. *Vit. Moys.* (*PG* 44. 360B). Cf. below, p. 432.

[3] See below, p. 454.

[4] See below, pp. 436; 447; 478–81.

[5] See below, pp. 455; 477. [On the divinity of soul in Plotinus see Part III (Plotinus), ch. 14, pp. 222–6. On the views of Porphyry and Iamblichus see Part IV (The Later Neoplatonists), ch. 18 B, pp. 288–91.]

[6] Contrast Plotinus, III 6 [26] 6, 71–2 with St Paul, II Cor. v. 4. See further below, pp. 447; 458; 489 n. 5

[7] See below, pp. 452; 473.

[8] Below, pp. 437; 485.

[9] Below, pp. 443; 458.

cal sciences at all, but must be a further activity or mode of existence of the ascending soul, leading to a perfection that transcends both sense and intellect. Three stages, therefore, were discerned in this ascent: the acquisition of the practical virtues, which are purificatory, since they remove sin and error;[1] the acquisition of the theoretical virtues, which are the wisdom conferred by illumination from above; and finally the soul's perfection, the end of all philosophy, in which the soul becomes one with God. For at this stage the approximation of knower and known, which is the measure of knowledge, culminates in their identification.[2] The ascent is typified in Moses' ascent of Mount Sinaï,[3] and the three stages by the three heavens, to the third of which St Paul was rapt.[4]

Since the soul is not divine, but a creature, her perfection, like her creation, lies beyond her own powers. Two forces operate the ascent, man's natural power and God's supernatural grace, of which the former declines as the latter prevails: nature is strong in the practical virtues, moderated in the theoretical, all but non-existent in the theological—for when the soul has acquired the theoretical virtues she has reached the limit of her powers, and must either fall back upon the 'likely hypothesis' or myth, or become the passive recipient of a truth she cannot climb up to, but which descends upon her, drawing her the rest of the way. At the limit of intellect Platonism gropes in the dark, but for the Christian, Truth itself enlightens the dark.[5] 'Divine wisdom differs from the worldly as the true from the verisimilitudinous.'[6]

The getting of wisdom is not, however, wholly passive. Moses, convinced that God is incomprehensible to the human mind, nevertheless perseveres in his attempt to penetrate the obscurity out of which he heard the Divine Voice.[7] The obstacles which the light encounters in its outpouring are of two kinds: the perversity of man's will in rejecting it, and the natural opacity of matter. Man, because his will is free, has power to remove the former, and by doing so purifies his vision for

[1] Below, pp. 443; 452.

[2] Below, pp. 444; 460; 464. [For a state of union with the divine higher than intellectual virtue in the Neoplatonism of Iamblichus see the preceding Part (IV, The Later Neoplatonists), ch. 18 C, pp. 294–5.]

[3] Below, pp. 442.

[4] Below, pp. 455.

[5] Cf. Aeneas, *Theophrastus* (*PG* 85. 996B), quoted below, p. 484.

[6] Athenagoras, *Supplication for the Christians*, *Corpus apologeticarum*, VII 130.

[7] St Clem. Alex. *Strom.* II 2 (*PG* 8. 933C–D).

theôria, and sharpens it so that it can penetrate the natural and material obstacles to see the light beyond and within them.[1] So enlightened he is drawn up by the divine rays into the source of that radiance, the perfection of deification.

Action, then, or purification, is the propaedeutic of contemplation, of which deification is the end. Of the three stages of the ascent, the Christian philosophy, though accompanied by the effects of the first and the prospects of the last, strictly speaking includes neither, but consists of rational deductions from the truths provided by the enlightenment to which the soul becomes receptive after purification and by which (as far as a creature may) it becomes God.

The enlightenment comes to her through two channels, the Scriptures (together with the oral tradition (τὰ ἄγραφα), which naturally tended to recede into oblivion,[2] but was still being invoked by Origen,[3] St Gregory Nazianzen,[4] and, as he claimed, the ps.-Dionysius[5]), and the observed phenomena of nature. The Scriptures, being divinely inspired, contain the truth which the philosophers seek to grasp by their own powers, though this may not be apparent to all, and can never be apparent to some. They are the divine Gnosis, the Wisdom of God revealed to man, and if all men had the capacity to understand what they reveal, they would receive through them the full radiance of the Light. They are the Christian oracles (*logia*),[6] instruction given by God to man rather than, or prior to, man's reasoning about God.[7]

The Gnosis is enshrined within the Old and New Testaments, of which the former is God's own explanation, delivered by the Holy Spirit through the *theologoi* (the 'mouthpieces of God'),[8] of human

[1] Cf. St Greg. Naz. below, p. 442, and George Herbert, *The Elixir*, 9–12 (*Works*, Oxford, 1953), p. 184:

> A man that looks on glasse,
> On it may stay his eye;
> Or if he pleaseth through it passe,
> And so the heav'n espie.

[2] See below, p. 439.
[3] Below, p. 432.
[4] Below, p. 439.
[5] Below, pp. 457; 514.
[6] Origen, *De princ.* IV 2. 4; V 312. 2 f.; Eusebius, *Praep. evang.* IV 21. For the use of this term by the pagans see Stiglmayr, *Römische Quartalschrift für christliche Altertumskunde und Kirchengeschichte*, XII, p. 373.
[7] Ceslas Pera, 'Denys le Mystique et la θεομαχία', *Revue des sciences philosophiques et théologiques*, XXV (1936), p. 12. See below, p. 440.
[8] Cf. St Athanasius, *De Incarnat.* LVI (*PG* 25. 195 A); Eusebius, *Praep. evang.* VII 7, 11, 15. See also below, p. 439.

history in terms of the Incarnation which he foretells, while the latter contains the records of those who have been in direct contact with the Incarnate Word who is also Incarnate Truth.[1] It is therefore called *Theologia*, which originally had a more general sense, embracing both the pagan and the Christian Gnosis,[2] but to which St Athanasius and St Basil, by identifying it with the Scriptures,[3] gave a specifically Christian value,[4] thus freeing it from the Neoplatonic associations which some would regard as inseparable from it.[5] The Christian Gnosis is thus a tradition handed down from God, through its recipients, to the Church at large, and supplies the premises from which the Christian philosopher philosophizes.[6]

But the first word of Scripture is that God created heaven and earth, and it is unthinkable that he should have contrived an illusion. The objects presented to man's natural sense and reason and intellect also supply an authoritative channel of enlightenment, open to pagan and Christian alike. For pagan and Christian alike, the cosmos is modelled on the Forms, which are located in the Mind of God.[7] Therefore a proper understanding of the creation leads to the knowledge of the Mind of the Creator, and therefore of the Creator himself. The discourse of Scripture and the variety of nature reveal the same truth because their unifying principle is the same. The Scriptures express the Word of God, which, like the Neoplatonic Intellect (Νοῦς),[8] is the

[1] Cf. Max. Conf. *I Ambig.* XXXVII (*PG* 91. 1304 D2–3).

[2] Ceslas Pera, 'I teologi e la teologia nello sviluppo del pensiero Cristiano dal iii al iv secolo', *Angelicum*, XIX (1942), p. 52.

[3] Idem, 'Denys le Mystique', pp. 12–13; 'I teologi', p. 74; R. Roques, 'Note sur la notion de "Theologia" selon le ps.-Denys', *Revue d'ascétique et de mystique*, XXV (1949), pp. 207–10; W. Volker, *Kontemplation und Ekstase bei ps.-Dionysius Areopagita* (Wiesbaden, 1958), p. 88; below, p. 434.

[4] J. G. Suicer, *Thesaurus ecclesiasticus* (Amsterdam, 1728), s.v. 'Theologia'; K. Gronau, *Poseidonios und die jüdisch-christliche Genesisexegese* (Berlin, 1914). For its use by the pagans see W. Jaeger, *Nemesios von Emesa, Quellenforschungen zum Neuplatonismus und seinen Anfängen bei Poseidonios* (Berlin, 1914); idem, *Theology of the Early Greek Philosophers* (Eng. tr.), pp. 4 f., 194 n. 7 (Plato, Aristotle); H. A. Koch, *Quellenuntersuchungen zu Nemesios von Emesa* (Berlin, 1921); M. J. Congar, 'Théologie', *Dict. théol. cat.* XV, 1 (1946), pp. 341–502, esp. pp. 341–53; A. J. Festugière, *La Révélation d'Hermès Trismégiste*, II (Paris, 1949), pp. 598–605 (Plato to Philo); V. Goldschmidt, 'Theologia', *Revue des études grecques*, LXIII (1950), pp. 20–42.

[5] Cf. H. Koch, 'Pseudo-Dionysius Areopagita in seinen Beziehungen zum Neuplatonismus und Mysterienwesen', *Forschungen zur christlichen Literatur und Dogmengeschichte*, I, 2–3 (Mainz, 1900), pp. 34, 41 f.

[6] See below, pp. 439; 446.

[7] See below, pp. 437; 476; 497; 526–7; Eriugena, *Periphyseon*, II 3 (*PL* 122. 529B1–2).

[8] Cf. Plotinus, V 9 [5] 8, 4–5; A. H. Armstrong, *Introduction to Ancient Philosophy*, p. 73; below, pp. 437; 447; 497.

pleroma of all the Forms (νοητά). St Maximus taught that the saints receive a perfect knowledge of created beings because when they attain to the contemplation of the Nature of God they contemplate in him the Forms of all things,[1] and that the identity of scriptural with scientific truth was the revelation which the apostles received on the mount of Transfiguration:

By means of the white garments they received a revelation of what they had learnt from the great works of creation and from the Scriptures as a single truth, and so in their contemplation (ἐπιγνώσει) of God they beheld that which the Holy Spirit revealed in the Scriptures and that which their science and wisdom had taught them about the created universe as one, and in that unified vision they saw Christ himself.[2]

The Word in its unity abides eternally in the Father, but its expression is the act of creation. The Forms in their plurality are neither inert nor transcendent, but dynamic and immanent. In separation they are only apprehensible to the intellect, but in composition they bring into existence the sensibles,[3] and therefore St Basil calls them 'intelligible impulses towards the coming into being of bodies', and St Gregory of Nyssa 'intelligible powers', constituting a 'luminous force' which God introduces into not-being and so brings it to being.[4] As power they are creative (οὐσιοποιοί),[5] as light they lead the creature back to its Creator: for they are the rays (φῶτα, ἀκτῖνες, αὐγαί) of which God is the Sun,[6] the apprehensible aspect of divinity, whether intelligible or visible, through which he communicates himself to the minds and senses of his creatures, and through that knowledge draws them back to him, for 'knowledge is a kind of conversion'.[7]

Thus the Christians shared with the Platonists the conception of universal nature as a rest-in-motion or motion-in-rest consisting of three aspects: the eternally abiding First Principle; a procession therefrom through the Forms into their effects; and a return of the effects through the Forms to their First Principle. The names given to these aspects, by

[1] V. Lossky, *Théologie mystique de l'Église d'Orient*, p. 73.
[2] Max. Conf. *I Ambig.* VI 31 (*PG* 91. 1160C12–D6).
[3] See below, p. 497.
[4] St Greg. Nyss. *De hom. opif.* XXIV (*PG* 44. 213B). See below, pp. 447–8
[5] Ps.-Dionys. *DN*, V 8 (*PG* 3. 824C10–15). See below, p. 461.
[6] See below, p. 442.
[7] E. R. Dodds, *Proclus: Elements of Theology* (Oxford, 1933), p. 219. See below, pp. 452–3.

Platonist and Christian alike, were *monê*, *proodos*, *epistrophê*;[1] but also, because every intelligible and creative principle abides what it is, and in order to accomplish its will emits power, which achieves its effect when the intention which emitted it is fulfilled, they were given the names *ousia*, *dunamis*, *energeia*.[2]

The latter triad, which does not feature prominently in Neoplatonism, tended, after the ps.-Dionysius, to be preferred by Christians, since it was more convenient than the other for the exposition of a doctrine of creation (God effecting his will) as opposed to one of emanation (an automatic process). Since the Divine Power is never ineffective, *dunamis* and *energeia* (or *proodos* and *epistrophê*) are in God, that is, in their ultimate reality, inseparable, and are sometimes used interchangeably. He creates by making known, and makes known by creation. What he makes known (in terms comprehensible to sense or intellect) is his own Nature. For the Forms are identical with the attributes of God whose names are recorded in Scripture, and which are thus seen to be no abstractions or metaphors,[3] but dynamic and concrete realities.[4] If, then, to make known is to create, God creates himself in the Forms. This was the solution of the central problem which confronted the philosophers studied in this Part: how a created universe can know, and love, and ultimately be reabsorbed into, a Creator who transcends it. It was stated in its most uncompromising form by the last of them: God, in creating all things, creates himself in all things.[5]

[1] Below, pp. 442; 459. [On the Neoplatonic triads see Part IV, ch. 19 B, pp. 308–13.]
[2] Below, p. 459 n. 4.
[3] Below, pp. 435; 461.
[4] Lossky, *op. cit.* pp. 77–8; 219.
[5] Below, p. 532.

CHAPTER 29

THE CAPPADOCIANS

A. *St Basil of Caesarea* (*c.* 330–79)

The Cappadocians inherited the Alexandrian Gnosis through Origen, though each departed from the position of their master, St Basil most of all. He was more interested in the moral and pastoral than in the philosophical implications of the Faith, distrusted allegory,[1] and clung to the literal interpretation of Scripture, to which the pagan learning was to supply rational corroboration as required rather than combine with it to form a synthesis. Therefore, as was to be the case with the Aristotelian Christians,[2] he made greater use of the physics of the pagans than of their metaphysics, and in his *Homilies on the Hexaëmeron*,[3] intended as a scientific defence of the Mosaic account of creation, he drew chiefly on the current cosmology, meteorology, botany, astronomy and natural history.[4]

As a consequence, the Christian theory of creation assumed certain pagan features, of which the most important were the implied identification of the Platonic Demiurge with Yahweh,[5] the Aristotelian division of the universe into the supralunar and sublunar spheres, and the notion of a universal harmony (συμπάθεια):[6] 'Although the totality of the universe is composed of dissimilar parts, he binds it together by an indissoluble law of friendship into one communion and harmony, so that even the parts that from the positions they occupy seem most distant from one another are yet shown to be united by the universal *sumpatheia*.'[7]

Nature is the work of God, who created her in time, or rather created time in the process of creating her.[8] Matter is a part of creation, for if it

[1] Cf. *Hex.* IX 1 (*PG* 29. 188B–C).

[2] Below, p. 478.

[3] *PG* 29. 4A–208C, ed. S. Giet, Paris, 1950 (*Sources chrét.* 26). References are to this edition by numbers of columns in *PG*.

[4] Giet, *op. cit.* 56–69. Cf. St Greg. Naz. *Orat.* XLIII (*PG* 36. 528A).

[5] Below, p. 439.

[6] Cf. Philo *ap.* É. Bréhier, *Les Idées philosophiques et religieuses de Philon d'Alexandrie* (Paris, 1925), pp. 158–61.

[7] *Hex.* II 2, 33A. Cf. Proclus, who taught that the Hierarchies are connected by love (ἔρως) or friendship (φιλία) which is ἑνοποιός (*In Tim.* 155–6, II 53. 24 – 54. 25 Diels (Leipzig, 1904)). See also below, p. 437.

[8] Cf. below, pp. 437; 447; 487; 501.

were uncreated God would have been dependent upon it for bringing his plan to fruition;[1] and if matter were independent of God there would not be that reciprocity between agent and patient which is everywhere apparent.[2]

Although Scripture does not speak of the four elements, it mentions earth and implies fire (for since Moses limits his theme to the created universe[3] he must mean by heaven the highest part of the physical world, of which the substance is fire[4]), and by speaking of the highest and the lowest it infers the two intermediaries.[5] Fire (or light) is the substance of heaven because, although the elements were originally intermingled, each tends towards its proper level: fire at the top, extending downward as far as the Firmament;[6] then air; then water; then earth at the base.

Each element also has its proper quality: fire is warm, air moist, water cold, earth dry.[7] But none is found wholly in its place or with its quality unmixed: fire is found below the Firmament, and there are waters above it;[8] earth, as it is experienced, is cold as well as dry, and so can combine with water; water moist as well as cold, and so can combine with air; air warm as well as moist, and so can combine with fire; and finally fire is dry as well as warm, and therefore can mingle with earth. This cyclic movement of the elements[9] produces the variety of combinations out of which all sensible beings are created.[10]

This is Aristotelian and Stoic doctrine, except for 'the waters above the Firmament', which is part of revealed truth. The Alexandrians interpreted these allegorically as the intelligible world, separated from the sensible by the Firmament, or First Heaven:[11] Basil characteristically insists on the literal sense on the ground that Moses is only concerning himself with the physical universe. There is water above the Firma-

[1] *Hex.* II 3, 32A–B. Cf. Origen, *De princ.* II 1. 4 (*PG* 11. 185C–D, 110. 1 – 111. 1 Koetschau).

[2] *Hex.* II 3, 33B–C. See below, p. 500.

[3] See below, p. 440.

[4] See below, p. 448.

[5] *Hex.* I 7, 20B–C. For air and water as intermediaries cf. Plato, *Tim.* 32B.

[6] See below, p. 448.

[7] Cf. Aristotle, *De gen. et corr.* II 3, 331a4.

[8] Gen. i. 6.

[9] Cf. Aristotle, *op. cit.* II 4, 331b2.

[10] *Hex.* IV 5, 89B–92A. See below, pp. 437; 448; 520. The doctrine that the elements pass into one another is a Stoic variation of the Heraclitean theory of flux.

[11] See below, p. 448.

ment to abate the fiery substance and prevent the Stoic conflagration (ἐκπύρωσις).[1]

The *Homilies on the Hexaëmeron* demonstrate that the truth discovered by man's reason is not different, so far as it goes, from the truth revealed by Scripture. But Scripture also reveals truths inaccessible to man's reason: the Nature of God, which is wholly incomprehensible, as well as the basic principles of the intelligible and sensible worlds. The incomprehensibility of the Divine Nature[2] was one of the points on which the Cappadocians were at issue with Eunomius, the champion of Arianism; for Eunomius,[3] following his master Aëtius,[4] contended that reason is equal in value and power to revelation, and that therefore if the Divine Nature is known through revelation it is also accessible to reason. He further argued that if what we know of God is his Essence, and if we know of him that he is Father, Son, and Holy Spirit, then each of the three is his Essence; but that, on the other hand, we deduce that God is not more than Trinity, and that therefore all names given to him by Scripture beyond these Three must be mere metaphor. For instance, the Begotten Word cannot literally be God since God is unbegotten. This line of reasoning imposed upon Basil and the other Cappadocians the task of examining the problem of the Divine Names.[5] Basil's answer was that any epithet could be applied to God, but that all fall into one of two classes: those that indicate what he is not (τῶν μὴ προσόντων), of which 'unbegotten' is an example; and those which affirm that he is not other than this (τῶν προσόντων ἐν θεῷ), such as 'righteous', 'judge', 'creator'.[6] The former can lead the reason to a partial knowledge of God by what the Neoplatonists called *aphairesis*, the progressive stripping away of every concept that the mind can form about God in the certainty that every one will be inadequate.[7] *Aphairesis* by itself, however, will lead to sheer negation;[8] and this would be all

[1] See below, pp. 479–80.

[2] See below, p. 460.

[3] Cf. Eunomius *ap.* Socrates, *Hist. eccl.* IV 7. 13–14, 482. 10–14 Hussey (Oxford, 1853); Theodoret, *Haeres. fat. comp.* IV 3; idem, *In Dan.* VIII.

[4] Cf. Aëtius *ap.* Theodoret, *Hist. eccl.* II 24 (*PG* 82. 1072C2–5).

[5] τὸ τῶν ὀνομάτων μυστήριον, St Greg. Naz. *Orat.* XXX 16 *ad fin.* (134. 17–18 Mason). See below, p. 441.

[6] St Basil, *Adv. Eun.* I 10.

[7] St Basil, *Ep.* CCXXXV 2 (*PG* 32. 869C1–2); *Adv. Eun.* I 14 (*PG* 29. 544A10–B15); cf. Plotinus, V 5 [32] 13, 11–13. See below, p. 440; ps.-Dionys. pp.468–70.

[8] Plotinus, V 5 [32] 6, 11–13. See below, p. 468.

hat could be known of God, did not Scripture reveal that he is, and that ıe possesses the Attributes with which it endows him. The Scriptural Names or Attributes are therefore outgoings (πρόοδοι) of God's Nature o the human understanding,[1] and are thus the authentic Names of his *Energeiai*.

The intelligible world is only accessible to reason in its function of ubstantiating the sensible. By revelation it is known as the angelic world,[2] outside time (ὑπέρχρονος, αἰωνία, ἀΐδιος),[3] not with the absolute eternity of God, but with that eternity which is consistent with its being a creature; for *aion* is a limit which precludes even the intellectual activity of man from being infinite.[4] The angels are substantial and occupy a substantial world, but one which does not share a common natter with the sensible world. It has an intelligible matter,[5] which Basil identifies with the light[6] which illuminates the material world, and s therefore the common ground of the whole universe, intelligible and ensible. This leads him to give to Ps. ciii. 4[7] a literal interpretation which St Gregory Nazianzen treats with reserve,[8] and St Gregory of Nyssa rejects.[9]

It follows that light is a more general nature than time,[10] for time is found only in the sensible world. Because light is not limited to time it was universally diffused at the moment of its creation,[11] as it fills the whole room in which a lamp is kindled. Between the intelligible and the ensible worlds the Firmament acts as a barrier, of which the solidity mplied by its name is such that light may pass through it (though in a diluted form), but time cannot break out to the world above.[12]

[1] This is the subject of the ps.-Dionysius' treatise *On the Divine Names*, for which see below, p. 461. Cf. above, p. 431.

[2] πᾶσα τῶν νοητῶν διακόσμησις; *Hex.* I 5, 13 A. Cf. St Greg. Nyss. below, p. 454 ps.-Dionys. below, p. 464.

[3] *Hex. loc. cit.* See below, p. .

[4] Cf. St Greg. Nyss. *C. Eun.* I (*PG* 44. 365 C (I 135 Jaeger)); Lossky, *op. cit.* p. 97.

[5] St Basil, *Hom. in ps. xlviii*, 8 (*PG* 29. 449 B (I 148 E ed. Maur.)).

[6] Idem, *Hex.* II 5, 40 C–41 A. See below, pp. 437; 507–8.

[7] Quoted by St Paul, Hebr. i. 7.

[8] St Greg. Naz. *Orat.* XXVIII 31 (70. 3–7 Mason) (*PG* 36. 72 A). See below, p. 443.

[9] According to Greg. Nyss. fire is intermediary between the intelligible and sensible nature (*C. Eun.* II (XII B/XIII) (*PG* 45. 1004 A, I 306 Jaeger); *In Hex. PG* 44. 80 D–81 A; 81 C–D; 116 B; 121 A), and therefore the angelic intelligences are of a higher order than fire. See below, p. 448.

[10] Proclus identified light with space, which he held to be an immovable, indivisible immaterial body: idem *ap.* Simpl. *Phys.* ed. Diels (Berlin, 1882), pp. 611–12.

[11] *Hex.* II 7, 45 A.

[12] See below, p. 437.

Bounded within the Firmament, time is the principle of the sensible world, which is more explicable to reason than the intelligible, but still not wholly so; otherwise there would be no purpose in the translucency of the Firmament. It is by revelation that we know that it is not eternal, for reason would suggest the contrary.[1] It was created with time, or as a logical consequence of time (ἀπὸ χρόνου), which is itself a necessary consequence of the creation of the Firmament rotating in space; for time, motion, and spatial extension[2] are mutually interrelated. Not only can there be no motion without time, but time is only time when measured by motion. Therefore, since there can be no motion that is not from one place or state to another, there can be no first moment of time, and Moses is careful to call the 'First Day' of creation not the first but 'one day':

> The God who created the nature of time appointed the periods of the days as its measures and marks, and ordains that the week, by returning upon itself, shall count the motion of time. The week is the fulfilment of the one day seven times returning upon itself: for this is the way of the circle, that it starts from itself and ends in itself. In this it resembles the aeon, which returns upon itself endlessly. Therefore he called the origin of time not a first day but one day, to show that time retains its kinship with eternity.[3]

But this does not mean that time and eternity are identical or that the physical universe is eternal. In the passage just quoted the last sentence (which is also reproduced in almost the same words by Johannes Lydus)[4] comes from a Pythagorean source, but whereas the Pythagoreans held that time was intrinsically eternal, Basil only claims for it an affinity (συγγενές) with eternity. He agreed with Plato[5] that it is the copy of eternity, but only in so far as what is created can be a copy of what is not. Eternity has no beginning: time has no beginning *in itself*. The beginning (ἀρχή) is 'not even the smallest part of time',[6] but quite outside the temporal process, and therefore no part of the creative act takes place

[1] See above, p. 426.

[2] St Bas. *Adv. Eun.* I 21 (*PG* 29. 560B, I 233A–B ed. Maur.). The identification of time and extension is Stoic: see Simplicius, *In Categ.* 350 Kalbfleisch; Plutarch, *Quaest. plat.* 1007; Philo, *Leg. alleg.* II 2.

[3] *Hex.* II 8, 49B–C.

[4] Ioan. Lyd. *De mens.* III 3, 39. 4–14 Wuensch. Cf. J. Daniélou, 'La typologie de la semaine au ive siècle', *Recherches de science religieuse*, XXXV (1948), p. 399. For Lydus, see also below, p. 522.

[5] *Tim.* 37D. Cf. Plotinus, III 7 [45] 13, 23–5.

[6] *Hex.* I 6, 16C.

within time. God creates 'in the beginning' (ἐν ἀρχῇ) and therefore not in time (ἐν χρόνῳ).[1] The Firmament is created 'before' the earth not in a chronological sense, but as the container precedes the content, and the light the shadow cast by an interposed body.[2] The creation of the extra-temporal circumference was necessarily the cause of the temporal content, and therefore of motion and extension. The effect of extension is that the divine *energeiai*, which in the intelligible world are one in the Nous or Logos,[3] now become many, and the effect of motion is to bring them into association to form sensible bodies,[4] and to separate them again to bring about the dissolution of those bodies. Basil agrees with Aristotle that whatever comes into being in time must perish in time,[5] for time, as we have seen,[6] cannot pass through the Firmament.

But Aristotle was wrong to apply this principle to the soul, for although the soul is involved in the spatio-temporal world, she is not of it, and therefore is destined to pass beyond it.[7] By nature she belongs to the intelligible world, and is like the angels a creature of light, to which the Firmament is not a barrier.[8] For the same reason the incarnate soul's mode of cognition, which is discursive, is not precluded from the knowledge which is the object of Nous. Since time is the offspring of eternity and resembles it, the content of the temporal world is a copy in this extended medium of the non-extended prototype, as that in its turn it is the expression of the Thoughts of the Divine Mind. Thus the entire universe is linked together by a chain of likeness and exhibits a harmonious sympathy.[9]

As time is co-existent with, and a kind of secondary substance of, the sensible world, so this sympathy is the primary substance of the whole

[1] *Hex.* IX 2, 189B.

[2] *Hex.* II 5, 41A–B.

[3] See above, p. 429.

[4] See above, p. 433.

[5] *Hex.* I 3, 9C. Cf. Aristotle, *De caelo* I 12, 288b4; St Greg. Nyss. *De hom. opif.* XXIII (*PG* 44. 209B); Baudry, *Le Problème de l'origine et de l'éternité du monde dans la philosophie grecque de Platon à l'ère chrétienne* (Paris, 1931), p. 111; below, p. 496.

[6] Above, p. 435.

[7] *Hex.* I 5, 12C.

[8] See above, p. 435. Cf. H. Urs von Balthasar, *Présence et pensée* (Paris, 1943), pp. 8–9.

[9] *Hex.* II 2, 33A. See above, p. 432. The idea comes from Plato (cf. *Tim.* 32A), and plays an important part in the philosophy of Posidonius: cf. Cleomedes, *De motu circ.* I 1, 4, 8 Ziegler; Sextus Empiricus, *Adv. math.* IX = *C. phys.* I 78–80; Karl Reinhardt, *Kosmos und Sympathie* (Munich, 1928), pp. 52 f. However, L. Edelstein, 'The physical system of Posidonius', *American Journal of Philology*, LVII (1936), p. 324, considers that its importance for Posidonius has been overrated.

creation, intelligible and sensible, being the mode in which the *energeiai* express the divine unity. Where it does not reach creation does not reach, and this is the realm of evil, which is no substance, but the absence of good.[1] It is probably to be identified with the darkness which covered the face of the earth 'before' its creation.[2]

For St Basil, as for every Christian philosopher, the central theme is God, his dealings with the world, and especially with man. God creates the world, and sets in it his own image, man.[3] But this is man's eternal, not his contemporary condition. Created in the intelligible order, he falls into the sensible; designed for eternity, he is enmeshed in time, and in danger of a further fall into the total dissolution which is a concomitant of temporality, that is to say, into absolute evil. The philosopher's task is to reverse this trend, converting the descent into an ascent, first by a purification of the carnal passions, which leads to the First Heaven, the Firmament; then by the acquisition of wisdom to which the soul, no longer clouded by these obscurities, now has access, and by which she rises, illumined, to the summit of the intelligible world, which is the Second Heaven; from which she is finally drawn up to the Third Heaven of deification.

B. *St Gregory Nazianzen (329/30–c. 390)*

In relation to Origen, St Gregory Nazianzen stands midway between St Basil and St Gregory of Nyssa. Origen inclined to the allegorical, Basil to the literal interpretation of the Scriptures. Gregory of Nyssa is closer to Origen in this respect, and will devote pages of mystical interpretation to an event,[4] to a book,[5] or to a symbol.[6] Gregory of Nazianzen, on the other hand, believed that all interpretations of the Scriptures are equally true, and that this showed their superiority over

[1] *Hex.* II 4, 37 C–D. This definition of evil, which derives from Plotinus (cf. I 8 [51] 11, 8–9; III 2 [47] 5, 25–6), was held in common by all the Cappadocians, and was developed at length in the Neoplatonic tradition that was drawn upon by Proclus and the ps.-Dionysius.

[2] *Hex.* II 5, 41 B.

[3] St Basil left his exposition of the theme uncompleted, for the *Homilies on the Hexaëmeron* break off at the point where God creates man in his own image. A treatise on this was promised, but the promise was long deferred. See below, p. 449.

[4] Cf. his *Life of Moses.*

[5] Cf. his *Commentary on the Song of Songs.*

[6] Cf. his exposition of the symbolism of the Cross, *In Christ. resurrect.*, *Orat.* I (*PG* 46. 621 C–625 B).

the books of the pagans.[1] 'He was not, like Basil, a realist, nor, like Gregory of Nyssa, a bold speculative.'[2]

He agrees with Basil that the cosmology of the *Timaeus* harmonizes with the account of creation in Genesis,[3] but sees no need to support the latter by reference to the former or to other physical theories of the pagans as Basil had done, for events recorded in Scripture are vouched for not by reason, but by faith. The language of Scripture does not reveal the truth directly, but a half-concealed version of it.

This is because the sensible world from which it draws its illustrations is an imperfect copy of the intelligible:[4] it displays shadows, and the intelligible world images, of the sole reality, which is God. Similarly the Old Testament displays shadows, the New images, of the ultimate Truth who is the incomprehensible God.[5]

The Scriptures are supplemented by the oral tradition,[6] which depends for its survival upon the fidelity of the disciple to his master.[7] Orthodoxy is related to heresy as health (παλαιὰ ὑγίεια)[8] to disease (καινὴ νόσος),[9] an indisposition (σύγχυσις, ἀναστροφή)[10] incurred when the Divine Logos, i.e. *theologia*, is displaced by the human logos, i.e. reason uncontrolled by faith.[11] The vehicle of the Tradition, both written and unwritten, is the Church, which is both the agent and the witness of the diffusion of enlightenment throughout the world.[12] Therefore, as a bishop of the Church, Gregory regards himself as one of the organs through which the Tradition is transmitted, a *theologos* in direct line with the *theologoi* who wrote the Scriptures.[13] He philosophizes as 'one of the bearers of God's Word (θεοφόρων) philosophized (ἐφιλοσόφησεν) a little before my time'.[14] Consequently he lays no claim to

[1] Greg. Naz. *Poem. ad Nemes.* 138 f. (*PG* 37. 1561 f.).

[2] Mersch, *Le Corps mystique du Christ*, II 440.

[3] *Orat.* XXVIII 5, 29–31. On this harmonization see Bréhier, *Hist. philos.* I 499 f. See above, p. 432.

[4] A notion deriving from Plato and Plotinus.

[5] See below, p. 444–5 .

[6] See above, p. 428.

[7] *Orat.* XXXII 21 (*PG* 36. 197C–D). Cf. 25–6 (*PG* 36. 201–3).

[8] *Orat.* XXI 21, 32.

[9] *Ibid.* 21.

[10] *Ibid.*

[11] Greg. Naz. *Poem on his Life*, 715 (*PG* 37. 1078).

[12] J. Plaignieux, *Saint Grégoire de Nazianze théologien* (Paris, 1951), p. 56.

[13] See above, p. 428.

[14] *Orat.* XXXI 28 (181. 3–7, *PG* 36. 163D). For the Theological Orations (*Orat.* XXVII–XXXI) the references in brackets preceding the *PG* references are to the edition of A. J. Mason, *The Five Theological Orations of Gregory of Nazianzus* (Cambridge, 1899).

originality.[1] Like Solomon, he would not wish to open his mouth without having first 'suffered' (παθεῖν)[2] divine instruction,[3] for otherwise he could not be a *theologos*, with authority to speak about God. For God is unnamable,[4] and authority alone acquaints us with certain facts about him, from which we tentatively draw for ourselves dim pictures of what he really is, and so endow the Unnamable with names.

Reason is certainly not without value, and Gregory is severe on those Christians who will have nothing to do with pagan learning, reviling that which they do not know.[5] The 'general education' (παντοία παιδεία), in which classical and Christian literature were associated, was a pearl of great price.[6] He is grateful for his education in the Athenian Schools: 'After divinity it is the first gift I obtained, and I keep it still.'[7] Especially does he praise the Platonists, 'who have thought best about God and are nearest to us'.[8] But reason derives its value from faith,[9] and the Platonic achievement is of no avail unless it is subordinated to faith and acknowledges its limits: 'Take for your guide faith rather than reason; from the realization of your weakness in regard to the things that are nearest to you judge the value of your reason and understand that there are things that are beyond it.'[10]

Faith tells us that the events recorded by Scripture are true, reason how they are true, and begins by dividing them into four categories: things which do not really exist but about which men speak; those which exist but about which men do not speak; those which do not exist and about which men do not speak; and those which exist and about which men speak.[11] To the first category belong the anthropomorphisms necessitated by the limitations of human discourse; to the second the concepts which are discarded by *aphairesis*;[12] to the third the

[1] See ps.-Dionys., below, p. 457. [2] See below, p. 468.

[3] *Orat.* XX 5 (*PG* 35. 1069 C).

[4] τὸ θεῖον ἀκατονόμαστον, *Orat.* XXX 17 (134. 19–20, *PG* 36. 125 B).

[5] *Orat.* XLIII 11 (*PG* 36. 507–9. See above, p. 425).

[6] *Orat.* XI 1 (*PG* 35. 832 B). [7] *Orat.* IV 100 (*PG* 35. 636 A).

[8] *Orat.* XXXI 5 (150. 3–4, *PG* 36. 137 B). Cf. XXVIII 4; 16 (26. 12–27; 46. 15 – 47. 3; *PG* 36. 29 C, 47 A; above, p. 426).

[9] *Orat.* XXIII 12 (*PG* 35. 1163 C–D); *Poem. ad Seleuc.* 245–9 (*PG* 38. 1593).

[10] *Orat.* XXVIII 28 (66. 15–19, *PG* 36. 68 A). Cf. Plato, *Laws*, IX 863.

[11] *Orat.* XXXI 22 (172. 1–3, *PG* 36. 157 A).

[12] See above, p. 434, below, pp. 468–70.

nihilum out of which God creates; to the fourth the events which are literally and historically true.[1] It is only in the last that reason is adequate by itself to reveal the truth: for the first contains no truth of its own; the second is above reason and the third below it: reason, proceeding from faith, begins from the one and ends in the other.

That which is, then, is the point from which reason starts; and That which is is the highest of the Divine Names[2] communicated by faith to reason. It is God's most 'proper' name: 'Being (οὐσία) is precisely that which is of God alone, and identical with him.'[3] Being is an attribute of the creature because it participates in the Being of the Creator,[4] but all the other attributes applied by Scripture to the Creator are taken from the creature, and therefore contain an element of anthropomorphism. *Theos*, for instance, derives either from run (θέειν),[5] or shine (αἴθειν).[6] The same is true in the case of the names of the Three Hypostases,[7] except that whereas *Theos*, by the accepted etymologies, denotes the Creator's relation to the creature, the names Unbegotten, Begotten, Proceeding, Father, Son, Spirit, denote those within the Divine Nature Itself.[8] They reveal that the universal triadic process of Beginning, Middle, End, or Being, Motion, Rest,[9] is already present, in a non-temporal and non-extended sense, in the One; and explain how from the immutable One is produced a multiple world moving through space and time: 'That which is the Monad from the beginning moved to the Dyad and comes to rest in the Triad.'[10]

'He came to rest in the Triad' because the names of the Three Hypostases are the last to be applied to God in his transcendent Nature. The other Divine Names designate his powers (ἐξουσίαι) or dispositions (οἰκονομίαι),[11] and constitute the hierarchy of functions he has imposed upon his work, an order (τάξις) which, whether in the harmony of the angelic choirs, or the courses of the heavenly bodies, or the round of the seasons, or the life-cycle of the body, alone supplies the force, the beauty,

[1] *Orat.* XXXI 22 (172. 7–8; 173. 2–4; *PG* 36. 157A–C).
[2] See above, p. 434.
[3] *Orat.* XXIX 11 (88. 13–14, *PG* 36. 88B).
[4] *Orat.* XXX 18 (136. 14 – 137. 2, *PG* 36. 125–8).
[5] Cf. Plato, *Cratylus*, 397C.
[6] *Orat.* XXX 18 (136. 1–10, *PG* 36. 128A; see below, p. 460).
[7] *Orat.* XXIX 12 (91. 1–2, *PG* 36. 89A–C).
[8] *Orat.* XXIX 16 (97. 10 – 98. 8, *PG* 36. 43–6).
[9] See below, p. 496.
[10] μονὰς ἀπ' ἀρχῆς, εἰς δυάδα κινηθεῖσα, μέχρι τριάδος ἔστη, *Orat.* XXIX 2 (75. 7–8, *PG* 36. 76B).
[11] *Orat.* XXX 19–20 (138. 3–4, *PG* 36. 128–32). See above, pp. 431; 435.

and the stability of the universe.[1] They are the 'latter' Nature of God (τὰ ὀπίσω θεοῦ) which Moses saw; for, unlike the 'former' Nature, they can be known.[2]

The degree in which they are known depends upon the degree of illumination of the knower. For whereas in the Divine Nature there are no gradations, it is in accordance with 'harmony and the general good' (τοῦ παντὸς εὐαρμοστία καὶ συμφέρον) that there should be superiors and inferiors in the extended world which is contemplated by discursive reason.[3] It is this which gives it its name, cosmos, and is to be venerated as its law (νόμος) and order (εὐταξία).[4] It must be recognized that there are those who teach and those who learn, so that Wisdom (φωτισμός), whose source is in God, may smoothly flow down to all levels of creation.

This Wisdom or enlightenment is the vehicle of the universal threefold rhythm of *monê*, *proodos*, *epistrophê*:[5] it abides in God; proceeds from God; and returns to God again.[6] In its procession it becomes first the luminous and jubilant wisdom of the angels and of those who enjoy the Beatific Vision;[7] then human wisdom which is the reflection of this. God is to the intelligible world what the Sun is to the sensible,[8] and the angels are his rays (ἀπορροαί),[9] which purified human souls reflect.[10] In the return, human wisdom is the dawn of the angelic, which brings in the full radiance of day: the opacity (παχύτης) of human nature is enlightened by the immaterial luminosity of the angels, and so introduced to the absolute purity (καθαρότης) of God.[11]

Like all intermediaries the angels have a triple aspect: with regard to the Source of Light (πρῶτον φῶς) above them they are intelligent powers (νοεραὶ δυνάμεις);[12] with regard to themselves they are intelligible natures (νοηταὶ φύσεις)[13] or 'intelligences' (νόες);[14] with regard to the nature below them they are purificatory (καθάρσιοι).[15] It is with reference to the last two aspects that they are called 'spirits' (πνεύματα) and

[1] *Orat.* XXXII 7–12 (*PG* 36. 181B–188D).
[2] *Orat.* XXVII 3 (*PG* 36. 28–9).
[3] See below, p. 466.
[4] See below, p. 444.
[5] See above, p. 431.
[6] See below, pp. 445–7.
[7] Eric Peterson, *Le Livre des anges* (Leipzig, 1935).
[8] *Orat.* XXVIII 30 (68. 8–12, *PG* 36. 69A). Cf. Plato, *Rep.* VI 508C; above, p. 430.
[9] *Orat.* XL 5 (*PG* 36. 364B).
[10] See below, p. 453.
[11] *Orat.* XXVIII 31 (70. 16 – 71. 5, *PG* 36. 72).
[12] *Orat.* XXVIII 31 (70. 14).
[13] *Ibid.* (70. 8).
[14] *Ibid.* (70. 14). See below, p. 476.
[15] *Ibid.* (70. 9–10). See below, p. 453.

'flames of fire',[1] expressions that cannot be taken literally unless the angels are corporeal, which Gregory hesitates to affirm.[2] They are either corporeal or the nearest spiritual thing to corporeality.[3] He also calls them 'ascents' (ἀναβάσεις),[4] a name which he does not explain, but which clearly implies that they are the means of man's return to God: they already possess that nature to which man ascends when he is purified, an intelligible nature and a ray (ἀπορροή) of the Divine Light.

Man becomes a ray by cleansing his soul so as to restore the original lustre which enables it, like a polished mirror, to reflect the light from above,[5] and 'light is added to light, our darkness opens up to brightness, awaiting the moment when we attain the Source of the reflections here below, the Beatific Vision where images dissolve into Truth'.[6] Illumination must be preceded by purification.[7] Gregory will not give instruction and forbids it to be received before purification, for 'it is as dangerous for the impure to touch the pure as for those with weak eyes to gaze on the Sun's rays'.[8] Solomon says that fear is the beginning of wisdom, but 'where there is fear there is observance of the commandments, and where there is observance of the commandments there is purification of the flesh, which is a cloud that envelops the soul and prevents her from having a pure vision of the Divine Splendour'.[9] In the *Lamentations on the Sorrows of his Soul*,[10] he recounts a dream in which he is first visited by Chastity and Temperance appearing as two women dressed in white, whose ornament is to have no ornament; and thereafter by 'the worshippers from the side of the Throne of God, who bring with them the first rays of the Divine Light, and communicate it to mortals'. The significance is made clear in a passage from *Orat.* XX:[11] 'You wish to become a theologian... observe the precepts, advance in the commandments. *Praxis* is the ladder to *Theoria*.'[12] St Basil was fit

[1] Hebr. i. 7 = Ps. ciii (civ). 4.
[2] See above, p. 435; below, p. 448.
[3] *Orat.* XXVIII 31 (70. 3–7).
[4] *Ibid.* (70. 14). See below, p. 445.
[5] See above, p. 442; below, p. 450.
[6] *Orat.* XX 1 (*PG* 35. 1065 A–B).
[7] See above, p. 427.
[8] *Orat.* XXVII 3 (4. 19 – 5. 2, *PG* 36. 13 D–16 A). Cf. Plato, *Phaedo*, 67 B. See below, ps.-Dionys., p. 465.
[9] *Orat.* XXXIX 8 (*PG* 36. 344 A).
[10] 229 f. (*PG* 37. 139 f.).
[11] *Orat.* XX 12 (*PG* 35. 1080 B). See also *Orat.* XXVI 9 (*PG* 35. 1240 A–B).
[12] See above, pp. 426–7. Boethius, *Cons. phil.* prose i, 4, describes a vision of a person whose garments are embroidered with a Π and a Θ, connected by a ladder. Boethius probably studied in Alexandria, and both he and Gregory may be using a common Alexandrian source.

to expound divine matters because he was first purified by the Holy Spirit.[1] He attained the episcopate (which, according to the ps.-Dionysius, corresponds to perfection in the Ecclesiastical Hierarchy) 'not by receiving baptism and instruction at the same time, as is the case with most of those who nowadays aspire to that office, but in accordance with the order and law of the spiritual ascent' (τάξει καὶ νόμῳ πνευματικῆς ἀναβάσεως).[2] The influx of unworthy persons to holy orders, the 'glossalgia' of heretics, the abominations of the pagan mysteries, all result from disturbing the sequence of purification, illumination, perfection,[3] which expresses the hierarchic harmony of the universe.

Each of these three stages of the ascent is again subdivided into three, typified in the first two cases by the three kinds into which the human race is divided according to whether it rejects, partially accepts, or totally receives the Revelation: pagan, Jew, and Christian. Pagans become Jews by renouncing idols but retaining sacrifices, Jews become Christians by renouncing sacrifices but retaining circumcision, and eventually Christians ascend from sensible to intelligible symbols by abandoning circumcision.[4] But each change represents a gradual withdrawal from the *sensibilia*, which a man may either regard as realities in their own right and so become an idolater,[5] 'or else, through the beauty and ordered hierarchy of the visible things, he gets to know God, using his power of vision to ascend to that which is beyond vision (τῶν ὑπὲρ τὴν ὄψιν), careful not to defraud God of his excellence by attributing it to things seen'.[6]

For to each suppression or purification there is a corresponding access of illumination:

I find the same sort of thing in the case of theology, but in the contrary sense: in the former case the changes were effected by suppression, while here perfection is acquired by additions . . . the Old Testament proclaimed the

[1] *Orat.* XLIII 65 (*PG* 36. 584A).

[2] *Ibid.* 25 (*PG* 35. 532A–B). Cf. above, p. 442.

[3] *Orat.* II 76 (*PG* 35. 484A–B); XX 4 (*PG* 35. 1069A–B); XXXVIII 7 (*PG* 36. 317B–C); XXXIX *ad fin.* (*PG* 36. 357D–360A); XLV 3 (*PG* 36. 528A). See above, p. 427; below, p. 452.

[4] *Orat.* XXXI 25 (177. 7–17, *PG* 36. 161B). Cf. above, p. 439, and for other patristic texts illustrating this theme, Thomassin, *Dogmata theologica*, *De Incarnatione*, X 3–4; Bonsirven, *Épître aux Hébreux*, p. 425.

[5] *Orat.* XXVIII 13 (43. 9–13, *PG* 36. 44A–B). See also chs. 14, 15.

[6] *Ibid.* (43. 13–16).

Father clearly, the Son obscurely; the New revealed (ἐφανέρωσεν) the Son, and implied (ὑπέδειξε) the divinity of the Holy Spirit; now the Holy Spirit dwells among us and is manifesting himself more clearly (ἐμπολιτεύεται... σαφεστέραν...παρέχον τὴν ἑαυτοῦ δήλωσιν). As long as the divinity of the Father was not yet recognized, it would not have been prudent to proclaim openly that of the Son; and as long as the divinity of the Son was not admitted, it would have been wrong, if I may say so, to impose upon men a new burden in speaking to them of the Holy Spirit...It was necessary to proceed by progressive additions...and ascents (ἀναβάσεις), and to advance from glory to glory.[1]

Finally, the revelation of the Spirit, which represents the perfection of the Divine Nature as Trinity,[2] also emerges by three stages: first as being sent by the Father at the request of the Son, demonstrating the Father's authority; then as being sent by the Son, showing that the authority of the Father and the Son are equal; finally as coming in his own authority, showing that he is equal to the Father and the Son in one Trinity.[3]

From these passages it is seen that the three degrees of the ascent are not temporally successive, but are three aspects, a negative and a positive, and a third which lies outside the human categories of negative and positive and relates to a corroborating activity within the Divine Nature itself. Christian baptism is not the only purification but the 'first', and at the same time the first illumination (φωτισμός);[4] and enlightenment is a second and continuing purification[5]—continuing because the closer one approaches to absolute Purity the more impure one discovers oneself to be, so that illumination includes a progressive revelation of fresh motives for purification.[6] Finally, neither purification nor illumination is annihilated in deification. Speaking to one well advanced in spirituality but suffering from discouragement Gregory says: 'Let us purify our intellect (νοῦς) by the experience brought by

[1] *Orat.* XXXI 26 (178. 1–15, *PG* 36. 161 C–D). The last phrase is taken from Ps. lxxxiii. 6–8 (lxxxiv. 5–7). For ἀναβάσεις see above, p. 443.

[2] It must be remembered that Gregory is writing at a time when the divinity of the Holy Spirit was still a matter of debate. From his point of view it was natural to identify the establishment of this truth (which was one of his major aims as a theologian) with the eventual perfection of man's knowledge of the Divine Nature.

[3] *Orat.* XXXI 26 (179. 6–19, *PG* 36. 164 A–B). He refers respectively to John xiv. 16; xiv. 26; xvi. 7.

[4] *Orat.* XL 3–7 (*PG* 36. 361–8).

[5] *Orat.* XXXVIII 16 (*PG* 36. 329 B–C); XL 3, 4, 8, 19, 26, 29, 32 (*PG* 36. 360–425); XLV 9 (*PG* 36. 633 B–636 A).

[6] Plagnieux, *op. cit.* p. 150 n. 99.

God upon us (θείαις ἐμφάσεσιν).'[1] 'Purification is illumination, and illumination is the accomplishment of all desires, at least for those who are bent on ascending to the heights, or rather, to the Most Highest, or better still, to him who is above every height.'[2]

In linking the three purificative–illuminative–perfective stages of the approach to the ultimate truth with the three stages of man's development, pagan, Jew and Christian, Gregory foreshadows the three hierarchies upon which the system of the ps.-Dionysius is constructed, the Legal, the Ecclesiastical, and the Celestial; for the abandonment of idols and the revelation of the Father constitute the ascent from paganism to the monotheism of the Law; the abandonment of sacrifices and the revelation of the Son, the ascent from the Law to the Gospel upon which the Church is founded; and the abandonment of earthly for celestial symbols which is in the process of being effected by the Holy Spirit[3] is the final ascent through the intelligible world of the angels to deification.[4] Gregory adumbrates the synthesis of the Christian revelation with the triadic structure of the Neoplatonic universe which the ps.-Dionysius was later to expound:[5] the triple rhythm of *monê*, *proodos*, *epistrophê*, God as the immutable source of enlightenment, the dissemination of enlightenment through the Christian Tradition, and the return of the creature through increasing degrees of purification, illumination, and perfection to the Creator; the triple nature of the Deity; the triple hierarchy of angels, the Church and the Law.

Gregory's assimilation of Christianism to Platonism is thus much more profound and has wider implications than Basil's. Both are Christian Platonists but they combine the two elements in different ways. Basil uses selected pagan doctrines to support the revealed truth where he considers it requires it; Gregory expounds the Scriptures which contain the whole truth adequately for faith in the terms of pagan thought as a whole so that the truth may be expressed, as far as possible, adequately for reason. A movement of spiritualization culminating in deification,[6] effected by the divine condescension which will

[1] *Epist.* CCXV. [2] *Orat.* XXXIX 8 (*PG* 36. 344A). [3] See p. 445 n. 2.

[4] *Orat.* XXXI 25 (176. 3–9, *PG* 36. 160B–161B). See below, p. 460.

[5] That the Dionysian writings are post-Cappadocian is about the only thing that can be said with confidence about their historical position: see below, p. 457 n. 8

[6] Cf. *Orat.* XI 6 (*PG* 35. 840); XLI 1 (*PG* 36. 428A–429B).

not cease until it has penetrated the whole of human, and even cosmic, reality, in co-operation with the aspiration of the human will and intellect, constitute an interaction of descent and ascent which is not far removed from the teaching of Plotinus.[1] But this philosophy, though expressed in Neoplatonic terminology, is embodied in the Incarnation: 'the descended God (ὁ κάτω θεός) became man that I may become God to the extent that he became man.'[2]

C. *St Gregory of Nyssa* (d. *394*)

St Gregory of Nyssa, closest of all the Cappadocians to Origen in thought,[3] restated St Basil's biblical exegesis in terms of the Alexandrian Gnosis.[4] Where his brother had interpreted the Hexaëmeron literally (ἱστορικῶς),[5] Gregory, in his commentary[6] and sequel to it,[7] interpreted it anagogically[8] as 'nothing less than the philosophy of the soul, with the perfected creature (τέλειον) as the final result of a necessary order of evolution'.[9] It is not necessary to follow the scriptural order of events since the Creation was a single act of the Divine Will outside time.[10] From it sprang instantaneously the potentialities of all things, which, being seminal (σπερματικαί),[11] develop, without further divine intervention,[12] successively[13] into all the phenomena which can and will constitute the world.[14]

Regarded as a single seminal power these potentialities (δυνάμεις) or 'surges' (ἀφορμαί) or causes (αἰτίαι)[15] are the Logos, whose unity is eternal and therefore is never wholly lost in the multiplicity of creation but holds it together and is the means by which it may in due course (διὰ βαθμῶν) ascend from the less to the more perfect,[16] from the minimal being of purely potential matter to its information,

[1] Cf. Plagnieux, *op. cit.* p. 148 n. 94.

[2] *Orat.* XXIX 19 (*PG* 36. 100A).

[3] J. Daniélou, *Platonisme et théologie mystique* (ed. 2, Paris, 1953), p. 144.

[4] Above, p. 429.

[5] Greg. Nyss. *Contra Eunomium*, II (XII/XIII), 255 (*PG* 45. 996D, I 300, 29) (references in brackets following the *PG* reference are to volume, page and line of Jaeger's edition, Leiden, 1960).

[6] *Apologia in Hexaëmeron* (*PG* 44. 61–124).

[7] *De hominis opificio* (*PG* 44. 126–256).

[8] Above, p. 438.

[9] Greg. Nyss. *Apol.* (*PG* 44. 64C f.). See above, p. 425.

[10] Above, p. 432.

[11] *Apol.* 77D.

[12] Greg. Nyss. *In ps. vi* (*PG* 44. 610B–C).

[13] *Apol.* 72B–C, 113B, 121D.

[14] Cf. Plotinus, III I [3] 7, 3–4. See above, p. 437.

[15] *Apol.* 72A–B.

[16] *De hom. opif.* VIII (*PG* 44. 148B).

vivification (ὕλη ζωοπλασθεῖσα),[1] sensitivization, rationalization and deification.

Created light, the first physical manifestation of the Divine Will,[2] inheres from the beginning in the particles of matter,[3] from which it naturally flows out (where it is not hindered by those elements which, because of their opacity, will not receive it)[4] to the Firmament or First Heaven which divides the sensible from the intelligible world.[5] Hence it is reflected back again, and this dilation and illation of light is the cause of the cycle of days and nights.

Each element seeks its proper place, the heaviest at the centre, the lightest at the circumference.[6] This is fire, which, because of the subtlety of its nature, is intermediary between the sensible and intelligible worlds.[7] Therefore the waters above the Firmament cannot be the sensible element[8] but represent the celestial intelligences.[9] They comprise the Second Heaven, which is the boundary of the whole creation, visible and invisible. There is no mention in Moses' 'historical account' of the Third Heaven to which St Paul was rapt[10] since this comprises 'all those things which cannot be explained in words, namely, the beauty of Paradise',[11] the uncreated powers[12] of which the intelligibles are the conceivable copies.

The only creature who is not confined to one side or other of the First Heaven which separates the sensible from the intelligible world is man. As animal he belongs to the one, as rational soul to the other. Therefore he is a 'borderline case' (μεθόριος)[13] and a means of transition from the one to the other.[14] Furthermore, since all higher powers include what is below them, man as rational animal is the summation of the

[1] Greg. Nyss. *C. Apollin.* (*PG* 45. 1256A).
[2] Above, p. 433.
[3] *Apol.* 72D.
[4] *Apol.* 76C.
[5] *Apol.* 76D.
[6] *Apol.* 80D–81A.
[7] *Apol.* 80D–81A, 81C–D, 116B, 121A. A Pythagorean idea taken over by Plotinus. Cf. Aristotle, *De gen. et corr.* 335a; Plotinus, I 6 [1] 3, 21–2; Burnet, *Early Greek Philosophy* (ed. 3, 1920), p. 109; A. H. Armstrong, *The Architecture of the Intelligible Universe in the Philosophy of Plotinus* (Cambridge, 1940), pp. 54–5. See above, p. 435.
[8] *Apol.* 84C–D, 124B.
[9] Above, p. 433.
[10] *Apol.* 64D. See above, p. 433.
[11] *Apol.* 121D. Below, p. 455.
[12] Above, p. 430.
[13] Greg. Nyss. *In ps. vii* (*PG* 44. 457B); *Orat. cat.* VI (*PG* 45. 25C–28A). Cf. Nemesius, *De nat. hom.* I (*PG* 40. 505B–517A (after Posidonius)); Eriugena, *Periphyseon*, II (*PL* 122. 531B); below, p. 530.
[14] Greg. Nyss. *In ps. vii*, *loc. cit.*

whole sensible world. Animal, vegetable, and inanimate matter are all involved in his creation,[1] which is therefore the fruit of which the visible world is the seed.[2]

But by origin he belongs to the intelligible world,[3] and therefore human nature, with the sensible and intelligible worlds which are fused together in it, may ascend to the Second Heaven, and through it to the Third, so that all things may partake in equal measure of the Beatific Vision.[4] It is man's duty and destiny to be the agent by which the whole universe, in himself, is restored to its pristine nature, and to present it in him as a unity to the One.[5]

Therefore the creation of man, omitted from Basil's account of the creation,[6] is the dénouement which reveals its significance. Gregory supplies the omission in the *De hominis opificio*,[7] and in doing so embarks upon a Christian version of the Neoplatonic theory of the descent and return of the soul, which is the basic theme running through his most important treatises, the *De hominis opificio* itself, *In Ecclesiastem*,[8] *De virginitate*,[9] *In canticum canticorum*,[10] and the *Life of Moses*.[11]

Man was first created in the Second Heaven[12] and therefore an intelligible and incorporeal being.[13] But since he was made in the image and likeness of God,[14] differing from his Prototype only as the created differs

[1] Idem, *De hom. opif.* XXX (*PG* 44. 252B–253A). Cf. Eriugena, *op. cit.* II 530D.

[2] Greg. Nyss. *De anima et resurrectione* (*PG* 46. 128A). Cf. Aeneas, below, p. 486.

[3] Below, pp. 453; 508

[4] Greg. Nyss. *De hom. opif.* VIII (*PG* 44. 144D–148C); *Orat. cat.* VI (*PG* 45. 25B–28A).

[5] Below, p. 504.

[6] Above, p. 438 n. 3.

[7] In fact Basil did eventually produce his promised homily on the creation of man, which survives in the form of lecture notes (printed in *PG* among the works of Greg. Nyss. under the title *In verbis, Faciamus*...), and in a revised version (printed among the works of Basil as *De structura hominis*), but Gregory does not seem to have known this. See S. Giet, 'Saint Basile a-t-il donné une suite aux homélies de l'Hexaéméron?', *Recherches de science religieuse*, XXXIII (1946), pp. 317–58; J. Bernardi, 'La date de l'Hexaéméron de s. Basile', *Studia patristica*, III (1961), p. 169.

[8] *PG* 44. 616 f.

[9] *PG* 46. 317 f.; ed. Jaeger, *Opera ascetica s. Greg. Nyss.* (1952), pp. 247 f.

[10] *PG* 44. 756–1120; ed. H. Langerbeck, Leiden, 1960, cited here with references in brackets following the *PG* reference.

[11] *PG* 44. 279–429; ed. J. Daniélou, *SC* I *bis*, used here with references to columns of *PG* which this edition retains.

[12] *De hom. opif.* XVII 189A; *PG* 44. 508C; *De virgin.* 324B; above, p. 448.

[13] *PG* 46. 41C; below, p. 453.

[14] For Gregory the two terms denote the substantival and verbal aspects of the same thing: εἰκών is the divine resemblance in its actuality, ὁμοίωσις the sustained effort to preserve it. See J. T. Muckle, 'The doctrine of St Gregory of Nyssa on Man as the Image of God', *Medieval Studies*, VII (Toronto, 1945), pp. 56, 59, 60; Daniélou, *Platonisme et théologie* (ed. cit.), p. 48. Contrast St Maximus, below, p. 503.

from the uncreated,[1] he is not only intelligible but also one. The image is found in the totality of human nature.[2] Plurality and composition come with corporeality, which is no part of the original image but 'comes from outside' (ἔξωθεν γενέσθαι).[3]

It comes, that is to say, from the sensible world, where man was created a second time[4] as the individual Adam on the Sixth Day. He is still in the image of God, a 'figure moulded of earth which is a copy (εἰκόνισμα) of the Supernal Power',[5] but now his nature reflects not only what is above but also what is below. He looks down upon the nature that has been created beneath him as well as upward towards the unmanifested God whose theophany he recognizes it to be.[6] The purpose of the First Creation was that he might in the Image, as in a mirror,[7] see and know the transcendent God, otherwise invisible and unknowable,[8] and so conform himself to him:[9] the purpose of the Second was to provide him with a means of knowing God in his immanence when the Fall, by obscuring the Image, should have concealed the knowledge of him in his transcendence.

But the descent from unity to multiplicity already preconditions the Fall. For although the accretions that the soul has received 'from without', the concupiscent and irascible passions, are a divine provision for life in the sensible world,[10] they form no part of the image of the Absolute Good. They are accidental to it,[11] and cast the first shadow on

[1] *De hom. opif.* XVI 184C.

[2] *De hom. opif.* XVI 185C; *De an. et res.* (*PG* 46. 160C); below, p. 463.

[3] *De an. et res.* (*PG* 46. 57B). Cf. Philo, *De opif. mund.* 134; Muckle, *art. cit.* p. 58 n. 9; below, pp. 463–4. Contrast Leontius, below, p. 508.

[4] *De hom. opif.* II 133B; XVI 181B. Cf. Maximus, below, p. 499.

[5] *Orat. cat.* VI (*PG* 45. 28B).

[6] *De hom. opif.* II 132D–133A; *In cant. cant.* XI (*PG* 44. 1009D, 335. 12 – 336. 1).

[7] Greg. Nyss. *De beatitudinibus* (*PG* 44. 1272A–C). See above, p. 443. The Mirror was an important symbol in the Dionysiac Mysteries for the fall from unity into multiplicity. Damascius (ps.-Olympiodorus, *In Phaed.* B III. 4 Norvin) expounds Plotinus, IV 3 [27] 12, 1–2, 'The souls of men, beholding images of themselves in the sensible world as in the Mirror of Dionysus, were drawn by desire towards them and so established themselves there', as follows: 'For the soul must first imprint an image of herself upon the body—that is what is meant by providing the body with a soul. Next she conceives a passion for the image as like is drawn to like. Finally she is shattered into fragments...and dispersed over the face of the world.' Both St Augustine and St Gregory are familiar with this imagery: see St Aug. *In ps. xcv, xv*; Greg. Nyss. *De an. et res.* (*PG* 46. 157A); εἰς πλῆθος κατεμερίσθη.

[8] *De beat. loc. cit.*

[9] *In cant. cant.* IV (*PG* 44. 833A–B, 104. 10–15).

[10] See p. 451 note 1 below.

[11] See below, p. 452.

its brightness. They are relative goods, and a relative good is a relative evil.

The concupiscent and irascible parts of the soul prepare the ground for further accretions which are the occasions of sin. To both series of accretions Gregory gives the name of 'passions' (πάθη), but when he wishes to distinguish the second he calls them 'vicious passions' (πάθη κατὰ κακίαν). For the first are neither good nor evil. In the animal kingdom they are virtues, protecting and preserving life,[1] and may become so for man too when he descends to that level.[2] Gregory uses a passage from Exodus[3] and Plato's Myth of the Charioteer to illustrate this. Reason is the lintel of the soul, and the concupiscent and irascible passions are the doorposts which, as long as they remain in position, far from introducing sin, prevent its entry:[4] or reason is the charioteer and the passions are his two horses. So long as he is in control and directs them towards objects that are real and good or away from those that are illusory or evil, then 'the irascible will generate the virtue of courage, and the concupiscent will desire what is divine and incorruptible'.[5] But if the gateway is overthrown 'so that what should be above is below, and reason is thrown to the ground...and the concupiscent and irascible dispositions are set above it, then the destroyer enters within':[6] 'if reason loses hold of the reins...and falls back behind the chariot and is dragged along by it wherever the irrational urge of the horses carries it, then the tendencies (ὁρμαί) of the soul are changed to the passions we observe in the animals'.[7] These are the vicious passions.

Thus, the soul's descent is marked by three crises: from her first creation in the intelligible world in the image of God she passes through her second creation in the sensible world, where she is clothed[8] in the passions required for her life there, to the Fall in which she becomes tarnished with the vicious passions. They divide the descent into three stages, entry into intelligible being, entry into sensible being, entry into

[1] A notion taken from Posidonius. See K. Gronau, *Poseidonios und die jüdisch-christliche Genesisexegese* (Leipzig, 1914); E. von Ivanka, 'Die Quelle von Ciceros De natura deorum ii 45–60 (Poseidonios bei Gregor von Nyssa)', *Archivium philologicum* (1935), pp. 1–62.

[2] *De hom. opif.* XVIII 192B.

[3] Exodus xii. 22.

[4] *Vit. Moys.* (*PG* 44. 353CD).

[5] *De an. et res.* (*PG* 46. 61B). Cf. Synesius, *De regno*, X A.

[6] *Vit. Moys.* (*PG* 44. 353C–D).

[7] *De an. et res. loc. cit.*; cf. Synesius, *loc. cit.*; Leontius, below, p. 491.

[8] See below, p. 452.

sin, which in the return must be traversed in the reverse direction,[1] by purification, illumination, and perfection in union with God.[2]

In the *De virginitate*[3] Gregory describes the three stages as the abandonment of marriage; purification from the thoughts of the flesh; and the recovery of confidence (παρρησία) to appear before the Creator. By marriage he means the sexual mode of propagation and, by extension, the lusts of the flesh.[4] It is a moral purification from the vicious passions that he has in mind.[5] Purification from the thoughts of the flesh, on the other hand, signifies the renunciation of the fantasies by which the senses beguile us into error. These represent the sensible phenomena as realities in themselves, whereas 'all things that are fair to the sensual eye are deceptive appearances: in their own nature they are inconstant and transitory, having neither existence nor substance'.[6] This renunciation is an enlightenment: 'The soul is alienated from the sleep of illusion when she has been enlightened by the truth.'[7] This light was the garment with which the soul was clothed when she was in the intelligible world, which she exchanged for the 'tunics of skin', i.e. the passions, when she descended into the sensible world,[8] and which she puts on again now that she returns to the intelligible.

Whereas the tunics of skin were a weight that kept the soul down at the sensible level, the garment of light is a winged chariot that carries her aloft.[9] The garment of light is identified with Christ,[10] the winged

[1] *De virg.* (*PG* 46. 373C–376C). The traditional view that the return must be by the same road as the descent (cf. *Corp. Herm.* X 16; Plotinus, I6[I] 7, 3–5; Proclus, *El. theol.* 38) probably originates in Heraclitus: 'The way up is the way down' (fr. 69 Bywater).

[2] Above, pp. 427; 444.

[3] *Loc. cit.*

[4] Probably Gregory's language was influenced by the subject of the treatise and the fact that it was delivered to a monastic audience. See Maximus, below, p. 503.

[5] Above, p. 427.

[6] *In Eccles.* (*PG* 44. 737C). Cf. *In ps.* (*PG* 44. 445B); Plotinus, IV 4 [7] 44, 5–6 and 25–7.

[7] *In cant. cant.* XI (*PG* 44. 996D, 317. 13–16). Cf. Valentinus, *Gospel of Truth*, Jung Codex ed. Malinine–Puech–Quispel (Zurich, 1956): 'They cast ignorance from them as they would sleep...they abandon (the phantoms of sensual experience) as they would a nocturnal dream.'

[8] Genesis iii. 21. Cf. Greg. Nyss. *Orat. cat.* VIII 4 (*PG* 46. 148D); above, p. 451. The analogy had long existed in pagan thought, applied to the body as the soul's vesture (see Empedocles, fr. 126: Diels, *Vors.* ed. 5, I 362), and is so used by Porphyry, *De abst.* I 31, 109. 17; II 46, 174. 29 Nauck (perhaps influenced by Genesis) and by the Valentinian gnostics: see St Iren. *C. haeres.* I 5, 5; VII 501 = Tertullian, *Adv. Valentinianos*, XXIV (*PL* II 578). For the inappropriateness of this application to Christianism see above, p. 426.

[9] *De virg.* (*PG* 46. 365B). Like the Charioteer, this is a notion borrowed from the *Phaedrus*, and is frequently used by the Neoplatonists. Cf. Proclus, *El. theol.* 209, 182. 16–23 Dodds.

[10] *In cant. cant.* X (*PG* 44. 1005A, 328. 11). Cf. Rom. xiii. 14; Maximus, below, p. 503.

chariot is the Holy Spirit in the form of a dove.[1] Both manifest themselves on the intelligible level as the rays (ἀπόρροιαι) or *energeiai* which come down from the 'Father of Lights' and are the exemplars of the virtues in the soul and of the reality which lies behind the illusions of the sensible world. Illumined by them the soul recognizes the phenomena to be the effects of the *energeiai* and in doing so contemplates the *energeiai* themselves.

'Those who have rejected the deceitful and unreal fantasy of worldly occupations shall behold the underlying reality (ὑπόστασις) of things, and become sons of light.'[2] The underlying reality of things is their likeness to God and their participation in him. Therefore the phenomena, dangerous to those they deceive, are for the illuminated soul signposts which point to that which they imitate and in which they participate.

When, in search of the Beautiful, the uninstructed mind sees something in which there is an appearance of beauty he supposes that this...is beautiful in itself, and sees no need to search further. But he who has purified the eye of his soul...dismisses the matter in which the Form (ἰδέα) of Beauty manifests itself, and makes of the visible object a vantage-point from which to contemplate that intelligible Beauty by participation in which all beautiful things are beautiful.[3]

The soul may then derive from her contemplation of 'the beauty of the heavens, the light of the stars and their swift courses about the pole, the earth which reflects them in the seasons which follow their revolutions, and the various species of animals and plants' symbols which enable her to conceive their Maker.[4]

By purification and illumination the soul has now attained the intelligible level, where the Image was first established: by purification she reached the First Heaven 'on the frontier (μεθόριος) between the human and the incorporeal natures',[5] and by illumination the Second Heaven where she has become one of the 'sons of light', for the restoration of

[1] *In cant. cant.* v (*PG* 44. 868D–869A, 150. 13 – 151. 2).
[2] *In cant. cant.* vi (*PG* 44. 884B, 170. 3–11).
[3] *De virgin.* (*PG* 46. 364B–C).
[4] *In cant. cant.* (*PG* 44. 1009C, 335. 1 – 336. 1). This is the art which, in the ps.-Dionys., becomes the Symbolical Theology. See below, pp. 462–3.
[5] Greg. Nyss. *Vita Macrinae* (*PG* 46. 972A). See above, p. 442.

the Image, the knowledge of God by participation, and the return of man to the society of the angels all mean the same thing.[1]

But the return of the soul to the point whence she set out does not, as in Platonism, mean her deification, for she never was divine.[2] There still remains the last stage of her journey to the Third Heaven.

The soul rises again and...goes about the intelligible and hypercosmic world[3]...where the Principalities dwell, and the Dominations, and the Thrones assigned to the Powers; she frequents the assemblies of the celestial beings...and mingles with the numberless throng, seeking her Beloved there...and...begins to question if even the angels can apprehend him whom she loves. They give her no answer, but by their silence make it plain that he is inaccessible even to them.[4] So...she abandons all that she has found there, and finds her Beloved in her very inability to grasp that which he is.[5]

Her situation would now seem to be tragic. The very light in which she was clothed after her purification and which gave her a clear view of the beauty of the universe, and through it of the virtues in which it was created, has become so intense that it is now a darkness[6] blinding her from him she seeks. She has climbed from peak to peak only to arrive at the verge of an abyss which offers no foothold or handhold.[7] When she renounced the senses, she was still aided by the intellect, which is her purified self, but now this too 'appears to undergo self-dissolution for it must divest itself of its essence. This advance evacuates the soul more completely than the moral renunciation, for while that affected the actions judged, this affects the judgement itself.'[8]

[1] Daniélou, *Platonisme et théologie mystique*, ed. cit. p. 161.

[2] See above, p. 426.

[3] Cf. ps.-Dionys., below, pp. 463–4.

[4] St Gregory's angelology owes much to Philo, for whom 'the sphere of pure intelligences is still not absolutely concentrated in God. It knows God through the multiplicity of the "Powers" which are at one and the same time aspects of the divine operation in the universe and the various and complementary modes under which we contemplate the divine unity. The Powers are not different from the intelligences...They are mediations, indispensable for the practice of the worship of God, though not for the explanation of the cosmos. If God operates directly upon the universe, it does not follow that souls ascend directly to God' (J. Trouillard, *La Purification plotinienne* (Paris, 1955), p. 175); cf. É. Bréhier, *Les Idées philosophiques et religieuses de Philon d'Alexandrie* (Paris, 1925), p. 175.

[5] *In cant. cant.* VI (*PG* 44. 893A–B, 182. 5 – 183. 3). Cf. *C. Eun.* II (XII) (*PG* 45. 920–1, I 235. 4 – 237. 10); I 345A, I 116. 18 – 117. 5; *Vit. Moys.* (*PG* 44. 377A). See ps.-Dionys., p. 470.

[6] Below, p. 470.

[7] *PG* 44. 729A–732A.

[8] Trouillard, *La Procession plotinienne* (Paris, 1955), p. 67.

But while the soul cannot ascend beyond the intelligible world by her inherent faculty of gnosis (for gnosis is of the Powers),[1] the moment she relinquishes it she is upheld by an external force which is something more than gnosis (ἐπίγνωσις). This is Faith, which reveals that the Deity surpasses every determining symbol:[2] 'It is by faith that I who have abandoned all intelligible aids have found my well-beloved.'[3] As Christ, revealing himself as light, brought gnosis, so Christ, communicating himself as faith, brings Love, in which alone the ascent from the many to the One is at last consummated: 'When the soul has become simple, unified (μονοειδής) and Godlike (θεοείκελος), she cleaves to this only true and desirable Beloved by the living *energeia* of Love',[4] for 'the end of love is physical union with the beloved'.[5] Like St Paul she is now rapt into the Third Heaven in super-intelligible unification.[6]

But the Third Heaven is not a station, like the First and Second. The soul 'is transformed into that of which the apprehension and discovery are eternal processes'.[7] The restored image, as perfect man, has become one with Christ the Perfect Man, but not one with Christ as God, for God is absolutely transcendent.[8] In Plotinus' philosophy transcendent and immanent coalesce in the divinity of the soul[9] and 'the transfiguration of the soul consists in the realization of its most pure activity, not in an addition to itself.... Therefore transcendence and immanence imply each other.'[10] But for Gregory the soul is the image of the Divine, not the Divine itself, and the mutual implication of transcendent and immanent is never realized in the soul, but in the consubstantiality of the Son. This remains a mystery: but though inaccessible to the intellect, it is grasped by faith, which reveals the Third Heaven as an insatiable joy,

[1] *Vit. Moys.* (*PG* 44. 380A). See below, p. 459.

[2] *C. Eun.* II (XII B/XIII) 89 (*PG* 45. 940D–941A, I 252. 24 – 253. 17). See ps.-Dionys., below, pp. 466–7.

[3] *In cant. cant.* VI (*PG* 44. 893B, 183. 7–8). Cf. *C. Eun.* II (XII B/XIII), 56–7 (*PG* 45. 928, I 242. 11–17); 90–1 (941B, 253. 18 f.). See above, p. 434.

[4] Greg. Nyss., *PG* 46. 93C.

[5] Idem, *PG* 44. 737D–740A. Cf. ps.-Dionys., below, pp. 470–1.

[6] See above, pp. 427; 448.

[7] Idem, *PG* 46. 93C. [For the origin of this idea in Plotinus see Part III (Plotinus), ch. 15, pp. 246–7.]

[8] Cf. Eriugena, below, p. 530.

[9] Cf. Plotinus, IV 8 [6] 1, 1–3 with Greg. Nyss. *De inst. Christ.* XL 1–9 (*PG* 46. 288A). For the divinity of the soul see Proclus, *De dec. dub.* 64. 10–12 Boese, and above, p. 426.

[10] Trouillard, *Proc. plot.* p. 65. Cf. idem, *Purif. plot.* pp. 14–15; Plotinus, V 1 [16] 11.

insatiable because the distance between the soul and God is infinite, joy because the soul has become one with her Beloved, who is one with God.

> The beauty (of the Beatific Vision) reveals itself with ever-increasing clarity, the divine majesty exceeds more and more as the soul advances, and the perpetual discovery of new delights in the transcendent realm makes each seem the beginning of a fresh ascent....He who makes the true ascent must ascend for ever, and for him who runs towards the Lord there will never be wanting a wide space in which to pursue this divine course.[1]

The *energeia* of love is called living because it never dies of satiety; and it is the joy of everlasting anticipation of further joy that makes the Beatific Vision the supreme end of man.

St Gregory of Nyssa is the first Christian philosopher. Upon the revealed truth which St Basil had defended and St Gregory Nazianzen expounded he constructed a philosophy which was as faithful to the Platonic tradition as that of Plotinus, which it closely resembles. It is directed towards the understanding of the Divine Nature as Transcendent, as true Being, and as Provident. The divine Transcendence assures the distinction between Creator and creature; the divine Being implies that the creature, whether sensible or intelligible, is but a participant in being; while the Divine Providence, through the Incarnation, effects the ultimate reunification, in man, of the whole creature, sensible and intelligible, with the Being in which it participates and from which it sprang.[2] The Providence removes the tragic element from the Transcendence, and justifies the claim of the Christians that their religion is a religion of joy.

[1] *In cant. cant.* v (*PG* 44. 876B–C, 159. 4–15). See ps.-Dionys., below, p. 470; Maximus, p. 501.
[2] See Maximus, below, p. 504.

CHAPTER 30

THE PSEUDO-DIONYSIUS

A. *Introduction*

Like the Cappadocians,[1] the ps.-Dionysius claims that he is not an innovator[2] but a communicator of the Tradition, which he presents as Christian, but which in fact comes from Christian and pagan sources. Of the former the only authorities he names are the Scriptures (including some apocryphal works),[3] but he is clearly indebted to the Cappadocians[4] and perhaps directly to the Alexandrians;[5] the pagan sources are disguised either as part of the 'unwritten tradition'[6] or under the name of his master 'Hierotheos', possibly a fiction invented to confer upon them the authority of one whom he represents as being an associate of the Apostles.[7]

The pagan element, apart from the Platonism which he inherited from his Christian sources, shows unmistakable affinity with the later Neoplatonism of which the most famous exponent was Proclus,[8] and the

[1] Cf. St Greg. Naz. above, p. 440.

[2] *CH* (= *De caelesti hierarchia*), VI 1 (*PG* III 200C10–11). The text of G. Heil (*Sources chrét.* 58, Paris, 1958) is used, but with references to column and line of *PG*, which are preserved in this edition.

[3] The Gospel of St Bartholomew (*MT* (= *De mystica theologia*), I 3, *PG* 3. 1000B11). Cf. A. Wilmart and E. Tisserant, 'Fragments grecs et latins de l'Évangile de Barthélemy', *Revue biblique*, X (1913), p. 161); the 'philosopher Clement' (*DN* (= *De divinis nominibus*), V 9, *PG* 3. 824D1), probably a conflation of the Clement mentioned by St Paul (Phil. iv. 3), St Clement of Rome with whom he was early identified (cf. Origen, *In Ioann.* VI 54; Eusebius, *Hist. eccl.* III 15; John of Scythopolis, *PG* 4. 329B), and St Clement of Alexandria, who is the author of the passage cited (below, p. 462); the 'holy Justus' (*DN*, XI 1, *PG* 3. 949A15), whom John Scyth. (*PG* 4. 393A) identifies with the Joseph Barsabbas who competed with St Matthias for the vacant apostolic throne (Acts i. 23).

[4] Especially St Gregory of Nyssa.

[5] See n. 3 above.

[6] Cf. *EH* (= *De ecclesiastica hierarchia*), I 4 (*PG* 3. 376B–C). Above, p. 428.

[7] H. F. Müller, *Dionysius, Proklos, Plotinus* (Munich, 1926), pp. 37–8; J. Vanneste, *Le mystère de Dieu* (Brussels, 1959), pp. 14, 41–2. It is perhaps significant that one of the works ascribed to Hierotheos bears the title of *Elementa theologica*, the work of Proclus which approximates most closely to the Dionysian philosophy in general principles. See below, pp. 466; 470. But I now incline to the view that Hierotheos was a real person. See I. P. Sheldon-Williams, *Studia Patristica*, VIII (*Texte und Untersuchungen* 93), 1966, pp. 108–17.

[8] Too little is known of the predecessors of Proclus to assert (as is often done), that the ps.-Dionys. depended on him directly. It can only be said that they lived in the same philosophical climate, which was that of fifth-century Neoplatonism. It follows that the known dates of Proclus do not provide evidence for dating the ps.-Dionys., a task not made easier by the fact that while

most distinctive feature the importance attached to theurgy, a special branch of *praxis* which, under the increasing weight of religious influence upon the schools of philosophy, tended to exclude the other branches in the same way as theology, a special branch of *theôria*, had already, for similar reasons, become dominant in that field.

Theurgy, like all *praxis*, was the utilization of sensible objects, but concerned itself not with their matter but with the inherent power which they were supposed to derive from the *sympatheia* which binds the whole universe together, the sensibles to the intelligibles and the intelligibles to the gods, and the control of which was therefore an automatic means of invoking divine and demonic assistance for practical ends.[1] Although the practice of theurgy had been advocated as early as Iamblichus, Christianism had hitherto been unaffected by this side of Neoplatonism, for Christians had already adapted *praxis* in their own way to the practice of the virtues.[2] The fact that they possessed scriptural authority for investing certain objects, the Sacraments of the Church, with supernatural qualities, was ignored by the early Christian philosophers. The ps.-Dionysius, however, believed in a Christian theurgy, and it is clear from the language he uses that the idea came to him from the Neoplatonists. The ascent of the soul, which in St Gregory is a gnostic process relying upon the perception of the theophanies first in the sensible and then in the intelligible worlds, is in the Dionysian system procured by the efficacy first of the rites and ceremonies of the Ecclesiastical Hierarchy, then of the orders and operations of the Celestial.

Nevertheless, on a less superficial view, the Dionysian theurgy is more closely related to the Gregorian anagogy than to the theurgy of the pagans. Since the *sympatheia* on which the latter relies was regarded as a force of nature, the demonic and divine powers inhere in the sensible objects naturally, whereas in the sacred objects of the Christian ceremonies they are there by sacramental grace; nor are they a substitute for gnosis, but supplement and confirm it.[3] In the *EH* the ps.-Dionysius is less concerned with the description of the rites than with their *theôria*, the isolation of their intelligible significance; and in the *CH* he

his pagan sources belong to the fifth, his Christian sources seem to belong to the fourth century. [On the philosophy of Proclus and his predecessors see Part IV (The Later Neoplatonists), ch. 19, pp. 302–5.]

[1] See below, p. 513. [2] Above, pp. 426; 427; 443. [3] See below, p. 463.

defines the gradations of the Hierarchy not only as orders and operations, but also as 'sciences' (ἐπιστῆμαι), i.e. prolongations of the gnosis which the soul acquires in the Ecclesiastical Hierarchy through which she will eventually arrive at the *agnôsia* (Gregory's *epignôsis*) of the Transcendent God.[1] On the other hand, the interpretation of *praxis* in theurgic rather than in moral terms has left the ps.-Dionysius, like the other late Neoplatonists, with no moral philosophy at all. Theology, which had already swallowed up the rest of *theôria*, has now engulfed *praxis* as well, a fact which the ps.-Dionysius recognizes by calling his theurgy the Symbolic Theology.[2]

If theurgy is the most distinctive feature which the Dionysian Christianism owes to the Neoplatonists, the most important is the conception of a universe which in origin and in structure, and at every level of its structure and in every part, is both monadic and triadic. The theory goes back to Plotinus, and had already influenced Christianism in formulating the doctrine of the Trinity, and in a wider application appears in the Cappadocians. But it is not obtrusive there, whereas for the ps.-Dionysius, as for the other late Neoplatonists, it is the basic principle of their system, is reflected in every detail of it, and organizes the whole throughout. Whether the subject is the universe in its totality, or God, or the Forms, or a particular Form, it reveals three aspects which are inseparable but can be treated separately: what it is in itself, which immutably remains what it is and in which nothing participates and which participates in nothing; what it is as efficient cause which can be participated in through the effects into which it proceeds; and what it is as final cause to which the effects by participation return. From the point of view of participation (or non-participation) this triad is called 'unparticipated' (ἀμέθεκτος), 'participated' (μεθεκτός), 'participating' (μετέχων); from the point of view of motion (or rest) *monê*, *proodos*, *epistrophê*;[3] from the point of view of action (or inaction) *ousia*, *dynamis*, *energeia*.[4]

[1] See below, pp. 470–1.

[2] On the Dionysian theurgy I follow in the main J. Vanneste, *Myst. dieu*, 33 f.; 'La théologie mystique du ps.-Denys l'Ar.', *Studia patristica*, v (Berlin, 1962), pp. 409 f., but depart from him in regarding it as an integral part of his theology.

[3] Above, pp. 431; 442.

[4] Above, p. 431. This triad, which must derive from Aristotle's teachings on potency and act, is first encountered in Porphyry (Iambl. *De myst.* p. xxxii Parthey) and is used both by Proclus and the ps.-Dionys. (see below, p. 466), all of whom write of it as of something too familiar to require

The writings of the ps.-Dionysius, consisting of the four treatises *DN*, *EH*, *CH*, *MT*[1] and ten *Epistles*,[2] are written with the purpose of expounding his 'theology', by which he means 'the methodical science of God'.[3] The whole work falls into three parts corresponding to the three aspects of the Divine Triad, or Thearchy, a term employed presumably because it combines the notions of plurality and singularity, and also because 'God' itself is merely one of the Names of God.[4] These three parts he calls the Cataphatic, Symbolic, and Mystical[5] Theologies. The Cataphatic Theology is the science of God as *proodos* or Efficient Cause of the Forms. It is so called because the Forms are the attributes which are affirmed of God. It is the subject of the *DN*.[6] The Symbolic Theology is the science of God as *epistrophê* or Final Cause, to Whom it ascends through sensible and intelligible symbols. The ps.-Dionysius mentions a treatise of this name, but if it ever existed it no longer survives: the subject is covered in the two *Hierarchies* and *Ep*. IX. The Mystical Theology is the science of God as *monê*, immutably inaccessible to sense and intellect, and is the subject of the treatise of that name. Each Theology falls into three sections: the Cataphatic deals with the Good, the Intelligible Triad, and a subsidiary triad which will be discussed later; the Symbolic with the Legal, Ecclesiastical and Celestial Hierarchies; the Mystical proceeds by the apophatic method,[7] so called because it denies that the affirmations applied in the Cataphatic Theology to God as Cause are relevant to God as Transcendent, through *agnôsia*, the unknowing of the Unknowable, to *henôsis*, the super-intelligible union with God. In the last two, which are anagogic, the three sections are respectively cathartic, illuminative, and unitive, and thus correspond to the three stages of the soul's ascent.[8]

explanation. John of Scythopolis is the first extant writer to feel that this was necessary, and St Maximus the first to expound this triad fully (below, pp. 492–3).

[1] To adopt the order in which they are discussed here. Internal evidence shows that the *MT* followed the *DN* and that the *EH* followed the *CH*. The probable chronological order is *DN*, *MT*, *CH*, *EH*, since *DN* seems to have been the earliest. See n. 6 below.

[2] Of these, I, II and V comment the *MT*, VIII the *EH*, and IX is a small treatise on the Symbolic Theology.

[3] *DN* I 8; II 1; III 1 *et al.*

[4] Vanneste, *Myst. dieu*, 24; see above, p. 441.

[5] Or Apophatic; but strictly speaking the Apophatic is only the first part of the Mystical Theology.

[6] The *DN* also contains matter relevant to the other theologies, and seems to have been a general introduction to the whole work.

[7] Below, p. 468.

[8] Above, p. 427; below, pp. 464–5.

B. *The Cataphatic Theology*

God as Efficient Cause is the object of knowledge (τὸ νοητόν),[1] the highest thing that can be known. The knowable is the nameable. The Divine Essence is unknowable and therefore cannot be named.[2] The name of One, employed by the Neoplatonists, in an attempt to utter what appears to be its most significant feature, is an inadequate way of saying what would be more accurately expressed by such unintelligible terms as 'that which is more unified than One' (ὑπερηνωμένη). The only 'intelligible Names of God' (θεωνυμίαι νοηταί)[3] are those of the νοητά or Forms. The first of these is his Name of Good (ἀγαθωνυμία),[4] for only this name expresses the boundless dispensation of the Divine Providence,[5] and therefore includes the notions both of efficient and of final cause:[6] it marks the point at which the divine 'unions' (ἑνώσεις) and 'separations' (διακρίσεις), that is, the modes under which the Thearchy may be regarded as one and the modes under which It may be regarded as many,[7] are still both a separation of unities and a unity of separations. It comprises the triad 'beginning' (ἀρχή), 'coherence' (συνοχή), 'end' (πέρας): *archê* and *peras* each represent one side of the double movement of separations and unions, or descent and return, of which the Good is the origin,[8] and *synochê* the bond which unites them.[9]

This triple function constitutes the hierarchic activity of the intelligible world which subsists because God 'holds together' (συνέχουσα) those things that are of the same order, and moves the higher to exercise providence over the lower and attach them to themselves, i.e. to descend to the lower that the lower may ascend to them.[10] These orders in the intelligible world result from the continuation there of the process of differentiation (διάκρισις), whereby Nous in turn becomes the triad Wisdom–Life–Being.[11] After the discussion of God as Wise, as

[1] Below, John Scyth., p. 476. [2] Below, p. 469.
[3] *MT* III (*PG* 3. 1033 A 13–14). Cf. *DN*, I 8; above, pp. 431; 435.
[4] *DN* III I (*PG* 3. 680 B 2). See below, p. 469.
[5] *DN* II I (*PG* 3. 636 C 1–12); IV 1–4, 693 B–700 C. Cf. St John Damasc. below, p. 508.
[6] *DN* I 2. [7] Below, Maximus, p. 494. [8] *DN* IV 35.
[9] E. von Ivánka, 'Der Aufbau der Schrift "Die diuinis nominibus" des ps.-Dionysius', *Scholastik*, XV (1940), pp. 389–99, shows that the sequence of Names, which it will be noticed have no biblical authority, closely resembles Plato's list of the attributes of the One in the *Parmenides*. With ἀρχή, συνοχή, πέρας cf. Maximus, below, p. 494.
[10] *DN* IV 12. See below, p. 471.
[11] *DN* II 5 (*PG* 3. 641 D 10–644 A 7). Cf. Proclus, *In Tim.* III 45.

Living, and as he who is,[1] two other names are introduced, Power and Peace.[2] They suggest a third triadization of Wisdom into Wisdom–Power–Peace, to which Constantine dedicated his three churches in Byzantium, Hagia Sophia, Hagia Dynamis and Hagia Eirene.[3] With this triad (if it can be read into the *DN*) the discussion of the Forms is brought to a close, for the remaining two chapters belong, properly speaking, to the Symbolic and Apophatic Theologies respectively, ch. XII being devoted to the Symbolic (and biblical) Names of God, King of Kings, Lord of Lords, God of Gods, while ch. XIII anticipates the *MT* by discussing the consummation of all things in the One. The triad, Wisdom–Power–Peace, appropriately sums up the discourse on the Cataphatic Theology by showing that even within its own limits it reflects the universal rhythm of *monê*, *proodos*, *epistrophê*: God is Wisdom because in him as the eternal dwelling-place of the Forms all possible being and not-being is pre-ordained; Power because he goes forth in his powers to confer existence on all things; and Peace because he brings conflict to harmony and restores the Many to the One.[4]

C. *The Symbolic Theology*

For the triad *monê*, *proodos*, *epistrophê* is reproduced in the world of Forms. As *paradeigmata*[5] they abide in the Divine Nature: as its conceivable Attributes which are studied in the Cataphatic Theology and which, as the means by which the Thearchy achieves its purpose of communicating to the Hierarchies all of it that can be known, are described as 'expressions of the Divine Providence' (πρόνοιαι ἐκφαντορικαί)[6] and 'Divine Volitions' (θεῖα θελήματα),[7] they proceed from it into

[1] *DN* V–VII.

[2] *DN* VIII and XI. Chs. IX and X consist of a digression on the applicability of the Categories to the Divine Nature.

[3] E. von Ivánka, 'Das Trias Sophia–Dynamis–Eirene im Neuplatonischen Denken und die Kirchengründungen Konstantinus des Grossen', *Communication to the 6th Congress of Byzantine Studies 1939*. The Congress was prevented by the outbreak of war, but the Communication was issued privately to delegates.

[4] *DN* XI 1 (*PG* 3. 948D1–949A1). See above, p. 461.

[5] *DN* V 9 (*PG* 3. 824C9–14). Cf. C. Kern, 'La structure du Monade d'après le ps.-Denys', *Irénikon*, XXIX (1956), pp. 205–9.

[6] *DN* III 1 (*PG* 3. 680B4–5). Cf. V. Lossky, 'La théologie négative dans la doctrine de Denys l'Ar.', *Revue des sciences philosophiques et théologiques*, XXVIII (1939), p. 208. See below, p. 475.

[7] *DN* V 9 (*PG* 3. 824C9–14). According to St Maximus (below, p. 498) this expression was first used by St Clem. Alex., probably in the *De providentia*; see Stählin, *loc. cit.* and above, p. 457 n. 3. Cf. Maximus, below, p. 498.

he intelligible and sensible worlds; and immanent there as *logoi*,[1] they re the means by which those worlds are drawn back to their Creator, nd are therefore described as 'ascensions' (ἐπιστροφαί).[2] Under the last spect they are the subject of the Symbolic Theology.

The Symbolic Theology is an ascent from the sensible to the intel-igible or knowable, to be prolonged in the Apophatic Theology from he knowable to the unknowable, culminating in the super-intelligible nion with the Transcendent One. The terms, sensible, knowable, un-nowable,[3] union,[4] have an objective as well as a subjective meaning. They may name either the attitude of the subject to the object or the uality of the object which conditions that attitude. The sensible niverse is, objectively speaking, that part of the universe which is acces-ible to the senses,[5] and as such could be the concern of the senses only. But once it is impregnated with the *logoi* as a consequence of the Divine πρόοδος, it becomes a world of symbols.[6] The *raison d'être* of a symbol loes not reside in its sensible matter which confines it to a corner of space nd time, but in its significant content. The Symbolic Theology is the cience of discarding the materiality and evoking the significance. Thus it s the first stage of the Apophatic Theology, for it proceeds by negations. But while the Symbolic Theology discards the material and retains the ignificant, the Apophatic discards the significant itself. Similarly, the Apophatic is a continuation of the Symbolic Theology, for both work rom the principle that every creature, sensible or intelligible, considered n its proper nature, and according to the capacity of its proper nature,[7] s, as St Gregory of Nyssa taught,[8] a theophany or manifestation or ymbol of the One.[9]

The *logoi* impose upon the created world the triadic structure of their ource. The symbols are therefore disposed on three levels or Hier-archies, the Legal, the Ecclesiastical and the Celestial, corresponding to

[1] C. Kern, *art. cit.* See below, pp. 467; 508.

[2] *DN* VII 3 (*PG* 3. 869 C 13–872 A 3); IV 4, 700 A 13–B 8. Cf. Proclus, *El. theol.* 39, 40. 27 – 42. 7. The secondary references to this work are to the edition of E. R. Dodds, Oxford, 1933.)

[3] See below, p. 470.

[4] See below, p. 472.

[5] R. Roques, 'Symbolisme et théologie négative chez le ps.-Denys', *Bulletin de l'Association Guillaume Budé*, ser. 4 (March 1957), pp. 98–9.

[6] Idem, *L'Univers dionysien* (Paris, 1954) (hereafter cited as *UD*), p. 53.

[7] V. Lossky, 'La notion des "analogies" chez le ps.-Denys l'Ar.', *Archives d'histoire doctrinale et littéraire du Moyen Âge*, V (1930), pp. 279–309.

[8] Above, p. 450.

[9] *CH* IV 3 (*PG* 3. 180 C 3–13).

the division of the world into things, men and angels. The ps.-Dionysius defines these as 'sacred orders (τάξεις),[1] sciences (ἐπιστῆμαι), and *energeiai*, approximating as closely as possible to deiformity, ascending towards the illuminations bestowed upon them by God in proportion to their capacity for imitating him'.[2] This definition, besides explaining the notion of theophany, shows that each Hierarchy reproduces within itself the triple movement of the Thearchy, for the 'sacred order' is permanently established, but as 'science' causes the divine radiance to descend to the order below it,[3] and as *energeia* is the means of ascent to its source. Again, in this last respect they are symbols of the three stages of the ascent of the soul to God;[4] the ascent from the Legal to the Ecclesiastical Hierarchy is a purgation of the materiality of the symbols which is irrelevant to their significance, the ascent from the Ecclesiastical to the Celestial an illumination which renders their multiplicity transparent so that through them the One can be discerned, while in the ascent from the Celestial Hierarchy to the Thearchy the Symbolic Theology is abandoned for the Apophatic, by which the soul is brought to the inexpressible union (ἕνωσις) which is the perfection of deification (θέωσις). But the three stages are not successive: each implies the other, and therefore each Hierarchy is also a triad of purifications, illuminations and perfections,[5] although the scheme is fully worked out only for the Celestial Hierarchy.

Although the ps.-Dionysius is not always consistent in his terminology,[6] he usually calls the orders within the Hierarchies *diacosmêseis*, a term also used by Alexandrians, Cappadocians and Neoplatonists.[7] In each Hierarchy the highest *diacosmêsis* consists of 'Mysteries' (τελεταί), the second of Initiators (ἐπιστήμονες, μύσται),[8] the third of those who are in the process of being initiated into the Mysteries (τελούμενοι).[9] The Mysteries are the immutable God-given Truth in so far as it can be

[1] See above, p. 442.

[2] *CH* III 1 (*PG* 3. 164D 1–10). See above, p. 443.

[3] See John Scyth, below, p. 476.

[4] Above, pp. 427; 460; below, p. 468.

[5] *CH* X 3 (*PG* 3. 273B 1–3); III 3 (168A 11–15). See above, p. 460.

[6] See, e.g. the titles of *CH* II, VIII, IX.

[7] Cf. Origen, *De princ.* I 6. 2, V 81. 3 f.; Basil, *Hex.* I 5 (*PG* 29. 13A); above, p. 435; Greg. Nyss. *C. Eun.* II 223 (I 290. 19–20); *De orat. dom.* II (*PG* 44. 1140B); *De an. et res.* (*PG* 46. 29A); Proclus, *El. theol.* 148, 130. 16–19 (διάκοσμος); Damascius, *De princ.* II 14, 136 Ruelle.

[8] An example in the Ecclesiastical Hierarchy is Hierotheos (above, p. 457), who is described as ἱερομύστης and ἱεροτελεστής.

[9] *EH* V 1 (*PG* 3. 501A 4–6).

manifested at the level of each Hierarchy,[1] which comes down through the Initiators to those who, being initiated, are converted to it. Thus the three definitions of the Hierarchy apply severally to its three *diacosmêseis*.

The sensible symbols are the most enigmatic theophanies,[2] furthest removed from their Prototype, concealing the *logoi* under a veil[3] to protect tender eyes from too strong a light.[4] This is how they appear to the Legal Hierarchy, in which the Mysteries are purely mechanical ceremonies, the significance of which is undisclosed, and the Scriptures interpreted only in their 'sensible', i.e. literal meaning.

It is in the Ecclesiastical Hierarchy that the symbols begin to be read. Its theurgy is the evocation of the significance of the rites it receives from sense and matter by the 'intelligible', i.e. anagogic interpretation of the Scriptures.[5] Its Mysteries, therefore, at once sensible and intelligible, are the the Scriptures and Sacraments,[6] its Initiators the priests who expound the one and administer the other, and its initiated the devout who receive them.[7] Each *diacosmêsis* is divided into three orders: the lowest into those who are undergoing purification (catechumens), those who are being illumined (confirmed Christians), and those who are being perfected (monks); the Initiators into those who purify (deacons), those who enlighten (priests), and those who perfect (the 'hierarchs',[8] i.e., bishops);[9] the Mysteries into the purification of Baptism,[10] the illumination of the Scriptures,[11] and the perfective and unitive rite of the Eucharist, which is the gateway to the intelligible world.[12]

The intelligible world is the highest of creatures, and therefore the purest of theophanies. The angels or intelligences (θεῖοι νόες)[13] are 'heralds of the divine Silence' bearing 'torches which light up the

[1] Cf. Proclus, *De dec. dub.* 17. 12–18 Boese.

[2] *EH* v 2 (*PG* 3. 501 B 11–14).

[3] *Ibid.*

[4] *Ibid.* 501 C. Cf. above, p. 443.

[5] Vanneste, *op. cit.* p. 28.

[6] *EH* I 4 (*PG* 3. 376 B 11–13).

[7] *EH* v 2 (*PG* 3. 501 D 4–8).

[8] This title, from which the ps.-Dionys. appears to have coined the word *hierarchia*, occurs in Greek inscriptions with the meaning of administrator of temple property and president of the sacred rites (*IG* VII 303 *ap.* Liddell and Scott (Jones)). No doubt it was because of the second function, with its clear theurgic implications, that the ps.-Dionys. prefers this name to 'bishop'.

[9] *EH* v 6.

[10] *EH* II. Cf. Roques, *UD*, ch. VIII, sec. 1; idem, 'Le sens du baptême selon le ps.-Denys', *Irénikon*, XXXI (1958), pp. 427–49.

[11] *EH* I 4 (*PG* 3. 376 B 9–14).

[12] Roques, *UD*, ch. VIII, sec. 2.

[13] Below, pp. 474; 476.

presence of him who dwells in inaccessible places'.[1] Whereas the triads of the Ecclesiastical Hierarchy are dispersed, so that the Mystery is separate from the Initiator who is separate from those he initiates who remain separate from the Mystery in which they are initiated, the intelligible triads, on a level closer to the One, co-inhere; for Nous is inseparable from its knowing and from the object of its knowledge: *ousia*, *dynamis* and *energeia* imply each other.[2] Therefore each *diacosmêsis* displays in its orders, besides its own function, those of the other two. The Mysteries consist of the Seraphim or 'burning ones',[3] so called because they are, within their Hierarchy, the source of light; the Cherubim, 'abundance of knowledge or effusion of wisdom',[4] who transmit the light;[5] and the Thrones, so called because they are the recipients of the light:[6] the Initiators, of the Dominations, who by fixing their eyes on what is above become *paradeigmata* of the Truth;[7] the Virtues (δυνάμεις), who communicate it;[8] and the Powers (ἐξουσίαι), who receive it:[9] the Initiated, of the Principalities, who, within the diminished scope of their *diacosmēsis*, have the same function as that of the Dominations;[10] the Archangels, whose name shows that they mediate between the Principalities (ἀρχαί) and the angels;[11] and the angels themselves, who are the Initiated within their own *diacosmêsis* and order, but as members of the Celestial Hierarchy share in its initiatory function towards the Ecclesiastical. 'They are initiated in the property of being messengers.'[12]

In the Dionysian Corpus the *EH* follows the *CH* for it is a copy of it in the extended world of matter, but in the logical order of the Symbolic Theology it comes first because the way of ascent is from copy to exemplar, and continues from the exemplar to the One. Always in the *EH* the initiated who is being instructed in the Scriptures or participates in the rites is invited to pass beyond the materiality to the discovery of the true and the One; by this process the theurgy of the Hierarchy as a whole participates in the intelligible operations of the

[1] *DN* IV 2 (*PG* 3. 696B 13–14).

[2] *CH* XI 2 (*PG* 3. 285D 5–6). Cf. Proclus, *El. theol.* 167 and 169; *De dec. dub.* 22. 13–19 Boese; above, pp. 455; 459.

[3] *CH* VII 1 (*PG* 3. 205B 5–6).

[4] *Ibid.* 6–7.

[5] *Ibid.* 205C 8–15.

[6] *Ibid.* 205D 6–8. Cf. Proclus, *Theol. plat.* VI 24.

[7] *CH* VIII 1 (*PG* 3. 237C 8–D 3).

[8] *CH* VIII 1 (*PG* 3. 240D 8–9).

[9] *CH* VIII 1 (*PG* 3. 240A 9–12).

[10] *CH* IX 1 (*PG* 3. 257B 6–12).

[11] *CH* IX 2 (*PG* 3. 257C 12–D 2).

[12] *CH* IX 2 (*PG* 3. 260A 3).

angels and so is set on the way from *theôria* to the transcendent gnosis which is inseparable from deification. Thus, at the very moment when the Church sets before our eyes the liturgical spectacle in all its ritual complexities, she has but the one aim, cathartic and anagogic, of encouraging, in the midst of the multiple and the sensible, the practice of the negative dialectic which tends first to the intelligible simplicity of the Celestial Hierarchy which it reflects, and thence to that of which the Celestial Hierarchy is itself a reflection, the super-celestial One.[1]

D. *The Mystical Theology*

The ascent from the Legal to the Ecclesiastical Hierarchy is a catharsis, that from the Ecclesiastical to the Celestial an illumination. St Gregory Nazianzen had already stressed the dangers of seeking illumination before purification,[2] and the ps.-Dionysius repeats the warning. If the methodical science of God does not evoke the significance of material objects from their materiality it will end in idolatry. If this is not done on the sensible plane, where the materiality of the symbol, that is to say, its unlikeness to what it symbolizes, is demonstrable to the intellect which is therefore deterred from worshipping it, it will be impossible to do on the intelligible plane where the symbols are no longer sensible objects but intelligible concepts whose likeness to what they signify is so close as to deceive the unpurified eye. The kinship (οἰκειότης, συγγένεια) which, by love, beauty, brightness, symmetry, serviceability for personal or social ends, aligns the symbol with the reality of which these qualities are affirmed by the Cataphatic Theology, allures the soul to a life lived wholly on the aesthetic, intellectual, rational or utilitarian level; and if she enters wholly into the universe of these values she will make it the exclusive object of her contemplation in the same way that sense devoid of reason is exclusively concerned with the material world. Therefore, even on the intelligible plane, the Symbolic Theology prefers to work with symbols transferred (not by human experience but on the authority of the truth revealed in the Scriptures) from the sensible to the intelligible world, rather than with those that are proper to the intelligible world and in the human view are indistinguishable from the *logoi* they conceal. The dissimilar symbol is a more dependable guide than the

[1] Roques, 'Symbolisme et théologie négative', p. 108.

[2] Above, p. 443.

similar, and the more dissimilar the more dependable. Things which belong to the lower or grosser or even monstrous and disordered levels of being are those which it is easiest to understand that God is not.[1] This principle, established by the Symbolic Theology, reaches its logical conclusion in the Apophatic which attributes to the Cause of being the name of Not-Being.

The ascent from the concept of God as Final Cause, where the Symbolic Theology arrives at the point from which the Cataphatic began, introduces the Mystical Theology, which in the medieval English version is accurately translated 'Hid Divinitie', for *mustikos* contained none of the psychological associations that have become attached to it, but simply means that, since it transcends conceptualization, it cannot be expounded but only experienced,[2] and therefore remains concealed. It is a complete anagogy in itself, in which the ascent from the Second to the Third Heaven, which St Gregory of Nyssa left unanalysed,[3] is disposed into its purificatory, illuminatory and perfective modes:[4] the discarding (ἀφαίρεσις)[5] of intellectual concepts, the transcendent gnosis which reveals that God is unknowable and is therefore *agnôsia*, and the union with the Unknowable which it implies.

The first mode is the Apophatic Theology[6] which proceeds by discarding the shapes and figures which the Cataphatic Theology derives from the First Cause and the Symbolic traces back to it again. It is still an intelligible operation, consisting of the successive negation of the Divine Names successively affirmed by the Cataphatic Theology: the two theologies operate in the same field, in contrary directions, each acting as a check upon the other. This can be most clearly seen at the end of each process: the Cataphatic Theology as expounded in the *DN* ends with such affirmations as 'King' and 'Lord', and requires the Apophatic to rescue it from anthropomorphism; the Apophatic ends with the negation that God is,[7] and requires the affirmation that God is

[1] *CH* II 3 (*PG* 3. 141 A–C). Cf. Roques, 'Symbolisme et théologie négative', pp. 101–3.

[2] Hierotheos, we are told, not only learnt but *felt* the Mysteries, οὐ μόνον μαθὼν ἀλλὰ καὶ παθὼν τὰ θεῖα (*DN* II 9, *PG* 3. 648 B 2–3). Cf. Aristotle, *fr.* 15 Rose; below, p. 470, Maximus,

[3] Above, p. 454.

[4] See above, p. 464.

[5] A Plotinian term: see above, p. 434.

[6] Above, p. 460.

[7] Cf. Plato, *Rep.* VII 519 C8–D1; 521 C1–8; Plotinus, V 3 [49] 10, 14; V 5 [32] 6, 13; V 5 [32] 13, 13; VI 7 [38] 38; above, p. 434.

the Cause of all being and therefore cannot simply not be. Even the negation that He is, is the affirmation that he is not.[1]

The Platonic view that Essence is not transcendent, but on the contrary the ground of immanence and the first manifestation at the level of exterior processions,[2] led to the dilemma of Plotinus: 'Even if we say that He is not we do not say that which He is.'[3] Although from the point of view of the Symbolic Theology Not-being may be, by virtue of its absolute dissimilarity from the Cause of being, the least deceptive symbol for the Divine Nature, yet the Cataphatic Theology shows that it is still a symbol and not totally expressive, for God is the Good, and the Good includes both being and not being;[4] and the Apophatic shows that far from being the most dissimilar, it is the most similar, and therefore the most deceptive, symbol. But the Dionysian sense of the Divine Transcendence is positive enough to withstand absorption within the categories of the similar symbolism. Although he will not, as the profane (ἄμυστοι) do, confound Creator and creation by attributing the concept of being to both,[5] neither will he, with the Platonists, stop short at the conclusion of the Apophatic Theology. He therefore introduces the term super-being (ὑπερούσιος),[6] which is neither being nor not-being, but transcends both. It is real, and therefore cannot be the object of ignorance; man is blinded by the vividness of its reality, and therefore it cannot be the object of knowledge;[7] it is God, and therefore cannot be an object at all.[8] It is not even One,[9] but a whole world filled with objects that are no objects, and which we can only name as though they were objects by the repeated use of the prefix *huper-* which, while not destroying significance, transcends it. The name which the ps.-Dionysius gives these super-objects, 'hidden objects of contemplation' (μυστικὰ θεάματα),[10] both affirms and denies that they are contemplable,

[1] See below, p. 493.

[2] E. Corsini, 'La questione areopagitica: contributi alla cosmologia dello ps.-Dionigi', *Atti della Accademia delle scienze di Torino*, XCIII (1958–9), p. 35.

[3] Plotinus, V 3 [49] 14, 6–7.

[4] Above, p. 461.

[5] See below, p. 497.

[6] For the history of this word see Corsini, *art. cit.* pp. 50–3. Below, Maximus, p. 493.

[7] V. Lossky, 'La théologie négative dans la doctrine de Denys l'Aréopagite', *Revue des sciences philosophiques et théologiques*, XXVIII (1939), p. 206. This goes further than the Cappadocians, who, like the Neoplatonists, deny only that God can be the object of knowledge. See above, pp. 434–5; 440; 454.

[8] *MT* V (*PG* 3. 1048A15–B1).

[9] Above, p. 461.

[10] *MT* I 1 (*PG* 3. 997B6).

and the *theôria* by which we do or do not contemplate them is *agnôsia*, which is the second mode or stage of the Mystical Theology.

In saying that the knowledge of God is the knowledge that he is unknowable the ps.-Dionysius agrees with the Cappadocians,[1] but he appears to be original in understanding the Divine *agnôsia* in an objective sense[2] as a quality inherent in the *mustika theamata*. The soul's satisfaction, or rather, her insatiable joy, in the discovery that to know God is to know that he is unknowable, is something more than an emotional experience, as St Gregory of Nyssa treats it.[3] It is a concrete reality. True, the *agnôsia* is not the Divine Essence itself, but only 'the place where God is',[4] like a treasure chest that may be possessed but never unlocked: yet in possessing the chest we possess the treasure.

The last stage of the Mystical Theology, the ascent from *agnôsia* to *henôsis*, is immediate, for the one implies the other. Once Moses had entered into the Divine Darkness[5] of *agnôsia* he was united in an eminent mode with him who is wholly unknowable.[6] In its subjective sense *agnôsia* is no more privative than it is in its objective sense. It does not mean a failure of the intellect, but its coalescence with God, and is thus mystical in the technical sense of the word.[7] But its role is rather passive than active.[8] *Agnôsia* excludes the sensible, and therefore cannot be demonstrated; excludes the intelligible, and therefore cannot be taught (διδακτόν); and yet is a vision of a unitive order,[9] ineffable and transdiscursive. It is indistinguishable from ecstasy and love. By ecstasy the ps.-Dionysius means not the abandonment of will and intellect but an extension of their capacities beyond their natures, where they can no longer rely upon themselves but, encountering the Divine Power which comes to meet them, that is to say, with the Divine Providence which pre-existed them,[10] the intimate force which moves the Thearchy to act,[11]

[1] Above, pp. 434; 454–5.

[2] Vanneste, *op. cit.* pp. 10, 50. Fr. Vanneste believes that this explains the choice of a pseudonym associated with St Paul's sermon on the Unknown God. See above, p. 463.

[3] Above, p. 456.

[4] *MT* I 3 (*PG* 3. 1000D6).

[5] See above, p. 454.

[6] *MT* I 3 (*PG* 3. 1001A9–10). See above, p. 459; below, p. 472.

[7] *DN* IV 13 (*PG* 3. 712A).

[8] *DN* II 9 (*PG* 3. 648B3); VII 1, 865D–868A; VII 2, 872A, *et al.*; above, p. 468.

[9] *DN* IV 6 (*PG* 3. 701B7).

[10] The ps.-Dionysius would have been familiar with the etymology of πρόνοια known to Proclus: πρὸ νοῦ, that which exists before Nous.

[11] *DN* IV 10.

in a word, Love (Ἔρως), become merged with it. The cycle of descent and return traced by the Cataphatic and Symbolic Theologies is enclosed within the erotic cycle which perpetually[1] proceeds from God through the Hierarchies, the intelligible, the sensible, the animate and the material, impressing its nature upon all,[2] and in a symmetrical return, as 'unifying power' (δύναμις ἑνοποιός), gathers together all things hierarchically into the One.[3] Since Eros is the Divine Nature Itself, and yet moves through creation, it is appropriately termed 'outgoing love' (ἔρως ἐκστατικός):[4] but it also causes ecstasy in others, for Love does not allow that those who love should belong to themselves.[5] So there are two ecstasies, or excursions from nature: God, as taught in the Cataphatic Theology, condescends from his proper Nature, which is One, to the limits of multiplicity in a theophany of innumerable symbols; and the soul, after ascending from the sensible to the intelligible in the Symbolic Theology, is in the Mystical Theology drawn out of her proper intelligible nature of the multiplicity of concepts into the absolute unity of God.[6] The product of the two ecstasies is the universal fusion in unity[7] which, with them, comprises the triad of *monê*, *proodos*, *epistrophê*.

Yet God does not depart from himself,[8] and the Divine Ecstasy is identified with the Divine Transcendence.[9] Furthermore, the bonds of love which bind the intelligibles together in their Hierarchy, and those which draw them up to the Thearchy above them to which their ascent is directed, and those which draw them down to the Hierarchy below to which they are providential,[10] do not destroy the natures which they bind together. It is only, apparently, the ascending soul that is capable of substantial ecstasy. In spite of this, however, there is no inconsistency between the 'theurgic' treatises which insist on the rigorous separation of the Hierarchies and the 'theological' treatises which seem to ignore it, for the Dionysian Hierarchies, unlike those of the Neoplatonists, are not potent in their own right but are the agents of the potency of God, who is not only the sole Efficient, but also the sole Final Cause, con-

[1] *DN* IV 14.
[2] *DN* IV 12.
[3] *DN* IV 13–17 (*PG* 3. 712A–713D).
[4] *DN* IV 13 (*PG* 3. 712A1).
[5] *Ibid.* 1–2.
[6] Roques, 'Symbolisme et théologie négative', p. 112.
[7] *DN* IV 15 (*PG* 3. 713A7–8; 17, 713D3).
[8] *DN* IV 13 (*PG* 3. 712B2–5).
[9] *Ep.* IX 5 (*PG* 3. 1112C6–14).
[10] *DN* IV 10 (*PG* 3. 708A8–10). See above, p. 461.

ditioning a return which is the same for all levels of being, the sensible world, men, and angels.[1] They are part of the material of the Symbolic Theology, the last and most similar of the symbols[2] to be rejected before the soul goes out of herself and enters the Divine Dark in ecstasy. As order, they symbolize the stability of the sequence, purification, illumination, perfection, in the ascent to God; as science the illumination which must precede the Beatific Vision; as operation the contemplation which is so intimate that she becomes what she contemplates.[3] But in the end she must pass beyond all order, all science, all operation, and the Celestial Hierarchy itself, which is the highest object of contemplation in the ordinary sense of the word,[4] and grasp the *agnôsia* of God, in which she enters upon a unity with him which is no abstract idea but his very One-ness:[5] for the super-intelligible *henôsis* denotes both her participation in God and that which he is.[6]

[1] Vanneste, *op. cit.* p. 28. See below, p. 504.

[2] Above, p. 464; below, p. 508.

[3] Above, p. 470.

[4] Above, pp. 465–6.

[5] Above, pp. 455; 468.

[6] Vanneste, *op. cit.* p. 200; H. Ball, *Die Hierarchien der Engel und die Kirche* (Munich-Planegg, 1955), p. 84.

CHAPTER 31

THE REACTION AGAINST PROCLUS

A. *John of Scythopolis*

No attempt is here made to intervene in the apparently interminable debate as to who the ps.-Dionysius was[1] and when he lived, though this must have been later than the Cappadocians, some of whose notions he developed,[2] and before 528, the latest possible date for the first historical reference to his writings. Obviously he had both Christian and Platonist sympathies, though it is difficult to assess their relative weight.[3] It is probably safe to say that he was a Christian philosopher who presented his beliefs in terms of the contemporary Neoplatonism both because it had a strong appeal for him and because these beliefs could best be defended by turning the arguments of what he considered the most satisfactory of the rival philosophies against itself.[4]

In this, his position was not unlike that of St Gregory of Nyssa: but the Neoplatonism of Gregory was that of Plotinus while the Neoplatonism of the ps.-Dionysius was that of Proclus. The trend from the one to the other was a deviation in the direction contrary to Christianism, and the ambiguities of the ps.-Dionysius are the symptoms of a tension between Christianism and Platonism that was nearing breaking point.[5] This was felt at once. No sooner had the *Corpus Dionysianum* been made public than commentators leapt to the task of defending not

[1] Candidates still in the field stretch back from the sixth century (with Peter the Fuller and the subject of this section) to the second (Ammonius Saccas).

[2] See above, p. 457.

[3] Vanneste, *op. cit.* p. 14. Contemporary opinion differs as to whether the author was a pagan who prudently disguised his thorough-going Neoplatonism under a thin Christian veneer, or a sincere Christian, and even a Christian mystic, who found the Neoplatonic formularies a suitable mode of expression for his thought.

[4] Corsini, *art. cit.* pp. 56–60; E. von Ivánka, 'La signification historique du Corpus areopagiticum', *Recherches de science religieuse*, XXXI (Paris, 1949), pp. 5–24.

[5] While the ps.-Dionysius is quite explicit on the peculiarly Christian doctrine of 'total salvation' (ὁλικὴ σωτηρία) of man, i.e. the resurrection of body and soul, he is not interested in such themes as original sin or the inherited corruptibility of man: indeed, anthropology is the most neglected part of his system. See, for the resurrection of the body, *EH* VII (*PG* 3. 533 A–B, 563 B); Roques, 'Symbolisme et théologie négative', p. 107; above, p. 426: for the deficiencies in Christian doctrine, Roques, *loc. cit.*; J. Gross, 'Ur- und Erbsünde in der Theosophie des ps.-Dionysius Areopagita', *Zeitschrift für Religions- und Geistesgeschichte*, IV (1952), pp. 34–42.

only its genuineness, but also its orthodoxy. In the first half of the sixth century commentaries were written by John and George of Scythopolis,[1] by St Maximus in the seventh, by Germanus I, Patriarch of Constantinople in the eighth,[2] and by other anonymous commentators who belong to these three centuries. Of the earliest commentaries probably all that survive is the series of glosses found in many MSS of the *Corpus* and printed in the *PG* under the name of Maximus,[3] but which, for the most part at least, are the work of John of Scythopolis,[4] written *c.* 530.

These Scholia seem to have been designed to reassure two sets of people:[5] Christians who suspected that the Dionysian doctrines were heretical; and Platonists, whether Christian or not, who were equally suspicious of, or perhaps merely unfamiliar with, the elaborations, often irrational and bizarre, of the Procline type of Neoplatonism. They contain attacks (in the name of the ps.-Dionysius) against all the current heresies: Nestorianism,[6] Arianism,[7] Eunomianism,[8] Simon Magus,[9] the Valentinians,[10] the Marcionites,[11] the Manichaeans,[12] the Origenists,[13] the Lampetians,[14] the Messalians,[15] the Acephaloi,[16] and the Adelphians.[17] On the other hand, affinities with Platonism, dissembled in the *Corpus* it-

[1] George's commentary no longer survives but a letter which he fabricated in which 'Dionysius' dedicates his work to Pope Sixtus II, and which was intended to give verisimilitude to the authorship, is published in J. B. Pitra, *Analecta sacra*, IV (Paris, 1883), pp. xxiii–xxiv and 414–15. See Urs von Balthasar, 'Das Scholienwerk des Johannes von Scythopolis', *Scholastik*, XV, 1 (1940), 19 n.; O. Bardenhewer, *Geschichte*, IV, 296–7.

[2] Mai, *Spicilegium Romanum*, VII (Rome, 1842), p. 74; *PG* 98. 87–8; *Dict. théol. cath.* VI, 1305; Krumbacher, *Geschichte der Byzantinischen Literatur*, p. 67.

[3] *PG* 4. 14–432, 527–76. See below, p. 519.

[4] Lequien (*Dissertatio damascenica* II, *PG* 94. 281 f.) and J. Pearson (*Vindiciae ignatianae*, I, 10, *PG* 5. 202 f.) both attribute the glosses to John. Balthasar, *art. cit.*, thinks that only the scholia attached to the Syriac version of the *Corpus* made by Phocas bar Sergius in the first half of the eighth century are by him, and that the rest are by Maximus. But the evidence that Maximus wrote any of the glosses at all is tenuous (P. Sherwood, 'Sergius of Rešaina and the Syriac Version of the ps.-Dionysius', *Sacris erudiri*, IV (1952), p. 181).

[5] J. M. Hornus put forward the intriguing suggestion, which he has only reluctantly abandoned, that John was himself the author of the *Corpus* and is expounding his own work. See 'Les recherches récentes sur le ps.-Denys l'Ar.', *Revue d'histoire de philosophie religieuse*, XXXV (1955), p. 448; 'Les recherches dionysiennes de 1955–1960', *Rev. d'hist. de phil. relig.* XLI (1961), 37.

[6] 57BC, 209D, 225D, 536B (all references to John Scyth. are from *PG* 4).

[7] 60B, 192C, 209D, 536B.

[8] 192C, 209B.

[9] 176A–B, 312A, 337C–D, 545C.

[10] 176A, 397C.

[11] 169D, 176A.

[12] 176A, 272D, 285B, 397C, 557B.

[13] 176A–B, 545C.

[14] 169D.

[15] 169D, 557B.

[16] 209D.

[17] 169D.

self,[1] are brought out: in calling the angels 'intellects' (νόες)[2] the author is following 'the philosophers of the Greeks' who also gave that name to the intelligible or angelic powers',[3] and when he calls the Forms *paradeigmata* he is following Plato.[4] Initiation (τελετή) is explained in terms of the pagan Mysteries.[5] But in drawing attention to these verbal parallels the scholiast is careful to indicate the change in significance.

The Celestial Hierarchy is not the same as, but replaces, the polytheistic hierarchies of the Neoplatonists:[6] God is called the Thearchy because 'he is the ruler of the so-called gods, that is to say, the angels and the saints'.[7] 'For the Cause of all things is one and not many, and it is One Godhead which brings (παράγουσα) all things into existence, the Holy and Blessed Trinity, not a plurality of creative divinities. This he says not incidentally, but in condemnation of the wise men of the Greeks and the Simoniacs, who say that there are degrees of divinities corresponding to the descending hierarchy of creatures, extending as far as that which underlies all things, namely matter.'[8] Again, the ps.-Dionysius' conception of *paradeigma* was different from Plato's: 'While Plato unworthily separated the *paradeigmata* from God, our Master (πατήρ), although employing the same term, gave it a worthier (εὐσεβῶς) meaning.'[9] While not categorically rejecting the Dionysian concept of *huperousios* (any more than any other of his 'Master's' doctrines), he prefers to speak of the Divine *ousia*, avoiding the ambiguities of the apophatic theology. At the same time, he avoids the confusion of Creator and creature,[10] for the Divine Essence is adequately differentiated from all other essence by its absolute unification with the Divine *dynamis* and the Divine *energeia*, whereas elsewhere there is always a degree of dispersal. The Divine Essence is One rather than being: creation is the process of dispersal.

In his casual reference to the Triad *ousia–dynamis–energeia*, the ps.-Dionysius states that *ousia* is by nature incorruptible, and *dynamis* corruptible.[11] To find this Triad in the Divine Nature, therefore, and in a pre-eminently unified mode at that, would seem to admit corruptibility into the heart of the Thearchy itself. But John explains that the destruc-

[1] Above, p. 457. [2] Above, p. 465. [3] 32A13–14.
[4] 329D3–6. [5] 32D3–5. [6] 32C1–2.
[7] 192C9–10. [8] 312A6–9. [9] 329D3–6.
[10] See above, p. 469. [11] *DN* IV 23 (*PG* 3. 724C9).

tion of *dynamis* is its passage into *energeia*.[1] 'Corruptibility' in the Divine means the descent (πρόοδος) of the powers into the Hierarchies, for the powers come to an end in the return (ἐπιστροφή) of the Hierarchies to the Divine Being which always remains what it is (μονή).

John interprets the Dionysian doctrine of Forms in terms of Middle Platonism:[2] they stand in relation to God as νοήσεις to Nous. For as God descends into the Forms (which are his δυνάμεις), Nous descends into thought.[3] But again, the destiny of δύναμις is to pass into ἐνέργεια, which is the ascent of Nous to God, and its proper activity.[4] From the point of view of this activity, God is the object of knowledge (τὸ νοητόν),[5] and the beings who contemplate him, the angels (νόες), whose substance is the Divine νόησις, an intelligible or immaterial 'matter',[6] are intellectual (νοεροί).[7] But the Celestial Hierarchy is in turn the object of contemplation of the Ecclesiastical, and therefore in relation to men the angels are intelligible (νοητοί). They may therefore be described as 'intellectual and intelligible' (νοητοί τε καὶ νοεροί).[8] But the Ecclesiastical Hierarchy is the lowest that is endowed with Nous. Therefore, since there is no order below men who can contemplate men, they cannot be *noêtoi* in relation to anything, and therefore, as contemplating the Celestial Hierarchy and God, they are *noeroi* only,[9] just as the Thearchy, having no order above it which it can contemplate, is *noêton* only.

In restating the Thearchy and the two Hierarchies as the triad *noêton–noêtoi te kai noeroi–noeroi* John has disposed of the theurgic element in the Dionysian system, and brought together the Cataphatic and Symbolic theologies. He has eliminated those features which had created the impression that the ps.-Dionysius had failed to bring his system into a consistent whole.[10] At the same time, not only in this, but

[1] 289A11–12. This idea need not have originated with John: it may have been latent in the mind of the ps.-Dionys., who did not consider that this triad, formulated at least as early as Porphyry, needed explanation. See above, p. 459 n. 4; below, pp. 492–3. For the destruction of δύναμις in ἐνέργεια see below, p. 499.

[2] 329C7–14; 332A4–B6.

[3] δύναμις τοῦ νοῦ τὸ εἰς νοήσεις κατιέναι, 289C5–6. See below, p. 526.

[4] 289C3–5.

[5] See above, p. 461.

[6] 317C4.

[7] 309C1–11.

[8] 344C13–D5; 325A11–13. Cf. ps.-Dionys. *Ep.* IX 2 (*PG* 3. 1108D1). See below, p. 507; above, p. 464.

[9] 344D5–9.

[10] See above, p. 471.

by introducing elements deriving from Aristotle (e.g. the reliability of sense experience) and from Middle Platonism and from the earlier Neoplatonism, he brought the Dionysian philosophy closer to the main stream of Platonism, and therefore closer to the Christian position.

B. *Alexandria: Johannes Philoponus*

The probable date of the Scholia of John of Scythopolis coincides with the closing of the Athenian Academy by Justinian in 529 and the appearance in the same year of the *De aeternitate mundi contra Proclum* of Johannes Philoponus.[1] The motives which prompted all three were essentially the same: a rejection of the teaching which the Academy had been putting out since Iamblichus and which reached its fullest expression under Proclus. This teaching could no longer be invoked to support the Christian themes, as in some measure the Neoplatonism of Plotinus could (the ps.-Dionysius was apparently the only writer who attempted to use it in this way), but was a dangerous rival directly opposed to it. Justinian's act was the gesture of a Christian prince silencing the enemies of the faith;[2] but the enemies were not Platonism or even Neoplatonism in their broad principles, but the Procline theology based on polytheism, and the Procline theurgy deriving from the belief in a supernatural power inherent in the phenomenal world.[3]

These two notions have as their common source the pagan dichotomy of reality into the intelligible and sensible worlds as opposed to the Christian dichotomy between Creator and creation.[4] It cannot be said that the Christian Platonists had established the latter position incontrovertibly, for until the Procline Neoplatonism had worked out those implications of the pagan concept which were demonstrably unacceptable the dangers in it had not been perceived. Although the Cappadocians and the ps.-Dionysius are explicit in asserting the absolute distinction between the One God on the one hand and the sensible–intelligible universe on the other, and although St Gregory of Nyssa is careful to avoid calling the human soul divine, and the ps.-Dionysius explicitly differentiates the Forms, which are the Thoughts of God, from the intelligibles of the Celestial Hierarchy, in no case is the distinction

[1] Ed. H. Rabe, Leipzig, 1899.

[2] Johannes Malalas, *Chronographia*, XVIII 18.

[3] B. Tatakis, *La philosophie byzantine* (Bréhier's *Histoire de la philosophie*, fasc. suppl. ii), ed. 2 (Paris, 1959), p. 20.

[4] See above, p. 426.

clearly expounded. Furthermore, since these philosophers paid little attention to the physical world (except St Basil, who avoids entering into this particular question),[1] they did not concern themselves with Aristotle's theory of the Quintessence to explain the dichotomy in physical terms.[2] Philoponus' great contribution to Christian philosophy was the demonstration by scientific arguments that the celestial matter was not different from the sublunar, and that therefore the whole phenomenal universe was corruptible, thus putting the Christian doctrine of a world created in time and to end in time on a scientific basis. From this it followed that it is not divine, and that the Procline hierarchies of gods descending into the phenomenal world are non-existent.

Johannes Philoponus was born between 475 and 480,[3] probably at Alexandria,[4] where he was a member of the philosophical school established by Hermeias, a pupil of Syrianus, and was himself the pupil (in company perhaps with Boethius)[5] of Ammonius, the fourth son and successor of Hermeias. Under Ammonius the school had turned from Platonic to Aristotelian studies, perhaps under ecclesiastical pressure.[6] Ammonius himself did not entirely abandon Plato,[7] but his lectures on Aristotle were the more popular and reached a wider public. Philoponus abandoned his master's Aristotelianism for Stoic theory, of which he was the most brilliant exponent in the sixth century.[8] At the same time he eliminated from his teaching everything that was incompatible with Christianism; for either he was always a Christian[9] or

[1] St Basil, *Hex.* I 11 (*PG* 29. 25 A–28 B).

[2] Aristotle, *De caelo* I 2, 269b13.

[3] P. Joannou, 'Le premier essai chrétien d'une philosophie systématique, Jean Philopon', *Studia patristica*, v (Berlin, 1962), p. 508.

[4] Nicephorus Callistas (s. vi), *Hist. eccl.* I 18. 47 (*PG* 47. 424).

[5] P. Courcelle, 'Boèce et l'École d'Alexandrie', *Mélanges de l'École française de Rome*, LII (1935), 185–223; idem, *Les lettres grecques en Occident* (Paris, 1948), p. 264; P. Chenu, *Revue des sciences philosophiques et théologiques*, XXVI (1937), p. 389; P. de Labriolle, *Histoire de l'Église depuis les origines jusqu'à nos jours*, IV (Paris, 1937), p. 566. [Also Part VII, ch. 35 D, pp. 553–4.]

[6] H. D. Saffrey, 'Le chrétien Jean Philopon et la survivance de l'école d'Alexandrie', *Revue des études grecques*, LXVII (1954), pp. 400–1. Cf. above, p. 432. [For a fuller study of the evidence for the attitude of the Alexandrian School to Plato and Aristotle see Part IV, ch. 19 C, pp. 314–19.]

[7] Damascius, *Vita Isidori*, ed. Asmus (Leipzig, 1911), 113, 37 n.; Olympiodorus, *In Gorgiam*, ed. Norvin (Leipzig, 1936), 183, 11.

[8] Bardy, *Dictionnaire de théologie catholique*, VIII, 834.

[9] E. Évrard, 'Les convictions religieuses de Jean Philopon et la date de son commentaire aux Météorologiques', *Académie royale de Belgique: Bulletin de la classe des lettres et des sciences morales et politiques*, ser. 5, XXXIX (1953), 356; Joannou, *loc. cit.*

became one during the course of his teaching career.[1] He died soon after 565.

The *De aeternitate mundi contra Proclum* was so called to distinguish it from another work of the same name which he wrote against Aristotle. This is lost, but from the long excerpts preserved by Simplicius in his *De caelo* and *In phys.* its purpose is seen to have been to refute the doctrine of the Quintessence and thence argue the contingency of the world. Aristotle had inferred the uniqueness of the substance of the stars from the uniqueness of their movement. For since this is circular, with the earth as the centre of the circle, it does not partake of the opposites of upwards and downwards, which are found in all sublunary motions.[2] But this theory had been undermined by subsequent advances in the science of astronomy:

> If Alexander is right in saying that Aristotle calls motion in the proper sense that which goes round the centre of the universe, the other motions are neither circular in the proper sense nor simple. But the astronomers have shown that each star has its specific motion, which is not homocentric with the universe. ...Therefore their motions are not simple, and upward and downward components can be observed in them.[3]

But even if the motion *is* circular, it is not unique, for 'though the starting and terminal points of circular motions are the same, there is still an antagonism of the opposites because the direction of the start of one is the direction in which the other ends'.[4] Therefore celestial motions, even if circular, are of the same kind as terrestrial.

The refutation of the Quintessence is part of the attack on the eternity of the world, which, like the related theory of the *ecpyrôsis*,[5] was rejected by others besides Christians. Aristotle taught that the world is eternal in the *De philosophia*.[6] Zeno dissented, but in turn was opposed by Theophrastus. Epicurus attacked Theophrastus with the arguments recorded by Lucretius[7] and used by St Basil:[8] a being whose parts are corruptible must itself be corruptible. Christians like Hippo-

[1] Tatakis, *op. cit.* p. 38.

[2] Aristotle, *De caelo* 270b32–271a29.

[3] Philoponus *ap.* Simplicius, *De caelo* 32, 2 Heiberg. P. Duhem, *Système du monde*, II (Paris 1914), p. 61, wrongly attributes the fragment to Xenarchus, another opponent of the Quintessence

[4] Philoponus *ap.* Simplicius, *op. cit.* 193, 11.

[5] See above, p. 434.

[6] E. Bignone, *L'Aristotele perduto e la formazione filosofica di Epicuro* (Florence, 1936).

[7] Lucretius, *De rerum natura*, V 235–59.

[8] Cf. *Hex.* I 3 (*PG* 29. 9C f.).

lytus, St Basil[1] and Procopius of Gaza, who regarded the *ecpyrôsis* as a reasonable hypothesis, could argue from it the non-eternity of the world: those who rejected it, the Alexandrians and St Gregory of Nyssa, were forced into accepting a kind of mundane eternity. If there is no *ecpyrôsis*, 'the elements continue to penetrate each other without interruption, transforming themselves one into another, without increase or diminution, each abiding for ever in its original measure'.[2] But this eternity is relative to the spatio-temporal sphere, and conditioned by the Divine Providence. It is eternal in the sense that it has no intrinsic cause of destruction. It is a rest (στάσις) in time, not an eternal rest (στάσις εἰς αἰῶνα).[3]

Philoponus deduces the same conclusion from the circular motion of the heavenly bodies. He does not disagree with Simplicius' comment: 'One could say that the heavens too, although they do not change from movement to rest, do rest with regard to their centre, axis and poles, remaining as a whole in their place.'[4] If it is true that the motion of the heavenly bodies is purely circular, then they move with the motion that most closely approximates to rest. 'As nature looks towards some state of perfection and moves so as to attain it, and once having attained it remains there, and as the heavens are perpetually in that state...and do not leave it, they persevere in that state which will never cease to be perfect.'[5] But that does not mean that the celestial beings are omnipotent, as Proclus held.[6] Even if they are durable to the point of permanence, all material objects and phenomena in the universe are still limited in power and duration by the Will of God: 'As long as God wants the universe to exist its principal parts have to be preserved, and admittedly the heaven as a whole and in its parts is the principal and most essential part of the universe.'[7]

The *De aeternitate mundi contra Proclum* may have been intended as a demonstration that the Alexandrian school dissociated itself from the teaching of Proclus which was now being proscribed,[8] or, if its author had by then abandoned the school, as an attack on it for persisting in it

[1] See above, pp. 433–4.
[2] St Greg. Nyss. *Apol.* (*PG* 44. 113 A).
[3] Idem, *In Eccles.* I (*PG* 44. 628 B–D).
[4] Simplicius, *In phys.* 264, 18 Diels.
[5] Philoponus, *In phys.* 198, 22 Vitelli. Cf. Maximus, below, p. 502.
[6] Proclus, *In Tim.* III 21, 1. Cf. I 294. 28 – 295. 12; II 131. 4 f.; 262. 5 f.
[7] Philoponus *ap.* Simplicius, *De caelo*, 142. 7.
[8] Saffrey, *art. cit.*

—which it certainly did under Olympiodorus, who was less compromising than Ammonius and his disciples.[1] It answers point by point the eighteen arguments which Proclus had assembled to show that the world is eternal. The second of these (the first is missing from the MSS) is that 'if eternity is found in the exemplar, then it must also exist in the image: for exemplar and image are a pair of relatives', the one of which cannot exist without the other. Philoponus accuses Proclus of misinterpreting Plato. Certainly Plato said that the Forms, which are eternal, are the Exemplar: but that does not mean that it is the essence of Forms to be exemplars. What did not exist before the image and will not survive its destruction is Form *qua* exemplar, not Form *per se*. The eternity of the world, therefore, does not follow from the eternity of the Form which, for the period of the existence of the Cosmos, is its exemplar.

The statement and counter-statement are of interest, for the eternity of relationship was one of the arguments used by the iconodules, who did not presumably realize its implications, in their defence of the veneration of images.[2] It is not surprising that Philoponus himself opposed the veneration of images, and that his christology is that of Severus of Antioch. He drew no distinction between nature and hypostasis,[3] and from the Aristotelian principle that nature does not exist apart from the individuals he concluded that the Humanity of Christ, having never existed independently, is not a nature. His last work, the *De opificio mundi*,[4] was dedicated to Sergius, Patriarch of Antioch 546–9, to whose influence may be ascribed the more tolerant attitude it adopts towards Aristotle, whose writings were highly esteemed by the monophysites, as may be seen from the frequency with which he was translated into Syriac. But it is not so much a piece of Aristotelian exposition as an attempt to reconcile Aristotelianism with Christianism. Moses teaches what Greek science discovered long afterwards. Where the Mosaic account conflicts with Aristotle, it is the former which is the more successful in 'saving the appearances'. But Moses did not pretend to be a physicist or astronomer. He does not answer such questions as: What are the material principles of things? Are they one or

[1] Westerink, *op. cit.* p. xiii.

[2] See below, p. 512.

[3] See below, p. 490.

[4] Ed. G. Reinhardt (Leipzig, 1897).

many? If many, how many? Are they the same in all things, or do they differ? What is the substance of heaven? Does it differ from that of the sublunar world? Is the movement of sublunar things accompanied by substantial change? These questions throw light on what was being debated in Philoponus' time, and not least by Philoponus himself in his earlier works; and the way in which they are dismissed in this work as being matters of secondary importance is an indication of his declining intellectual powers. For he is now in sympathy with what he claims to have been Moses' own intention: first, to lead men to a knowledge of God, and then to teach them to live in conformity with it. It is the attitude of St Basil in the *Hexaëmeron*, which is his principal source.[1]

Professor Sambursky[2] suggests that Philoponus' demonstration that the celestial bodies are composed of the same matter as the sublunary world would have caused as much indignation among Christians as among pagans. But the effect was rather to emphasize the distinction between God and the created universe, as he recognizes elsewhere:[3]

> The unique position of Philoponus in the history of scientific ideas is given by the fact that through him a confrontation of scientific cosmology and monotheism took place for the first time. The very idea on which all monotheistic religions are based implies of course the belief in the universe as a creation of God, and the subsequent assumption that there is no essential difference between things in heaven and on earth.

In comparison with Philoponus, the other members of the Alexandrian school are of secondary importance. Olympiodorus, born between 495 and 505,[4] scholarch before 541,[5] and still teaching in 565, was, on his own admission,[6] a pagan, and lectured both on Plato and Aristotle.

[1] Bardy, *art. cit.* pp. 835–6.

[2] S. Sambursky, *The Physical World of Late Antiquity* (London, 1962), p. 174.

[3] Idem, *op. cit.* p. 157.

[4] Westerink, *op. cit.* p. xiii.

[5] *Ibid.*

[6] L. Skowronsky, *De auctoris Heerenii et Olympiodori Alexandrini scholis cum universis tum iis singulis quae ad vitam Platonis spectant capita selecta* (Breslau, 1884); W. Norvin, *Olympiodorus fra Alexandria* (Copenhagen, 1915), p. 319. The belief that he was a Christian arose from his being confused by Anastasius Sinaïta (*PG* 89. 936 and 1189) with a deacon and exegete of the same name, *c.* 510, who wrote commentaries on Ecclesiastes, Job, and Jeremiah, and a treatise against Severus of Antioch (*PG* 89. 13–780); and from the doubtful attribution to him of a Christian alchemical treatise. See Tannery, 'Sur la période finale de la philosophie grecque', *Revue philosophique*, XLII (1896), p. 277; K. Prächter, 'Richtungen und Schulen im Neuplatonismus', *Genethliakon Carl Robert* (Berlin, 1910), p. 151; Westerink, *op. cit.* p. xv; R. Devréesse, *Dict. de la Bible* Suppl. I, 1137, 1141, 1164 *et passim*. For Olympiodorus on images see below, p. 513.

Elias,[1] who, if he is to be identified with the Prefect of Illyrium of that name to whom Justinian addressed his *Novella* CLIII of December 541, must have been, to hold that office, a Christian, shows little sign of it in his surviving works, which consist of commentaries on the *Organon* and perhaps the *Prolegomena to Platonic Philosophy* which survives in a MS of the tenth century copied from a prototype owned by Arethas.[2] The same could be said of his younger contemporary David,[3] whose surviving Commentary on the *Isagoge*[4] may have been known to Eriugena.[5] Mention should also be made of the Christian Commentator of the *Parmenides*, whose work replaces the missing part of Proclus' Commentary in the MSS,[6] and of the Christian author of a preface to the *Isagoge* which may also have been known to Eriugena.[7]

Of more importance than these is Philoponus' pupil Stephanus,[8] who, on the accession of Heraclius in 610, was appointed Director of Studies of the restored Imperial Academy of Byzantium,[9] where, less than a century after the closing of the Athenian Academy, he was lecturing on Plato, Aristotle, geometry, arithmetic and astronomy.[10] He must have been one of the principal links between the Alexandrian School and the Aristotelian Renaissance of Byzantium which was already beginning to emerge.[11]

C. *Gaza*

The Academy whose studies Stephanus came to direct had been founded by Constantine, and greatly enlarged by Theodosius II in 425,[12] but it

[1] Westerink, 'Introduction to Elias on the Prior Analytics', *Mnemosyne*, ser. 4, XIV (1961), 126–39.

[2] MS Vienna phil. gr. 314, ed. Westerink, *Anonymous Prolegomena to Platonic Philosophy* (Amsterdam, 1962).

[3] Sometimes confused with the fifth-century theologian David the Armenian because biographical data concerning him are preserved in an Armenian MS.

[4] Ed. Busse, *C.A.G.* XVIII 2. Another recension, closer in thought to Elias, is preserved in MS Paris Bibl. Nat. gr. 1939 printed by J. A. Cramer, *Anecdota graeca e codd. manuscr. Bibl. Reg. Paris.* IV (Oxford, 1841), p. 442. See Busse, *Die neuplatonischen Ausleger der Isagoge des Porphyrius* (Berlin, 1892), pp. 20–3; idem, *C.A.G.* XVIII 2, XX–XXIV.

[5] See below, p. 525 n. 4.

[6] *Procli opera*, ed. Cousin (1864), 1257–1314.

[7] Printed by Cramer, *op. cit.* p. 430, from MS Paris Coislin 387. See below, p. 525 n. 4.

[8] H. Usener, *De Stephano Alexandrino* (Bonn, 1879); R. Vancourt, *Les derniers commentateurs alexandrins d'Aristote* (Lille, 1941), pp. 26–42; Tatakis, *op. cit.* pp. 50–1; below, p. 492.

[9] Usener, *op. cit.* pp. 4–5.

[10] Idem, *Stephani alexandrini opusculum apotelesmaticum* (Bonn, 1879), p. 17.

[11] See below, p. 490.

[12] Fr. Fuchs, *Die höheren Schulen in Constantinopel*, p. 2; L. Bréhier, *La civilisation byzantine*, pp. 457 f.

is clear from his constitution that it was not a philosophical school in the sense that Athens and Alexandria were. Of the thirty-one chairs that were established, only one was allocated to philosophy.[1] During the sixth century Christian Platonism, outside Alexandria, is represented by the School of Gaza and, in Byzantium itself, by Leontius the Hermit. In both cases, the extravagances of Procline Neoplatonism have ceased to be a problem, the conflict between Christianism and Hellenism is mild or non-existent, and in the case of Leontius the former has become invigorated by the influence of Aristotelian logic.

The school of Gaza was an offshoot of Alexandria as Alexandria had been an offshoot of Athens. Its founder Aeneas was a pupil of the Alexandrian Neoplatonist Hierocles.[2] He spent most of his life in Gaza as a professor of rhetoric, concerned as much in stating the Christian position in Platonic style as supporting it by Platonic thought. A sincere admirer of Plato, he invokes the authority of Plato himself to justify the composition of a Platonic dialogue in support of his Christian convictions: 'Plato himself has said that Plato must be followed until one appears who is wiser than he: but there is no one wiser than God.'[3] But for this very reason, *Theophrastus*, *or*, *On the Immortality of the Soul and the Resurrection of the Body*,[4] although it shows his mastery of the Platonic style, cannot maintain the Platonic technique. It opens with a display of Socratic irony: the Christian interlocutor comes to seek wisdom from the pagan philosopher. But the irony has to be abandoned because Socratic agnosticism has been replaced by Christian certitude: 'Among good Christians there is no dogma which depends on verbal proof: it derives its certainty from the very works.'[5]

Therefore, the dialogue develops as a criticism of the Platonic Myth: for if the hypothesis is destroyed the philosophy is refuted. For instance, if it were true that the soul has fallen from a higher state to a lower, this would provide the sinner with a further occasion for sinning, for whatever it was that caused the soul to fall from there would be all the more

[1] Theodosian Code, XIV 9. 3.

[2] Tatakis, *op. cit.* p. 27.

[3] Aeneas of Gaza, *Theophrastus* (*PG* 85. 1001 C).

[4] *PG* 85. 865–1004: his only surviving work apart from 25 short letters written in the rhetorical style, ed. R. Hercher, *Epistolographi graeci* (Paris, 1873), pp. 24–32; L. Massa, *Collana di studi greci dir. da V. de Falco* (Naples, 1950). Cf. idem, *Giornal. ital. filol.* V (1952), pp. 205–7.

[5] Aeneas, *op. cit.* 996 B. See above, p. 427.

effective in causing her to fall here where she is enslaved to the passions.[1] But this would be contrary to justice, which by nature is remedial.[2] Again, if the soul has vacated a higher state, this would dislocate the order of the Cosmos, which is universal and eternal. If, on the other hand, the soul enters one body from another, it would imply that God required of the soul more than one incarnate life on which to form his judgement.[3] Furthermore, pre-existence of the soul would imply its continued existence after the dissolution of the body, and where would that existence be passed? If the good souls are continually passing into the Elysian Fields and the wicked into Hades, a time must come when there will be no more souls for the visible world.[4]

On these grounds he rejects the Platonic theory of the soul for one based on Aristotle[5] and St Gregory of Nyssa. Humanly speaking, the number of souls is infinite, but finite in the eyes of God. The universe is filled with rational powers which it contains in their totality and is filled totally by each. The soul is not divine, and not pre-existent, but comes into existence with the body, as St Gregory teaches: 'Since man is one in his composition of soul and body, his being can have but one and common origin.'[6]

On the other hand, the soul is immortal.[7] For every living body is composed of matter and form. The latter, as an active and directive Idea and a rational substance, must remain immortal, for the Creator, who is always identical with himself, does not cease to confer immortality on all rational beings. At death the soul, which is the form of the body, leaves in it a vestige of its immortality which, with the co-operation of the Divine Providence, has the power to assemble to itself the dissipated particles of the deceased body, and reforms it by bestowing upon it that disposition which it had before its dissolution, so that even the material body, revived at a given time by the divine power, rediscovers its soul and becomes immortal.[8] Even matter has a degree of immortality, and will at some date be immaterialized,[9] since all created things have a

[1] The argument is taken from St Greg. Nyss. *De hom. opif.* XXVIII (*PG* 44. 232B).

[2] Aeneas, *op. cit.* 896A.

[3] Aeneas, *op. cit.* 956C.

[4] Aeneas, *op. cit.* 956B.

[5] See above, p. 426.

[6] St Greg. Nyss. *De hom. opif.* XXIX (*PG* 44. 233D).

[7] Aeneas, *op. cit.* 949B.

[8] Cf. St Greg. Nyss. *op. cit.* XXVII (*PG* 44. 225BC, 228AB).

[9] Tatakis, *op. cit.* p. 32.

natural tendency towards perfection. For the whole of creation has a moral end, and is in travail for the perfection and happiness of man.

But the sensible world is not eternal but created. To the Neoplatonic objection that if so, its creation must have been at a given moment, and if the Creator did then what he had not done before, creation would be accidental to him, Aeneas agrees that since God is pure Act he could not at any time be inactive: but he has been Creator from all eternity since he has had about him from all eternity the Intelligible World, which he created.[1] The sensible world is the appearance by which we contemplate it: 'When a painter has a beautiful archetype he makes many copies of it so that no part of its beauty shall escape him. Similarly by the variety of objects and their coming into being we are led to a better contemplation of the *logoi* which are concealed behind the appearances'.[2]

The sensible world is a reality in which may take place radical change and events, including dissolution: 'The stars are the most beautiful things in the sky, but they are mortal'.[3] But the history which all these compose is an ascent from the mortality of the sensible to the immortality of the intelligible.[4] Of this sensible world man is the centre and consummation,[5] not only now but also in the future life, since immortal souls, requiring body, also require place,[6] though these will be different from sensible place and sensible body; they will be spiritual and dematerialized.

Zacharias, the friend and fellow-citizen of Aeneas, was a convert from monophysitism to orthodoxy who became bishop of Mitylene and died before 553. He wrote, besides a number of historical and polemical works,[7] *Ammonius, or, On the Creation of the World*,[8] which covers much the same ground as the *Theophrastus* and may have been written before it. As its subtitle suggests, it also has the same purpose as the *De aeternitate c. Proclum* of Philoponus of attacking the doctrines of Proclus and Ammonius. These take creation to be merely a causal relation: the world's coming into being means that it is the effect of a cause,

[1] See Zacharias below, p. 487.
[2] Aeneas, *op. cit.* 969B.
[3] Idem, *op. cit.* 961B.
[4] See Procopius, below, p. 488.
[5] Cf. St Greg. Nyss. above, p. 449.
[6] Aeneas, *op. cit.* 957B.
[7] Ed. E. W. Brooks, *Corpus scriptorum christianorum orientalium*, LXXXVII–LXXXVIII (Paris, 1924); new imp. XXXVIII and XLI (1953). See Bardy, *dict. théol. cath.* XV, 3676–80; E. Honigmann, *Patristic studies* (= *Studi e testi*, Rome, no. 173) (1953), pp. 194–204.
[8] *PG* 85. 1011–1144. See Nyssen, *Byzant. Zeitschr.* (Munich, 1940), pp. 15–22.

apart from which it has the same dignity with the Creator and is co-eternal with him.[1] In his reply to this Zacharias sets forth a fully Christian concept of God[2] as intelligible, incorporeal, incorruptible, immortal, always in the same state, incircumscribable, transcending all definition and relation. He has been Creator from eternity because he possesses in himself the creative Logos.[3] As a doctor is still a doctor even when not engaged upon curing a disease, so God is Creator even when not engaged in the act of creating.[4] But in fact he is always creating by virtue of his Providence which sustains the universe.

Creation is *de nihilo*. God provides for the Forms the matter required for their expression. '*We* say that God is the Creator of the substances themselves, and not, as *you* say, of their form only. *Your* creator merely supplies form and specification to unformed and unspecified matter.'[5] God's eternal will to create includes the will to create each nature at the time when it is good for it to come into being—not for some advantage to himself, as the Platonists say, but because he is the Good.[6]

It follows that the sensible world is not eternal, as God is. Gesius, an iatrosophist who was a friend of Aeneas,[7] argued that if it is true that everything that comes into being comes into being in time, then time itself does not come into being: for if so it would itself come into being in time, which is absurd: therefore time does not have a coming into being,[8] and neither does the temporal world.[9] But it is not true that everything that comes into being comes into being in time, so that it need not be that time comes into being in time. It comes into being in eternity, for it is the creation of an eternal God, and so is the temporal world, which is his sensible image. Another argument which the pagans use is that the sensible world is a sphere, and a sphere has neither a beginning nor end. But 'it is only for you and me that the sphere has no beginning—it must begin somewhere just as when we describe a circle we begin at some point'.[10]

Procopius, probably the brother of Zacharias, died *c.* 538. His philosophy emerges from the introductions to a series of catenae, a form of

[1] Zacharias, *op. cit.* 1021 B.
[2] Idem, *op. cit.* 1048 f.
[3] See Aeneas, above, p. 484.
[4] Zacharias, *op. cit.* 1068 A.
[5] Idem, *op. cit.* 1076 B.
[6] Idem, *op. cit.* 1093 C.
[7] Tatakis, *op. cit.* p. 28.
[8] See above, p. 436.
[9] Zacharias, *op. cit.* 1081 C.
[10] Idem, *op. cit.* 1104 D.

commentary which he seems to have invented. The eternity of the world is refuted in his *Commentary on Genesis*,[1] which like all works of the kind derives mainly from St Basil's *Hexaëmeron*. If matter were eternal it would have to be immutable, for if mutable its mutability would have to apply to its eternity, since matter has neither quality, quantity nor form to which it could refer: but mutable eternity is a contradiction in terms.[2] Again, if God and the world are both eternal, the composite would not be subsequent to the simple, nor act to potency, nor the perfect to the imperfect; but this would be contrary to the law of nature, by which the adult succeeds the child, the fruit the seed, increase that which has not increased.[3] In fact, nothing could happen in the world at all.[4]

It can be seen here that Procopius shared with Aeneas the concept of a universe having a history and a progress. But he makes it clear that the history and the progress do not go beyond the limits of its nature, by denying the notion of ecstasy as an annihilation of the intellect.[5] It is rather its energization:

> The prophet (Isaiah) sees...not, as some believe, by going out of the intellect, as though the Holy Spirit veiled the intellect....The Divine effects the perfection, not the deprivation, of the natural powers....Light does not cause blindness, but on the contrary incites the faculty of vision to action: similarly God incites the purified intellect to spiritual contemplation. Only a malignant power would induce ecstasy to the detriment of the ecstatic.[6]

What is called ecstasy is really inspiration, and when the prophet receives it he does not cease to be a rational being: he is a human being who has achieved perfection.

D. *Byzantium*

The philosophers of Gaza do not have the profundity of a Philoponus. Their merit is that, unaffected by his revolt from Aristotle, they could supplement from Aristotle his arguments against the eternity of the world, while at the same time employing Aristotelian notions to define and defend the doctrine of the immortality of the soul, stripping it more successfully than the Cappadocians had done of any suggestion of pre-existence or divinity. Soul cannot exist before its body, nor does it in

[1] Procopius, *In Gen.* (*PG* 87. 1, 29 A).
[2] Idem, *op. cit.* 29 B.
[3] Idem, *op. cit.* 33 A–B.
[4] *Ibid.*
[5] See above, p. 470.
[6] Procopius, *In Esaiam* (*PG* 87. 2, 1817 A f.).

ecstasy depart from its own nature into the nature of God. Its perfection lies not in deification but in intellectualization. On the other hand, being a rational nature, the soul is immortal; and since it is the form of the body and therefore cannot exist apart from body, its immortality ensures the resurrection of the body.[1]

But Aristotle's theory is not wholly satisfactory from the Christian point of view since it presents the soul as little more than the mode of the body's organization. A more satisfactory theory was that which the Neoplatonists had evolved in refutation of the Stoic argument that since the soul associates with a corporeal substance it must itself be corporeal. But such an association must either be a juxtaposition, in which the two substances do not become one but remain two as they were before;[2] or a mixture, in which the two components would be destroyed and be replaced by a third substance different from either.[3] But spiritual substances are indestructible and therefore cannot enter into a union of this kind. The solution of the dilemma lies in the possibility of a third kind of union, a union without confusion (ἕνωσις ἀσύγχυτος), in which the identity of each component is fully preserved.[4] This is suggested in Porphyry's *Quaestiones commixtae*,[5] where he may be recording Plotinus' explanation of the association of body and soul,[6] which in turn may have been learnt from Ammonius Saccas.[7] Nemesius and Priscianus Lydus find an example of such a union in the association of light and air: 'Light is united to air by being mingled together with it without confusion (ἀσυγχύτως).'[8] Among the Neoplatonists the theory is first fully expounded by Proclus,[9] and among the Christians by Leontius the Hermit.

Leontius was born in 475 and died in 543/4. Although his work shows that he was well-grounded in the Aristotelian logic and was particularly familiar with Porphyry's *Isagoge* and a commentary on the

[1] See. above, p 426. [2] Nemesius, *De nat. hom.* (*PG* 40. 593B). [3] Idem, *op. cit.* 592B.

[4] E. L. Fortin, 'The Definitio fidei of Chalcedon and its philosophical sources', *Studia patristica*, v (Berlin, 1962), p. 493. The author shows that only on this theory could the analogy between the two Natures of Christ and the association of soul and body be made. [For Augustine's use of the same doctrine see the preceding Part (v, Augustine), ch. 22, pp. 357–9.]

[5] Idem, *Christianisme et culture philosophique au cinquième siècle* (Paris, 1958), p. 119.

[6] Porphyry, *Life of Plotinus* 13, 10–11. Cf. Plotinus, I 1 [53]; IV 3 [27]; IV 7 [2].

[7] Nemesius, *op. cit.* 603B.

[8] Idem, *op. cit.* 592C; cf. Prisc. *Solutiones*, ed. Bywater, *Supplementum aristotelicum*, I 2, 21. See below, p. 504. [9] Proclus, *In Tim.* 131B; 199A; 218C.

Categories written either by Porphyry or a disciple, and is sometimes called the founder of Byzantine Aristotelianism,[1] the substance of his teaching is Platonist or Neoplatonist.[2] Our impression of the world is general but vague, not revealing the truth; and if we attempt to particularize by division into genera and species and individuals, although the vagueness is reduced the general view is lost: we are heading not towards the truth but towards an infinite regress.[3] The truth can be revealed by faith alone, through the Word of God, which is not pronounced but initiates the elect by voiceless discourse.[4] It contains all knowledge since its source is God who is identical with being. By this silent illumination the intellect apprehends the realities which would otherwise be inaccessible to it, and in that sense transcends its own nature. Leontius, like St Gregory Nazianzen and the ps.-Dionysius, renounces all claim to originality:[5] his object is to interpret the Scriptures and deepen his knowledge of them.

In speaking of the relationship of soul and body he distinguishes between nature and hypostasis, which Philoponus had identified.[6] The nature, or substance, of a thing is something which concerns its being:[7] its definition is not affected by the number of individuals which participate in it:[8] it is the universal considered in relation to its individuals.[9] The hypostasis is the particular being,[10] as nature or substance is universal being.[11] It is not absolute being since it is conditioned by its particular existence.[12] The relation between nature and hypostasis is not reciprocal: all hypostasis is nature, but not all nature is hypostasis.[13] The hypostasization of nature makes it one thing of that nature that is not another,[14] and is characterized by a grouping of accidents peculiar to itself.[15]

But when it is said that not all nature is hypostasis, this does not mean that there can exist a nature independent of hypostasis.[16] Natures that

[1] E.g. by Rüganer, Loofs, Ernoni, Harnack. Cf. Bulgakov, *The Lamb of God* (YMCA Press, 1928), p. 82 (in Russian).
[2] Ueberweg, *Die patristische Philosophie*, pp. 125 f.
[3] Leontius, *Libri tres contra Nestorianos et Eutychianos* (*PG* 86. 1, 1296B).
[4] Idem, *op. cit.* 1300B.
[5] Leontius, *op. cit.* 1344D.
[6] Above, p. 481.
[7] Leontius, *op. cit.* 1280A.
[8] Idem, *Solutio argumentorum Severi* (*PG* 86. 2, 1917A–B).
[9] Idem, *Libri tres*, 1280A.
[10] *Ibid.*
[11] Idem, *Solutio*, 1917A–B. See Maximus, below, p. 497.
[12] Idem, *op. cit.* 1945A.
[13] Idem, *Libri tres*, 1280A.
[14] Idem, *Solutio*, 1917B.
[15] Idem, *op. cit.* 1917B–C.
[16] Idem, *Libri tres*, 1280A.

are not hypostases exist in hypostases: they are *enhypostaseis*.[1] The enhypostasis is intermediate between accident, which is *anhypostasis*, and hypostasis. The hypostasis denotes the individual, the enhypostasis its substance (οὐσία). Soul and body are examples of the last. United in man, each is a complete substance: considered apart each is a hypostasis. Therefore soul and body are divided in their natures and united in their hypostases.[2] On the other hand, soul is united in its nature but divided in its hypostasis.

The hypostatic union of soul and body, not being a union of nature,[3] is an operation of the Divine Power.[4] In it neither of the separated natures is destroyed or impaired:[5] soul *qua* soul is perfect, and body *qua* body is perfect. But neither is perfect in relation to the man, since of him they are parts.[6] Man is not his soul, as Plato teaches, but the substantial composite of soul and body.

The nature of soul is a self-moving incorporeal substance, and therefore immortal and incorruptible.[7] But it is not proper to her nature to be impassible, for she possesses by nature the affective faculties,[8] and therefore she is affected by the passions concomitant to corporeal existence. Since these are of her nature, and not accidents acquired in the course of her fall, and since her nature is good, they too are essentially good, and properly used serve good purposes: the appetite (ἐπιθυμητικόν) yearns lovingly for God, the energy of the will (θυμοειδές) co-operates with the will of God, the reasoning faculty (λογιστικόν) receives without shadow the immaterial impressions of reality and is illumined within by the unification of thought. It is the soul's abuse of the passions, not something inherent in the body, which is the cause of ignorance and evil.[9] Leontius, admitting an element of composition into the very nature of the soul, and placing upon the soul, rather than the body, the responsibility for evil,[10] removes the last trace of divinity from the soul, which still lingers in the doctrine of St Gregory of Nyssa.[11]

[1] Idem, *op. cit.* 1277D, 1280A–B.

[2] Leontius, *Solutio*, 1925C; *Libri tres*, 1293D f.; 1300B; 1301D–1306B.

[3] Idem, *Solutio*, 1940B.

[4] Idem, *Libri tres*, 1280B, 1340B.

[5] *De sectis* (*PG* 86. 1, 1248). The *De sectis* may not be by Leontius, but by a disciple, perhaps Theodore of Raithu. See Diekamp, *Analecta patristica* (Rome, 1938), pp. 176–8. It will, however, reflect his teaching (Tatakis, *op. cit.* 62–3).

[6] Leontius, *op. cit.* 1281A.

[7] Idem, *op. cit.* 1281B.

[8] Idem, *op. cit.* 1284C.

[9] Cf. St Greg. Nyss., above, pp. 451–2.

[10] Leontius, *op. cit.* 1285A–B.

[11] Above, p. 450.

CHAPTER 32

ST MAXIMUS THE CONFESSOR

A. *Introduction*

Born in Constantinople *c.* 580, Maximus was thirty when Stephen of Byzantium became director of studies at the Imperial Academy and taught, among other things, the philosophies of Plato and Aristotle; but whether he was educated there or at the Patriarchal Academy, he would have found already established the curriculum which Stephen inherited;[1] for since the time of Leontius an Aristotelian renaissance had been under way, and the two philosophies were taught side by side. Leontius himself shows the effects of this programme, and they are to be seen again in Maximus.

Maximus, however, was closer in temperament to the Cappadocians and the ps.-Dionysius, and his achievement was to present doctrines that were basically theirs in terms of the Aristotelian logic which was more congenial to the intellectual temper of the time, and which, by rationalizing without rejecting their mysticism, rendered it less susceptible to misinterpretation. The universe of Maximus is that of the ps.-Dionysius with a place found in it for the anthropology of St Gregory of Nyssa. The rigid formularies of the one are quickened by the historicism and dynamism of the other, a synthesis made possible by the critical examination to which the philosophers who preceded them had subjected the Aristotelian theories of time and eternity, motion and rest.

It is still a triadic universe, but the triad upon which it is constructed is no longer defined in the Plotinian and Procline terms of *monê–proodos–epistrophê*, but as Being, Power, and Act (οὐσία–δύναμις–ἐνέργεια). This terminology may be described as Porphyrian, since Porphyry is the first known to have referred to this triad, but Maximus is the first to explain it fully.[2] In principle it is nothing more than the triad under which the human mind contemplates every conceivable process: beginning, middle, end.[3] A being is (οὐσία), is capable of

[1] P. Sherwood, *Date-List of the Works of Maximus the Confessor* (*Studia anselmiana*, xxx) (Rome, 1952), pp. 1–2. See above, p. 483.

[2] See above, pp. 459; 466; 476; below, p. 494.

[3] See Eriugena, below, p. 524.

doing something (δύναμις), and does it (ἐνέργεια). The importance of this innovation is that in the earlier triad two members, *proodos* and *epistrophê*, belong to the category of motion, and one, *monê*, to the category of rest, while in the later, one (Power) belongs to motion, and two (Being and Act) belong to rest. Motion is no longer a composite of descent and return, but a simple link between Being and its fulfilment. It provides Maximus with a universal principle which he can apply to the Deity without a suggestion of emanationism and to created nature without denying it stability; to the intelligible or eternal world without making it co-eternal with God, and to the physical or contingent world without denying it immortality.

B. *The Triad*

God by his Nature (οὐσία) is; and is omnipotent and therefore has the capacity (δύναμις) for all act; and is perfect and so brings all act to perfection (ἐνέργεια). The Nature of God is transcendent. Like the ps.-Dionysius Maximus declares him to be 'above being itself',[1] and therefore literally inexpressible and imparticipable. To say that he is, is inadequate: to say that he is infinite, still more so, for infinity is a quality of being.[2] *A fortiori*, he has no other attributes. He neither moves nor is at rest,[3] is neither active nor passive,[4] can neither be affirmed nor denied:[5]

Negation and affirmation, which are opposite to each other, are reconciled in God, in whom each absorbs the other. The negation that signifies that God is not a being but a not-being agrees with the affirmation that this not-being is:[6] and the affirmation that he is, which does not affirm what he is, agrees with the negation that denies that he is something. Affirmation and negation in relation to each other display opposition, but in relation to God the affinity of meeting extremes.[7]

[1] ὑπὲρ αὐτὸ τὸ εἶναι, Max. Conf. *I Ambig.* VI 38 (*PG* 91. 1180B9–10) (The *Ambigua*, which appear as a single work in most MSS and are so reproduced in *PG*, consist of two distinct works, widely separated in time. *PG* follows the MS tradition of placing the later *Ambig.* (*II Ambig.*) before the earlier. *I Ambig.*, the longer and more important, occupies *PG* 91. 1062–1417, and consists of 67 chapters, of which ch. 6 is of exceptional length, containing 51 sections (these divisions are not indicated in *PG*). *II Ambig.* is contained in *PG* 91. 1032–60). See above, p. 469.

[2] Idem, *op. cit.* XI (*PG* 91. 1220C8–10). See below, pp. 495; 497.

[3] See below, p. 500.

[4] Max. Conf. *I Ambig.* XI (*PG* 91. 1221A10–B1).

[5] See below, p. 504.

[6] See above, p. 469.

[7] Max. Conf. *op. cit.* XXX (*PG* 91. 1288C1–11).

The apophatic and cataphatic theologies complement each other: 'He who by the infinity of his proper excellence is inexpressible and incomprehensible...is manifested and multiplied in all things which come from him with the good that is proportionate to each, and resumes all things into himself.'[1] In saying something of anything, if it be true, we say something of its Creator. Nor does what we say contradict the Apophatic Theology: an affirmation made about the Creator is a negation made about the creature, and *vice versa*. If the former is, the latter (in that sense of being) is not; if the latter is, the former (in that sense) is not.[2]

He is who he is and becomes all things to all men in their being and their becoming, but in himself he is not nor ever becomes in any way anything which is or which becomes, because never in any way is he associated naturally with any essence....If we are to understand the difference between God and his creatures, the affirmation of a Superessence is the negation of being, and the affirmation of beings is the negation of the Superessence.[3]

The Cataphatic Theology is concerned not with the *ousia* of God, which is Superessence, and ineffable, but with his Power and his Act, with what he can do and what he does. Since God does not act but as he wills, and, being omnipotent, has no will that he does not accomplish, his power is identical with his will,[4] and will (θέλημα) may replace *dunamis* as the middle term of the triad.[5] The divine Powers fall into two classes, corresponding to the Dionysian modes of unification (ἑνώσεις) and division (διακρίσεις),[6] which Maximus calls Providence (πρόνοια) and discrimination (κρίσις): 'By Providence I understand... that which maintains the cohesion of the whole[7]...by discrimination ...the maintenance of the difference between things...which safeguards to each creature its connexion with the *logos* after which it was conceived...and the inviolability of its individuality.'[8]

These Powers are exercised by God as Bestower of Being (τοῦ εἶναι

[1] Max. Conf. *I Ambig.* III (*PG* 91. 1080A12–B4). [2] See below, p. 497.

[3] Max. Conf. *Mystagogia* (*PG* 91. 664A4–C3). Cf. the *Gnostic Century* published by S. L. Epifanovič in *Materials to Serve in the Study of the Life and Works of St Maximus the Confessor* (Kiev, 1917: in Russian), I, 33. [4] See below, p. 495.

[5] E.g., Max. Conf. *Opuscula theologica et polemica*, IX (*PG* 91). See above, p. 492.

[6] See above, p. 461. [7] See above, p. 461.

[8] Max. Conf. *I Ambig.* VI, 18 (*PG* 91. 1133D3–1136A4). Cf. *Op. theol. et polem.* (*PG* 91. 36D5–7).

δοτήρ),[1] Creator of becoming (γενεσιουργός),[2] and Prime Mover (for no creature initiates its own movement):[3] that is to say, he is the Efficient Cause (ἀρχή) of the eternal or intelligible world, which starts from being; and of the contingent or physical world which starts from becoming; and of that motion which, as discursive reason, brings thought to its conclusion, and as mutability is the means by which the contingent world reaches its end, in which mutability, becoming, and being will be reabsorbed into him as Final Cause or *energeia*. The creation of the eternal world is the first, that of the contingent world is the second, of the five ramifications which comprise the multiplicity of the created universe. The third is the division of the contingent world into heaven and earth, the fourth the division of the earth into paradise and the inhabited region, and the fifth the division into male and female.[4]

Being, the mode of existence of the intelligible world, is a process between two terms which are identical, for both are God: God as Efficient Cause and God as Final Cause.[5] Here the triad of Being, Power, and Act takes the form of Being–Well-Being–Eternal Being (τὸ εἶναι–τὸ εὖ εἶναι–τὸ ἀεὶ εἶναι):[6] Being is the immediate product of the Divine Power, proceeds through Well-Being, and in Eternal Being returns to God as Final Cause. The first manifestation of the Divine Power or Will is Nous, which, because it is a product of the Cause of Being, is naturally (κατὰ φύσιν); and may be good if it wishes (κατὰ γνώμην, by direction of the will), that is to say, is good potentially; and if it so directs its will and actualizes its good, achieves eternity. Thus, the middle term, *dynamis*, is again identified with the will.[7] It is also, like the Divine Power, a movement from what it is to what it effects,[8] and a creative movement, for Being, at the moment of passing into Well-Being, produces Becoming (γένεσις), the first member of the triad

[1] Max. Conf. *I Ambig.* III (*PG* 91. 1073C6).

[2] Idem, *op. cit.* XV (*PG* 91. 1217C5–6). See below, pp. 496; 498.

[3] Idem, *op. cit.* XV (*PG* 91. 1217B14–15).

[4] Idem, *op. cit.* XXXVII (*PG* 91. 1304D3–1305B2). See below, p. 503.

[5] Max. Conf. *I Ambig.* VI 3 (*PG* 91. 1116B5–6).

[6] Idem, *op. cit.* VI 3 (*PG* 91. 1116A15–B4). For this triad see H. U. von Balthasar, *Liturgie cosmique* (Paris, 1946), p. 95. It derives from the ps.-Dionys., for whom the Universal Providence is ὁ τοῦ εἶναι καὶ τοῦ εὖ εἶναι τὰ πάντα αἴτιος (*Ep.* IX 3, *PG* 3. 1109C6).

[7] Max. Conf. *Op. theol. et polem.* I (*PG* 91. 12C4–7); III (45D3–48A1); XVI (185D1–5). Cf. John Damasc. *De fid. orth.* II 22 (*PG* 94. 944B).

[8] Max. Conf. *I Ambig.* III (*PG* 91. 1073B15–C5).

of the contingent world, which, through its own non-productive movement (κίνησις), reaches its end (στάσις) by passing into Eternal Being. Well-Being, the central term of the intelligible triad, is thus coterminous with the contingent triad. The extreme terms, Being and Eternal Being, are identical, for Being extends infinitely before *genesis* as Eternal Being extends infinitely after *stasis*.

Becoming, the mode of existence of contingent being, is conferred upon it out of Being (τὸ εἶναι) by God as *genesiourgos*.[1] It is the beginning of a process in space and time, that is to say, of physical movement. Since all movement which has a beginning in space and time must have an end in space and time,[2] physical movement is potential rest, and this rest, when realized, is the final term of the contingent triad of Becoming, Movement, Rest (γένεσις–κίνησις–στάσις).

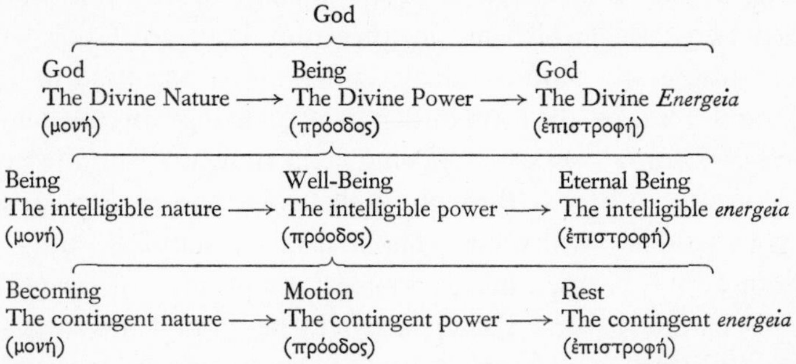

God

God The Divine Nature ⟶ (μονή)	Being The Divine Power ⟶ (πρόοδος)	God The Divine *Energeia* (ἐπιστροφή)
Being The intelligible nature ⟶ (μονή)	Well-Being The intelligible power ⟶ (πρόοδος)	Eternal Being The intelligible *energeia* (ἐπιστροφή)
Becoming The contingent nature ⟶ (μονή)	Motion The contingent power ⟶ (πρόοδος)	Rest The contingent *energeia* (ἐπιστροφή)

Since *genesis* is the product of Being, and Being the product of God; and since *stasis* is absorbed into Eternal Being, which is the *energeia* of God, the whole process, contingent becoming and eternal being, begins from God, takes place within him as his *dynamis*, sustained by him at every point, and returns to him in the end.[3] Contingent becoming lies, as it were, at the heart of eternal Being, for it is the middle term of eternal Being which transcends it; and eternal Being lies at the heart of, and is the middle term of, the Divine Triad of Being, Power, and Act, which is contained within the Unity of God.[4] At the same time, the sense of the triad *monê–proodos–epistrophê* is preserved, for the Divine

[1] See above, p. 495. [2] See above, p. 437.

[3] Max. Conf. *I Ambig.* III (*PG* 91. 1084A14–B7); XV (1217C15–D3).

[4] Idem, *op. cit.* X (*PG* 91. 1184B10–1185A1); *Centuriae gnosticae*, I 2 (*PG* 90. 1084A9–11).

Nature, Intelligible Being (before it 'moves' into Well-Being), and even *genesis* before motion are immutable: the divine and intelligible Powers and physical motion are processes from the Divine Nature, intelligible Being and contingent becoming respectively; and the Divine *energeia*, eternal Being, and rest are returns to the position from which each process began. The diagram shown on p. 496 will make this clearer.

C. *The Eternal World*

When God is said to be beyond being, 'being' is understood in the sense of intelligible being. There is no danger in calling God himself Being if it is understood that the intelligible world is not being in the same sense.[1] The same terms can be used of each level of existence, but only in relation to that level. In relation to the level above it the meaning will be qualified, for the formulation of each triad is a definition. The superessential Unity is not even defined as infinity,[2] for the mode of existence of God as being is Three: 'The Trinity is truly a Monad, for such is its nature (ὅτι οὕτως ἐστί); and the Monad is truly a Trinity, for that is its hypostasis (ὅτι οὕτως ὑφέστηκεν).'[3]

The qualification is not conferred at the moment of the triad's formulation but develops within it. God, as creator of being, confers upon the intelligible world simple being (τὸ ἁπλῶς εἶναι); but to be one thing rather than another (εἶναί πως) belongs to Nous as the exercise of the intelligible will (γνώμη), which chooses between virtue (τὸ εὖ εἶναι) and vice (τὸ φεῦ εἶναι).[4] Simple being is unbounded, or bounded only by itself;[5] being something is bounded because it does not contain its principle[6] or definition within itself.[7] This is illustrated by the difference between the *logoi* and the intelligibles. The former are the principles of existence which eternally pre-exist in the Divine Mind.[8] In their unity they are the Second Person of the Trinity,[9] hypostatically but not essen-

[1] See above, pp. 469; 494.

[2] Max. Conf. *I Ambig.* VI 41 (*PG* 91. 1184B14–D1). See above, p. 493.

[3] Max. Conf. *II Ambig.* (*PG* 91. 1036C1–3); *I Ambig.* III 1077C1–1080A5. See above, p. 490.

[4] Max. Conf. *I Ambig.* (*PG* 91. 1392B1–4). Cf. Eriugena, below, p. 529.

[5] Max. Conf. *cit.* VI 38 (*PG* 91. 1180C3–9). [6] Idem, *loc. cit.* 1180D1–3.

[7] Idem, *op. cit.* LXIII (*PG* 91. 1400C15–18).

[8] ἐν τῷ θεῷ προϋπάρχουσι παγίως ὄντες οἱ λόγοι, Max. Conf. *I Ambig.* XXXVIII (*PG* 91. 1329A1–6).

[9] Idem, *op. cit.* III (*PG* 91. 1081D1–4). See above, p. 429.

tially, and therefore not essentially God: they are not the Divine Nature but the Divine Powers or Wills (θελήματα).[1] But the intelligibles come into being, so that in relation to the nature of the *logoi*-wills their own nature is a *genesis*, whose principle is outside itself: 'Of those things of which the existence...cannot, *once they have come into being* (μετὰ τὴν γένεσιν), pass from being into not-being (i.e. the intelligibles), the *logoi* are permanent (μόνιμοι) and firmly established, having as the one origin of their being Wisdom, from which and through which they exist, and by which they are given power to be.'[2] The eternal world is the efflorescence of the Idea which in the Logos is monomorphic[3] and is its beginning and end. The *logoi* are actually one, the Being of the intelligible triad Being–Well-Being–Eternal Being, and potentially many, the evolution of the triad: the intelligibles are actually from the moment of their *genesis* many, potentially one when through Well-Being they pass to the Eternal Being of the *logoi*.

D. *The Contingent World*

Qualified being falls into two classes, the intelligibles and the sensibles, of which the former once they have come into being do not relinquish their being and are subject to the process from being through well-being to eternal being, and the latter to the process from becoming through motion to rest. Both are equally dependent on God, who is not only creator of being but creator of becoming:[4] 'God gives to all things their being and their perseverance in the mode of being particular.'[5] But in the same way as the Divine Nature contains the intelligible world which is hypostatically united to his Powers, the intelligible world contains the sensible. Here again, the hypostatic unity they share is not identity: the intelligible world is a dyad consisting of being and particular formative properties, the sensible a dyad consisting of form (in the Aristotelian sense) and matter, its form being the effect of the formative properties (the powers, i.e. the well-being) of the intelligible world, and its matter the principle of individuation which differentiates it therefrom.

[1] Max. Conf. *op. cit.* III (*PG* 91. 1085 A 7–12, B 7–12). See above, p. 462.
[2] Idem, *op. cit.* XXXVIII (*PG* 91. 1329 B 14–C 4).
[3] Idem, *op. cit.* III (*PG* 91. 1081 B 10–C 1).
[4] See above, p. 495.
[5] Max. Conf. *Op. theol. et polem.* (*PG* 91. 36 D 5–7).

Therefore the sensible world stands to the intelligible, as the intelligible to the Divine Powers, in the relation of qualified to simple being. The Celestial and Ecclesiastical Hierarchies of the ps.-Dionysius are replaced by the Aristotelian classifications of universal (καθόλου) and particular (καθ' ἕκαστον). But because 'being' as well as 'being a particular' is a gift of God, the universal retains the reality of the Platonic Form, with which it had already been identified by St Gregory of Nyssa, while the individual is as substantial as it was for Aristotle. For Gregory the universal denotes both the unity and the *logos* of all the individuals it includes and their summation in the whole;[1] consequently, the Forms have a real existence in the particulars. But he applies the principle only to the relation between Humanity (or the first, unitary creation of man) and particular men and women (or the second creation).[2] Maximus extends it to cover his whole philosophy. The fabric of the world is an oscillation between the universal and the particular, which reproduces in created nature the unity-in-diversity of the Logos-*logoi*. It is also equivalent to the *proodos* and *epistrophê*, and illustrates the relation between *dynamis* and *energeia*: 'And again the universals are destroyed (φθείρεται) by the particulars (τὰ μερικά) in segregation (κατ' ἀλλοίωσιν), and the particulars are destroyed by the universals in *analysis*:[3] the birth of the one is the death of the other.'[4]

Proodos and *epistrophê* are not two opposing motions, however closely associated, but a single unity-in-tension[5] between the intelligible and sensible worlds. For the ps.-Dionysius, God is the 'Father of Lights' which descend through levels of increasing opacity: for Maximus they illumine the boundary between the two worlds, of which the mutual attraction constitutes the physical universe, and where the Transcendent appears, in the world of immanence, as Wholly Other.[6] In this meeting of sense and symbol, the subordination of the Ecclesiastical to the Celestial Hierarchy disappears, and with it the need for a distinct Symbolic Theology: 'The world is one because it is not divided by its parts; because, on the contrary, it circumscribes the natural

[1] H. U. von Balthasar, *Présence et pensée* (Paris, 1942), pt. 1.
[2] See above, p. 450. [3] See above, p. 496.
[4] Max. Conf. *I Ambig.* VI 32 (*PG* 91. 1169C1–5). Cf. Heracleitus, fr. 62 Walzer (67 Bywater).
[5] See above, p. 493.
[6] Balthasar, *Liturgie cosmique*, 48–9.

differentiation even of the parts themselves by its relation (ἀναφορᾷ) to the indivisible unity of itself.'[1]

The principle of unity-in-diversity applies not merely to the relationship of the intelligible and sensible worlds, but to the whole of reality, including the Creator himself: 'Ever remaining himself without change or alteration, without increase or decrease, he makes himself all things to all men...humble to the humble, lofty to the lofty, Very God to those who become gods (θεουμένους).'[2] Thus, not only is man the image of God, but in a certain sense God permits himself to become the image of man: 'for [St Gregory Nazianzen] says that God and man are each the image of the other'.[3] Man is not related to God as passive to active, but as that in which passive and active are opposed to one another is to that in which their opposition is transcended. The antithesis of active and passive constitutes the duality of created being.[4] The passivity of the sensible world and the activity of the intelligible are equidistant from the Deity who transcends activity and passivity.[5]

In the sensible or contingent world the triad Being–Power–*Energeia* takes the form of Becoming–Motion–Rest (γένεσις–κίνησις–στάσις). This triad is the extension in space and time of the intelligible Power or Well-Being as the intelligible triad of Being–Well-Being–Eternal Being is the extension into multiplicity of the Divine Power or Logos. *Genesis* is a beginning in time, and what begins in time must begin somewhere; therefore place and time are the *sine qua non* (ὧν ἄνευ) of contingent being:[6] 'Leaving aside the fact that the being of beings is particularized being, not simple being...who does not know that in every being... the first thing to be known is the Where, to which is always and everywhere attached the knowledge of the When?'[7] They are the diversification of the Divine *status mobilis* in contingent being, for place belongs to the category of rest, and time to motion.[8]

But although time, with its concomitant, place, is the *sine qua non* of contingent being, it is not a new creature but the condition of being set

[1] Max. Conf. *Myst.* II (*PG* 91. 629B5–8).
[2] Max. Conf. *I Ambig.* XVII (*PG* 91. 1256B4–9).
[3] Idem, *op. cit.* VI 3 (*PG* 91. 1113B10–11).
[4] Idem, *op. cit.* XXXIII (*PG* 91. 1296A5–B4). See above, p. 433.
[5] Idem, *Cent. gnost.* II 2 (*PG* 90. 1125C6–14).
[6] See below, p. 501.
[7] Max. Conf. I *Ambig.* VI 38 (*PG* 91. 1180B4–12).
[8] Idem, *Quaestiones ad Thalassium*, LXV (*PG* 90. 757D7–10).

in motion. Therefore it is not annihilated when motion is concluded in rest, but reverts to being as eternal being, in which motion becomes eternal motion (ἀεικινησία) or rest eternally moving (ἀεικίνητος στάσις). Time is eternity measured by the march of movement, and eternity is time which has ceased to move.[1]

The new element, then, is motion, in association with which being becomes time.[2] Maximus' doctrine of motion is his most important divergence from Origenism, by which his philosophy is powerfully influenced. Origen shared with the pagan philosophers the view that all movement must be a departure from the immutable Good, and to that extent evil. For Maximus it is the predetermined concomitant of existence between *genesis* and rest, and the field in which the will has room to exercise its choice between good (τὸ εὖ εἶναι) and evil (τὸ φεῦ εἶναι). It is only when the latter is chosen that movement is evil, and becomes a deviation (τροπή) from the path that leads from being to eternal being: 'The cause of *tropê* lies not in the nature of movement but in false judgement.'[3] It is *tropê*, not *kinêsis*, which is annihilated when the process comes to rest, for, not being created by God, it is not eternal.[4]

E. *The Return*

The *aeikinêsia* or *aeikinêtos stasis* into which the motion of contingent being is absorbed is not a rapture beyond nature and the world, nor a journey which intervenes between these and God, but the process by which the intelligible creature fulfils its fundamental structure (and that of the whole created nature). The difference between the *stasis* which concludes the triad of the contingent world and the *telos* of the whole of creation into which it is absorbed is that the former is limited by the conditions of the *genesis* out of which it developed, a coming to fruition of the seeds of its particularized being, i.e. space, time and movement, while the latter is unlimited since it is simple being and eternal being.[5] It corresponds to the difference between the *genesis* of the contingent world and the principle of the intelligible world which is undifferenced

[1] Idem, *I Ambig.* VI 31 (*PG* 91. 1164B14–C1). See above, pp. 432; 437; 447; 487.
[2] Idem, *op. cit.* LII (*PG* 91. 1377D–1340A3). See above, p. 496.
[3] Max. Conf. *Ep.* VI (*PG* 91. 432A4–6).
[4] Idem, *Quaest. ad Thalas.* Prooem. (*PG* 90. 252B8–C1).
[5] Max. Conf. *Quaest. ad Thalas.* LXV (*PG* 90. 757D3–760A11).

being (τὸ εἶναι). The *telos* is not unlike Gregory of Nyssa's conception of the Third Heaven as an endless and yet not hopeless quest.[1] Repose in God is not a *stasis*, which connotes the end of a motion and is the appropriate term for the end of contingent being, but something beyond *stasis*, a 'state' which is not rest because it is more than rest, and not movement because it is more than movement.[2] In describing this state Maximus uses language similar to Gregory's: 'God, by reason of the infinity of his Nature, enlarges to infinity the appetite of those who delight in him through participation.'[3] But whereas Gregory does not resolve the paradox of a *stasis* which is at the same time a *dromos*,[4] Maximus, by the use of such terms as *aeikinêsia*, suggests the analogy of the unchanging motion of the heavenly bodies.[5]

In so far as it is movement it is a passage from the particular *logos* to the Divine Logos: 'If the soul does not freely prefer anything to her own *logos*, she will not fall away from God, but rather move towards God and become God (θεὸς γίνεται).'[6] The tendency to the realization of her own *logos* is her natural movement through the contingent triad of *genesis*–movement–rest, which in that case is well-being: the *aeikinêsia* from the *logos* to the Logos is of Grace.[7] Like Gregory of Nyssa,[8] Maximus relates it directly to the Incarnation. The Logos is not only the end, but also the Way, both through the contingent world, where it enables man to choose the good and reject the evil, and through the intelligible world, where it illumines the Nous and enables it to contemplate the Beatific Vision.

In addition to the gift of being from which contingent nature takes its *genesis*, and of eternal being in which it should find its rest, it is offered two additional gifts, the acceptance or rejection of which constitutes man's freedom of choice which intervenes between his becoming and his coming to rest. These are virtue and wisdom, which, with being and eternal being, comprise the four characteristics (ἰδιώματα) of

[1] See above, p. 456.
[2] Max. Conf. *I Ambig.* XI (*PG* 91. 1221A15).
[3] Max. Conf. *I Ambig.* III (*PG* 91. 1089B11–14). Cf. *Centuriae caritatis*, III 46 (*PG* 90. 1029C6–8); St Greg. Nyss. *Vit. Moys.* (*PG* 44. 405B–C).
[4] St Greg. Nyss. *loc. cit.*
[5] See above, p. 480.
[6] Max. Conf. *I Ambig.* III (*PG* 91. 1080C2–7). Cf. 1081B8–11, D8–9, and M. T. Disdier, 'Les fondements dogmatiques de la spiritualité de s. Maximus le Confesseur', *Échos d'Orient*, XXXIII (1930), 296–313.
[7] Max. Conf. *Cent. gnost.* LXVII (*PG* 90. 1108B13–14).
[8] See above, p. 452.

man.[1] Being and eternal being are natural characteristics, virtue and wisdom are conditioned by will and judgement. The natural characteristics constitute the Image of God, the conditioned characteristics his Likeness. For unlike Gregory of Nyssa,[2] Maximus distinguishes between the Image and the Likeness: the Image is what we are as existing and eternally existing creatures, the Likeness is what we may achieve when by practice of the virtues and the pursuit of wisdom we restore the Image to its pristine brightness.[3] The conditioned characteristics are the path which links our beginning and our end, which are the natural characteristics. But this path of virtue and wisdom is Christ, whom Origen[4] and Gregory of Nyssa[5] had already identified with substantial righteousness, and whom Maximus, on the same scriptural authority,[6] by implication identifies with Wisdom.[7] The conditioned characteristics are the means by which the natural characteristics are purified; the one conduces the human will to the will of God, the other brings human knowledge to that 'not-knowing' which the ps.-Dionysius teaches is the non-conceptual knowledge of the Divine. As in his system, purification and illumination are the steps to perfection; but they are interdependent rather than successive. Baptism is an illumination as well as a purification, for the stains which it removes concealed the light of the Image. This is why St Gregory Nazianzen calls the flesh a cloud and a curtain.[8]

Christ leads the many back to the One through the five ramifications out of which it developed:[9] the synthesis of male and female,[10] of Paradise and the inhabited world, of heaven and earth, of the intelligible and sensible worlds, to the final restoration of the complete unity of creature and Creator.[11] In the last synthesis intelligible being reaches its 'end' (τέλος) in eternal being, in which all human activity ceases. What follows is a 'rapture' (ἀνάληψις) or ecstasy of the Nous out of its own

[1] Max. Conf. *Cent. carit.* III 25 (*PG* 90. 1024B6–10). The term comes from Philo: see H. A. Wolfson, *Philo*, II (Cambridge, Mass., 1948), pp. 130 f.

[2] See above, p. 449 n. 14.

[3] Max. Conf. *Cent. carit.* III 25 (*PG* 90. 1024C1–8).

[4] Origen, *In Ioann.* [i 14], 6. 40 and [xiii 2], 32. 11, *GCS Origen*, IV 115. 1–2 and 444. 2–3 (Preuschen); idem, *In Ierem.* 15. 6, *GCS Origen*, III 130. 12 (Klostermann); *In Esaiam*, 5. 1, *GCS Origen*, VIII 263. 9 (Baehrens).

[5] St Greg. Nyss. *In Eccl.* VII (*PG* 44. 724D *ad fin.*).

[6] I Cor. i. 30.

[7] Max. Conf. *I Ambig.* III (*PG* 91. 1081C14–D7).

[8] Idem, *op. cit.* VI 2 (*PG* 91. 1112B5–12); VI 12 (1124B2–7).

[9] See above, p. 456.

[10] Cf. St Greg. Nyss. above, p. 452.

[11] Max. Conf. *Quaest. ad Thalas.* XLVIII (*PG* 90. 436A11–B8); *I Ambig.* XXXVIII (*PG* 91. 1308D11–1312B7).

nature into the Divine *energeia*: 'rapture is a *pathos* of the rapt and an *energeia* of him to whom we are rapt (τοῦ ἀναλαμβάνοντος)'.[1] It is a πάθος of the rapt because the soul has reached the end of her activity:

There is nothing left for the soul to conceive (νοῆσαι) after she has conceived all that it is in her nature to conceive. Thereafter, beyond *nous* and *logos* and *gnôsis*, she is united with God in a simple encounter without thought or knowledge or word...for God is not an object of knowledge which she can relate to her capacity for knowing (νόησις), but is without relation (ἄσχετον), and a unity which transcends knowledge, and a word which cannot be spoken or interpreted, and which is known only to God Who bestows this ineffable grace upon those who are worthy.[2]

Since the rapture does not annihilate *pathos*, but is itself a *pathos*, it is not the upper part of the soul only which is absorbed into the Divine *energeia*, but her whole tripartite nature:

Therefore, says [Gregory Nazianzen], if I make myself one with those who stand before God and enjoy the Beatific Vision, wholly possessed of peace and sanctity, I shall unite myself to the indivisible Deity by identifying my will with his (κατὰ τὴν γνώμην ταὐτότητι) and by rationalizing the irrational faculties of the soul, that is to say, the irascible and concupiscent, and by bringing them through reason to Nous and assimilating them to Nous, changing the irascible to love (ἀγάπην) and the concupiscent to joy (χαράν) like that of John when he leapt in his mother's womb and of David when he danced before the Ark as it rested.[3]

It is a true and total return of the whole creation, soul and body, with all its experiences and emotions, all the variety of God's work, his contingent and his eternal creation, to the unity and harmony of the One God from whom it proceeded.

Maximus' doctrine of motion and created nature derives from Aristotelian as well as from Neoplatonic sources. While his description of the Return owes much to Gregory of Nyssa and the ps.-Dionysius, the concept of unconfused unity (ἕνωσις ἀσύγχυτος) which had been revived in the theological context by the Council of Chalcedon in 451, and of

[1] Max. Conf. *I Ambig.* XVI (*PG* 91. 1237D7–9).

[2] Idem, *op. cit.* XI (*PG* 91. 1220B8–C3). Cf. the *Gnostic Century* published by S. L. Epifanović in *Materials to Serve in the Study of the Life and Works of St Maximus the Confessor* (Kiev, 1917: in Russian), LXXII, 48. 9.

[3] Max. Conf. *I Ambig.* II (*PG* 91. 1065D4–1068A10).

which the philosophical implications had been worked out by Leontius in the following century, enabled him to propose a theory of ecstasy which avoided the criticisms brought by Procopius against ecstasy of the Dionysian type. For Maximus it is not a brusque and violent contravention of the norms of nature, but the accomplishment of its perfection, at once an *ekstasis* and an *ektasis*.

CHAPTER 33

THE PHILOSOPHY OF ICONS

A. *The Natural Image*

It was said at the outset that Platonism and Christianism adopted different attitudes towards corporeal nature, the one regarding it as an obstacle to the soul's perfection, the other as an aid, and itself perfectible.[1] The statement requires modification on both sides. Plato in his later works taught that the sensible world, being a copy of the intelligible, was a guide to the understanding of it, and his successors, under the influence of the Asiatic cults, adopted the same attitude to man-made images; while the early Christians, inheriting the Jewish abhorrence of idolatry, regarded as sacrilegious the representation of spiritual things through the medium of matter. Paganism and Christianism reacted to the same stimulus in contrary ways: the pagan cults which infected Platonism with theurgy stiffened the resistance of the Christians and turned their monotheism, for a time, into iconoclasm.

In the sensible world natural images are distinguished from artificial images by their causes. The causes of the former are the Forms: 'The Idea', says Xenocrates,[2] 'is the exemplary cause of things which subsist naturally (κατὰ φύσιν).' The causes of the latter are concepts in the mind of the artist: 'Every artist possesses wholly the *paradeigma* in himself, and confers its shape upon matter.'[3] But if the Forms are themselves concepts in the Divine Mind,[4] then both kinds of cause are concepts or thoughts, and the difference lies in the thinker, in the one case divine, in the other human.

Mind is manifested in its thought. Therefore the concepts which are the archetypes of the images, whether divine or human, are in turn images of the mind which conceives them, whether divine or human. For this reason Philo calls the Logos, which is the pleroma of the Forms,[5]

[1] Above, pp. 426.

[2] Fr. 30 Heinze.

[3] Albinus, *Didasc.* IX 1, ed. P. Louis (Paris, 1945), p. 51.

[4] Above, p. 429.

[5] *Ibid.*

the Image of God (ἡ εἰκὼν τοῦ θεοῦ),[1] which in turn is the archetype of all else: as God is the Father of the Image, the Image is the pattern of other beings.[2] There is thus a hierarchy of natural images: the intelligible world which is the image of God, and the sensible world which is the image of the intelligible. Christians identified the Logos with Christ, who is also called Image of God,[3] and who in turn is the pattern of man, for man is created 'in' the Image (κατ' εἰκόνα), i.e. in the image of Christ, the Image of God.[4] Here again, then, there is a hierarchy of natural images, but man is not the lowest order of it, for being a creature endowed with mind he produces thoughts which are the patterns of the memorials and monuments of literature and art.[5] Likeness, the relation of image to archetype, is equivalent to participation,[6] the relation of the lower to the higher order of a hierarchy. In so far as an image is like its archetype it is equal and identical with it, for it participates in its nature.[7] Therefore every order of the hierarchy except the highest and the lowest can exist in three different ways: in its cause (κατ' αἰτίαν ἀρχοειδῶς), or in itself (καθ' ὕπαρξιν) or by participation (κατὰ μέθεξιν εἰκονικῶς).[8] Thus the Logos (and the Forms of which he is the pleroma) pre-exists eternally in the Father; exists in the Person of Christ; and exists *eikonikôs* in every human being created in his image. The three modes of existence belong to the brand of Platonism to which both Proclus and the ps.-Dionysius adhere. The latter gives as an example the fiery substance of the firmament:[9]

The superessential God is given the name of fire (πῦρ), and the intelligible oracles of God[10] are said to be afire (πεπυρωμένα),[11] and yet again the God-like orders of intelligible and intelligent angels (τῶν νοητῶν ἅμα καὶ νοερῶν)[12] are

[1] Philo, *De confusione linguarum*, 147 f., ed. L. Cohn and P. Wendland, *Philonis Alexandri opera*, II (Berlin, 1896), p. 247. For the same idea in St Greg. Nyss. see above, p. 455.

[2] Idem, *Leg. Alleg.* III 96, I 134 Cohn and Wendland.

[3] II Cor. iv. 3; Col. i. 15 *et al.*

[4] Col. iii. 9 f. See R. Leys, *L'Image de Dieu chez s. Grégoire de Nysse* (Brussels and Paris, 1951); W. Dürig, *Imago: Ein Beitrag zur Terminologie und Theologie der Römischen Liturgie* (Munich, 1952); D. Cairns, *The Image of God in Man* (New York, 1953); G. Ladner, 'Die mittelalterliche Reformidee und ihr Verhältnis zur Idee der Renaissance', *Mitteilungen des Instituts für Oesterreich. Geschichtsforschung*, LX (1952), 31 f.

[5] St John Damascene, *De sacris imaginibus*, I and III.

[6] Below, p. 509.

[7] Proclus, *In Tim.* II 81 B f. (on Plat. *Tim.* 28 A f.). Cf. K. Borinski, *Die Antike in Poetik und Kunsttheorie*, I (Leipzig, 1914), pp. 1–21.

[8] Proclus, *El. theol.* LXV. See below, p. 509.

[9] See above, p. 435.

[10] I.e. the enlightenment transmitted through the Scriptures: see above, p. 428.

[11] Cf. Deuteronom. iv. 33.

[12] See above, p. 476.

delineated . . . by fiery shapes (ἐμπυρίοις σχηματισμοῖς), and the same image of fire has one meaning when it is applied to the God who transcends every concept (νόησιν), another when applied to his intelligible 'providences' (προνοιῶν) or *logoi*,[1] and another when applied to the angels. For in the first it is in its cause, in the second in itself, in the third by participation,[2]

for the angels partake of the fiery substance.[3]

In the Dionysian terminology, the *logoi* are not only 'Providences' or precognitions, 'things known beforehand', but also pre-definitions (προορισμοί),[4] 'things marked out beforehand',[5] a term also used by St John Damascene.[6] They are analogous to the line drawn by the artist to delimit and thus create the shape of his artefact. According to Methodius of Olympus, *c.* 300, Christ assumed a human body in order that man might the better imitate him, as though he had painted his picture for us so that we could liken ourselves to the Painter.[7] The notion of Christ the Iconographer is at least as old as the second century,[8] but by the early Greek Fathers it was interpreted in the spiritual sense in which the Platonists understood the image–archetype relationship of the sensible to the intelligible world. Following Philo,[9] they identified man created in the image of God with the human *nous*,[10] to which corporeality is an accidental accretion.[11] Like Plato, they were concerned only with the natural image, which, having an eternal archetype, cannot be seen in the transient accidents, but in the eternal substance.

B. *The Artificial Image*

The artificial image was useful, however, as an illustration to explain the natural. What the image is here below by imitation (μιμητικῶς), writes

[1] See above, p. 463.

[2] Ps.-Dionys. *Ep.* IX 2 (*PG* 3. 1108C11–D6). For the existence of the archetype in the image see also idem, *EH* IV 3. 1 (*PG* 3. 473C5–6).

[3] See above, pp. 435; 443.

[4] Ps.-Dionys. *DN* V 8 (*PG* 3. 824C).

[5] Cf. Rom. viii. 29; Eph. i. 5.

[6] In Damasc. *De sacr. imag.* I 10 (*PG* 94. 1240D); III 19 (1340C).

[7] Method. Olymp. *Symposium*, I 4 (24), *GCS* (i.e. *Griechische christliche Schriftsteller*, ed. by the Kirchenväterkommission der Preussischen Akademie, Berlin), *Methodius*, XIII.

[8] Cf. *Acta Ioannis*, 28 f. ed. R. A. Lipsius and M. Bernet, *Acta Apostolorum apocrypha*, II (Leipzig, 1888), 166 f.

[9] Philo, *De opif. mund.* I 69, I 23 Cohn and Wendland.

[10] Cf. St Clem. Alex. *Strom.* II 109 (102. 6), *GCS Clem. Alex.* II 169; V 14 (94. 5), II 388; Origen, *In Gen.* I 13, *GCS Orig.* VI 15; *De princ.* IV 4. 10, *GCS Orig.* V 363; *Contra Celsum* VI 63, *GCS Orig.* II 133; VII 66. ii. 216; *Selectiones in Gen.* (*PG* 12. 93 f.); *In cant. cant.* Prologus, *GCS Orig.* VIII 64; St Greg. Nyss. above, p. 449; ps.-Dionys. *EH* IV 3. 1, 473B15–C10.

[11] Cf. St Greg. Nyss. above, p. 450.

St Basil,[1] the Son is by nature (φυσικῶς) above; and as in the painter's work the likeness (ὁμοίωσις) is according to shape, so in the Godhead is the unity (ἕνωσις), as a consequence of which 'honour rendered to the image passes to the prototype'.[2] Man, when he produces an artificial image, produces it out of corruptible matter; it cannot therefore be more than *like* its archetype, which is an immaterial concept: the Divine Image is *one* with its Archetype because it is of its essence.

The Divine Image and the artificial image differ, then, both in form (or cause), which in the one case, as in that of all natural images, is God, and in the other is man; and in matter, which in the one case is again God, and in the other is a corporeal substance; and consequently they also differ in relation to their respective archetypes, which in the one is unity and in the other likeness. But likeness does not exclude unity, it is unity-in-unlikeness, participation[3] though not identification. In every like thing there is an element that is one with that which it is like. This element is what Proclus called the existence of the archetype in the image *eikonikôs*.[4] In doing so he was anticipated by St Basil, who notes that we give the name of 'Emperor' both to the Emperor himself and to his statue, although there are not two Emperors but one. Therefore it can in a sense be said that the Emperor exists in his statue.[5] St Basil is still only employing a physical illustration of the way in which the Divinity of the Father is present in the Son, but the same illustration was later used by St John Damascene (*c.* 675–749)[6] to justify the veneration of images, which he was the first to defend on philosophical grounds, and in the Acts of the Second Council of Nicaea (the 7th General Council, 787),[7] at which the iconoclasts were finally defeated. The proposition that 'honour rendered to the image passes to the prototype' could be applied as well to the artificial as to the natural image.

But the iconoclasts argued that not only should images of Christ not be venerated: they should not, and indeed cannot, even be made. They

[1] St Basil, *De Spiritu Sancto*, XVIII 45 (*PG* 32. 149C). Cf. St Greg. Nyss. *De hom. opif.* V (*PG* 44. 137A).

[2] St Basil, *loc. cit.*

[3] See above, p. 507.

[4] See above, p. 507.

[5] St Basil, *De Spiritu Sanct.* XVIII 45 (*PG* 32. 149C). Cf. St Athanasius, *Orat. III c. Arianos* 5 (*PG* 26. 332A f.); Plotinus, V 9 [5] 5, 12–19.

[6] St John Damasc. *De sacr. imag.* III (*PG* 94. 1405A).

[7] Mansi, *Concilia*, XIII 69B f.

should not be, because to represent the Divine in a material substance is not to venerate but to dishonour him. But such an argument would inhibit all worship of whatever kind: for the very Tablets of the Law (which were held to prohibit images) were of stone, and the whole cult consists of holy objects made by human hands, which through matter lead to the immaterial God.[1] The argument is based on the conception of matter as an essence independent of God, which was certainly not St Basil's view,[2] although he is not concerned on this occasion to refute it. For the Christian, there is nothing in wood, wax, or stone that is not created by God, and to that extent divine; for him, material objects stand both above and below the status of the artificial image: above, as creatures of God and not of man (as Plato said, a bed is better than a picture of a bed);[3] below, in relation to what the image is εἰκονικῶς. The artist does not debase God, but exalts matter, and thereby co-operates with the divine purpose that all things, including matter, shall in the end be assimilated to their Creator.

It was claimed by the Christians that their images were genuine because they represented historical personages whose forms had been seen by human eyes, whereas the pagans made images of invisible powers:[4] for what Plato considered to be the prerequisite for evaluating an image, prior knowledge of the archetype,[5] was even more so for the making of one. Consistently with this, the more moderate iconoclasts (those not influenced by the Semitic prejudice against any kind of representation of the human form) objected only to such images as representations of the angels, or of the Holy Spirit in the Form of a dove; but above all to images of Christ, which were the crux of the iconoclastic controversy.

For Christ was an historical personage only in respect of his humanity, and therefore an image of Christ represents his humanity segregated from his Divinity. To venerate such an image is to make of the humanity of Christ a 'Fourth Hypostasis'; not to venerate it is to suggest that the humanity is no essential part of the Divine Logos, but a

[1] St John Damasc. *op. cit.* II 23 (*PG* 94. 1309C).

[2] See above, pp. 432–3.

[3] Plato, *Republic*, X 597.

[4] John of Thessalonica (*c.* 630), *Contra paganos et Iudaeos*, cited at the 2nd Council of Nicaea; Mansi, *Concil.* XIII 164–8.

[5] ὅ τί ἐστι πρῶτον γιγνώσκειν, Plato, *Laws*, II 669A–B.

'robe' which he put on for a time.[1] The only escape from this dilemma was to show that the image represents not only the humanity but also the divinity of Christ. 'Together with the King and God', writes St John Damascene,[2] 'I worship the purple[3] of the body, not as a robe (ἱμάτιον) nor as a Fourth Person (τέταρτον πρόσωπον)...but as being God also....Therefore I boldly represent the invisible God not as invisible but as having become visible for our sakes.'[4]

It is just this, the iconoclasts argued, that cannot be done: the invisible cannot be circumscribed, and what cannot be circumscribed cannot be depicted. In this argument the proposition is a fallacy, and the conclusion, though valid, is a *non sequitur*. The angels, who are invisible, can be circumscribed by time, because they have a beginning, and by apprehension (κατάληψις), for, since they are intelligences,[5] they must apprehend one another's natures and each is circumscribed by that apprehension. Therefore it is not true that the invisible cannot be circumscribed.[6]

But it still does not follow that everything that can be circumscribed can be depicted. 'Pictorial representation (γράφεσθαι, εἰκονίζεσθαι) is contained in circumscription (περιγράφεσθαι), while circumscription is not contained in it.'[7] The statue of the Emperor does not circumscribe the Emperor, but only one or more of his properties, and in the image of Christ it is not his Nature, or even his human nature, that is circumscribed,[8] for it reigns in heaven, but his *Energeiai*.

The iconoclasts identified pictorial representation with circumscription because they believed that a true image must be consubstantial (ὁμοούσιος) with its archetype,[9] as in the case of Christ, the Image of the Father. They saw the relation of image to archetype in terms of identity and otherness, instead of similarity and dissimilarity; for the former terms belong to the category of substance while the latter belong to the

[1] Constantine V (741–75), *frs.* 4–15 ed. G. Ostrogorsky, *Studien zur Geschichte des byzantinischen Bilderstreits* (Breslau, 1929), pp. 8–11.

[2] St John Damasc. *De sacr. imag.* I (*PG* 94. 1236B = III *PG* 94. 1325B).

[3] ἁλουργίς, the purple robe of the Emperor.

[4] See below, p. 513.

[5] See above, p. 442; below, p. 514.

[6] Nicephorus Patriarch of Constantinople (806–15), *Antirrheticos* II 7 (*PG* 100. 345C).

[7] Nicephorus, *Antirrh.* II 12 (*PG* 100. 360A–B). Cf. Eriugena on definition and place, below, p. 527.

[8] Idem, *op. cit.* 357A–B.

[9] Constantine V, *fr.* 2.

category of quality.[1] If image and archetype were consubstantial, they would come under the same definition, and the image would be its own archetype. An anonymous commentator on St John's Gospel,[2] writing before 812,[3] after distinguishing the natural from the artificial image,[4] contrasts Christ, who as the natural Image of the Father[5] contains the full truth of the Father both in form and matter, with the artificial image which contains the form but not the matter of its archetype,[6] and consequently does not have its full identity, and 'where there is not full identity, but an otherness of substance and shape, there is not room for the full truth'.[7]

But the image is the effect of which the archetype is the cause. Whoever destroys the effect destroys the cause,[8] and worship offered to the effect affects the cause.[9] Image and archetype are correlative, and therefore simultaneous: 'Artificial images, and even more so, natural images, introduce and take away the existence of the archetype to which they are related. For where there is an image, there the archetype must necessarily appear; and when the image is removed, the archetype is altogether removed with it.'[10] The commentator does not introduce these arguments as novelties, and they must have been current for a considerable time, perhaps from within a decade of the Second Council of Nicaea.[11] Although he was a monk of Studium,[12] and his arguments are reproduced by Theodore Studites in his second *Epistle* written in 814,

[1] Nicephorus, *Antirrh.* I 31 f. (*PG* 100. 281 A). The argument is Aristotelian (cf. Arist. *Cat.* VIII, 11 a 15), and indicates the way in which the iconodules, during the period when the works of St John Damasc. were proscribed by the iconoclastic Emperors, had recourse to the Aristotelianism which had been taught in Byzantium for over a century. See P. J. Alexander, *The Patriarch Nicephorus of Constantinople* (Oxford, 1958), p. 14 n. 1; K. Schwartslose, *Der Bilderstreit* (Gotha, 1899), p. 183; G. Ostrogorsky, review of E. J. Martin, *A History of the Iconoclastic Controversy* (London, 1930) in *Byzantinische Zeitschrift*, XXXI (Munich, 1931), p. 391: above, p. 483.

[2] Brit. Mus. Addit. MS 39605, ed. Karl Hausmann, *Ein neuentdeckter Kommentar zum Johannesevangelium* (Paderborn, 1930). Cf. W. Jaeger, 'Der neuentdeckter Kommentar zum Johannesevangelium und Dionysius Areopagites', *Sitzungsberichte der Preussischen Akademie der Wissenschaften* (1930), pp. 569–94.

[3] Alexander, *op. cit.* p. 197.

[4] *Comm. in Ioann.* 184. 32–5 Hausmann. See above, p. 506.

[5] See above, p. 507.

[6] *Comm. in Ioann.* 187. 25–33 Hausmann. Cf. Nicephorus, *Antirrh.* I 17 (*PG* 100. 228 D).

[7] *Comm. in Ioann.* 188. 6–8 Hausmann.

[8] Contrast Philoponus, above, p. 481.

[9] *Comm. in Ioann.* 190. 34–8. Cf. St Basil, above, p. 509.

[10] Idem, 191. 5–9.

[11] Alexander, *loc. cit.*

[12] Hausmann, *op. cit.* p. 84.

they were not peculiar to that monastery, for Nicephorus, who also made use of them,[1] had little contact with it. They must have been part of the Byzantine Aristotelian tradition.[2]

C. *The functions of Artificial Images*

Granted the possibility and the venerability of sacred images, it still remains to indicate their use. For pagan and Christian alike, the artificial image had both a symbolic value, and inherent powers, proper to itself and talismanic in the case of the pagans, communicated and sacramental in the case of the Christians.

The image is the visible means by which the invisible Deity can be sensibly worshipped.[3] Athenagoras, in his *Supplication for the Christians*[4] addressed to Marcus Aurelius and Commodus *c.* 177, cites the pagan argument: 'Although these are only likenesses, yet there exist gods in honour of whom they are made; and the supplications and sacrifices presented to the likenesses are to be referred to the gods, and are in fact made to the gods; and there is not any other way of coming to them, for "'tis hard for man to meet in presence visible a god".'[5] 'Who but an utter fool', asks Celsus,[6] 'considers them to be gods, and not dedications and statues *for* the gods?'; and there are similar passages in Porphyry,[7] Olympiodorus,[8] and Julian the Apostate.[9]

The same arguments with which the pagans defended themselves against the Christians were used by the Christians against the Jews and other opponents of the images. The ps.-Dionysius borrows from Plotinus the illustration of the priest who, when he has entered the sanctuary, has an intelligible knowledge (ἐπιγνωσόμεθα) of the invisible things of

[1] Nicephoros, Ἔλεγχος καὶ ἀνατροπὴ τοῦ ἀθέσμου καὶ ἀορίστου καὶ ὄντως ψευδωνύμου ὅρου τοῦ ἐκτεθέντος παρὰ τῶν ἀποστατησάντων τῆς καθολικῆς καὶ ἀποστολικῆς ἐκκλησίας καὶ ἀλλοτρίῳ προσθεμένων φρονήματι ἐπ' ἀναιρέσει τῆς τοῦ θεοῦ λόγου σωτηρίου οἰκονομίας, MS Paris Bibl. Nat. gr. 1250, f. 224 v, *ap.* Alexander, *op. cit.* p. 204.

[2] Alexander, *op. cit.* p. 198.

[3] Cf. St John Damasc. above, p. 511.

[4] Athenag. Πρεσβεία περὶ χριστιανῶν XVIII 1, ed. E. J. Goodspeed, *Die ältesten Apologeten* (1914).

[5] Homer, *Iliad* XX 131.

[6] Origen, *Contra Celsum* VII 62. Cf. E. R. Bevan, *Holy Images* (1940).

[7] Porphyry, *Against the Christians*, ed. A. Harnack, *Abhandlungen des kgl. Preussischen Akad. der Wissenschaften*, phil.-hist. Kl. (1916), 1, *fr.* 16, pp. 92 f.

[8] Olympiod. *In Gorgiam* 225, 17–20 Norvin. See above, p. 482.

[9] Julian, *Ep. ad Theodorum*, ed. J. Bidez, *L'Empereur Julien: Œuvres complètes*, I 2 (Paris, 1924), pp. 160–2.

which the images in the main body of the church give a visible impression.[1]

The substance and orders above us [the Celestial Hierarchy]...are incorporeal and their hierarchy is intelligible and hypercosmic:[2] but...our own Hierarchy [the Ecclesiastical] is filled with a variety of sensible symbols appropriate to our condition (ἀναλόγως ἡμῖν αὐτοῖς), by which symbols we ascend through the hierarchies (ἱεραρχικῶς) to the uniformity of deification. ...They, as intelligence,[3] have intelligible knowledge as of right: we ascend to the contemplation of the Holy Mysteries through sensible images (εἰκόνες) as best we may.[4]

The chiefs of our Hierarchy...have given us the super-celestial Mysteries by means of sensible symbols[5]...and divine things by means of human, and immaterial by means of material, and the super-essential by means of what is familiar to us, through their revelations both written and unwritten.[6]

St John Damascene was perhaps the first to call the images the books of the unlettered.[7] As the ineffable may be communicated in words, so the invisible may be honoured in visible objects:

And we set up his figure perceptibly everywhere, and hallow the first sense, sight, as we also hallow the sense of hearing by speaking. For the image is a memorial, and what the book is to the lettered, the image is for the illiterate, and what speech is to hearing, the image is to sight. Through it we are spiritually united with God.[8]

The superiority of sight over the other senses, which is an Aristotelian doctrine,[9] is also used by Nicephorus to justify the use of images.[10] The images offer to the faithful the tradition and the history of the Faith without mediation, the things themselves as though they were present; whereas words, although they are also images of things, present them

[1] Ps.-Dionys. *EH* III 3 (*PG* 3. 428D1–4); II 8. 2 (397C5–8). Cf. Plot. VI 9 [9] 11. See above, p. 463; see St Greg. Nyss., above, p. 453.

[2] Cf. St Greg. Nyss. above, p. 454.

[3] See above, p. 511.

[4] Ps.-Dionys. *EH* I 2 (*PG* 3. 373A7–B3). See above, p. 465.

[5] Cf. Julian, *loc. cit.*: 'Our fathers established statues...as symbols of the presence of the gods.'

[6] Ps.-Dionys. *EH* I 5 (*PG* 3. 376C10–D10). For the unwritten tradition see above, p. 428.

[7] St John Damasc. *De sacr. imag.* III 9 (*PG* 94. 1332B).

[8] St John Damasc. *De sacr. imag.* I 17 (*PG* 94. 1248C). Cf. below, p. 516.

[9] Cf. Aristotle, *Metaph.* A 1, 980a1–24; *De sensu*, 437a; Themistius *ap.* Plutarch, *De recta ratione audiendi* 2; ps.-Aristotle, *De mundo* IV, 397a17.

[10] Nicephorus, *Apologeticus maior* LXII (*PG* 100. 748D–749B); *C. Eusebium et Epiphanidem*, ed. Pitra, *Spicilegium*, IV (Paris, 1858), pp. 301 f.

indirectly, for after having received the words by the ear, reflection is required to arrive at the truth they represent.[1]

There is here an implication that the image is more than a mere memorial of an archetype which is no longer there. The presence of the archetype in the image, although not substantial, is a real presence. Christians shared with pagans the belief that material objects can be the seat of a spiritual power communicable by physical contact.[2] The earliest images to be venerated by Christians had some physical connexion with their archetype, such as the clay tablets which the Stylites of the fifth and sixth centuries made from the sweat and dirt scraped off their bodies and handed down to the pilgrims who visited them,[3] or the 'images not made with hands' (ἀχειροποίητοι) which originated from materials such as a towel or cloth imprinted with the effigy of the sacred original by physical contact,[4] or reliquaries in the form of the saint whose relics they contained, to which the power in the relics was communicated by contact.[5] It is perhaps significant that the earliest recorded statue of Christ (seen by Eusebius, who did not deny its genuineness) was believed to have been erected by the woman with an issue of blood, whose faith in the efficacy of physical contact was justified.[6]

Here the value of the image is not didactic but is due to the fact that it is a repository of the power transmitted to it by a primary repository, who is the subject of the image. It is natural that with the passage of time images of this type, like that other kind of 'unwritten tradition', the oral,[7] should disappear, and be replaced by images in which the presence of the archetype is established by similarity. But although both types of image are used by pagans as well as Christians, the Christian veneration of images is not to be identified with the pagan worship of idols, and therefore is not a breach of the commandment which forbids the latter.[8] For the pagan the power brought to the idol by contact or assimilation is an automatic effect of the law of *sympatheia* as

[1] Idem, *Antirrh.* I (*PG* 100. 377B–C, 380A). [2] Cf. above, p. 458.

[3] K. Holl, 'Der Anteil der Styliten am Aufkommen der Bilderverehrung', *Gesammelte Aufsätze zur Kirchengeschichte*, II (Tübingen, 1928), pp. 388–98.

[4] E. von Dobschütz, *Christusbilder* (Leipzig, 1899), pp. 277–9.

[5] A. Grabar, *Martyrium: recherches sur le culte des reliques et l'art chrétien antique*, II (Paris, 1946), pp. 343–57.

[6] Eusebius, *Hist. eccl.* VII 18. Cf. Matt. ix. 20–2. [7] See above, p. 428.

[8] St Germanus of Constantinople (d. 733), *Epistola dogmatica* II (*PG* 98. 180–1).

the apple falls by the law of gravity: for the Christian the power in the image is the divine *energeia* which, in the contingent world, works with the co-operation of man.[1] As man's free will is required for the fabrication of the image, so it is required for its efficacy. The *haemorrheousa* would have touched the hem of Christ's garment in vain if she had not had faith in the power which would cure her. The external act is ineffective without the internal sentiment.[2]

Indeed, the theory of the veneration of images, to which Christendom is committed by the Seventh Oecumenical Council,[3] brings the sensible world fully within the scope of the descent and return of the divine *dynameis* and *energeiai* from and to the divine Transcendence. The Divine Powers descend into the intelligible world and make God knowable to the intellect and so bring back the intellect to God; they descend into the sensible world and are the means by which the senses perceive God and are so brought back to him; but the recognition of God in the natural image is still an operation of the intellect, not of sense. It is only when man, realizing within the sensible world the creative powers with which he is endowed by virtue of being created in the image of the Creator, himself creates the artificial image that the Divine Power,

[1] Cf. above, p. 515.

[2] St Germanus, *op. cit.* II (*PG* 98. 180–1).

[3] Christendom: it is a common view that the theory and practice of the veneration of images is confined to the Roman Communion and the Eastern Orthodox Churches. But Hooker, the first important theologian of the Church of England, reflects, almost verbally, the teachings of St John Damascene and Nicephorus: 'Men are edified, when either their understanding is taught somewhat whereof in such actions it behoveth all men to consider, or when their hearts are moved with any affection suitable thereunto; when their minds are in any sort stirred up unto that reverence, devotion, attention, and due regard, which in those cases seemeth requisite. Because therefore unto this purpose not only speech but sundry sensible means besides have always been thought necessary, and especially those means which being object to the eye, the liveliest and the most apprehensive sense of all other, have in that respect seemed the fittest to make a deep and a strong impression: from hence have risen not only a number of prayers, readings, questionings, exhortations, but even of visible signs also.... Words, both because they are common, and do not so strongly move the fancy of man, are for the most part but slightly heard: and therefore with singular wisdom it hath been provided, that the deeds of men which are made in the presence of witnesses should pass not only with words, but also with certain sensible actions, the memory whereof is far more easy and durable than the memory of speech can be' (*Ecclesiastical Polity*, v, ed. Keble, Church and Paget, *The Works of Richard Hooker*, I (Oxford, 1888), pp. 418–19. It is true that Hooker is speaking not of images but of ceremonies, but the reasoning covers both, and images are found in churches of the Anglican Communion, and sometimes venerated. The proposition that the essential elements of Christian teaching have been determined 'in the old symbols and decisions of the seven Ecumenical Synods' (of which the 7th promulgated the veneration of images) has been accepted by Anglicans in conversations on reunion held with the Orthodox and Old Catholics (Archbishop Germanos in *Faith and Order*, ed. H. N. Bate (London, 1927), pp. 21–2).

through matter moulded into some semblance of itself, becomes apprehensible to the physical sense as well as to the intellect, and 'sight is hallowed'[1] and turned, with the intellect, to God.

[1] St John Damascene, above, p. 514. [For the Carolingian criticism of this whole doctrine of images see the following Part (VII, *Western Christian Thought from Boethius to Anselm*), ch. 36, pp. 566ff.]

CHAPTER 34

JOHANNES SCOTTUS ERIUGENA

A. *Introduction*

The Christian Platonism of the Greeks, shaped by the Alexandrians, the Cappadocians, the ps.-Dionysius and St Maximus the Confessor from material that continued to the end to be drawn from the pagan schools, had grown apart from that of the Latin West, which, except for Alexandrian influence reaching it through Boethius, was largely unaffected by any pagan thought later than Porphyry. But the defeat of iconoclasm in the East at the Second Council of Nicaea caused a flow of iconoclastic refugees to the West, bringing their books with them. The works of the ps.-Dionysius became available even if they were not read. In 758 Pope Paul I sent a copy to Pepin the Short,[1] and Hadrian I may later have sent another to Abbot Fulrad of S. Denis.[2] But there is no evidence of any use being made of these books. It was the gift of a third codex[3] from the Emperor Michael the Stammerer presented to Louis the Debonair at Compiègne in September 827[4] that initiated the

[1] Paul's letter accompanying the gift is preserved in MS Vienna Staatsbibl. 449 (the *Codex Carolinus*), edited by I. Gretser, *Volumen epistolarum quas romani Pontifices Gregorius III, Stephanus III, Zacharias I, Paulus I, Stephanus IV, Adrianus I et ps.-Papa Constantinus miserunt ad Principes et Reges Francorum Carolum Martellum, Pipinum et Carolum Magnum* (Ingolstadt, 1613), p. 121; Caj. Cenni, *Monumenta dominationis pontificiae sive Codex Carolinus iuxta autographum vindobonense*, I (Rome, 1760), p. 148; W. Gundlach, *Epistola ad Pippinum*, *MGH*, *Ep.* III (Berlin, 1892), p. 529. Cf. D. Bouquet, *Recueil des historiens des Gaules*, I, p. xxviii; v, p. 513; C. Prantl, *Geschichte der Logik im Abendlande*, II (Leipzig, 1870), p. 3 n. 6; P. Jaffé, *Bibliotheca rerum germanicarum*, IV, *Monumenta carolina* (Berlin, 1867), pp. 101–2; J. B. de Rossi, 'De origine historia indicibus scrinii et bibliothecae Sedis Apostolicae', in H. Stevenson, *Codices palatini Bibliothecae Vaticanae* (Rome, 1886), p. lxxxiii; L. Traube, *MGH*, *Poet. lat. aevi Caroli*, III (Berlin, 1896), p. 520 (521) n. 3; P. G. Théry, *Études dionysiennes*, I (Paris, 1932), pp. 1–3. For the date see P. Kehr, 'Über die Chronologie des Briefes Pauls I.', *Nachrichten der Göttinger Gesellschaft der Wissenschaften* (1896), pp. 102 f. Jaffé and Gundlach date the document between 758 and 763.

[2] The authority for this is J. Mabillon, *Annales Ordinis s. Benedicti*, II (Lucca, 1739), Bk XXXI, n. xlii, p. 536, but he supports it by no documentary evidence. See J. de Ghellinck, *Le Mouvement théologique du xiie siècle* (Paris, 1914), pp. 70–1. For Fulrad see Félibrien, *Histoire de l'abbaye royale de s. Denis en France* (Paris, 1706), pp. 19, 42.

[3] Now MS Paris Bibl. Nat. gr. 437. See H. Omont, 'MS des œuvres de s. Denys envoyé de Constantinople à Louis le Debonair', *Revue des études grecques*, XVII (1904), p. 230; Sauzay, *Musée de la Renaissance*, Notices des ivoires, no. 53.

[4] *Rescriptum Hilduini abbatis ad serenissimum Imperatorem Ludovicum... de notitia excellentissimi martyris Dionysii*, *PL* 106. 16; Baronius, *Histoire de l'abbaye de s. Denys en France* (1825),

study of the ps.-Dionysius in the West and led to the transplantation of Greek Christian Platonism into Europe.

After an abortive translation by Hilduin,[1] the abbot of S. Denis where the codex was deposited, a new version was requisitioned in or about 860[2] by Charles the Bald from Johannes Scottus, an Irishman who some time in the first half of the century had been driven from his country by the depredations of the Danes,[3] and who like so many of his compatriots had brought with him the reputation for a knowledge of Greek exceeding what could be found on the European continent at that time. Considering the imperfections of the text from which he had to work and the fact that even among the Irish the knowledge of Greek was, by modern standards, limited both in vocabulary and in understanding of the rules of grammar and syntax, Eriugena's[4] achievement was remarkable; not so much for the translation itself, of which the style is marred by his concern to give a word-for-word rendering of so venerable an author, as for his insight into the meaning of the original. He discovered in himself an instinctive sympathy for the Greek way of thinking, and embraced it with enthusiasm.

He was given the opportunity to indulge his taste further: for Charles, who had learnt from Anastasius the Librarian of the Vatican of the glosses on the ps.-Dionysius attributed to St Maximus the Confessor,[5] set Eriugena to translating the latter's earlier *Ambigua*; and, on his own initiative apparently, he also made a translation, under the title *De Imagine*, of the *De hominis opificio* of St Gregory of Nyssa, perhaps in the belief that the author was St Gregory Nazianzen, whose teachings

pp. 212, 1218; Ivo de Chartres, IV, 104 (*PL* 161. 289 f.); Dom Maïeul Cappuyns, *Jean Scot Érigène, sa vie, son œuvre, sa pensée* (Paris and Louvain, 1933), pp. 150 f.

[1] Ed. Théry, *op. cit.* II (Paris, 1937). He dates it between 832 and 835, *op. cit.* I, 20.

[2] I. P. Sheldon-Williams, 'A bibliography of the works of Johannes Scottus Eriugena', *Journal of Ecclesiastical History*, X, 2 (1960), p. 203.

[3] J. Colgan, *Life of St Buo* (Louvain, 1645), p. 256, *ap.* F. E. Warren, *Antiphonary of Bangor*, I (London, 1893), n. 3. [On the earlier philosophical and theological activities of Eriugena see Part VII, ch. 36 C–D, pp. 576–86.]

[4] Johannes used the name Eriugena ('Irishborn' on the analogy of the Virgilian *Graiugena*) only for the Dionysian translations, but it is more distinctive than his proper name, which by a widespread custom it replaces. 'Eriugena' is more correct than the commoner 'Erigena', which is not found before the thirteenth century.

[5] Anastasius, *Epistola ad Carolum Calvum* (*PL* 122. 1027/8, 21–35). See above, p. 474.

Maximus expounds in the *Ambigua*.[1] Thus he fortuitously became acquainted with three of the most characteristic and important documents of the Greek Christian Platonism; the effect of their influence upon him was to bring him as wholly into the Greek tradition as if he had been a Byzantine writing in Greek, and to make of him the agent through whom the Western world came into this valuable inheritance.

B. *The four aspects of Nature*

When he was asked to translate the ps.-Dionysius he was probably already engaged upon a work of his own to which he eventually gave the name *Periphyseon*.[2] It was intended to be an investigation of the universal nature which should achieve a synthesis of a number of ideas drawn from sources which were exclusively Latin: the Neoplatonism of St Augustine, the Aristotelian logic and physics which came to him through Boethius and others, and more recondite theories which, Greek in origin, can also be found in Latin intermediaries.

The inquiry opens with a division of universal nature (all that is and all that is not) into four 'aspects':[3] that which is not created and creates; that which creates and is created; that which is created and does not create; that which does not create and is not created. The pattern is clearly suggested by the doctrine of the syzygies in which Eriugena had shown interest in earlier works,[4] according to which each of the four

[1] Except for the first six chapters of the *Ambigua*, neither of these translations has been published. See Sheldon-Williams, 'Bibliography', pp. 203–6. Evidence has come to light to suggest that Eriugena also made a translation of another work of St Maximus, the *Quaestiones ad Thalassium*. See Dom Paul Meyvaert, 'The Exegetical Treatises of Peter the Deacon and Eriugena's Latin rendering of the Ad Thalassium of Maximus the Confessor', *Sacris Erudiri*, XIV (1963), pp. 130–48.

[2] The earliest extant MS is superscribed in Greek περὶ φύσεως μερισμοῦ, which in the twelfth-century MS (Camb. Trin. Coll. O 5 20) from which the first edition was edited is taken for the title and Latinized as *De divisione naturae*, by which consequently the work is generally known. But it is probably the title of the first section only: in its Latin form it appears as the first lemma (perhaps in Eriugena's autograph) of MS Bamberg Ph 2/1 which was copied from the Rheims MS, and which, like all the early MSS except Rheims, is given the title περὶ φύσεων (in the same hand as the lemmata). See Sheldon-Williams, 'The title of Eriugena's Periphyseon', *Studia patristica*, III (*Texte und Untersuchungen* 78) (Berlin, 1961), pp. 297–302.

[3] Eriugena calls them *species* and *theoriae*.

[4] *Annotationes in Marcianum*, 4. 3–28 Lutz; *Comm. in Boeth. Cons. Phil.* III 9. 8–9, ed. H. Silvestre, 'Le commentaire inédit de Jean Scot Érigène au mètre ix du livre III du "De consolatione philosophiae" de Boèce', *Revue d'histoire ecclésiastique*, XLVII (1952), pp. 44–122. Cf. St Basil, above, p. 433; but Eriugena's source is probably Macrobius, *Somn. Scip.* I 6, 489–90 Eyssenhardt.

elements is connected with, and can pass into, the element adjacent to it: fire is dry and warm, air is warm and moist, water is moist and cold, earth is cold and dry. There are also two syzygies by opposition: the first aspect is opposed to the third, and the second to the fourth[1] for the same reason that fire is opposed to water, and air to earth:[2] none of these pairs has a quality in common. Although Eriugena is careful not to omit these two syzygies (he makes Alumnus ask Nutritor to repeat his description of them),[3] they do not play an important part in his system; but he is anxious to show that this system is basically a dialectic. The doctrine of the syzygies is an application to the physical world of the dialectician's table of contraries and contradictories which he would have known from Boethius.[4] The original purpose of the *Periphyseon* was to show that it can be applied to metaphysics as well.

C. *The fourth aspect of Nature*

In the physical world the opposites are still syzygies because they are linked by intermediaries: the heat of fire can pass into the coldness of water through the moisture of air, and the moisture of air into the dryness of earth through the coldness of water;[5] but when Eriugena attempts to establish similar relationships between the four aspects of universal nature he encounters a difficulty. The first three give no trouble:[6] they can be plainly discerned in the Neoplatonic trichotomy of the Universe into God, the Forms, and sensible matter. God, as Efficient Cause, is the uncreated Creator; the Forms are his first creatures through whom he creates the sensible world, and are therefore created creators;[7] the sensible world, created by God through them,

[1] *Periphyseon*, I 1, 441B10–442A12. (For the *Periphyseon*, references are to book, chapter, column and line of *PL* 122.)

[2] *Annot. in Marc.* 4. 16–26 Lutz; *Comm. in Boeth. ad loc.* Cf. Aristotle, *De gen. et corr.* II 4.

[3] The *Periphyseon* is a dialogue between a preceptor and his pupil. In the earliest MSS these are called respectively N and A, which are usually taken to stand for Nutritor and Alumnus. In later MSS A was read as a Greek delta (= Discipulus), causing M (= Magister) to be read for N, as in the printed texts.

[4] Cf. Boethius, *In Arist. De interpretatione*, I, ed. Meiser (Leipzig, 1877), p. 87.

[5] Eriugena, *Annot. in Marc.* 4. 19–22 Lutz; *Comm. in Boet.* III, met. 9, 8–9.

[6] Idem, *Periphyseon*, I 1, 442A14.

[7] Dean Inge (*Philosophy of Plotinus*, I, ed. 3 (London, 1941), p. 75) calls the Forms 'formative principles in the world of appearance....They are seen by Plato and all Platonists to be also creative forces.' 'In the *Sophist* the *dynamic* character of the Ideas is strongly insisted upon' (idem, *op. cit.* p. 76); cf. above, p. 431. For the Forms as creatures see below, p. 529.

creates nothing, and is therefore the uncreative creature. Indeed, these three aspects are taken directly from St Augustine:

The Cause, then, that makes all and is not made itself is God [causa itaque rerum, quae facit nec fit, deus est]. The other causes do both effect and are effected [aliae vero causae et faciunt et fiunt]: such are all created spirits.... The corporal causes which are rather effects than otherwise are not to be counted as efficient causes because they come but to do that which the will of the spirit within them doth enjoin.[1]

It is the fourth aspect which presents difficulties;[2] for it is not apparent that the opposition of that which neither creates nor is created to that which both creates and is created is mediated by that which is created and does not create in the same way as the opposition of the last to that which is not created and creates is mediated by that which both creates and is created; nor does it seem to form part of the chain of cause and effect which unifies the Augustinian triad. It stands apart.

Eriugena presents the fourth aspect as an innovation,[3] but it is already to be found in the numerological theory of the Pythagoreans, who divided the numbers into four categories: that which begets without being begotten, the Monad; that which is begotten and begets, the Tetrad; that which is begotten and does not beget, the three-dimensional Ogdoad of the sensible world; and that which is neither begotten nor begets, the Hebdomad. The source of this information is Philo,[4] who goes on to argue that since begetting involves motion both in the begetter and the begotten,[5] only the Hebdomad is immutable, and is therefore the Master of all.[6] He quotes a passage from Philolaus[7] which Lydus also uses in the same context,[8] indicating that the theory was known in Neoplatonic circles.

The argument that since God is immutable, he neither is begotten nor

[1] St Aug. *De civ. dei* V 9, ed. Kalbfleisch, I (Leipzig, 1928), p. 207, tr. John Healy, Everyman edition, I (London, 1945), p. 154. Cf. Eriug. *Periphyseon*, I 1, 442A15–B3.

[2] *Periphyseon*, I 1, 442A12–13.

[3] *Op. cit.* I 1, 442A13–14.

[4] *De opif. mund.* C–CI, ed. Cohn (Berlin, 1896), 33. 26 – 34. 19. For the Monad as Begetter (of life and soul) see also *Quaest. in Gen.* II 46. 12.

[5] Cf. Plotinus, VI 3 [44] 21, 39.

[6] Philo, *De opif. mund.* 34. 12 Cohn. See also *De Abr.* XXVIII; *Leg. alleg.* I 46; *Quod deus immut.* XI; *De decal.* CII–CVI; *De Septen.* I and VI; *Quaest. in Gen.* II 12. 91 and 93; II 41. 119; II 78. 162; *Vit. Moys.* II 210; *De opif. mund.* LXXXIX f.

[7] Philolaus, fr. B. 20 = Diels, *Vors.* I (Berlin, 1950), 416. 8–22.

[8] Lydus, *De mensibus*, II 12, Wuensch (Leipzig, 1898), 33. 8 f.

begets is used by Candidus in his dispute with Marius Victorinus,[1] which Eriugena had almost certainly read, for at the end of the only ninth-century MS of the Letter of Candidus with Marius' reply[2] there is a note in the hand which is widely thought to be his;[3] while he could have known of the Pythagorean theory through Macrobius,[4] another author with whom he was acquainted.[5] Since for the Pythagoreans numbers are the universal principles of nature, he would feel justified in combining it with the Augustinian triad, and thus arriving at his own theory *de divisione naturae*.

D. *St Maximus the Confessor*

But although Eriugena might find in his Latin sources a precedent for a fourth aspect of nature related to the other three by a dialectical device, he is still left with the task of integrating it with them ontologically. It inherits from the Pythagorean Hebdomad a uniqueness which isolates it from the rest of nature: 'But the fourth aspect', says Nutritor, 'is set among the impossibles; its distinguishing feature (*differentia*) is that it cannot be.'[6] When Alumnus asks for elucidation he is put off with a digression which lasts for the rest of the book.

Eriugena is rescued from his embarrassment by the Greeks. The second book begins with a long quotation from the *Ambigua*, and he at once notices that in Maximus his four aspects are reduced to three by the identification of the first and the fourth.[7] For Eriugena this becomes the

[1] Candidus, *Epistola ad Marium Victorinum de generatione divina*, I 4–11, ed. P. Hadot, *Marius Victorinus: Traités théologiques sur la Trinité*, I (Paris, 1960: *Sources chrét.* 68), pp. 112–24.

[2] MS Bamberg 46 (*olim* Q. VI 32), f. 41 r.

[3] L. Traube, 'Paläographische Forschungen, V: Autographa des Johannes Scottus, aus dem Nachlass herausgegeben E. K. Rand', *Abhandl. d. kgl. bay. Akad. d. Wiss., philos.-philol. Kl.* XXVI, I (Munich, 1912), pl. XI. An affinity between the plan of the *Periphyseon* and certain themes of Marius Victorinus is indicated by Mlle D'Alverney, 'Le cosmos symbolique du xiie siècle', *Archives d'histoire doctrinale et littéraire du Moyen Âge*, XX (Paris, 1953–4), pp. 39 n. 5, 42 n. 1).

[4] Cf. Macrobius, *Somn. Scip.* I 5, 16, 494. 27–30 Eyssenhardt.

[5] Although it has been denied that Eriugena had read Macrobius (Duhem, 'La physique néoplatonicienne au Moyen Âge', *Revue des questions historiques* (Louvain, 1910), p. 15; Cappuyns, *op. cit.* p. 216 n. 2; Silvestre, *art. cit.* p. 116), he mentions him twice by name in the *Annot. in Marc.* (22. 154 Lutz), and once in his *Expositiones super Ierarchiam caelestem* (III 4, ed. H. Dondaine, *Arch. d'hist. doctr. et litt.* XVIII (1951–2), p. 254), where *Somn. Scip.* I 4 (489 Eyssenhardt) is cited.

[6] *Periphyseon*, I 1, 442 A 2–4.

[7] Professor Tatakis finds the doctrine of the four aspects of nature in the ps.-Dionysius and Maximus (*Philosophie byzantine*, ed. 2, p. 86), but from the passages to which he has kindly drawn my attention it cannot be deduced without difficulty, and evidently was not by Eriugena.

first of a succession of syntheses which carry him beyond his objective of rationalizing the quadripartition of nature to the reduction of the quadripartite nature itself to the unity which is God.

Already in the first book, again following upon a citation of Maximus, God is stated to be the Final as well as the First Cause, with the assumption that he is therefore also all that lies between:

> For he is the Principal Cause of all things which are made by him and through him, and therefore is also the end of all things that are from him. So he is Beginning, Middle and End:[1] Beginning, because all things that participate in being are from him; Middle, because in him and through him they subsist; End, because towards him move all things which seek rest from their movement and the establishment of their perfection.[2]

But this is an isolated passage, attached to a discourse on the first aspect of nature, where it breaks the continuity of the thought, and like the other passages in the first book which are obviously Greek-inspired reads like a subsequent addition. The application of Maximus' triad to the whole quadripartite nature is made in Book III: the Divine Nature as Beginning is the 'creative and not created nature';[3] as Middle, it is first 'created by itself in the Primordial Causes, and thus creates itself, that is, begins to appear in its theophanies',[4] and then is properly said to be created—though not to create—in the final effects of the Primordial Causes;[5] as End, 'we rightly say that it is neither created nor creative'.[6]

E. *The ps.-Dionysius*

What is said about the first aspect of nature can with equal propriety be said of the whole of nature because the first aspect (God) contains the whole. Strictly speaking, Eriugena's division of nature is not the division of a whole into parts which the physicists apply to the sensible world, nor the division of genus into species which the dialecticians apply to the intelligible world,[7] but a kind of meta-dialectics which alone is applicable to the whole of nature (inclusive of Creator and creature),[8] and which he finds it hard to define: *intelligibili quadam universitatis contemplatione.*[9] But as the intelligible species are more unified

[1] Cf. Maximus, above, p. 492.
[2] *Periphyseon*, I 11, 451D1–452A1. Below, p. 530.
[3] III 23, 688D3.
[4] *Ibid.* 689A15–B2. See below, p. 527.
[5] *Ibid.* 689B9–11.
[6] *Ibid.* 688D7–8.
[7] *Periphyseon*, II 1, 523D2–3.
[8] *Ibid.* 524D4–5.
[9] *Ibid.* 524D3–4.

in their genus than the physical parts in their whole, so the four aspects are more unified in universal nature than species in a genus. If, then, it is true that the genus only becomes manifest and thinkable in its species, it is *a fortiori* true that the universal Cause only becomes manifest and contemplable in its divisions. Apophatically speaking, God is not a genus any more than he is a whole:[1] cataphatically speaking, he is that before all else 'for all things may rightly and reasonably be predicated of him'.[2]

Therefore throughout his discourse on universal nature Eriugena remains a dialectician. The terms species, which he explicitly uses of the four aspects, and genus, which by implication denotes the universal nature, are transferred from the dialectics of the intelligible world to the universal meta-dialectics which embraces both the intelligible and the sensible worlds.

Dialectics is still the 'science of disputation',[3] proceeding by the division (διαιρετική) of genera into species and of species into individuals, and the reduction (ἀναλυτική) of individuals into their species and species into their genera,[4] but it is concerned not merely with thought but with the whole of reality (οὐσία):

> The art which the Greeks call Dialectic...is first and foremost concerned with *ousia* as its proper principle, from which every division and multiplication of its subject takes its start, and descends (*descendens*) from the most general...to the most particular, and ascends again...by the same stages... until it attains the *ousia* from which it began, and in which it never ceases to seek its rest.[5]

This is the very language in which he summarizes the teaching of Maximus:

> The Universal Cause, which is God, is both simple and multiplex; what is meant by procession, that is, the multiplication of the Divine Goodness, is all

[1] *Ibid.* 523D3–7.

[2] *Ibid.* 524D1–3. The last two citations are from an insertion in the margin of MS Rheims 875 in the hand reputed to be Eriugena's.

[3] *Periphyseon*, V 4, 868D7–869A1; cf. *De praedestinatione*, VII 382B12–13.

[4] *Periphyseon*, I 14, 463B1–4; *Expos.* VII 2, 183A3–184C12. In the *De praed.*, philosophy is regarded as a dialectic of four branches: διαιρετική, ὁριστική, ἀποδεικτική, ἀναλυτική (358A4–15), a classification which is only found elsewhere in the writings of the Alexandrian School: the preface to Porphyry's *Isagoge* by an unknown Christian author, printed by J. A. Cramer (*Anecdota graeca e codd. manuscr. Bibl. Regiae Parisiensis*, IV [Oxford, 1841], p. 430) from MS Paris Coislin 387; and David (for whom see above, p. 483), *Comm. in Isag.*, printed by Cramer (*op. cit.* p. 442) from MS Paris Bibl. Nat. gr. 1938. See above, p. 483.

[5] *Periphyseon*, V 4, 868D7–869A11; cf. IV 4, 749A1–6.

things that are, descending from the highest to the lowest, first through the general essence of all things, then through the most universal genera, then through the less universal, through the less particularized species to the most particularized: and then this same Divine Goodness returns (*reversio*) by gathering itself together (*congregatio*) from the infinitely varied multiplicity of the things that are, through the same stages to that most unified unity of all things which is in God and which is God; so that on the one hand God is all things and, on the other, all things are God. The divine procession into all things is called *resolutio* (ἀναλυτική),[1] and the return is called *deificatio* (θέωσις).[2]

Thus, the dialectical processes of division and reduction are identified with the *proodos* and *epistrophê* of the ps.-Dionysius, whose treatise on the Divine Names 'admits us into the most subtle and secret mysteries of the unity and the trinity of the Divine Nature, explaining first the procession of the One Universal Cause into the Primordial Causes, and then through them its manifold manifestation (*theophania*) in the genera, species, and individuals of invisible and visible natures'.[3]

F. *The Primordial Causes*

The universal *proodos* and *epistrophê* are the *divisio* and *reversio* of the divine dialectics which is the exemplar of the intelligible dialectics practised by the human mind. The division of genus into species and the reversion of species into their genus are not imposed upon nature by the mind but are discovered by the mind to be the way in which the principles of nature are disposed in the Divine Mind.[4] Were it not for this disposition, neither God nor the intelligible world would be knowable at all: for mind is only known in the distinguishing of its thoughts,[5] and these in turn depend on the distinctions in nature; and similarly the Mind of God (which is God himself) is only known in its thoughts, which are the principles of those distinctions, the Forms[6] or, as Eriugena calls them, the Primordial Causes, which constitute his second aspect of nature.

Therefore *proodos* (or *divisio*) is a process of self-manifestation. At

[1] This must be a slip. Elsewhere ἀναλυτική and *resolutio* are identical with *reversio*.

[2] *Versio Maximi Ambiguorum*, prooem. (*PL* 122. 1195 A8–1196 A2).

[3] *Versio Dionysii*, prooem. (*PL* 122. 1034 C6–14); cf. *Periphyseon*, III, 678 D2–4.

[4] *Periphyseon*, IV 4, 749 A1–6. Below, p. 529.

[5] II 23, 577 B.

[6] Above, pp. 437; 476; 497.

the beginning of the *Periphyseon* Eriugena discusses five different ways of distinguishing that which is from that which is not, and decides that the most adequate is that which predicates being only of what is apprehensible to sense or intellect.[1] On this definition, self-manifestation means self-creation: the mind, which has no being outside its thoughts, creates itself in thinking, and God, who transcends being, creates himself in the Primordial Causes. Therefore, the second aspect of nature which is created and creates, like the first which includes it, is an aspect of the Divine Nature, 'created by itself in the Primordial Causes and thus creating itself in beginning to appear in its theophanies'.[2]

God in his first aspect as the uncreated Creator of all things is the First Person of the Trinity: in his second aspect as created Creator he is the Second. The Logos or Divine Wisdom[3] is the pleroma of the Divine Thoughts or Primordial Causes: *quidquid enim in dei verbo substantialiter est...non aliud praeter ipsum verbum est.*[4] Since the Logos is eternal they too (in their true, unitary nature) are eternal,[5] and since the Logos is potentially infinite they too (when actualized in their effects) 'extend to infinity: for as the First Cause of all, from whom and in whom and through whom and for whom they are created, is infinite, so they too know no limit which encloses them'.[6]

G. *The Effects*

The infinity of the Primordial Causes is distributed into the multiplicity of their effects by a process of segregation which in the intelligible world is called definition and in the sensible world place. While all definition is not place (for place requires corporeality, whereas definition does not), all place is definition;[7] and all definition is division, all division is dialectic, and dialectic, like all the arts, is in the mind.[8] But whereas the divisions which the human mind discovers in universal nature are in the Mind of God, the definitions and localizations of the intelligible and sensible worlds are in the mind of man. Man is therefore

[1] *Periphyseon*, I 3, 443A9–D4; III 2, 628B–C.
[2] *Periphyseon*, III 23, 689A15–B2. See above, p. 524.
[3] Cf. *Periphyseon*, II 23, 568B1: *sapientiam patris, filium dico.*
[4] III 9, 642A5–7. See above, p. 526; below, p. 528.
[5] II 20, 556C14–D3. Cf. II 31, 561B; III 5, 635C; III 16, 667C; V 24, 909D–910A.
[6] III 1, 623D5–9.
[7] See above, p. 511.
[8] *Periphyseon*, I 28, 475B10–13.

a kind of subsidiary creator. His thought is the spatio-temporal becoming of nature as the Divine Wisdom is its eternal essence. As the Primordial Causes are in, and are, the Divine Logos, so their effects are in, and are, the human reason. The human logos, like the Divine, is all that it knows.[1] Furthermore, as all the Primordial Causes are one in the Divine Logos, so all the effects are one in the human reason.[2] Finally, since unity always precedes differentiation, and God is prior to his thoughts and man to his knowledge, the effects exist in a truer and better sense in the unity of human nature than in the multiplicity of their sensible manifestation in the same way as the Primordial Causes have a higher existence in the unity of the Divine Logos than in the multiplicity of their effects.

But since human nature itself is a Primordial Cause, *notio quaedam intellectualis in mente divina aeternaliter facta*,[3] the totality of defined and localized effects which that Primordial Cause is is likewise in the Mind of God. Therefore the definitions and localizations applied to the effects are not their essence as the divisions of universal nature are its essence, but distinctions imposed by the mind upon an essence which, being divine, is prior to it. Only God creates *ex nihilo*.

The *nihilum* out of which God creates is his own Nature,[4] which he creates in the created and creative nature of the Primordial Causes and, through man, in the non-creative and created nature of the effects.[5] Therefore the third aspect of nature, like the second and the first, is an aspect of the Divine Nature. These three aspects are the manifestation in universal nature of the Trinity. The first, the Father, is, by generation, the Cause of the Son, who is therefore God's first manifestation and self-creation, embracing all the rest;[6] and, by conferring subsistence, is the Cause of the Spirit,[7] who proceeds from him through the Son;[8] the Son is the Cause of the creation of the Primordial Causes;[9] the Spirit (operating through man) of their distribution into their effects,[10] 'into genera, species, and individuals...whether of the heavenly and intelligible essences...or of the sensible essences of this visible world,

[1] IV 9, 779B7–13.

[2] IV 9, 779B14–C4.

[3] *Periphyseon*, IV 7, 768B9–10.

[4] III 17, 678D2–679A5; III 19, 681B14–C6.

[5] II 23, 577B11–C3. Above, p. 527.

[6] See above, p. 527.

[7] II 30, 600–1.

[8] II 31, 603A5–7.

[9] II 22, 566A7–B4; II 36, 616A. See above, p. 527.

[10] II 36, 616A.

both the universals and the particulars which are separated in place, move through time, and differ in quantity and quality'.[1]

H. *The Return*

But it is also true that the Primordial Causes and, through man, their effects are created in God. The *Periphyseon*, which explores the traces of the Divine Nature in the world, finding nothing in the world that is not a trace of the Divine Nature, seems to teach that God and his creation are one. But there is a real distinction between them. God contains all things: but that which contains cannot be identical with that which it contains[2] for the latter is defined or localized while the former is not. All things which after God are endowed with being possess not simple but particularized being, *non simpliciter sed aliquo modo esse*.[3] As has already been said,[4] the divisions of universal nature, of which this is the most significant, are real because they are made not by the human mind but by God.

Nevertheless, when the human mind practises dialectics, it is imitating the divine activity, and if in the intelligible dialectics division must be balanced by reversion, it is because in the Divine meta-dialectics the *proodos* is balanced by the *epistrophê*. There comes a point in human thought where specification reaches its limit and it must retrace its steps towards generalization. So too the Divine *processio* into creation does not descend to the absolute dissipation of nothingness, for it subsists in the Superessence and is therefore entirely and eternally preserved. The limit is reached with matter, which is not absolute nothingness, but a not-being seeking to become, 'a motion which abandons total not-being and seeks its rest in that which truly is'.[5] It is at the beginning of the *epistrophê* which counterpoises the *proodos* of the Not-being which condescends to being.

This aspiring motion which starts from matter is the universal life-principle or *vita communis* which Eriugena identifies with the World-Soul:[6] for life is the name for soul from the moment when, as it were, it

[1] II 22, 566 A 12–B 4.
[2] *Periphyseon*, III 17, 675 C 14–D 1. Cf. G. C. Capelle, *Autour du décret de 1210: iii: Amaury de Bène: Étude sur son panthéisme formel* (Paris, 1932), p. 54.
[3] I 39, 482 A 1–2. See Maximus, above, p. 497.
[4] Above, p. 526.
[5] II 15, 547 B 9–12.
[6] III 36, 729 A.

utters its first cry on issuing from the womb of matter until, after ascending to form and clothing itself in body where it is manifested in the constant shifting of the elements until they resolve themselves into their incorporeal natures and ascend to the life of sensitive beings (fishes which derive their life from water, birds from air impregnated with water), it arrives at the rational nature of man,[1] who is the Final Cause in relation to the sensible universe. For it is man's function to be the agent of the lower part of the process by which God as the true Final Cause[2] withdraws the effects into their Causes, and the Causes into himself.[3] Man, created head and, as it were, God of the realm of effects, withdraws the sensible world into the intelligible,[4] and both into himself, so that in returning to God he brings the whole of creation with him.

The divinity from which the created universe is distinguished by particularized being is the end to which the universe returns when the particulars are resolved into the universal. Eriugena is following Maximus when he illustrates the deification of nature from the association of air and light: 'Nature with its Causes shall enter into God as air enters into light.'[5] In both cases it is a unification without confusion of natures.[6] When nature, resumed in man, is deified, it is not therein destroyed.[7] But that to which it returns is not the very nature of God, which is imparticipable and is related to nature neither as its creator nor as that in which nature is created. When the Scriptures speak of the Vision of God, they refer to his theophanies: 'We do not mean by this that any creature other than the Humanity of the Word can transcend all the theophanies...but that there are theophanies so exalted that they are known by the highest contemplation to which the Divine Nature can be subjected (*proxima deo contemplatione*) to be above every creature and are regarded as theophanies of theophanies',[8] that is, the revelation of God which the theophanies themselves enjoy. Cataphatically speaking, not only the Primordial Causes and their effects, the second and

[1] Cf. II 13, 542A11–13, 'non solum rationabilem *animam* verum etiam...vitam nutritivam et auctivam'.
[2] Above, p. 524.
[3] II 2, 528C–D; III 4, 632C9–11. See above, pp. 527–8.
[4] II 23, 577C–D.
[5] V 8, 876A15–B2.
[6] I 10, 451B3–9.
[7] V 8, 876B2–10.
[8] V 23, 905C2–10. Cf. I 8, 448B15–C5; V 27, 926D; above, p. 455.

third aspects of nature, the self-manifestations and self-creations of God in the intelligible and sensible worlds, but the whole dialectic of universal nature is God: 'He himself is the *divisio* and *collectio* of the universal creature, and its genus and its species and its whole and its part.'[1] Apophatically speaking, he is the fourth aspect of nature which eternally and immutably contemplates itself; and which, contrary to the case of the other aspects, is distinguished from the first not by nature but in the mode under which the divine is contemplated.[2]

I. *Conclusion*

In the *Periphyseon* Eriugena set out to write a dialectical treatise, and although the discovery of Greek Christian thought changed and presumably enriched the original conception, he retained its dialectical framework. Throughout he continually refers to the structure of the universe and the structure of thought in identical terms, for the divisions which man sees in the created universe are the divisions which articulate his thought about it, and this is so because they are the divisions into which God articulates his own thought through which it was created. In both cases division is a *proodos* from the One to the Many. Similarly when human thought reassembles the individuals into their species and the species into their genera, it is bringing back the multiplicity of the corporeal world into the unity of the intellect, and when God brings back the sensible and intelligible worlds into the unity of universal nature, he completes, on the supra-intelligible level, the same dialectical operation. If Eriugena 'hypostasizes the *Tabula logica*',[3] he does so because it is the plan upon which the universe is created. That plan is discovered by thought because thought placed it there, and indeed it is thought, the Thought of the Creator of the Universe, which is the substance of the Universe. That man should think, imperfectly but essentially, what God thinks, is a necessary consequence of his having been created in the Image of God.

Eriugena is conspicuous not so much for the originality of his thought as for his boldness in expressing it and his skill in synthesizing the doctrines in which he had been brought up with those that came to him

[1] II I.
[2] II 2, 527D–528A.
[3] Ueberweg criticizes him for this in his *History of Philosophy*.

later from his Greek sources. By this synthesis he not only was able to solve problems arising out of his own system but, in accommodating to the latter the teachings of the Cappadocians, the ps.-Dionysius and St Maximus concerning the descent and return of the soul, he clarified these also. Difficulties regarding the status of the divine *dunameis*, which are not creatures and yet not identical with the Creator,[1] are resolved in Eriugena's conception of the Primordial Causes as created by God and yet creative because they are God creating himself, and through them their effects which are also self-creations of the Divine; and the deduction from that that the first three aspects of nature are aspects of God, who yet remains distinct from his creation under his fourth aspect, reveals the essential unity of the two triads which Christianism took over from Neoplatonism: *monê*, *proodos*, *epistrophê* and *ousia*, *dynamis*, *energeia*. Finally, if the actualization of the Divine Power is the return to the Divine Nature in the same way as the actualization of man's intellectual powers is a return to the unified concept, then the fourth aspect of nature, the imparticipable One, is fitted into a rational scheme, and the mystical exposition of the return is included in a rational framework.

Both as a translator and as an original writer Eriugena's influence was to prove considerable. The Dionysian versions form the basis for those of Saracenus and Grosseteste (written in clearer Latin and from better texts), and therefore underlie the curriculum of the philosophical schools where the ps.-Dionysius was the chief authority until superseded by Aristotle in the thirteenth century, and the tradition of Western mysticism which also derives from the ps.-Dionysius. The doctrines of the *Periphyseon* were taught by Eriugena's disciples and their followers, such as Remigius, Heiric of Auxerre and the mysterious 'Icpa'.[2] The work was epitomized by Honorius of Autun[3] (Augustodunensis) and others.[4] It was widely read among the Cathars, and was supposed

[1] See above, p. 431.

[2] The author of glosses on Porphyry's *Isagoge*, MS Paris Bibl. Nat. lat. 12949, s. ix, sometimes attributed to Eriugena himself.

[3] Under the title *Clauis physicae*, MSS Paris Bibl. Nat. lat. 6734, Gottweig 103, Lambach 102, all of the twelfth century.

[4] E.g. MS Oxford Bodl. Auct. F. iii 15, ff. 31–68. See Sheldon-Williams, 'An epitome of Irish provenance of Eriugena's De divisione naturae', *Proceedings of the Royal Irish Academy*, LVIII, C 1 (June 1956).

to have inspired some of the heresies of Almeric of Bena and David of Dinant, and was condemned in the thirteenth century in consequence.

And yet it continued to be influential; for although no further copies were made after the twelfth century and many then existing must have suffered the fate of heretical works, and although the first printed edition, which appeared in 1681,[1] was immediately placed upon the Index, much of the text was preserved in glosses to the Latin Dionysius,[2] in which form it was studied by, among others, St Albert the Great.[3] Eriugena, therefore, though banned and unacknowledged, has been a formative influence in the tradition not only of Western mysticism, but also of medieval scholasticism.

[1] Ed. by Thomas Gale, Regius Professor of Greek at Cambridge. See Sheldon-Williams, 'Bibliography', pp. 211–12.

[2] Over 6 per cent: see H. F. Dondaine, *Le Corpus dionysien de l'Université de Paris au xiiie siècle* (Rome, 1953), pp. 88, 135–8.

[3] Dondaine, *op. cit.* pp. 88, 138–9.

PART VII

WESTERN CHRISTIAN THOUGHT FROM BOETHIUS TO ANSELM

BY

H. LIEBESCHÜTZ

ABBREVIATIONS

BOETHIUS

Isag. Porph. ed. pr./ed. sec.	*In Isagogen Porphyrii commenta (editio prima/editio secunda)*
De Trinitate	*De Sancta Trinitate ad Symmachum*
De consol.	*De Consolatione Philosophiae*

ANSELM OF CANTERBURY

Ep.	*Epistolae*
Ep. de Incarnatione	*Epistola de Incarnatione Verbi*

CHAPTER 35

BOETHIUS AND THE LEGACY OF ANTIQUITY

A. *The last Roman and the medieval tradition of logical studies*

When we try to draw a borderline between antiquity and Middle Ages, in order to define the point where the history of medieval philosophy begins, the work of Boethius comes immediately to our mind.[1] The last Roman and the first schoolman, the two titles with which he is normally introduced, express in their combination clearly his position between the two periods. His link with the Middle Ages is obviously very strong. Translations of two treatises from Aristotle's *Organon*, his introductions for the beginners and his commentaries and monographs for the advanced student of logic, have deeply influenced the course of medieval thought. In this development the gradual absorption of the Boethian legacy remained an important aspect up to and including the rise of early Scholasticism in the twelfth century. Through all the centuries of the Middle Ages *De consolatione philosophiae*, the Roman senator's final account with life, was a standard book, stimulating discussions among scholars, and a source of spiritual strength in critical situations. Hundreds of manuscripts, originating from the eighth to the fifteenth century, prove the importance of the Boethian corpus of writings in the libraries of Western and Central Europe.

But the history of his influence in the medieval world shows clearly that the Roman interpreter of Aristotle was not himself a part of it, but rather an intellectual force radiating from a distance. In life and thought Boethius still belonged to Christian antiquity. There is no doubt that he and his contemporaries felt the possibility of the end approaching

[1] On Boethius' environment and achievement: E. K. Rand, 'Boethius the Scholastic', in: *Founders of the Middle Ages* (Cambridge, Mass., 1920), pp. 135–80.—*In categorias Aristotelis II*; *PL* 69. 201 B: 'Et si nos curae officii consularis impediunt quominus in his studiis omne otium plenamque operam consumamus, pertinere tamen videtur hoc ad aliquam rei publicae curam elucubratae rei doctrina cives instruere.'

and certainly such foreboding had a stimulating influence on their studies and literary activities. At this time Italy was ruled by a Germanic king, and his Ostrogothic retainers represented the power in the state as a warrior class. Theodoric, in his attitude to learning, may appear rather similar to Charlemagne, if we do not compare them too closely. Boethius was favoured by the court for many years and reached finally a high position as *magister officiorum* in this society, in which military power and administration were divided between the Gothic swordsmen and the literary Romans. But Boethius, in contrast to representatives of learning in the medieval world was not only a layman—examples of this type existed still in the Carolingian period—but he did not write for the education and religious instruction of the Germanic society by their clergy; he expected his readers to come from the educated class of the landowning aristocracy, to which Anicius Manlius Severinus Boethius himself belonged by his family. Symmachus, his father-in-law, who had also been the mentor of his youth, was the great-grandson of the man who had pressed the claim to restore the altar of Victory to the council chamber of the Senate. At this time that meant conflict with Ambrosius in the name of belief in the classical tradition and in Roman greatness. The fifth century had brought about a definite change. The national pride of this class, the feeling of continuity with the past was still alive. But now they found their ancient ideal represented in the position of Rome as the head of the Christian world. They were eager to defend such aspirations against rival claims from Constantinople and in the secrecy of their hearts they refused to recognize the Gothic rulers as legal representatives of the *res publica*, because of their adherence to a heretical creed, Arianism. Their zeal for orthodox belief had a background of Roman patriotism.

This social environment is relevant to the understanding of Boethius' thought. To the modern reader of his books he certainly appears as a trained scholar and man of letters. But he did not see himself merely as a professional writer, but rather as a late follower of Cicero, for whom literary activities were an appropriate occupation for the leisure hours which high office and politics allowed him. After 550 years he intended to complete the great task which the master of Latinity had started, to renew philosophical learning in his own mother tongue.

Boethius was conscious of the fact that his great predecessor in this task had already faced the problem of finding the adequate equivalents for Greek terminology in a language which had grown by describing the concrete world of an agricultural community not originally interested in the theoretical aspects of things.

This task was carried on in schools, where literature was taught as a part of rhetorical education. Martianus Capella offers examples for the period about 400. The patristic writers of the Latin Church from Tertullian to Marius Victorinus and Augustine did the corresponding work in the service of speculative theology. But it was finally Boethius who established the vocabulary of abstraction with which the schoolmen of later generations could do their work.[1]

The programme by which the Roman senator in Gothic Italy intended to complete Cicero's work was very comprehensive. He planned to translate the whole Aristotelian corpus, as far as it was still available to him. In this way he hoped to bring all three sections of philosophy, logic, ethics and natural science, in their full range to his countrymen. The next step in his scheme was the translation of all Platonic dialogues as basis for a synthesis of Platonism and Aristotelianism. He wished to refute the majority opinion, that the two great teachers of Greek philosophy were opposed to each other in the essentials of their thought.[2]

When, in consequence of a radical change of political conditions, Theodoric's will brought violent death to Boethius, while he was still in his forties, all his work in this field had been restricted to the logical doctrines of Aristotle; nothing lasting had been accomplished regarding the translation of the Platonic dialogues. But this does not imply any siding with Aristotle. His disinclination to define an opinion on an issue which to most people seemed to contain the essential difference between the two systems, is expressed in a clear refusal to declare one master right and the other wrong. We read this famous passage in two versions, which appear in the first and second edition of his interpretation of Porphyry's Isagoge, the introduction to the elementary concepts of logic. In the Greek text the question of the nature of species and

[1] M. Grabmann, *Gesch. d. scholastischen Methode*, 1 (Freiburg i. Br., 1909), pp. 156 f.

[2] *In librum de interpretatione (editio secunda)*, 1, cap. 2 (*PL* 64. 433).

genus had been raised; the alternatives are surveyed: either they are, as concepts, mere products of the human mind, or they exist, either as material or as immaterial beings. Their existence may be inherent in the things which are the objects of our senses, or they may be separate. Porphyry had refused to discuss this question, because it would have led him to an investigation beyond his literary purpose of writing an elementary book on philosophy.[1] Boethius goes beyond the text he explains by refuting the objection that universal propositions are fictitious, because nobody can see them. Nobody would maintain that a geometrical line is the same kind of fiction as the centaur, a compound of man and horse. We think of this mathematical conception as of something outside corporal existence, but we are conscious of the fact that we have abstracted it from our sense experience. In the same way 'species' exists in the objects of our observation, from which we collect the impression of similarity between different things. This similarity becomes a thought in our mind and so a 'species'. When we go on to compare different species and find similarity between them, 'genus' arises in the same way as a mental phenomenon. While we observe the similarity in single things it remains an object of our sense experience; but when it leads to an act of generalization it is transformed into the mental process of understanding: species and genus are inherent in objects of observation. But as instruments in the process of understanding reality they belong to the sphere of the mind as separate entities.

Boethius concludes this chapter by stating that Plato went beyond this view when he maintained the existence of species and genus not only in the act of understanding, but in reality. Aristotle's opinion is identical with the doctrine Boethius himself was giving as further explanation to Porphyry's text. He did so because the *Isagoge* is an introduction to an Aristotelian treatise.[2] But Boethius emphasized that by doing so he did not mean to give a judgement on the question as such, which must be decided on a higher level of philosophical reflection.

This abstention from a subject-matter which seemed to lie beyond

[1] *Isag. Porph.*, *ed. pr.* I, cap. 10 Brandt, p. 24.—*ed. sec. loc. cit.* I, cap. 10, p. 159.

[2] *Isag. Porph.*, *ed. sec.* I, cap. 11, p. 17, *loc. cit.* p. 167: 'idcirco vero studiosius Aristoteli sententiam executi sumus, non quod eam maxime probaremus, sed quod hic liber ad Praedicamenta conscriptus est, quorum Aristoteles est auctor.'

the scope of the endeavour which the author has in hand, corresponds well with the carefully organized programme in which one stage of work was planned to follow the other in logical sequence. Boethius, while writing these paragraphs in his commentary to Porphyry, could not foresee that 600 years later the alternatives, which he had left side by side without definite conclusion, would form the centres around which the opposite views of realists and nominalists in the important debate on the nature of concepts would crystallize.

But the impact of Boethius' logical work on the development of Western thought is no product of historical chance. The bias of higher education towards rhetoric, which can be traced back to the sophist and the early Hellenistic period, had brought dialectic into the service of literary activities as a part of the trivium. The subject was planned to train the student in the shaping of a persuasive forensic argument rather than in methods for establishing truth scientifically. Boethius, as an author of textbooks on the liberal arts, avoided dealing with the trivium. He translated and compiled from the Greek in order to produce up-to-date Latin textbooks for the quadrivium, the mathematical sciences of numbers and bodies, of immobility and motion.[1] The manuals on Arithmetic and on musical theory survived and had a long history in the schools. In connexion with these scientific interests he was also considered as an expert on a technical problem. Theodoric thought him well equipped by his studies to design a water-clock, which he wished to send to the Burgundian King Gundobad, his brother-in-law.[2]

This attitude of mind, unusual in the Latin West, had also an influence on his extensive logical studies; they were taken out of their usual literary context and brought back to their original philosophical meaning of examining man's instrument for the understanding of his world. The function of higher education in the earlier Middle Ages was essentially to preserve a class of men capable of understanding Latin. The emphasis was no longer on speech-making but on the writing of letters and documents, but the general aim of rhetorical training, which had made logic a part of the trivium, remained valid. We shall see later how

[1] P. Courcelle, *Les Lettres Grecques en Occident. De Macrobe à Cassiodore* (Paris, 1943), pp. 261–4.

[2] Cassiodorus, *Variae* I, 45, § 4 in: *Mon. Germ. Hist., Auctores Antiquissimi*, XII, p. 40.

the existence of Boethius' logical writings in the libraries and their use in schools was fitted into this framework of education. But their potential force as instruments for the investigation of truth did not remain latent for ever. Their fuller assimilation during the eleventh century was a factor in the rise of the scholastic method, and prepared the way for the full understanding and use of the whole Aristotelian organon during the twelfth century.

B. *A statesman as lay theologian*

The strongest reason for tracing the origin of scholasticism back to Boethius is derived from his application of Aristotelian terminology to the definition of trinitarian doctrine.[1] Not only Carolingian scholars and Gilbert de la Porée, but also Thomas Aquinas wrote commentaries to his theological treatises, and E. K. Rand went so far as to say that Boethius was perhaps only prevented by his early death from anticipating in his own way the great synthesis brought about by the Dominican master of the thirteenth century. In our context we cannot attempt to define the position of Boethius in the history of theological thought by measuring the distance which separates the Roman author at the end of Antiquity from his commentator in the thirteenth century. But we must try to sketch the relationship between philosophy and Christian belief in Boethius' mind as a necessary presupposition for the understanding of the book *De consolatione philosophiae*, which, on the strength of its theistic piety and Christian ethics, became a medieval classic. It is well known that its author has avoided any formulation which would declare an exclusively Christian belief and any clear reference to biblical or ecclesiastical authority. As long as the authorship of the theological treatises was disputed, this character of his final confession could be explained by the assumption that Boethius had always been a Christian only in name in order to fulfil the legal condition for holding high office in Rome. But the discovery of a short fragment from a writing by Cassiodorus about the men of letters related to his own family, has barred this easy way out of the difficulty.[2]

[1] On the influence of Boethius' theological writings on the Middle Ages: M. Grabmann, *Die theologische Erkenntnis- und Einleitungslehre d. H. Thomas v. Aquin. auf Grund seiner Schrift In Boethium de Trinitate* (Fribourg, Switzerland), pp. 1–32.

[2] H. Usener, *Anecdoton Holderi, Ein Beitrag zur Gesch. Roms in Ostgothischer Zeit* (Bonn, 1877), p. 4: 'scripsit librum de sancta trinitate et capita quaedam dogmatica et librum contra Nestorium'.

The situation in which the Roman senator and philosopher entered the field of theological controversy has been reconstructed by recent research. Between 513 and 519 negotiations were going on for liquidating the schism between east and west, which more than thirty years earlier had arisen out of controversies about the definition of the two natures in Christ. A complicating element in the dispute of doctrines was the appearance of an ethnic group of monks from the lower Danube who, in order to reconcile the monophysite opinion of the East with Roman teaching, pressed for the inclusion of the formula *unus de trinitate passus est* in any proposed agreement. To the subject of this dispute, which combined subtle questions of doctrine with problems of political control and power, Boethius contributed four short theological treatises in 512 and 522.[1] They were a kind of experiment, in which he applied the philosophical concepts, to which he had dedicated his studies, in order to define more clearly and persuasively the doctrine, once proclaimed by the council of Chalcedon under the influence of Pope Leo I. In this way he gave his support to the programme on which his Roman circle under the leadership of Symmachus wished to establish unity between east and west. They were successful in 519, when, after the death of the Emperor Anastasius, the new Byzantine regime under the influence of the future ruler Justinian decided to give in to Rome on the question of doctrine.

Boethius' intervention in the dogmatic debate was encouraged by Augustine's interpretation of the Trinity in philosophical terms.[2] Boethius uses the concepts of substance and relation, which he had discussed thoroughly in his Aristotelian studies, to explain the dogma. The divine *substance* represents unity, relation within this unity is the presupposition of Trinity.

An investigation of the concepts *natura* and *persona* leads to the definition that nature is the specific peculiarity of every substance, while

[1] V. Schurr, 'Die Trinitätslehre des Boethius im Lichte der "skythischen Kontroversen"', in: *Forschungen z. christl. Literatur- und Dogmengesch.* XVIII, cap. 1 (Paderborn, 1935).

[2] *De Trinitate, Prooemium*, Stewart, Rand, p. 4: 'Idcirco stilum brevitate contraho et ex intimis sumpta philosophiae disciplinis novorum verborum significationibus volo ut haec mihi tantum vobisque conloquantur;...Sane tantum a nobis quaeri opportet quantum humanae rationis intuitus ad divinitatis valet celsa conscendere....Neque enim medicina aegris semper adfert salutem; sed nulla erit culpa medentis, si nihil eorum quae fieri opportebat, omiserit.... Vobis tamen etiam illud inspiciendum est, an ex beati Augustini scriptis semina rationum aliquos in nos venientia fructus extulerint.'

persona is the indivisible substance of a *rational* nature. In this way philosophical terminology renders Nestorius' doctrine of the two persons in Christ meaningless. At the end of one of the three treatises which were dedicated by Boethius to the deacon John, he asks his clerical friend whether he thinks these arguments agree with the teaching of the Church. In case John should not be able to give such assurance, he is requested to work out, if possible, another and more correct rational interpretation of faith.[1] Boethius is conscious of the fact that this philosophical inquiry about theological questions cannot go beyond a certain point, but he adds that such a borderline also exists in other fields.

He knows well that he comes to theology as an outsider, who sees an opportunity of applying the resources of his own field of study, and cannot expect anything like general recognition. But he feels strongly that his own philosophical approach gives him superiority over the average ecclesiastic, the figure that dominates the council discussions, which do not even touch the surface of the subject. He gives in one preamble a short report on such a meeting, where he fell silent, because the pretensions of the ignorant controversialists impressed him like madness. But the problem of defining the right position between the heresies of Nestorius and Eutyches made his mind work; finally he formed a logically organized argument, which he submitted to the judgement of John, his theological expert.[2]

There is no sign that any form of conversion or of spiritual progress has led Boethius at this stage definitely away from philosophy, demoting his former studies to the stage of preparatory exercises. The concepts which he applies have not become for him mere reminiscences from the propaedeutics of his rhetorical school or from reading, which have led him on the way to the Church, to ecclesiastical duties or monastic vocation. He remains a man of the world who writes theological treatises. In this respect his mentality is different from that of the authors who represent our main sources for the history of religious thought

[1] 'Utrum Pater et Filius et Spiritus Sanctus de Divinitate substantialiter praedicentur' (Final conclusion); *loc. cit.* p. 36: 'Haec si recte et ex fide habent, ut me instruas peto; aut si aliqua re forte diversus es, diligentius intuere quae dicta sunt et fidem si poterit rationemque coniunge.'

[2] *Contra Eutychen et Nestorium*, *Prooemium*, Stewart, Rand *loc. cit.* p. 74; M. Cappuyns, 'Boèce', in: *Dictionnaire d'Histoire et de Géographie Ecclésiastique*, IX, cols. 352–61.

in the Latin world of Christian antiquity and the Middle Ages. This peculiarity of Boethius' career may be relevant to the understanding of his intention in writing *De consolatione philosophiae*.

C. *Philosophy as man's guide*

We summarize first the relevant facts about the circumstances which led to Boethius writing this book in prison, while waiting for Theodoric's decision on his own fate after his condemnation to death. The ecclesiastical settlement between Rome and Constantinople in 519 had removed a strong motive for the city aristocracy's loyalty towards the Gothic regime. But the situation in Italy did not deteriorate immediately. Three years later co-operation between Byzantium and Ravenna still seemed better than before. But in 523 the charge was raised against Boethius of having given support to a plot of Roman aristocrats with Constantinople to overthrow the Gothic dynasty; the judgement of a special court was confirmed by a frightened and compliant senate.

The story of the catastrophe is given without consideration for personalities in high position by Boethius to personified Philosophia in the first book of *De consolatione*. The outbreak of open hostility against Arianism and its freedom of worship in the Byzantine empire came after the end of Boethius. But we can assume that Theodoric at the moment of his action against the senatorial group had already some information about the preparation for this turn of religious policy and its impact on the loyalty of the Romans. Under these circumstances the reunification which ended the conflict between Constantinople and Rome, a result which Boethius had tried to strengthen by his theological writing, took on a different and more sinister look. The ecclesiastical element in the political conflict which led to Boethius' catastrophe is the genuine core in the ancient tradition that Boethius died as a martyr.[1]

The idea that philosophy is called in to help in mastering a grave misfortune suffered by the author himself did not represent the usual convention of shaping the literary genus of *consolatio*. Normally such tractates were dedicated to another person in distress. When Cicero,

[1] The problem is discussed by W. C. Bark, in *American Hist. Rev.* LIX (1944), pp. 410–26, and *Speculum*, XXI (1946), pp. 312–17.

after the death of his daughter, retired for some time from public life in order to recover quietness of mind by philosophical reflections, he observed that nobody before him had done so. Cicero had been an inspiring influence for Boethius in the earlier stages of his intellectual career, and he remained also the most important example for his final retreat to philosophy.[1]

The book is a great dialogue between Boethius and Philosophia. When a certain result is reached, the preceding section is summarized in the form of a poem, in which the author tries to adapt the metre to the contents.

The same literary form had been taken up a hundred years earlier in the pseudo-apocalyptic introduction to Martianus Capella's encyclopaedia. The aim of the whole work is to discover the motives of the human soul's alienation from its genuine self and to point the way back from shadow to truth.

Philosophia starts with the assumption that the man whom she finds in prison still believes in the power of divine providence to establish and preserve the cosmic order, but that he sees in his personal fate only the cruel work of Fortuna's varying moods. But there is no real change in the character of this power when a good time is followed by evil days. Every gift of fate which makes the external life richer, contains necessarily an element of instability and induces man to forget what gives its real value to human existence. This theme is developed with the examples and the framework which were readily available from antiquity in the popular ethics of the diatribe. This section reaches its final conclusion with the statement that the good things of the world can only be right if they are accepted as gifts from the divine creator. In this context the fundamental idea of Plato's *Timaeus* is introduced in the poem III m. 9 which praises the creation of heaven and earth, man and animals in the harmony of the elements, as a witness to the goodness without envy which defines God. The medieval scholars in their commentaries have often seen in this poem, in which modern analysis has traced the influence of pagan liturgical literature, the core of *De consolatione*. It certainly offers the transition from the critical examination of secular values to theological ideas. The poem ends with a request that

[1] G. Misch, *Gesch. d. Autobiographie* (Leipzig, 1931), I, pp. 205, 220.

the divine creator may give strength to the human mind to find the way back out of the world to its origin.[1]

The creation of the world by God means that there is no room for evil as a genuine reality, because there can be no being in opposition to divine providence. In defence of this optimistic interpretation against everyday experience, exemplified by Boethius' situation in the dungeon, Plato's argument in the *Gorgias* is used: there are evildoers in the world so powerful that they are beyond punishment. Nobody will stop their doings. But God has created man in such a way that evil itself is punishment, because it destroys the essence of the human soul and leaves only an empty shell.

This argument leaves unsolved the question why visitations, which are intended as chastisements for the criminal, strike the just man, who would prefer to continue his way of life undisturbed and in honour. This objection leads to the first of two metaphysical investigations on the structure of providence, which form the last part of *De consolatione*. At this point Philosophy emphasizes that a new line of thought has to be taken up.[2] The transient affairs of our life have their origin in the stability of divine nature and its lasting simplicity. This centre of all events is providence in its purity. When we turn our observation to the periphery and try to see the realization of God's will in the changing pattern of things, we use quite correctly the ancient term 'fate'. All the infinite variety and multitude of phenomena in macrocosmos and microcosmos are comprehended in providence, but fate is the instrument allocating to every individual thing its special place and its special moment in time. Divine providence knows neither the one nor the other type of differentiation. This hierarchical subordination of fate to divine will and the concepts by which they are contrasted points clearly to a Neoplatonic origin.

But this philosophical doctrine appears here in a very simplified form,

[1] Ed. G. Weinberger, p. 64, 10–12: 'Da pater augustam menti conscendere sedem,/ da fontem lustrare boni, da luce reperta / in te conspicuos animi defigere visus.' On the structure of this poem: G. Klingner, 'De Boethii consolatione philosophiae', in: A. Kieszling and M. v. Wilamowitz-Möllendorff, *Philolog. Untersuchungen*, XVIII (1921), pp. 37 ff. K.'s analysis of the whole work and the preceding analysis by E. K. Rand, *Harvard Studies in Classical Philology*, XV, pp. 1–28, are now supplemented by P. Courcelle, *Les Lettres Grecques*, pp. 278–300.

[2] *De consol.* IV, pr. 6, § 1, *loc. cit.* p. 95, 20 f.: 'Ad rem me, inquit, omnium quaesitu maximam vocas, cui vix exhausti quicquam satis sit.' § 4: 'In hac enim de providentiae simplicitate, de fati serie, de repentinis casibus, de cognitione ac praedestinatione divina, de arbitrii libertate quaeri solet, quae quanti oneris sint ipse perpendis.'

which allows it to avoid any deviation from biblical monotheism. Boethius emphasizes in this context the irrelevance of all concepts which describe the forces mediating between God and the variety of experience.[1] Man's life is placed under the power of fate, but he is nevertheless able to turn from the periphery to the centre and to approach God directly without the intervention of cosmic forces, and so to escape from the pressure of necessity into freedom.

This idea of freedom also remains the theme in the long investigation by which *De consolatione* is concluded. The objection is raised that God's infallible prescience, which is an undeniable aspect of his providence, must frustrate man's liberty to act according to his own decisions. The answer starts with some reflections on the causal effect of knowledge on the event which forms its object. When we see a charioteer in the circus drive his horse as he thinks fit so as to win the race, our observation of his activities will in no way restrict his freedom of decision. Prescience does not differ from observation of events in the moment when they happen, as far as the lack of causal effect is concerned.

Against this argument the objection is raised that prescience of an event, which possibly might not happen, cannot be classified as knowledge, but only as opinion,[2] and would therefore be quite unacceptable as an aspect of divine providence. But to argue in this way would mean misinterpreting the character of divine prescience, which is determined by eternity as an inherent quality. The implication of this attribute is made clear by a discussion of its contrast, the time process, which recalls very much the corresponding passages in Augustine's *Confessiones*. It is impossible for the individual existence to comprehend itself as a whole in one of the fleeting moments through which it passes from past to future. If one believes in the infinity of time, as Aristotle did, eternity is only imitated, without its essential quality. The quietness of eternity is

[1] IV, pr. 6, § 13, *loc. cit.* p. 97, 10: 'Sive igitur famulantibus quibusdam providentiae divinae spiritibus fatum exercetur seu anima seu tota inserviente natura seu caelestibus siderum motibus seu angelica virtute seu daemonum varia sollertia seu aliquibus horum seu omnibus fatalis series texitur, illud certe manifestum est, immobilem simplicemque gerendarum formam rerum esse providentiam, fatum vero eorum, quae divina simplicitas gerenda disposuit, mobilem nexum atque ordinem temporalem.'

[2] V, pr. 3, § 26, *loc. cit.* p. 113, 4: 'Quid enim divina providentia humana opinione praestiterit, si uti homines incerta indicaret, quorum est incertus eventus?'

transformed into a movement which has no beginning and no end. Unchanging simplicity appears degenerated into an infinite variety. For this reason it is wrong to blame Plato, because in his *Timaeus* he has not linked the process of creation to a definite time. His critics are wrong when they assume that the Attic philosopher, in doing so, makes the world co-eternal with God.[1] Their assumption presupposes that the difference between creator and creature can be measured by the duration of time, while in reality eternity can only be understood as something beyond and above the course of time.

For this reason the character of God's knowledge is not influenced by the fact that every human action is preceded by a moment of uncertainty, in which the freedom of choice is exercised. The degradation of knowledge to opinion cannot take place in God's eternity. For the same reason divine prescience does not interfere with the sequence of human decision and action, which runs its course as a part of the time process.

The conversion, from the dependence on Fortuna and her external goods, to God as the only final value, does not imply a surrender of human freedom to a power which predestinates everything by knowing it before it happens. In God's view there is no difference of before and after. So ends Philosophia's message to the prisoner.

D. *The problem of Boethius' religious allegiance*

The most controversial question raised by the book in the mind of readers was always about the religious tendency of Boethius' philosophy. The range of the modern solution is marked by two answers at the opposite ends. Rand, who had done a great deal of spadework for the understanding of Boethius' writings, does not admit any serious problem. For him the Christian spirituality of this theistic philosophy disperses any serious doubts about the author's faith and intention which the lack of quotations from the Bible and ecclesiastical writings might raise. Boethius has tried out how far unaided reason is able

[1] v, pr. 6, §§ 9–11, *loc. cit.* p. 123, 3 f. § 9: 'Unde non recte quidam, qui, cum audiunt visum Platoni mundum hunc nec habuisse initium temporis nec habiturum esse defectum, hoc modo conditori conditum fieri coaeternum putant. Aliud est enim per interminabilem duci vitam, quod mundo Plato tribuit, aliud interminabilis vitae totam pariter complexam esse praesentiam, quod divinae mentis proprium esse manifestum est.'

to approach religious truth. If Theodoric had spared his life, Boethius might have supplemented the *De consolatione* by a second book demonstrating the complete harmony between the religious conclusions of his reason with revealed truth. This assumption implies that the design of Boethius' *De consolatione* was dictated by a methodical consideration of the parallelism of reason and revelation, which would have anticipated the thought-form of medieval scholasticism. The other alternative was recently formulated by Professor Momigliano, according to whom Boethius abandoned Christianity at the end of his life and, under the pressure of his experiences, returned to philosophy as the pagan way to human salvation.[1]

The principle that Christian truth can be proved by philosophical argument, without any recourse to ecclesiastical tradition, had been established by the apologists in their attempts to win over educated opinion outside the Church. Lactantius' discreet circumscriptions of Christian concepts in his first treatise *De opificio Dei* is a good example of the tactical purpose of this method of defending the faith. Boethius had certainly no reason to introduce Christian truth in such disguise, and the situation which determined his work excludes any idea that he might have had in mind a plan to redevelop the doctrinal contents of revelation in a second work parallel to *De consolatione*. That in his four genuine theological treatises he attempted to find philosophical expressions for the central doctrine of the Christian faith, when it seemed helpful for the ecclesiastical cause to do so, does not form any basis for the assumption that *De consolatione* was designed as the section on rational theology in a system of revealed truth.

On the other hand, we cannot well overlook the fact that for his final confession he selected those ideas from the philosophical tradition which expressed essential features of Christian spirituality and ethics. Augustine's theoretical world-picture was still near to his thought, although he avoided any application leading to definite ecclesiastical doctrine. It is difficult to imagine that in the sixth century a former Christian should have written such a work in order to express renunciation of his faith by identifying philosophy with paganism in his mind as

[1] Rand, *Founders*, p. 178; A. Momigliano, 'Cassiodorus and the Italian culture of his time', in: *Proceedings Brit. Acad.* XLI (1955), p. 212.

Symmachus in the fourth century had linked rational theism with the traditional worship of the Roman people.

The assumption of a real break at the end of Boethius' life would have greater force if we had to accept the treatise called *De fide Catholica*, which summarizes the history of salvation in theological, not philosophical terms, as a genuine work expressing Boethius' attitude a few years before he wrote *De consolatione*. The manuscript evidence allows for arguments on both sides. Differences of vocabulary and style between *De fide* and the four genuine treatises have been accounted for by the contrast in the subject-matter. But, while such differences can be easily understood in a case like that of Tacitus writing both the dialogue on the rhetor's education and the two small historical essays, it would be very difficult to find room for a purely theological composition in Boethius' intellectual career.

We saw that his literary activity in all periods of his life had centred around the task of preserving the legacy of ancient philosophy. His preference for the abstract problems of Aristotelian logic made any possibility of conflict between rational thought and the doctrines of Christian faith remote. When he used his intellectual equipment to give literary support to the cause of Roman orthodoxy and ecclesiastical unity, religious and patriotic motives were inseparably fused in the loyalty of his allegiance. We saw how this contribution to the unity of West and East by a prominent Roman aristocrat became politically suspicious at the moment when the future of the Gothic dynasty was menaced.

But we do not know whether the abstention from anything definitely ecclesiastical in doctrine and language was caused to some degree by the author's hope of turning his fate by giving the impression of philosophical neutrality to the Arian court at Ravenna. The very outspoken style of his political justification in book I seems, however, to contradict the assumption that such considerations of prudence played a predominant part in the shaping of *De consolatione*. On the other hand, the feeling of deep disappointment with the attitude of the Roman senate is clearly reflected in the work. Boethius had once applied philosophy to theology, acting as speaker for this body, who now had forsaken him. This experience did not change his deepest conviction, the belief in the harmony of philosophy and religious faith, but it made him refrain from the treatment of such problems and the use of any terminology which could lead a man into the sphere of political controversy. It was certainly the purpose of *De consolatione* to show the way of liberation from entanglement in the strife for power. His limitation to the expression of his faith in theistic universalism allowed him to avoid all problems which had become issues in the conflict between individuals and groups. That he knew patristic writings which followed a similar course, especially the early dialogues of Augustine, made this attitude easier. Boethius could neglect the fact that his circumstances and motive were different from those of the Fathers of the Church. That he was able to undertake such a task in the way he did was made possible by his contacts with the Hellenic East; here lies the key to his entire achievement.

The assumption that he was once a student in Athens has been ruled out by the consideration that it was based on a *metaphorical* description of his renewal of philosophy in the eulogistic letter of Cassiodorus. A further hypothesis that he spent his youth in Alexandria, where his father would have held high office, cannot be firmly established and does not fit in very well with the documentation of Boethius' life and career.[1] On the other hand, the evidence that the Roman senator's unique intellectual position can only be accounted for by an intimate contact with Alexandrian thought and learning is very strong.

We must admit, it seems, that we simply do not know the way by which the Roman aristocrat acquired his extensive knowledge of language, methods and doctrines characteristic of contemporary Hellenic scholarship: in any case, the results were of lasting historical importance.

The spirit of scientific inquiry was very lively in Alexandria during the late fifth and the first half of the sixth century. The principles on which the right understanding of nature must be based were subjects of eager discussion. John Philoponus, who disputed Aristotle's dichotomy of heaven and sublunar world and aimed at a uniform explanation of the cosmos in physical terms, was a younger contemporary of

[1] *Variae* I, 45, § 3, *loc. cit.* 40, 5: 'sic enim Atheniensium scholas longe positus introisti, sic palliatorum choris miscuisti togam, ut Graecorum dogmata doctrinam feceris Romanam'. Quoted with critical observations by P. Courcelle, *Lettres Grecques*, p. 260; on study in Alexandria: Courcelle, pp. 298–300.

Boethius, but in no way the first who introduced such themes among the scholars of this late period of Greek Alexandria. When the Roman philosopher's scientific interest enabled him to emancipate logic from the purely literary scope of the trivium, he did so in harmony with the ideas prevalent in the Greek thought of his days.[1] But recent research, especially by Courcelle, has proved that the contacts between Boethius and the leading teachers of the Alexandrian school have left much more concrete results. The Egyptian centre of philosophical studies had shown a strong tendency to concentrate its main effort on the textual interpretation of the two classical authors, Plato and Aristotle. This approach corresponded to the interest in the critical study of authors which was rooted in local tradition of long standing. Moreover, there was the influence of an important section among the pupils, who wished to supplement their Christian belief by a training in abstract thought. Their purpose could easily collide with the tendency in the development of Neoplatonic speculation of combining philosophy with the defence of Polytheism. The safest way to avoid such serious friction was the return to the objective task of explaining the classic masters. This situation led also to emphasis on Aristotelian studies, especially on his *Organon*; while the tradition of the Alexandrian school prevented any refutation of Plato in favour of his master pupil.[2] It is obvious that the comprehensive programme for his life's work, which Boethius has drawn up, corresponds to the syllabus of Alexandrian studies.

But the most intimate influence of the Alexandrian masters can be traced in *De consolatione*. The simplification of the hierarchical world picture, by which Boethius removed an important difference between the Neoplatonic theory of emanation and Christian monotheism, was already prepared for him by his Alexandrian sources. Here the theological interpretation of the demiurge in Plato's *Timaeus* by Ammonius allowed man to face God without mediating powers. The same author, a pupil of Proclus, had incorporated in commentaries to Aristotle's logical and scientific works speculations on the relationship of God's eternal

[1] S. Sambursky, *The Physical World of Late Antiquity* (London, 1962), pp. 254–75. [On John Philoponus, and on the relationship between Christianity and philosophy in the School of Alexandria in general, see Part VI (The Greek Christian Tradition), ch. 31 B, pp. 477–83.]

[2] K. Praechter, 'Christlich-neuplatonische Beziehungen', in: *Byzant. Ztschr.* XXI (1912), pp. 1–27; 'Richtungen und Schulen im Neuplatonismus', in: *Genethliakon f. Carl Robert* (Berlin, 1910), pp. 147–56.

decision to the fluctuations of fate, as well as the investigation on the compatibility of divine providence and human freedom which made it possible for Boethius to find an adequate expression for his Christian piety in purely philosophical concepts. Fifth-century Alexandria had also brought forth reinterpretations of Plato's *Gorgias*; the tendency of this dialogue corresponded closely to what *De consolatione* intended to teach about the relationship of human sin and happiness. While denying that the world's creation had happened in time, Boethius safeguarded an important axiom of theism by differentiating between God's eternity and the permanence of the world.[1] By doing so, he accepted again a tradition from Alexandria as consistent with his own religion. His whole plan excluded the possibility of discussing in his context the Church's difficulty with a theory which would not allow the first two chapters of Genesis to be understood literally. In this way Boethius' discipleship to the Alexandrian school offered to later generations in a less sophisticated world stimulating but also puzzling problems.

E. *Isidore of Seville and philosophical lore at the beginning of the Middle Ages*

Philosophical learning came to the world of the Earlier Middle Ages as a section of the encyclopaedic surveys by which knowledge and ideas were transferred from the secular schoolrooms of late antiquity to the medieval libraries of monasteries and cathedrals. When the Greeks had formulated philosophical doctrines as controversial solutions to questions about the essential nature of world and man, free debate between individuals and schools was an important presupposition of this intellectual enterprise. In the comprehensive framework of general knowledge they became neutralized and seemingly without strength to interfere with the ecclesiastical purpose of studies in the rising world of the Middle Ages.

The fact that, even in this context, the fragments of ancient speculation did not lose all their potentialities for stimulating fresh thought whenever an individual mind and the problems of his environment combined to bring about the right constellation, initiated philosophy in

[1] P. Courcelle, 'Boèce et l'École d'Alexandrie', in: *Mélanges de l'École française de Rome*, LII (1955), pp. 204–15.

the Middle Ages. It is well known that the work of Isidore of Seville (560–636) played a prominent part in this process. We consider his life, his world and the philosophical subject-matter of his writings in an attempt to understand his position.[1]

He grew up as the youngest son of a family whose names make their origin from Romanized stock probable. His father Severianus had left Cartagena under the pressure of the upheaval caused when Justinian's policy of imperial restoration reached Spain. Finally the rule of the Visigoths survived this period of trial stronger than it had been before, and in 589 King Reccared replaced Arianism, the more loosely organized form of Christianity, which the whole group of Gothic peoples and the tribes related to them had originally adopted, by Roman Catholicism. In this way he ended the religious division which had separated the ruling race from the Latin speaking native population. Isidore's elder brother Leander was, as Archbishop of Seville, Reccared's main adviser during the third council of Toledo, which established the new order. His own Latin style shows some traces of contact with a living tradition from antiquity, as it still lingered in the upper ranks of Mediterranean society; Isidore, whose education had been directed by Leander, conforms with the simplification of literary standards characteristic of ecclesiastical learning and writing in the age of Gregory the Great. But there is one important difference between Visigothic Spain and Italy after Justinian's invasion: Benedict of Nursia and Gregory had been sceptical about the value of secular knowledge and literary skill for their work in safeguarding some continuity of Christian life in the midst of the breakdown of civilization which surrounded them: Cassiodorus had a more positive attitude towards learning as the general background of sacred studies, but he also thought only of a narrow circle of men giving refuge to books and scholarship. In contrast to him, Isidore, who about 599 became his brother's successor as metropolitan in the province of Seville, continued Leander's work in organizing the Spanish church by writing treatises on ecclesiastical discipline and government and creating a doctrinal basis for conformity by the compilation of patristic teaching in his three books of Sentences. In

[1] Jacques Fontaine, *Isidore de Séville et la culture classique dans l'Espagne Wisigothique*, I and II (Paris, 1959). This comprehensive work has placed Isidorian studies on the broad basis of Hellenistic and late Latin literature.

contrast to Gregory, he included extensive introductions to secular studies in his literary work, intended to establish Catholic Christianity for the coming generation in the Germanic kingdom.

This aspect made his legacy the model for those scholars who, during the five hundred years following his death, again and again renewed contact with the ancient store of learning. This tradition was felt as a necessary element of life in society, both ecclesiastical and secular, which was liable to be extinguished by powerful forces of more robust character. The development of medieval philosophy remained during this period closely connected with the more comprehensive efforts to preserve the connexions with the ancient sources of learning. Philosophy in the sense of a coherent system of thought on man's position in the world, as understood by the post-Aristotelian schools, does not as such form part of Isidore's encyclopaedic work. In its twenty main sections it brings together all knowledge from ancient books which the bishop thought relevant to the educational work of the Church.[1] Books I–III deal with the liberal arts. Dialectic which, after rhetoric, fills the second half of Book II is introduced by a chapter defining the content and the divisions of philosophy. Book VIII is dedicated to the Church and her antagonists, the sectarians and their heresies. These manifold aberrations are shown to have had their parallels in the various opinions formulated in the philosophical schools. Books XIII and XIV offer a cosmography, which begins with two chapters summarizing the theories of atoms and elements as the substance behind the visible world. The anthropology of Book XI is concentrated on explaining how all human organs are exactly adapted to their purpose, and so continues a theme which was very popular in philosophical literature since the Hellenistic period.[2] During the later centuries of antiquity the idea of divine providence in the creation, revealed in the parallelism of macrocosmos and microcosmos, recommended this approach to nature as a part of Christian scholarship.

The one concept which gives Isidore's diverse material a certain

[1] I quote the Oxford edition: W. M. Lindsay, *Isidori Hispalensis episcopi Etymologiarum sive Originum Libri XX* (1911) (no pagination); *PL* 82.

[2] The treatise *De natura rerum*, a monograph on the same theme, was written about 612, while the *Etymologiae* belong to the final part of Isidore's career. New edition with French translation and valuable introduction and notes: J. Fontaine, *Isidore de Séville, Traité de la nature* (1960), *PL* 83. 964–1018.

unity is formulated by the two titles of the work, *Etymologiae* or *Origines*. One question remains the starting-point throughout all books and chapters. From what is the name of the subject under discussion derived, and what does this linguistic explanation contribute to the understanding of the real thing? It is well known that Isidore's etymological statements about the formation of nouns are in most cases rather like fairy tales without any reliable evidence. But this approach as a whole was very natural in a period of book-learning, which had to be satisfied with the knowledge and ideas of a remote past, and needed the 'grammarian' as the natural mediator. Moreover, this basic idea is not quite without philosophical implications. For Isidore the understanding of the name is the first step to knowledge, because by doing so, we separate the subject under discussion, as a definite entity, from other objects. The term *differentia*, which was offered by the tradition of the school as a concept of elementary logic, was introduced by Isidore as the grammarian's instrument for distinguishing between phenomena which have certain qualities in common, like king and tyrant. Isidore is aware of the fact that not all names are given by the ancients in accordance with the nature of the thing to be described. He knows from his everyday experience that slaves and possessions are sometimes given arbitrary names by their possessor. Moreover, in certain cases the learned tradition offers descriptions derived from the vocabulary of nations whose language does not reveal any meaning to the pupils of Greece and Rome.[1] But this experience does not impair the validity of the principle that the name alone, correctly understood, allows us to know the character and significance of a thing.

The authority of the Old Testament, with its emphasis on the power of the divine name and its general interest in etymological interpretations, encouraged Isidore's belief in the soundness of his approach. The exegesis of the Alexandrian schools, both Jewish and Christian, which reached Seville through the Latin Fathers, especially through Ambrosius, exercised its influence in the same direction. But it remains true that this building up of a world-picture on the basis of etymology had its origin in the thought of the Stoics. They had from their beginnings proclaimed the belief that the strength of the logos in the human mind

[1] *Etymol.* I, cap. 29, *PL* 82. 105 B–C.

had brought primitive men so close to the essence of the things they met in nature, that their name-giving expressed the truth, even if they believed themselves to have acted arbitrarily.[1] Isidore could not well be aware of the fact that the design of his encyclopaedia followed the doctrine of one philosophical school, because this piece of Stoic teaching came to him as a part of the syncretistic knowledge in which the student of rhetoric was trained in the Roman Empire's centres of higher learning. But the question how far the concepts of human language do express reality was implied in the design of the *Etymologiae*; in this way a manual of general knowledge could become a starting-point for fresh philosophical investigation.

Problems of this type were raised in the medieval schools when the possibility of defining ecclesiastical doctrine in rational concepts was discussed. Such a thought-provoking effect of the *Etymologiae* on its readers at a later period came about without intention on the part of its author to emphasize the value of philosophy as an essential part of Christian scholarship.

We shall find in Isidore's work formulations which stress the antagonism between philosophy and Christian belief, which he found ready at hand from a succession of patristic teachers in the Latin world, reaching from Tertullian to St Jerome. But this attitude does not dominate the whole work, which he intended as a means for safeguarding the continuity of education as it was understood at the end of antiquity, and that meant including elements of philosophy in the syllabus. The bishop has allowed such fragments to pass into his work without any depreciatory remark. His lack of consistency in this respect is not merely caused by the loss of direction characteristic of compilations of a late epoch, but reflects also the result of a long and complicated development summarized in this encyclopaedic survey. On the one hand, there was an old conflict between the Church and the philosophical schools, sharpened during the critical period of the last persecutions: the faith based on Biblical revelation and its authorized explanation stood against the claim of reason to find the truth by coherent argument. On the other hand, since the second century the Church herself had stressed the harmony between her teaching and genuine philosophy. The great

[1] M. Pohlenz, *Die Stoa*, I (1948), pp. 40–2.

leaders of the Church in the fourth century had confirmed the truth of this apologetic position by their own experience. There was good sense in the fact that Isidore's framework provided for sections which would serve either the one or the other of these two tendencies.

Dialectic is introduced as a valuable instrument for scholarly investigations, a discipline invented to discuss the causes of things. The other name of this part of philosophy, Logic, expresses its rational character displayed in the capacity to raise questions and to discuss them methodically. In this school is learnt the discrimination of truth from falsehood. Aristotle had established this discipline as a system, after the first philosophers had made casual use of its possibilities.[1]

Some general remarks on philosophy, of which logic is a branch, are offered as introduction. In this context we find a passage on two degrees of certainty, which can be obtained in different spheres. Real knowledge must be based on the firm ground of rational argument, by which truth can be established.[2]

But when we investigate the size of the sun, whether it corresponds to appearance or in reality surpasses that of the earth, or when we try to decide the question whether the stars are fixed to a sphere or move freely through the air, we shall never establish a firm case for our solution of these problems of natural philosophy. We shall only be able to make an *opinion* probable.[3]

The traditional tripartite division of philosophy into the doctrine of nature, ethics and logic is applied by Isidore in the *Etymologiae* to the books of the Bible, which are classified accordingly with regard to their doctrinal content.[4] The idea came to him through Jerome from the Alexandrian school, and he uses it in this context of secular learning to narrow down the gap between theology and philosophy.

The same chapter leads also to a first digression into the history of ancient philosophy. The inventors of the three branches are listed: Thales is given first place in the investigation of nature, followed by

[1] *Etymol.* II, cap. 22, §§ 1, 2, *PL* 82. 140 A.

[2] II, cap. 25, § 1: 'continens in se demonstrationem primarum rationum de qualibet re quid sit, suaque certa ac substantiali definitione declaretur', *PL* 83. 143 A.

[3] Cap. 24, § 2: 'Scientia est, cum res aliqua certa ratione percipitur; opinatio autem cum adhuc incerta res latet et nulla ratione firma videtur, ut puta sol utrumne tantus quantus videtur, an maior quam omnis terra', *PL* 82. 141 A.

[4] *Etymol.* II, cap. 24, § 8, *PL* 82. 141 D.

Plato, who brought the discoveries of his predecessor into a system by establishing the quadrivium. The third began with Socrates, who pointed the way to a good life by defining the four cardinal virtues. Logic is again traced back to Plato, who distinguished its two branches, dialectic and rhetoric.[1] Aristotle does not appear in Isidore's classification as an inventor of philosophy, although he is praised some paragraphs later as an eloquent master of dialectic.[2] This placing of Aristotle as an expert in one highly technical branch within the range of literary studies and outside the sphere of natural science—a description which deprives him of his qualification as one of the founders of philosophy—is probably not merely an accidental outcome from a compilation of extracts. It may reflect the eclipse of his system as an intellectual force in the Latin world during the age of St Augustine, when Aristotle's name appeared mainly in treatises which were, before Boethius, more closely connected with training in rhetoric than with the study of philosophy.

Isidore has another more detailed chapter on ancient philosophers. Both reports became the most important source of information on this subject for the following centuries, while sporadically in monastic and cathedral schools the rise of scholasticism was prepared. The second of these chapters introduces philosophy in the context of a report on the Church and her antagonists. Some observations on the theological aspect of ancient thought lead on to a paragraph describing how the deviations from correct belief were derived from these teachings of the philosophical schools on God and world.[3] Their splitting up of the one truth into contrasting opinions had been used as a strong argument in controversial writings since the early days of the Church and could be equally well applied to the many heretical interpretations of ecclesiastical dogma. Isidore built up his chapters from summaries taken from this type of apologetic literature starting from Tertullian. It is obvious that time and deeply rooted changes in environment had established

[1] Cap. 24, §§ 4–7, *PL* 82. 141 B–C.

[2] *Etymol.* cap. 27, § 3: 'Hanc Aristoteles vir in rerum expressione et faciendis sermonibus peritissimus, Perihermenias nominat, quam interpretationem nos vocamus', *PL* 82. 145 C–D.

[3] *Etymol.* VIII, cap. 6, §§ 1–6: 'Introduction, origin of the name "philosophy", its divisions according to subjects and schools'; §§ 7–17: 'The founders of schools and their doctrines'; §§ 18–21: 'Opinions on God and world'; §§ 22–3: 'Influence on heresies', *PL* 82. 305 B; 308 A.

a screen between seventh-century Seville and the Athens of the philosophers.

In Isidore's survey of ancient philosophy there is no place for the concept of development and no attempt to construct a history of thought. Consequently there is in this context no interest in chronology. The Stoic school is identified with its founder Zeno, who taught the identity of virtue and beatitude; this school does not allow any difference between great and small sins; they do not believe in the immortality of the soul, but desire for themselves eternal glory. The most severe criticism, well prepared already by the controversies of pagan antiquity, is directed against Epicurus, who did not accept the reality of anything immaterial and proclaimed bodily pleasure as the highest good. For this school God is completely separated from all action; there is no divine providence in the world, which exists as the accidental result from the movement of atoms.[1]

It is significant for the character of Isidore's work that the same Epicurean theory of the atom reappears as a useful piece of information in a context in which cosmography is the theme. The philosophers, Isidore reports in this connexion, trace the origin of this world down to particles which can neither be seen nor divided. The word atom expresses the peculiarity that these smallest units in the universe cannot be further reduced by cutting. They move through empty space and produce, according to the teaching of some pagan philosophers, all phenomena of the visible world. They do so by moving relentlessly and without definite direction, like the fine dust which the rays of the sun make visible.[2]

The main source for Isidore is Lactantius, who himself used Cicero's *De natura deorum* and Lucretius' great poem for his information about the materialistic philosophy.[3] The apologist reports on the Epicurean school, in order to obtain a basis for his attack on its consistency. They account for variety by assuming a basic matter, which is defined by its lack of differentiation. In order to make the agglomeration of this light and smooth substance plausible they assume variety of surface,

[1] §§ 15 f.; § 20, *PL* 82. 306D; 307C.

[2] *Etymol.* XIII, cap. 2, §§ 1–2, *PL* 82. 472D f.

[3] Lactantius, *De via*, cap. 10, §§ 2–4 (*CSEL* 27, 1, p. 85 f.; *PL* 6. 101A f.). On Lactantius' use of Lucretius: H. Hagendahl, *Latin Fathers and the Classics* (1958), pp. 3, 70–5.

allow even hook-like excrescences and do not notice that by such addition they deny the nature of atoms as originally defined.

Isidore has cut out this criticism of his source. But within one short paragraph he says twice that such theories represent the teaching of pagan philosophers. This remark shows that he still has a feeling for the daring character of the doctrine. The traditional stigma on Epicurean philosophy remained very relevant for him, when he was dealing with the theme 'Church and Heresies'. But when he intends to gather the concepts for a cosmographic survey, there is nothing to stimulate discussion and controversy.

When Lactantius wrote his apologetic treatises during the decade preceding the recognition of Christianity by Constantine, the world picture of Epicurus, proclaimed by Lucretius' great poem, was still a competitor of the Bible and of ecclesiastical doctrine. Three centuries later their thought could be considered as more or less acceptable material of learning.

Some reflections on the Latin and Greek terms for matter led to the alternative theory of the four *elements* as the substances behind the variety of our experience.[1] The main concept of this doctrine was recommended for Isidore by the Latin text of the Solomonic book of Wisdom, where he read that the biblical king as author thanks God for his ability to understand the forces of the elements.[2] Moreover, there was the broad acceptance of the theory of four elements as the key for the understanding of macrocosmos and microcosmos by the patristic writers of the fourth century. Isidore presents this doctrine in the form of a *tripartite* scheme of qualities, the contrasts referring to: density, penetration and mobility.

Earth is obtuse, dense and immobile, while fire, dominating the opposite side of the cosmos, is penetrating, rarefied and mobile. The middle elements, water and air, close the chain because the arrangement of their qualities enables them to act as link from one stratum of the world to the others. Fontaine has shown that the particular form in

[1] *PL* 82. 472D f.

[2] *Etymol.* XIII, cap. 2. *De natura rerum*, *praef.* § 2, ed. Fontaine pp. 167 f.: 'Quin immo, si ab investigatione veri modis omnibus procul abessent, nequaquam rex ille sapiens diceret: ipse mihi dedit horum quae sunt scientiam veram, ut sciam dispositionem caeli et virtutes elementorum...', *PL* 83. 964–6.

which Isidore presents this theory is nearest to the formulation which Calcidius in his commentary on the *Timaeus* has given to the Platonic doctrine of elements.[1]

Isidore does not attempt to establish any logical consistency between the atoms of the one chapter and the theory of four elements in the next. They stand side by side. This kind of composition had become customary since the philosophers of the Hellenistic period had included cosmological theories in their treatises for the educated public.

The patristic commentaries on Genesis in this respect also followed the example of the pagan schools. For Isidore's encyclopaedic intention this procedure was completely natural. But when early in the twelfth century at Chartres medieval scholars pondered on the meaning of such a succession of theories, they felt challenged to bridge the gap between the different doctrines by a logically consistent theory. The world which we know through our senses was produced at a further stage by the mixture of the elements and their qualities. Before this process took place the elements, as mere atoms, could not be perceived.[2] Such problems did not come into the orbit of Isidore's encyclopaedia. He was no philosopher, but he offered the material for later theoretical thought.

[1] The complete scheme: *De natura rerum*, cap. 11, ed. Fontaine, p. 43, *PL* 83. 979B f.; a possible link between Calcidius and Isidore: Fontaine, *Isidore...et la culture*, p. 258.

[2] On atomism and the elements in the school of Chartres see T. Gregory, *Anima mundi, La filosofia di Guglielmo di Conches*, pp. 201–12. Already Eriugena had pondered on conflicting theories in this field: *De divisione naturae* I, cap. 53, *PL* 122. 495D f.: 'Videmur nam eis contra nos agere, contrariaque et nobis adversantia firmare, dicentes, aliquando quattuor elementorum coitum materiam gignere, aliquando quantitatis atque qualitatis ousiae conventum causam materiae esse. Nec mirum quoniam illos latet, non aliunde mundi huius elementa, nisi praedictorum ousiae accidentium concursu componi.' Cf. *loc. cit.* III, 32. 711D f. on the position of the pure elements as the mediators between spirit and matter.

CHAPTER 36

DEVELOPMENT OF THOUGHT IN THE CAROLINGIAN EMPIRE

A. *Frankish criticism of Byzantine theories of sacred art*

Up till now we have surveyed the type of literature which formed a link between the legacy of late antiquity and the new civilization of the West. We must admit that important representatives of the Carolingian revival of letters were mainly concerned with continuing this compilatory work by shaping the traditional lore of learning into textbooks for monastic and cathedral schools. But the question remains, whether such activities represented the whole intellectual achievement of the period. It has been shown in an earlier chapter by P. Sheldon-Williams that John Eriugena brought about a genuine renewal of Greek speculation in the ninth century, and there is no doubt that by this achievement he established himself as the first in the great sequence of medieval thinkers. His teaching and writing took place during the years 845–70, that means at a time when Carolingian society, in which institutions of learning had formed a vital element, dissolved under the impact of barbaric invasions and internal disintegration. This chronological paradox could perhaps be explained by Hegel's saying about the owl of Minerva, whose flight starts at dusk. But by doing so we should accept the assumption of a theory of history according to which the earlier stages of a civilization produce all the tendencies and impulses which finally find their expression in the conceptual language of philosophy. The course of the ninth century does not offer a genuine proof of the deductions of this idealistic system, nor would its author have sought such confirmation within this period. But nevertheless we can trace preparatory movements of thought since the time of Charlemagne, which made the work of the philosopher at his grandson's court possible. About 790 the *Libri Carolini* were written, in which, at the king's command, scholars of his circle drew up a picture of Frankish mentality as the expression of a Christian civilization. They were designed to define the attitude of the West towards the cult of images, which, after sixty years of iconoclasm, had been restored in the Byzantine Empire by the synod of Nicaea in 787. The pope Hadrian had been consulted by the Empress Irene; the Frankish Church and the Frankish king, who controlled Rome politically, had not. The *Libri Carolini* are meant to answer this challenge by comparing the state of mind in West and East as the source of the right and the wrong attitude. No individual authorship can be established, yet phrases and vocabulary on the one hand and types of quotations on the other point in different directions.[1]

It is certain that several hands were active in producing the final version. But the design and the vigorously sustained tendency of the argument seem to show that the main task had been the responsibility of one author. There is, however, in the writings of this generation no parallel to the ideas of this book to back any identification. We may conclude that the king, who appears as the nominal author, really gave impulse and direction, when he allotted this unusual theme to one of his men of letters.

In this controversy the West had to face the use of Neoplatonic speculation by the Byzantine theologians, who endeavoured to justify the religious interpretation of images as an expression of the spirit's urge to make itself visible by descending into matter. At this stage the West had no interest in this type of speculation and no understanding of this emphasis on symbolism. But the claim to intellectual superiority implied in such theories was clear. The Carolingian scholars built up a counterposition by outlining a theory of Frankish kingship in contrast to what they felt as a continuation of ancient emperor-worship immanent in the Byzantine regime. By fitting their criticism of the antagonistic philosophy of art into this framework they tried to demonstrate its essentially pagan character and lack of religious meaning. The general attitude taken is simply the middle line, or, as they like to call it with a favourite biblical quotation of Alcuin, the *via regia*: images must not be destroyed as the Iconoclasts decreed in 754. But they must not,

[1] The question is discussed by L. Wallach, *Alcuin and Charlemagne* (Ithaca, N.Y., 1959), pp. 169–77. [For the doctrine of images against which the *Libri Carolini* were directed, see the previous Part (VI, 'The Greek Christian Tradition'), ch. 33, pp. 506–17, 'The Philosophy of Icons'.]

either, be adored.[1] They are useful but not necessary for salvation; they adorn the churches and help the uneducated to learn certain facts about the history of salvation. The East lacks the moderation needed to find such a solution. This lack of balance is traced back to its origin in the spirit of the Byzantine regime. It is established by a critical examination of a phrase used by the Empress in a letter: She invokes God as someone who reigns together with her. This means, according to the critic, that she does not understand the nature of the gulf between creature and creator. God is eternal and does not belong to any particular period, which can only be a fragment of his eternity. The change from the future through the present into the past, which dominates all periods through which human life passes including the reign of kings, has no application to God, who by his very nature cannot be thought to share in any human status or activity bound to the time process. Here we see Augustine's philosophy of time called in to refute the Byzantine claim to leadership in orthodox government.

The East had defended image-worship in Christian cult with the analogy of honours proffered in public places to figures representing the secular rulers. The Carolingian writer took this Byzantine practice as a survival from the time of the Babylonian and Roman empires, two regimes distinguished by the ruthless energy with which they carried through their programme of conquest. They produced statues or paintings of their rulers, dispatched them to various localities and forced the inhabitants to worship them as substitutes. Consequently, the Byzantine argument implies the belief that God himself is also restricted to a certain place and not all-powerful; also no image would be necessary to serve as link with a distant power. The Byzantine attitude is clearly described as belonging to the *Civitas terrena*.[2]

In striking contrast the Frankish monarchy is characterized as a regime in which the borderline between God and ruler, spirit and matter is carefully kept. The king is only commissioned to be the shepherd of men with the task of allotting punishment and reward according to merit. Honours which would create a barrier between him and humanity, and would reduce the distance between him and God, must

[1] Ed. H. Bastgen, *Mon. Germ. Hist.*, *Concilia*, II. *Supplementum* (1924), *praefatio*, pp. 3, 15 – 6, 12; IV, 4, p. 179, 17. On *via regia*: Wallach, *loc. cit.* pp. 67–72, 171.

[2] II 19; III 15, pp. 77, 25; 133, 33 ff.

be avoided. Examples of such humility have been given by the leading apostles. This political theory, with which the Frankish court intends, at this moment of conflict, to counter the claim of the Byzantine empire to represent dominion on higher levels, amounts to a negation of myth as basis of kingship. The monarch is the administrator of God's law, following the rule drawn up for the ideal king in the Old Testament, in contrast to the pagan despotism of the oriental empires. This ideal of kingship has remained valid under the New Testament and its genuine traditions are guarded by the teaching and customs of St Peter and his deputies on earth.[1] To this recognition of the gulf between God and ruler corresponds the contrast between spirit and matter which underlies the Frankish criticism of the metaphysical interpretation of art by the Byzantine theorists.

The cult of images is defended by the assertion that the forces of sanctity gathered in a saint by a life of devotion are transferred from his portrait, through the eyes of the man who looks on it, into his soul. But what we really see is the material shaped into an imitation of life. The saint's virtues were in his soul. The assortment of dyes which compose a picture does not represent any equivalent to the soul. There is no moment in the process by which a work of art is created, when sacredness could grow out of its wooden basis under the hand of the artist by the application of his tools. Observations on the use of everyday speech are quoted to illustrate the lack of identity between an image and its object. In different sentences we frequently use the same subject without implying any identity of meaning. 'Augustine was a most prominent philosopher'; 'Augustine must be read'; 'Augustine is portrayed in a church'; 'Augustine is buried at a certain place'. The subject in every one of these four sentences has a link with Augustine. But only in the first sentence has the word the meaning of a living person, the real Augustine. But the exhortation to read, points to a book, the church contains a painting, the tomb a corpse. An equal relationship exists between the real and the painted man; their link is the name. The artist has the free choice to produce the *impression* of a fighting, speaking or observing being, while in reality none of these actions takes place as the effect of the artist's combination of colours. A statement of truth has no

[1] I 1; III 16, pp. 10, 33; 137, 20.

such liberty; one way is forced upon it by a reality to which it must conform, else it would lose the character of truth.[1]

The *Libri Carolini* accepted the teaching of Gregory the Great that there is a potential value in paintings as an instruction on historical facts, giving a knowledge to the illiterate relevant to their salvation. But in all cases of *abstract* subject-matter the visible instrument for teaching can only be letters, which form words and so recall the meaning in the reader's soul. Words like 'Hear O Israel: The Lord our God is One' cannot be expressed by paintings. The exhortations of the Gospels, the teaching of the apostles cannot be demonstrated by painting. Man's morality depends on the way he chooses to act. This decision is an act of his internal life, which by its very nature cannot be the subject of painting. Therefore images can never present any model of human behaviour and cannot help in teaching morals, which must be left to the word, as the Bible shows. Only language can reach that part of man on which good and evil action depends.[2]

Genuine discrimination between the value of paintings depends on the place we allocate to them on a scale ranging from beauty to ugliness. This fact proves that the believers in images which transfer the power of sacredness from the saint's likeness to the pious observer, are under a deception. Their real experience brought about by the beauty of the painting depends purely on the artist's skill andis in no way the result of religious devotion, which characterized the man used as the portrait's subject. If, however, people worship less beautiful or even ugly pictures their deception is complete, because the painting offers no reason at all for their emotion. God's power safeguards the coherence of the world; in comparison with this monument of his strength no painting can be considered of any relevance. In the period after the creation of the world no pictorial art existed. Neither Abel nor Enoch could worship God in images, because there was no experience of any mundane art of painting. There are still regions where human beings are ignorant of it, but it would be unreasonable to assume that the inhabitants do not adore the power of God.[3] It does not seem probable that this clause of the argument was formulated without any consideration for the vast superiority

[1] I 2, p. 13, 30 ff. Cf. I 17, p. 41, 20 f.; IV 27, p. 225, 36 f.

[2] III 23, p. 153, 5.

[3] IV 2, p. 175, 6.

in the number of works of art which the east could muster in comparison with the north-west under Carolingian rule. We may add that also the centre of the argument in this philosophy of art, that moral action cannot be taught by visual impressions, has some link with the realities of the Frankish regime. Charlemagne, who had added the task of teaching the rudiments of religion to the traditional duties of a Germanic king, used the *missi dominici*, his delegates in the provinces, to shape the minds of his subjects *by word of mouth*. It seems that this experience of governmental practice is reflected in the argument of the *Libri Carolini*. From the Carolingian point of view the most serious objection the Byzantine controversialists had directed against the critics of image-worship was the saying in Genesis that God had created man in his likeness. This was taken in the last instance as recognition of the human form as a revelation of divinity on a lower level, in preparation for the second great action of God's Wisdom, the Incarnation. The representation of Christ was taken as the final link in the chain created by God according to his decision to descend and express himself visibly to his creatures. The image remains connected with its prototype like the shadow with the body. The Carolingians at this stage had no sympathetic understanding of this interpretation of the creed in terms of Neoplatonic hierarchy. But they felt this challenge to their orthodoxy strongly and emphasized that Christology was the centre of their faith. Yet they denied that from this attitude any need for a material mediation between man and God could arise. The saying in Genesis is interpreted on the authority of St Ambrose and Augustine: The qualities of the soul, not the forms of the body, represent the similarity to God. There is no task for the painter's brush. In the autobiographical report of his *Confessions* Augustine had emphasized this piece of exegesis, by which the bishop of Milan had dispersed the deeply rooted doubts of his youth concerning the theology of the Old Testament. The Father's teaching fitted in well with the spirit in which the Carolingian authors fought this controversy.[1] The characterization of the Eastern mentality as a revival of pagan superstition created the right background for the representation of the Frankish monarchy as both orthodox and rational.

[1] I 7, pp. 22 ff.

The treatise itself shows in some passages that this picture does not cover all aspects of reality. The *Libri Carolini* draw a sharp line between Byzantine images, as purely man-made objects of cult, and relics, that is the bodies and garments of saints, which are recognized by Frankish theologians as rightful objects of adoration. But we should not guess from these marginal remarks how vitally important the belief in the help by the forces radiating from these relics was everywhere in the Carolingian empire as motive power and local centre of popular piety.[1] But it remains nevertheless true that the *Libri Carolini*, by rationalizing the viewpoint of a monarchy which saw the building up of religious morality and education as a part of its task, reflected a genuine aspect of the period. The idea of scholarly criticism, which the Carolingian authors played out against the miracle-stories of the east, can be traced back to Charlemagne's interest in the genuine text of the Bible and other classical religious writings, on which he intended to base the spiritual unity of the various nations in his empire. This aspect of his policy, in which the biblical idea of kingship served as his model, was at the root of the voluntaristic philosophy of the *Libri Carolini*: Man has to face God and his will directly. No belief is allowed in any intermediate zone determined by its own natural forces, on which man might exercise some influence. The external world is created as a stage for human action only. In this way the beginning of western thought is determined by the impact of the Bible; there is not much room for the application of ideas from ancient philosophy: some fragments of Platonic philosophy have helped to formulate the contrast of soul and body, and there are some logical concepts from the textbooks of the seven arts to support the argument, but there is no sign in the *Libri Carolini* that two generations later a scholar of a royal Court would attempt to solve the problems of his days with the help of a comprehensive assimilation of Greek thought.

B. *Political and theological discussions after Charlemagne's death*

The death of Charlemagne, an event which marks the beginning of his empire's dissolution, had no detrimental influence on learning and

[1] Einhard's realistic description illustrates this aspect very well: 'Translatio SS. Marcellini et Petri', *Mon. Germ. S.S.* xv, pp. 239–64.

thought. The work of copying and studying texts, which he had encouraged, went on in the scriptoria and libraries of the great ecclesiastical institutions. Moreover, his impulse showed its best results only in the decade after 814. The man of the eighth century who had taken up the new learning and exercised it in the writing of prose and poetry struggled with the difficulty of restoring language, literary tradition and forms of thought belonging to an earlier civilization rooted in very different conditions of life. It was only after the death of Charlemagne that Latinity became an adequate instrument for expressing freely the reactions of the contemporary élite to contemporary experience. It was this tendency in the intellectual development of the ninth century which gave Charles the Bald his only real chance of success when in 843, by the treaty of Verdun, he was legally recognized as king in the Western part of his grandfather's empire. He had to face an endless struggle in order to maintain himself against feudal disobedience, barbarian invasion and rival claims from the East-Frankish Carolingians. But he was able to revive the ideal of a royal court as a centre around which creative minds in scholarship and fine arts would gather. But just because during the Carolingian period the influence of the monarchy on learning was a more active force than in almost any period of the later Middle Ages, the changes in the social and political scene necessarily made their impact on intellectual life. During Charlemagne's reign scholarship had remained in close contact with the ideas by which the ruler kept secular and ecclesiastical institutions under his unifying control. Controversial topics of importance could only arise out of conflict with an outside power like the one which produced the *Libri Carolini.*

Soon after 814, in the reign of Charlemagne's son Louis the Pious, the rise to power of self-seeking factions of secular aristocracy created as reaction an opposition among the prelates, which found its expression in publicistic literature *freely* discussing the *internal* conflicts. Thus, for some time, the experience of social disintegration stimulated thought in men; they looked back to the Golden Age of the Frankish Empire, and in doing so transformed the motives of Charlemagne's political actions into a logical, coherent system. Archbishop Agobard of Lyons was the most prominent writer in this group. For him his contemporaries represented the Old Age of the world: as symptoms of such decay he pointed to various types of superstitious actions in his environment, both secular and ecclesiastical: men tried to exercise magical influence on the created world, which in reality, as matter in God's hand, must remain beyond their reach. We see that here the biblical philosophy of the *Libri Carolini* is carried on under very different circumstances. A good example of this attitude is the proposal, addressed to the Emperor Louis, to abolish ordeal by single combat as a means to force God to reveal his judgement on right and wrong. He describes this institution, authorized in his ecclesiastical province by a codification of Burgundian tribal law, as a means to expose old and weak people to blackmail. Such legal usage fosters the opinion that God assists the man who intends to ruin his fellows by his superiority in physical strength. Agobard bases this argument on a conviction, which he shares with St Augustine, that victory does not prove the conqueror to be on God's side. Neither King Necho of Egypt, who killed the pious King Josias in battle, nor the Saracens, who conquered Jerusalem, were so distinguished. The reality of God's will can be traced neither from great decisions in politics nor from events of everyday life. The emperor ought to abolish this variety of tribal rights, which favour wrong religious conceptions, and ought to replace them by a uniform law.[1]

The increase in the freedom of critical discussion, which had originated in the political sphere, spread to the more theoretical field of theological questions. The progress of patristic studies led to the discovery that the synthesis of revelation and philosophy in the classical period from St Ambrose to Boethius offered strong inducements to simplify or isolate certain ideas by eliminating others which were, or seemed to be, contradictory. This was done by the application of dialectical conceptions taken from the textbooks of rhetoric. During the forties and fifties King Charles the Bald encouraged such intellectual activities by dispatching questionnaires on points of dispute among contemporary scholars. Theoretically the purpose remained the traditional aim that finally *one* true answer must be found to which all the subjects of the king had to adhere. But the monarchy no longer had the authority established by the earlier Carolingians, to enforce unity, and probably King Charles himself was quite satisfied to stimulate various

[1] *De unitate legis*, §§ 6–9: *Mon. Germ. Hist., Epist.* v, p. 160, 21 f.

opinions based on different readings from the Fathers. About 850 he sent a questionnaire to the cathedral school of Reims, in which the problem was raised whether God must be considered the only being without material basis. This question arose out of the more general problem of the soul's relation to space. At the same time Ratramnus, a prominent scholar and controversialist, whom we know as a monk in the Benedictine community of Corbie (830–68), collected and examined patristic passages in a treatise *De anima* in answering a similar inquiry from the royal court.[1] It was ten years later, but probably not without knowledge of Ratramnus' first treatise *De anima*, that his diocesan bishop Odo of Beauvais asked him to defend sound ecclesiastical doctrine against the theory that the soul derives its qualities from a universal substance, with which it is linked by a process of emanation. This piece of speculation, based on Neoplatonic concepts, came originally from an Irishman, Macarius, and had recently been renewed by an anonymous pupil, monk in a monastery for which the bishop had a special responsibility.[2] Ratramnus, after preliminary exchanges with bishop and monk, answered this call by writing a second treatise *De anima*. The starting-point of this discussion was a paragraph in St Augustine's *De quantitate animae*. This book, a dialogue between master and pupil, was written in 388, soon after the author's conversion, and was intended to establish the spiritual interpretation of man's soul against the materialism of the Manichean sect. The passage on which Macarius had based his metaphysical theory describes a philosophical dilemma: the unity of all souls seems to be excluded by the simple consideration that one and the same soul cannot be at the same time both happy and unhappy, a coincidence which is normal among different men. On the other hand, the denial of any bond between the souls seems to Augustine ridiculously wrong, while the middle way, the idea that souls partake equally in unity and diversity, seems so hard to grasp that any attempt to affirm it would not be taken seriously by the audience.[3] Macarius' theory is offered as a precise definition of such an intermediate position, which, as he and his pupil suppose, was not worked out by the Father, because he

[1] A. Wilmart, 'L'opuscule de Ratramne sur la nature de l'âme', *Rev. Bénédict.* XLIII, pp. 207–23.

[2] Ph. Delhaye, *Une controverse sur l'âme universelle au IXe siècle* (Namur, 1950), pp. 7–18.

[3] *De quantitate animae*, cap. 32, § 69, *PL* 32. 1073.

considered this solution too difficult for his rude audience. According to Macarius the species 'soul' is divided up and allocated to individual bodies, but remains in existence as the source from which the individual entities continue to derive their separate existence. Ratramnus characterizes this position as the assumption of an *anima universalis* and declares it a falsehood in contrast to Christian doctrine and not supported by philosophy. To prove this point Ratramnus made use of Boethius' discussion on the reality of the universals. Of the two alternatives offered in the famous passage of Boethius, Ratramnus chooses the negative solution. Species do not exist in reality, they are abstractions from a number of particular phenomena. Therefore a species can never be the cause of the existence of an individual. The thesis that the particular soul cannot exist apart from the species, the universal soul, can only be described as a perversion of truth. In reality there is no species which does not result from the activity of the mind, which perceives different individual beings and groups them according to their similarity. Consequently, soul as species exists only in thought and cannot carry accidental qualifications, while particular souls allocated by God to single human bodies have an existence and qualification of their own. While talking of a single man's soul, for instance Cicero's, we use the concept of a species; yet we do not make a statement about many but about one single soul. And as long as we talk about souls, as they exist in diversity, we pronounce only about their common features and do not refer to the peculiar existence of one soul. Therefore Augustine's statement, that we cannot affirm substantial unity and individual diversity as being together in man's soul, is completely serious and completely correct.[1]

In this way Ratramnus applies Boethius' logical theory to restore a satisfactory interpretation to a patristic paragraph. Sound philosophy, and that means for him logic, has eliminated dangerous speculation.

[1] *Liber de anima ad Odonem*, ed. Dom D. C. Lambot (Namur, 1952), cap. 9, p. 131: 'Sic igitur fit ut genera seu species non causa sint existendi eorum quae dicuntur individua, sed potius individua causam praestent existentiae speciebus seu generibus. Male igitur dixit particulares animas non posse subsistere, non existente specie, id est, anima universali....' Pp. 136 f.: 'Etenim anima cuiuscumque singulariter hominis utpote Ciceronis, quamvis in eo quod est anima species enuncietur, in eo tamen quod dicitur Ciceronis anima, non multae, sed una singulariter praedicatur.'

C. *John Eriugena and his cosmological interpretation of Martianus Capella*

Among these controversies the question of predestination aroused the most intense and the most widely spread interest. It was concerned with a part of St Augustine's teaching which seems a purely theological interpretation of the Bible remote from his philosophical interests. Nevertheless this problem gave a strong impetus to the rise of philosophical thought in the final phase of the Carolingian period by its impact on the development of John Scottus Eriugena (*c.* 820–70). A sketch of his career will show why. His second and his third name describe him as an Irishman. But we know him only on the continent, where he must have joined the court of Charles the Bald as a teacher of grammar soon after 840. Locally he seems to have been linked to the cathedral of Laon; the influence of his studies and learning on the next generations of scholars could be traced in manuscripts from this region. The royal estate of Quierzy, which belongs to the same neighbourhood, was an important place of residence for Charles' court.[1] Our most important witness for Eriugena's activities at this period is Prudentius of Troyes, who until his elevation to the bishopric in 846, was John's friend and companion at court. Five years later, when he was driven to write against his former friend, he reports that, when they lived together, he had heard from Eriugena himself, as well as from others, that the grammarian was led to the teaching of daring cosmological theories in the course of his study of Martianus Capella.[2]

It seems now that we possess at least for the first book of Martianus Capella that draft of his annotations which corresponds to Prudentius' critical observations. The theme, the journey of Mercury and Virtus through the celestial spheres, allows us to trace the development of the author's interests to this early stage in his career.[3] Martianus' inclination to use Greek terminology freely gave great scope to display know-

[1] M. Cappuyns, *Jean Scot Érigène: Sa vie, son œuvre, sa pensée* (Louvain–Paris, 1933), pp. 59–66.

[2] *De praedestinatione, contra Joh. Scotum, PL* 115. 1293D.

[3] L. Labowsky, 'A new version of Scotus Eriugena's Commentary on Martianus Capella', *Mediaeval and Renaissance Studies*, I (1943), pp. 187–93; the MSS discussed is Bodleian MS. Auct. T. 2. 19.

ledge which Eriugena shared with other scholars who had come to the continent from Ireland. They liked to compile polyglot vocabularies of sacred languages, which combined the Latin of the Western Church with Greek from Septuagint texts and added sometimes a third column with Hebrew parallels from St Jerome's writings. Moreover, the text of Martianus offers a good opportunity for the Latinist to explain a language made artificially difficult in vocabulary, style and antiquarian subject-matter. More characteristic seem the cosmological excursions to which John is stimulated by a special peculiarity of his text. In the introductory part of his encyclopaedia Martianus uses the Olympian gods in a double capacity. The reader is made to think of them both as the anthropomorphic figures of Greek mythology and as planets. When Mercury visits Apollo, taken as sun-god, in his celestial spheres, both change easily from one part to the other. Martianus' raw material for this tale had some links with the cosmic religion of late antiquity, in which the planets combined the character of abstract physical forces with human personality. This ambiguity, which fitted in well with the general trend of interpretation offered by the mythological manuals from late antiquity in medieval libraries, gave Eriugena his chance. He certainly did not share the suspicious attitude of the earlier generation of Carolingian scholars towards the philosophical interpretation of mythology. Mercury wishes to consult Apollo about his intended engagement; the annotations explain that the short distance between the planet and the sun makes such co-operation necessary, and add the theory that Mercury and Venus move around the sun. In two lengthy excursions Eriugena deals with the souls' journey from their celestial home through the planetary spheres into the body and with their identical way in the opposite direction after death. The corruptions originating in their stay on earth are purged in the zones of the planets before each soul is allowed to return to the world of the stars. Eriugena's description quotes as its main source Macrobius' interpretation of Cicero's *Somnium Scipionis*. In his excursus on the souls' celestial journey, Eriugena emphasizes that the Platonic school, to whom he ascribes this doctrine, does not allow for any space outside the cosmos, where the soul could receive punishment or reward. This statement reflects Macrobius' intention of proving that Cicero's description of man's position in the world represents sound Platonic doctrine.[1] Eriugena's interest in the philosophical interpretation of pagan mythology is again shown in his note on a theory which identifies God with the *anima mundi*, while the single gods represent the different strata of the universe from ether to earth. The direct source, St Augustine's polemic against the Roman antiquarians, is not mentioned.[2] Prudentius, in his polemic, emphasizes this deficiency strongly, documenting his criticism with a long quotation from St Augustine's *De civitate Dei*. In this context he denounces Eriugena as a man who used the Father's work, the model for the defence of Christianity, as a source of information for the spreading of pagan superstition. The bishop traces this attitude to Eriugena's absorption in the study of Martianus. By this work he was entangled in those theories which destroy the Christian doctrine of man's ultimate destiny by accepting nothing outside the natural space of the universe.[3]

A Paris manuscript edited by C. Lutz represents a redrafting, probably finished about 860; it shows Eriugena's reaction to the theological attack on his cosmological interests.[4] Varro's reinterpretation of the pagan gods as representing parts of the *anima mundi* is now withdrawn and the statement that, according to Platonic doctrine, nothing outside the cosmos exists, is cut out. But these recantations are strikingly tactical; they concern only formulations which offer an easy target of attack. Eriugena's links with ancient cosmic religion have become even more obvious. Now Martianus himself is considered as Platonist, and the theory of the sun as the soul of the world, radiating all forces of life, irrational and rational, into the world, which Eriugena knows from Macrobius and Calcidius, is discovered in his text. This doctrine inspired the philosophically minded grammarian to construct a new theory of planetary movement around the sun to fit in with his understanding of Martianus' text.[5]

[1] Fol. 10 v: 'quia Marcus Tullius in somnio Scipionis dicit quod omnes animae descendunt de celo.... Primum enim descendunt in circulum Saturni.' Cf. Macrobius *in somnium Sc.* I, cap. XII, 14 f. Fol. 15 v: 'et quoniam extra mundum nihil putabant esse ad eosdem planetarum meatus, per quos animas ad corpora lapsas machinabantur, easdem redire putabant...'.

[2] Fol. 24r: 'Marcus Varro definit deum esse animam mundi cum suis partibus. Pars in aere juno, pars in aethere jovis...pars in terra diana.' The source is *De civ. Dei* VII, cap. 5; 6.

[3] Prudentius, *De praedestinatione*, *PL* 115. 1011; 1293 f.

[4] *Johannis Scoti Annotationes in Martianum* (Cambridge, Mass., 1939), pp. 22, 4; 38, 2.

[5] Lutz, 22, 30: 'Ac per hoc bis necesse erat Virtuti cum Mercurio planetarum circulos transire, primum quidem dum sint infra solem secundo vero...dum sunt supra.' Cf. H. Liebeschütz, 'Texterklärung u. Weltdeutung bei Johannes Eriugena', *Arch. f. Kulturgesch.* XL (1958), pp. 69–73, 90–3.

D. *A philosopher's reinterpretation of St Augustine*

The intensity of Eriugena's cosmological interests was a personal feature of his own; but the task itself, the explanation of a difficult text, fitted well into the framework of contemporary scholarship. It was this aspect of his work on Martianus which brought him into the controversy about the right interpretation of St Augustine. This controversy arose from an individual's radical insistence on one aspect of the patristic doctrine: Gottschalk's faith in the absolute determination of man's fate by divine decision was perhaps in its origin linked with the young Saxon nobleman's rebellion in 829 against his subordination to monastic life in Fulda. His creed, as it developed, implied a reduction of any institution's relevance to human salvation. But in the extensive texts which we now possess of his writings we do not find anything pre-Christian or Germanic in his concepts and ideas. In his combination of grammatical and theological studies and his poetry he is definitely a scholar of the Carolingian period in its maturity. He is distinguished by the power of the impact which Augustine's doctrine of predestination, understood according to the teaching of Fulgentius of Ruspe, had on his mind. Gottschalk represents a revival of the Father's religious experiences in his later life. They seem to form a paradoxical contradiction to those ideas from Platonic sources by which Augustine had once liberated himself from his allegiance to Manichaeism. With the stress laid on the significance of God's unaccountable Will this doctrine remained impenetrable to philosophical understanding. The two archbishops, Hrabanus Maurus of Mayence, Gottschalk's former abbot in Fulda, and Hincmar of Reims, always remained his enemies and kept him as a prisoner during the later part of his life. Their main motive for this was the challenge to all ecclesiastical institutions and to the moral discipline they wished to exercise, which could be implied in the former monk's teaching. The prelates were well entitled by contemporary conditions to consider the Church as the only power capable of preserving a fragment of Carolingian order in a disintegrating monarchy. It was for this reason that Hincmar made himself the advocate of free will and moral responsibility. But he discovered that Gottschalk was isolated from the theologians' opinion of his time more by the temperament which inspired his formulations than by the substance of his Augustinian discipleship. Both the development of patristic studies and the chaos in the surrounding world fostered a serious and sympathetic interest especially in the later stages of the Father's thought. Hincmar had to face the resistance of scholars in the neighbouring ecclesiastical province of Sens and, being himself stronger in canon law than in theology, turned to obtain the support of experts. But they did not produce satisfactory evidence in his favour: his suffragan Pardulus, bishop of Laon, suggested employing the court-grammarian resident in his neighbourhood.[1] Eriugena was a layman at this time (about 850), and quite unknown as a student of patristic theology. Hincmar may have been aware of a possibility that this move might strengthen his relation to the court; King Charles was very much interested in the problems raised by this controversy. But the main motive lay in the character of the dispute. Against the assertion that Hincmar had misunderstood Augustine he needed a scholar capable of showing with dialectical skill, persuasively, that the doctrine of double predestination to good and to evil had no basis in the Father's teaching. This was the task which Eriugena took on and which led him finally from his original cosmological interest to Neoplatonic philosophy. It meant for him that the stratum in the Father's writings in which the emphasis was on free will and on the negation of substantial reality in evil, had to be isolated from the rest and to be established as the only genuine meaning of his whole teaching. Gottschalk, whose Augustinism was scarcely less one-sided, had a parallel, but easier, task of abstraction. His creed was based on those aspects of Augustine's doctrine which were emphasized in the later period of his life as an answer to the Pelagian challenge. It was from this point of view that Augustine had critically reviewed much of his earlier work in his *Retractationes*. So Gottschalk, having quoted some Augustinian passages on the origin of both *civitates* in God's will, could well feel entitled to present these formulations as the patristic master's final view: in his habit of careful revision and retractation, Augustine would not have left such sentences unchanged without the

[1] The history of the controversy: M. Cappuyns, *loc. cit.* pp. 102–27. Pardulus' defence of bringing in Eriugena is quoted: *PL* 121. 1052A: 'Sed quia haec inter se valde dissentiebant, Scotum illum, qui est in palatio regis, Johannem nomine, scribere coëgimus.'

conviction that they were completely true and in full agreement with Catholic faith.[1]

Gottschalk very rarely expresses a difference of opinion from St Augustine's doctrine, but the whole philosophical aspect of his work is passed over in silence. Obviously Gottschalk takes it as one stage in the man's development, which the Father has sufficiently criticized himself and which therefore cannot represent divine truth. Gottschalk did not feel that the task of harmonizing the different aspects of St Augustine's work offered any appeal to his dialectical powers.

In clear contrast to him, Eriugena, who intends to demonstrate patristic teaching as one uniform philosophy of religion, cannot avoid dealing with those passages which the defenders of the double predestination used to give as authority for their thesis. He employs the theory of rhetorical topics to eliminate the literal meaning of such texts. Neither prescience nor predestination can be attributed to God as a genuine predicate. These concepts presuppose an interval of time between vision and event. But no difference between past, present and future exists in God. When Augustine expresses the truth in terms of human eloquence he has to use metaphors and his reader must try to understand distinctly what is implied in their application. If we speak of God's foresight in planning we assume the possibility of an *analogy* to human action, that means an element of similarity.[2] But the second possibility, which it would be dangerous to overlook, is an emphasis on contrast brought about by the use of strikingly inadequate concepts in defining God's action. Faced with passages dealing with predestination to death Eriugena proposes to account for them as figurative expressions intended to make the reader conscious of the gulf between God and evil. In this context the court-grammarian quotes examples used by Isidore in a paragraph on allegorical speech, like 'lucus a non lucendo'; in this way he demonstrates that his interpretation of Augustine's pas-

[1] *Confessio prolixior*, D. C. Lambot, *Œuvres théologiques et grammaticales de Godescalc d'Orbais* (Louvain, 1945), p. 65, 12: 'Nempe haec omnia...si tantus auctor iste veracissima et catholicae fidei per omnia congruentissima non esse perspexisset, nullatenus incorrecta relinqueret sed ea potius, quando libros suos diligentissime retractando recensuit, corrigere studuisset...si quid itidem periculi inesse cognovisset.'

[2] Eriugena, *Liber de praedestinatione*, cap. 9, §§ 5, 7, *PL* 122. 392B–C; 393B–C.

sages corresponds to the rules of the school.[1] The tendency is clear: Eriugena could not pass over those patristic statements which were in the centre of contemporary discussion. He quoted them, but he eliminated their doctrinal content and consequently there was no need to exercise dialectical skill in harmonizing Augustine's philosophical doctrine, as Eriugena reconstructed it, with the theology of Grace. In this final result his own proceeding was not very different from Gottschalk's, when he ignored the Platonic element in his master's teaching.

Eriugena's positive teaching points mainly in two directions. First, he intends to characterize double predestination as a pernicious attempt to connect God's will with evil and to destroy the free will of man. Secondly, the genuine content of St Augustine's teaching has to be established as contrary to such predestination. That means that Eriugena draws mainly on the set of ideas which the Father had developed in opposition to the Manichean doctrine of evil as the natural substance of world and man.

In his preface, addressed to the two prelates who had commissioned his work, Eriugena requests his readers not to think him blasphemous when he seems to restrict God's foreknowledge by denying the possibility of a real link between the divine mind and intention on the one hand and all those objects of human experience on the other, which must be understood as negations of substance and therefore as a contradiction of God's nature. In our daily life we meet with phenomena which cannot become objects of knowledge in any positive sense, because they are only the negation of what we could observe. Darkness has this relation to light, and silence to sound, but stupidity and wisdom can also be quoted as examples. These negatives must be what Augustine in *De civitate Dei* calls 'a kind of not knowing'.[2]

All actions which we call evil, and their consequences, fall under the same logical category. They exist in us as a corruption of good. Sin is a deficiency of justice, punishment the negation of beatitude. Therefore we cannot allocate the character of true being to such experiences; they have no genuine element of truth in themselves. That makes it impos-

[1] *Loc. cit.* cap. 9, §§ 2 f.; cap. 11, § 4; cap. 15, §§ 6–7, *PL* 122. 390B f.; 399B f.; 415A–C—Isidorus, *Etymolog.* I, cap. 37, §§ 22, 24.

[2] *PL* 122. 375; cap. 10, §§ 4 f., *loc. cit.* 396A f., where Eriugena quotes Augustine, *De civ. Dei* XII 7 as basis for a similar argument.

sible to characterize them as a potential content of God's mind. Every object of God's foreknowledge must have its origin in himself, the Creator, and not in the element of nothingness, with which God's creation of the world started.

The most characteristic section of the treatise is perhaps the final chapters, which have the purpose of eliminating the assumption that God has designed places of eternal damnation for a considerable part of mankind. This threat of punishment after death was a very important object of reflection, and in some circumstances a powerful motive for action among the philosopher's contemporaries. Eriugena establishes his opposition by offering alternatives which represent his tendency in a different degree of decisiveness. The more radical negation of a preconceived place of punishment in God's creation follows from Eriugena's conception of a sin as an action by which man fails his destiny. A way of life, by which he misses truth for ever and moves in the direction opposite to his vocation, cannot fail to create a lasting feeling of misery in the depth of man's soul which will serve as his self-inflicted punishment.[1] The second interpretation is given in connexion with the word from the Gospel on the fire prepared for all who follow Satan. To avoid the assumption of hellfire as part of the creation, Eriugena proposes its identity with the fourth element. In the higher strata of the cosmos, where this element is concentrated, are the regions in which both the evil and the pious souls gather. But the same environment means something different to each group, just as the sun's light is beneficent to the healthy eye, and painful when the sight is impaired.[2] There is a reminiscence of Augustine's *De ordine* in this statement: the dark sides of life have their place in the cosmic order and in its beauty. But in the main the subject-matter of this brief sketch of eschatological thought shows the impact of other sources. The connexion with his earlier Martianus studies, which had offered Eriugena a bridge to the cosmic religion of antiquity, is clear; Prudentius knew the ways of his old companion well. Another influence, mentioned in passing by the bishop of Troyes, is more important: Rufinus' Latin translation of

[1] Cap. 16, § 6, col. 423c: 'In omni enim peccatore simul incipiunt oriri et peccatum et poena ejus, quia nullum peccatum est, quod non se ipsum puniat, occulte tamen, in hac vita, aperte vero in altera, quae est futura.'

[2] Cap. 19, §§ 1, 2, col. 436c f.

Origen's *De principiis* offered him a Christian system which could give him much stronger encouragement for his daring transformation of an article of faith which was of the highest importance to his environment.[1] The way in which Eriugena's arguments are compiled by a very one-sided selection from St Augustine's works, supplemented from other sources, and the lack of complete consistency in his doctrines, must not hide the fact that, already at this stage, he is guided by a definite idea of man's position in the world. For him, as for Origen, the world is a place of education, where with the help of God's Grace man may learn to repair the damage which the abuse of his free will has wrought on him.

It was this philosophy which had brought him into the controversy about predestination. Man's free will was the theoretical presupposition for Hincmar's attempt to carry on the Carolingian idea of a society shaped by Christian morality under ecclesiastical leadership. From this point of view the Archbishop and the royal grammarian could consider themselves potential allies. The character of this controversy as a discussion about the interpretation of Augustine was certainly an important reason why in *De praedestinatione* Eriugena based his doctrine mainly on Latin tradition. The use of Origen is visible only in the short paragraphs on the punishment after death; Gregory of Nyssa, whom Eriugena knew already in the forties, is only mentioned in passing.[2] But the mental climate of his first book shows clearly that it was not only the contact with fresh literary material from Byzantium in Abbot Hilduin's St Denis which brought about the achievements of Eriugena's final period. Without the *corpus areopagiticum* he would not have become the champion of a hierarchical world-picture to which Carolingian thought two generations earlier had been antagonistic. But his pamphlet on the question of predestination shows that his mind was

[1] Origen, *De principiis* II, 10, §§ 4, 8, *PG* 11. 236, 240.

[2] *Lib. de praed.* cap. 17, § 8, col. 429B: 'Sive itaque ignis ille corporeus, ut ait Augustinus, sive incorporeus, ut Gregorio placet....' Gregory of Nyssa is quoted by Eriugena for the first time in the Oxford text of the Martianus notes: Fol. 11r f.: 'gregorius nyseus, germanus basilii ait, quia iuvenis quidam dicebat se esse aliquando sicut uir aliquando sicut femina uel etiam sicut uolatile uel sicut piscis uel sicut rana. Ideo dicit hoc propter nimiam miseriam animarum.' This passage abbreviates *De hominis opificio*, ch. 29, *PG* 44. 232A f. Eriugena explains his emphasis on Augustine as a tactical necessity: ch. 11, § 2, col. 398B: '...necessarium duximus, et utiliter ad rem pertinere videmus, illius auctoris dicta ponere, cui maxime G. haereticus sui nefandi dogmatis causas solet referre'.

already well prepared for this change. The grammarian's intervention in the debate on predestination was felt on all sides as an alien intrusion into the field of patristic theology. The influence of Origen was not quite overlooked, but the main criticism was directed against the revival of Pelagian heresy as the most characteristic feature of the book. Prudentius emphasized that the same spirit can be traced both in Pelagius and in Julian of Eclanum, the ardent defender of Pelagius. Possibly this equation was stimulated by a passage in Gottschalk's *De praedestinatione*, where he observes that this main champion of the Pelagian school had used a sentence by John Chrysostom out of its context to support the errors of his own sect.[1] A corresponding judgement would certainly apply to Eriugena's interpretation of Augustine, as Prudentius saw it. The disclosure of such a compromising relationship caused the Archbishop of Reims to pretend that he did not know anything reliable about the origin and author of these nineteen chapters, which had been dedicated to him. To characterize their contents he took up a jest coined originally by St Jerome against Pelagius himself, and applied to Eriugena in two council decisions, by complaining that his colleagues were feeding him, an innocent man, with this Irish porridge. Eriugena had anticipated such criticism. He had mentioned Pelagius as a man who had denied divine grace all power, and had placed him near to Gottschalk, who substituted necessity for grace.[2] The passage about Pelagius may very well be a symptom of Eriugena's early awareness of his position as an outsider among contemporary scholars. This experience caused him to cover up or withdraw certain exposed aspects or compromising relationships of his philosophy, without yielding anything of importance to him. The same attitude appears certainly as a characteristic feature in the later draft of his Martianus notes.

There is no doubt that Eriugena and Pelagius were near to one another as representatives of faith in Man's power and responsibility for determining the course of his actions by free will. In this attitude both were the disciples of the ancient moralists. Pelagius' commentaries on

[1] Prudentius in the introductory letter to Wenzilo of Sens, *Mon. Germ. Epist.* v, p. 632, 10 f. Gottschalk, *De praedestinatione*, ed. Lambot, p. 192, 5.

[2] Hincmar, *De praedestinatione*, preface, *PL* 125. 50 A. In ch. 31, 296 A he denies having any reliable knowledge about the author of the nineteen chapters; Eriugena, *Lib. de praedest.* ch. 7, § 1, 2, col. 370 C f.

the letters of St Paul, which were well within the reach of the Carolingian scholar from Ireland, intended the same sort of transformation of the apostle's thought as did Eriugena's interpretation of St Augustine. And when the Carolingian philosopher read in Augustine's *Retractationes* the complaint that the author's early writings, with their emphasis on free will, had been misunderstood and quoted in support of the Pelagian position, he may well have taken up these remarks in a sense opposite to the great bishop's intentions. Charlemagne would certainly have repudiated such a daring course. But Eriugena's theoretical radicalism in working out the principle does not eliminate the fact that the educational ideas closely connected with the great emperor's government gave the first impetus to the emphasis on Man's freedom of action in the thought of the philosopher at his grandson's court. That the Greek Fathers allowed him to elaborate this idea and to justify it as traditional and orthodox doctrine determined the final phase of his development.[1]

[1] [On this final phase see Part VI (The Greek Christian Tradition), ch. 34, pp. 518–33.]

CHAPTER 37

THE DEBATE ON PHILOSOPHICAL LEARNING DURING THE TRANSITION PERIOD (900–1080)

A. *The discussion on the character of Boethius: Platonic or Christian philosopher?*

The impetus given to speculative thought by the existence of a court interested in intellectual activities petered out with the beginning of the tenth century. The invasions destroyed a good deal of the economic presuppositions on which centres of learning had to rely, and interrupted their lines of communication. There is good reason for the name of the 'Dark Age' given to the decades which followed the end of Carolingian civilization. While the importance and influence of the French monarchy was reduced by the rise of feudal principalities, and remained so during this period, after 950 the Ottonian dynasty were capable of re-establishing monarchical power in Germany and of reviving literary activities as the true heirs of Charlemagne. Under their rule Latin writing in prose and verse was cultivated in those Saxon lands where Christianity had been introduced only a few generations earlier. But their court never reached such importance as a forum where speculative questions were debated as had distinguished the circle of scholars round Charlemagne and his grandson. Single centres in West and Central Europe kept up a certain continuity of philosophical learning. In some monasteries and cathedrals the libraries, collected under the impulse of the Carolingian revival, were preserved, and so the tradition of study, linked to the keeping and copying of manuscripts, remained alive. Some of these books, handed on from antiquity, raised disturbing questions about the relationship of rational thought to Christian revelation in the mind of the monk or canon who read them. It was Boethius' *De consolatione philosophiae* which stimulated reflections of this type. With its tendency to lead Man back from his entanglement in the affairs of the world to his true vocation, it was felt to be a valuable instrument of Christian teaching. The great number of existing manuscripts from this period and the famous translations into the vernacular by King Alfred and Notker the German are witnesses of its popularity. It was natural that such a textbook of the right way of life should become the object of studies in libraries and schools. Remigius of Auxerre, who by his teacher Heiric was linked to the school of Laon and finally to Eriugena's grammatical teaching, wrote the standard commentary. The theoretical content of Boethius' book was most intensely studied in special commentaries to *metrum* III 9 where the Roman philosopher describes the connexion between God and cosmos in concepts taken from Plato's *Timaeus*.[1] It seems now that Eriugena himself, in the early phase of his studies when his work was mainly dedicated to the explanation of Latin authors, annotated the philosophical doctrine of this poem. The most interesting feature in the work done during the dark age is the first discovery of the problem which still divides the modern critics: Does *De consolatione* belong to the Christian writing of Boethius or does it represent pagan philosophy? Bovo of Corvey in Saxony and Adalboldus of Utrecht are the protagonists on both sides of this controversy. Bovo, who was abbot of his monastery during the last sixteen years of his life (†916), had studied the literary legacy of Boethius since the days of his youth. Therefore he feels entitled to assert that both the treatises on Christian Theology and *De consolatione* show identical brilliance of style and therefore must be ascribed to the same author. On the other hand, the ideas of *De consolatione*, and especially the cosmogony of the *metrum* III 9 on which he comments, seem to him rather those of a Platonic philosopher than the work of a Christian author. Bovo underlines these doubts by emphasizing his hesitation to annotate such a text. He raises the question whether work of this type is appropriate to his status as a monk, and he safeguards his conscience by asking for the censorship of the bishop, his namesake, relative and former pupil, who had encouraged this work.[2] But with all these reser-

[1] H. Silvestre, 'Comment. inéd. de J. Scot Érigène', *Rev. hist. ecclés.* XLVII (1952), pp. 49–122. The main study on the history of *De consol.* during the Middle Ages: P. Courcelle, *Étude crit. s. l. Commentaires d. l. Consolat. de Boèce* (IX–XIV s.), *Arch. d'hist. doctr. et lit. du M.A.* XII (1939), pp. 5–140.

[2] *PL* 64. 1239–46; R. B. C. Huygens, 'Mittelalterl. Kommentare z. "O qui perpetua"', *Sacris erudiri*, VI (1954), pp. 383 ff. offers a critical edition.

vations Bovo does not really repudiate *De consolatione*. When he sets out to explain the cosmological theories, he cannot hide his serious interest.

For the solution of questions raised by the passage in which Boethius describes the power inherent in numbers to bring about linkages between the elements, he turns to another source of Platonic tradition; Macrobius, in his commentary on the *Somnium Scipionis*, offers a theory about the arrangement of the four elements in the cosmos. Earth and fire form the outer layers, while water and air in the middle are keeping them together; their qualities hot and cold, dry and wet are so distributed, that each element shares one quality with its neighbour. It is the number four which brings about this unbreakable chain, uniting the contrasts of earth, which is dense and heavy, with fire, which is rarefied and light. In this paragraph of Macrobius Bovo finds the explanation for the passage in Boethius, and so anticipates the method applied by the masters of Chartres, when they built up their cosmological philosophy as a well designed mosaic from a wider range of similar sources. All this source-material is finally derived from the ancient doctrines on macrocosm and microcosm gathered for the explanation of Plato's *Timaeus*. Boethius' concept of the *anima mundi* is explained by the commentator as the driving force in the universe and as a characteristic feature of a specifically philosophical theory remote from Christian doctrine. But it is dealt with at length as a probable hypothesis to account for the opposite movements of planets and stars.[1] In other passages the contrast between Christian truth and pagan error is more strongly emphasized. When Bovo mentions the world-picture in which the earth is placed in the centre of the universe with the celestial spheres moving around it, he is eager to avoid any impression that he is offering such Platonic theories as established facts; otherwise his readers might assume that he also confirms Macrobius' teaching on the existence of the antipodes, which is so clearly in contrast to the faith. Again Macrobius is quoted to reveal the danger behind Boethius' statement in Book v, that the souls enjoyed great freedom of contemplation before they went down to earth and were incorporated into bodies. In this seemingly edifying reflection reported by Macrobius Bovo sees a link with the

[1] § 8, col. 1241 B; § 17, cols. 1244 f.

emphatically pagan doctrine of the soul's descent through the celestial spheres which, by their radiating influence, determine man's character on earth. Faced with such aspects of Boethius' work the learned abbot of Corvey finds his task similar to that of Augustine, who studied pagan ritual in order to defend Christianity.[1]

A clear contrast to Bovo's attitude towards the *De consolatione* can be traced in the annotations to the same cosmogonic poem by a prelate, who during the last quarter of the tenth century was brought up in the learned tradition of Liège cathedral. The author, Bishop Adalbold of Utrecht (+1026), was a man of many-sided activities in his diocese, his territory and at court, representing a type not infrequent under the Ottonians.[2] For him Boethius was a Christian philosopher. The beginning of the poem, an abstract appeal to God as the eternal wisdom ruling the world, is accepted by Adalbold as an appropriate definition of the creator, whom, as the Bible teaches, no simile can describe adequately. Hermes and Plato have approached the truth in their discourses, but they did not succeed in penetrating it. Boethius proved superior, because he did not try to describe a picture seen by the body's eye, but felt the essential core of the cosmos in his heart. When Boethius speaks of God's mind, in which the beauty of the world had been anticipated, the Ottonian bishop takes that as a description of Christ, the Word, by which everything came into existence. The passage on the souls brought down from heaven to earth by the creator, which Bovo had associated with pagan myth, was very differently understood by Adalbold. For him the text may intend to define the moment when the individual souls have been created, a question discussed but not decided by Jerome and Augustine; Adalbold does not wish to go beyond this abstention. The description of God as *summi forma boni* poses another problem to the bishop, wishing to defend the Christian character of Boethius' theism. The Roman Platonist seems to have reduced the distance between God and creature; form demands the supplement of matter. Adalbold avoids this consequence, which would make God a part of this world, by

[1] § 22, col. 1246A. Bovo's biography: M. Manitius, *Gesch. d. lat. Literat.* I (1911), pp. 526–29.

[2] Manitius, II (1923), pp. 143–8; Courcelle, pp. 73 ff.: T. Gregory, *Platonismo Medievale* (1958), pp. 1–15 discusses both Bovo and Adalboldus. Critical edition of the text in C. T. Silk, 'Pseudo-Johannes Scottus, Adalbold of Utrecht and the early commentaries on Boethius', *Mediev. and Renaissance Studies*, III (1954), pp. 14–24.

understanding the form as the creator's instrument, by which he makes his perfect goodness visible to the human eye. God does not enter the creation he shapes, but its form is the sign of the Master. It has been recently demonstrated by Gregory, that Adalbold took this solution of his difficulty from Eriugena's idea of the world as *theophania.*[1]

With Manegold's theological criticism of ancient cosmology we reach the second half of the eleventh century and so the age of the ecclesiastical reform. Activity in this sphere was not restricted to the field of canon law and the problems raised by the new ideas about the relationship of sacerdotal and secular office. The lasting influence of this movement on the development of medieval thought is obvious: the rise of scholasticism during the twelfth and thirteenth centuries cannot be separated from the problems raised by the ecclesiastical reform, which was one of the great forces ushering in the second period of civilization in the Middle Ages. Here we have to trace the modest beginning of this process.

The fragments of ancient cosmological teaching and the idea of philosophical understanding, which had survived through the Dark Age as a part of ecclesiastical learning, and had produced the discussion about the meaning of Boethius' *De consolatione*, became now the target of deeply emotional criticism. For it was considered to be the origin of a mentality from which resistance to the right order had sprung.

Manegold of Lauterbach had been a teacher in the liberal arts, famous in West and Central Europe for his learning. After his conversion to the regular life he became the most passionate champion of Gregory VII in the war of pamphlets, denouncing ideas and persons in the imperial camp. About 1085 he wrote against Wolfhelm of Cologne, who as a Benedictine defended orthodox belief against Berengar in the eucharistic controversy, but was in politics a follower of the anti-Gregorian party.[2] Manegold draws his antagonist as a man who finds

[1] Silk, pp. 14, 22, 16. Eriugena III 19, *PL* 122. 681 A is discussed by Gregory, *loc. cit.* pp. 12 f. [On Eriugena's idea of the world as *theophania* see preceding Part (VI, 'The Greek Christian Tradition'), ch. 34, pp. 523–31.]

[2] *Opusculum contra Wolfelmum coloniensem*, *PL* 155. 147–76. Wolfhelm's letter against Berengar: *PL* 154. 412 ff. Manegold's conversion from the life of a secular master of arts to that of a regular is acclaimed by Ivo of Chartres, *Correspondance*, ed. J. Leclerq, I (1949), no. 38, pp. 156 ff. On Manegold's career: J. A. Endres, *Forschungen z. Gesch. d. frühmittel. Philos.* (1915), pp. 87–113; T. Gregory, *loc. cit.* pp. 17–30; E. Garin, *Studi sul Platonismo Medievale* (1958), pp. 23–33.

scarcely anything in the Platonic tradition, as offered by Macrobius, which would harm a Christian's soul. Manegold traces inborn ferocity in such statements. The intention to obey God's will has been expelled from the mind by the study of philosophy. In this way an attitude originates, which produces the principle: 'We have no pontiff but Caesar.' Manegold emphasizes the impact which a man's ideas about his soul and about his own responsibility for his fate after death must have on his actions. It will not help him to read in Macrobius the incredible Pythagorean story of punishment by transmigration to animal bodies, nor will the variety of opinions on this matter, represented by the doctrines of the different philosophical schools, encourage the Christian student to take the right decision. Greek philosophy at its best produced Plato's doctrine on the origin of the soul at the moment of creation. But the details of this theory are so obscure that Macrobius' attempt at an explanation means trying to achieve the impossible.[1]

Manegold, however, admits that some subjects of philosophical teaching might be above his criticism. As example he quotes the classification of virtue. He knows very well that some ethical doctrines formulated by the Platonists have been taken over by the Fathers, who adapted them to the needs of the Christian communities.[2] This differentiation made by Manegold between acceptable and dangerous aspects of philosophical teachings reflects, as has been observed recently, a contrast between the approach to Platonism by the Fathers on the one hand and the attitude of the schools in the earlier Middle Ages on the other. In the ancient Church the Athenian thinker was seen mainly as the antagonist to Homeric mythology and as the main representative of the Socratic emphasis on philosophy as the search for moral values. He was therefore, with some necessary reservations, accepted as an ally in the defence and explanation of faith. This view of Platonism reached the medieval world mainly through the writing of St Augustine. But there was, as we know, another stream of tradition connected with the name of Plato, which came to the Middle Ages from the *Timaeus* and those

[1] Preface, *PL* 155. 149 f.; ch. 23, 172C; ch. 2, 153D f.

[2] Ch. 22, 170; the Neoplatonic classification of virtue in Macrobius *Somnium Scipionis*, I 8. [On the patristic use of Platonic moral teaching see Parts II, V and VI.]

writings of late antiquity which reflect the influence of this cosmogonic treatise on popular philosophy. This body of doctrine, representing an important part of the available philosophical lore, with its parallelism to Genesis, could easily be taken as reason's challenge to revelation. Manegold found this dangerous aspect of philosophy symbolized by Macrobius' speculation on macrocosm and microcosm. To search for the understanding of the fabric of the universe or for the relations between the elements means for him seeking the sun in a cave —the Platonic flavour makes this deprecation slightly paradoxical. What was true in the wisdom of the philosophers came from the Bible; but in this process of adoption the genuine meaning was lost. Thus the idea of the Trinity was debased into the triad of intelligible form, matter and demiurge, the latter responsible for the combination of the three; there was no room left for God's omnipotence in such an account of the world's origin. Manegold does not overlook the fragments of astrological determinism in Macrobius. He speaks of people who believed themselves able to trace a chain of causes from planets and constellations to events linked to them by necessity. The doctrine that mankind was separated into four groups by barriers of climate and other insuperable obstacles, which had aroused objections since the eighth century, was also noted by Manegold as contrary to the message of the gospels, that the coming of Christ would save all men.[1]

Errors like that are not a product of chance but originate in a wrong assessment of human reason. Even after the Fall man has remained capable of establishing uniformity or diversity among the objects he encounters in his environment. But when the philosopher's self-confidence ventures beyond this natural field allocated to human understanding, he is liable to be rushed from wrong presuppositions into deceptive arguments.[2]

B. *Dialectical skill as a scholar's showpiece*

It has been observed that Manegold's sceptical attitude towards the human intellect did not prevent him in his fight for the cause of Gregory VII from using that dialectical skill which he had exercised as a

[1] On Astrology, ch. 7, 157B–C; on the antipodes (Macrobius II 5), ch. 4, 154D.
[2] Ch. 1, 152C.

teacher of the liberal arts in the early stages of his career. When he discusses the deposition of Henry IV in his treatise on ecclesiastical politics,[1] he emphasizes the necessity of analysing precisely the texts quoted as authorities by the antagonist on the royalist side: no single phrase can be accepted as part of the argument without examination of context and style. When Pope Gregory the Great speaks of his obedience towards the Byzantine emperor, the reader ought not to forget that such an expression is formed by the language of the court, where voluntary actions and attitudes are described as expressions of obedience and loyalty. To invalidate a quotation from the first letter of St Peter prescribing obedience to the king, Manegold examines what is meant by the word 'king'. It does not describe a natural quality permanently inherent in man, but an office, which can be taken away from him. Consequently, the apostle's word does not apply to Henry IV, who has broken the contract which formed the basis of his authority.[2] If Manegold's temperament had allowed him any reflection on his own consistency, he might have defended his use of rational analysis throughout his political treatise by his former statement about the capacity of the human intellect to distinguish and to subsume.

But Manegold's application of dialectical technique is not merely a survival from the earlier stage of his individual career. In the great controversy about monarchy and church government two systems of legal thought faced each other. This condition produced on both sides an unprecedented effort to build up persuasive arguments by appropriate interpretation of texts quoted as authorities. The method developed under this impulse became, after the success of the ideas of reform, an important motive behind the rise of scholastic philosophy throughout the twelfth century.

This development had been prepared during the earlier part of the Middle Ages by the fact that dialectic had remained an established part in the curriculum of learning, as it was pursued in monastic and cathedral schools. The task of writing Latin letters and documents, for which the students were prepared, seemed to demand a logical training. We possess two documents which demonstrate in a lively manner the

[1] *Ad Gebehardum liber*, *Mon. Germ. Hist.*, *Libelli de lite*, I (1891), pp. 308–430. Cf. C. Mirbt, *Publizistik im Zeitalter Gregors VII.* (1894), pp. 26–9, 227–35, 483–8.

[2] Ch. 45; 43, *loc. cit.* pp. 388, 15; 385, 15.

use of this type of philosophical exercise as a testing ground for a scholar's capacity to form an effective argument. Gunzo's open letter to the monks of Reichenau, written probably after 965, and the eighty years later *Rhetorimachia* by Anselm of Besate are both pamphlets meant to demonstrate the competence of the two Italian authors against the sceptical assessment of their capacities they experienced north of the Alps.[1] In order to emphasize the naïvety with which the German monks in St Gallen had commented on a mistake in his Latin speech, Gunzo emphasizes that genuine learning does not always lead to one definite solution of a given problem. Boethius' passage dealing with the controversy on the existence of universal concepts is quoted as an example in this context. Gunzo refers to the antagonism between Plato, who affirmed, and Aristotle who denied, such existence. He draws the conclusion that nobody can make a decision when two authorities of such standing disagree.

A discussion on the meaning of accident and substance serves the same purpose. Primitive dogmatism would assume that all the phenomena of the world can be summarized under these two concepts. But closer examination shows that this is not the case. When we point to something as a *difference* we have not in mind a *substance*, because we do not think of the being of something, but neither is *accidens* meant, because *difference* contributes to the shaping of a substance.[2]

Anselm's *Rhetorimachia*, and the dedicatory letters which serve as introduction and an epilogue, are designed to show the world his competence as teacher of rhetoric within the framework of a fantastically fictitious case against his cousin. His emphasis on logic, as the instrument by which an argument is made probable, is expressed in the additional name Peripateticus, by which he attaches himself to the school described by Boethius as dominating the ancient tradition of dialectic. Anselm quotes from Boethius' logical proposition, that the combination of two species will never produce a third one; nothing that we observe as uniform in itself can contain two contrasting elements. The

[1] A critical edition of both treatises was recently published with full introduction and commentary: Karl Manitius, *Gunzo Epistola ad Augienses und Anselm von Besate Rhetorimachia* (*Mon. Germ. Hist. Quellen z. Geistesgesch. d. M.A.* II, 1958). On the subject-matter cf. G. Misch, *Geschichte d. Autobiographie*, II, 2 (1955), pp. 402–15.

[2] Manitius, p. 40, 10–23.

Italian dialectician hesitates to doubt a statement behind which he recognizes Aristotle's authority. But he mentions Man, who is composed of a rational and a mortal part, and whose colour originates from the combination of black and white, as a phenomenon which seems opposed to the Aristotelian theorem. In the epilogue to his work Anselm returns to this argument in a report on the part he played in an assembly of prelates in Mayence. He served at this period as a notary in the chancellery of the emperor Henry III, so this meeting can be dated in 1049. Anselm wishes to prove that the lukewarm attitude of the city towards his masterpiece, the *Rhetorimachia*, cannot be defended.[1]

The people of Mayence pretended that they had kept to the middle line by refraining both from praise and from blame. Such reticence represented—according to Anselm's report—a combination of praise and blame comparable to the origin of red from a mixture of black and white; he means that his antagonists wanted to move in two contrasting directions at the same time. The objection that the citizens' lack of positive appreciation was not the outcome of a combination of blame and praise, but the result of abstention from either, is countered by a further observation on such neutrality. The negation, on which it is based, has no limits; it refers to anything in heaven and on earth as well as to praise and blame. There is no possibility of defining it by any predication; it remains nothing, which can certainly not be defended. It is no accident that these treatises have two Italian masters of literary and logical studies as authors. It was in the towns of the Lombard plain that this kind of activity kept some contact with the affairs of the citizens and notaries, because here fragments of Roman law had remained the basis of business life. Under these circumstances learning was connected with a secular purpose promising prosperity to the successful teacher. This special combination during this earlier period of the Middle Ages made writings possible in which questions of religion and theology appear to be removed to an isolated corner of the discussion. These conditions did not exist quite in the same way in other parts of Western or Central Europe. Therefore we find in Italy the uninhibited

[1] Manitius, p. 134, 1–14; p. 180 f.; on Anselm's biography cf. C. Erdmann, *Forschungen zur polit. Ideenwelt des Frühmittelalters* (1951), pp. 119–24.

expression of pride in intellectual superiority, which contrasts strikingly with the style of humility accepted since the patristic epoch. But the fact that medieval politics employed the literary and dialectical skill of letter-writers as an instrument for promoting co-operation, accounts for similar developments in other parts of Europe, where the special background prevailing in Northern Italy was missing. It is evident that this attitude of trust in the power of reasoned argument, which had spread with the increase of political correspondence since the end of the tenth century, worked as a factor contributing to the revival of philosophical thought, which had to be based on a similar confidence. The foremost representative of intellectual brilliance among men of action during the earlier part of the Middle Ages, Gerbert of Aurillac, was not yet very remote from the stage where philosophical reasoning functions mainly as a showpiece. He was born in Aquitania about 945 and ended his eventful career as Pope Silvester II (†1003). The names of his parents are unknown to us; it was only the power of his mind which carried him through the vicissitudes of his life, in which his elevation to the archbishopric of Reims (991–6) was only an episode, followed by exile.[1]

When, in 972, he was appointed by Archbishop Adalbero to the mastership of the cathedral school in Reims, he was the first teacher, of whom we know, to give a full course on the introductory treatises of Aristotelian logic (*Logica vetus*) as it was represented by Boethius' commentaries and monographs. His teaching of logic was given in the normal framework as part of the course in liberal arts, described in detail by his pupil Richer; thus the students went on from logic to rhetoric, a subject intended as the training ground for future notaries and writers of Latin letters and so nearest to the practical purpose of the school. In Gerbert's Reims, as 150 years later in Chartres, the pupils were well grounded in the reading of poets, Roman comedy, satire and epic, to broaden their command of the language. On the other hand they practised controversial arguments with a specialist in this art. The second part of the arts course, the quadrivium, as directed by Gerbert,

[1] His biography in F. Picavet, *Gerbert ou le pape philosophe* (1897); M. Uhlirz, *Untersuchungen über Inhalt und Datierung der Briefe Gerberts v. Aurillac, Papst Silvester II.* (1957); a brilliant description of his personality, based on analysis of some letters in E. Auerbach, *Literatursprache und Publikum in der lat. Spätantike u. im Mittelalter* (1958), p. 128.

was distinguished by the use of instruments, made to illustrate the movements of planets and constellations across the sky, and by the introduction of the abacus to mechanize arithmetical operations. In Gerbert's astronomical interests we can probably trace contacts with Arabic science, which he was able to establish after he had spent some years as student in Vich, a cathedral-city in the Spanish March.[1]

There is no sign in Richer's enthusiastic description of his teacher's effectiveness that it was Gerbert's aim to link the different subjects of his curriculum, and so to present a deeper insight into the structure of the world. But the chronicler emphasizes that the master of Reims was very well known in the world as the philosopher whose knowledge comprised both the human and the divine sphere. It was for this reason that Otric, who had been active in the cathedral school of the metropolitan see of Magdeburg and was at the time permanently attached to the court of the emperor Otto II, challenged his colleague Gerbert to debate the question how the different branches of knowledge, which make up the whole of philosophy, are dependent on each other. This disputation took place in 980 in Ravenna and, according to Richer's report, filled a day. Finally Otto had to bring proceedings to an end, because the distinguished audience was tired out.

The problem of this disputation came from a paragraph in Boethius' first commentary to Porphyry's *Isagoge*, where a division of philosophy is sketched. Here theology, mathematics and physics, by which is meant the doctrine of nature, form the three theoretical species of the genus philosophy. Gerbert feels the need to subordinate mathematics to the more comprehensive concept of physics, but recognizes the difficulty of doing so, because both physics and mathematics are equally species of the same genus and stand therefore on the same level. No solution is reached to the problem, because Otric starts a digression by raising the question about the purpose for which philosophy came into being. Gerbert's answer, that philosophy is intended to give knowledge of things human and divine, leads off to a dispute on the possibility of

[1] Richer, *Histoire de France*, éd. et trad. R. Latouche, II, *Les classiques de l'histoire de France au Moyen Âge*, XVII (1937), lib. III, chs. 46–54, pp. 54–64. On G.'s position in the history of medieval logic: A. Van de Vyer, 'Les étapes du développement philosoph. d. Haut Moyen Âge', in: *Revue Belge de Philolog. et d'Histoire*, VIII (1929), pp. 441–3.

giving self-sufficient definitions by one single noun.[1] It seems, however, that the logical problems connected with subordination of genus and species formed a serious challenge to Gerbert's thought. The short treatise *De rationali et ratione uti*, written after the French scholar had joined the imperial court in 997, is the only product of his pen which we may call philosophical; its problem points in the same direction as the main topic in the debate with Otric.

Generally it is considered contrary to rule to define a concept of a wide range by one restricted within narrower limits. It would be correct to describe both horse and man as animals, because the concept of a living being comprises one and the other, but the application of 'use of reason' as predicate to characterize a rational being raises doubts: somebody in possession of reason may not use this capacity permanently, therefore *uti ratione* covers a narrower range than *rationale*. Under which condition would it be considered a valid element of a proposition defining 'man'? Some dialecticians attempted to avoid this difficulty by emphasizing that *rationale* points to the mere potentiality, while *uti ratione* affirms the realization of this capacity and so represents a quality of higher order, which compensates for the narrower range by its dignity. But this defence appears as a mere sophism, when we consider that a genus by its very nature can comprise different degrees of dignity without losing its universal validity: the same concept 'animal' can be applied both to a human being and a donkey, and both God and man are equally classified as rational beings.

Gerbert proposes to solve this problem by a simple distinction. When we describe the substance of anything, every attribute, either positive or negative, must be valid independently of time or circumstance. Therefore no predicate is admissible which covers a narrower range of meaning than the subject which it describes. But the case is different when the proposition deals with phenomena which are only accidental. The sentence 'fire warms' remains true as long as the fire exists, because it deals with its substance. But the statement 'Cicero is sitting' concerns only an accident; the permanent possibility of being in such a posture, has been made actual at a given moment. On the other hand, the definition of Cicero as a rational being points to a substantial differentia-

[1] Richer, II, chs. 55–65, pp. 64–80. Boethius, *In Isagogen Porphyrii commenta*, ed. Brand, p. 8.

tion, defining his lasting character as a man. When we describe him as using his reason, we speak of something which at any given moment may be either happening or not, because it concerns an accidental differentiation.[1] The most frequently quoted part of this treatise is the highly polished dedication to Otto III. Here Gerbert emphasizes that his enterprise in dialectics adds an essential element to the court life of a Roman emperor who can claim Greek origin from his mother. This introduction is more than mere ornament, because it defines well the limitation of the author's intention in his philosophical exercise. His attempts to apply the analysis of elementary logical concepts in Porphyry's and Boethius' treatises to the solution of a problem remains for him mainly a test of intellectual superiority intended to counterbalance the well-established claims in this field raised by the Byzantine rival for imperial power.[2] Gerbert was distinguished by his capacity to make contemporary politics articulate by the adaptation of classical ideas from ancient literature. His extensive knowledge of mathematical and logical writings gave him a prominent place among the scholars of his time. But his philosophical interests were not essentially different from the type represented in the two programmes by Italian masters of the liberal arts, which we considered above.

C. *Berengar of Tours: an attempt at applying logical analysis to theological doctrine*

The more intense study of the Boethian corpus of logical writings, which Van de Vyer could trace in the manuscript tradition, gave a fresh impulse to philosophical analysis of topical questions in the course of the eleventh century. Men became aware that the method of logical discussion exercised in the classroom could be applied to more concrete and more vital subjects. The possibility of understanding things which form man's environment in clearly defined concepts acted as an impulse to the human mind. In this context we must understand the attempt by Berengar of Tours (1010–88) to apply his dialectical training to an interpretation of the Eucharist by discussing one aspect of the sacra-

[1] *PL* 139. 159–68. The definition under discussion: 'rationale id est, quod ratione utitur' came from Augustine, *De ordine* II, ch. XII, § 35, *CSEL* LXIII, p. 172, 10.

[2] On the political influence of Gerbert's ideas: P. E. Schramm, *Kaiser, Rom und Renovatio*, I (1929), pp. 96–100; K. Erdmann, *Polit. Ideenwelt*, pp. 107–11.

mental doctrine as a metaphysical question.[1] But there were additional circumstances in his biography and in the history of his time, which contributed to shape this fresh start in the development of the medieval mind. Berengar, who had begun his career of learning as pupil of Bishop Fulbert of Chartres, was most of his life master of the ancient school of St Martin in Tours. His literary fame as writer of Latin was so far spread among the experts in this art that a group of his letters found their way to the cathedral school of Hildesheim and were incorporated into a collection of writings intended as models for the scholars.[2] The middle of the century, when Berengar turned his skill to the understanding of an important, but not yet officially defined, piece of ecclesiastical doctrine, was the time when the reform of ecclesiastical institutions raised controversies and offered a new challenge to men's minds.

The question of the right administration of the sacraments can be traced as the background both on the theological and the popular level. Berengar's speculations were not linked to either of the antagonistic sides. His attitude appears to be that of a scholarly individual who, fortified by his learning and his fame as teacher, feels sure about his ability to approach the greatest subject without any risk of fundamental error.

The attitude of a dialectician, who uses the force of his argument to demonstrate the strength of his learning to the world, can certainly be traced in the formation of Berengar's personality. He could declare his readiness to retract his teaching, if anybody could prove him at variance with the classical texts on which the authority of the Church was based. But Berengar's humility remained superficial, because he was convinced that his philosophy was based on an interpretation of these documents which no other man could challenge. He was a pioneer in applying dialectical methods to biblical exegesis. Despite this element of egocentric daring in his intellectual make-up, he could expect, or at least pretend, to be entitled to protection by Hildebrand, the future Pope Gregory VII. Political conditions in the Angevin land, with which the

[1] R. W. Southern, 'Lanfranc of Bec and Berengar of Tours', in: *Studies in Medieval History presented to M. Powicke* (1941), pp. 27–49, esp. p. 34.

[2] Ed. in C. Erdmann, N. Fickermann, *Briefsammlungen d. Zeit Heinrichs IV.*, *Mon. Germ. Hist.*, *Briefe d. Kaiserzeit* (1950), v, pp. 132–72.

coming leader and prophet of ecclesiastical reform had to deal as a legate in 1054, gave rise to this paradoxical combination, which critical examination of Berengar's reports has reduced in scale but not eliminated. Twice the master of St Martin's school was forced to revoke his doctrine (1059 and 1079) at Roman synods under the guidance of the reformed papacy, but he was allowed to live out his long life peacefully in the neighbourhood of Tours.[1] His controversial doctrine was frequently quoted and attacked in letters of the time; in some cases Berengar's answer has been preserved. We know of two more elaborate writings from his pen on this theme both designed as defence against the criticism of Lanfranc (1010–89).[2] When this controversy started about the middle of the century his antagonist was master at the rising school of the Norman monastery of Bec. As a scholar of Lombard origin he could feel entitled to be Berengar's equal in dialectical skill.[3] Both applied this form of thought to biblical exegesis. But Lanfranc, perhaps under the impact of his Benedictine environment and his personal inclination to eremitical life, put a definite limitation to the application of this method to theological subject-matter, in order to avoid any possible encroachment on established authority. He became an innovator in doctrine only by attempts to find precise orthodox answers to questions to which no well defined solution existed. Berengar used his grammatical learning about the distinction of words and meanings of syntactic forms for the explanation of texts to support his experiment in theological speculation. He never doubted the basic assumption of his epoch, that truth must be found in authorized texts, if correctly interpreted. But he was strongly conscious of the fact that his own title to do such work had to be based on his erudition. Again and again he raises the objection against Lanfranc that his antagonist's doctrine cannot be reconciled with its author's justified claim to be an educated man. Even Pope Nicholas II,

[1] A. J. Macdonald, *Berengar and the Reform of Sacramental Doctrine* (1930); C. Erdmann, 'Gregor VII. und Berengar von Tours', in: *Quellen u. Forschungen aus italien. Arch. u. Bibl.* XXVIII (1937), pp. 48–74.

[2] The first is only preserved in a quotation by Lanfranc, *De corpore et sanguine Domini*, *PL* 150. 407–42; the second treatise *De coena Domini* was discovered by G. E. Lessing in a MS of the Wolfenbüttel library in 1770 and commented on with the learned enthusiasm of eighteenth-century enlightenment. Newest edition by W. H. Beekenkamp, *Kerkhistorische Studiën* (1941), vol. II.

[3] On Lanfranc's and Berengar's exegetic work: B. Smalley, 'La Glossa Ordinaria', *Rech. Théol. anc. méd.* IX (1937), pp. 372–99.

who had given too free a rein to Berengar's enemy, the Lorraine Cardinal Humbert, is stigmatized as lacking both in character and in education.[1]

In this context we must understand Berengar's praise of dialectic as the effective instrument in the search for truth. Reason is the best part of man, the permanent sign of his creation in God's image and by his wisdom. To prohibit its use means to take from man his honour and dignity. Authority alone is not good enough as an argument, because it will always be offered in the form of a text which must be understood correctly, that is, by the application of the right method. Against Lanfranc's rule of caution against the use of syllogistic forms in biblical exegesis Berengar emphasizes the use of dialectic art, while eschewing the deceit of eristic altercations. Berengar adds that no man of courage would subscribe to his antagonist's statement, asserting his preference for yielding to authority rather than perishing by the use of reason. He quotes Augustine's *De ordine* in support of such a declaration, which has a very personal meaning for him. He confesses that at the Roman synod of 1059, when Cardinal Humbert and his group acted against him 'without the moderation of human rationality', he was prevented by fear of death from making a stand for his own conviction; he compares his own situation with that of Aaron, when from the same motive he yielded to the people's demand for the golden calf, and so makes his reflection about his personal record still more emphatic.[2]

What we may call Berengar's philosophical interest in the eucharistic doctrine is centred in his critical discussion about the transformation of the sacramental matter, bread and wine. The discovery that the Aristotelian concepts which describe the character of substance, available to him in the logical textbooks of Boethius, made a firmer grasp of the

[1] *De coena Domini*, ch. 34, ed. Beekenkamp, p. 86: (addressing Lanfranc) 'Revera manifestissimum habere debuit *eruditio* tua rem gestam de Moysi virga et de aquis Egipti nulla prorsus similitudine convenire cum conversione panis et vini mensae dominicae'. B. assumes that Charlemagne has turned to Eriugena: 'ne *ineruditorum* carnaliumque illius temporis prevalere ineptia, erudito viro Johanni illi imposuit colligere de scripturis quae ineptiam illorum destrueret', printed in: Erdmann, Fickermann, *Briefsammlungen*, Nr. 88, p. 154, 3.

[2] Ch. 23, Beekenkamp, p. 47: 'Maximi plane cordis est per omnia ad dialecticam confugere, quia confugere ad eam ad rationem est confugere, quo qui non confugit, cum secundum rationem sit factus ad imaginem Dei, suum honorem reliquit.' P. 48: '... nec sequendus in eo es ulli cordato homini ut malit auctoritatibus circa aliqua cedere quam ratione, si optio detur, perire'. His own enforced revocation, ch. 14, § 23: Augustine, *De ordine* II, 13, § 38.

visible world possible, is the driving force of his controversial teaching. In his reflections on the meaning of material change Berengar discusses the meaning of the word 'being'; first it affirms the existence of a subject and secondly it links certain qualities together. But these two meanings are connected. Every statement which we make about quality presupposes the existence of the subject to which the quality is allocated. The proposition 'Socrates is just' has no meaning if we do not include the assumption that such a man exists. This reflection is offered as objection against Humbert's thesis, as defended by Lanfranc, that after consecration bread and wine become the true body and blood of Christ while keeping those accidental qualities of the original status which we observe. But for Berengar no quality can survive the existence of the subject to which it belongs. If justice is attributed to Socrates it will not outlast his existence.[1] Change means for him the disintegration of one subject and the creation of a new one out of it. We differentiate things by forms or qualities, which make up their appearance. But this process is impossible without matter underlying qualities or forms. Pure forms are no object of observation. No colour exists without something which is coloured. White, red or brown do not form entities in themselves. When the subject goes, every attribute predicated fades out too. It is obvious that Berengar uses the Aristotelian concept very loosely. Form is for him not a constitutive element of substance, but the comprehensive term for all qualities which determine the image of things observed by our senses. These cannot exist without the matter of which they are accidents. Colour is for him the most favoured example, because his antagonist asserts that the colour of bread and wine persists after the substance has gone.[2]

Berengar's theory of substantial change does not admit any differentiation between invisible essence and the surface which presents the subject's picture to observation. If a man's body is changed into marble, or Lot's wife into a pillar of salt, the original outline of the body may be

[1] Ch. 16, p. 29. Cf. R. Hunt, 'Studies on Priscian in the eleventh and twelfth centuries', in: *Mediev. and Renaissance Studies*, I (1943), p. 226.

[2] Ch. 34, pp. 91 f.: 'Et apud eruditos enim constat...nulla ratione colorem videri nisi contingit etiam coloratum videri...cum constet omne, quod in subjecto est, sicut ut sit, ita etiam ut videatur non a se habere sed a subjecto in quo sit, nec visu vel sensu aliquo corporeo comprehendi colorem vel qualitatem nisi comprehenso...et colorato.'

preserved, but it is no longer the outline of a living body, it is the form of a block of stone or salt. The similarities do not in any sense mean identity, because the underlying subject, which they characterize and to which they are allocated, has undergone a radical transformation.[1]

In the course of this argument Berengar considers a second type of material change which could be used as another line of defence for his antagonist's theory. There are cases in which a change of surface gives the impression of a transformation of matter. No destruction of the original substance takes place. As example he quotes reports, according to which ebony and coral represent matter petrified under the prolonged influence of seawater. The normal outside of wood, which easily yields to the artisan's instrument, is overlaid by the firmness of stone. A similar process happens with water, when under the impact of low temperature its surface is transformed into ice. In contrast to such phenomena Lanfranc's theory of transformation asserts the destruction of the original substance, the creation of a new one, while former accidental qualities continue to exist on the surface.[2]

It is evident that in these arguments the sacramental matter is considered as part of the *visible* world. This approach implies a eucharistic theory based on a strict separation between the spiritual force and the material appearance of the sacrament. The visible things on the altar cannot be more than the *sign* of the divine presence. Consecration does not physically change their character. The argument that Christ cannot be brought back from heaven to earth as the result of any transformation of matter, which can only produce a new object, occurs again and again. The reality which is added to the sacramental matter by the consecration, is purely spiritual but nevertheless an effective instrument of salvation.[3]

An important part of Berengar's writing on the subject is devoted to demonstrating that his teaching is supported by the authority of St Augustine: he applies the skill of his dialectic to prove that the other great teachers of the Church, especially Ambrosius, agree on this point with the African master and are antagonists to the doctrine of any change in the sacramental material.

[1] Ch. 35, p. 98. [2] Ch. 21, p. 44.

[3] On the theological aspect of Berengar's doctrine: I. Geiselmann, *Die Eucharistielehre der Vorscholastik* (1926), pp. 290–404.

Modern study has on the whole confirmed Berengar's view as far as Augustine is concerned, whose differentiation of *signum* and *res* in the sacrament expresses his interest in the symbolic interpretation; only during the Father's later years do we find a changed emphasis also in this part of his doctrine under the impact of his conflict with Pelagian teaching.[1] We know, however, from Berengar's own reports that it was not the direct contact with Augustine's writings which stimulated his interest in this problem. The impulse came to him from the theological debate in the circle of Charles the Bold. The defence of the symbolic interpretation of the eucharistic sacrament, written by the monk Ratramnus of Corbie as answer to the emphasis on the transformation of bread and wine in a treatise of his abbot Paschasius Radbertus, was Berengar's starting-point into the field of theological speculation. He and his contemporaries took Ratramnus' book for the work of Eriugena.

A letter, in which Berengar vigorously defended the orthodoxy of the Irish philosopher, brought the conflict between him and his colleague at the monastery of Bec into the open. The authority of Rome was soon involved. Soon afterwards the master of Tours tried to protect Eriugena in another letter to an acquaintance at the court of the French king, placing the philosopher at the court of *Charlemagne*. This great ruler had not only been strong in action, but also eager in the cause of religion. Therefore he called in John Scottus, as a man of education, to dispel the superstition of the illiterate by his superior knowledge.[2] It appears from a letter addressed to Acelin, Canon of Chartres, that Berengar knew that there were other controversial writings by Eriugena and he had seen something of them, but his unreserved pleading was dedicated to the pseudo-Scottus, who was in reality Ratramnus.[3] In what way did the eleventh-century master of dialectic go beyond the representative of Augustinian doctrine in the ninth century?

[1] K. Adam, *Die Eucharistielehre des hl. Augustin* (1908), pp. 50 ff., 100–6, 163.

[2] To Lanfranc, *PL* 150. 63 C. The quotation of Charlemagne in defence of Eriugena belongs to B.'s letter mentioned in note 2, p. 602, which was addressed to a courtier of the French king Henry I.

[3] *PL* 150. 67 B: Berengar says of Eriugena: *Omnia illius non pervidimus*, and adds that his knowledge has not become more complete at the moment of writing. It is not likely that this observation points to the comparatively short treatise on the Eucharist, and can be much more easily understood to mean the extensive genuine work of Eriugena.

Ratramnus' treatise was written as an answer to a questionnaire of Charles the Bold, like the one which had initiated his investigation of the place of the soul in the world. The king had first asked whether the terms *in mysterio* or rather *in veritate* were rightly applied to the Eucharist, and secondly, whether the *corpus Christi* was to be understood as the historical body. Ratramnus started with chapters clearly defining concepts like *figura*, *veritas*, and the distinction of outer appearance and spiritual meaning. In this investigation he writes as a faithful student of Augustine, but his treatise comes to more definite decisions than would result from a summary of the Father's corpus of writings on this subject. The sacrament represents a simile, not a physical transformation, a memory of the event, not the suffering itself. There is nothing of the anatomical features of a human body, nothing of its physiological life or of the impetus which the soul gives to the natural body, in the *corpus Christi* of the Eucharist. Sacrament remains bread made out of grain. But consecration adds to it *virtus*, the power which connects the believer in spirit with Christ in his glory.[1]

Ratramnus draws a clear line between Augustine's symbolism, by which he is guided, and any doctrine of material transformation. We may say that this more precise definition was already implied in the king's questionnaire, which he answered, and represented the tendency characteristic of late Carolingian interpretation of patristic writing. But Ratramnus remains half-way between Augustine and Berengar; his use of the term *species* or *substantia* never leads to an analysis of the process of material transformation. The difference between the essence of a thing and its appearance does not form part of his problems, while such investigation constitutes the basis of Berengar's criticism of the doctrine of transformation; he does not accept the doctrine that the accidents remain when the substance has gone. With Ratramnus there is no reflection on the character of the physical change that takes place when something new is created out of the disintegration of an existing phenomenon. The eleventh century did not, however, restore from the study of Boethius its exact meaning to Aristotelian terminology. We saw that for Berengar form was not a constitutive aspect of substance, but the comprehensive name for accidental peculiarities which charac-

[1] *De corpore et sanguine Domini*, *PL* 121. 125–70; ch. 72, 154A.

terize the appearance of an object. But the impulse to interpret the material element of the sacrament as a part of the visible world and to reflect on its structure came from this source. Seen from this point of view Berengar's application of dialectic to the theory of the Eucharist represented a preparatory experiment on the way to the interpretation of theological doctrine in the framework of a metaphysical system. To his contemporaries it was an audacious challenge, to which the next reaction was firmly negative.

D. *Petrus Damiani: conversion from dialectic to ascetic life*

Petrus Damiani became the strongest representative of an attempt to refute philosophy's intrusion into the theological field by means of dialectic. Damiani (1007–72) started his working life as a teacher of grammar and dialectic, the same kind of studies which Gunzo and Anselm of Besate paraded in their writings. In the cities of Northern Italy such activity opened a career to men without inherited property. About 1035 Damiani left the world, since he was converted to an eremitical life, the severest form of monasticism, which had taken root in Italy.[1] He became a leader in this movement. An important element of their life was the complete break with any effort to learn and to investigate. All understanding of man and world, as far as it was useful for finding the right path to salvation, would come as God's gift in reward for ascetic achievement. All skills in acting and thinking required in school have no value beyond a restricted purpose and always imply the risk of increasing human pride. Damiani was not able to throw out the gifts and mental capacities on which he had started his career—it was no chance that he was forced into the office of cardinal bishop of Ostia in 1057—but he used these literary skills to write impressive pamphlets, in which he passed judgement on the moral deficiencies of his time, both in the world and in the Church, and fought the intrusion of reason into the secrets of religious doctrine by means of the instruments of dialectic. His writing on God's omnipotence was implicitly the most comprehensive counter-attack against Berengar's attempt to bring the sacrament within the limits of philosophical understanding. It was written in 1067

[1] Jean Leclerq, *St Pierre Damien, érémite et homme d'église* (1960). His attitude to rational understanding was recently discussed by J. Gonsette, *Pierre Damien et la culture profane* (1956).

after a conversation with Desiderius of Montecassino about an argument of St Jerome, in which he tried to establish the irreplaceable value of female chastity.[1] From this beginning Damiani developed the problem, whether it would be possible to assume that God may cancel out events and achievements which have taken place in the past. Could the foundation of Rome be so nullified by divine decision, as if the city had never existed?

Damiani stresses that the application of the concept 'impossible' to God is always wrong. There is no borderline between past events which exist in our knowledge, and those which we witness in the present or expect in the future. Such difference has no place in consideration of God's omnipotence.[2] Man, whose whole existence is placed in the time process, carries such differentiation into his reflection on God's power, which, by its very nature, is beyond time in lasting eternity. For God's knowledge and action the infinite chain of events is simultaneous. Everything we observe as possessing existence in our world derives its being from God's will only. Nobody doubts that God could prevent the building of Rome, but such a statement is true not only for what we see at the moment of the city's foundation, but for the whole length of human history. The withdrawal of the divine will does not turn an event or any feature of our experience into the past but deletes it without trace, as if it had never come into being. This paradox that something, which once had come into being, might be reduced to the state of having never existed points to the fact that logic, which prevents our mind from accepting such happenings, is itself created by God for the human understanding of nature's common order. Therefore it remains entirely subjugated to the divine will. Its application becomes thoroughly misleading when we try to reflect on the links between God and world. No concept, which is taught in the schools, can be used to understand God without a grave distortion of his nature. Something created to serve as a proposition in a syllogistic deduction is quite unsuitable as an intrument to penetrate the secret of divine power.[3]

Man's mind can take this lesson of humility from many stories reported in the Bible. Human experience has come to the conclusion that fire turns wood into ashes; therefore a man who sees a piece of timber

[1] *PL* 145. 596C. [2] 619D. [3] 603D.

burning has no doubts about the single case that meets his eye. But the Bible teaches us that the burning bush of Moses was not destroyed in this process, because God's will went in the opposite direction. In the same way the general validity of the statement that no fruit can come from a piece of wood detached from its tree, is refuted by the biblical report on Aaron's flowering staff. Not only Scripture, but also everyday life, offers examples which contradict conclusions from our normal experience; so the brightly glowing fire which blackens everything that is touched by it. In this context Damiani uses a collection of natural phenomena which are of a miraculous character, compiled by Augustine from manuals of late antiquity.[1] The inspiration of the African Father is noticeable throughout Damiani's treatise: the question of evil in God's world brings up the argument that evil as such does not possess the quality of being with which the creation is endowed. Augustine's philosophy of time is used as basis for the proof that the experience by which we separate past, present and future remains below divine level. From this starting-point Damiani's radical criticism directed against the transfer of dialectical method into the field of theology is developed. This sophisticated background of Damiani's fight against intellectualism made his formulations influential. It seems very probable that, when Manegold in Southern Germany wrote his Christian polemic against classic cosmology, his main argument was shaped by Damiani's fight against the theological use of dialectic.

[1] 610D. Augustine, *De civitate Dei* XXI, ch. 4. Cf. H.-J. Marrou, *St. Augustin et la fin de la culture antique* (1938), pp. 148–57 on interest in curiosities in late antiquity.

CHAPTER 38

ANSELM OF CANTERBURY: THE PHILOSOPHICAL INTERPRETATION OF FAITH

A. *The impact of the Berengarian controversy*

Anselm of Canterbury (1033–1109) in his literary work opened a new and highly individual chapter in the great controversy about the relationship of reason and belief. Before he became Primate of England in 1093 he had lived, studied and taught as a Benedictine in the Norman abbey of Bec, in contact with the spiritual and intellectual movements which at this time had their centre in the French-speaking countries of Western Europe. He had come from Aosta in the south-east corner of ancient Burgundy near the Lombard border. From his mother's side he was related to an important family of dynasts ruling in these parts. As a young man he was attracted by the revival of learning in France, like the Lombard Lanfranc before him, who in the fifties was prior of the newly founded monastery of Bec and had established there a school of some renown. Anselm joined him, first as a secular student and in 1060 as a monk.[1] At this moment Lanfranc was deeply involved in the controversy with Berengar; he had attended the council of Rome, where the teaching of the famous master of Tours was condemned. When Anselm joined the monastic community this had been the great event of the previous year. Lanfranc himself was considered a pioneer in the revival of dialectical studies, and he was certainly anxious to strike the right balance between loyalty to the authority of biblical and ecclesiastical tradition and interest in a technically correct argument. Anselm remained in intimate contact with him for three years and became his successor as prior and head of the school, when Lanfranc left Bec on his appointment as abbot of St Stephens in Caen.

We know from Anselm's own report that he did not enjoy the teach-

[1] Eadmer, *De vita et conversatione Anselmi archiepiscopi Cantuariensis*, I 5, ed. Rule, *Scr. rer. Brit.* vol. 81, pp. 317 f.; *PL* 158. 52. Cf. Southern, *Eadmer*, pp. 8 f.

ing of elementary Latin to the boys, who filled the classroom as *oblati*, and the attraction of Bec for students from outside the cloister faded with Lanfranc's departure. Anselm developed his genius mainly in contact with the younger monks, whose character and spiritual life he influenced by the example of his personality and by his sympathetic understanding of their intellectual problems. He was inclined to reflect on his educational practice in the monastery, and so he attempted to define the reasons why adolescence is the right period for giving its lasting shape to the human mind.

The philosophical writings composed in Bec after 1070 have their origin in the discourses and conversations which he dedicated to this purpose.[1] Anselm himself has given us the documents, which allow us to revive the atmosphere of this circle in which this thought developed.

The exchange of letters in the service of friendship was a well-established feature in the ecclesiastical world of the Middle Ages. Already in the eighth century Boniface's collection give us striking examples of this cultivation of human relationships among the Anglo-Saxon missionaries in Germany. In the eleventh century we find this attitude in various letter collections of the German cathedral schools. The social functions of an educated élite had brought the writers together in common training and subsequently dispersed them in the course of their lives and careers. In Anselm's case a similar situation arose, when Lanfranc, since 1070 Archbishop of Canterbury, took some Norman monks to England who had been in close contact with Anselm. But this part of his correspondence, while he was prior, and since 1078 abbot of Bec, is distinguished from previous writings of this type by the emotional intensity with which he expressed his belief in the spiritual importance of the fellowship between himself and the receiver of the letter. The fact that they are remote from each other in space serves to put the common purpose in stronger relief.

The community of prayer needs friendship, but is also able to create it between men unknown to one another personally and linked only by their trust in a common friend. In some cases the affirmation of such spiritual intimacy serves as introduction to a serious warning against

[1] Dom F. Schmitt, 'Zur Chronologie der Werke des hl. Anselm v. C.', *Rev. Bénéd.* XLIV (1932), pp. 322–50.

concrete dangers which a monk might experience in everyday life to the detriment of his mental stability. But even in these cases there is no contradiction between the appeal to friendship in the preamble and the emphasis on the needs of discipline in the main text, because the spirit of personal humility pervades both parts. He does not command, but always tries to *persuade* and so to fulfil the rule of St Benedict. This education of ethos remains an important motive for his work as philosophical writer.[1]

For his place in *intellectual* history we shall look back to the controversy between Berengar and Lanfranc. Anselm found his own solution to the problem so eagerly discussed in his youth. A methodically correct argument based on spiritual experience would serve men to find the right way in life and thought. Anselm's design of applying the technique of philosophical debate to the definition of religious truth went not only beyond Lanfranc, but was also much more comprehensive than Berengar's attempt to introduce the skills of logical training into the discussion of one theological problem.

Berengar had opposed a reinterpretation of the eucharistic theory with considerations concerning the nature of changes in matter, to which he had been stimulated by the ontological content of Boethian concepts. He tried to refute the possibility of a theological doctrine, because it seemed to contradict his understanding of the nature of matter; moreover, he used the dialectical skill of a fully trained grammarian in his own defence in order to prove that the authority of the ecclesiastical tradition was on his side. From the theological point of view his approach to the problem under discussion offered a philosophy of negation; he excluded a solution, because it was in contrast to his analysis of matter. The analysis of the visible world was not coordinated with a comprehensive survey of theological doctrine before the middle of the thirteenth century after the full assimilation of Aristotle. When Anselm took up his task he felt safely separated from Berengar, whose theory he never discussed. Between him and the daring champion of reason stood his own intention, which he once formulates as 'faith seeking understanding'.

[1] *Ep.* 37 to Lanzo on *stabilitas loci* is a characteristic example, Schmitt, III, pp. 144–8. *PL* 158, *ep.* I, 29. 1093–1101. On his own limitation as teacher of Latin: *ep.* 64, Schmitt, III, pp. 180 f.; *PL* 158, *ep.* I, 55. 1125 f.

B. *The meaning and purpose of understanding faith*

Anselm was very ready to explain this principle to his readers in his writings as well as orally in his addresses and conversations with his brethren in the cloister. We find remarks about the meaning of his own method in his writings on various topics and from all periods of his life.

Anselm emphasizes equally two aspects of his programme. On the one hand, he intends to establish his case by arguments which have in themselves the power to convince. He wishes to teach his doctrine in a way which makes its inherent *necessity* evident. On the other hand, he will not allow his readers to forget his own awareness that he would be unable to carry on his argument if he were not a believer himself *before* he started. The combination of these two apparently contrasting motives in his thought is probably its most characteristic feature and therefore the key-point for the understanding of his philosophy.

The intention of guiding his readers by rational analysis is clearly expressed by the style of his writings. He avoids basing his deductions on authorities; even Augustine, whom he knows so very well and confesses to be his main source for the principles and content of his speculation, is not quoted in the texts to confirm his teaching. Moreover, the argument itself is designed so as to be independent even of the sayings of the Bible. The result of every single investigation must be proved true by the force and clarity of reasoning. At the end of the theological discussion in *Cur Deus homo* we hear that the offered proof would be conclusive, even if the few passages from Christian authorities had been omitted. The difference between Anselm and the main stream of twelfth- and thirteenth-century philosophy, in which the classical form of *quaestio* and *summa* was developed, is striking. The search for a final unity in the divergent doctrines of the Fathers is not a driving force behind Anselm's dialectic. We find in his writings objections and doubts playing an important part in the progress of the argument. But they are represented as natural stages in reaching the truth and they reflect the author's experience from his philosophical conversations with his monastic audience in Bec.[1] Anselm declares that nothing in his own

[1] *Monologion*, *Prologus*; Schmitt, I, p. 7; *PL* 158. 142 f.: 'Quidam fratres saepe me studioseque precati sunt, ut quaedam, quae illis de meditanda divinitatis essentia et quibusdam aliis huiusmodi meditationi cohaerentibus usitato sermone colloquendo protuleram, sub quodam eis meditationis exemplo describerem.'

deductions must be left ambiguous and that every objection, however weak, will be taken into account, so that even the slowest mind may be able to see the evidence of the argument.[1]

But the force of the 'credo' as the factor which gives the framework to Anselm's philosophy is certainly not less important for the shaping of his thought than his belief in the value of rational demonstration. Anselm was firmly convinced that no teaching relevant to the spiritual needs of mankind could make any genuine addition to the wisdom contained in Scripture and in the writings of the Fathers. The final decision about truth and error lies here. Nothing clearly contradictory to this tradition can be acceptable, however strongly it seems to be supported by our reason. That means that the results of philosophical deductions can only claim a hypothetical validity. Any demonstration that they are in contradiction to authorized tradition would invalidate them.[2] This emphasis on obedience to established tradition must not be understood as the outcome of a supplementary adaptation to the circumstances of his existence in the ecclesiastical and monastic world, but represents his genuine attitude of mind; his declaration that 'all his philosophical statements carry no definite truth in themselves' allows him to combine the intellectual ambition of a thinker with Benedictine humility.

He has tried to define the place left for intellectual attempts like his own beside the existing authorized tradition of doctrine. He assumes that the biblical text implies ideas which are not articulated and developed. The Fathers' restricted span of life did not allow them to exploit these potentialities fully; moreover, divine grace will always allow later generations to see new aspects of the eternal truth. Everything which reason deduces from presuppositions contained in Scripture, which cannot be demonstrated to be in contradiction to its authority, must be true, because the Bible cannot be assumed to favour falsehood by allowing it to go undetected.[3]

[1] *Monologion*, ch. 6; Schmitt I, p. 19; *PL* 158. 152A: 'Quoniam namque ad magnum et delectabile quiddam me subito perduxit haec mea meditatio, nullam vel simplicem paeneque fatuam objectionem disputanti mihi occurrentem negligendo volo praeterire.'

[2] *De concordia praescientiae et praedestinationis et gratiae dei cum libero arbitrio* III, 6. Schmitt, II, p. 272; *PL* 158. 528B–C: 'Ac si ipsa [auctoritas] nostro sensui indubitanter repugnat: quamvis nobis ratio nostra videatur inexpugnabilis, nulla tamen veritate fulciri credenda est.'

[3] *Commendatio operis ad Urbanum II*, printed by Schmitt, II, pp. 39–41 as preface to *Cur Deus homo*; *PL* 158. 259 f.

Anselm stated clearly that his method of teaching religious truth was not designed to convert Christians who had lost their faith and therefore would not recognize biblical authority. After baptism men are bound by the duty of obedience to accept the faith; therefore they are not entitled to demand a demonstration of belief by reason alone, because they do not recognize the authorities.[1] By this statement Anselm intends to explain his intention in writing his treatise against Roscelin. A philosophical challenge had to be answered. The refutation was meant, as we shall see later, to show that the logical theories of the 'modern' school and their application to theological problems led to views which bar the understanding both of God and the world. The literary form used in Anselm's treatises conveys the impression that his deductions of religious truth were addressed to unbelievers outside the Church. But it was not his real intention to write a *summa contra gentiles*. He had not the intense intellectual contact with non-Christian thought which the thirteenth-century thinkers had as a presupposition of their own investigations. Although two letters show a warm and active interest in the fate of a Jewish convert, there is no sign that he wrote any treatises to meet real objections from this camp. Aquinas' observation that for this purpose interpretation of passages from the Old Testament would be appropriate must have been just as obvious for Anselm. In this respect too he does not write apologetics.[2]

But the patristic application of philosophy to the explanation of the faith, Anselm's classic model, had as its starting-point the justification of Christian belief as the superior rational interpretation of the world for people still accustomed to choose between various schools of thought without any regard to authority. Correspondingly, the monk Boso, the interlocutor in *Cur Deos homo*, who later became abbot of Bec, had to assume the part of a perfect outsider to Christian faith, who does not believe anything unproved by reason. Every reader was expected to recognize this literary design as fiction, planned to form a background to Anselm's method. But what was the real purpose of his philosophy of belief? Whom did Anselm really address?

Anselm has formulated his final aim throughout his work. By lead-

[1] *Ep.* 136, Schmitt, III, pp. 280 f.; *PL* 158, *ep.* II, 41. 1192D f.

[2] *Ep.* 380 f., Schmitt, V, pp. 323 f.; *PL* 159, *ep.* III, 117. 153B f.; *ep.* IV, 71. 238B.

ing his audience in the cloister and his readers to understand the belief they held in clear and coherent concepts, he intended to give them the pure feeling of joy in contemplating their own creed as *evidently true*. As a young monk he had witnessed how dialectical skill gave the man who mastered it the capacity for holding an unassailable position. The discussion on the bounds within which the application of this method to theological questions could be admitted created an exciting experience.[1] Berengar had used logical concepts for the limitation of belief by forming theories on the nature of matter and its changes. Anselm discovered that a much more positive use of dialectic was possible if it was more intimately linked to religious doctrine. If the main principles of faith were taken as axioms from which deduction were made according to logical rules, a religious philosophy became thinkable. The self-sufficiency of its argument would be similar to the force which masters in the schools derived for their pleading on controversial subjects from the use of concepts from the Boethian corpus, while his starting-point would exclude as a matter of principle any deviation from ecclesiastical tradition.

The impulse for this experiment in philosophy came to him from his study of Augustine's thought. Here he found his solution to the problem which was causing the great controversy in his world. Anselm's definition of his programme *credo ut intellegam* was taken from the African Father's version of a verse from Isaiah, which Augustine liked to quote in defence and in definition of his own thoughts on religion.[2] But in the text of his arguments Anselm never refers to the patristic source which had inspired him as authority for the truth of his deductions.

This deviation from the normal usage of contemporary scholarship was caused by his conviction that such documentation would falsify the idea behind his work. Anselm held on to this attitude against what must have been the strongest possible opposition. When, about 1076, he had for the first time put his philosophical interpretation of the creed into writing, he sent this treatise as *exemplum meditandi de ratione fidei* to

[1] *Monologion*, ch. 6; Schmitt, I, p. 19; *PL* 158. 152A: '...ad magnum et delectabile quiddam me subito perduxit haec mea meditatio...'.

[2] The main passage: *De doctrina Christiana* II, 12, § 17; *PL* 34, col. 43. [See Part V (Augustine), ch. 21, p. 351.]

his old master, Lanfranc, now Archbishop of Canterbury, but did not succeed in eliciting an immediate reply. An explanatory letter, sent slightly later, made Anselm's intention more explicit: Lanfranc was requested either to approve or to condemn the whole. If his objections were raised against single passages, proposals for alteration are asked for. The archbishop is also requested to find a suitable title. This letter was evidently answered by the archbishop. But he did not commit himself to any definite judgement or to concrete proposals for the title or for alterations. But he must have shown that he found the prior's experiment daring, and he certainly emphasized that most fundamental questions were discussed without any support by texts carrying the authority of the ecclesiastical tradition. Anselm answered in a letter from which we can reconstruct the archbishop's criticism. He reminded Lanfranc, respectfully, that the essence of his treatise came from Augustine's books *De Trinitate*. He added that he did not emphasize this point in his own defence, but in order not to claim something as his own achievement which he has taken from another man's book. He ends this letter with thanks for the archbishop's cautionary advice.[1] But by continuing on his way he showed that he did not consider it his duty, in obedience to his superior's suggestion, to change the style of his thought and writing.

He composed a preface to the *Monologion*, which stressed the agreement of his ideas with patristic and especially Augustinian doctrine, and he declared his wish that this introductory remark should be added to every copy of the *Monologion*, in order to avoid rash judgements.

In a later, but still early, edition of this treatise he added some lines to the first chapter expressing a reservation about the provisional character of his deductions, however evident they might appear.[2] This qualification, which was repeated in his later writings, represents certainly a genuine aspect of his thought and has not the character of a retraction. In the oldest manuscripts the *Monologion* still shows a link with Lanfranc

[1] *Ep.* 72, 77 to Lanfranc, Schmitt, III, pp. 193 f., 199 f.; *PL* 158, *ep.* I, 63, 68, 1134C f., 1138C f., The final titles of *Monologion* and *Proslogion* show already the same fashion of giving composite names made up from Greek words, which we find in the works of John of Salisbury. Anselm, in his report on this question of titles to Archbishop Hugh of Lyons, avoids giving the reason for his final choice. *Ep.* 109, Schmitt, III, p. 242; *PL* 158, *ep.* II, 17. 1159A.

[2] Schmitt I, p. 14: 'In quo tamen, si quid dixero quod maior non monstret auctoritas: sic volo accipi ut, quamvis ex rationibus quae mihi videbuntur, quasi necessarium concludatur, non ob hoc tamen omnino necessarium, sed tantum sic interim videri posse dicatur.'

by its dedication. But Anselm seems to have never again submitted anything he had written in Bec to the criticism of Lanfranc in Canterbury.

The relationship of Anselm's ideas on philosophy and belief to Augustine's thought is perhaps most precisely expressed in the justification of his literary work which he sent to Urban II. The concluding paragraph gives a transformation of a passage in the Father's *De doctrina Christiana*. Here Augustine tries to show that the version in which he normally quotes Isa. vii. 9: *Nisi credideritis, non intelligetis*, which came to him through his African Latin text from the Septuagint, teaches essentially the same as the version in the Vulgate, which replaces *intelligetis* by *permanebitis*: both biblical texts presuppose the contrast between the transient world here and the vision of eternal truth in the world to come. To both, belief is the indispensable guide to man's final goal, as long as his existence on earth lasts. *Intellectus* belongs to the eternal kingdom. Faith is the necessary preparation for man's permanent life in heaven where he is able to exercise his spiritual possibilities fully. In this sense for Augustine the two verbs in the two versions have the same meaning. Anselm has reproduced the patristic distinction in more clearly defined outlines. By giving understanding a middle position between simple faith and eternal vision, he brings it clearly within the reach of Man in his temporal existence, while his master had only implied that human faith and moral purification may foreshadow the approach to truth.[1]

C. *The transformation of Platonism*

We shall now try to see what Anselm meant by allocating to Man a capacity for understanding beyond the sphere of secular affairs. In what way did he apply dialectical methods for defining God's relation to the world, and how far did the link between philosophy and belief influence the working of reason? Did it simply establish a limitation acting as a protecting barrier for the innermost mysteries of faith against the intrusion of the human mind, or does this *credo ut intelligam* shape Anselm's thought from the start? We shall seek for the answers to these

[1] Schmitt, II, p. 48; *PL* 158. 261 A–B: 'inter fidem et speciem intellectum quem in hac vita capimus esse medium intelligo'.

questions mainly from Anselm's early writings *Monologion* and *Proslogion* and especially from their relation to each other.

The observation that Man's image of his environment is very much shaped by judgements of good and evil, beautiful and ugly, is the starting-point of Anselm's investigation. Such qualifications have an infinite variety in degree and in kind. A horse may be good, that means in this case useful for men by his speed or his courage. A robber may also possess the same qualities of speed and courage which, in the context of his way of life, characterize him as evil. Actions of just men can be very different in type, justice itself is the only link between them. We use *greatness* in a meaning which has nothing to do with extension in space, for describing something as supreme in goodness.[1] The scheme of our value judgements remains simple in strong contrast to the variety of objects and events to which they are attached. From this observation Anselm goes on to a metaphysical statement. That we know a boundless variety of phenomena as good can only be understood on the assumption that they possess this common character by participation in something which is goodness itself. The differentiation in kind and degree, the possibility that good may be turned into evil, is brought about by the nature of the changeable world. Even the most common experience which our everyday world offers us, that of being, cannot be understood without the assumption of a creative force beyond our normal environment, with its causal connexions.

When we follow up the observation of everyday life we are finally forced to the conclusion that one thing's existence is caused by another's action, which in itself is again finally the result of the first. To break this absurd circle we have to abandon the acceptance of plurality of causes for the existence of the phenomena around us.[2]

Moreover there is a natural hierarchy in the mere existence of things. A piece of wood is less than a horse, a horse is less than a man. If there were no break between the world of experience and the sphere in which it has its origin, this stratification from low to high would have no end, because there is nothing absolutely supreme thinkable in the reality in

[1] *Monologion*, ch. 2; Schmitt, I, p. 15; *PL* 158. 146 f.

[2] *Monologion*, ch. 3; Schmitt, I, p. 15; *PL* 158. 146 c f.: 'Ut vero plura per se invicem sint, nulla patitur ratio, quoniam irrationabilis cogitatio est, ut aliqua res sit per illud, cui dat esse. Nam nec ipsa relativa sic sunt per invicem.'

which we exist. This result, which everybody would describe as absurd, can only be avoided by the derivation of this stratification from perfection itself, which does not tolerate subordination to anything else.[1]

This world-picture, in which God's sphere of ideas and Man's everyday reality are sharply divided, but linked by the Platonic concept of participation, which, in this context, replaces causation, remains the basis of Anselm's philosophy. Anselm himself has pointed to Augustine as his source and model. This connexion is very obvious. The master of Latin ecclesiastical thought had intended to make his readers see the vestiges of the trinitarian Godhead in the created world, both in macrocosm and microcosm. Everything's existence is borrowed from God's unchangeable essence. That we are able to apply the predicate 'good' to the unstable phenomena of our surroundings, is only possible by their participation in goodness itself. When Anselm discovered this interpretation of the relationship between God and his creation in Augustine's works, especially in the books *De Trinitate*, he became convinced that the essential outline of belief could be understood and described as a logically coherent doctrine. Such an exposition, it seemed to him, would have the same cogency as any striking deduction in the schools of dialectic.

This great project is circumscribed by the programmatic word *credo ut intellegam*, again inspired by various passages in Augustine's writings.[2] But the African bishop at the end of antiquity used philosophical deductions mainly as *analogies*, in order to guide his hearers and readers one way or the other to the right solution of the numerous questions and controversies which occurred in his time. Therefore he was less interested, at least in the years of his maturity, in the construction of a strictly conclusive argument. For Anselm the compass of problems which challenged his mind to analytical activity was much narrower, and for this reason allowed a more intense concentration. This singleness of purpose determines the character and style of his writings. He does not quote Augustine explicitly in the course of his deductions, because he has assimilated the Father's thought as the one

[1] *Monologion*, ch. 4; Schmitt, I, p. 17; *PL* 158. 148C.

[2] For instance: *sermo* 44, § 4; *PL* 38. 255: 'Dixit mihi homo: Intelligam ut credam; respondeo: Crede ut intelligas.' See A. Koyré, *L'idée de Dieu dans la philosophie d'Anselme d. C.* (Paris, 1923), ch. VII. [Cf. also Part V (Augustine), ch. 21, pp. 544–53, 'Christianity and Philosophy'.]

philosophy which has made his own attempt at expressing the truth of belief in the language of human reason possible. In principle Anselm's deductions always remain liable to be disproved by demonstration of their opposition to biblical and ecclesiastical tradition. In this sense Anselm would recognize the authority of Augustine as a possible witness against himself. But the doctrines he had adopted from the Father's writing must stand by the strength of their own reason. In this context we must have in mind that Anselm's conviction of his own teaching as a vocation and divine gift excluded for him any personal claim to merit, acquired by literary achievements.

Although Anselm never mentioned the name of Augustine in his writings, except for these introductory remarks, he certainly always thought of him. The modern reader of Anselm might be inclined to look beyond the African master of Christian thought and find in the Norman cloister an echo of Plato's Academy.[1] There is certainly no sign that the Benedictine philosopher himself felt any impulse to trace his own teaching to such an origin. He must have known about Plato's importance from *De civitate* and from the textbooks in his library. We saw that cosmological ideas derived from the *Timaeus* had attracted the interest of medieval scholars since Carolingian times, and they were going to do so increasingly in the decades after Anselm's death. Interest in the phenomena of nature was not completely absent from his mind, but remained subordinated to his main aim, the task of understanding the ideas directly linked to religious doctrine. His own Platonism was always dependent on Augustine's completion of the long process by which the theory of ideas was adapted to monotheistic doctrine. Pagan and Christian Neoplatonists had placed the emphasis on the spiritual aspect of a philosophy which, in its beginning, had had the closest links with the political and scientific problems, as well to the habits, of a society in a leading city state of the fourth pre-Christian century.

But all these obvious facts do not quite prevent the impression that Anselm's philosophical search for the proof of religious truth comes nearer to the spirit which we trace in the Socratic dialogues, than most of the literature classified by us as medieval Platonism, even if we include

[1] On the Platonic structure of Anselm's thought: Cl. Bäumcker, *Witelo* (Münster, 1908), pp. 290–5.

the lively speculation of the School of Chartres in our comparison. It is due to the intensity with which Anselm exercises his dialectical skill on ancient concepts, his single-mindedness in attempting to dissolve any objection which may block his pupil's mental and spiritual progress, that we are reminded of the philosophical conversations of Athens.

After *Monologion* and *Proslogion* Anselm used the form of dialogue for a group of his monographs. This literary form had been accepted in the medieval school since the time of Charlemagne, as a vehicle for instruction. The pupil asks briefly and the master answers at length, according to requirements. Anselm developed this form as Eriugena had done before him. The pupil becomes a junior partner in the investigation: the Boso in *Cur Deus homo* represents the climax of this line. The philosophical conversation shows the way from theoretical doubt to certainty. This situation is different from the experience Plato had portrayed by the creation of his Socratic dialogues, but the belief in the educative power of thought is strong on both sides and forms perhaps the most important link between the two.

D. *Human speech and theological concepts*

Anselm had shown that Man's environment borrows its values and its very existence from God and cannot be understood without his lasting presence. Both the Bible and the philosophy of the Fathers led him on to the problem of origin. He passes over the theories on the four elements or on form and matter. They are answers to less radical questions than his own, when they presuppose the existence of primitive matter and describe the rise from chaos to cosmos. Anselm intends to understand how the whole dualistic structure, this combination of the eternal with the transitory, came into being. He cannot accept a process of evolution, in which the visible world grows out of the highest being, because such an assumption would involve the eternal truth in a course of change leading to deterioration and corruption.[1] That the visible came

[1] *Monologion* ch. 7; Schmitt, I, pp. 20 f.; *PL* 158. 153C: 'Non autem dubito omnem hanc mundi molem cum partibus suis sicut videmus formatam, constare ex terra et aqua et aere et igne, quae scilicet quattuor elementa aliquomodo intelligi possunt sine his formis quas conspicimus in rebus formatis, ut eorum informis aut etiam confusa natura videatur esse materia omnium corporum suis formis discretorum; non inquam hoc dubito, sed quaero, unde haec ipsa quam dixi mundanae molis materia sit.... At si ex summae naturae materia potest esse aliquid minus ipsa, summum bonum mutari et corrumpi potest; quod nefas est dicere.'

into existence *ex nihilo* seems to him the only acceptable condition, and he emphasizes, in this context, that nothingness 'must in no way be understood as a kind of matter'.[1] This critical remark is probably aimed at Augustine's derivation of evil from the element of nothing at the root of the world.

Even so the doctrine that the visible world came into being from a state of non-existence is only partially true. It excludes the part of the creator. In his Word the universe was always in being beyond time, an aspect of divine eternity. This Christian tradition of the Logos as the creator of the world stimulated Anselm to insert in this context some observations on the nature of human language as an illustration of his thought. He brought a special interest in this subject from his studies of dialectic. Anselm distinguishes three ways in which we identify things. We can do so with signs expressed in words, which we hear or see when they are pronounced or written down, we can secondly recall these words in our mind and identify our object with this mental concept or we can do without any mediatory signs, by thinking the object itself; for instance, either the concrete form 'man' or the general concept: an animal, which is rational and mortal. Real words are only in exceptional cases identical with the object which they define. This happens when we pronounce the vowel 'a'. But such identification, independent of any difference of language, is always reached when we think the object directly without any mediation of words. This kind of signification is the nearest image of a world as it exists in the creator's mind.[2]

The production of a work of art offers an additional analogy, but points at the same time to a characteristic difference. The artist needs not only material but also, for his design, observation from existing reality. When we see a fabulous monster sculptured or painted it represents a strange compound, of which we can see every single part in various living animals. There is no analogy to such imitations in God's creative power, which reflects only his own essence.

[1] *Monologion*, ch. 8, *loc. cit.* p. 23; *PL* 158. 156B–C: 'Alia significatio est, quae dici quidem potest, vera tamen esse non potest; ut si dicatur aliquid sic esse factum ex nihilo, ut ex ipso nihilo, id est ex eo quod penitus non est, factum sit; quasi ipsum nihil sit aliquid existens, ex quo possit aliquid fieri. Quod quoniam semper falsum est: quotiens esse ponitur, impossibilis inconvenientia consequitur.'

[2] *Monologion*, ch. 10, *loc. cit.* p. 25; *PL* 158. 158B f.

The demonstration that the world cannot be understood without God as its centre and creator included for Anselm the trinitarian nature of Divinity. Augustine offered all the concepts he needed. On the other hand, Anselm felt clearly that with this problem he came to a limit in the application of his method. The internal relations between the persons of the Holy Trinity must remain a mystery which will always be beyond the reach of human reason. This admission does not exclude a rational argument in proof of the *existence* of something whose final nature must remain incomprehensible; but it creates a special problem. The object of a demonstration must be described in words, while the incomprehensible cannot be subjected to the process of abstraction and generalization on which language is based. The result of any investigation about its existence must be put into words which cannot signify the reality of their object. Anselm finds the solution to this problem in the everyday experience of metaphorical speech, comparable to showing a person's form in a mirror. In such cases, what we say and what we see is not identical with the subject we have in mind. No doubts about the truth of our statement arise from such indirect approach in ordinary usage. Nothing prevents us from signifying divine nature in the same way metaphorically. Words used in this context are kept at a very great distance from their subject, but they are similes and not falsehood.[1]

We shall see that considerations of this type were in Anselm's mind when he reshaped his speculation in order to render it more conclusive.

E. *The argument for God's existence*

We have Anselm's own report in the preface to the *Proslogion*, which confirms in essential features Eadmer's narration in his biography, about the development of his thought after the completion of the *Monologion*.[2] In this case his Benedictine loyalty, in all phases of his life an important motive for his attitudes and actions, did not compel him to accept the guidance of Lanfranc. He was not to be deflected from his course of finding a philosophical expression for the truth of belief which made it evident for human reason, unsupported by the authority of revelation. The parallelism of diverse chains of arguments, which he had offered in

[1] *Monologion*, ch. 64; 65, *loc. cit.* pp. 75 ff.; *PL* 158. 210B f.

[2] *De vita et conversatione* I, 19 ed. Rule, pp. 333 f.; *PL* 158. 63A f. Southern, *Eadmer*, pp. 29 ff.

his first treatise on the subject, did not satisfy him completely. He started to search for an argument which would give at once intellectual certainty both that God exists, and that all the attributes which belief has taught us are logically connected with this existence. For some time this task proved too frustrating, and Anselm tried to liberate himself from what seemed to him now an obsession which absorbed all his strength. Suddenly a formula came to his mind which he recognized as a solution. His inspiration was based on memories of passages from Augustine which must have suddenly come back to his mind, and in which the idea of God is described as something in comparison with which nothing better and more sublime can be thought.[1]

Anselm takes as basis the axiom that nothing greater than God can be thought. It is obvious that in this context 'greatness' has a metaphorical meaning, independent of extension in space as already defined by Anselm, in the *Monologion*. The fool whom the Psalmist quotes as saying to himself 'there is no God', would be able to listen to his definition and understand its literal meaning. But in this process he would not understand that God is real. At this point the difference between something which is grasped by our intellect and the same thing existing as a real object becomes relevant. A painter who considers a design for his work, but has not yet executed it, is in position similar to the fool, for whom the words about God form an understandable sentence, but do not describe reality. However, what we imagine in our mind can also be thought to exist both in mind and in reality.

In this case it would be greater than it would be as a mere content of our mind. Consequently, according to the basic definition, God cannot be restricted to the existence of a concept without reality. He cannot be *thought* as non-existing. But how do we account for men who speak and think in the way represented by the fool of the Bible?[2] Here Anselm goes back to the difference he has drawn in the *Monologion* between thinking a word and thinking its object. The type quoted by the

[1] For instance: *De moribus Manichaeorum* II, 1; *PL* 32. 1345: 'vellem quidem, ut tam serenam mentis aciem homines ad haec investiganda deferrent, ut possent videre illud summum bonum, quo non est quidquam melius aut superius.... Hoc enim intellecto... simul viderent id *esse*, quod summe ac primitus esse rectissime dicitur... cui si contrarium recte quaeras nihil omnino est. Esse enim non habet nisi non esse.' Anselm's basic argument is developed in chs. 2–4 of the *Proslogion*.

[2] Mentioned in the same context by Augustine, *De libero arbitrio* II, 2, § 5; *PL* 32. 1242.

psalmist have only the word for God in their thought and therefore they feel it possible to say 'God does not exist'. This same proof of God's existence serves also as basis for the reality of his attributes.

Modern judgement on this argument, which was discussed by the philosophers throughout the centuries, has been directly or indirectly influenced by Kant's criticism of what he called 'the ontological proof for the existence of God'. The predicate of existence does not belong to an object as such, but derives its validity from the pattern of things of which this object forms a part, witnessed by our sense-experience. This means that existence cannot make an object more perfect. There is no value added to 100 coins in our imagination, when we see them lying on the table.[1]

But had Anselm really overlooked the fact which forms the elementary core of this criticism, the contrast between the logical concept and the reality to which it is applied? There is a passage at the beginning of his argument which seems to imply that he did not make this transition from one to the other without knowing the clear dividing line between them, but he seems to ignore the consequence for his argument.[2]

As a way out of this difficulty, we may consider Karl Barth's strictly theological interpretation of Anselm's thought. According to his assumption, the Benedictine thinker had no intention to establish a *metaphysical* truth by his rational argument, but wished only to elucidate the ecclesiastical doctrine. Criticism, such as that represented by Kant, would thus lose its target. There would be no question of Anselm not having clearly differentiated between a verbal concept on the one hand and the reality of the object so described on the other. With obedience to the tradition authorized by the Church, he accepted both the conceptual definition of God and the duty to believe in his existence. Anselm would have seen his task as constructing a bridge between these two ends, in an attempt to understand how these ideas of the sacred texts possessed reality by their very nature.[3]

[1] *Kritik der reinen Vernunft: Von der Unmöglichkeit eines ontologischen Beweises vom Dasein Gottes*, ed. of the Berlin Academy, III, pp. 401 f. (1904). K.'s polemic is directed against Descartes' and Leibnitz' renewal of the argument.

[2] *Proslogion*, ch. 2; Schmitt, I, p. 101; *PL* 158. 227D: 'Aliud enim est rem esse in intellectu, aliud intelligere rem esse.'

[3] K. Barth, *Fides quaerens intellectum. Anselms Beweis der Existenz Gottes* (München, 1931), esp. pp. 16 ff.; 36, 82 f.

A recent analysis of the *Proslogion*'s literary form by Dom Schmitt seems to offer support for this interpretation. Anselm gives his argument as part of a prayer to God for illumination. The book's title summarizes the writer's situation, which underlies his reflections. God is approached with the request to reduce the distance in which Man is held away from him by his sin. This motive is repeated when, in the progress of the reflections, difficulties arise about the understanding of the divine attributes and their mutual consistency. God himself must dispel the darkness and disturbances of a mind frustrated in its attempt to understand the divine harmony and enjoy its logical evidence.[1]

It is evident that here Anselm has again taken Augustine as his model, who in the *Confessiones* shaped the philosophical analysis of his life into a book of prayer to God, as a gift of thanksgiving. This literary form, which he adopted, gave Anselm the possibility of reminding his readers again and again of the religious meaning of his thoughts.

The argument of the *Proslogion* on the existence of God meant for Anselm a definite progress in the establishment of his method of teaching a religious truth conclusively by dialectical exposition. In adopting the basic structure of Augustine's autobiography, he counterbalanced any impression of personal achievement which otherwise might be suggested by his philosophical deductions. But this link with Augustine gives no decision on the character of Anselm's argument. The *Confessiones* contain important pieces of their author's philosophical experiences, as for instance the refutation of astrological belief or the contact with Neoplatonism, which had played a part at important turning points of his life; in addition the discussion on the character of time is intimately connected with the intention and structure of Augustine's whole work. The idea that all these mental discoveries have been brought about by the grace of God determines the atmosphere of the *Confessiones*, but does not reduce the philosophical character of these sections.

The same observation applies to the argument which forms the core of the *Proslogion*. The definition of God as something in comparison with which nothing greater can be thought, is taken as a self-evident presupposition, from which deductions are made with a claim to rational necessity. The counter-argument of a contemporary critic, whom

[1] Dom F. S. Schmitt, O.S.B., *A. v. C. Proslogion* (Stuttgart, 1962), Introduction, pp. 15–34.

Anselm took very seriously, as we shall see immediately, discussed exclusively this section of the *Proslogion* which, in contrast to the modern theologian, he understood as an attempt at basing religious truth on demonstration by reason.

Moreover, the *Proslogion*'s argument for the existence of God is constructed with complete abstraction from everything which could be considered as a part of his incomprehensible essence. This means that it was kept completely within the limits which Anselm himself had defined earlier in the *Monologion* for the possibility of a rational proof in this sphere.[1] The difficulty which both the theological and the empiricist critic have found in this argument are rooted in the centre of Anselm's position. He took his religious experience, which he knew to be determined by the acceptance of ecclesiastical tradition, as the basis of deduction for which he claimed logical necessity. He became a philosopher, because he began with the conviction that his interpretation of religious doctrine could command the same degree of logical necessity as the masters of the schools of dialectic claimed for their deductions about things or events from Man's environment. Anselm's reservation concerned only the experimental character of his speculations in face of the ecclesiastical tradition and the obligation to respect an innermost sphere of religious mystery.

The possibility that the concepts used in his arguments may lose their meaning when applied outside sense-experience did not come to his mind. His world-picture, both in his personal roots and its intellectual elaboration under the influence of Augustine, had no room for the recognition of the material world as an independent object of man's thought; it could never be for him a final object of investigation by human reason.

That does not mean that Anselm did not take any interest in natural phenomena, and it is perhaps useful in our context to illustrate his approach in this direction. In the dialogue *De veritate* he mentions the experience that a staff standing in water gives the appearance of being broken, and goes on to discuss the phenomenon that an object seen

[1] *Monologion* 64, Schmitt, I, p. 75; *PL* 158. 210B: 'Sufficere namque debere existimo rem incomprehensibilem indaganti si ad hoc ratiocinando pervenerit ut eam certissime esse cognoscat, etiamsi penetrare nequeat intellectu quomodo ita sit.'

through glass of sufficiently strong colour loses its own. The optical delusion which results in both cases, is, as Anselm emphasizes, not the fault of the senses, which act as they ought, but a failure of our soul misjudging the circumstances by which the images have been transformed before they reached the eye.[1] Anselm takes an interest in nature in order to illustrate and justify creation. Any search for causes not connected with the achievement of this aim would, as he emphasizes, not be worth while. The highest rectitude and truth is the final cause of all existence. That nature possesses only a reflected reality, derived from its divine origin, is the basic presupposition of this thought.

This position prevented Anselm from seeing that the concepts of ancient logic, which he used to demonstrate religious truth, had been abstracted to 'save the appearances'; that is, to transform sense experience into lasting knowledge. After the full reception of Aristotle's philosophy of nature in the thirteenth century the situation changed. St Thomas in his criticism of the argument in the *Proslogion* did not accept Anselm's definition of God as self-evident for the non-believer and emphasized that such a 'divine name', grasped in its meaning by the intellect, does not offer any basis adequate to carry the affirmation of existence in the reality of things. Behind this methodical reflection lies a new idea of nature as an object of rational investigation.[2] Anselm's philosophical impulse, his search for necessary reasons, was concentrated on the interpretation of belief. The standard by which he finally measured the rectitude of his own argument, was its adequacy to express his faith. But this aim did not mean for him any reduction in the rational character of his deductions. He simply would not take into account any criterion based on the model of sense-experience, which in his view of the world did not form an independent sphere for Man's understanding.

F. *Defence against Gaunilo and Roscelinus*

For the full appreciation of Anselm's position we must include his own comments written in defence of his doctrine or with the intention of

[1] *De veritate*, ch. 6; Schmitt, I, pp. 184 f.; *PL* 158. 474A f.

[2] *Summa contra gentiles* I, 10 f.; *Summa theologica* I, quaest. 2, art. I. The historical truth of Anselm's argument is emphatically vindicated by W. v. d. Steinen in his comprehensive survey of the philosophical debate from the thirteenth to nineteenth century, *Vom heiligen Geist des Mittelalters* (Breslau, 1926), pp. 56–118.

clear demarcation. On the whole, contemporary reaction to his writings did not foreshadow the long-lasting effect of his thought on the discussion of the philosophers. But he found himself involved in two important controversies. The first arose when he was still an abbot; its subject was the argument of the *Proslogion*; the second developed during the years of transition from Bec to Canterbury, when Anselm felt the necessity to make clear his attitude towards the intellectual challenge to Christian tradition coming from Roscelin's use of dialectic.

In defence of the *Proslogion* Anselm wrote against the Benedictine monk Gaunilo of the great abbey of Marmoutier near Tours († 1083) who had written down his doubts about the argument as an appendix to Anselm's work. A common friend brought the manuscript back to Normandy; Anselm added his reply and made the request that in future all copies should include both Gaunilo's criticism and his own answer.[1]

Gaunilo defended the logic of the fool of the Bible, and tried to show that the *Proslogion*'s argument did in no way force him out of his position. The critic fully recognized the pious impulse which had dictated Anselm's work, but remained of opinion that the belief in God had its firm basis in the loyal recognition of ecclesiastical tradition only. Reason had not the power to compete in this sphere. The discussion between the two Benedictines centres therefore round the question, whether human understanding is capable of grasping the idea of God adequately enough for his reality to be represented in Man's *thought*. For Gaunilo Anselm's argument against the Psalmist's fool must necessarily remain a sequence of empty words which the listener has to fill with his imagination of something quite unknown. There is not even an appeal to analogy, because experience does not offer any similar object. Gaunilo summarizes his own point of view by an imitation of Anselm's argument in more concrete terms.

He takes up the story of the most wonderful island in the midst of the ocean, which is now out of mankind's ken. Its existence, however, cannot be doubted, because it is characterized by an excellence surpassing everything in the world. Otherwise we should be free to imagine another country with all the qualities allocated to the island, which would

[1] Eadmer, *Vita* I, ch. 19, ed. Rule, p. 334; *PL* 158. 68 A, Southern, *Eadmer*, p. 31.

be more eminent by possessing reality. This conclusion would be in contradiction to the story's presupposition.[1]

In his answer Anselm has not altered the essentials of his argument, but in his repartee he placed fresh emphasis on the impossibility for our thinking to combine the idea of God with non-existence. We can consider everything else as potentially not real, because we know of places or periods in which there is or was no trace of such things. The same experience arises when we distinguish parts in an object, which exist either side by side or successively in the course of time.

One place contains only a fragment of the whole, while the rest is missing, or one moment brings its whole content into reality, which is lacking in the stages that have passed or are still to come in the future. In contrast to such phenomena, God's superior greatness is based on the fact that we face his wholeness in every fragment of space and time. Our mind is brought into the right direction towards him, because our environment presses upon us the recognition of a hierarchical order, by the different degrees of good which we observe. But the idea of God remains completely different from any other phenomenon in Man's knowledge or imagination. Therefore the story of the lost island is merely a fairy-tale without any possible application to the argument. Anselm is ready to promise it as reward to anybody who may find an object besides God to which the *Proslogion*'s formula would fit.[2]

But an understanding of God's existence is possible, although his essence must remain impenetrable for our mind; we are able to see the daylight although our eyes do not stand facing direct sunshine. Anselm upholds the validity of his argument, because it expresses adequately his belief, or as we may say in modern terms authorized by Anselm himself, his religious experience.[3] For him the words by which it is formed reach the reality on which his life is based. Therefore he feels his thought in conformity with the fundamental truth from which every rectitude in theory and action is derived. Nothing else in human experience is on the same level; therefore no refutation from this direction can carry conviction. In contrast to him, his contemporary critic felt, and the

[1] *Quid ad hoc respondeat quidam pro insipiente*, ch. 4; 6, Schmitt, I, pp. 127–8; *PL* 158. 244B ff.

[2] *Quid ad hoc respondeat editor ipsius libelli*, ch. 1; 3, Schmitt, I, pp. 130–1; *PL* 15. 253A ff.

[3] *Ep. de incarnatione*, ch. 1, Schmitt, II, p. 9; *PL* 158. 264B: 'Nam qui non crediderit, non experietur.'

philosophers since the thirteenth century knew, that the logical concepts by which Anselm proceeded had their origin in abstractions from sense-experience.

For Anselm the impulse behind his philosophical analysis came from a combination of his belief with dialectical demonstration, which he found early in his life confirmed by his study of Augustine. Therefore he felt called to oppose a development of dialectic which obviously destroyed the presupposition of his philosophical interpretation of faith. Roscelin (1050–1125) was a secular master of the liberal arts, first in his native town of Compiège, later in Loches (Britanny), where Abaelard was one of his students. In 1092 a council of Soissons under the presidency of Rainald, archbishop of Reims, condemned his philosophical speculations on the character of the Trinity and forced him to withdraw this part of his teaching. As we learn from a gravely monitory letter by Ivo of Chartres addressed to him, Roscelin did not feel bound by this judgement, but immediately after the decision continued his attempt to win over new followers for his doctrine.[1] Despite this defiant attitude he was not left without ecclesiastical support; he became canon of Besançon cathedral and preserved connexions with the great Church of St Martin in Tours, where Berengar had resided one generation earlier. There is no report about a second condemnation.

From Roscelin's writings only a lengthy invective against Abaelard is preserved; it is in its style near to those rhetorical showpieces of self-assertion, such as were produced in the schools.[2] But it contains also some pages defending the author's trinitarian doctrine by quoting suitable patristic authorities. No textbook offering his dialectical teachings has survived; but Abaelard has quoted his opinions on points of detail.

The most important source both for Roscelin's intellectual attitude and for the character of his doctrine remains Anselm's polemic in his *Epistola de incarnatione*, which is twenty-five years earlier than the surviving text from Roscelin's own pen. The first version of this treatise was drafted when its author, then still abbot of Bec, was warned that Roscelin had claimed both the recently deceased Lanfranc and himself

[1] J. Reiners, *Der Nominalismus in der Frühscholastik* (Münster, 1910), pp. 24–40. Yves de Chartres, *Correspondance*, 1, ed. Dom J. Leclercq (Paris, 1949), *ep.* 7, pp. 22–6; *PL* 162. 17 f.

[2] J. Reiners, *loc. cit.* pp. 62–80; *PL* 178. 357 ff.

as sharing essentially the same trinitarian doctrine which he had established. This information came to Anselm just before the council of Soissons. When one year later Anselm, who had just crossed over to England, heard that Roscelin had not changed his line of approach, he wrote to his friends in Bec for the material he needed for this controversy, in order to take the task up again, which he had left unfinished the year before.[1]

In his pamphlet against Abaelard Roscelin emphasizes his recognition of Anselm's wisdom and piety and justifies his own critical attitude towards Anselm's argument for the *necessity* of salvation, but he does not dispute the quotations from his own teaching which Anselm had once taken as the basis for his refutation. This reticence makes it at least probable that he had no striking objections in this direction.[2] Anselm's attack against Roscelin was intended to counter his tendency of considering as three separate substances the three persons, whose mutual relationship within the divine unity is stated by ecclesiastical doctrine. He had been informed that his antagonist had used the example of three angels or three souls as similes in order to make his opinion on their separate existence clear. Anselm allows for the possibility that these similes had been added as comment by the man who had reported on Roscelin's teaching to him.[3]

He traces the intellectual origin of Roscelin's unsound doctrine to his emphasis on sense-impressions as the starting-point for man's understanding of his environment. His attitude expresses his incapacity to control the power of the images which the senses transmit from the outside world into man's consciousness. For Roscelin no logical concept is available which would allow him to place colour, and the object to which it belongs, on two different levels. This means that he does not recognize as real the contrast between the whole and its parts, which language uses for its descriptions. Roscelin's own remark, that we may define an individual as soul and bodies, by which are meant the parts

[1] *Ep. de incarnatione, prior recensio*, Schmitt, I, pp. 280–90; *ep.* 129 to monk John; *ep.* 136 to Fulco, bishop of Beauvais; *ep.* 147 to the prior of Bec, Baldric. Schmitt, III, pp. 271 f., 279 f., 293 f.; *PL* 158, *ep.* II, 35; II, 41; II, 51: 1181 f.; 1192D f.; 1206B.

[2] Reiners, *loc. cit.* p. 66; *PL* 178.

[3] *Ep. de incarnatione*, ch. 4, Schmitt, II, pp. 16 f.; *PL* 158. 270B: 'Sed forsitan ipse non dicit "sicut sunt tres angeli aut tres animae", sed ille, qui mihi eius mandavit quaestionem, hanc ex suo posuit similitudinem.'

which make up the body, seems to confirm Anselm's opinion that his antagonist sees the material world as a conglomeration, and does not recognize the reality of any organizing principle.[1] Anselm concludes that this attitude excludes any understanding even of this world, which is ruled by the laws of space and time, and illustrates his judgement by the example of the Nile. He has heard that this river appears in three different aspects, as source, stream and lake, but these different parts form together one natural phenomenon, the water of the Nile. In this way experience offers us a phenomenon in which one exists in three, and three are one. The different stages through which a river passes can be compared with the changing periods of life. Both are never complete at any given moment or place, before they have reached the end of their run. Moreover, there is a certain likeness with human speech, which is never experienced as a whole, as long as it is coming from the speaker's mouth.[2] Here again the influence of Augustine is obvious. The Father's philosophy of time is used as material for Anselm's own argument, by which he demonstrates that Roscelin's presuppositions exclude the understanding of Man's environment, which is dominated by time and space and divided into parts. This statement is meant to show how great must be the remoteness of his mind from the mystery of divinity, which is beyond the categories of everyday experience.

Roscelin's daring logical theory, on which his fame as the first champion of nominalism is based, identifies the general concepts, the universals, with the spoken words; his teaching was much talked about in schools down to the middle of the twelfth century.[3] Anselm finds his statements characteristic of the whole group, whom he calls briefly the 'modern teachers of dialectic'. They do not understand how several men can be considered as representatives of the species and from this point of view of one unit, man. He is interested in this development of dialectic, because Roscelin's logical attitude of isolating every single

[1] *Ep. de incarnatione*, ch. I, Schmitt, II, p. 10; *PL* 158. 265 C: Roscelinus, *ad Abaelardum*; J. Reiners, p. 73; *PL* 178. 365 D: 'ut hominis, quia alia pars est corpus, alia anima, unam animam dicimus, sed plura corpora propter corporis partes diversas'.

[2] Ch. 13, Schmitt, II, pp. 31 f.; *PL* 158. 289 C ff.

[3] John of Salisbury, *Policraticus* VII, 12, ed. Webb II, 142: 'Fuerunt et qui voces ipsas genera dicerent esse et species; sed eorum iam explosa sententia est et facile cum auctore suo evanuit' (written 1159); the name of Roscelinus is given by John in the same context, *Metalogicon* II, 17, ed. Webb, p. 92.

phenomenon under consideration blocks in his view all possibility of approach to the theological problem of the Trinity. Roscelin is for him a 'heretic using dialectic'.[1]

The learned tradition in the Boethian corpus, the passages commenting on Porphyry and the observations which explain Aristotle's *Categories* as verbal terms, were certainly well known to Anselm. In the earlier stages of his teaching at Bec the technicalities of dialectic had been so much in his mind, that he wrote a dialogue on the question how far the skills a man uses in his profession form a part of his substance or remain an additional quality. The argument in this writing is very much concerned with the structure of the positions and syllogistic conclusions which are used on both sides to prove and to refute.[2] At the time of his maturity Anselm's interest in the formal character of thought depended more and more on its function for the philosophical interpretation of faith. Anselm did not discuss Roscelin's position in the school and his relationship to Boethius or Isidore. He concentrated on those features which expressed for him Roscelin's mentality, the starting-point of a philosophy which excludes all possibility of religious truth as basis of thought. For Roscelin and his fellows use concepts which can be proved defective even as instruments for the understanding of the world in space and time and are completely inadequate for application to their author's faith. This situation leads them to dispute the truth as taught by the Fathers. They have become like owls and bats, animals moving through the night, when they quarrel on the nature of the light at midday with the eagle, who can focus the sun without drawing back.

G. *The pre-scholastic form of thought*

Anselm's attempt at thinking and teaching the content of faith in the form of philosophical arguments is not based on a clear distinction between subject-matter for which thirteenth-century scholasticism considers such treatment adequate and other doctrines for which essential knowledge is claimed from revelation only. We saw already, when we dealt with Anselm's methodical principles, that the great treatise *Cur Deus homo*,

[1] *Ep. de incarnatione*, ch. 1; Schmitt, II, p. 10; *PL* 158. 235 A: 'Denique qui non potest intelligere aliquid esse hominem, nisi individuum, nullatenus intelliget hominem, nisi humanam personam.'

[2] 'Quomodo grammaticus sit substantia et qualitas', chs. 1–4; Schmitt, I, pp. 145–8; *PL* 158. 561 ff.

dealing with the theological problem of the necessity for incarnation, is especially rich in observations relevant to such general questions. Anselm did not change his approach while discussing a strictly dogmatic subject-matter. The reservations by which he safeguarded the ecclesiastical correctness of his thought from the start seemed to him to cover the whole field. Boso as interlocutor has, as we saw, the part of the unbeliever who demands the consistency of a rational argument. On the other hand, he also occasionally raises some doubts against Anselm's deductions which are based on biblical passages, which the master has to disperse by his interpretation. The argument must be made safe on both fronts vital to Anselm. After the discussion has reached a conclusion on the main topic, Boso declares why he, a loyal believer, requested such argument as would be acceptable to the unbeliever: he aimed at enjoying the confirmation of his faith through the evidence of understanding.[1]

That brings us back to the same motive as stimulated Anselm's thought from the beginning. This tendency is emphasized when Anselm makes Boso refuse to accept as *argument* the traditional typological co-ordination of Eve and the tree in Paradise on the one hand and St Mary and the cross on the other. Such correspondences could have the value of pictures illustrating something already in one's possession. But separated from the authority of the Church, and at the same time without the solid basis of truth established by reason, they would have no more strength than pictures painted on clouds.[2]

[1] *Cur Deus homo*, II, 15; Schmitt, II, p. 116; *PL* 158. 416B: 'Sed hoc postulo, ut, quod quasi non debere aut non posse fieri videtur infidelibus in fide christiana, hoc mihi, qua ratione fieri debeat aut possit, aperias; non, ut me in fide confirmes, sed ut confirmatum veritatis ipsius intellectu laetifices.'

[2] *Cur Deus homo* I, 3 f.; Schmitt, II, p. 51; *PL* 158. 364C f. Boso rejects the use of this parallelism as a rational argument. Ch. 4, pp. 51 f.: 'Omnia haec pulchra et quasi quaedam picturae suscipienda sunt. Sed, si non est aliquid solidum, super quod sedeant, non videntur infidelibus sufficere. ...Nam qui picturam vult facere, eligit aliquid solidum, super quod pingat, ut maneat, quod pingit....Quapropter, cum has convenientias, quas dicis, infidelibus quasi quasdam picturas rei gestae obtendimus, quoniam non rem gestam, sed figmentum arbitrantur esse, quod credimus, quasi super nubem pingere nos existimant. Monstranda ergo prius est veritatis soliditas rationabilis, id est necessitas, quae probet....' It has frequently been overlooked that *convenientia* in this passage obtains a special meaning by the typological context, which is in contrast to Anselm's normal usage; *conveniens et necessarium* are normally only different in degree, sometimes *conveniens* is even used to describe the conclusions of Anselm's argument. *Proslogion*, ch. 3, Schmitt, I, p. 102; *PL* 158. 228B: 'Quare si id quo maius nequit cogitari, potest cogitari non esse; id ipsum quo maius cogitari nequit, non est id quo maius cogitari nequit; quod *convenire* non potest.'

But, as Anselm saw, this search for reasons which would give the character of logical necessity to incarnation and crucifixion, called for a clear distinction in order to prevent the metaphysical consequence of placing Divinity under the domination of an external motive force. Anselm attempted to solve this problem by differentiating between an external *necessity of causation*, such as that which we can trace behind the movements of the celestial sphere, and the *subsequent necessity* describing an event as the *given* result of a situation. Only the latter type, for which a man's spontaneous speech is given as example, which does not imply any external force, can be used as analogy for the understanding of divine action.[1]

In such a world picture as is outlined in the *Monologion* the problem of evil was very urgent. It was for Anselm closely connected with the question, how to combine the free will of Man with the necessity of sin after the Fall, which had been discussed by the Abbot of Bec in a group of dialogues during the eighties. In this context the basic problem of *Cur Deus homo* is formulated in *De veritate*, where we read the following reflections: sometimes we see striking contrasts within the same event when we look at it from different points of view, as if it were possible to say of the same thing that it ought to be and that it ought not to be. When we consider the Passion of Christ it is evident that the perpetrators were evil and the suffering quite improper; therefore it ought not to have happened. But a more comprehensive view will lead to the conclusion of the necessity of this event in the history of salvation.[2]

From such passages we see that not only identity of method, but also coherence in problems and solutions, links Anselm's important dogmatic contribution to the doctrine of atonement with his earlier writing on speculative themes. This absence of demarcation characterizes his approach to philosophy.

Chronology and even more the dramatic events in Anselm's life as archbishop might tempt us to see him as the man who represented in his thought the tendency of the ecclesiastical reform connected with the name of Gregory VII. But he did not feel himself as the discoverer or, as the style of the period would have called it, the restorer of the prin-

[1] *Cur Deus homo* II, 17. Schmitt, II, p. 125; *PL* 158. 424A f.
[2] *De veritate* 8, Schmitt, I, pp. 186 f.; *PL* 158. 476A.

ciples which led to a transformation of the Church's position in Christian society. His emphasis was on the traditional concepts of obedience towards the papacy and on the honour and rights of Canterbury, which were not allowed to be infringed while he was responsible. That he had no interest in the investigation and reconciliation of conflicting views in the legal and doctrinal tradition of the Church, points in the same direction. It was the rising scholasticism which represented the mentality necessary for the administration of ecclesiastical institutions after Gregory VII. The more intense study of Boethius' logical corpus since the eleventh century was connected, both as cause and as effect, with this movement, and was at the same time a presupposition of Anselm's work. But the way he assimilated this ancient legacy into his work eliminated any potential relationship with the dominant contemporary current.

Perhaps we can say that he had his genuine roots in the development of Benedictine piety towards a more articulate expression of the ideas behind their way of life. In the philosophical elements of Augustine's teaching he found the instrument for this task. When, in the next generation, the Cistercians undertook a parallel attempt, they also could not avoid using conceptual language. But in the meantime the rise of philosophical schools had made intellectual pride a very visible feature of the period, and this was felt by Bernard of Clairvaux and his circle to be antagonistic to their life and thought. This situation destroyed the harmony between belief and understanding, as Anselm had experienced it, and so gave him the unique but also isolated position by which his work is characterized in the history of medieval philosophy.

PART VIII

EARLY ISLAMIC PHILOSOPHY

BY

R. WALZER

Dedicated to Sir Hamilton Gibb for his 70th birthday

CHAPTER 39

INTRODUCTORY

A. *Approaches to the study of Islamic philosophy*

It appears premature, at the present time, to embark on a history of Islamic philosophy in the Middle Ages.[1] Too many of the basic facts are still unknown. New texts are constantly being discovered. Not all the manuscripts known are available in critical editions, or indeed published at all. Very few commentaries of any standing exist and scarcely any monographs on essential topics. Very few texts—apart from those translated centuries ago into medieval Latin—can be read in translation. It would be of some use, it is true, to survey the information available at present, to list the main facts which have been established beyond doubt and to show where future work should start and which are the most urgent tasks.[2] But this would scarcely agree with the purpose of the present publication. It seems to be more appropriate to discuss the essence of what the Muslims called 'philosophy' (*falsafa*), to explain how, on one side, it depends on Greek thought as taught in the philosophical schools in the later centuries of the Roman Empire, and how on the other side it answers the needs and questions of a new and different world—whose inhabitants speak a different language, Arabic, and adhere neither to the religion of classical Greece nor to Christianity which had taken its place, but follow a Hebraic religion of a new type, Islam.[3] I shall, therefore, confine myself to a minimum of indispensable general

[1] Cf. S. Munk, *Mélanges de philosophie juive et arabe* (Paris, 1859) (reprinted); T. J. de Boer, *The History of Philosophy in Islam*, English translation by E. R. Jones (London, 1903) (reprinted); É. Gilson, *History of Christian Philosophy in the Middle Ages* (London, 1955), pp. 181–220; Jean de Menasce, *Arabische Philosophie* (*Bibliographische Einführungen in das Studium der Philosophie*) (Bern, 1948); Julius Guttmann, *Philosophies of Judaism*, English translation (London, 1964), pp. 47 ff.; R. Walzer, *Greek into Arabic* (Oxford, 1962), pp. 1 ff.; R. Walzer, *Encyclopedia Britannica* (1963), *s.v.* Arabic Philosophy; W. Montgomery Watt, *Islamic Philosophy and Theology* (Islamic Surveys, 1) (Edinburgh, 1964); H. Corbin, *Histoire de la philosophie islamique*, I (Paris, 1964). General reference works: *Encyclopedia of Islam*, 1st edn (Leiden, 1913–39), 2nd edn (1954 ff.); C. Brockelmann, *Geschichte der arabischen Literatur*, 2nd edn (1943–9), two volumes; three supplementary volumes (1937–42); G. Sarton, *Introduction to the History of Science*, 4 vols. (1927–48).

[2] Cf. R. Walzer, *Correspondance d'Orient*, v (Bruxelles, 1962), pp. 347 ff.

[3] Cf. e.g. H. A. R. Gibb, *Mohammedanism*, 2nd edn (Oxford, 1953).

facts, so as to concentrate mainly on giving a fuller picture of one outstanding early Muslim philosopher, al-Fārābī, with a view to trying to indicate how and why philosophy never succeeded in reaching in the Islamic world the position which it had maintained in the ancient world for more than a thousand years.

It is pertinent to begin by inquiring what attitudes can be adopted to this body of philosophy by the modern scholar. The study of this Muslim medieval philosophy is of course no longer part of any philosophical syllabus in Western universities, as it was—in Latin translation—from the twelfth century until the eighteenth. Plato and Aristotle and Plotinus are no longer associated with al-Fārābī (died A.D. 950), Avicenna (980–1037: Ibn Sīnā) and Averroes (Ibn Rushd: 1126–98) in the minds of those who study them, nor is it realized, as it used to be, that the Muslim thinkers themselves stand on the shoulders of their Greek predecessors and, in a very real sense, continue their work. These days have definitely passed now. But nonetheless we do not need to resign ourselves to taking a predominantly antiquarian interest in the subject. On the contrary, there are various very good reasons why it should be attractive for scholars of our days to embark on a study of medieval Muslim philosophy and why non-specialists also should be drawn to become acquainted with the progress of that study.

Firstly, to become familiar with the essence and history of medieval Islamic philosophy (*falsafa*) is obviously relevant for the student of Islam. Although philosophy is by no means a dominant feature of this very widely spread civilization it is certainly an important element of it, and students of Islam who refrain from taking due notice of it will certainly miss something essential. It has of late become less unusual to consider Greek philosophy as part of the whole of Greek civilization—as a kind of conscious self-expression of the whole of Greek life—rather than to be satisfied with looking at it in isolation and referring it to absolute truth. Yet the same cannot be done in the case of Islam, or at least not in the same way, because the position of philosophy in the Islamic world is different. Philosophy was brought into it from the outside and naturalized, but it was no genuine growth. We are still very remote from an adequate understanding of Islamic philosophy as a special feature of Islamic civilization. Only patient interpretation of the available texts will help and comparison with other manifestations of Islamic life, theology, law, literature, etc. No sociological short-cut can relieve us of this task. Yet we may, eventually, succeed in gaining a better understanding of the differences between Islam and the Western world precisely by looking at it from the point of view of philosophy.

Another perfectly legitimate approach is, secondly, to treat medieval Islamic philosophy exclusively as part of the legacy of classical Greece. It is, after all, based on an impressive number of good translations of Greek philosophical texts. Translations of Greek philosophy—together with translations of all kinds of sciences, mathematics and medicine, etc.—had never been undertaken before on such a scale and are a considerable achievement in their own right. The Greeks themselves, for instance, had done very little to acquaint Greek readers with works written in a foreign idiom: the Septuagint, the Jewish translation of the Old Testament into Greek, had not become known to educated Greeks in general before the triumph of Christianity. It is quite possible, too, to search for otherwise lost Greek texts in Arabic disguise; this has in fact been done not unsuccessfully already, and still more results can confidently be expected. One can also recover such material, by careful analysis, from the texts of Arabic philosophical works. Similarly, the textual establishment of extant Greek writings—and indeed the mere lexicographical understanding of individual Greek words—gains from comparing Greek texts with their Arabic translations.[1] Moreover, some new appreciation of the total achievement of Greek thought may ultimately follow from the study of the works of the Muslim heirs of Greek philosophy.

Thirdly, the study of the history of Western philosophical terminology in general, not too eagerly pursued at present, will certainly benefit considerably from the analysis of Arabic philosophical terms, especially when the classical Greek and Latin terms and their Arabic equivalents are taken together with both the new Arabic terms and the terms used in the numerous medieval Latin translations from Arabic.[2] Progress in this very promising field of study is very slow

[1] Cf. R. Walzer, *Greek into Arabic*, pp. 29–174 and below, p. 649.

[2] Terms coined by the Arabs are, for instance, *māhiyya–quidditas–quiddity*, *qabliyya-prioritas–priority*. Cf. M. T. d'Alverny: 'Aniyya-anitas', *Mélanges É. Gilson* (1959), pp. 59 ff.

at present, one of the reasons being the widespread neglect of late Greek philosophy in contemporary classical studies.

Fourthly, it is, moreover, obvious that a first-hand knowledge of the Arabic originals of the medieval Latin versions of al-Fārābī, Avicenna, Averroes and others is relevant both to a deeper understanding of that section of medieval and post-medieval Western philosophy, and to a historical appreciation of the achievement of the Schoolmen and their more immediate successors.[1] It is, again, surprising how little attention is being given to this comparatively easy task. Western scholars, brought up in the classical tradition, are shy of taking up oriental languages. Students of medieval Jewish philosophy (which depends wholly on the Muslim *falāsifa* and is available in both Arabic and Hebrew) have been far more ready to make themselves familiar with the language of the Muslim thinkers.[2]

Fifthly, Islamic philosophy may also be appreciated as an interesting stage in that perennial debate between a philosophical truth which claims to base itself exclusively on human reason—as the ancient Greeks had discovered it—and the Hebrew concept of a religious revelation believed to be due to a supernatural agency, as Jews, Christians and Muslims maintained with the same strength of conviction. Since these views clashed seriously for the first time in late antiquity—Galen's criticism of Jews and Christians and Porphyry's voluminous attack on the Christians are the first landmarks of this struggle[3]—that debate has been going on uninterruptedly. The Arabic Muslim contribution to it is both interesting and ingenious and it differs radically from the way in which Greek Patristic writers looked at the problem—since they were connected with and dependent on the dogmatic decisions of their coun-

[1] M. Steinschneider, *Die europäischen Übersetzungen aus dem Arabischen bis Mitte des 17. Jahrhunderts* (Graz, 1960) (reprinted); E. Renan, *Averroès et l'Averroïsme*, 2nd edn (Paris, 1861); H. A. R. Gibb, 'The influence of Islamic culture in medieval Europe', *Bulletin of the John Rylands Library*, XXXVIII (1955), pp. 82 ff.; M. T. d'Alverny, 'Avendauth', *Homenaje a Millas-Valliscrosa*, I (Barcelona, 1954), pp. 19 ff.; 'Notes sur les traductions médiévales des œuvres philosophiques d'Avicenna', *Archives d'histoire doctrinale et littéraire du Moyen Âge* (1952), pp. 337 ff.; *ibid.* (1961), pp. 281 ff.; (1962), pp. 217 ff.; (1963), pp. 221 ff.; 'Avicenne et les médecins de Venise', *Studi in onore di Bruno Nardi* (Firenze, 1955), pp. 177 ff.

[2] M. Steinschneider, *Die hebräischen Übersetzungen des Mittelalters und die Juden als Dolmetscher* (Berlin, 1893) (reprinted); Maimonides, *The Guide of the Perplexed*, translated with an Introduction and Notes by S. Pines; with an introductory essay by L. Strauss (Chicago, 1963).

[3] Cf. R. Walzer, *Galen on Jews and Christians* (Oxford, 1949); W. Jaeger, *Early Christianity and Greek Paideia* (Cambridge, Mass., 1961); H. Chadwick, *Origen Contra Celsum* (2nd edition).

cils whereas no comparable authority ever existed within the religious organization of Islam.[1] The main Muslim protagonists of this controversy are al-Ghazzālī (d. A.D. 1111), who made a determined and very able attack on all the main tenets of philosophy in his *The Incoherence of the Philosophers*,[2] and Averroes who subtly and vigorously defended it in *The Incoherence of the Incoherence*.[3] The debate moves on a very high level and is conducted with the utmost fairness and consistency, and its level within the Islamic world had indeed been high and impressive all the time.

Sixthly, it is perhaps even more tempting to try to look at all these different sides of Islamic philosophy from a comprehensive and more general point of view, since Islamic philosophy is also a particularly interesting and instructive phenomenon in the continuity of the tradition of Western civilization as a whole. As far as philosophy in general is concerned, it fills a conspicuous gap in the history of many fundamental ideas which had originated in classical Greece and which succeeded in surviving its downfall, taking a new lease of life after having been divorced from their native soil. Moreover, since, in a large number of cases, both the Greek and the corresponding Arabic philosophical evidence is available, Islamic philosophy lends itself to a more detailed comparison with its predecessors than is possible, say, in the case of the fragments of the Presocratics and the very incomplete remnants of the Babylonian and Egyptian civilization of the Ancient East.[4] We can follow the transmission of the Greek tradition within the Arabic world almost step by step, as it were, and watch its gradual adaptation to new surroundings and to circumstances and problems of a totally different world: we can ascertain—and not just guess—how it was turned to fresh use in answer to questions which it had never been intended to tackle. In addition, this study may help towards the understanding of historical continuity between different civilizations in general, quite apart from its value for the historian of specifically European ideas: it

[1] Moreover, Neoplatonic Greek philosophy was amply used in support of the dying pagan religion.

[2] *Al-Ghazali's Tahafut Al-Falasifa* (*Incoherence of the Philosophers*), English translation by Sabih Ahmad Kamali (Lahore, 1958).

[3] S. van den Bergh, *Averroes' Tahafut al-Tahafut* (*The Incoherence of the Incoherence*), translation with Introduction and Notes, 2 vols. (London, 1954).

[4] Cf. e.g. W. K. C. Guthrie, *A History of Greek Philosophy*, I (Cambridge, 1962), pp. 32 ff.

may thus contribute to the consideration of one of the most harassing problems of the present day, I mean, how continuity can be preserved in a world which is in a state of constant and increasingly rapid change.

B. *Islamic and Greek philosophy: al-Kindī and al-Rāzī*

Islamic philosophy is, in the following pages, to be understood as that trend of Muslim thought which continues the type of Greek philosophy which the later Neoplatonists had created: a blend of Aristotelian and Platonic views as understood by philosophers in the later centuries of the Roman Empire. Like its Greek model, it is not restricted to any particular branch of knowledge, but concerns itself with every aspect of the world and of human life. It culminates and finds its ultimate justification in a theistic philosophy—a natural theology, based on human reason, whose beginnings can be traced back to the Presocratics and whose mature form had been more and more refined since Plato's and Aristotle's days.[1] It is fascinating to follow up how these Muslim philosophers who believed in the absolute truth of Greek philosophy tried to give this foreign legacy a prominent place in their own civilization which had become a political and cultural entity in its own right thanks to the unconditional acceptance of the authority of the divine Qur'ān, as communicated to them by the prophet Muḥammad. Their intention needs to be clearly distinguished from the aim of the Muslim apologists, the so-called *mutakallimūn* who take the truth of Islam as their starting-point and can be described as dialectical or speculative theologians. The philosophers themselves, especially al-Fārābī and his like, insist on emphasizing this difference and pointing to the shortcomings of this movement.[2] It seems to me wrong to make this speculative theology—the *kalām*—part of a historical discussion of Islamic philosophy by considering it as a kind of philosophy of religion. It rather belongs to a comprehensive history of Muslim thought in general —which may take account of 'philosophy' as well—together with the development of religion, tradition, Holy Law, mysticism, etc. I also find

[1] Cf., for instance, W. Jaeger, *Theology of the Early Greek Philosophers* (Oxford, 1947). A second volume was never written. It was to be concerned 'with the period from Socrates and Plato down to the time when, under the influence of this tradition of Greek philosophical theology, the Jewish-Christian religion transformed itself into a theological system in the Greek manner, in order to force its admission to the Hellenistic world' (*op. cit.* p. v).

[2] Cf. L. Gardet–M. M. Anawati, *Introduction à la théologie musulmane* (Paris, 1948), pp. 102 ff.

it misleading to understand Muslim philosophy as a prelude to the theosophy of thinkers like the Persian Suhrawardī (1155–91), a contemporary of Averroes. To confound philosophy and theosophy seems to me equal to rating Iamblichus or Hermes Trismegistus as the greatest philosophers of antiquity.

The Muslim philosophers had at their disposal a very rich legacy of translations of those Greek texts which had still been studied in the late Greek schools. Much of this late Greek syllabus had in fact survived for a considerable time in Egyptian and Syrian cities after they had been conquered by the Muslim advance in the seventh century, and it had even found a place in the new Abbasid capital of Baghdad. The work of the Arab translators starts about A.D. 800; it can be followed up till about A.D. 1000. There are numerous translators, and different centres and schools are to be distinguished. The translations are partly made from the Greek original, partly from the intermediate Syriac versions; they constantly improved in quality as the techniques of translation were perfected and a definite standard was established. Many of them are extremely good, others are lacking in understanding and style, but on the whole it may fairly be said that they are very reliable and served their purpose extremely well. The most renowned of these translators were the Nestorian Syrian Ḥunain son of Ishāq, and his pupils.[1] One may well doubt whether Islamic philosophy would ever have come into existence if these translations had not been commissioned by philosophers and other public figures who felt the need of them and acted accordingly. At any rate it would have taken a very different course.

The texts which became in this way best known to Arabic readers were the lecture courses of Aristotle—the *Politics* excepted—and an impressive number of commentaries of late antiquity.[2] Plato's *Timaeus*, *Republic* and *Laws*—and probably some other of his dialogues—were also available and were actually studied.[3] Porphyry (A.D. 232–after 300)[4] and Proclus[5] (A.D. 410–85) were more than mere names to them, and they knew John Philoponus (6th cent. A.D.) better than we can know him today. They became acquainted with many minor

[1] M. Meyerhof, 'New light on Ḥunain ibn Isḥāq', *Isis*, VIII (1926), pp. 685 ff.; G. Bergsträsser, *Ḥunain ibn Isḥāq, Über die syrischen und arabischen Galenübersetzungen* (Leipzig, 1925).

[2] Cf. *Encyclopedia of Islam*, 2nd edn, *s.v.* Arisṭūṭālīs.

[3] *Ibid. s.v.* Aflāṭūn. [4] *Ibid. s.v.* Furfūriyūs. [5] *Ibid. s.v.* Buruḳlūs.

Neoplatonic treatises which are unknown to us. More philosophical writings of Galen were read in ninth-century Baghdad than anywhere in the later Western world.[1] This brief list is not meant as an exhaustive survey of all the Greek philosophical works which the translators made accessible to Arab students of philosophy, but simply as an indispensable prelude to our examination of al-Fārābī in particular.[2]

Al-Fārābī presupposes, however, not only the existence of a philosophical literature in Arabic translation but also a philosophical movement which had begun about two generations before him. Two of its outstanding representatives seem to deserve some attention, however superficial, namely the Arab Ya'qūb ibn Isḥāq al-Kindī (died after A.D. 870) and the Persian Muḥammad ben Zakariyyā al-Rāzī (d. 923 or 932).

Al-Kindī lived in the first half of the ninth century and dominated the philosophical scene for about a hundred years. It is mainly due to him that philosophy was established as a new discipline of Muslim learning; the comparatively recent discovery of one large manuscript of his writings has given us at least some idea how this was done. He appears to be convinced that revelation and human reason ultimately come to the same conclusions although they follow different ways; he is prepared to subordinate philosophy to Scripture, and does not proclaim the absolute superiority of philosophy as al-Fārābī does. Alone among the great Muslim philosophers he maintains that the creation of the world from nothing—a tenet which appears so utterly foolish to the commonly accepted Greek view—can be demonstrated scientifically; he depends in this respect on the great Christian Aristotelian John Philoponus of Alexandria. Otherwise he follows the conventional Aristotelian analysis of reality combined with Neoplatonic tenets in metaphysics and a rather radical negative theology. His method of exposition and the structure of his arguments still lack the refinement which we observe in the writings of al-Fārābī, Avicenna and Averroes.[3]

[1] Cf. *Encyclopedia of Islam*, 2nd edn, *s.v.* Djālīnūs.

[2] M. Steinschneider, *Die arabischen Übersetzungen*, cf. above, p. 646; F. Rosenthal, *Das Fortleben der Antike in Islam* (Zurich–Stuttgart, 1965).

[3] Critical edition of 24 works of different size by Abū Rīda, 2 vols. (Cairo, 1950–3). Arabic text, Italian translation and commentary on two works in M. Guidi–R. Walzer, *Studi su Al-Kindi*, I (Roma, 1940); H. Ritter–R. Walzer, *Studi su Al-Kindi*, II (Roma, 1938); A. Nagy, *Beiträge zur Geschichte der Philosophie des Mittelalters* (Münster, 1897) (Latin translations); R. Walzer, *Greek into Arabic*, pp. 175 ff.

Al-Rāzī[1] is better known as an outstanding and by no means entirely bookish physician, who is proud of his own judgement and his original observations. He was not less original as a philosopher. He did not follow the line started by al-Kindī and continued by al-Fārābī, Avicenna and Averroes. He claimed to be a Platonist; he maintained that the world was shaped by the Creator out of shapeless eternal matter and is in due course destroyed periodically—whereas al-Fārābī and his successors assumed the world to be eternal. There are five eternal principles: the Creator, the soul of the world, matter, absolute time and absolute space; matter is of atomic structure. Revealed religion was to him identical with superstition. He has no use for the universally recognized prophets: Moses, Jesus and Muḥammad, the founders of three widely spread religions, have according to him brought nothing but misery and war into the world. They contradict each other and are self-contradictory, mere impostors. Philosophy is the only true way to salvation, and it is accessible to everybody. Not much of al-Rāzī's refreshingly lively and original work has survived; it did not find much favour with orthodox Muslims and it was frowned upon by Neo-platonic-Aristotelian philosophers and Muslim speculative theologians.

[1] Cf. *Encyclopedia of Islam*, 1st edn, *s.v.* Al-Rāzī; 1st edition of a number of treatises by R. Kraus as *Opera Philosophica*, I (Cairo, 1939); S. Pines, *Beiträge zur islamischen Atomenlehre* (Berlin, 1936), pp. 34 ff.; 'Rāzī critique de Galien', *Actes du 7e Congrès International d'Histoire des Sciences* (1953), pp. 480 ff.; *Mémoires de la Société des Études Juives*, I (Paris, 1955), pp. 55 ff.; English translation of his 'autobiography' by A. J. Arberry, *Asiatic Review* (1949), pp. 703 ff. (cf. P. Kraus, 'Raziana, I,', *Orientalia*, IV (1935), pp. 300 ff. Translation of another treatise, A. J. Arberry, *The Spiritual Physick of Rhazes* (London, 1950).

CHAPTER 40

AL-FĀRĀBĪ AND HIS SUCCESSORS

A. *Life and writings: political philosophy*

We know next to nothing about al-Fārābī's personal life. He preferred to be remembered by his work alone. He did not write an *apologia pro vita sua*, as Plato had done in antiquity and al-Rāzī among the Muslims[1] and al-Ghazzālī after him,[2] who described his own conversion to mysticism. Nor did he compose an autobiography for the use of a close pupil, like Avicenna,[3] nor did any of his intimates record significant details of his life, as Porphyry had done in the case of his master Plotinus. The salient facts we have are these: al-Fārābī spent the greater part of his life in the capital of the Abbāsid caliphate, Baghdād, where he had come from his birthplace in a Turkish district of Transoxania; during his later years he stayed at the court of a minor Shiʿite ruler in Aleppo. He is supposed to have died as an old man A.D. 950.[4]

Many of al-Fārābī's writings survived and were studied in the East until recent times. He wrote numerous elementary introductions to philosophical topics—like the later Greek treatises composed for beginners (τοῖς εἰσαγομένοις). Since he did not address a sophisticated audience which had been imbued with Greek philosophy for centuries, these treatises became more popular than we would be inclined to expect.[5] He also wrote many monographs on special questions, as for instance on the One and the Intellect,[6] on dreams and on various kinds of political associations,[7] such works, apparently, being meant as prelim-

[1] Cf. p. 651 n. 1.

[2] 'Deliverance from Error', available in an English translation by W. Montgomery Watt, *The Faith and Practice of Al-Ghazzālī* (London, 1953).

[3] Translated by A. J. Arberry, *Avicenna on Theology* (London, 1951), pp. 10 ff.

[4] Cf. *Encyclopedia of Islam*, 2nd edn, *s.v.* Al-Fārābī.

[5] For treatises of this kind, which are published and translated, cf. the article referred to in p. 646 n. 1. N. Rescher, *Al-Fārābī's Short Commentary on Aristotle's Prior Analytics* (Pittsburgh, 1963); cf. A. Sabra's review, *Journal of the American Oriental Society*, 85 (1965).

[6] Cf. also É. Gilson, *Archives d'Histoire doctrinale et littéraire du moyen âge*, IV (1929), pp. 113 ff.

[7] *Aphorisms of the Statesman* (*fuṣūl al-madanī*), ed. D. M. Dunlop, with English translation and notes (Cambridge, 1961); *Compendium Legum Platonis*, ed. F. Gabrieli, with Latin translation and notes, *Plato Arabus*, III (London, 1952).

inaries for more comprehensive studies. In addition, he composed commentaries on Aristotle's lecture courses in which he followed the late Greek way of interpreting Aristotle—which he knew from translations—without a gap. One of these commentaries—on the *De interpretatione*—has recently been edited for the first time:[1] Averroes, whose commentaries on Aristotle (written in Muslim Spain during the twelfth century) became so important for so many generations of later Western scholars, was simply following al-Fārābī's example in this respect; Avicenna did not write any commentaries of this kind but preferred to deal with the various topics of Greek thought in a more systematic way and write comprehensive encyclopedias of philosophy. It is obviously not of primary importance to deal with this side of al-Fārābī's philosophical activity for its own sake, interesting as it is for the continuity of Greek philosophical studies as a whole. It shows the extent of his familiarity with Greek thought and the considerable depth of his understanding—especially if one compares him with his contemporaries in the Western Latin world. But Islamic philosophy is more than a mere handing on of Greek tradition. Like all the great Islamic philosophers, al-Fārābī aimed at being more than a teacher of ancient thought for students of philosophy. This was, it is true, indispensable: but it was meant as a preliminary introduction to something else, as an activity which was not considered to be self-contained and final. Al-Fārābī tried to show how this philosophy, which he was proud to represent within the Muslim world, was to be related to his own tradition—to specifically Muslim sciences, such as the study of the Holy Law or dialectical theology, the *kalām*. He did not believe that reason is limited to theoretical issues only, he was convinced that true reason, when applied to practical issues, must express itself in moral demands which would conform to the results of theoretical reasoning: that true politics would have to agree with metaphysical truth. Hence it so happened that he embarked—though without entering practical politics himself—on a programme of political reform of the Islamic world which was in a critical state in his days. This reform was to be conditioned and determined by philosophy: Plato's demand for a philosopher-king was to be applied to the circumstances of tenth-century Islam, no longer to a small city-state like Athens: as had already

[1] W. Kutsch–H. Marrow, *Al-Fārābī's Commentary on Aristotle's* Περὶ ἑρμηνείας (Beyrouth, 1960).

happened in late antiquity, the ideal had to be adjusted to much larger political entities, such as the Imperium Romanum or the vast Muslim Empire, and to a state which would embrace the whole inhabited world, the οἰκουμένη.[1] But these philosophical ideas could not be made acceptable to Muslims unless it could be shown at the same time that they provided the best answers to the main questions about God, the world and man and society, which were discussed outside the narrow circle of philosophers: i.e. by Muslims who had no previous knowledge of Greek philosophical thought and had remained unaware of the truth conveyed by these foreign thinkers.

Al-Fārābī's insistence on the political task of philosophy, and his conviction that the true nature of philosophy demands this integration of the philosopher's personality, are as unique in the history of Islamic philosophy as Plato's call had been within the Greek world. Neither al-Kindī nor Avicenna nor al-Rāzī shows any traces of a similar interest. For al-Fārābī, however, it is, to quote his own words, beyond doubt that 'if at a given time no philosophy at all is associated with the government, the state must, after a certain interval, inevitably perish'.

B. *Philosophy and religion*

Al-Fārābī dedicated several works of his to this topic,[2] and for the purpose of this discussion we may choose 'The principles of the views of the citizens of the excellent state (ἀρίστη πολιτεία)' to examine in some detail.[3] I propose to give a survey of its contents and to show, as this review progresses, which lines of Greek thought al-Fārābī has chosen to continue or to modify (a task which cannot always be carried

[1] R. Walzer, 'Aspects of Islamic political thought: al-Fārābī and Ibn Khaldūn', *Oriens*, XVI (1963), pp. 46 ff.

[2] I refer (*a*) to his *Survey of Sciences*, which is available in Arabic and medieval Latin (cf. above, p. 646, n. 1); (*b*) to a work in three books: (1) *On Attaining Felicity*, English translation by M. Mahdi, *Alfarabi's Philosophy of Plato and Aristotle* (New York, 1962), pp. 13 ff; (2) *On the Philosophy of Plato = Plato Arabus*, II, with Latin translation and notes, by F. Rosenthal and R. Walzer, *op. cit.*, English translation by M. Mahdi pp. 53 ff; (3) *On the Philosophy of Aristotle*, ed. and translated by M. Mahdi *op. cit.* pp. 71 ff.; (*c*) *On Political Government*, partial translation in R. Gerner–M. Mahdi, *Medieval Political Philosophy* (New York, 1963), pp. 39 ff. German translation by F. Dieterici (Leiden, 1904).

[3] A German translation (F. Dieterici, *Der Musterstaat*, Leiden, 1900) and a French translation (by R. P. Janssen and others, Cairo, 1949) are available, both based on an unsatisfactory edition of the Arabic text. My references are to the French translation and—in brackets—to F. Dieterici's edition of the Arabic text (1895, recently reprinted).

out conclusively, since his immediate predecessors are unknown), considering at the same time the way in which he has succeeded in connecting his very abstract looking statements with definite non-Hellenic and Islamic questions.

A chapter towards the end of the book provides the key for the right understanding both of this particular book and of much of al-Fārābī's thought in general. Al-Fārābī says:[1] 'The results of philosophical research can be acquired in two ways: either they are imprinted in the souls of men as they are, or they are represented in them analogically so that symbols arise in their souls, which "imitate", reproduce, the abstract truth'; it is important to note that they may be verbal or visual symbols or symbols of any other conceivable kind—and not merely artistic symbols.

Now the philosophers are those who become aware of the truth through rigid demonstrations and their own insight. Those who follow them closely know reality as it is, making full use of the insight of the philosophers: they follow them, assent to their views and accept them on trust. But all the others know true reality through symbols which reproduce it analogically, since no natural or acquired disposition of their minds would enable them to understand it as it is. Both these kinds of knowledge are to be recognized as legitimate; but the knowledge of the philosopher is undoubtedly of a superior rank. Some of those who know the truth only through symbols know it through symbols which are very near to the truth, some through symbols which are slightly more remote, some through symbols which are still more remote than those, and some only through symbols which are very remote indeed.

There can be no doubt, I assume, that al-Fārābī points in this very abstract way to very definite religious beliefs and symbols with which his Muslim contemporaries were familiar. He continues:

Now truth—properly known to philosophers only—is reproduced for each nation (*umma*) and for the people of each city by those symbols which are most apt to be understood by them; but what is most apt to be understood is, in general, not the same among all nations; most, or at least part, of it varies. Hence the truth is expressed for each nation in symbols which are not the same as those used by any other nation. Thus it is possible that several

[1] Pp. 95 (69) f.

excellent nations and several excellent cities exist whose religions (*millal*) are unlike—although they all have as their goal one and the same felicity and one and the same purpose.

Al-Fārābī, obviously, distinguished between a philosophical truth, which is the same for all mankind but accessible to philosophical minds only, and religious symbols which express the same truth: these symbols, however, vary from nation to nation and are not universally valid, though they may be widely recognized. Like all the great Greek philosophers down to Porphyry, al-Fārābī is in no doubt about the primacy of philosophy. He chose neither to subordinate it to a revealed truth which he felt unable to recognize as such, as did al-Kindī (or later on, al-Ghazzālī), nor to identify religion and philosophy, as did Avicenna, the most influential Islamic philosopher. Nor, on the other hand, did it occur to him to follow the few Muslim outsiders like al-Rāzī, who set out to condemn religion altogether as superstition.

In looking at the position of philosophy in this way al-Fārābī follows a time-honoured Greek tradition which he makes completely his own and which he adapts to a contemporary situation which none of his Greek predecessors could ever have foreseen. To understand traditional Greek religion and myth as an approach to truth through symbols was an idea familiar to Greek philosophers since the days of Plato. It had, however, also been used for the understanding of foreign non-Greek religions. When, about the first century A.D., the traditional balance of Greek life was disturbed by the influx of oriental religions such as the Egyptian worship of Isis, and again later on, when faced by the increasing diffusion of Judaism and Christianity in the higher strata of society, this outlook had proved particularly useful for meeting this unexpected challenge. 'There is', says Plutarch[1] about A.D. 100, 'one divine mind which keeps the universe in order and one providence which governs it. The names given to this supreme God differ; he is worshipped in different ways in different religions; the religious symbols used in them vary, and their qualities are different, sometimes they are rather vague, and sometimes more distinct.' Plutarch is also very much aware of the danger of being conducted to truth solely by religious symbols: it may result either in abiding by superstition or by agnosticism and atheism.

[1] *De Iside et Osiride* 67, pp. 377 f.

A philosophical superstructure of religion—a natural theology—is therefore indispensable. Akin to Plutarch's attitude is, about a century later, Celsus' argument against Jews and Christians.[1] There can be no doubt that al-Fārābī was in sympathy with ideas of this kind. He actually appears to have found his own way to philosophy—which had as yet no recognized position in the Islamic world of his days—by patient and consistent criticism of different levels of symbolic representation and by determinedly turning away from religious fundamentalism, from scepticism and from atheism. These ideas remained quite popular in the later centuries of antiquity and appealed to the Neoplatonic way of thought. It is obvious that al-Fārābī had the same ideas as Plutarch in mind, when he distinguished between philosophy and the various religions in almost the same way. But the scene had changed in the meantime. Greek and Roman paganism had disappeared, and no traces of the pre-Christian religions of the Near East were left. Their place had been taken by Islam and Judaism and Christianity, by Zoroastrianism and Manichaeism, by Hinduism and Buddhism—religions which were all more or less known to educated Muslims in the tenth century of the Christian era. And al-Fārābī is not a Greek philosopher who tries to fit hitherto unknown religions into the established framework of Greek philosophy, but a Muslim who is for the first time undertaking to give philosophy a position within Islam comparable to the position which it had in the glorious but definitely bygone days of ancient civilization.[2] This attitude, in which I make bold to assert that the true originality of al-Fārābī really lies, manifests itself throughout the work we are considering.

C. *The world, man and society*

The book deals point by point with all the principal topics common to ancient philosophy. Like all later Greek philosophical works it contains views of different origin which are blended with each other and form a relatively harmonious compound. By uniting Peripatetic and Neoplatonic tenets, it represents a type of thought not uncommon in late antiquity, yet it is not identical with any particular school we know—but then we do not know very much about this period. Al-Fārābī's

[1] Origen, *Contra Celsum* I 24 (p. 74, 4 ff. Kötschau): cf. R. Walzer, *Galen on Jews and Christians*, pp. 44 ff.

[2] Cf. *Plato Arabus*, II, p. ix.

Aristotelianism is of the dogmatic kind, it conforms to the closed system which Peripatetic scholars of the Imperial age, Alexander of Aphrodisias and his like, had built up on Aristotelian foundations.[1] Neoplatonic features, the law of emanation in particular, prevail in the treatment of the First Cause and the world above the moon and the description of human perfection, but none of the more subtle and sometimes abstrusely complicated ideas of Iamblichus and Proclus and their companions have been adopted by al-Fārābī. Whereas most of the physical world below the moon is described according to orthodox Peripatetic views, the discussion of organized society, of the state, and of the qualifications of the ruler, is based on an otherwise unknown late Greek interpretation of Plato's *Republic* and *Laws*. Doubtless al-Fārābī will have had some Greek predecessor who likewise combined these heterogeneous trends of thought in this particular manner: this seems, at any rate, to be a very likely guess.

The double aim of the book is to show that human society in general must be organized in conformity with the hierarchical structure of the universe as discovered by the theoretical insight of the philosopher and that this general rule should be applied to Islamic society in particular. Hence it is not surprising that this twofold interest reflects itself in its composition, especially in so far as certain topics are treated at great length, and others just mentioned or deliberately skipped altogether. Al-Fārābī has himself divided the book into six sections (or 2 + 1 + 6 + 5 + 3 + 2 chapters) of varying size. The first[2] is exclusively concerned with metaphysics. The First Cause is one and unique; it is a mind which unceasingly thinks itself and in doing so enjoys itself. A continuous overflow of its substance makes it at the same time the eternal cause of the eternal existence of the universe and of everything in it. In the second section,[3] a rather short one, the eternal higher world above the moon is described. There are nine spheres. A separate, transcendent 'intellect' (νοῦς) is assigned to each of them, and other intellects reside within each of the spheres—which, in their turn, are the result of the self-thought of the respective 'separate' intellects. The lowest 'separate intellect' has no material sphere as its

[1] [For an account of the Peripatetic system of Alexander of Aphrodisias see Part I, ch. 6 B, pp. 116–23.]

[2] Pp. 13–33 (5–18).

[3] Pp. 34–5 (19 f.).

counterpart but serves as intermediary between the eternal world and the human mind. It is a late Greek metamorphosis of the Peripatetic 'active intellect'—the expression νοῦς ποιητικός is post-Aristotelian—and developed out of Alexander of Aphrodisias' interpretation of the rather ambiguous term. In section III[1] al-Fārābī deals with the transient sublunar world of becoming, of coming-to-be and passing away. He shows, like Aristotle and the later Peripatetics, how it depends on the higher world, to which it owes its perfection and its arrangement according to providential justice.

Section IV[2] is dedicated to man. Like section III, it is based on a very sensible late Greek co-ordination of several disciplines which had still been kept separate in the original Corpus Aristotelicum: the biological treatises, the different lecture-courses on psychology, and the *Nicomachean Ethics*. First, an analysis of the soul is provided which mainly follows Alexander of Aphrodisias' *De anima*; a nutritive faculty, sense perception, representation (φαντασία) and reason are distinguished. The fixed and unchangeable order of rank of these four faculties of the soul is stressed, reason ruling supreme. But whereas the maintenance of this order depends on the free decision of man, the hierarchy within the body is guaranteed by nature: all its organs and limbs are ultimately ruled by the heart, not by the brain. All the faculties of the soul are closely related to their bodily counterparts, their ruling activities are situated in the heart, with the exception of intuitive reason (which is in no need of a material substratum). Perfect human felicity results from the most accomplished activity of the human mind, but lower grades of felicity exist as well, provided that the respective individuals recognize the truth either by agreeing with the views of the philosophers or by accepting appropriate symbols. All these people are granted immortality and eternal bliss after their souls have been released from the body. The 'contact' of exceptional souls, i.e. the minds of perfect philosophers, with the absolute in the guise of the active intellect is defined, and it is unambiguously shown that they remain below the rank of this transcendent entity. Much space is taken up by a rational explanation of divination and of an apparently supranatural knowledge which is concerned with the realm of the transcendent as well as with particular events in

[1] Pp. 36–54 (20–34).

[2] Pp. 55–75 (34–53).

the future and in the present time. It reproduced an Aristotelian Hellenistic theory of divination and divine possession (μαντική and ἐνθουσιασμός) which has been slightly modified by Neoplatonic thought. Prophecy of this kind is definitely inferior to reason but it may come to its support. Prophets are then individuals of a peculiar excitability and of an unusual range of imagination, of a rare perfection of the faculty of representation.[1] The man who has reached the most perfect grade of humanity and who should, as we are told in section v, for this very reason be made the ruler of the perfect state, will be philosopher and prophet in one. Whoever is endowed with prophetic gifts only, without being an accomplished philosopher at the same time, can never be called perfect and never be considered worthy of governing the perfect state.

The fifth section no longer deals[2] with man in isolation but considers him now as a social being. Organized society—in the form of city-state, empire and universal state comprehending the whole inhabited world—becomes now the main topic. The philosopher-ruler is discussed at length, but, as by Plato himself, the 'citizens' are not neglected. (Al-Fārābī says 'the people': classical Arabic has no word for the 'citizen', the idea not being found in the Islamic world.) The same 'geometrical equality', the same justice which has been shown to exist by nature in the universe and in the human body, can, as a result of the choice of the enlightened human will, be established in human society as well, and the best and most perfect state can thus be brought about. The best ruler—and failing him the second and third best ruler—are described, and it is pointed out, in the Platonic way, that no state can survive in whose government philosophy has no share. A survey of those cities (or 'states') which al-Fārābī cannot commend follows: they are divided—Platonic distinctions having been developed in later centuries—into four groups, described from various points of view. In the tradition which eventually reached the Arabs, they will originally have corresponded to realities of the Greek and Roman scene; but it is not easy to make out how far they are meant by al-Fārābī to indicate special Islamic political circumstances at the same time.

[1] Cf. also *Greek into Arabic*, pp. 206 ff.

[2] Pp. 74–97 (53–71).

The sixth section, an important appendix to the main body of the work, deals in a very impressive way with the mistaken views of two of the states to be rejected, the states called 'ignorant'—with which we are familiar from Plato's *Republic* VIII–IX, and which were evidently discussed afresh by later Platonists—and the states said to be 'going astray', whose inhabitants despise the earthly life altogether, adhere to a kind of pseudo-revelation and hanker exclusively after felicity in the world-to-come. St Augustine's *City of God*, had it been known to al-Fārābī, would have fallen under this verdict. Citizens of 'ignorant' cities believe, for instance, that concord and unity of a state can be based exclusively on common descent from the same ancestor or on common language and history and the national character. Formal alliances cannot guarantee that leagues of tribes or nations are permanent. Furthermore, an 'affluent' society which would comprehend a major part of the earth and in which peace would prevail throughout—like the Roman Empire—would likewise fall short of the demands of true philosophy, since its scope would not go beyond the material welfare of its citizens.[1]

D. *Natural theology*

It would need a full-sized commentary, if one were to try to give a complete account of this well reasoned but by no means easy book. In the context of this necessarily brief chapter it must suffice to have indicated some essential features in the work of this pioneering Arabic thinker: al-Fārābī aimed at convincing a rather sophisticated Muslim public of the superiority of his new philosophical approach, by showing the interplay of philosophical truth and religious symbolism in his own peculiar way. He did not intend to hold forth on philosophy as such and was not satisfied to impart information about Greek philosophy for its own sake. He achieved his aim partly by pointing explicitly to the Islamic parallel, partly by letting the reader guess how his abstract statements might be related to the circumstances of his world and of his own day. We are reasonably well informed about the non-philosophical Muslim discussion during al-Fārābī's lifetime. It was widely concerned with issues which had troubled the ancient Greek philosophers as well, with God as the cause of this Universe of ours, with the origin of the

[1] Pp. 98–113 (71–85).

world, with man and the extent of his responsibility for his actions and his connexion with the higher world of the divine, but it had not yet become familiar with philosophical methods and with the kind of answers which philosophy alone could provide. The apparent miracle of prophecy and revelation had to be explained in the face of various criticisms and doubts; the fashioning of Muslim society according to the tenets of Scripture and Holy Law was seriously debated and so were the qualities which the Caliph (the successor of the Prophet as both spiritual and secular ruler of the realm of Islam) should possess. The most progressive leaders of this discussion were the Muslim speculative theologians the *mutakallimūn*. Al-Fārābī seems to have been the first to see the limitations of their scriptural and dialectical theology (which relied on Scripture and the faith of one particular religion). He is proud to represent a natural philosophical theology, which is the outcome of human reason and philosophical demonstration alone, and is deemed to be universally valid. Its answers are therefore superior to the answers given by the *mutakallimūn*, although their views are certainly nearer to philosophy than the fundamentalist orthodox tenets. Here are some examples:

The First Cause of Greek natural theology is, according to al-Fārābī, the same as Allāh in the symbolic language of the Qur'ān[1]—or Zeus in the pagan religion of the ancient Greeks[2] who no longer exist. The description of the First Cause as an immaterial self-thinking intuitive mind (νοῦς νοῶν νοούμενον), is not too far remote from the contemporary speculative theology of the so-called Mu'tazila,[3] which did away with Allāh's anthropomorphic features and established the Oneness and Uniqueness of God in a more subtle and refined way—although it did not come up to the requirements of philosophy. The epithets given to Allāh by the representatives of this advanced theology are still less precise and less comprehensive than the philosopher's statements about the First Cause, but they are recognized as pointing in the right direction. Whereas al-Kindī had agreed with the miraculous creation from nothing, in which all the Muslim theologians believed, and had given it a philosophical substructure (cf. above, p. 650), al-Fārābī replaced it by a

[1] Cf. p. i (i). [2] Cf. *Plato Arabus*, III, p. 5 (4).

[3] Cf. *Encyclopedia of Islam*, 1st edn, *s.v.* Mu'tazila, and 2nd edn, *s.v.* Allah.

timeless and unwilled emanation from the First Cause, as the Neoplatonists taught it; the creation from nothing may well have been considered by al-Fārābī as a symbolic description of a metaphysical process which cannot be grasped by ordinary minds.

Al-Fārābī equates the 'separate' intellects and the transcendent intellects placed within the various spheres of heaven with the 'angels' and 'spiritual beings' of the Muslim faith.[1] There exist no angels in reality, but only those entities of which we are informed through philosophy.

To provide a philosophical view of revelation and inspiration (ἐνθουσιασμός, *waḥy*) becomes an important feature of this natural theology. The answer given provides a substantial threat to cherished religious convictions. According to al-Fārābī, the Holy Spirit and the Trustworthy Spirit of the Qur'ān, the angel of revelation in the religious terminology, is the same as the 'active intellect' whose transcendent existence is demonstrated by human reason; they are just less precise terms.[2] Like the angel, the 'active intellect' intermediates between the First Cause and the divine world above the moon on one side, and man on the other. But man cannot establish a lasting contact with the higher world by coming close to the 'active intellect' unless he reaches the highest perfection of his mind which a human being can attain. A mystical union in the Plotinian way is expressly rejected as an old women's fairy-tale;[3] it is impossible as long as the 'intellect', the νοῦς, is not yet fully detached from the body. 'Revelation', 'divine inspiration' is thus nothing miraculous, but necessarily linked with the activity of human reason, and it should by no means be understood as being due to some inscrutable supranatural agency. The state of mind which Islam—like the other Hebraic religions—describes as 'the indwelling of the deity', as inspiration or revelation, is in fact nothing else but the result of the most perfect reasoning of the metaphysician, and it is in this way that Islam and cognate religions can be fully and most adequately understood in terms of Greek philosophy. According to al-Fārābī, prophecy is by no means man's supreme quality but is subordinate to philosophy and assists it. It does not reside in the rational faculty of the soul but is confined to a lower stratum, the faculty of representation. If the philo-

[1] Cf. p. 3 of Dieterici's translation of the 'Staatsleitung'.
[2] Cf. p. 665.
[3] Cf. p. 659.

sopher happens to be a prophet—in this sense—as well, he will be able to translate abstract metaphysics into religious symbols and thus become the founder of a religion. A philosopher-prophet of this type is the most perfect human being, and as such he is at the same time meant to be the ruler of the perfect state. He also would, according to the Platonic tradition, be the supreme legislator and be capable of convincing the common man of truth through the right form of oratory and of arranging his education in the proper way.[1] It is fascinating to observe how these Greek ideas can be made to fit the Islamic scene. It is not explicitly said, but can be almost with certainty be inferred from al-Fārābī's statement, that Muḥammad was such a man: only people mostly do not realize that he was primarily and mainly a philosopher, and prophet, legislator, orator and educator only in addition. The Qur'ān is nothing but a translation of philosophical truth into a symbolical language which non-philosophical Arabs can understand. It thus takes the place of Greek poetry in Plato's *Republic* or of the Gospels in Christianity.

The Caliph is the successor of the Prophet without being a prophet himself. It was not conceivable from an Islamic point of view that any other philosopher-prophet like Muḥammad should come after him. But it seems that the Greek tradition on which al-Fārābī drew also did not envisage that somebody like the first ruler of the perfect state would appear again and put things right. The good Caliph—who, however, could never reach the level of the founder of the religion—seems then to correspond to the second-best ruler of the best state of al-Fārābī's Greek political theory. He would be a philosopher, i.e. a Peripatetic metaphysician with strong Neoplatonic leanings, lacking in prophetic gifts but endowed with all the other qualifications of the perfect ruler. Al-Fārābī seems, as far as Islam is concerned, to have compared those second-best rulers to the four so-called orthodox caliphs, the immediate successors of the Prophet—who were always idealized in the Islamic tradition. The other possibilities of a philosophical government which he mentions, read rather like practical proposals for a change and can scarcely be referred to any special situation in Islamic history. A philosophical government could be brought about when a philosopher and a

[1] Cf. p. 59 (94).

politician could agree to work together—as Plato himself had tried to do (and failed) in Sicily. Should this prove to be impractical, the perfect state could be run by a team of persons each of whom would display one of the qualities required—a proposal vaguely comparable to the nocturnal council of Plato's *Laws*. Al-Fārābī, like Plato, says most emphatically that if there came to be a government without philosophy altogether, the caliphate would come to an end—unless it were saved and put right by philosophy.

E. *Greek philosophy and Muslim theology*

In this way, al-Fārābī's abstract book comes to life, once it is seen in the light of topics discussed in his own day: the time-honoured Greek treasure house of truth, whose contents he knows to perfection, provides him with answers to questions which no Greek philosopher had ever foreseen since no similar experiences could ever have occurred to him. This is, certainly, not the only achievement of Muslim philosophers—by commenting on the translated set books and rethinking the Greek doctrines they were also led to make additions to the inherited tradition—but it is a highly interesting and important new feature in the history of the Greek legacy outside the Greek world, and therefore deserves the special interest of the historian of philosophy. Another example: it is well known that Aristotle proclaimed man's responsibility for his own actions, and that the later Peripatetics maintained this view and restated it against the Stoic belief in a predetermined fate. Al-Fārābī followed them without apologizing for implicitly disagreeing with the very widespread Muslim belief in predestination. He must, however, have realized that in doing so he came very close to the advanced theology of the Mu'tazilites[1] who, though for different reasons, insisted that man alone is the author of his acts and will, moreover, be rewarded or punished for them in the after-life. It is not surprising that al-Fārābī's thoughts about the immortality of the soul—he does not even discuss the resurrection of the body, as al-Kindī does—come, again, very near to the convictions of the Mu'tazilite theologians. Recompense and eternal bliss in the after-life are reserved for those who have lived a good life according to the tenets of Greek philosophy,

[1] Cf. p. 662 n. 3.

either as active philosophers or as believers in their teachings, or as accepting the truth of philosophy on the level of religion through symbols. The souls of those who on their own initiative act against the truth, although they know it to perfection, will survive as well and meet eternal punishment. This again is, apart from the restriction of immortality to the soul, in full agreement with the Muʿtazilite view. Al-Fārābī, however, holds a view of his own—derived from Peripatetic sources—about the after-life of the people who, through no fault of their own, live in ignorance of the true good in every form in which it possibly could be presented to them: their souls disintegrate together with the body and are completely annihilated. But those who have deliberately misled them—al-Fārābī may think of the founders of false religions or of the obstinate Meccan adversaries of Muḥammad—will be punished as voluntary wrong-doers. Al-Fārābī thoroughly dislikes Hermetics and Gnostics and rejects the Neoplatonic trend represented by men like Iamblichus and Proclus. He adheres to a philosophical tradition which is nearer to the spirit of classical Greek thought. It is a mistaken view, he says, to assume that one can aim at attaining eternal bliss in the after-life while forgetting that a good life on earth is a necessary and indispensable stepping-stone to it. To take part in building up the excellent state is a major concern of the philosopher; he should not withdraw from politics as Plotinus had recommended. Asceticism is a wrong path to the eternal life—and in rejecting this, al-Fārābī was turning away at the same time from the rising tide of Muslim mysticism, which was to become very influential in the following centuries. Aristotle and the 'political' Plato appear to him as the appropriate guides for this world, whereas Plato the metaphysician—as the moderate Neoplatonists understood him—teaches men to prepare themselves for the world to come. Like Porphyry and other late Greek thinkers al-Fārābī is aware that humanity is in need of both, Plato and Aristotle. He represents, in this respect, a variant of the same tradition with which we are familiar from Raphael's 'School of Athens'—where Plato and Aristotle appear together on a higher level than all the other philosophers.

F. *The successors of al-Fārābī*

So much about al-Fārābī as the most outstanding representative of early Muslim philosophy. It seems to be due to him that philosophy became definitely naturalized in the Islamic world. Ibn Sīnā (Avicenna: A.D. 980–1037) and Ibn Rushd (Averroes: 1126–98)—to mention only his most eminent successors—built mainly on the foundations laid by him; they developed and modified these according to their own inclinations, the circumstances of their own days, and the conditions prevailing in the parts of the Islamic world in which they lived—Avicenna in different cities of Persia, Averroes mainly in Cordova in the later days of Muslim Spain. Avicenna's work continued to be studied intensely later on, particularly in Shi'ite surroundings in the East; also the achievement of al-Fārābī, who was highly appreciated by him, was not forgotten. Avicenna's impact on the Western Latin Schoolmen and on later European thought is likewise well known, although much detailed research is still needed to describe it fully and to understand its meaning. Averroes—who disagrees with Avicenna on many important issues and is, on the whole, much nearer to al-Fārābī's thought, was much less known in the Islamic world than Avicenna but became very influential in the West, especially through his commentaries on Aristotle. Both he and Avicenna are placed by Dante in Limbo (*Inferno*, IV, 143–4),[1] together with the distinguished heathen philosophers who could not receive baptism since they lived before the advent of Christianity—while Muḥammad and his son-in-law 'Alī are confined to the ninth bolgia in the eighth circle of Hell, as heretics and propagators of discord. Averroes' and Avicenna's true role in the West will, however, be more adequately understood once they have come to be properly appreciated in their own setting and in their own right.

Avicenna differs from al-Fārābī (apart from many minor features) in so far as his thought corresponds rather to a different trend in late Greek philosophy, the Neoplatonism of Plotinus and his followers in the more scholastic form which was given to it by Porphyry and others—which includes, however, a thorough study of Aristotle as well. He shows a deeper sympathy for mysticism than al-Fārābī and tries to explain it

[1] Al-Fārābī appears in Raphael's 'School of Athens'.

in philosophical terms. He also assesses the relation between Islam and philosophy in a way which reminds us of the Neoplatonic attitude to Greek religion: he neither subordinated philosophy to revelation—as did al-Kindī—nor did he, like al-Fārābī, give the second place to Islam by upholding the primacy of reason. Avicenna identified Islam and philosophy as it were, and maintained that Islam could not be adequately understood except in terms of philosophy. The prophetical gifts are no longer confined to the faculty of representation; the prophet has, in addition, become a kind of super-mind, he is *qua* prophet the most accomplished philosopher. The highest form of the ritual prayer of the mystic is for Avicenna identical with the silent contemplation of the Neoplatonic philosopher which is the outcome and the consummation of intense and protracted philosophical studies. Avicenna does not treat ethics and politics in his great philosophical encyclopaedia, which was so eagerly studied in the West. Unlike al-Fārābī, he prefers to concentrate on theoretical philosophy. The foundations of the perfect society are laid down by Qur'ān, Traditions and the Holy Law.

The position of philosophy in the Muslim world did not remain unchallenged for long. Things had been different in ancient civilization. The position of philosophy, as it had been established there in the centuries after Aristotle, was not attacked on its own level before the sixth century A.D., when the Christian Aristotelian John Philoponus voiced his disagreement. The pagan Greeks were not aware of a supranaturally revealed truth, nor did they believe in an omnipotent God who could override the laws of nature. John Philoponus' attack is ingenuous and yet impressive, but it seems to have been of little immediate consequence, and did not lead to the establishment of a Christian Aristotelianism on the lines suggested by him. In Islam, a comparable reaction against the supremacy of philosophy arose after a much shorter interval, about a generation after Avicenna's death, and it was probably helped by the precedent created by John Philoponus (whose works against Proclus and against Aristotle were known in Arabic in translation). The leader of this both spirited and highly competent opposition was al-Ghazzālī (058–1111) from Ṭūs in Persia, who undertook it while using all the tools provided by philosophy. He belongs to a movement which eventually led to the definite political ascendancy and consolidation of Sunnite Islam; as a theologian of the first order, he made a very outstanding and well-known contribution to this development. He came to reject al-Fārābī and Avicenna as unbelievers. The religious mind was dissatisfied with an intellectual and merely (or mainly) rational understanding of the world. This is not the place to describe his refutation of the philosophers' incoherence in detail, but he singles out three main points for reproach. The philosophers deny the resurrection of the body and thus differ not only from all the Muslims but from Jews and Christians as well; their view of divine providence is defective, since they say that God knows only universals but no particulars, and thus make God ignorant of individuals and not concerned with caring for them; they maintain that the world is everlasting, and in doing this misinterpret the omnipotence of the creator-god. On the whole, they are unaware that the religious life, and mystical experience in particular, represent a higher degree of knowledge than the certainty which human reason can attain. Al-Ghazzālī would in fact prefer to look at God as an immortal man instead of making him, with the followers of the philosophers, a dehumanized principle. 'His heart submits to a truth his reason cannot establish, for his heart has reasons his reason does not know.'[1]

Al-Ghazzālī's attack made little impact on the Shi'ite section, whereas it was, on the whole, successful within the orbit of Sunni Islam—i.e. in the greater part of the Muslim world. This fundamental difference appears less surprising if we keep in mind that a clear-cut and definite decision on the conflicting aims of Sunna and Shi'a is characteristic only of the centuries after al-Ghazzālī. Averroes' *Incoherence of the Incoherence*—in which he sets out to refute al-Ghazzālī—is certainly one of the most impressive and most accomplished of all Arabic philosophical works and has rightly attracted the attention of outstanding modern students of Islamic philosophy. But as far as medieval Islam is concerned, Averroes was fighting a losing battle. Philosophy, at least within the Sunnite tradition, could never again claim to be the best or the unique interpretation of Islam. It had to be satisfied with the place of a specialist and slightly suspect inferior kind of knowledge.

[1] Cf. S. van den Bergh, *Averroes* (above, p. 647 n. 3), 1, p. xxxvi.

SELECT BIBLIOGRAPHY

This bibliography makes no pretension to completeness. References to fuller bibliographies are given in the appropriate places in the several sections. The arrangement is as follows. First come a number of general works (including works on special subjects or problems relevant to more than one section). General histories of philosophy are not included: nor are general histories of the Church, the later Roman Empire, or medieval Europe, which often contain sections of varying length and value dealing with the subject-matter of this *History*. The bibliographies for each Part follow: each of them is divided into two parts, the first containing texts and some important translations, arranged in the order in which they are referred to in the Part, the second, other literature arranged by chapters, the order in each chapter-list being alphabetical. In addition to the books listed in the general section the following works of reference contain numerous relevant articles (some of the more important are listed individually in the appropriate places). *Paulys Realencyclopädie der classischen Altertumswissenschaft*; *Reallexicon für Antike und Christentum*; *Dictionnaire de Spiritualité*; *Dictionnaire de Théologie Catholique*; *Encyclopedia of Islam*; *Patristic Greek Lexicon*: this last is of fundamental importance for the understanding of Greek theological terms.

General

Altaner, R. *Patrology*. Freiburg–Edinburgh–London, 1960.

Aubin, P. *Le Problème de la 'conversion'*. Paris, 1962.

Bardenhewer, O. *Geschichte der altchristlichen Literatur*, 5 vols., 2nd ed. Freiburg, 1913–32 (reprinted 1962).

Courcelle, P. *Les lettres grecques en Occident*. Paris, 1948.

Entretiens Hardt, III. *Recherches sur la tradition platonicienne*. Vandœuvres–Genève, 1957.

Festugière, A. J. *La Révélation d'Hermès Trismégiste*, 4 vols. Paris, 1944–54.

Geffcken, J. *Der Ausgang der griechisch-römischen Heidentums*, with appendices. Heidelberg, 1929.

Gilson, E. *History of Christian Philosophy in the Middle Ages*. London, 1955.

Goodenough, E. R. *Jewish Symbols in the Greco-Roman Period*, 11 vols. New York, 1953–64.

Harnack, A. von. *Lehrbuch der Dogmengeschichte*, 3 vols. 4th edn. Tübingen, 1909–10. (English tr. of 3rd edn. *History of Dogma*, 2nd edn. New York, 1958.)

Huber, G. *Das Sein und das Absolute*. Basel, 1955.

Ivánka, E. von. *Plato Christianus. Übernahme und Umgestaltung des Platonismus durch die Väter*. Einsiedeln, 1964.

Jonas, H. *Gnosis und spätantiker Geist*. Göttingen. Vol. I, 3rd edn. 1964; vol. II, I, 1954; vol. II, 2, 1965.

Knowles, D. *The Evolution of Medieval Thought*. London, 1962.

Misch, G. *Geschichte der Autobiographie*, 3 vols. in 5. Frankfurt (1st vol. in 3rd edn.), 1949–62.
Overbeck, F. *Vorgeschichte und Jugend der mittelalterlichen Scholastik*. Basel, 1917.
Pépin, J. *Théologie cosmique et théologie chrétienne*. Paris, 1964.
Praechter, K. 'Richtungen und Schulen im Neuplatonismus', in *Genethliakon C. Robert*. Berlin, 1910.
Prestige, G. L. *God in Patristic Thought*, 2nd edn. London, 1952.
Rist, J. M. *Eros and Psyche: Studies in Plato, Plotinus and Origen*. Toronto, 1964.
Sarton, G. *Introduction to the History of Science*, 3 vols. in 5. Baltimore, 1927–48.
Spanneut, M. *Le stoïcisme des Pères de l'Église*. Paris, 1957.
Studia patristica. Papers presented to the International Conferences on Patristic Studies in Oxford. 7 vols. so far published. Berlin, 1957–66.
Totok, W. *Handbuch der Geschichte der Philosophie*, vol. I. Frankfurt, 1964.
Ueberweg, F. and Praechter, K. *Die Philosophie des Altertums*. 13th edn. Basel, 1953. (Photographic reprint of 12th edn. Berlin, 1926.)
Ueberweg, F. and Geyer, B. *Die patristische und scholastische Philosophie*, 11th edn. Berlin, 1928.
Vogel, C. J. de. *Greek Philosophy*, III, 2nd edn. Leiden, 1964.
Zeller, E. *Die Philosophie der Griechen*. 3 vols. in 6: various editions cited; last reprinted Hildesheim, 1963.

Part I. Greek Philosophy from Plato to Plotinus

[Editions of the works of Plato and Aristotle are not included in this bibliography. For editions of the works of Plotinus see Part III.]

SPEUSIPPUS *Fragments*, ed. P. Lang in *De Speusippi Academici scriptis*. Bonn, 1911 (reprinted Frankfurt, 1964).
XENOCRATES *Fragments*, ed. R. Heinze. Leipzig, 1892.
ANTIOCHUS *Fragments*, ed. G. Luck in *Der Akademiker Antiochus*. Bern, 1953.
PLUTARCH
Moralia, ed. G. N. Bernardakis, 7 vols. Leipzig, 1888–96.
Moralia, ed. C. Hubert, M. Pohlenz, etc.: in progress. Leipzig, 1952–.
Moralia, ed. and tr. F. C. Babbitt, etc. (Loeb Classical Library): in progress. London, 1927–.
ALBINUS
Ed. C. F. Hermann in *Platonis Dialogi*, 6 vols. Leipzig, 1921–36; vol. VI, pp. 147–89.
Épitomé, ed. P. Louis. Paris, 1945.
ANONYMOUS COMMENTARY ON THE THEAETETUS Ed. H. Diels and W. Schubart. Berlin, 1905.
APULEIUS *De Philosophia libri*, ed. P. Thomas. Leipzig, 1908.
ATTICUS *Fragments*, in Eusebius, *Praeparatio evangelica* XI 1–2; XV 4–12; ed. J. Baudry. Paris, 1931.
OCELLUS LUCANUS Ed. R. Harder. Berlin, 1926.

NICOMACHUS *Introductio arithmetica*, ed. R. Hoche. Leipzig, 1866.

NUMENIUS *Fragments*, ed. E. A. Leemans. Brussels, 1937.

THEOPHRASTUS *Metaphysics*, ed. and tr. W. D. Ross and F. H. Fobes. Oxford, 1929.

PERIPATETICS *Fragments*, ed. F. Wehrli (*Die Schule des Aristoteles*), 10 vols. Basel, 1944–59.

ARISTOCLES *Fragments*, ed. H. Heiland, *Aristoclis Messenii reliquiae*. Giessen, 1925.

ALEXANDER OF APHRODISIAS Commentaries on Aristotle, in *Commentaria in Aristotelem Graeca*, I–III. Berlin, 1891–9. Minor Works, ed. I. Bruns, in *Supplementum Aristotelicum*, II, 1–2. Berlin, 1887, 1892.

THE OLDER STOA *Stoicorum Veterum Fragmenta*, ed. J. von Arnim, 4 vols. Leipzig, 1903–24.

POSIDONIUS *Fragments*, ed. I. Bake. *Posidonii Rhodii reliquiae*. Leyden, 1820.

PANAETIUS *Fragments*, ed. M. van Straaten, 3rd edn. Leyden, 1962.

PSEUDO-ARISTOTLE *de mundo* Ed. and tr. D. J. Furley (Loeb Classical Library). London, 1955.

[For works on Plotinus containing discussions of the influence on him of earlier philosophers see Part III* and for works on later Neoplatonism Part IV, 1.]

Chapters 2–7

Baeumker, C. *Das Problem der Materie in der griechischen Philosophie*. Munich, 1890 (reprinted Frankfurt, 1963).

Krämer, H. J. *Der Ursprung der Geistmetaphysik*. Amsterdam, 1964.

Merlan, P. *From Platonism to Neoplatonism*, 2nd edn. The Hague, 1960.

—— *Monopsychism, Mysticism, Metaconsciousness*. The Hague, 1963.

Robin, L. *La théorie platonicienne des idées et des nombres d'après Aristote*. Paris, 1908 (reprinted Hildesheim, 1963).

Theiler, W. *Die Vorbereitung des Neuplatonismus*. Berlin, 1930.

—— 'Plotin und die antike Philosophie', in *Museum Helveticum*, 1 (1944), 209–25.

Chapter 2

Gercke, A. 'Eine platonische Quelle des Neuplatonismus', in *Rheinisches Museum*, 41 (1886), 226–91.

Vogel, C. J. de. 'On the Neoplatonic Character of Platonism and the Platonic Character of Neoplatonism', in *Mind*, 62 (1953), 43–64.

—— 'La théorie de l'ἄπειρον chez Platon et dans la tradition platonicienne', in *Revue Philosophique*, 149 (1959), 21–39.

Chapter 3

Bignone, E. *L'Aristotele perduto e la formazione filosofica di Epicuro*, 2 vols. Florence, 1936.

* In particular, several of the essays in *Entretiens Hardt*, v, *Les Sources de Plotin* are relevant to this Part.

Hamelin, O. *La théorie de l'intellect d'après Aristote et ses commentateurs*. Paris, 1953.

Kampe, F. F. *Die Erkenntnistheorie des Aristoteles*. Leipzig, 1870.

Chapter 4

Dodds, E. R. 'The *Parmenides* of Plato and the Origin of the Neoplatonic "One"', in *Classical Quarterly*, 22 (1928), 129–42.

Dörrie, H. 'Der Platoniker Eudoros von Alexandreia', in *Hermes*, 79 (1944), 25–39.

—— 'Kontroversen um die Seelenwanderung im kaiserzeitlichen Platonismus', in *Hermes*, 85 (1957), 414–35.

Freudenthal, J. *Der Platoniker Albinos und der falsche Alkinoos*. Berlin, 1879.

Lueder, A. *Die philosophische Persönlichkeit des Antiochos von Askalon*. Göttingen, 1940.

Praechter, K. 'Nikostratos der Platoniker', in *Hermes*, 57 (1922), 481–517.

—— 'Severos' and 'Tauros', in *Paulys Realencyclopädie*. Stuttgart, 2.2 (1923) and 5.1 (1934).

Sinko, T. *De Apulei et Albini doctrinae Platonicae adumbratione*. Kraków, 1905.

Strache, H. *Der Eklektizismus des Antiochos von Askalon*. Berlin, 1921.

Witt, R. E. *Albinus and the History of Middle Platonism*. Cambridge, 1937.

Ziegler, K. 'Plutarchos', in *Paulys Realencyclopädie*, 21.1 (1951).

Chapter 5

Beutler, R. 'Okellos' and 'Numenios', in *Paulys Realencyclopädie*, 17.2 (1937) and Suppl. 7 (1940).

Bickel, E. 'Neupythagoreische Kosmologie bei den Römern', in *Philologus*, 79 (1924), 355–69.

—— 'Senecas Briefe 58 und 65', in *Rheinisches Museum*, 103 (1960), 1–20.

Boyancé, P. 'Fulvius Nobilior et Le Dieu Ineffable', in *Revue de Philologie*, 29 (1955), 172–92.

Puech, H. C. 'Numénius d'Apamée et les théologies orientales au second siècle', in *Mélanges Bidez*, II (Brussels, 1934), 745–78.

Chapter 6

Immisch, C. 'Agatharchidea', in *Sitzungsberichte der Heidelberger Akademie d. Wissenschaften, philos.-hist. Kl.* 1919.7 (1919).

Moraux, P. *Alexandre d'Aphrodise*. Paris, 1942.

—— 'Quinta essentia', in *Paulys Realencyclopädie*, 24.1 (1963).

Thillet, P. 'Un traité inconnu d'Alexandre d'Aphrodise sur la Providence dans une version inédite', in *Actes du Premier Congrès International de Philosophie Médiévale : L'Homme et son destin* (Louvain, 1960), pp. 313–24.

Chapter 7

Jaeger, W. *Nemesios von Emesa*. Berlin, 1914.

Pohlenz, M. *Die Stoa*, 2 vols., 3rd edn. Göttingen, 1964.
Reinhardt, K. 'Poseidonios', in *Paulys Realencyclopädie*, 22.1 (1953).
Schmekel, A. *Philosophie der mittleren Stoa.* Berlin, 1892.

PART II. PHILO AND THE BEGINNINGS OF CHRISTIAN THOUGHT

PHILO

Works, ed. L. Cohn and P. Wendland, 6 vols. Berlin, 1896–1915 (works extant in Greek only).
Works, ed. and tr. F. H. Colson, G. H. Whitaker and R. Marcus: index by J. W. Earp (Loeb Classical Library), 12 vols. London, 1929–62.
Works, ed. and tr. R. Arnaldez, C. Mondésert and J. Pouilloux. Paris, 1961–.
The Fragments of Philo Judaeus, ed. Rendel Harris. Cambridge, 1886.
Neue Philontexte in der Überarbeitung des Ambrosius. H. Lewy. Berlin, 1932. (*Sitzungsberichte der preussischen Akademie*, IV, 23–84.)
In Flaccum, ed. H. S. Box. London and New York, 1939.
Legatio ad Gaium, ed. E. M. Smallwood. Leiden, 1962.
Latin translation of works extant only in Armenian paraphrase. Aucher. Venice, 1822; reprinted, Leipzig, 1830 and 1853 (Tauchnitz edition).

THE GREEK APOLOGISTS

PG 6.
Die ältesten Apologeten, ed. E. J. Goodspeed. Göttingen, 1914.
Theophilus of Antioch, ed. and tr. G. Bardy (*Sources Chrétiennes*). Paris, 1948.
Epistle to Diognetus, ed. and tr. H. I. Marrou (*Sources Chrétiennes*), Paris, 1951.
Justin, *Apologies*, ed. A. W. F. Blunt. 1911.

CLEMENT OF ALEXANDRIA

Works, *PG* 8–9.
Works, ed. O. Stählin, 4 vols. Berlin, 1905–36 (3rd edn. of *Stromata*, I–VI by L. Früchtel. Berlin, 1960).
Protrepticus, etc., ed. and tr. G. W. Butterworth (Loeb Classical Library). London, 1919.
A number of individual works in the series *Sources Chrétiennes.*

ORIGEN

Works, *PG*, 11–17.
Works, *Die Griechischen Christlichen Schriftsteller*, 12 vols. Berlin, 1899–1955.
Entretien d'Origène avec Héraclide, ed. and tr. J. Schérer (*Sources Chrétiennes*). Paris, 1960.
Philocalia, ed. J. A. Robinson. Cambridge, 1893.
De Principiis, translation and commentary by G. W. Butterworth. London, 1936.
Contra Celsum, translation and commentary by H. Chadwick. Cambridge, 1953.
A number of individual works in *Sources Chrétiennes.*

Select Bibliography

Chapter 8

[For literature on Philo prior to 1937 an exhaustive list is given by H. L. Goodhart and E. R. Goodenough, 'A general bibliography of Philo', in E. R. Goodenough, *The Politics of Philo Judaeus* (1938). For literature 1937–62 see L. H. Feldman, *Scholarship on Philo and Josephus* (New York, 1963).]

Bousset, W. *Jüdisch-christlicher Schulbetrieb in Alexandria und Rom.* Göttingen, 1915.

Bréhier, E. *Les idées philosophiques et religieuses de Philon d'Alexandrie*, 3rd edn. Paris, 1950.

Daniélou, J. *Philon d'Alexandrie.* Paris, 1958.

Goodenough, E. R. *By Light, Light.* New Haven, 1935.

—— *Introduction to Philo Judaeus*, 2nd edn. Oxford, 1962.

Heinemann, I. *Philons griechische und jüdische Bildung.* 1932 (reprinted 1962).

Lewy, H. *Sobria Ebrietas.* Giessen, 1929.

Pohlenz, M. 'Philon von Alexandreia', in *Nachrichten von der Akademie der Wissenschaften in Göttingen, Phil.-hist. Klasse*, 1942, Heft 5.

Völker, W. *Fortschritt und Vollendung bei Philo von Alexandrien.* Leipzig, 1938.

Wolfson, H. A. *Philo*, 2 vols. Cambridge (Mass.), 1947.

Chapter 9

Andresen, C. *Logos and Nomos.* Berlin, 1955.

Daniélou, J. *Message évangélique et culture hellénistique.* Tournai, 1961 (English tr. London, 1965). (Also for chapters 10 and 11.)

Geffcken, J. *Zwei griechische Apologeten.* Leipzig, 1907.

Pellegrino, M. *Studi sull'antica apologetica.* Rome, 1947.

Puech, A. *Les apologistes grecs.* Paris, 1912.

Chapter 10

Bigg, C. *The Christian Platonists of Alexandria*, 2nd edn. Oxford, 1913 (also for chapter 11).

Camelot, T. *Foi et Gnose.* Paris, 1945.

Faye, E. de. *Clément d'Alexandrie*, 2nd ed. Paris, 1906.

Mondésert, C. *Clément d'Alexandrie. Introduction à l'étude de sa pensée religieuse à partir de l'Écriture.* Paris, 1944.

Osborn, E. F. *The Philosophy of Clement of Alexandria.* Cambridge, 1957.

Tollinton, R. B. *Clement of Alexandria.* 1914.

Völker, W. *Der wahre Gnostiker nach Clemens Alexandrinus.* Berlin, 1952.

Chapter 11

[An almost exhaustive, classified bibliography of 643 items will be found in H. Crouzel, *Origène et la Connaissance Mystique* (Paris, 1961).]

Cadiou, R. *La jeunesse d'Origène.* Paris, 1935.

Crouzel, H. *Théologie de l'Image de Dieu chez Origène.* Paris, 1956.

—— *Origène et la philosophie*, Paris, 1962.

Daniélou, J. *Origène*. Paris, 1948 (English translation London, 1955).

Faye, E. de. *Origène*, 3 vols. Paris, 1923–8.

—— *Esquisse de la pensée d'Origène*. Paris, 1925 (English translation: *Origen and his Work*, 1926).

Hanson, R. P. C. *Allegory and Event*. London, 1959.

Harl, M. *Origène et la fonction révélatrice du Verbe incarné*. Paris, 1958.

Koch, Hal. *Pronoia und Paideusis: Studien über Origenes und sein Verhältnis zum Platonismus*. Leipzig, 1932.

Kerr, H. T. *The First Systematic Theologian, Origen of Alexandria*. (Princeton Pamphlets, 11). Princeton, N.J., 1958.

Lubac, H. de. *Histoire et Esprit*. Paris, 1950.

PART III. PLOTINUS

PLOTINUS *Enneads*

Ed. E. Bréhier (with French translation, introductions and notes), 7 vols. Paris, 1924–38.

Ed. R. Harder, continued by R. Beutler and W. Theiler (with German translation and notes: vols. I–III and V so far published: IV still to appear). Hamburg, 1956–.

Ed. P. Henry and H. R. Schwyzer (vols. I–II (*Vita Plotini* and *Enn.* I–V) so far published, vol. III (*Enn.* VI) still to appear). Paris and Brussels, 1951–.

Ed. P. Henry and H. R. Schwyzer (ed. minor, extensively revised: vol. I (*Enn.* I–III) so far published. Oxford, 1964–.

French translation by M. M. Bouillet (of value only for its extensive commentary), 3 vols. Paris, 1857–61.

Italian translation, with critical commentary, by V. Cilento, 3 vols. (the last contains an extensive bibliography by B. Mariën). Bari, 1947–9.

Latin translation by Marsilius Ficinus. Florence, 1492.

German translation by R. Harder (first edition of the translation later revised and reprinted with text and notes: see above), 5 vols. Leipzig, 1930–7.

English translation by S. MacKenna, 3rd edn., revised by B. S. Page. Introduction by P. Henry. London, 1962.

An English translation, with notes, of the revised Henry–Schwyzer text, by A. H. Armstrong, is appearing in the Loeb Classical Library (vols. I–II. London, 1966).

Chapters 12–16

Armstrong, A. H. *The Architecture of the Intelligible Universe in the Philosophy of Plotinus*. Cambridge, 1940.

—— 'Was Plotinus a Magician?', in *Phronesis*, I, 1 (1955), 73–9.

Arnou, R. *Le Désir de Dieu dans la philosophie de Plotin*. Paris, 1921.

Aubin, P. 'L'"Image" dans l'Œuvre de Plotin', in *Recherches de Science Religieuse*, 41, 3 (1953), 348–79.

Bourbon de Petrella, F. *Il Problema dell'Arte e della Bellezza in Plotino.* Florence, 1956.

Bréhier, E. *La philosophie de Plotin.* Paris, 2nd edn. 1961.

Crouzel, H. 'Origène et Plotin, élèves d'Ammonios Saccas', in *Bulletin de Littérature Ecclésiastique de Toulouse* (1956), 4, 193–214; (1958), 1, 3–7.

—— 'Encore Origène et Ammonios Saccas', in *Bulletin de Littérature Ecclésiastique de Toulouse* (1956), 4, 193–214; (1958), 1, 3–7.

Gandillac, M. de. *La Sagesse de Plotin.* Paris, 1952.

Keyser, E. de. *La signification de l'art dans les Ennéades de Plotin.* Louvain, 1955.

Dodds, E. R. 'Tradition and Personal Achievement in the Philosophy of Plotinus', in *Journal of Roman Studies*, 50 (1960), 1–7.

Hadot, P. *Plotin.* Paris, 1963.

Harder, R. 'Plotins Leben, Wirkung und Lehre', in *Kleine Schriften*, ed. W. Marg. Munich, 1960, 257–74.

—— Zur Biographie Plotins, in *Kleine Schriften*, ed. W. Marg. Munich, 1960, 275–95.

Entretiens Hardt, v. *Les sources de Plotin.* Vandœuvres–Genève, 1960.

Henry, P. 'La dernière parole de Plotin', in *Studi Classici e Orientali* (Pisa), II (1953), 113–30.

Himmerich, W. *Eudaimonia: die Lehre des Plotin von der Selbstverwirklichung des Menschen.* Würzburg, 1959.

Heinemann, F. *Plotin.* Leipzig, 1921.

Inge, W. R. *The Philosophy of Plotinus*, 2 vols., 3rd edn. London, 1929 (reprinted 1948).

Kristeller, O. O. *Der Begriff der Seele in der Ethik des Plotin.* Tübingen, 1929.

Lloyd, A. C. 'Neoplatonic and Aristotelian Logic', in *Phronesis*, 1 (1955–6), 58–72 and 146–59 (also for Part IV, ch. 19).

Merlan, P. 'Plotinus and Magic', in *Isis*, 44 (1953), 341–8.

Rist, J. M. 'Plotinus on Matter and Evil', in *Phronesis*, 6 (1961), 154–66.

Schwyzer, H. R. 'Plotinos', in *Paulys Realencyclopädie*, 21.1 (1951).

Trouillard, J. *La Purification Plotinienne.* Paris, 1955.

—— *La Procession Plotinienne.* Paris, 1955.

—— 'Valeur critique de la mystique plotinienne', in *Revue philosophique de Louvain*, 59 (1961), 431–44.

Part IV. The Later Neoplatonists

PORPHYRY

Life of Plotinus. Printed in all editions and translations of Plotinus listed in previous section: with German translation and notes in Harder vc (1958).

De philosophia ex oraculis haurienda librorum reliquiae, ed. G. Wolff. Berlin, 1856 (reprinted Hildesheim, 1962).

Against the Christians, fragments, ed. A. Harnack, in *Abhandlungen der preussischen Akademie der Wissenschaften, phil.-hist. Kl.* 1916, I (additions in *ibid. Sitzungsberichte*, 1921, I, 266–84 and II, 834 ff.).

Ad Gaurum, ed. K. Kalbfleisch, in *Abhandlungen der preussischen Akademie der Wissenschaften, phil.-hist. Kl.* 1895, 33–62 [authenticity disputed]: French translation by J. M. Festugière, *La Révélation d'Hermès Trismégiste*, III, app. I.

Letter to Anebo, ed. and tr. A. R. Sodano. Naples, 1958 [reconstructed from Iamblichus, *De Mysteriis*].

De abstinentia: in *Porphyrii Opuscula Selecta*, ed. A. Nauck, 2nd edn. Leipzig, 1886 (reprinted Hildesheim, 1963).

Ad Marcellam: in the same.

Ad Marcellam, French translation by A. J. M. Festugière, in *Trois dévots païens*, II. Paris, 1934.

Sententiae ad intelligibilia ducentes, ed. B. Mommert. Leipzig, 1907.

Isagoge sive quinque voces, ed. A. Busse, in *Commentaria in Aristotelem graeca*, IV, I. Berlin, 1887.

Isagoge sive quinque voces, French translation with notes by J. Tricot. Paris, 1947.

Commentary on the Timaeus, fragments, ed. R. Sodano. Naples, 1964.

ANONYMUS TAURINENSIS Ed. W. Kroll, 'Ein neuplatonischer Parmenidescommentar in einem Turiner Palimpsest', in *Rheinisches Museum für Philologie*, 47 (1892), 599–627.

IAMBLICHUS

On the Soul, French translation [of Stobaeus's extracts] with notes by A. J. M. Festugière, *La Révélation d'Hermès Trismégiste*, III, app. I.

De vita pythagorica, ed. L. Deubner. Leipzig, 1937.

Protrepticus, ed. L. Pistelli. Leipzig, 1888.

Theologumena arithmeticae, ed. V. de Falco. Leipzig, 1922.

De communi mathematica scientia, ed. N. Festa. Leipzig, 1891.

De Mysteriis, ed. G. Parthey. Berlin, 1857.

De Mysteriis, German translation with introduction and notes by T. Hopfner (Quellenschriften der griechischen Mystik, I). Leipzig, 1922.

De Mysteriis. A critical edition by M. Sicherl is in preparation.

JULIAN

Ed. F. C. Hartlein, 2 vols. Leipzig, 1875–6.

Ed. and tr. W. C. Wright (Loeb Classical Library), 3 vols. London, 1913–23.

PROCLUS

In Platonis Rempublicam commentarii, ed. W. Kroll, 2 vols. Leipzig, 1899–1901.

In Platonis Cratylum commentarii, ed. G. Pasquali. Leipzig, 1908.

Commentary on the First Alcibiades of Plato, ed. L. G. Westerink. Amsterdam, 1954.

Commentary on the First Alcibiades of Plato, English translation with notes by W. O'Neill. The Hague, 1965.

Commentarius in Parmenidem, ed. V. Cousin, 2nd edn. Paris, 1864 (reprinted Hildesheim, 1961).
Commentarius in Parmenidem: pars ultima adhuc inedita, interprete Guillelmo de Moerbeka, ed. and tr. R. Klibansky, C. Labowsky, E. Anscombe. London, 1953.
In Platonis Timaeum commentarii, ed. E. Diehl, 3 vols. Leipzig, 1903–6.
In Platonis Timaeum commentarii. A French translation by A. J. M. Festugière is in preparation.
Elements of Theology, ed. and tr. E. R. Dodds, 2nd edn. Oxford, 1963.
Elements of Theology, French translation by J. Trouillard. Paris, 1965.
In Platonis Theologiam, ed. A. Portus. Hamburg, 1618.
In Platonis Theologiam, Italian translation by A. Turolla. Bari, 1957.
In Platonis Theologiam, A new critical edition, with French translation, by H. D. Saffrey and L. G. Westerink, is in preparation.
Tria opsucula (*De Decem Dubitationibus*, *De Providentia et Fato*, *De Malorum Subsistentia*), ed. H. Boese. Berlin, 1960.
On the Hieratic Art, ed. and tr. J. Bidez, in *Catalogue des manuscrits alchimiques grecs*, VI (appendix). Brussels, 1928.
Hymni, ed. E. Vogt. Wiesbaden, 1957.
Eclogae de philosophia chaldaica, ed. A. Jahn. Halle, 1891.

MARINUS *Vita Procli*, ed. J. F. Boissonade. Leipzig, 1814 (reprinted in *Procli opera inedita*, ed. V. Cousin, 2nd ed. Paris, 1864 and *Diogenes Laertius*, ed. C. G. Cobet, Paris, 1878).

DAMASCIUS
Life of Isidoros, ed. and tr. R. Asmus. Leipzig, 1911 [extracts from Photius, *Bibliotheca* cod. 242. (Migne, *PG* 103)].
Life of Isidoros, ed. E. Zintzen. Hildesheim, 1965.
Dubitationes et solutiones de primis principiis, ed. C. A. Ruelle, 2 vols. Paris, 1889. A new critical edition is in preparation.

HIEROCLES
De Providentia et Fato [extracts] in Photius, *Bibliotheca* cod. 214 and 251 (Migne, *PG* 103).
Commentarius in aureum carmen, ed. F. W. A. Mullach, in *Fragmenta philosophorum graecorum*, I. Paris, 1883.

SYNESIUS *De Providentia*, ed. N. Terzaghi, in *Synesii Cyrenensis opuscula*. Rome, 1944. Migne, *PG* 76.

HERMIAS ALEXANDRINUS *In Platonis Phaedrum scholia*, ed. P. Couvreur. Paris, 1901.

OLYMPIODORUS
Commentary on the First Alcibiades of Plato, ed. L. G. Westerink. Amsterdam, 1956.
In Platonis Phaedonem, ed. W. Norvin. Leipzig, 1913.
In Platonis Gorgiam, ed. W. Norvin. Leipzig, 1936.

SIMPLICIUS. *Commentarius in Epicteti Enchiridion*, ed. F. Dübner, in *Theophrasti characteres*, etc. Paris, 1877.

Ed. J. Schweighäuser, in *Epicteti philosophia*, IV. Leipzig, 1800.

[The Alexandrian Neoplatonist commentaries on Aristotle are published in *Commentaria in Aristotelem graeca*. Berlin, 1882–1907.]

EUNAPIUS. *Lives of the Sophists*, ed. J. Giangrande. Rome, 1956.

CHALDAEAN ORACLES. Ed. W. Kroll, *De Oraculis Chaldaicis*. Breslau, 1894 (reprinted Hildesheim, 1962).

Chapter 17

Bidez, J. *La vie de l'Empereur Julien*. Paris, 1930.

Dodds, E. R. 'Theurgy and its relation to Neoplatonism', in *Journal of Roman Studies*, 37 (1947), 55–69 (reprinted in *The Greeks and the Irrational*, Berkeley (Cal.), 1951, app. II).

Geffcken, J. *Der Ausgang des griechisch-römischen Heidentums*. Heidelberg, 1920.

Lewy, H. *Chaldaean Oracles and Theurgy*. Cairo, 1956.

Westerink, L. G. 'Proclus, Procopius, Psellus', in *Mnemosyne*, ser. 3, 10 (1942), 275–80.

Whittaker, T. *The Neoplatonists*, 2nd edn. Cambridge, 1928.

Chapter 18

Beutler, R. 'Porphyrios', in *Paulys Realencyclopädie*, 22.1 (1953).

Bidez, J. *Vie de Porphyre*. Ghent–Leipzig, 1913 (reprinted Hildesheim, 1964).

—— 'Le philosophe Jamblique et son école', in *Revue des études grecques*, 32 (1919), 29–40.

Dörrie, H. *Porphyrios' 'Symmikta Zetemata'*. Munich, 1959.

Fronte, S. 'Sull'autenticità del 'De Mysteriis' di Giamblico', in *Siculorum Gymnasium* (Catania), N.S. 7 (1954).

Hadot, P. 'Fragments d'un commentaire de Porphyre sur le Parménide', in *Revue des études grecques*, 74 (1961), 410–38.

Rasche, C. *De Iamblicho libri qui inscribitur de mysteriis auctore*. Diss. Münster, 1911.

Chapter 19.

[The most important modern work on Athenian Neoplatonism is the commentary of E. R. Dodds on Proclus, *Elements of Theology* (see above, p. 679).]

Courcelle, P. 'Boèce et l'école d'Alexandrie', in *Mélanges de l'école française de Rome*, 53 (1935), 185–223.

Grondijs, L. H. 'L'âme, le nous et les hénades dans la théologie de Proclus', in *Mededelingen der koninklijke nederlandse Akademie van Wetenschappen, Afd. Letterkunde*, N.R. 23 (1960), pp. 29–42.

Joseph, H. W. B. *An Introduction to Logic*, 2nd edn. Oxford, 1916.

Lloyd, A. C. 'Neoplatonic and Aristotelian Logic' (see above, p. 677).

Lovejoy, A. O. *The Great Chain of Being*. Cambridge (Mass.), 1936.

Marrou, H. I. 'Synesius of Cyrene and Alexandrian Neoplatonism', in A. Momigliano (ed.), *The Conflict between Paganism and Christianity in the Fourth Century*. Oxford, 1963.

Rosán, L. J. *The Philosophy of Proclus*. New York, 1949 (with extensive bibliographies).

Saffrey, H. D. 'Le chrétien Jean Philopon et la survivance de l'école d'Alexandrie au VIe siècle', in *Revue des études grecques*, 72 (1954), 396–400.

Sambursky, S. *The Physical World of Late Antiquity*. London, 1962.

Shiel, J. 'Boethius' commentaries on Aristotle', in *Mediaeval and Renaissance Studies*, 4 (1958), 217–44.

Tatakis, B. *La philosophie byzantine*. Paris, 1949.

Trouillard, J. 'Le sens des médiations proclusiennes', in *Revue philosophique de Louvain*, 55 (1957), 331–42.

Vancourt, R. *Les derniers commentateurs alexandrins d'Aristote: l'école d'Olympiodore, Étienne d'Alexandrie*. Lille, 1941.

Westerink, L. G. *Anonymous Prolegomena to Platonic Philosophy*. Amsterdam, 1962.

PART V. MARIUS VICTORINUS AND AUGUSTINE

MARIUS VICTORINUS

Ad Candidum, in *Traités théologiques sur la Trinité*, ed. P. Henry and P. Hadot [with introduction, French translation and notes] (*Sources Chrétiennes*). Paris, 1960.

Adversus Arium, in *Traités théologiques sur la Trinité* (see above).

Ars grammatica, ed. H. Keil, *Grammatici latini*, vol. 6 (Leipzig, 1874), 1–184.

Candidi Epistola I and II, in *Traités théologiques sur la Trinité*.

Explanationes in rhetoricam Ciceronis, ed. O. Halm, *Rhetores latini minores* (Leipzig, 1863), pp. 153–304.

Hymns, in *Traités théologiques sur la Trinité*.

In epistolam Pauli ad Ephesios, *PL* 8, 1235–94.

In epistolam Pauli ad Galatas, *PL* 8, 1145–98.

In epistolam Pauli ad Philippenses, *PL* 8, 1197–1236.

Liber de diffinitione, *PL* 64. 891–910 [ps.-Boethius].

AUGUSTINE For list of Augustine's works referred to in this Part see pp. 329–30. There is a full list in Andresen's bibliography (see below).

Chapter 20

Benz, E. *Marius Victorinus und die Entwicklung der abendländischen Willensmetaphysik*. Stuttgart, 1932.

Hadot, P. '*De lectis non lecta conponere* (M. Victor., adv. Ar. II 7)', in *Studia Patristica*, I (*Texte und Untersuchungen*, 63). Berlin, 1957, pp. 209–20.

—— 'L'Image de la Trinité dans l'âme chez Victorinus et chez saint Augustin', in *Studia Patristica*, 6 (*Texte und Untersuchungen*, 81). Berlin, 1962, pp. 409–42.

Henry, P. 'The *Adversus Arium* of Marius Victorinus: the first systematic exposition of the doctrine of the Trinity', in *J. Theol. Stud.* N.S. 1 (1950), 42–55.

Chapters 21–7.

[A very full Augustine bibliography is C. Andresen, *Bibliographia Augustiniana.* Darmstadt, 1962.]

Baynes, N. H. *The Political Ideas of St Augustine's 'De civitate Dei'.* London, 1936.

Bonner, G. *St Augustine of Hippo.* London, 1963.

Boyer, C. *Christianisme et néo-Platonisme dans la formation de saint Augustin.* Paris, 1920.

—— *L'idée de vérité dans la philosophie de saint Augustin*, 2e éd. Paris, 1941.

Burnaby, J. *Amor Dei.* London, 1938.

Cayré, F. *Initiation à la philosophie de saint Augustin.* Paris, 1947.

Courcelle, P. *Recherches sur les Confessions de saint Augustin.* Paris, 1950.

Deane, H. A. *The Political and Social Ideas of St Augustine*, New York and London, 1963.

Deman, P. T. *Le traitement scientifique de la morale chrétienne selon saint Augustin.* Paris, 1957.

Dinkler, E. *Die Anthropologie Augustins.* Stuttgart, 1964.

Fuchs, H. *Augustin und der antike Friedensgedanke.* Berlin, 1926.

Gilson, E. *The Christian Philosophy of Saint Augustine*, transl. by L. E. M. Lynch. London, 1961.

Guitton, J. *Le temps et l'éternité chez Plotin et saint Augustin*, 2e éd. Paris, 1955.

Hessen, J. *Augustins Metaphysik der Erkenntnis*, 2te Aufl. Berlin.

Holte, R. *Béatitude et Sagesse: St. Augustin et le problème de la fin de l'homme dans la philosophie ancienne.* Paris, 1962.

Jolivet, R. *Dieu soleil des esprits.* Paris, 1934.

Kamlah, W. *Christentum und Geschichtlichkeit.* Stuttgart, 1951.

Lauras, A. and Rondet, H. 'Le thème des deux cités dans l'œuvre de s. Augustin,' in *Études augustiniennes* (Paris, 1953), pp. 97–160.

Lorenz, R. 'Die Wissenschaftslehre Augustins', in *Zeits. f. Kirchengesch.* 67 (1955–6), 29–60, 213–51.

Maier, F. G. *Augustin und das antike Rom.* Stuttgart, 1956.

Marrou, H. I. *Saint Augustin et la fin de la culture antique.* Paris, 1938 [and *Retractatio*, Paris, 1949].

—— *Saint Augustine and his Influence through the Ages.* London, 1957.

Mausbach, J. *Die Ethik des heiligen Augustinus.* Freiburg, 1909.

Mommsen, T. E. 'Augustine's theory of progress' and 'Augustine and Orosius', reprinted in *Medieval and Renaissance Studies.* New York, 1959.

O'Meara, J. J. *The Young Augustine.* London, 1954.

Ratzinger, J. *Volk und Haus Gottes in Augustinus' Lehre von der Kirche.* München, 1954.

Schmaus, M. *Die psychologische Trinitätslehre des Heiligen Augustinus.* Münster, 1907.

Straub, J. 'Christliche Geschichtsapologetik in der Krisis des römischen Reiches', in *Historia,* 1 (1950), 52–81.

—— 'Augustins Sorge um die regeneratio imperii', in *Histor. Jahrb.* 73 (1954), 36–60.

Wachtel, A. *Beiträge zur Geschichtstheologie des Aurelius Augustinus.* Bonn, 1960.

Collective works

Augustinus Magister: Congrès international augustinien, 3 vols. Paris, 1954.

Recherches augustiniennes, 1. Paris, 1958.

PART VI. THE GREEK CHRISTIAN PLATONIST TRADITION FROM THE CAPPADOCIANS TO MAXIMUS AND ERIUGENA

ST BASIL

Works, PG 29–32.

Homiliae in Hexaëmeron, ed. and tr. S. Giet (*Sources Chrétiennes*). Paris, 1950.

On the Holy Spirit, ed. and tr. B. Pruche (*Sources Chrétiennes*). Paris, 1947.

ST GREGORY NAZIANZEN

Works, PG 35–8.

Orationes 27–31 (*Orationes theologicae*), ed. A. J. Mason. Cambridge, 1899.

ST GREGORY OF NYSSA

Works, PG 44–6.

Works, ed. W. Jaeger, H. Langerbeck, etc. Leiden, 1952–, in progress.

Oratio catechetica, ed. J. H. Srawley. Cambridge, 1903.

De Vita Moysis, ed. and tr. J. Daniélou (*Sources Chrétiennes*). Paris, 1956.

PSEUDO-DIONYSIUS

Works, PG 3.

De caelesti hierarchia, ed. and tr. R. Roques, G. Heil, M. de Gandillac (*Sources Chrétiennes*). Paris, 1958.

JOHN OF SCYTHOPOLIS *Works, PG* 4.

JOHN PHILOPONUS

De aeternitate mundi contra Proclum, ed. H. Rabe. Leipzig, 1899 (reprinted 1964).

De opificio mundi, ed. G. Reinhardt. Leipzig, 1897.

AENEAS OF GAZA *Theophrastus, PG* 85. 865–1004.

ZACHARIAS OF GAZA *Ammonius, PG* 85. 1011–1144.

PROCOPIUS OF GAZA *Works, PG* 87.

LEONTIUS THE HERMIT

Libri tres contra Nestorianos et Eutychianos, PG 86. 1. 1268 ff.

Solutio argumentorum Severi, PG 86. 2. 1916ff.

ST MAXIMUS CONFESSOR

Works, PG 90–1.

'Gnostic Century', in S. L. Epifanović, *Materials to serve in the Study of the Life and Works of S. Maximus Confessor*. Kiev, 1917.
Ascetic Life and *Centuries on Charity*, tr. and annotated by P. Sherwood. Westminster (Mld) and London, 1955.

ST JOHN DAMASCENE *De Sacris Imaginibus Orationes*, *PG* 94. 1232 f.

NICEPHORUS OF CONSTANTINOPLE
Works, *PG* 100.
Contra Eusebium et Epiphanidem, ed. J. B. Pitra, *Spicilegium solesmense* (Paris, 1852–8), I, 371–503; IV, 292–380.

ST GERMANUS OF CONSTANTINOPLE *Epistola dogmatica*, II, *PG* 98. 156 ff.

ANONYMOUS COMMENTATOR ON ST JOHN'S GOSPEL Ed. K. Hausmann. Paderborn, 1930.

JOHANNES SCOTTUS ERIUGENA
Works, *PL* 122.
Periphyseon, ed. I. P. Sheldon-Williams. (In preparation.)
Annotationes in Marcianum, ed. C. Lutz. Cambridge (Mass.), 1939.
Commentary on Boethius, '*De consolatione Philosophiae iii met. 9*', ed. H. Silvestre, in *Revue d'histoire ecclésiastique*, 17 (1952), 44–122.
Expositiones super Ierarchiam caelestem iii–vii, ed. H. F. Dondaine, in *Archives d'histoire doctrinale et littéraire du Moyen Âge*, 18 (1951), 252–301.

Chapter 28

Fortin, E. L. *Christianisme et culture philosophique au 5ème siècle*. Paris, 1959.
Ivánka, E. von. *Hellenisches und Christliches im frühbyzantinischen Geistesleben*. Vienna, 1948.
Jaeger, W. *Nemesius von Emesa*. Berlin, 1914.
Koch, H. 'Ps.-Dionysius Areopagita in seinen Beziehungen zum Neuplatonismus und Mysterienwesen', *Forschungen zur christlichen Literatur und Dogmengeschichte*, I, 2–3. Mainz, 1900.
Lossky, V. *Théologie mystique de l'Église d'Orient*. Paris, 1944 (English translation, London, 1956).
Lot-Borodine. 'La doctrine de la déification dans l'église grecque', in *Revue d'histoire des religions* (1932), pp. 5 ff., 525 ff.; (1933), pp. 8 ff.
Stephenson, A. A. 'St Cyril of Jerusalem and the Alexandrian Christian Gnosis', in *Studia Patristica*, I (Berlin, 1957), 142–56.

Chapter 29

Balthasar, H. von. *Présence et pensée: Essai sur la philosophie religieuse de Grégoire de Nysse*. Paris, 1942.
Daniélou, J. *Platonisme et théologie mystique*, 2nd edn. Paris, 1953.
Plagnieux, J. *Saint Grégoire de Nazianze théologien*. Paris, 1951.
Tatakis, B. 'Η συμβολὴ τῆς Καππαδοκίας στὴ Χριστιανικὴ σκέψη (*The contribution of Cappadocia to Christian Thought*). Athens, 1960.
Völker, W. *Gregor von Nyssa als Mystiker*. Wiesbaden, 1955.

Chapter 30

Hornus, J. M. 'Les recherches récentes sur le ps. Denys l'Aréopagite', in *Revue d'histoire et de philosophie religieuse*, 35 (1955), 404–8.

——'Les recherches dionysiennes du 1955–60', *ibid.* 41 (1961), 22–81.

Lossky, V. 'La notion des "analogies" chez le ps. Denys l'Aréopagite', in *Archives d'histoire doctrinale et littéraire du Moyen Âge*, 5 (1930), 279–309.

—— 'La théologie négative dans la doctrine de Denys l'Aréopagite', in *Revue des sciences philosophiques et théologiques*, 28 (1939), 204–21.

Roques, A. *L'univers dionysien.* Paris, 1954.

Rutledge, D. *Cosmic Theology* (commentary on the *Ecclesiastical Hierarchy*). London, 1964.

Sheldon-Williams, I. P. 'The Ecclesiastical Hierarchy of Ps.-Dionysius', in *Downside Review*, 82 (1964), 293–302 and 83 (1965), 20–31.

Vanneste, J. *Le mystère de Dieu. Essai sur la structure de la doctrine mystique du ps. Denys l'Aréopagite.* Brussels, 1959.

Völker, W. *Kontemplation and Ekstase bei ps. Dionysius Areopagita.* Wiesbaden, 1958.

Chapter 31

Balthasar, H. von. 'Das Scholienwerk des Johannes von Scythopolis', in *Scholastik*, 15, 1 (1940), 16–38.

Sambursky, S. See Part IV, chapter 19.

Tatakis, B. See Part IV, chapter 19.

Vancourt, R. See Part IV, chapter 19.

Chapter 32

Balthasar, H. von. *Kosmische Liturgie*, 2nd edn. Einsiedeln, 1961 (French translation of 1st edn. Paris, 1947).

Sherwood, P. *The Earlier Ambigua of St Maximus the Confessor and his Refutation of Origenism.* Rome, 1955.

Tatakis, B. See Part IV, chapter 19.

Chapter 33

Alexander, P. J. *The Patriarch Nicephorus of Constantinople.* Oxford, 1958.

Baynes, N. H. 'Idolatry in the Early Church', in *Byzantine Studies* (London, 1955), pp. 116–43.

—— 'The Icons before Iconoclasm', in *Byzantine Studies* (London, 1955), pp. 227–39.

Ladner, G. B. 'The Concept of the Image in the Greek Fathers and the Byzantine Iconoclastic Controversy', in *Dumbarton Oaks Papers*, 7 (1953), 3–34.

Ostrogorsky, G. *Studien zur Geschichte des byzantinischen Bilderstreites.* Breslau, 1929.

Tatakis, B. See Part IV, chapter 19.

Chapter 34

Cappuyns, M. *Jean Scot Érigène: Sa vie, son œuvre, sa pensée*. Louvain and Paris, 1933 (with full bibliography of works printed before that date) (reprinted 1964).

dal Pra, M. *Scoto Eriugena ed il neoplatonismo medievale*. Milan, 1941.

—— *Scoto Eriugena*. Milan, 1951.

Mazzanella, P. *Il pensiero di Giovanni Scoto Eriugena*. Padua, 1957.

Sheldon-Williams, I. P. 'A Bibliography of the Works of Johannes Scottus Eriugena', in *Journal of Ecclesiastical History*, 10, 2 (1960), 198–224.

Théry, P. G. *Études dionysiennes*. Paris, 1932–7.

PART VII. WESTERN CHRISTIAN THOUGHT FROM BOETHIUS TO ANSELM

BOETHIUS

Works, *PL* 63–4.

In Isagogen Porphyrii commenta (*editio prima; editio secunda*), ed. S. Brandt. *CSEL* 48.

Theological Tractates, ed. and tr. H. F. Stewart and E. K. Rand (Loeb Classical Library). London, 1918 (last reprinted 1953).

De Consolatione Philosophiae, ed. and tr. H. F. Stewart and E. K. Rand (Loeb Classical Library). London, 1918 (last reprinted 1953).

De Consolatione Philosophiae, ed. Weinberger. *CSEL* 67.

De Sancta Trinitate ad Symmachum, ed. H. F. Stewart and E. K. Rand, *in Theological Tractates*, Loeb Library, 1918 (see above).

ISIDORE OF SEVILLE

Works, *PL* 81–4.

Etymologiarum sive Originum libri XX, ed. W. M. Lindsay, 2 vols. Oxford, 1911.

Traité de la nature, ed. and tr. J. Fontaine. Bordeaux, 1960.

'LIBRI CAROLINI'

PL 98, 99–1248.

Ed. H. Bastgen. *M.G.H.*, *Concilia*, II, Suppl. 1924.

AGOBARD OF LYONS

PL 104, 29–350.

M.G.H., *Ep.* V, pp. 153–238.

GOTTSCHALK *Œuvres théologiques et grammaticales*, ed. D. C. Lambot (*Spicilegium sacr. Lovaniense*, 20). Louvain, 1945.

RATRAMNUS OF CORBIE

PL 121, 13–346.

M.G.H., *Ep.* V, pp. 149–58.

Liber de Anima ad Odonem, ed. D. C. Lambot. Namur and Lille, 1952.

JOHANNES SCOTTUS ERIUGENA See Part VI.

ADALBOLD OF UTRECHT

Ed. E. T. Silk, *Pseudo-Johannes Scottus, Adalbold of Utrecht and the early commentaries on Boethius. Mediaeval and Renaissance Studies*, III (1954), 14–24.

Ed. R. B. C. Huygens, 'Mittelalterliche Kommentare zum "O qui perpetua"', *Sacris erudiri*, 6 (1954), 373–427 (with Bovo of Corvey).

BOVO OF CORVEY *Ad Boethium De Consolatione philos. III metr. 9. PL* 64, 1239–44 (see also under ADALBOLD).

MANEGOLD

Opusculum contra Wolfelmum, PL 155, 147–76.

Opusculum contra Wolfelmum. Introduction and chs. 22–4, ed. K. Franke, *M.G.H.*, *Libelli de lite*, 1 (1891), pp. 303–8.

Liber ad Gebhardum, loc. cit. pp. 358–430.

ANSELM OF BESATE (AND GUNZO) Ed. K. Manitius, *Gunzo ad Augienses und Anselm von Besate, Rhetorimachia. M.G.H. Quellen z. Geistesgeschichte d. M.A.* II, 1958

GERBERT (SILVESTER II)

PL 139, 57–338.

Letters, ed. J. Havet. Paris, 1889, ed. and trans H. P. Lattin. N. Y. 1961

BERENGAR OF TOURS

De sacra coena adversus Lanfrancum, ed. A. F. and F. T. Vischer. Berlin, 1834 (reprinted W. H. Beekenkamp, *Kerk. histor. studien*, 2, 1941).

Ed. C. Erdmann and N. Fickermann, *M.G.H.*, *Briefe d. deutschen Kaiserzeit*, V, (1950), 132–72.

LANFRANC *Works*, *PL* 150, col. 1–640.

PETER DAMIANI *Works*, *PL* 144–5.

ANSELM OF CANTERBURY

Works, *PL* 158–9.

Works, ed. F. S. Schmitt, 6 vols. London and Edinburgh, 1946–51.

EADMER *Vita Sti. Anselmi*, ed. and tr. R. W. Southern. London and Edinburgh, 1962.

GAUNILO 'Liber pro insipiente', ed. Schmitt, in *Anselmi Opera*, I, 125–9.

ROSCELIN 'Ad Abaelardum', ed. J. Reiners, *Der Nominalismus in der Frühscholastik* (Münster, 1910), pp. 63–80.

Chapter 35

Bidez, J. 'Boèce et Porphyre', in *Revue Belge de Philologie et Histoire*, 1 (1923), 189–201.

Cooper, L. *A Concordance of Boethius*. Cambridge (Mass.), 1928.

Courcelle, P. *Les lettres grecques en Occident de Macrobe à Cassiodore*, 2nd edn. Paris, 1948.

Favey, C. *La consolation latine chrétienne*. Paris, 1937.

Fontayne, J. *Isidore de Séville et la culture classique dans l'Espagne wisigothique*, 2 vols. Paris, 1959.

Klingner, F. *De Boethii consolatione philosophiae*. Berlin, 1921.

Momigliano, A. *Cassiodorus and Italian Culture in his Time*. Proceedings of the British Academy, 41. London, 1955.

Praechter, K. 'Christlich-neuplatonische Beziehungen', in *Byzantinische Zeitschrift*, 2, 1 (1912), 1–27.

Rand, E. K. *Founders of the Middle Ages*. Cambridge (Mass.), 1928 (ch. 5, 'Boethius the Scholastic').

Schmekel, A. *Die positive Philosophie in ihrer geschichtlichen Entwicklung*, II. *Isidor v. Sevilla*. Berlin, 1914.

Schur, V. *Die Trinitätslehre d. Boethius im Lichte der skythischen Controverse*. Paderborn, 1935.

Stewart, H. T. *Boethius*. Edinburgh, 1891.

Chapter 36

Cabannis, A. *Agobard of Lyons*. New York, 1953.

Cappuyns, M. See Part VI, chapter 34.

Delhaye, P. *Une controverse sur l'âme universelle au IXe siècle*. Lille and Namur, 1950.

Ehrhardt-Siebold, E. v. and Ehrhardt, R. v. *Cosmology in the 'Annotationes in Martianum'*. Baltimore, 1946.

Laistner, M. L. W. *Thought and Letters in Western Europe A.D. 500–900*, 2nd edn. London, 1957.

Liebeschütz, H. 'Martianus Capella bei Eriugena', in *Philologus*, 104 (Berlin and Wiesbaden, 1960), 127–37.

Vielhaber, K. *Gottschalk der Sachse*. Bonn, 1956.

Wallach, L. *Alcuin and Charlemagne*. Ithaca, N.Y., 1959.

Chapter 37

Endres, J. A. *Forschungen z. Geschichte d. frühmittelalterlichen Philosophie*. Münster, 1910.

—— *Petrus Damiani und die weltliche Wissenschaft*. Münster, 1910.

Gonzette, J. *Pierre Damien et la culture profane*. Louvain, 1956.

Gregory, T. *Platonismo medievale, Studi e Ricerche*. Rome, 1958.

Macdonald, A. J. *Berengar and the Reform of Sacramental Doctrine*. London, 1930.

Picavet, F. *Gerbert ou le pape philosophe*. Paris, 1897.

Southern, R. 'Lanfranc of Bec and Berengar of Tours', in *Studies Presented to M. Powicke* (Oxford, 1948), pp. 27–49.

Chapter 38

Barth, K. *Anselm: Fides quaerens intellectum*, tr. J. W. Robertson. London, 1960.

Koyré, A. *L'idée de Dieu dans la philosophie de St. Anselme*. Paris, 1923.

McIntyre, J. *St Anselm and his Critics: a re-interpretation of the 'Cur Deus homo'*. Edinburgh and London, 1954.

Reiners, J. *Der Nominalismus in der Frühscholastik*. Münster, 1910.

Southern, R. *St Anselm and his Biographer*. Cambridge, 1962.

Steinen, W. v. d. *Vom heiligen Geist des Mittelalters* (Breslau, 1926), pp. 1–143.

Select Bibliography

PART VIII. EARLY ISLAMIC PHILOSOPHY

A. ḤUNAIN IBN ISHĀQ

Über die syrischen und arabischen Galenübersetzungen, Arabic text and German translation by J. Bergstraesser. Leipzig, 1925.

J. Bergstraesser, *Neue Materialien zu Hunain ibn Ishāq's Galen-Bibliographie.* Leipzig, 1932.

AL-KINDĪ

First edition of 24 mostly small writings by Abu Rida, 2 vols. Cairo, 1950 and 1953.

Arabic text, Italian translation and commentary of two treatises: M. Guidi and R. Walzer, *Studi su al-Kindi*, I (Accademia dei Lincei, Roma, 1940).

H. Ritter and R. Walzer, *Studi su al-Kindi*, II (Accademia dei Lincei, Roma, 1938).

Latin translations of two treatises, ed. A. Nagy. *Beiträge zur Geschichte der Philosophie des Mittelalters*, II 5. Münster, 1897.

AR-RĀZĪ

First edition of a number of treatises by P. Kraus as *Abi Bakr Mohammadi filii Zachariae Rhagensis Opera Philosophica*, Pars Prior. Cairo, 1939.

French translation of his autobiography by P. Kraus, Raziana, I, *Orientalia*, 4 (1935), 300 ff.

English translation by A. J. Arberry, *Asiatic Review* (1949), pp. 503 ff.

English translation of the *Spiritual Physick of Razes*, by A. J. Arberry. London, 1950.

MAIMONIDES *The Guide of the Perplexed*

Editions of the Arabic text by S. Munk, Paris, 1856–66 and I. Joel, Jerusalem, 1930.

English translation with introduction and notes (and an introductory essay by L. Strauss) by S. Pines. Chicago, 1963.

AL-GHĀZALĪ

Al-Munqidh min ad-Dalāl, ed. F. Jabre (with French translation). Beirut, 1959.

English translation by W. Montgomery Watt, *The Faith and Practice of Al-Ghazali*. London, 1953.

AVICENNA'S BIOGRAPHY Translation by A. J. Arberry, *Avicenna on Theology* (London, 1951), pp. 10 ff.

AVERROES *The Incoherence of the Incoherence* (*Tahāful at-Tahāful*)

Edition of the Arabic text by M. Bouyges, S.J. Beirut, 1930.

Sixteenth-century Latin translation, ed. B. H. Zedler. 1961.

English translation, with introduction and notes, 2 vols., by S. van den Bergh. London, 1954.

AL-FĀRĀBĪ

N. Rescher, *Al-Farabi. An Annotated Bibliography*. Pittsburgh, Pa., 1962. (Cf. *Journal of the Royal Asiatic Society*, 1963, p. 99.)

Aphorisms of the Statesman (*Fusūl al-madanī*), edited with English translation, introduction and notes by D. M. Dunlop. Cambridge, 1961.

Compendium Legis Platonis, edited with Latin translation and introduction by F. Gabrieli, *Plato Arabus*, III. London, 1952.

Survey of the Sciences (*ihsā' al-'ulūm*), edition of the Arabic text by 'Uthmān Amīn, Cairo. Latin translations by Gerard of Cremona and Guilielmus Camerarius (1638), edited by A. González Palencia. *Al-Farabi*, *Catálogo de las Ciencias*, 2nd edn. Madrid–Granada, 1953.

On Attaining Felicity (*fi taḥṣīl as sa 'āda*), English translation by Muḥsin Maḥdi. New York, 1962.

On the Philosophy of Plato: De Platonis philosophia, edition of the Arabic text with Latin translation, introduction and notes by F. Rosenthal and R. Walzer, *Plato Arabus*, II. London, 1943. English translation by Muḥsin Maḥdi. New York, 1962.

On the Philosophy of Aristotle, edition of the Arabic text by Muḥsin Maḥdi. Beirut, 1961. English translation. New York, 1962.

On Political Government (*K. as siyāsa al madaniyya*), English translation in R. Lerner and M. Mahdi, *Medieval Political Philosophy* (New York, 1963), pp. 39 ff. German translation by F. Dieterici, *Die Staatsleitung von Al-Farabi*. Leiden, 1904.

Principles of the Views of the Citizens of the Excellent State (*K. mabādī' arā ahl al-madīna al-fādila*), Arabic text edited by F. Dieterici. Leiden, 1895; by A. Nadir. Beirut, 1959. A critical edition will be published by the present writer. German translation by F. Dieterici, *Der Musterstaat*. Leiden, 1900. French translation by R. P. Jaussen, Youssef Karam and J. Chlala, *Al-Farabi, Idées des habitants de la cité vertueuse*. Cairo, 1949.

Chapters 39–40

Brockelmann, C. *Geschichte der arabischen Literatur*, 2nd edn., 2 vols. Leiden, 1943–9.

—— *Geschichte der arabischen Literatur, Supplement*, 3 vols. Leiden, 1937–42.

Corbin, H. *Histoire de la philosophie islamique*, I. Paris, 1964.

d'Alverny, M. T. 'Anniyya-Anitas', in *Mélanges Gilson* (Paris, 1959), pp. 59 ff.

—— 'Avendauth', in *Homenaje a Millas Valiscrosa*, I (Barcelona, 1954), 19 ff.

—— 'Avicenne et les médecins de Venise', in *Studi in onore di Bruno Nardi* (Firenze, 1955), pp. 177 ff.

Boer, T. J. de. *The History of Philosophy in Islam* (translated from the German). London, 1903.

Menasce, J. de. 'Arabische Philosophie' (*Bibliographische Einführungen in das Studium der Philosophie*, 6). Bern, 1948.

Gardet, L. and Anawati, M. M. *Introduction à la théologie musulmane*. Paris, 1948.

Gibb, H. A. R. 'The Influence of Islamic Culture in Medieval Europe', in *Bulletin of the John Rylands Library*, 38 (1955), 82 ff.

Select Bibliography

Gilson, E. 'Les Sources Gréco-Arabes de l'Augustinisme Avicennisant', in *Archives doctrinales et littéraires du Moyen Âge*, 4 (1929), i.

Guttmann, J. *Philosophies of Judaism* (translated from the Hebrew). London, 1964.

Macdonald, D. B. *The Development of Muslim Theology, Jurisprudence and Constitutional Theory*. New York, 1903.

Meyerhof, M. 'New Light on Hunain ibn Ishāq', in *Isis*, 8 (1926), 685 ff.

Munk, S. *Mélanges de philosophie juive et arabe*. Paris, 1859.

Pines, S. *Beiträge zur islamischen Atomenlehre*. Berlin, 1936.

Rahman, F. *Prophecy in Islam*. London, 1958.

Renan, E. *Averroès et l'Averroisme*, 2nd edn. Paris, 1861.

Steinschneider, M. *Die arabischen Übersetzungen aus dem Griechischen*. Graz, 1960.

—— *Die Hebräischen Übersetzungen des Mittelalters und die Juden als Dolmetscher*. Berlin, 1893.

—— *Die europäischen Übersetzungen aus dem arabischen bis Mitte des 17. Jahrhunderts*. Graz, 1956.

Montgomery Watt, W. *Islamic Philosophy and Theology*. Edinburgh, 1962.

Walzer, R. *Greek into Arabic. Essays on Islamic Philosophy*. Oxford, 1962.

—— *Encyclopaedia Britannica*, 1963, *s.v.* 'Arabic Philosophy'.

—— 'The Achievement of the Falasifa and their Eventual Failure', in *Correspondance d'Orient*, 5 (Bruxelles, 1962), 347 ff.

—— *Encyclopedia of Islam*, 2nd edn., vol. 1 (Leiden, 1960), *s.vv.* Aflātūn, Akhlāq, Arisṭuṭālīs, Buruklus; vol. 2 (Leiden, 1965), *s.vv.* Djālīnus, al-Fārābī, Furfuriyūs.

INDEXES

I. INDEX OF ANCIENT AND MEDIEVAL WORKS REFERRED TO IN THE TEXT

This index includes only titles named in the text or, in a few cases, in a note which makes directly a point of some substance: it is not an *Index Locorum*. (For Old and New Testament books see General Index)

II. GENERAL INDEX

III. INDEX OF GREEK TERMS

Greek terms transliterated in the text will be found in the general index

See also table on p. 314